Wines of France

A Guide to 500 Leading Vineyards

Also by Benjamin Lewin

Claret & Cabs:
the Story of Cabernet Sauvignon

In Search of Pinot Noir

Wine Myths and Reality

What Price Bordeaux?

Wines of France

A Guide to 500 Leading Vineyards

Benjamin Lewin MW

Vendange Press
Dover, 2015

Copyright © 2015 by Benjamin Lewin

All rights reserved. Published in the United States
by Vendange Press.

Library of Congress Cataloging-in-Publication Data
Lewin, Benjamin
Wines of France
A Guide to 500 Leading Vineyards
Benjamin Lewin
Includes bibliographical references and index.

ISBN 978-0-9837292-4-2

Library of Congress Control Number: 2015902645

Printed in China
1 2 3 4 5 6 7 8 9 10

Contents

For my Anima Figure

Preface

You shall find Calais engraved on my heart, said Mary Tudor. I feel the same way, well not exactly about Calais, which is too far north to have vineyards, but about France in general with regards to wine. I am omnibibulous: I taste and drink wines from everywhere, but time and time again I come back to the classics of France as defining my points of reference. I regard the biggest misfortune ever in English foreign policy as the loss of Bordeaux resulting from defeat in the Hundred Years' War. You get the idea.

The wines of France have changed enormously since wine production expanded from Europe into the New World. Some changes have been forced upon France by the competition, others result from natural forces, most notably global warming, and yet others are self-inflicted by the political environment. But everywhere the scene is different from ten or twenty years ago. It's fair to say that the wines of France have never been collectively better than they are today, but the more interesting questions are how they have changed, how much they are driven by tradition or competition, and how the styles will evolve in the future. If there's any change common to France as a whole, it is the trend to riper styles that is found worldwide.

France retains its leadership for the top wines in many regions; Bordeaux, Burgundy, and Champagne are the most obvious examples of essential reference points. Yet the moment you move below the top level, France is constantly challenged by the New World imperative for varietal labeling. The New World produces more approachable, more fruit-forward, more overtly delicious wines, with which it is hard for France to compete on either sheer fruit power or price. Aided by more reliable climates, and less hindered by tradition, the New World is able to respond more rapidly (if not indeed to create) market forces that drive wine styles at all price levels. This competition in export markets is certainly one major factor influencing styles in France. Decline in domestic support is another; even within France, *Le Monde* has reported the end of the French love affair with wine.[1] How will the (remaining) traditionalists in France hold out against the forces of modernism? But above all, my question is: why has France retained my allegiance through all these changes, and will it continue to do so?

The first part of the book describes the wine regions of France. Their traditions, the nature of the terroirs, the types of grape varieties that are grown, the driving forces for change, all contribute to the character of each region, as does its division into appellations or IGPs (and sometimes Vins de France). At the end of each section, the reference wines identify examples that seem to me to typify the area; in some cases, where there is a split between, for example, modernists and traditionalists, there may be wines from each camp. These are intended to be recommendations for wines that are generally available, and which offer a sense of the character of the appellation, not necessarily to identify the top wines. Of course, at the end of the day, it's the individual producers who define what the region stands for, so the vineyard profiles are intended not only as points of reference for finding wines, but also to amplify the account of each region. Reference wines for individual producers in the guide are not necessarily the producer's best-known wines, but those that offer a good representation of the style, to provide a starting point for trying the producer.

"Leading vineyards" has no single definition: it is a relative list rather than based on absolute judgment (if such a thing were possible). Leading producers range from those who are so prominent as to represent the common public face of an appellation to those who demonstrate an unexpected potential on a tiny scale. The list is naturally biased towards the major regions, with Bordeaux and Burgundy well in the lead, but I have tried to represent as many appellations as possible. It can be hard to convey the full sense of commitment you get when visiting vineyards, but I have tried to give a sense of each producer's aims for his wines, of the personality and philosophy behind them—to meet the person who makes the wine, as it were, as much as to review the wines themselves. It's hard to contain the list—there's always one more example popping up—but as a whole it should represent the best of both tradition and innovation in wine in France. And I owe an enormous debt to the hundreds of producers who cooperated in this venture by engaging in discussion and opening innumerable bottles for tasting. This book would not have been possible without them.

Benjamin Lewin MW

Illustrations for Chapter Headings

Chapter 1: Stone bas-relief showing transport of wine across the river Durance near Avignon in the Roman era

Chapter 2: Clos St. Jacques in Gevrey Chambertin

Chapter 3: Vineyards in the Médoc overlooking the Gironde

Chapter 4: Champagne maturing in the cellars at Krug

Chapter 5: Vineyards overlooking Riquewihr

Chapter 6: Muscadet vineyards close to the river Loire

Chapter 7: Vines overlooking Châteauneuf-du-Pape
Courtesy Inter-Rhône, Christophe Grilhé.

Chapter 8: Vineyards at the city of Carcassonne.

Chapter 9: The vineyard in Angers castle.

CARTE VITICOLE DE LA FRANCE

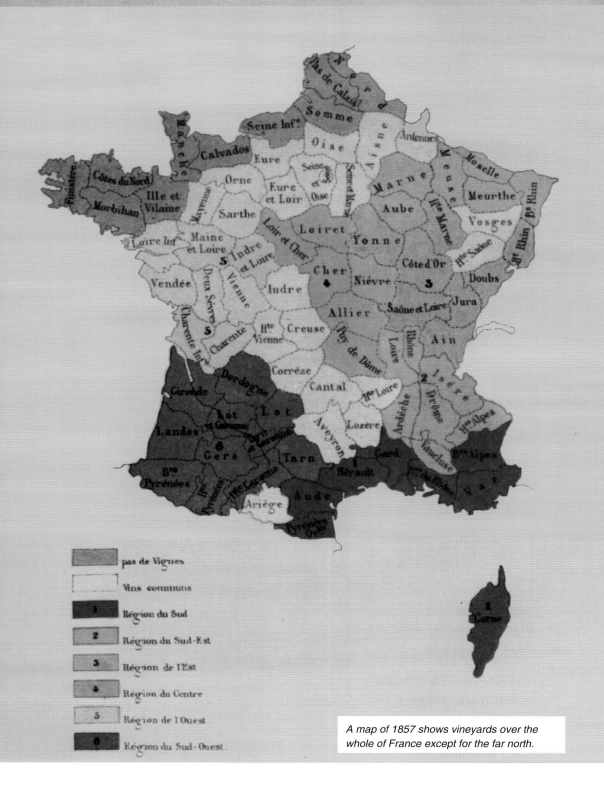

Légende:

- pas de Vignes
- Vins communs
- **1** Région du Sud
- **2** Région du Sud-Est
- **3** Région de l'Est
- **4** Région du Centre
- **5** Région de l'Ouest
- **6** Région du Sud-Ouest

A map of 1857 shows vineyards over the whole of France except for the far north.

1

The State of France

It Works in Theory

I was lost in France
And the vines were overflowing...
I was lost in France in love
(Bonnie Tyler)

"How can anyone govern a nation that has two hundred and forty-six different kinds of cheese?" asked General Charles de Gaulle. He might have been even more perplexed if he had considered wine: spread across France are 467 different AOPs (*appellation protégées*, formerly appellation contrôlées or AOCs) for wine. In Bordeaux alone, there were 57 AOCs at one point. Altogether there are more than 500 different official classifications in France, identifying the geographical origins of every wine.

The AOPs are both the glory and the despair of French winemaking. The glory because they set a standard and preserve tradition: the AOP system maintains a certain quality, for example, by limiting how much wine can be produced from each vineyard; and by restricting the choice of grape varieties, it prevents producers from abandoning regional traditions to jump on the same bandwagon of fashion. But the other side of this coin is that over-regulation can stifle innovation. This makes producers less flexible in responding to changing conditions such as global warming or foreign competition.

The intellectual framework for wine production in France is probably unique. The demand for a theoretical construct is typical. "Yes, it will work in practice, but will it work in theory?" was the famous response of a French diplomat to an Anglo-Saxon initiative.[1] Only in Bordeaux have they thrown away the theoretical surround and gone for a system based on that crude Anglo Saxon construct: the market. But even there it has been enveloped in a wrapper of official classification.

The big question is whether France has lost its way in practice.

Alsace	15,000 ha
Bordeaux	20,000 ha
Burgundy	29,000 ha
Beaujolais	22,000 ha
Champagne	31,000 ha
Languedoc	212,000 ha
Loire	64,000 ha
Provence	42,000 ha
Rhône	78,000 ha
Southwest	20,000 ha
Pyrenées	13,000 ha
Others	9,000 ha

Almost every part of l'Hexagone, as the French call France, makes wine. Only the far north is a grape-free zone (but it produces eaux-de-vie from other fruits). Climate change from north to south gives France perhaps the widest range of any wine-producing country.

France produces more than one half red wine, and less than a third white wine. Most of the white comes from the north; progressively more red wine is produced going from Alsace to the Loire to Burgundy, but white wine remains in the majority. Moving south, the tipping point is between Burgundy, where white wine production still dominates, to Beaujolais, which is largely red wine. South of Lyon, production is almost 90% red. Provence is the largest region for producing rosé.

In the most northern wine-producing region of France, the invention of Champagne was an act of sheer genius. Until the sixteenth century, the Champagne region produced still red wines that were the major source of supply for Paris; however, the temperature plunge of the mini ice age was followed by sustained cooler temperatures, making it impossible to ripen the grapes fully. Even white grapes give no more than a fairly thin, acid wine: but perform a second fermentation to introduce bubbles and increase alcohol, then add a little sugar before bottling, and you have the perfect sparkling wine.

On roughly the same challenging line of latitude as Champagne, but tucked into the northeast corner of France adjacent to Germany, Alsace grows a series of cool-climate white grape varieties (and some Pinot Noir). Riesling is the unchallenged leader here, planted in the best spots. Spicy Gewürztraminer and fat Pinot Gris come next. Almost all wines are vinified as single varieties.

The Loire is at the northern limit for viticulture; in fact only the ameliorating influence of the river makes it possible to grow grapes. The wine-producing regions follow the river all the way from the coast near the old fishing town of Nantes to the vineyards of Sancerre. The Loire is really four separate sub-

The wine-producing regions of France extend from just south of the 50° limit of latitude to the far south.

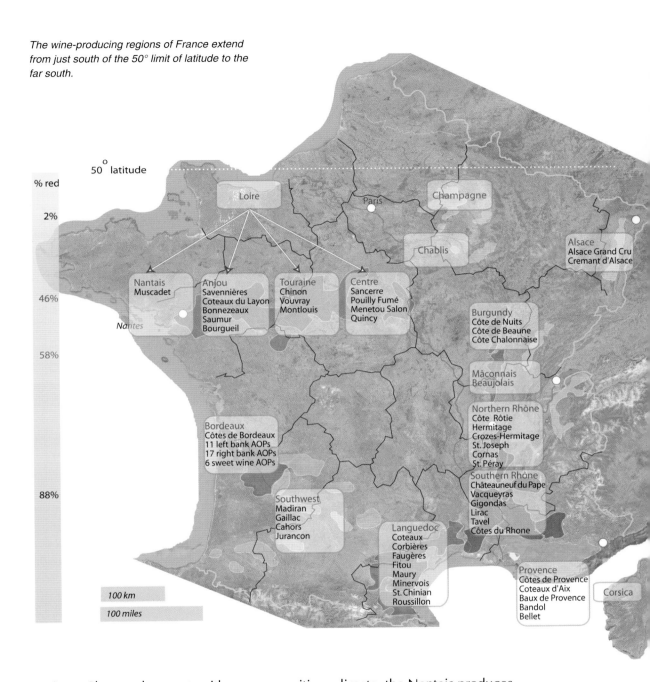

% red

50° latitude

2%

Loire

Paris

Champagne

Chablis

Alsace
Alsace Grand Cru
Cremant d'Alsace

Nantais
Muscadet

Anjou
Savennières
Coteaux du Layon
Bonnezeaux
Saumur
Bourgueil

Touraine
Chinon
Vouvray
Montlouis

Centre
Sancerre
Pouilly Fumé
Menetou Salon
Quincy

46%

Nantes

Burgundy
Côte de Nuits
Côte de Beaune
Côte Chalonnaise

58%

Mâconnais
Beaujolais

Northern Rhône
Côte Rôtie
Hermitage
Crozes-Hermitage
St. Joseph
Cornas
St. Péray

Bordeaux
Côtes de Bordeaux
11 left bank AOPs
17 right bank AOPs
6 sweet wine AOPs

Southern Rhône
Châteauneuf du Pape
Vacqueyras
Gigondas
Lirac
Tavel
Côtes du Rhone

88%

Southwest
Madiran
Gaillac
Cahors
Jurancon

Languedoc
Coteaux
Corbières
Faugères
Fitou
Maury
Minervois
St. Chinian
Roussillon

Provence
Côtes de Provence
Coteaux d'Aix
Baux de Provence
Bandol
Bellet

Corsica

100 km

100 miles

regions. Close to the coast, with a more maritime climate, the Nantais produces Muscadet, a light, refreshing wine; at one time there was an upper limit for alcohol of 12.3% to maintain lightness in the wine. Extending around the cities of Angers and Tours, Anjou and Touraine focus on the Chenin Blanc grape, vinified in all styles from completely dry to extremely sweet late harvest wines. There is also red wine from Cabernet Franc, as well as rosé and sparkling wine.

Vineyards in Alsace have tightly packed trellises of vines on slopes that catch the sun.

At the far eastern end of the Loire, the Central Vineyards focus on crisp Sauvignon Blanc, with an increasing amount of Pinot Noir being made today. If there is any unifying thread to the Loire as a region, it is that the dry wines tend to have fresh acidity and moderate alcohol.

Burgundy extends from its northernmost outpost in Chablis (northeast of Sancerre), through the major vineyards of the Côte d'Or, to the southern areas of the Chalonnaise and Mâconnais. White wines in Burgundy almost all come from Chardonnay; reds come from Pinot Noir. Chablis historically has made crisp white wine, but with increasingly warmer vintages, is becoming more like the richer white Burgundies of the Côte d'Or. The Côte d'Or divides into the northern part of the Côte de Nuits (south of Dijon), which focuses on red wine, and the southern part of the Côte de Beaune, around Beaune, which is split between red and white wine. Immediately to the south, the Chalonnaise makes both red and white wines, and then at the southern end, the Mâconnais is almost exclusively white.

Immediately to the south of the Mâconnais, Beaujolais produces almost entirely red wine, exclusively from the Gamay grape. From there it is only a short hop past Lyon to the Rhône, which is really two separate regions. The significant climatic divide going from north to south in France is between the two

halves of the Rhône: the Northern Rhône is not that much warmer than Beaujolais, but the Southern Rhône begins to approach the heat of the south. Both focus on red wines. Starting not far south of Lyon, the northern Rhône is Syrah country, with the best-known appellations being Hermitage and Côte Rôtie. The southern Rhône consists largely of blended wines, but with a wide quality range from the peak of Châteauneuf-du-Pape to the broad range of Côtes du Rhône, offering simpler wines for every day drinking. Grenache is the dominant grape all over the Southern Rhône. The small minority of whites come from grape varieties tending to be more aromatic or perfumed than those of the north.

Vineyards in Châteauneuf-du-Pape have rocky soils with individual bush vines pruned low to resist the wind.

The Languedoc in the far south is so large and disparate that it's hard to group under a single heading. Originally known as Languedoc-Roussillon, but now simplified just to Languedoc, it stretches around the Mediterranean, from the eastern Languedoc past Montpellier, through the western Languedoc around Toulouse, into the Roussillon region close to the Pyrenees. Formerly known as the Midi, a source of cheap red wines from characterless, overcropped grapes, it has made great strides towards quality in the past couple of decades. The region as a whole accounts for about a third of France's wine production. Although inferior grapes still dominate plantings, there are increas-

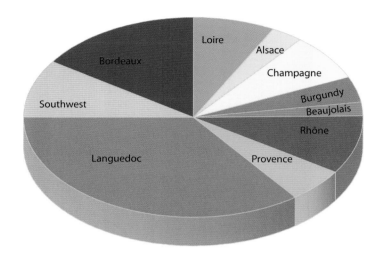

More than half of French wine is produced in the south (Languedoc, Provence, and the southern Rhône).[2]

ing amounts of Grenache, Syrah, and Mourvèdre (giving rise to the common blend known as GSM).

There are several rising AOP regions in the Languedoc, but its main impact is made at the level of IGP (the next level down in the classification system), where the Languedoc is by far the largest producer in France. The umbrella of the IGP d'Oc, a vast region with 90,000 ha of vineyards stretching across the Languedoc, accounts for 10% of all grapevine plantings in France, and 60% of IGP production for the country as a whole. Every sort of wine is made in the Languedoc: dry red, white, and rosé, and sweet and fortified (mostly in the area of Roussillon).

Famously divided into the Left Bank and Right Bank, Bordeaux is really two regions. The Left Bank remains the reference point for Cabernet Sauvignon, or more precisely, for wines based on blends of Cabernet Sauvignon with Merlot and Cabernet Franc. On the Right Bank, the wines are blends of Merlot with Cabernet Franc. Dry white wines, blended from (a majority of) Sauvignon Blanc with Sémillon, have been less successful, and Bordeaux became increasingly red-centric in the latter part of the twentieth century. Similar blends to the Right Bank are found in the area of the Southwest close to Bordeaux, together with holdouts for other grape varieties (notably Malbec in Cahors). The small area of Sauternes, to the south of the city of Bordeaux, is famous for its sweet wines, based on a blend of (a majority of) Sémillon with Sauvignon Blanc.

Perhaps the major stylistic dividing line is whether wines are Atlantic or Mediterranean. Wines under Atlantic influence, most directly the Loire and Bordeaux, but indirectly the entire cool north, tend to high acidity, and achieving ripeness historically has been a problem. For wines under Mediterranean influence, including the Languedoc, Provence, and Southern Rhône, the need to control ripeness has been the main problem. Perhaps not surprisingly, considering the easier climate, the Mediterranean regions produce more wine in total; but France's reputation for leadership in great wines comes from the Atlantic regions. The world's classic wine varieties originated here: Pinot Noir and Chardonnay in Burgundy, Cabernet Sauvignon and Merlot in Bordeaux, Sauvignon Blanc and Chenin Blanc in the Loire, and of course Syrah in the

Northern Rhône. It is easier to produce wine in warmer climates, but perhaps for that very reason, greatness is harder to achieve. As France has been moving in the direction of quality, the balance has shifted, with relatively less production in the south, due principally to a large decline in the Languedoc.

The wide variation in the reputations of different regions is evident from the average price of a bottle of AOP wine. There's been a considerable reordering, and widening of the gap, over two centuries.[4] Champagne is far and away the most successful, essentially twice that of Burgundy or Bordeaux. The vast area of Languedoc is almost at the bottom, beaten only by Beaujolais. The most prestigious regions are as successful as ever, but it's an open question whether France can compete with the New World at the lower end of the market.

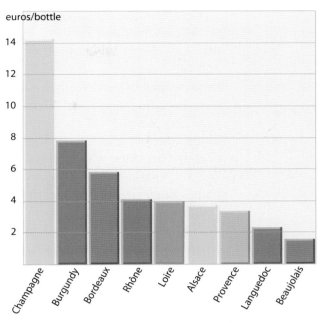

The average price of AOP wines varies widely.[3]

The average figures can hide considerable differences within a region. The contrast between the leaders and the struggling is typified nowhere better than Bordeaux, where the 2010 vintage sold with top wines over €500 per bottle, while generic Bordeaux fetches scarcely more than €3 per bottle, below the cost of production. The range is narrower in the regions at the top and bottom of the hierarchy: there is little cheap wine in Champagne and little expensive wine in Beaujolais.

"At its inception, the system of Appellation Contrôlée was elaborated with admirable rigor. Here was a noble idea. But when they set their minds to it the French can outwhore anybody… The current bunch in control of the INAO [the regulatory body for wine production in France] would have us accept the notion that a slope is flat. This is more than preposterous, it is legalized fraud," says Kermit Lynch, the well-known American importer of French wines.[5]

AOP (AOC)
470,000 ha
240 million cases
50,000 producers

IGP (Vin de Pays)
180,000 ha
140 million cases
13,000 producers

Vin de France
130,000 ha
130 million cases
7,000 producers

Control is the operative word in "Appellation Contrôlée." It has been taken far beyond the original intention, which was to ensure authenticity of origin, so that now almost every aspect of viticulture and vinification is tightly regulated. The big question is whether the system preserves a rich patrimony from the depredations of modern industrial development, or whether it precipitates decline by failing to adapt to the modern world.

France was the first country to classify its vineyards systematically. The roots of the system go back to the first part of the twentieth century when wine production in France was in dire straits. Infestation with Phylloxera, a louse that kills the vines, had reduced production, quality was impacted by a series of poor vintages, and demand for wine was suppressed by a world recession. Fraud was rife, and wines from inferior sources, including substantial imports from Algeria, were routinely relabeled with the names of more famous regions.

Spurred in the traditional French manner by riots in wine-producing regions, regulations were finally introduced to ensure that a geographical name on the label identified the real origin of the grapes. The concept of appellations originated with the law of 1905 that attempted to suppress fraud in food and wine production. The first proper regulations came into effect in 1919 (they had been delayed by the war), and further legislation followed, until the national system of Appellation d'Origine Contrôlée (AOC) was introduced in 1935. The name describes its purpose: wines in the system have controlled origins, as named on the bottle. This is intended to protect the producer (and more incidentally the consumer) by ensuring authenticity. An organization was created to administer the appellation laws, and this developed into INAO, the Institut National des Appellations d'Origine, in 1947.

The most notable feature of wine production in France is the emphasis on identifying wines by place of origin. The heart of the AOC system was the insistence that this should be the primary identification for every wine. The emphasis on origin is taken to the point that, except for Alsace, AOP wines have not usually been allowed to mention grape varieties on the label. However, under competitive pressure from the varietal-labeled wines of the New World, INAO has slowly been allowing more varietal descriptions; generic Bourgogne AOP can be labeled "Pinot Noir," for example.

Every AOP (formerly AOC) wine in France has a name on its label describing its place of origin. This is its *appellation*. Each region has a hierarchy of appellations of ascending quality, organized like Russian dolls. The details vary, but each AOP region is a pyramid, with a broad base of wines that can come from anywhere in the particular region, narrowing to a peak of top wines that can come only from more restricted sites. In ascending order, the hierarchy goes from region, to district, to commune, and finally (sometimes) to individual vineyards.[6] (Not all levels are used in all regions.) Individual AOPs vary in size from the tiny Château-Grillet, a single estate in the northern Rhône, to the broad region of the Côtes du Rhône, which sprawls over 45,000 hectares across most of the southern Rhône. Outside of the broad generic AOPs, the average AOP is about 1,000 hectares.

Only the top wine-producing regions were originally included in the AOC. Other classification systems cover the remaining wines. Vin de Pays was introduced in 1976 to allow more flexibility in producing and labeling for areas that could not make wine up to AOC standard. This also reflected the French love of hierarchy. Five Vin de Pays Regionale included wine from very broad areas; within them were 50 departmental Vin de Pays, each including wine coming from a specific Département (an administrative and political unit); and within these were much smaller Vin de Pays de Zone. But in fact the hierarchy has little significance for even an informed consumer; practically speaking, the various classes of Vin de Pays offered few differences in quality. Most French wine-growing regions were covered by both AOP and Vin de Pays (the most notable exceptions until recently being Bordeaux, Burgundy, and Alsace, which had only AOCs).[7]

When the AOC system was introduced, Vin de Table was created as a description for basic wine. It was not allowed to have any geographical description or statement of vintage; just about the only limitation for wine to be described as Vin de Table Français was that all the grapes should come from France. With the recent change in nomenclature, it is now known as Vin de France, the difference being that varieties and vintage can now be stated on the label.

The descriptions of AOC and Vin de Pays were replaced by AOP and IGP from 2011. AOP stands for appellation d'origine protégée, and, indeed, the drift of modern politics in France makes me wonder whether liberté, égalité, fraternité should be replaced

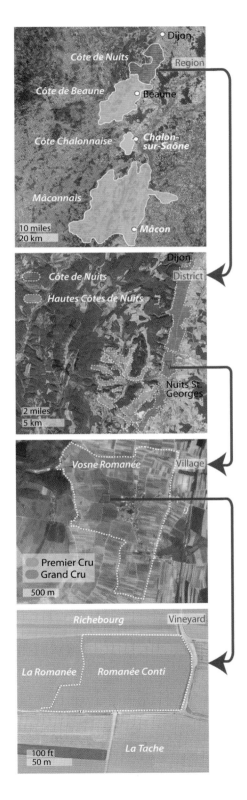

In the Burgundian hierarchy, the regional Bourgogne AOP (30,000 ha) includes districts such as the Hautes Côtes de Nuits (1,600 ha) and Côte de Nuits, which includes villages such as Vosne Romanée (150 ha), which includes individual premier and grand crus such as Romanée Conti (1.8 ha).

Overlooking the Rhône, Château-Grillet is one of the smallest appellations in France. Only 3.8 ha, it produces white wine from the Viognier grape. Its sole domain was under ownership of the Neyret-Gachet family from 1830 until François Pinault acquired it in 2011.

by liberté, égalité, protégé. Aside from the gobbledygook of the official description of AOP, it's hard to see any difference with the AOC, as AOCs have been directly replaced by AOPs of the same name. The IGP (Indication Géographique Protégée) is generally similar to the Vin de Pays that it replaces, but there has been some amalgamation so there are fewer IGPs (around 75, which is roughly half of the number of former Vin de Pays).

IGPs still nominally form a hierarchy, but the vast majority of IGP wines come from the six regional IGPs. Their large size makes it difficult for them to develop clear identity. Within them, the Départemental IGPs have boundaries defined by the politics of 1789 rather than geology, emphasizing the lack of focus on terroir compared with AOPs. The zonal IGPs are more coherent, but generally rather obscure. There is something of a north-south divide in the system. Most production in the northern half of the country is AOP. Most of the IGPs are in the south, concentrated in Languedoc, Provence, and the Pyrenees. Languedoc is the major region where AOP production is in a minority.

An important difference in regulation is that AOPs are highly restrictive about what grape varieties are grown, and IGPs are more relaxed. And IGPs (like Vin de Pays before them) allow varietal labeling; in fact the major source

of varietal labeled wines in France comes from the IGP d'Oc (in the Langue-doc).[8] Production of varietal-labeled wines has been constantly increasing, and now accounts for nearly 40% of all IGP production; this includes more than 90% of wines labeled by variety in France.[9]

The 70 individual AOCs created in 1936 were a small elite, including about 12% of the vineyards in France. For a long time, production was miniscule: until the late 1950s, AOC production remained only around 10% of the total. But the system has expanded steadily. Over the next thirty years, as more vineyards entered the AOC system, the proportion of AOC production increased from 100 to 250 million cases against a background of total production of 700 -800 million cases. Up to a point, this was simply recognition of improving standards. But in the 1980s the expansion gathered such pace that today the 467 AOPs cover about 60% of the vineyards. The vastly increased proportion represents an increase of areas classified as AOC, from 180,000 ha in 1950 to 470,000 ha today; total vineyards in France have decreased from 1,300,000 ha to 800,000 over the period. AOC production has somewhat leveled off, but its proportion has continued to increase because the general decline has reduced total production to around 500 million cases.[10] So the AOC system has increas-

With vineyards stretching as far as the eye can see, the Côtes du Rhône is one of the largest AOPs in France, encompassing more than 45,000 ha.

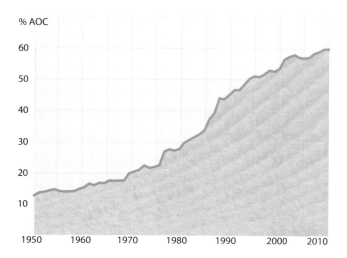

% AOC

The irresistible rise of the AOC has seen its proportion of vineyards in France increase from 12% in 1950 to 60% today.[12]

ingly become the face of French viticulture.

According to Michel Bettane, one of France's most respected tasters, "When the AOC represented 10% of the volume of wine produced in France, there was an equivalent 10% of the population interested in the cultural and historic elements of wine. But the immense farce which consisted of transforming the entire wine-producing territory of France into AOC areas led to the creation of false AOCs. Actually a certain amount of professional discipline is required for a wine to genuinely deserve this label. Paying the producer less than €2 per bottle is not sufficient to maintain this discipline. So 90% of French wines carry an AOC label, but the products do not meet the label's criteria."[11]

Perhaps the numbers are a little exaggerated, but it is fair to say that, with the possible exception of Champagne, every AOP region has a bottom level (usually the generic appellation) with a large proportion of wines at such low prices that it's hard to believe they can represent appellation character. In Provence and Beaujolais, the *average* price is below Michel Bettane's limit.

The major quality difference between AOP and IGP lies with the control of yield—the quantity of fruit produced by each plant. The theory is that a vine puts a certain amount of energy into producing berries. At lower yields, the vine puts its energy into a smaller number of berries, which therefore have more concentrated juice, and make better wine. The belief that low yields are associated with higher quality is one of the reasons why production from old vines is so highly valued, because yield decreases with age.

Every AOP has its own rules, but limits are mostly under 50 hl/ha.[*] Limits in the IGPs are usually around 90 hl/ha. Putting yields in context, if a vineyard is planted with 6,000 vines per hectare (equivalent to planting in a grid 1.3 x 1.3 m), a yield of 45 hl/ha means that each vine is producing one bottle of wine. In top vineyards, where the number of vines is more likely to be closer to 10,000 per hectare (a spacing of 1 m x 1 m), and yields may be even lower, a single vine produces only part of a bottle of wine. As yields increase above (say) 40-50 hl/ha, concentration and quality go down in the wine.

---

[*] hl/ha means hectoliters per hectare: a hectoliter is about 133 bottles, a hectare is 2.47 acres.

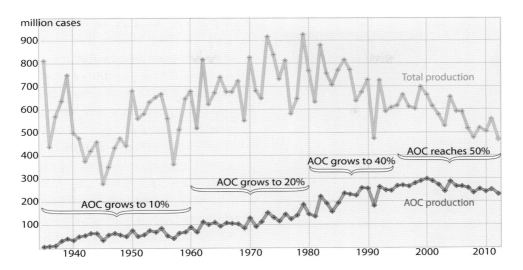

million cases

AOC production has increased steadily to around 250 million cases, while total production has fallen back to around 500 million cases.[13]

Today the 60% of vineyards in the AOP system represent around half of all production, because yields are lower than in the IGPs. Perhaps one of the best effects of the AOP system, aside from the guarantee of authenticity, is the reduction in yields. And where there is a hierarchy within an AOP, higher-level appellations have lower yield limits than lower-level appellations. Certainly in many cases the limits are too high, certainly an annual farce of increasing the limits undercuts the whole scheme,[14] but even so, yields are lower than they would otherwise have been. The average yield in France has doubled over a century, but the increase in yields of AOP wines has been much less than the increase outside of the AOP system.

In the first half of the last century, the low yields in France, mostly in the range of 30-40 hl/ha, represented the poor quality of the vineyards. The struggle was to get enough crop for production to be economic. Since 1945, yields in and outside the AOP have steadily diverged. Within the AOP system, the increase from about 30 hl/ha to 50 hl/ha largely represents improvements in viticulture. Outside the AOP system, the increase from 50 hl/ha to as much as 100 hl/ha represents the same over-cropping found everywhere in production of bulk wines that don't have much character.

It's not enough simply to have vineyards in an AOP, to cultivate the permitted grape varieties in an approved manner, and to make wine. To use the AOP description on the label, a producer has to obtain an *agrément*. This means submitting a sample of the wine for approval.[15] The nominal purpose of the exercise is to ensure that the wine satisfies "usages locaux, loyaux et constants," meaning that it truly represents the appellation for quality and *typicité* (representing a certain character). The fact that 99% of all submissions are approved casts some doubt on the value of the exercise. Can the standard of production in the AOPs be so universally high? Even worse, among the few

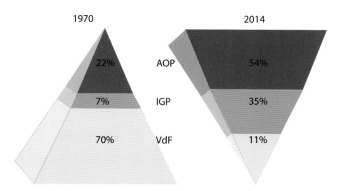

Has the huge increase in the AOC stood the entire system on its head? The doubling of AOC production has produced an inverted quality pyramid. Will it topple over?

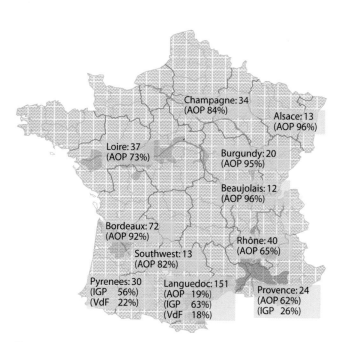

Production is predominantly AOP except in the far south, especially the Languedoc, which has most of France's IGP and some Vin de France (VdF). Numbers are in millions of cases.[16]

wines that are rejected is a significant number where the issue is *typicité* rather than quality.

Now this is a thorny question. The name of an AOP creates a certain expectation, and it's not unreasonable that wines should at least present some common features. A counter view comes from Jean-Marie Guffens at Verget: "Typicity is the accumulation of mistakes across the generations." At a minimum, there's a tendency to freeze current practice in place, if not to define typicity in terms of the lowest common denominator. (You might wonder whether Bordeaux would have been able to make the transition from Malbec to Merlot after phylloxera if the AOP system had existed at the time.)

Certainly, some AOPs are very definitely more equal than others, and in some typicité might even be equated with lack of character. Wines have been denied the agrément because they use techniques that aren't typical for the region or because their appearance is unusual. These include a fair number of "natural" wines made by reducing or eliminating sulfur. The common thread is that in each case the producer was striving to achieve a quality or bring out a character that might risk putting the other wines of the AOP to shame. There's certainly more than a tendency for the AOP to squash innovation by focusing on the "same old, same old." Three stories give the picture.

Marc Angeli had problems when he arrived in Anjou. "When I came here, I was very proud and my aim was to put Anjou very large on the label. We had problems with the agrément, first with the rosés and then again when I started to make dry white wines. With the rosé it was painful because they said it was not the right color, it was either too dark or too pale. And they said that dry white wines should not be made in this style, the problem was that they were too powerful." Putting it mildly, the generic Anjou AOP does not exactly have the highest reputation, and it is scarcely helped by keeping out some of its most interesting and characterful wines.

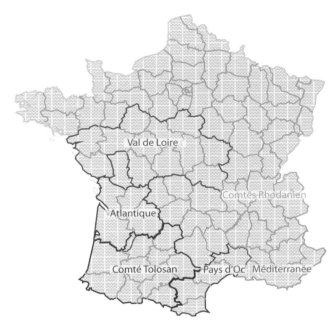

Six regional IGPs account for most IGP production. There are also 28 départemental IGPs and 41 smaller zonal IGPs.

Jean-Paul Brun, at Domaine des Terres Dorées at the southern tip of Beaujolais had problems with the agrément because he prefers to vinify his wines following Burgundian practices rather than the local methods. They taste like *wine*, with a supporting structure, instead of the alcoholic fruit juice found in much of Beaujolais. But, "There are the laws in the official description and the application. It's a matter of politics. You can make very good wine, everyone buys it, but they are breaking our heads. It's excessive," he says. Beaujolais is in the doldrums: excluding wines of real character won't help.

When Patrice Lescarret at Domaine Causse Marines received criticism of his wine from the authorities in the Gaillac appellation that described "some oxidative notes," his reply captured the issue. "Who are you to suppose that you hold the key to the sacrosanct typicity? Who authorized you to prevent the consumer from experiencing the real taste of wine? Who taught you to taste? Do not confuse 'oxidation' with 'very low sulfur'."[17] Gaillac actually has a wide range of styles, from dry to semi-sweet, from still to sparkling: only "oxidation" is a problem, it seems.

Some growers have been pushed by such problems into taking their wines out of the AOP; others do so because they want to use grape varieties that are not permitted, or to vinify in styles that are not allowed, by the appellation rules.[18] In fact, the constrictions of the AOP system are leading an increasing number of producers to label their wines as IGP, or even as Vin de France.[19]

Conventional
80,000 producers
730,000 hectares

Organic
5,000 producers
65,000 hectares

Biodynamic
165 producers
10,000 hectares

Viticulture is agriculture with a twist, because the grapes are not consumed directly, but are produced in order to be turned into wine. The character of the wine is influenced by the conditions of cultivation, especially the yield and the degree of ripeness determined by the timing of harvest. When you produce fruit to be eaten, the objective is simply to achieve ripeness, but with winegrapes the *level* of ripeness has an important influence on style. Whereas Sauvignon Blanc is usually harvested sooner, in order to maintain freshness, harvesting of Cabernet Sauvignon today is pushed later than it used to be, in order to avoid herbaceousness. Viticulture is now seen as the starting point for the winemaker to create the desired style of wine. "Wine is made in the vineyard," is the current buzz.

The grapevine is not a demanding plant: all it needs are more than 1,500 hours of sunshine and more than 700 mm of water per year. It is quite sensitive to cold: it stops growing below 10 °C and is killed by temperatures below −25 °C. It is also sensitive to too much heat: photosynthesis slows down over 30 °C and stops completely above 40 °C. These requirements translate into a band for growing fine wine grapes between latitudes of 50° and 30°. France occupies the cooler half of this band, touching the 50° northern limit; and until the recent warming trend, ripening was a problem in Champagne, Alsace, and the Loire. The warm south is still well within the grapevine's band of comfort (the southernmost vineyards around Perpignan are at about 42° latitude), and there is usually plenty of sunshine: sometimes there is not enough rain. These parameters play out in viticulture.

Vast improvements in viticulture over the past two decades are reflected in a changed appearance of the vineyards. The majority used to have a clean, scrubbed look, with bare earth maintained by herbicides, insects eliminated by pesticides, and yields increased by fertilizers. While this is still common, especially for larger and more "commercial" vineyards, many vineyards now have cover crops growing between the rows (to help restrain growth of the grapevine and to fix nitrogen in the soil); and pesticides and fertilizers have been cut back. Most viticulture in France remains conventional, with chemicals routinely employed; but there is a growing movement towards "lutte raisonnée," meaning sustainable viticulture in which treatments are applied only when necessary, rather than as a matter of routine. The urgency of the need to reduce use of pesticides is indicated by a study showing that 90% of wines have traces of pesticides used in the vineyards.[20]

There is increased use of organic viticulture, which means eliminating synthetic herbicides, pesticides, and fertilizers. Unlike organic food, where the description organic has been hijacked as a marketing term, organic viticulture really does mean something. It has grown rapidly over the past decade, reaching 9% of the vineyards and 4% of the producers in France. The proportion is greatest in Provence (helped by the dry climate), and is smallest in Champagne, where the vineyards are most broken up (it's more difficult for a small vineyard to be organic, because of the problem of sprays spreading from neighbors who are not organic). The only downside is the difficulty of controlling fungal diseases; this requires using copper (for mildew) and sulfur (for oïdium), neither exactly natural, and with the risk that accumulation of copper in the soil may be damaging in the long term. This makes organic viticulture more problematic in humid climates, such as Bordeaux. Although a great deal is heard about the move to organic viti-

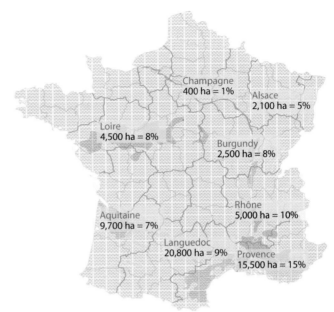

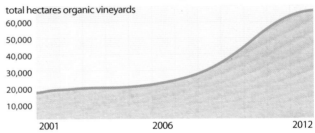

Organic vineyards are increasing steadily in most regions. [21]

culture, the fact remains that it still represents only a small minority.

Biodynamic viticulture is a step further. Based on the ideas of Rudolf Steiner, a twentieth century mystic, it calls for all the restrictions of organic viticulture plus the addition of a series of treatments consisting of homeopathic sprays (including nettle and chamomile tea). Its most famous procedure is to bury a preparation of silica in a cow's horn in the middle of the vineyard in winter; the contents are sprayed over the vines in the Spring. All agricultural activities follow the lunar calendar. Sounds nutty as hell, and we might ignore it altogether if it weren't for the fact that many top winemakers are following biodynamic principles. The number of certified biodynamic producers is quite small, but there are others who follow biodynamics without seeking certification. Certainly many of the biodynamic producers are in leadership positions. They account for almost 20% of the producers profiled in this book.

Biodynamic producers are turning back to horses to plough between the rows as at Château Pontet-Canet in Bordeaux.

One of the leading proponents of biodynamics, Nicolas Joly at the Coulée de Serrant in the Loire, believes it is necessary to reverse the damage done by modern agriculture in order to restore the meaning of the AOC. "There was something wonderful in the idea that a specific place brings a specific taste. An appellation is the sun taken by the leaves, and the soil taken by the roots," he says. "Conventional treatments involve weed killer, which creates the need for fertilizers, which creates the need for systemics, which kills flavor. All this is an argument for organic viticulture. The next question is whether organic is enough... If we do not understand that the whole process from flowering to grapes must be natural, wine will become artificial, an industrial product."

Given the lack of any scientific underpinning for biodynamics, not to mention its astrological connections, my own view is that it is the infinite care and attention these producers bring to bear on their grapevines that's responsible for their success. I suspect they would get the same results if they used water instead of the biodynamic treatments and ignored the lunar cycle. An experiment at Château Margaux seems to have vindicated this view. A small plot in the vineyard was divided into three parts, which were treated with conventional, organic, and biodynamic viticulture. I tasted the wines (blind) from these plots from the 2012 and 2011 vintages.[22] In each year, two of the wines were

closely similar, sharing brighter fruits and acidity, more sense of aromatic uplift, more presence on the finish; the third wine had a flatter profile with less
finesse. The last wine was the result of conventional viticulture. I could not see
any consistent difference between the organic and biodynamic wines.

*Conventional
viticulture uses
regular spraying of
pesticides and
herbicides by row-
straddling tractors.*

Is the attitude towards regulation in France wholly consistent? Irrigation of
vineyards is not allowed anywhere. In the northern half of the country, this is
rarely a problem. In fact the problem is more likely to be with too much rainfall, or with rainfall at the wrong time, especially during harvest, which has
spoiled many vintages in Burgundy and Bordeaux. The theoretical reason why
irrigation is not allowed is that rainfall is part of the typicity of the appellation;
the more practical reason may be that in the fertile conditions of the south, irrigation would certainly to lead to an increase in the wine glut. But if irrigation is
banned because it would reduce differences between terroirs, why is fertilization allowed? One of the features of organic and biodynamic viticulture is that
eliminating artificial fertilizers and weed killers tends to reduce yields, which in
itself may increase quality.

Besides methods of cultivation, the major advance in viticulture has been
in canopy management, the art of pruning the grapevine to get the right balance between leaf area (required for photosynthesis) and exposure of berries to

the sun (required for ripening). Getting the right balance requires different approaches in the north (where usually the objective is to get enough sun on the developing berries) and in the south (where it's more important to limit exposure to prevent over-ripeness). And of course pruning is the major tool for controlling yield. The development of canopy management is largely responsible for limiting damage in poorer vintages to the point at which good, if not outstanding, wine can be made.

One of the major developments in yield control has been the development of "vendange vert" (green pruning), in which excess fruit is trimmed off the plant at an early stage, some time after flowering, but most often at the point when the berries are small and green and the yield can be predicted. When introduced in the eighties, it was a controversial technique much favored by a group of producers on the right bank of Bordeaux, the so-called *garagistes*, who used it to help decrease yields dramatically. One of the first major châteaux to use it was Pétrus, the most famous wine of Pomerol. Christian Moueix crept out with friends to trim the vines at night to avoid attracting attention, but all the same, the story goes that he was denounced in the local church for wasting God's bounty.[23] Green pruning remains controversial because the vine tends to compensate by increasing the size of the remaining berries, but it has spread far beyond Bordeaux to become common practice everywhere, to the point at which you see the ground littered with berries that have been cut off in mid-season.[24]

The critical connection between harvest and winemaking is getting the berries from the vineyard to the fermentation vats in the best possible condition. Until the 1960s, there was only one choice for picking berries: pickers had to descend upon the vineyard and cut the bunches of grapes off the vine. The first mechanical harvesters were relatively crude tractors that moved along the rows, beating or shaking the vine to get the fruit to drop. They have become steadily more sophisticated, especially when the vineyard is designed from the start with mechanical picking in mind, but the human eye still offers better discrimination as to which bunches are ready to pick. Top vineyards continue to use manual picking, which today represents about one third of the vineyards and two thirds of the producers in France.[25]

One of the greatest improvements in quality has been the introduction of sorting before the grapes go into the fermentation vat. The first simple sorting tables were rolling belts that moved the grapes along under the eagle eyes of human sorters, who would remove unripe grapes or MOG (material other than grapes). Today there are increasingly sophisticated optical sorters that scan the grapes with lasers to direct the machine to accept or reject individual berries. This makes for much greater uniformity in the berries that go into the vat. As the focus is generally on excluding unripe berries, this is a contributing factor in the march to increasing ripeness.

Winemaking is a mixture of science and art. The essential process that creates all wine, alcoholic fermentation, when yeasts convert sugar into alcohol, has been understood in increasing detail since its discovery by Louis Pasteur in 1856. Almost all red wines and some white wines also go through a second process that softens the wine, the malolactic fermentation (MLF), when bacteria convert malic acid into lactic acid. Although the chemistry of these fermentations is now well defined, other questions, such as the effects of performing them in stainless steel versus wooden containers, remain in the realm of opinion rather than fact. And the maturation of wine is more art than science, with the effects of exposure to new oak very much a pragmatic choice of the winemaker. Winemaking is a series of decisions—whether conscious or not—every one of which affects the ultimate character of the wine. Even the decision of whether a wine should be bottled under cork or screwcap will have a definite effect on the style of the wine.

Red wine :	260 million cases
White wine :	140 million cases
Rosé wine :	55 million cases
Grapes :	7,000 million kg
Added sugar :	35 million kg
New oak barriques :	1.2 million

The big divide in winemaking is between red and white wine. Color comes from the skins: no fine wine-grape has colored juice. Contact between the juice and the skins of black grapes, before, during, and after fermentation extracts color and tannins into red wine. Control of this maceration is one of the major factors determining the character of red wine. The remnants of the grapes are pressed only at the end of this process to release their residual juice.

In white winemaking, pressing takes place at the very beginning, and the clear juice is run off into fermentation vats. There can be variations on the theme, allowing a little skin contact with the juice before fermentation starts, pressing whole clusters of berries, or taking individual berries off the stems first, but basically white wine come from the juice inside the grape.

Rosé is a compromise. Perhaps for that reason it is often viewed with some disdain. "Rosé is not wine," said the sommelier in a Michelin-starred restaurant in London when I mentioned that I was visiting rosé producers in France. But a great deal depends on whether rosé is the objective of winemaking or is a side product. Sometimes the quality of red wine is improved, especially when there has been some dilution in the grapes by rain before harvest, by a saignée—bleeding off some of the juice at the very start of winemaking, to increase the concentration in what is left. Because there has been only a short period of time for skin contact, the juice is pale-colored: it can be fermented to make rosé wine. But the best rosés are made by using white winemaking

Introduced in the 1960s, stainless steel fermenters gave producers much greater control over fermentation.

methods with black grapes: after immediate pressing, the juice is kept in contact with the skins for a short period before it is run off to start fermentation.

Fermentation is an extremely vigorous, not to say violent, process that releases carbon dioxide and lots of heat. The introduction of temperature control in the sixties and seventies was one of the century's major technical improvements in vinification. Its most important consequence was to stop fermentation being spoiled by excess temperature, but it also allows the process to be controlled to influence the character of the wine. As temperature increases, more volatile compounds are released, but (in the case of red wine production) more extraction occurs from the skins. Playing off these balancing factors gives significant control over style.

The yeasts that catalyze fermentation are Saccharomyces cerevisiae—brewers' yeast—and their influence goes well beyond merely providing a machine to turn sugar into alcohol. A major proportion of the compounds in wine are created by yeasts during fermentation; different strains of yeast can vary quite widely in the panoply of compounds they create. Producers have different opinions on whether it is best to let fermentation be conducted by indigenous yeasts—naturally present on the grapes and in the winery—or whether to add a culture of a specific yeast to start fermentation. The traditional

view is that indigenous yeasts are part of the character of the wine. The alternative view is that leaving fermentation to indigenous yeasts runs the risk of spoilage (because there are bad as well as good yeasts), and it's more reliable to add a cultured yeast that's known to give good results. Organic and biodynamic producers leave fermentation to the indigenous yeasts, not because there's anything nonorganic about cultured yeasts, but because they believe that relying on cultured yeasts leads to homogenization of wine flavors.

Alcohol and acidity are the most important targets for "adjustment" in winemaking. In cooler, northern, areas, it has been common to increase alcohol levels by adding sugar at the start of fermentation. (All the sugar is converted to alcohol during fermentation.) The increase resulting from this *chaptalization*[26] is legally limited to 1.5% alcohol (reduced from the former limit of 2%). Until the recent warming trend, a wine with, say, 12.5% alcohol might have had only 11-11.5% potential alcohol[27] at the time of harvest. Warmer conditions have reduced the need for chaptalization. Also, alternative methods are now available to increase alcohol, such as reverse osmosis, which can be used to extract water from the juice before fermentation. This is relatively common in Bordeaux (the apparatus is too expensive for the smaller producers in Burgundy). At the other end of the country, in the south, grapes

Introduced in the eighteenth century, aging in oak barriques has become the standard for maturation of fine wine.

may lack sufficient acidity. The natural acidity in grapes is due to tartaric acid and malic acid, and when the total is too low, tartaric acid may be added at fermentation. In regions such as Burgundy, where climatic variation can result in the need to adjust in either direction, the rule is that a wine may be either chaptalized or acidified, but not both.

Acidity is almost as essential a component of wine as alcohol. A wine with acidity that is too low will be flabby and lifeless; and wine with acidity that is too high may be unpleasantly piercing. When wine comes out of the fermentation vat, it contains the acids that were in the grapes. By converting malic acid to lactic acid, malolactic fermentation reduces the overall acidity (because lactic acid is weaker than malic acid); MLF also introduces a range of other aromas and flavors, most notably a creamy or buttery quality. Before the great oenologist Emile Peynaud defined the process in the 1960s, malolactic fermentation was a mysterious process that started spontaneously in the Spring, when the cellars warmed up to a temperature that activated the malolactic bacteria. (This could cause consternation: the wine had been resting quietly for months, and suddenly it would start bubbling.) Today MLF is usually performed by inoculating the wine with the bacteria. It's necessary for almost all red wine to avoid a clash with the taste of green apples that comes from malic acid, and it's usually performed with white wines such as Chardonnay, but not with varieties such as Sauvignon Blanc or Riesling, where the creamy flavors it produces would clash with the natural aromatics of the grape. The only area where MLF usage varies significantly among producers is Champagne, where opinion is split on whether it suits sparkling wine.

After fermentation, the most significant factor affecting style is whether the wine is matured in oak, and what sort of oak is used. When oak is new, it imparts a very decided set of aromas and flavors to the wine, including vanillin and spices, as well as adding wood tannins to the grape tannins. These effects decline quite rapidly as the oak ages; by the time barriques are used for the third year, they become quite neutral as a container. New oak is a major contributor to the style of the great red wines of Burgundy, Bordeaux, and the Northern Rhône, as well as to white Burgundy; but for more aromatic whites, such as those of Alsace or the Loire, only old oak is used (giving a softer, gentler result than maturation in stainless steel, mostly because there is more exposure to oxygen). A general tendency towards increasing use of new oak in the last two decades of the twentieth century has been reversed in the past ten years. Oak barriques are about as traditional as winemaking gets—they were used for transporting wine long before they were used for aging[28]—but they are expensive and one of the issues in France is when and to what extent cheaper alternatives (invented in the New World) should be allowed, such as placing staves of oak inside steel tanks or even dunking oak chips in the wine. Alternatives are allowed in some IGPs, but not so far in AOPs.

The final stage in wine production is bottling. Putting wine into a neutral container for consumption might seem to be a technical matter with no stylistic implications, but not a bit of it: within a short period in bottle, wine bottled under cork tastes different from wine bottled under screwcap.[29] In blind tastings, virtually everyone can tell the difference, although usually there is a more or less equal split on preference. Young wines, especially white wines, bottled under screwcap have a livelier, more vibrant taste, but it remains an open issue what will happen with aging in the bottle. Screwcaps are still regarded as an indication of inferior wine in France, where almost all fine wine is bottled under cork. It's a measure of the strength of this tradition that in Burgundy, where for the past two decades there have been major problems with premature oxidation of white wine, presumably connected with the corks, there has been no move to screwcaps.

Concentrated in the north, white wine production is divided roughly equally between Alsace, the Loire, and Burgundy. In all these regions, white wines are produced from single varieties. There is almost no overlap between the varieties grown in the different regions. There is also still a significant amount of white wine production in Bordeaux, where the wine is a blend. There are far fewer plantings of white grapevines in the south, where the traditional varieties are quite different from those of the north, although Chardonnay and Sauvignon Blanc have now spread into the Languedoc.

White Grapes

Ugni Blanc	84,000 ha
Chardonnay	45,000 ha
Sauvignon Blanc	27,000 ha
Muscadet	12,000 ha
Sémillon	11,500 ha
Chenin Blanc	10,000 ha
Colombard	8,000 ha
Muscat	7,500 ha
Grenache Blanc	5,000 ha
Viognier	4,500 ha

More than forty varieties of white grapes are planted in France, but quality is not the leader. The nondescript Ugni Blanc, the same grape as Trebbiano of Italy, is far and away the most planted white variety. But this is a bit deceptive, because most of it is planted in the Charentes, where it is used to make a characterless white wine for distillation into Cognac.[30] Excluding these plantings, however, it would still come in ninth place on the most planted list, which is not an indication of a rush to quality.

The most planted grape variety for making dry white wine is Chardonnay. Burgundy, where Chardonnay originated, has the most plantings, but now is only just ahead of the Languedoc. The other major area for plantings is Champagne. It's an indication of the desirability of Chardonnay that it is the most planted white variety in both the coolest and warmest areas of France. There are also significant amounts in the Loire and the Rhône. Basically it is found everywhere in France, except for

Aquitaine where it is banned.[31] (It's an interesting question whether it's banned because it's felt Chardonnay would not make a great white wine in Bordeaux or for the opposite reason.)

I call Chardonnay the chameleon grape, because it is so versatile. It is grown all over the world, and France has about a quarter of the total plantings. It grows best on calcareous soils, reaching its apotheosis on the Kimmeridgian chalk soils of Chablis and the limestone soils of the Côte de Beaune. It has a natural affinity for oak, and the top wines of the Côte de Beaune usually use significant amounts of new oak. The only other white grape in Burgundy, grown in diminishing amounts, is Aligoté, which tends to be more herbal and acidic (and rustic) than Chardonnay.

The runner up white grape, Sauvignon Blanc, is also widely distributed. Usually considered a cool climate variety, its traditional locations are the vineyards at the eastern end of the Loire around Sancerre, where it makes a varietal wine, and Bordeaux, where it is blended with Sémillon. However, changes in the Languedoc have seen a great deal of Sauvignon Blanc planted there, and today there is more Sauvignon Blanc in the Languedoc than in any other part of France.[32] The fact that the Languedoc now has almost as much Chardonnay as Burgundy, and more Sauvignon Blanc than either the Loire or Bordeaux, might be taken as an indication of its push towards quality, or perhaps viewed more skeptically as a tendency to plant popular varieties irrespective of suitability for the climate (filling the vacuum created by the lack of any traditional high quality white variety in the Languedoc).

Sauvignon Blanc has a very characteristic combination of herbaceousness with citrus and tropical fruits. The natural herbaceousness of Sauvignon Blanc was the argument for blending with the softer Sémillon in Bordeaux, where dry white wines are traditionally 80% Sauvignon Blanc to 20% Sémillon. The proportions are reversed for the sweet white wines, where Sémillon's susceptibility to botrytis leads to a lushness that is just cut by the more herbaceous quality of Sauvignon Blanc.

The distribution of other white varieties is more clearly aligned with climatic constraints. Muscadet (or more formally Melon de Bourgogne) is confined to the western end of the Loire, where it makes a relatively neutral wine, usually on the acid side. One nice thing about Muscadet is that alcohol is rarely high. The signature grape of the Loire might be regarded as Chenin Blanc, because although there is less planted than Sauvignon Blanc, in France it is found only in the Loire. And Chenin is made in a wide variety of styles, from the dry, mineral wines of Savennières, to the semi-sweet and sweet wines of Vouvray, and the botrytized wines of Quarts de Chaume or Coteaux du Layon. Chenin is a grape with high acidity and sugar (which plays out into high alcohol). The high acidity can turn to bitterness at anything short of ripeness; and the nose can be flat, with notes of wet wool.

Across in the northeastern corner of France, the grape varieties grown in Alsace have more in common with neighboring Germany than with the rest of France. The greatest grape of Alsace, Riesling, does not make it into the list of the top ten planted varieties in France; even in Alsace, although it is the most common grape, it is well under a quarter of all plantings. The competitors for Alsace Riesling in fact are in Germany and Austria (with Australia producing Riesling in a somewhat different style). At one time, Riesling from Alsace was usually dry, but with warmer vintages there has been a trend to production of slightly sweet wines. Riesling is the pur-

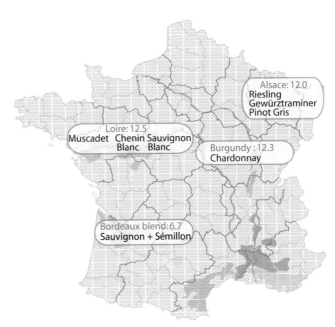

AOP white wine production is concentrated in the northern half of France. Numbers are in millions of cases per year. [33]

est of grapes, vinified in neutral conditions (old oak or stainless steel), without malolactic fermentation, and more directly expressing its terroir than any other variety.

Gewürztraminer, the next most important grape of Alsace, is planted in slightly smaller amounts. It has a spicy quality and expresses a characteristic perfume of lychees. There is some ambiguity about its character, because although the wine is white, the grape is classified under black varieties in official French records. At full ripeness, the skin is actually salmon pink. Another ambiguous grape is Pinot Gris, a variant of Pinot Noir that has partially lost color. It gives a fat, oily, white wine, with high alcohol. All three of these varieties—Riesling, Gewürztraminer, and Pinot Gris—are found in a range of styles from fully dry to sweet late harvest. The other varieties in Alsace are Pinot Blanc (a fully white variant of Pinot Noir), Muscat (perfumed and "grapey"), and Chasselas and Auxerrois (in whose favor there is not much to be said).

It's curious that the more perfumed white grape varieties are concentrated at the northern and southern extremes of France. The Rhône has three characteristic varieties: Viognier, Roussanne, and Marsanne. With a flavor profile slightly resembling Gewürztraminer, Viognier has an aromatic, perfumed, sometimes oily, quality. Low acidity restricts its capacity for aging. Quite a bit is now also grown in the Languedoc. The best indigenous white grapes in the Northern Rhône are Roussanne and Marsanne, often blended together, as Marsanne gives body and weight, and Roussanne adds finesse (disguising Marsanne's tendency to rusticity). The wines are savory, herbal, and nutty. In the south, Grenache Blanc and Clairette are more common, but neither is exactly known for quality. The problem with the south (meaning Languedoc and the Rhône) is that the planted white grapes are mostly relatively inferior varieties; and it's unclear whether the dominant plantings of quality grapes (Chardonnay and Sauvignon Blanc in Languedoc) are really suited to the climate. It's difficult to find quality white varieties for warm climates.

Moving into more specialized territory, Muscat, mostly used to produce sweet dessert wines, is concentrated in the warm climates of the Languedoc and Southern Rhône. The Southwest of France also has its own grape varieties in the form of Petit Manseng and Gros Manseng. Petit Manseng forms smaller berries than Gros Manseng, is especially low yielding, and makes fine sweet botrytized wines.

Adding it all up, just under half of the white wine grapes of France might fall into the quality category.[34]

Black varieties show more restriction to specific geographical areas than white varieties, and there's a fairly clear connection between variety and climate. Moving progressively from the cooler north to the warmer south, Pinot Noir dominates Burgundy, Merlot and Cabernet Sauvignon occupy Bordeaux, Syrah is the grape of the Northern Rhône, and Grenache is the grape of the Southern Rhône. The warmest region of all, Languedoc, is a grab-bag of varieties.

Official statistics list 165 varieties of black wine grapes grown in France, but the top ten varieties account for almost 90% of the total. Fewer than thirty varieties occupy planted areas greater than 1,000 ha.[35]

Merlot is by far the most grown black variety, concentrated in two areas: two thirds is in Bordeaux (or surrounding areas), and one third is in the Languedoc.[36] It is a hard variety to pin down. Relatively versatile, it grows in a variety of conditions, although in Bordeaux it is usually planted on the soils with higher clay content. One problem is that the period for perfect ripeness, between herbaceousness and over-ripeness, can be quite short. Merlot can be grown in large yields to give respectable, if uninteresting, wine. It tends to give high alcohol, and sometimes an impression of lacking refinement, which in Bordeaux is countered by blending with Cabernet Franc in the Merlot-dominated wines of

Black Grapes

Merlot	116,000 ha
Grenache	85,000 ha
Syrah	59,000 ha
Cabernet Sauvignon	53,000 ha
Carignan	49,000 ha
Cabernet Franc	35,000 ha
Gamay	30,000 ha
Pinot Noir	30,000 ha
Cinsault	18,000 ha
Pinot Meunier	11,000 ha

the Right Bank, although there are some famous wines, most notably Pétrus, that are 100% Merlot. On the Left Bank, it is perfect for fleshing out the more austere Cabernet Sauvignon.

Cabernet Sauvignon vies with Pinot Noir for the reputation of the greatest black variety, but the approach to winemaking could not be more different. The great grape of Bordeaux, Cabernet Sauvignon is always blended with Merlot, and the blend may also include Cabernet Franc and Petit Verdot. There is now also a significant amount of Cabernet Sauvignon in the Languedoc (well, there is a significant amount of almost every variety in the Languedoc).[38] A good proportion of the Cabernet Sauvignon in the Languedoc goes into varietal-labeled wine. A major characteristic of Cabernet Sauvignon is the production of

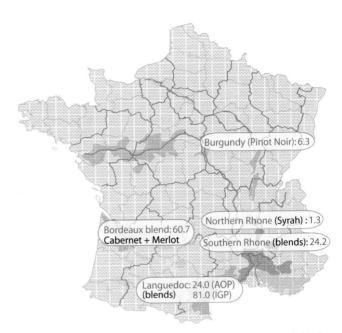

AOP red wine production is concentrated in the southern half of France. (In the Languedoc, IGP production is more significant.) Numbers are in millions of cases per year.[37]

pyrazines (inherited from its parent Sauvignon Blanc), which make it herbaceous at any level short of full ripeness. The greater ripeness resulting from warmer vintages and later harvesting has much reduced herbaceousness in Bordeaux, where Cabernet Sauvignon now more often shows the blackcurrant fruits of full ripeness, but by itself it can be a little narrow in its flavor focus: blending with other varieties broadens its range, an effect which becomes more evident as the wine ages. This is especially important because Cabernet Sauvignon has the most potential of any black grape for becoming increasingly interesting as the wine gets older.

The other parent of Cabernet Sauvignon, Cabernet Franc is only occasionally the dominant component of a blend in Bordeaux, but is the dominant black variety in Anjou and Touraine of the Loire. At full ripeness, it produces a delicious tobacco-driven palate, and can be most refined, although it rarely develops the depth of Cabernet Sauvignon. As with Cabernet Sauvignon, the flavor spectrum can be a little narrow.

Pinot Noir is almost confined to Burgundy, but with significant outliers of increasing quality in Alsace and Sancerre; and, of course, a substantial amount is planted in Champagne, which in fact has more than Burgundy.[39] Pinot Noir is most definitely a (relatively) cool-climate variety, and it has made little impact in warmer regions. Everywhere that it makes dry red wine, it is vinified alone (with the sole exception of a small amount of blending with Gamay in Bourgogne Passe-Tout-Grains or Coteaux Bourguignons). In terms of expressing variations in terroir, Pinot Noir is unparalleled among black varieties. At its best, it is marvelously sensuous. The other grape of the Bourgogne region, Gamay, is more versatile, but also more rustic: originating in Beaujolais, it is also grown in the Loire and the Rhône.

In second place in plantings in France, Grenache originated in Spain (where it is known as Garnacha). It is definitely a grape of the south, with the main plantings in France split more or less equally between Languedoc and Provence, with a substantial minority in the southern Rhône.[40] It's well adapted to the climate because it withstands dry conditions well and is relatively prolific; in fact, it's usually necessary to restrain its yields. A fair amount is used for producing rosé. It is the dominant variety in most appellations of the Southern Rhône. It tends to high alcohol and low acidity, sometimes giving a blowsy impression: which is why it is most often blended with other varieties. It's an oxidative variety, which is to say that it oxidizes easily, which can reinforce a jammy impression.

Definitely a noble variety in the great wines of the Northern Rhône, Syrah is almost always vinified as a single variety (following an old tradition, sometimes a small proportion of white grapes is also included). In its best locations, Hermitage and Côte Rôtie, Syrah makes a wine with faintly aromatic overtones, sometimes a slightly spicy or peppery impression, and an ability to age interestingly that is second only to Cabernet Sauvignon. Aging somewhat along the lines of Bordeaux, it becomes more savory with time. Syrah is a reductive variety, which is to say that it becomes more austere in the absence of oxygen, so it is often matured in small barrels to increase its oxidative exposure.

Today there is far more Syrah in the Languedoc, where it has become a "cépage ameliorateur," improving the quality of blends. In the past decade, plantings of Syrah have increased about a third in the Languedoc, while plantings of the Carignan grape that was a mainstay of the wine lake have been reduced to less than half. Even so, Carignan remains in fifth place on the list of black varieties. Opinions are mixed on Carignan: aficionados of the region believe that it is part of its original character, and a useful component of the blend, but I find that unless the vines are very old indeed, the flavor profile tends to be rather flat.

The majority of inferior black grape varieties in France have always been located in the Languedoc, including large amounts of Aramon and Cinsault. Aramon has almost disappeared now, but there's still a good deal of Cinsault, with the remaining plantings split between Languedoc and Provence.[41] Cinsault is officially well regarded, and classed as one of the three varieties (with Syrah and Mourvèdre) that should be blended with Grenache, but I am not completely convinced that it adds much character to the blend.

Below the top ten varieties, the most interesting black grapes all have local geographical distributions. Malbec, a variety that died out as part of the Bordeaux blend after phylloxera, is the basis for the "black wine" of Cahors. Mourvèdre, which gives a very dense, spicy wine, is grown in Bandol; they say of Mourvèdre that it likes to have its feet in the water but its head in the sun, which fits Bandol on the Mediterranean coast perfectly. Tannat gives a very intense, tannic wine in the southwest. Petit Verdot, intense and spicy, is used as a very small part of the blend with Cabernet Sauvignon in Bordeaux.

For a long time it was thought that the major varieties had either been brought to France from quite different places or had originated by different lines of descent from Vitis vinifera, but DNA mapping now suggests that many are interconnected. Many of the varieties of the northern half of the country originated in a series of independent crosses between Pinot (either Pinot Noir or a variant) and an almost extinct variety called Gouais Blanc, which originated in central Europe.

Most of the varieties of Bordeaux and the southwest are related to Cabernet Franc, which is a descendent of a variety called Txakoli that came across the Pyrenees. Merlot and Carmenère are direct descendents of Cabernet Franc, and Malbec is related. Cabernet Franc is one parent of Cabernet Sauvignon, and Bordeaux is connected to the northern varieties by the other parent, which is Sauvignon Blanc. Several important varieties in the south came independently from Spain, including Grenache and Mourvèdre (known as Monastrell in Spain).

These connections are an unexpected demonstration of the mobility of grapevine species. They have migrated up across the Pyrenees in one direction, and from central Europe in the other, meeting in France to form the world's most impressive se-

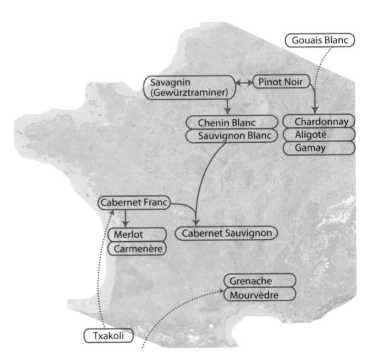

Many important varieties are related. The northern group is related to Pinot Noir, while the southwestern varieties have Cabernet Franc as a common denominator; some southern varieties came directly from Spain.

Vertical lines with arrows indicate parentage; horizontal lines indicate that the direction of the parent-progeny relationship is unknown; dashed lines indicate migration of varieties.

lection of noble varieties. With more than two hundred indigenous winegrape varieties, France has greater diversity than anywhere except Italy.[42] However, there is increasing concentration on planting the best known varieties. Indeed, for all the romantic concern to preserve indigenous varieties, there is a reason why many of them are now reduced to residual vineyards: the wines they make are not very interesting.

The importance of France goes far beyond simply providing variety of grapevines: it is the source of the cultivars that are the basis for almost all the great wines of the world. Every European country has its own great grape varieties—Nebbiolo or Sangiovese in Italy, Tempranillo in Spain, Touriga Naçional in Portugal, Assyrtiko in Greece, for example—but the notable feature about these varieties is that none is successful outside of its original area. Compare this with Chardonnay and Sauvignon Blanc, or with Pinot Noir, Cabernet Sauvignon, Merlot, and Syrah which originated in France but have spread worldwide. Only French varieties have been exported to the New World, and their universal expression has sown the seeds of a powerful challenge.

Phylloxera changed everything in France, and indeed in Europe generally. When phylloxera was introduced inadvertently on grapevines imported from America towards the end of the nineteenth century, it destroyed almost all existing grapevines in Europe as it spread from its starting point in the Rhône. Phylloxera is a louse that feeds voraciously on the roots of European grapevines, weakening plants to the point at which within only a few years they die from other infections. The fatal outcome is inevitable; even a century later, no cure for the disease has been found. The only solution is to bypass the problem by grafting European grapevines on to rootstocks of American grapevines; because phylloxera is indigenous to the eastern half of North America, the native grapevine varieties are resistant to it.

Before phylloxera, wine was produced all over France. Because all the grapevines had to be replanted after phylloxera, the less successful areas abandoned production, and others changed their varieties. Total production decreased dramatically: between 1875 and 1879, it crashed by half, and did not recover until 1900. Replanting tended to focus on varieties that were easiest to cultivate and which gave the greatest yields. The style of planting changed from complantation (intermingling grape varieties) to blocks planted with single varieties. And vineyards previously had consisted of a haphazard array of vines,

Phylloxera

Before phylloxera (1870-1875)

Vineyards : 2.4 million ha
 (own roots) 2.4 million ha
Production: 650 million cases
Vines :   14,000/ha

After phylloxera (1890-1895)

Vineyards : 1.7 million ha
 (own roots) 0.7 million ha
Production: 375 million cases
Vines :   8,000/ha

each supported by its own wooden stake, with vines propagated simply by sticking a shoot in the soil. By contrast, grafted plants were usually planted in tidy rows (making it easier to work the vines with horse-drawn equipment), but also involving a reduction in the density of vines. The decreased density of plantation, together with the greater productivity of grafted vines, led to higher yields. A measure of the increase is that by 1914, when the majority of vines were grafted, production had reached the same level as in 1870, but from only 60% of the land area.

Vines growing on their own roots are propagated by sticking a shoot into the ground until it roots; then the connection to the mother plant is cut.

Various attempts were made to keep vines on their own roots when phylloxera first arrived. Phylloxera does not do well on sandy soils, so vineyards in sandy areas were not so seriously affected. Drowning kills phylloxera, so flooding vineyards was tried, but was really effective only where there was ready access to a large water supply. Unfortunately neither sandy soils nor areas prone to flooding are associated with high quality wine production. However, these are the features of the major areas of vines that remain planted today on their own roots.

The largest area of ungrafted vines in France is almost certainly at Listel, where there are extensive vineyards on a large sandbar close to Sète, between the Mediterranean and the lake of Thau. Wine has been made here since the start of the fifteenth century.[43] Today the 260 ha vineyard largely produces rosé. The wine is labeled as IGP Sable de Camargue (Sands of the Camargue). Just a little to the north, the Domaine de la Ferrandière is situated on the site of an ancient maritime lagoon (between Corbières and Minervois). The soils are salty, and in order to reduce salt content, the vineyards are flooded for 40 days every year in the Spring. An incidental result is that the flooding kills phylloxera, so the vineyards have remained planted on their own roots.[44]

Elsewhere in France, in better known appellations, there are a few small plots of ungrafted vines. Some are very old vines that pre-date phylloxera; others are vineyards that have been planted more recently in attempts to recreate

The vast vineyards at the lido of Sète are on an isthmus (left) with sandy soils on which phylloxera cannot survive (right: courtesy Bernard Boost).

the original plantings. Wine made from these plantings is often labeled "Franc de Pied," indicating that the vines are on their own roots. (Often this is a short-lived endeavor as the vines inevitably succumb to phylloxera after twenty or so years.)

There are two contenders for the oldest vines in France. Just north of Madiran is the appellation of Saint Mont, planted with local varieties.[45] Saint Mont has the unique distinction of an 0.2 ha parcel of vines that has been classified as a historic monument. Planted on their own roots, these vines predate phylloxera, and are probably 150-200 years old. Part of the 12 ha Pédebernarde estate, the plot includes more than twenty varieties, including several that remain unidentified. There are about six hundred vines altogether. The grapes go to the Plaimont cooperative, and until recently there was no possibility of tasting wine made just from the oldest grapevines in France, but in 2011 the cooperative produced a cuvée of "Vignes Préphylloxériques".

Another contender for the oldest vines comes from the Loire. "These vines give wines that are completely different—they have more body, more depth, more density," says Jean-Sébastien Marionnet of his Provignage and Vinifera cuvées at Domaine de la Charmoise in Touraine. A few years ago, Jean-Sébastien purchased a small vineyard from a neighbor, and discovered in it a tiny patch of Romorantin, an old local variety, that was planted in 1850. The grapes had been sent to the local coop, but now form the basis for his splendid Provinage cuvée, which achieves a ripeness of flavor that is rare for Romorantin. Encouraged by the results, Jean-Sébastien then planted a few hectares with several local varieties on their own roots, on soils that vary from clay to com-

pact-silex or sand. So far they are doing well, and are the basis for the Vinifera cuvées.

Occasionally it's possible to compare wine made from ungrafted vines with wine made from similar vines on rootstocks in the same plot. "We are astonished by the minerality of this wine, it has more purity, more concentration. The grapes come to maturity one week earlier," says Catherine Delesvaux, comparing the Cuvée Authentique, from vines on their own roots, with a cuvée of the same Chenin Blanc from an adjacent vineyard on rootstocks at Domaine Philippe Delesvaux in Anjou. I find that wine from the ungrafted vines has more intensity and character.

The same impression comes from comparing two Bourgueils at Pierre & Catherine Breton, where the Franc de Pied comes from the same soil as the Le Galichets cuvée, and was planted twenty years ago on a parcel of virgin soil; perhaps the survival of the ungrafted vines (so far!) is due to the fact that grapevines had not previously been cultivated on this plot. "It is a barometer; it expresses the vintage conditions more clearly," says Catherine.

In these and other similar cases, part of the effect may be due to lower yields from ungrafted vines, but at Domaine de la Charmoise, the Vinifera cuvées come from ungrafted vines that actually give the same yield as those on rootstocks, yet there is still that extra purity. Perhaps it's imagination, perhaps it's due to extra stress on the vines, but it seems to me that in almost every case of pairwise comparisons, the Franc de Pied wines show increased purity of fruits. Their additional complexity makes you wonder what French wine would have been like if phylloxera had not arrived…

Wines from pre-phylloxera vines			
Saint Mont	Plaimont Producteurs (Vignes Préphylloxériques)	0.2 ha	1840
IGP Pays du Loire	Domaine de la Charmoise (Provignage)	0.4 ha	1850
Médoc	Clos Manou (Cuvée 1850)	0.1 ha	1850
Touraine	Marc Plouzeau, Clos de Maulévrier (Ante Phylloxera)	0.4 ha	1865
Corsica	Clos Canarelli, Tarra d'Orasi	0.5 ha	1874
Wines from ungrafted vines (Franc de Pied)			
Champagne	Tarlant (La Vigne d'Antan, Blanc de Blancs)	0.5 ha	1955
Champagne	Bollinger (Vieilles Vignes Françaises)	0.3 ha	1970
Champagne	Maillart	0.3 ha	1973
IGP Pays du Loire	Domaine de la Charmoise (Le Vinifera) (Chenin Blanc, Sauvignon Blanc, Gamay)	6 ha	1979-2000
Pouilly-Fumé	Didier Dagueneau (Asteroide)	0.2 ha	1989
Bourgueil	Catherine & Pierre Breton (Franc de Pied)	0.2 ha	1993
Chinon	Bernard Baudry (Franc de Pied)	0.3 ha	1994
Montlouis	François Chidaine (Les Bournais, Franc de Pied)	0.5 ha	1998
Anjou Blanc	Domaine Philippe Delesvaux	1 ha	2000
Saumur-Champigny	Domaine des Roches Neuves (Franc de Pied)	0.2 ha	2002
Côtes du Roussillon	Domaine Gauby (La Foun)	0.4 ha	1870-1970

Harvest

Before 1982
Flowering :   Jun 23
Harvest :   Sep 29
Hang time :   99 days

2000s
Flowering :   Jun 3
Harvest :   Sep 21
Hang time :   110 days

Mechanical:
36% of producers
72% of vineyards

There are three critical dates in the lifecycle of the grapevine: bud break, flowering, and harvest. The vine is dormant in the winter. The season starts with bud break, when the temperature rises above 10 °C (50 °F) and the first shoots push out, usually in late March. The vine grows vigorously for the next three months. Flowering is a sensitive period when any adverse weather—especially rain or wind—can disrupt the formation of berries (the grapevine is self-fertilizing). And then of course harvest occurs when the berries are judged to have reached ripeness.

The tradition in France was that harvest takes place 100 days after flowering. An average flowering date in the last week of June would lead to harvest at the end of September. But since the 1980s, global warming has been moving the cycle of the grapevine steadily forward. In the past decade, flowering has advanced about three weeks, and now occurs in the first week of June instead of the last. Harvest has also advanced, but the move to pick later to obtain more ripeness has increased the average hang time from 100 to 110 days. So harvest occurs after the

middle of September instead of at the very end. Of course, these dates vary with the region, and with the vintage: there is wide variation from year to year. But the trend is clear and has two important consequences: harvest occurs later in the grapevine cycle than it used to; but the entire cycle has been shifted earlier in the year.[46]

Anyone who doubts the reality of global warming should look at vineyard records. The main factor in determining when the grapes reach ripeness is the temperature during the growing season (the period from April through October). Records show an increase everywhere in France. Since the 1980s, the average temperature during the growing season has risen by 1 °C, more than the historic difference between regions. So the average growing season temperature in Burgundy today is comparable to the average in Bordeaux fifty years ago. The average in Bordeaux is comparable to the Rhône in the mid twentieth century. The temperature in every region in France has been shifted so that today it is similar to that of the region to its south fifty years ago. What does this mean for typicity? Up to this point, it has been beneficial in the north, allowing wines to have natural alcohol levels that previously could be achieved only by chaptalization. But limits are beginning to show, with wines in Alsace showing residual sugar, châteaux on the Right Bank of Bordeaux worrying that Merlot is becoming too ripe, and Châteauneuf-du-Pape producing wines at a brutal 16% alcohol.

Grape varieties historically have been planted in Europe at their northern limits, where ripening is difficult. Growing at the limits means that the growing season is longer. This is beneficial because grapes that ripen more slowly make better wine. The trade-off from working at the limits may be that the best vintages are better—but they occur less frequently. Often no more than two or

Three critical stages in the vine cycle (from left to right) are bud break (when the first new shoots begin to push through the old wood, typically in March), flowering (when flowers form, typically in June, followed by fruit set as they self-fertilize), and harvesting (still performed by hand at top domains and vineyards, usually in September).

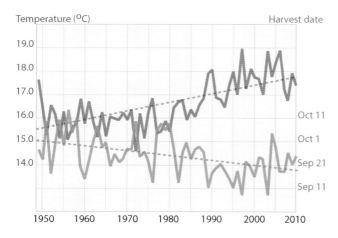

Temperature (°C)   Harvest date

Harvest dates are inversely correlated with average growing season temperatures.[48]

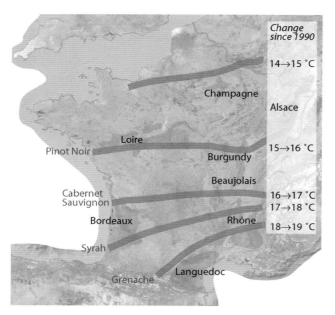

Red lines plot isotherms (lines of equal temperature). Average growing season temperatures have increased about 1 °C since 1990.[47] Grape varieties are identified with the isotherms at which they ripen best.

three vintages are really good each decade. The trend to warmer vintages over the past couple of decades so far has meant more reliable harvests with riper grapes. Pinot Noir, for example, does best with an average growing season temperature close to 16 °C: that line used to run through the Beaujolais, south of where Pinot Noir is actually grown, but now has shifted to run through Burgundy.

The main cause of poor vintages used to be cool weather (often accompanied by too much rainfall at the wrong time), but it's a sign of changing conditions that the most problematic vintage nationally across France in the 2000s was 2003, the year of the canicule (heat wave) when it was simply too hot and dry in the winegrowing regions. "Terroir shows itself in the wine only when development is very slow; there was no typicity in 2003," says Yves Gras at Domaine Santa Duc in Gigondas. Along those lines, if the trend continues, Burgundy could become too warm for Pinot Noir, and Bordeaux could become too warm for Cabernet Sauvignon.

The worldwide trend to harvesting grapes at greater maturity reflects the replacement of sugar level as the main criterion for harvest by the new idea of "phenolic ripeness." This somewhat imprecise concept means waiting until the tannins are more mature (judged mostly by tasting the grapes), rather than harvesting as soon as an acceptable sugar level is reached.[49] Later harvesting means higher sugar levels, which translate into higher alcohol levels in the wine.[50]

The trend is exacerbated when the growing season is shorter, because sugar levels respond more quickly to temperature than phenolic development.[51] The warmer (and shorter) the growing season, the faster sugar accumulates relative to phenols. The dilemma is that if you harvest by the old criteria of sugar levels that give acceptable alcohol levels, the tannins will not be ripe; but if you wait for ripe tannins, alcohol will be much higher.[52] Seeking phenolic ripeness has previously been more of a factor in driving the trend to higher alcohol levels in warmer regions, but the effects of global warming are now making it more of an issue for cool climate varieties also.

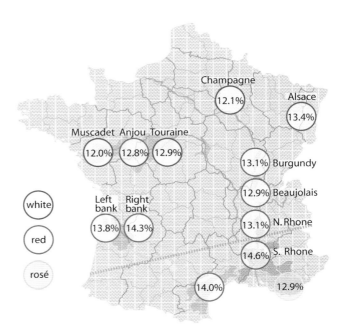

Alcohol levels in French wines today are typically above 13%, with a tendency to increase going south.[53] Chaptalization is allowed north of the dashed orange line.

The proportion of good years has been increased by warmer vintages, and the proportion of poor years has been decreased by improvements in viticulture, allowing good wine to be made when previously a vintage might have been written off. The combination has narrowed the gap, but there is still significant variation between vintages; and one striking feature of wine production in France is the high individuality of regions. (Before 2013, the last year that was uniformly poor in France was 1984; the last year that was uniformly good was 1990.) There is nothing so simple as a gradient from north to south; wine-making is far more local than that.

In the first decade of the twenty first century, for example, the best year in Champagne was 2002, but in neighboring Alsace it was 2001. On similar latitudes, the Loire in the west performed best in 2002, but Burgundy gave its best performance in 2005; and only just to the south of Burgundy, the Beaujolais was most notable in 2009. The Northern Rhône was at its best in 2009, but the Southern Rhône excelled in 2007, and the Languedoc in 2010. Looking at the classic regions of Bordeaux and Burgundy, both had excellent vintages in 2005 and 2009, but 2002 was very good in Burgundy and one of the poorer vintages of the decade in Bordeaux, whereas 2000 was average in Burgundy but hailed as a vintage of the century in Bordeaux.

Producers : 87,400

50% of harvest
Cooperatives : 690
(Growers) : 84,000

70% of wine production
Negociants : 1,050

One indication of the state of wine production in France is that while there are still more than 80,000 individual producers, there's an almost equivalent number of growers, who produce grapes but do not make wine. This half of the winegrape harvest goes to cooperatives, often representing situations in which wine production is simply not economic for the individual grower. Cooperatives account for 40% of AOP wine and more than half of IGP wine.[54] There's an approximate correlation between the reputation of a region and the proportion of production handled by cooperatives. The proportion is lowest in Burgundy and Bordeaux, and highest in Provence, Rhône, and Languedoc.[55]

The major divide in wine production is between estates that grow the grapes and then make wine from them, as opposed to negociants (the négoce as they are called in the trade), who buy either grapes for vinification or wine in bulk for bottling. The descriptions of Château and Domaine are reserved for estates; names such as Maison indicate a negociant activity. The negociants are somewhat prone to exaggerating their importance—the web site of one representative organization claims responsibility for more than 100% of the exports of French wine![56]—but they are by far the dominant face of French wine, accounting for total sales of almost three quarters of all wine, and for the majority of exports.[57]

Negociants come in all shapes and sizes, from vast enterprises handling wines from all over France to small businesses specializing in local regions. (The largest cooperative, Val d'Orbieu, would make into the list of the largest ten producers in France.[58]) Some negociants own vineyards and so also make estate wines, and some growers run negociant businesses, so the lines are not always completely clear. Usually a producer who has both activities will have different labels for the estate and negociant wines.

At the extremes, most wines at the top level come from estates, whereas generic brands come from negociants. There are some regional differences. In Bordeaux, all the top wines come from individual châteaux, but in Burgundy the lines are the most blurred, with some top wines coming from negociants who have estates. Overall, only about a quarter of French wine comes from estate production, but in terms of world markets, French influence comes from the top estates. Trend-setting brands tend to come from the New World.

One complaint about France is that it's difficult to compete with the New World because of the smaller scale of wine production. This is more an issue in terms of vineyard size than producer size. The average vineyard is only 8 ha,[59]

Most French wine is not artisanal. The construction of a new facility for producing bag-in-box at Grand Chais de France in Petersbach shows the scale of the operation. The building cost €28 million. Courtesy SIB-Etudes.

biased by many small growers who sell their grapes to cooperatives or negociants.[60] In terms of production, the largest negociants have become international conglomerates, with interests including vineyards outside France.[61] The consequence is that most of the names you might recognize on bottles are now parts of much larger organizations: JP Chenet belongs to Grand Chais de France, Ginestet belongs to Taillan, Barton & Guestier is part of Castel. Few of the old negociants are still independent, but the names of the holding companies are often unknown.

The top half dozen groups control production of around 100 million cases per year, roughly twenty per cent of all production. With extensive vertical integration, they extend far beyond the traditional distinction between negociants and growers. Difficulties in competing with the New World are due more to the organization of viticulture, in particular the regulations for AOP and IGP that define production in terms of relatively smaller areas, and to the economics of running a business in France, than to the size of the producer.

Negociants and cooperatives are most important at the lower levels of Vin de France and IGP;[62] the higher prices of AOP wines afford more scope for growers to bottle their own wine. There are sometimes conflicts between growers and negociants about AOP rules: growers tend to be in favor of regulations focusing on the development of a hierarchy that highlights the top wines, while negociants more often are against anything that will increase their costs. In Muscadet, for example, where growers see the development of a Cru system as essential for survival of the region, it took some time to persuade the

Cooperatives in France vary from old-fashioned and struggling or defunct, to large, dynamic organizations that are a driving force in their appellation.

negociants to go along. "Initially the négoce were refractory about the Crus but now they have a more positive attitude; they can see the potential advantage of the halo effect," says François Robin of the producers' organization, Inter-Loire.

Is there a unique character to French wine? Well, wine in France runs a complete gamut from bag-in-box sold at less than a euro for the equivalent of a bottle to the wines of top AOPs sold for several hundred euros a bottle (if you can obtain them at all). In terms of French wine as a reference point, the distinction made by many grower-producers is between artisanal wines and what they refer to disparagingly as "industrial" wines. "I don't think there is any more a competition between Old and New World wines, it is more a competition between artisanal and industrial wine. One is the recognition of terroir in wine, the other is market driven," says Frédéric-Marc Burrier, president of the grower's association in Pouilly-Fuissé. Sometimes the implication, stated or unstated, is that New World wines fall into the industrial category, and it is France that carries the flag for artisanal production against all odds. Encapsulating a common view, "In the New World, they produce wines in huge volume, they adjust them to the tastes of the consumer, they have done studies. Young people find it difficult to make the transition to vrai [true] vins," says Bernard Fouquet of Domaine des Aubuisières in Vouvray. The question then is more what makes a "vrai" wine? And if we accept that definition, is there something distinctive or even unique about *French* vrai wine?

Vintage Ratings	
***	universally agreed to be a classic vintage
**	a very good vintage without rising to the absolute heights
*	a good vintage with interesting wines
no stars	a vintage with few wines of interest

	2013	2012	2011	2010	2009	2008	2007	2006	2005	2004	2003	2002	2001
Champagne	*	**		*	*	**			*	**		***	
Alsace	*	*	**	**	**	*	***		**	*			*
Loire			*	**	*	*			***			***	
Burgundy	*	**		**	***	*			***			***	*
Beaujolais		*	**	**	***	*			***	*	*		
Bordeaux				**	***	*			***	*			*
Northern Rhone	*	*		***	**		**	**	***				*
Southern Rhone	*	*		***	**		***	*	***	*			**
Languedoc			*	**	**	**	**	*	**	*			*

| Total Harvest million cases | 650 550 450 | | | | | | | | | | | | |

	2000	1999	1998	1997	1996	1995	1994	1993	1992	1991	1990
Champagne	*	*	**	*	***	**			*		***
Alsace	**	*	**		*	**	*	*			***
Loire	*			*	**	**					***
Burgundy	*	**			*	**		*			***
Bordeaux	***	*				**	**				***
Northern Rhone		**	*			**				*	***
Southern Rhone	**	**	**			**					***

| Total Harvest million cases | 650 550 450 | | | | | | | | | | |

The map of Cassini from 1757 shows a narrow strip of vineyards from north of Dijon to south of Beaune.

Burgundy & Beaujolais

Terroir and Cépage

They leave kisses in the wine, I found one inside of mine
When the rhythm's really fine, rare and sweet as vintage wine
(Grateful Dead)

I'm not sure anyone's actually described Burgundy in terms of kisses in the wine, but if there's any wine for which this is appropriate, it's red Burgundy. At its peak, the Pinot Noir of Burgundy has a sublime, sensuous quality that no other wine in the world can match. Of course, while Burgundy remains unchallenged as the pinnacle for Pinot Noir, production of white wine, almost exclusively from Chardonnay, is more important in the region as a whole. As an area devoted principally to vinifying Pinot Noir and Chardonnay as individual varieties, Burgundy is the place to ask which is more important, terroir or winemaking, and just how far the intrinsic qualities of place and grape variety can be influenced in vineyard and cellar.

"You must also transplant the soil and the sun," the Prince de Condé was told, when he was disappointed with the results of transplanting vines from Volnay to his estate at Chantilly.[1] The soil and the sun are the key parts of terroir: the concept that every piece of land expresses its characteristics in the wine that is produced from the grapes grown on it. Nowhere is this concept better fulfilled than in Burgundy. Two adjacent vineyards, separated by no more than a track, if even that, may have different characters and reputations. Making wine from only a single grape variety, there is no way to hide differences in soil or climate, or the effects of vintage variation.

Burgundy stretches from Chablis in the north to Beaujolais in the south.

Total production of 16.5 million cases (excluding Beaujolais) is divided between regions as shown in the chart.

Chablis is 100% white, Côte de Nuits is 97% red, Côte de Beaune is 67% red, Côte Chalonnaise is 58% red, and Mâconnais is 90% white. Generic Bourgogne is 58% red.

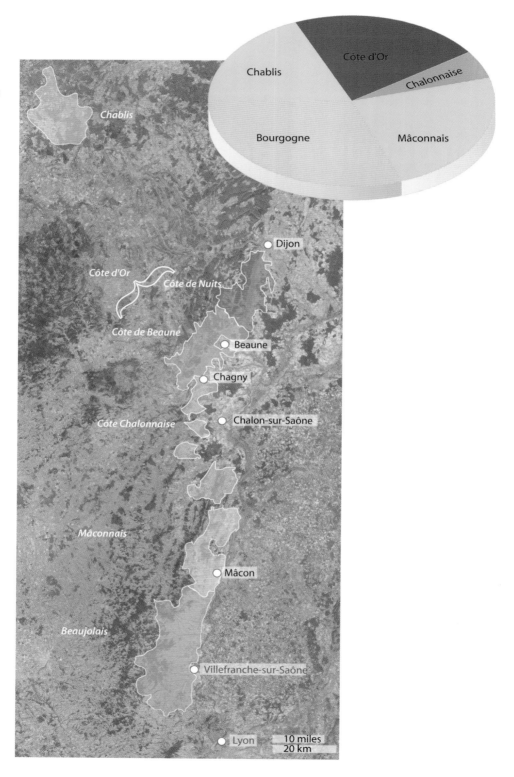

Burgundy originated as a distinct region in the fifth century. With Dijon as their capital from the ninth to fifteenth centuries, the Dukes of Burgundy ruled from the eastern end of the Loire (around Sancerre) to Auxerre in the north (the present area of Chablis), across to the Dijon-Mâcon axis. So far as winegrowing is concerned, Burgundy today includes most of this region; it has lost Sancerre (which split off in the fifteenth century), but retains Auxerre, the Côte d'Or, and Mâcon. It's a consequence of these historical divisions that Sancerre is part of the Loire, but Chablis is part of Burgundy. It's unclear why and when Beaujolais came to be connected with Burgundy.

No one knows exactly when wine production started in Burgundy, but there was a vineyard in Gevrey Chambertin by the first century.[2] Vines were well distributed in Burgundy by 312, when Emperor Constantin visited Autun and discussed the economic difficulties of producing wine in the region.[3] During the thousand years following the fall of the Roman Empire, the Church became the driving force for viticulture. Many of today's top vineyards were established in the first millennium. Founded near Mâcon in 910, the Benedictine abbey of Cluny was a major influence, until it declined and was replaced by the Cistercian abbey of Cîteaux.[4] The monks kept busy, and the region from Auxerre to Beaune was described as "une mer de vignes" [a sea of vines] by 1248.[5]

By the thirteenth century, the wines of Beaune and Bourgogne were known in Paris (Beaune referring to the region around today's Côte d'Or,[6] Bourgogne to the region farther north around Auxerre).[7] The notion that Burgundy should be devoted to producing wine of high quality goes back at least to the end of the fourteenth century, when Philip the Bold issued his famous edict requiring "bad and disloyal" Gamay grapes to be uprooted, and to be replaced by Pinot. The basic objection to Gamay was that it was too productive (giving at least twice the yield of Pinot Noir). Like many other such attempts at regulation, the edict was ineffective.[8] Attempts to eradicate Gamay recurred every century or so, but were generally ignored.[9]

Until the twentieth century, Pinot Noir and Chardonnay were concentrated in the Côte d'Or, essentially a narrow strip of vineyards running south from Dijon through Beaune to Chagny; other, inferior varieties (mostly Gamay for the reds and Aligoté for the whites) were planted in the surrounding areas.[10] Following the destruction of the vineyards by phylloxera, varieties were simplified, and plantings withdrew to the better terroirs. After replanting, Burgundy focused on Pinot Noir and Chardonnay for top quality; the proportion of Gamay and Aligoté declined. The Côte d'Or was almost completely replanted, but growers in some of the other areas gave up production altogether.[11]

Excluding Beaujolais, Burgundy produces 65% white wine and 26% red wine: another 9% is Crémant (sparkling wine). About 10% of the white grapes are Aligoté, and about 2% of the red are Gamay, both used only in generic Bourgogne.[12] But there are significant differences between the parts of Burgundy, with much of the white wine coming from the northern and southern extremities.

A mere sliver of land, the Côte d'Or is the heart of Burgundy. It is divided into two parts: in the north, the Côte de Nuits produces almost exclusively red wine; in the south, the Côte de Beaune is split between red and white. Chablis is an outpost well to the north and west, where the cooler climate supports only white wine.[13] To the south, the Côte Chalonnaise follows the Côte d'Or in style, but with less concentration and complexity. Then farther south the Mâconnais is devoted almost exclusively to Chardonnay. Over the border from the Mâconnais lies Beaujolais, almost entirely producing red wine, but with a switch to Gamay as the sole black grape.

The view that terroir determines the potential of every vineyard is the basis for Burgundy's highly hierarchical appellation system. The spine of the Côte d'Or consists of 5,000 hectares (12,000 acres), divided into 27 communes, mostly between 100 and 300 ha each. They include 470 premier crus and 32 grand crus, mostly less than 10 ha.[14] The classification system is organized into a relatively steep pyramid, steadily narrowing from the base of two thirds of regional AOPs, to a quarter in village appellations, with 11% of premier crus and 1.4% of grand crus at the peak.

Officially the AOPs are divided into Regionale and Village. Some of the Regionale AOPs are more regional than others, as George Orwell might have said, and for that matter there is even wider variation in the reputations of the villages. But never mind the official terminology, which covers a multitude of sins: think about Burgundy in terms of five levels: generic, regional, subregional, villages, and top villages.

Generic Bourgogne AOPs can come from anywhere in the entire region of Burgundy, and this is where Gamay and Aligoté are used. Crémant de Bourgogne is Burgundy's sparkling wine. Just a touch above them are Bourgogne classifications restricted to specific areas, such as Hautes Côtes de Nuits or Beaune. Then come the subregional AOPs, such as Côte de Beaune, Côte de Beaune Villages, Côte de Nuits Villages, Mâcon, and Mâcon Villages.

Bourgogne AOP includes a very wide range of wines. For growers located in the top villages, it may indicate a wine coming from vineyards just outside the village. In Puligny Montrachet, for example, the village more or less marks the bound-

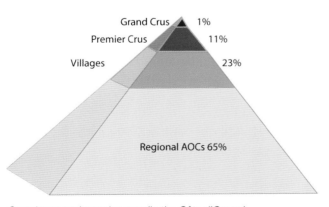

Grand crus and premier crus (in the Côte d'Or and Chablis) are only a small part of production.

Grand Crus 1%
Premier Crus 11%
Villages 23%
Regional AOCs 65%

Côte de Nuits Villages	Côte de Beaune		Mâcon	
	Coteaux Bourguignon Bourgogne Aligoté Bourgogne Passe-Tout-Grains Crémant de Bourgogne			*Generic*
	Bourgogne Hautes Côtes de Nuits Bourgogne Hautes Côtes de Beaune Bourgogne Côte Chalonnaise Bourgogne Côte d'Or			*Regional*
Côte de Nuits Villages	Côte de Beaune Côte de Beaune Villages		Mâcon Mâcon Villages	*Subregional*
Fixin Marsannay	Auxey-Duresses Blagny Chorey-lès-Beaune Ladoix Maranges Monthelie Pernand-Vergelesses Saint Aubin Saint Romain Santenay Savigny-lès-Beaune	Givry Mercurey Montagny Rully	Pouilly-Fuissé Pouilly-Loche Pouilly-Vinzelles Saint-Véran Viré-Clessé	*Villages*
Chambolle Musigny Gevrey Chambertin Morey St. Denis Nuits St. Georges Vosne Romanée Vougeot	Aloxe Corton Beaune Chassagne Montrachet Meursault Pommard Puligny Montrachet Volnay			*Top Villages*

Appellations are divided by hierarchy and geography. Columns show AOPs for Côte de Nuits, Côte de Beaune, Chalonnaise, Mâconnais; Chablis is not shown. The official hierarchies are Regionale (gray) and Village (pink and red).

ary of the appellation, and the vineyards beyond are mere Bourgogne; the difference between a Puligny village wine and a Bourgogne Blanc from immediately across the border is less than you might expect from the names of the appellations. But Bourgogne can also represent vineyards far away from the famous villages, indeed far away from the Côte d'Or itself. The name of the producer is the only guide to the potential quality of Bourgogne: it's a funny thing to say about Burgundy, where there seem to be infinite layers of appellations, but really Burgundy could do with more precision at this level. The latest idea is to have an appellation specifically for the Côte d'Or (outside of the famous communes), but it's controversial. As things stand, the first question you ought to ask about any Bourgogne Blanc is: "where does it come from?"

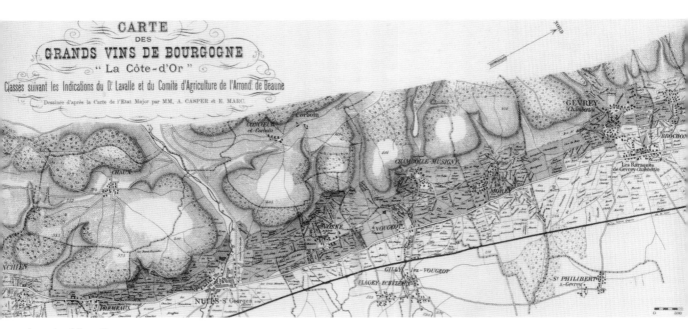

An extract from the map of the Côte d'Or prepared in 1860 could be used as a guide to the appellations today.

The important villages are the communes of the Côte d'Or and Côte Chalonnaise, and also some of the Mâconnais. Of course, there is significant variation in quality among them. Within each area there's a more or less continuous gradation of quality from the lesser to the best regarded villages; any classification placing all villages at the same position in a hierarchy is inevitably only a rough approximation. But the villages are only the start of detailed classification in Burgundy: within each village, the best plots are assigned to premier or grand crus. The definition of the crus goes back to the nineteenth century, when the best vineyards were singled out as "têtes de cuvée," followed in short order by a more detailed classification into première, deuxième, and troisième cuvées. An official map was drawn up in 1860, color-coded with pink for first class vineyards, yellow for second class, and green for third. Only minor changes have occurred in the classification since then, although price differences across the range have widened enormously.[15]

When the AOCs were defined in 1935, grand crus (more or less equivalent to the old tête de cuvée) were officially defined as appellations in their own right. Standing at the very top of the hierarchy, Grand Crus are considered so grand that they do not need to include the village name: I suppose this is a way of saying that each is unique. In fact, there is a reversal here. The greatest grand cru of Gevrey Chambertin, Le Chambertin, had its name when the village was simply called Gevrey. Later the village became Gevrey Chambertin to reflect the glory of the famous grand cru.

The premier crus are another story altogether, and owe their creation to an accident of war. As part of Occupied France during the second world war,

Burgundy became a major source of wine for the occupying forces, who introduced regulations allowing them to requisition ordinary wines. In effect, this excluded those wines that had been classified as crus. To protect their better wines, the Burgundians hastily introduced a system of premier crus, again pretty much following the old map.[16] The individual premier crus in each village were regarded as comprising part of a single Village Premier Cru AOC, and never officially became appellations in their own right. The system requires both the village name and the premier cru to be stated on the label.

The high number of premier crus gives Burgundy its complexity. On the official list of AOPs, the premier crus of each village count as a single entry, but if you counted the several hundred individual premier crus separately, they would be more or less equal to the total number of AOPs for the rest of France! Almost all the villages have premier crus,[17] but of course their significance is relative to the village appellation. A premier cru in the Côte Chalonnaise will probably not be as interesting as (say) a village Vosne Romanée. Wide variation in quality among premier crus is due partly to the intrinsic difficulties in classification on such a scale, and partly to political compromises.

There are many lieu-dits (individually named vineyards) in Burgundy, and their names may be used on the label when the wine comes from the specific vineyard, even if it is only classified at village level. Some of them are well respected and considered to be better than a communal AOP as such. But beware: casual brand descriptions for cuvées are also used, and no distinction is made between them and the authentic lieu-dits. So when you see an additional name on the label under the communal AOP, you have no means of knowing whether it really represents wine from a special vineyard. It is probably too much to expect this practice to be stopped, as of course it should be.

Appellations are an accurate guide insofar as a producer's premier cru will almost always be better than his village wine, and any grand crus will always be better than premier crus. The hierarchy is only a relative guide, however, as it's certainly true that a top producer's village wine may be better than another producer's premier cru. We had better not get into the issue of whether one producer's Bourgogne can be better than another producer's village wine.

The Gevrey Chambertin village wine (left) has the name of the village; the premier cru Cazetiers has the name of the Cru in smaller letters than the village name, and states Appellation Gevrey Chambertin Premier Cru (center); and the grand cru (right) just has the name of the Cru without any village name.

"I have 20 ha and I make 20 different wines," really tells the story of Burgundy: when you ask a producer how many hectares he has and how many different appellation wines he makes, the answers are often pretty much the same. (The average total size of about 1 ha may be made up of several smaller plots, however.) This means that the typical wine is made in quite small quantities—around 15-20 barrels or 5,000 bottles. And just to top it all off, sometimes a producer has such tiny amounts from several premier crus within a village that it's not worth maturing them separately, in which case a label may simply say premier cru, without an individual name, meaning that the wine comes exclusively from premier cru vineyards within the village, but not from one specific premier cru.

The areas for red and white wines are more or less segregated. Most villages of the Côte de Nuits have only scattered plots of white grapevines, and Gevrey Chambertin is exclusively red. The most northern parts of the Côte de Beaune, Aloxe Corton and Beaune, produce both red and white wines. South of Beaune, Pommard and Volnay turn back to red, but when you reach the Montrachets and Meursault, there is almost no red wine (although some parts of Chassagne Montrachet might in fact be more suited to growing black grapes).

In the mid nineteenth century, Puligny was more or less equally divided between red and white; Chassagne Montrachet produced very largely red wine.[18] Does the change reflect increased understanding of terroir or adjustment to the market? The Clos des Mouches premier cru in Beaune historically has been divided between red and white wines, but Philippe Drouhin fears that Drouhin may soon be the only producer left for red Clos des Mouches, as most producers are replanting with Chardonnay, which is cheaper to produce and offers higher yields. "It's a response to market demand," he says. Terroir has its limits.

Burgundy's focus on terroir followed a clash between growers and negociants in the 1930s. Negociants wanted to emphasize blending to develop brands; growers wanted to express individual terroirs. The growers finally won when the Appellation Contrôlée came into effect in 1936.[19] Domain bottling had begun when growers, led by the Marquis d'Angerville, began bypassing the negociants because of the dispute. Domain bottling stayed a relatively small proportion until after the second world war; it increased in the 1960s and 1970s, becoming common with the most valuable wines. Roughly a quarter of premier and grand cru production was probably domain-bottled in 1969, increasing to almost half by 1976.[20] Actually this was a mixed bag in terms of results, as the quality of bottling, often under contract, was variable.[21] By the 1970s, growers were installing their own equipment and gaining expertise. Then domain bottling spread to become common for village wines also.

Growers are responsible for only a minority of production. Overall, the major part of production in Burgundy, around 60%, comes from negociants. Another 25% is made by cooperatives, leaving only 15% for the artisan vignerons.[22] (The proportion of independent producers is higher on the Côte d'Or.) But the boundaries are less fixed than the numbers might suggest. Negociants in Burgundy are not usually mere traders in finished wine: as *negociant-éleveurs*, they buy grapes, must, or wine, and are responsible for the major production decisions. Today the major negociants usually also own vineyards and produce wines from their own estate as well as from grapes bought from outside growers. The six largest houses collectively own more than 400 hectares on the Côte d'Or,[23] including around 15% of the premier and grand crus. And at the other end of the scale, many growers who formerly produced only estate wine have small negociant businesses in which they extend their range by buying grapes.

The price of land has become a major issue. A single hectare of village land in Vosne Romanée runs for more than $2 million, premier crus achieve a multiple of that, and the peak, at Montrachet, commands around $20 million. This makes it difficult for newcomers to afford to buy land, but also accentuates the trend to break up holdings (to pay inheritance taxes) when one generation passes the estate to the next. It's a driving force for small family estates to sell out to larger organizations.

The Côte d'Or consists of the Côte de Nuits (from Nuits St. Georges to the north) and the Côte de Beaune (from Aloxe Corton to the south).

Gevrey Chambertin, Morey St. Denis, Chambolle Musigny, Vougeot, Vosne Romanée, and Nuits St. Georges are the great communes in the Côte de Nuits, all producing red wine.

In the Côte de Beaune, Aloxe Corton and Beaune produce more red than white, Pommard and Volnay are exclusively red, while Meursault, Puligny Montrachet, and Chassagne Montrachet are white.

The AOPs of the Hautes Côtes and Côtes de Nuits and Beaune lie on either side of the narrow line of communes.

Even if you don't have the capital to buy land, you can probably buy grapes. New negociants come from a variety of sources: winemakers at established estates who would like to strike out on their own; people from winemaking families who didn't obtain inherit land, or who left the family firm; and outsiders whose passion is to make wine in Burgundy. Some negociants started small and grew to significant sizes, such as Olivier Leflaive, who left Domaine Leflaive in 1994, and now has headquarters in Puligny across the village square from the domain. Some start as negociants with the aim of renting or acquiring vineyards later, such as Benjamin Leroux, formerly winemaker at Comte Armand in Pommard, whose negociant operation is based in a shared facility in Beaune, and now has some small plots of his own. Even for people who have inherited or successfully established domains, expansion can be problematic given the price of land, so adding a negociant business is a way to grow: Jeremy Seysses at Domaine Dujac, and Alix de Montille from Domaine Hubert de Montille have both followed this route. "The lines between the traditional domains and the *négoce* have become blurred," says Alex Gambal, who started as a negociant but now owns vineyards that provide a third of his supply.

The latest trend in Burgundy is the micro-negociant, so named not just because of their small size, but because they tend to make many different cuvées in very small amounts. One factor is that grapes from top appellations may be scarce. "Many (of my wines) are made in small quantities, sometimes only 1-3 barrels. If we were anywhere else it would be a total nonsense, but that's how it is in Burgundy," says Pascal Marchand in Nuits St. Georges. On the other hand, Patrick Piuze, a micro-negociant in Chablis, feels that, "The essence of the place depends on the mosaic of soils, when you realize this you want to make lots of cuvées not just one." In some ways, because they are not committed to estate vineyards, micro-negociants have a freer hand. Some remain faithful to the notion of only purchasing grapes, such as negociant Lucien Le Moine, established by Mounir Saouma, who makes a wide range of micro-cuvées (none as much as 1,000 bottles). Unlike most micro-negociants, who aspire ultimately to control and own vineyards, Mounir prefers to stay with buying grapes. "I trust my growers," he says. "We have the best growers in the world here."

Some of the new negociants really don't like the term. "We are at the border of the domain and the micro-negociants. I don't like the word negociant, it means you buy juice and you raise it, but there are three different métiers—farming, winemaking, and élevage—a traditional negociant is only the last. But in my opinion you have to control all three of the métiers. We are not really a micro-negociant because we are doing the same work as the domain," says Olivier Bernstein, a micro-negociant in Beaune. "I make the wine, from the beginning of vinification to bottling, I'm a winemaker, even though there's no word for it in French," says Olivier Leflaive. "I view myself as a winemaker, not as a negociant."

One of the common criticisms of the large negociants is that house style tends to be more noticeable in the wines than nuances of place. Refuting the argument, Olivier Masmondet of Maison Jadot says, "The style of the house does show beyond terroir, but this is just as true of small producers as the large negociants." It's just that when a producer only has a few wines, the differences between them may be more evident than the similarities. Indeed, you could find half a dozen "minimalist" producers in, say, Chambolle Musigny, all claiming to allow the grapes to speak clearly in the wine, and yet every one of their village wines will be different. The key thing is not so much whether styles are distinct from producer to producer as whether a particular producer's wines show relative differences reflecting each individual terroir.

Before the French Revolution, most vineyards were owned by the Church or large landowners. After they were confiscated as "biens nationaux," they became subdivided. The situation has since been exacerbated by French inheritance law, which requires that an estate must be split equally between all the heirs. Today most premier and grand crus are divided between multiple owners. Clos Vougeot's 50 hectares are distributed among roughly 80 growers; the largest has only 5.5 ha, and the smallest has only a few rows of vines.[24] In Chambertin, the largest proprietors have a couple of hectares, producing less than 10,000 bottles per year, and the holdings of the smallest proprietors are measured in ares (a hundredth of a hectare or 100 square meters), producing at most a few hundred bottles. Of course, each proprietor has other holdings, perhaps extending from generic Bourgogne in the vicinity of the village, some village AOP, and parcels of separate premier or grand crus. But each wine has to be vinified and matured separately.

Within the appellation hierarchy, differences between village, premier cru, and grand cru wines are intricately connected with yields. The principle is that vineyards classified at higher levels are restricted to lower yields. In Burgundy, the nominal limits for red wines are 55 hl/ha for generic or regional Bourgogne, 40 hl/ha for village wines and premier crus, and 35-37 hl/ha for grand crus.[25] (Values are slightly higher for white wines.) Curiously, village wines have the same yield limits as premier crus. Yet for my money, the sharpest increase in quality level when I taste Burgundy is going from village wine to premier cru.

The key to Burgundy is understanding that apparently imperceptible differences in vineyards consistently produce significant differences in the wines. A great illustration of terroir came from a tasting with Mounir Saouma at Lucien Le Moine. "There is an intersection where four grand crus from three villages come together: Clos Vougeot, Musigny, Echézeaux, and Grands Echézeaux. We are going to taste these four side by side, they are completely different," Mounir explains. Indeed they are. The Vougeot shows some fleshiness, with a

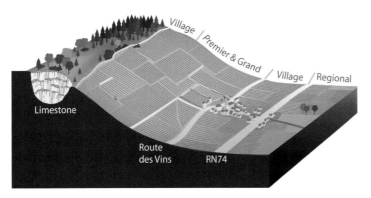

The best terroir lies in the middle of the slope along the Côte d'Or. The grand crus have an elevation of 250-300 m. Courtesy Ecole des Vins de Bourgogne, L. Groffier.

2,614 hectares

10 communal AOPs

135 premier crus

24 grand crus

1.2 million cases

97% red

warm, nutty background, the Echézeaux is broader with liquorice on the finish and an impression of roasted nuts, then the Grands Echézeaux makes a lighter impression, more precise and mineral. Finally the Musigny is just the height of elegance, classic femininity, almost delicate, infinitely refined. Yet the wines come from plots of land within a couple of hundred meters of one another. How differences in soils and microclimates determine the characters of the wines is not at all obvious, but over and over again there are examples of adjacent vineyards seeming all but identical, but producing consistently different wines. This is the mystery of terroir. Each village has its own character. Of course, this is only an approximation, as each producer also has his own style, and the relative characters of villages, or premier or grand crus within them, are interpreted through the prism of the producers' styles.

Côte d'Or might perfectly well mean "hillside of gold" judging from the prices that Burgundy fetches today, but for all its fame, the exact derivation is unknown. The name originated after the Revolution,[26] but it is unclear whether it was based on an abbreviation for Côte d'Orient, meaning a slope facing east,[27] or was a reference to the fame of the vineyards. The Côte is an escarpment running roughly south to north, with hills sharply defining its western boundary, and a plain opening out to the east.

The Northern half, the Côte de Nuits, used to stretch farther north, but today the most northern vineyards have disappeared under the urban sprawl of Dijon.[28] The Côte de Nuits is quite narrow; at some points, the band of vineyards is only a couple of hundred meters deep; even at its widest it is not much more than a kilometer. The common features giving the region its general character are the gentle slope and southeast exposure. Burgundy is a land of geological faults that create intricate variations in terroir. A myriad of small faults cause the underlying structure to change rapidly, but the major defining feature is the Saône fault, a large break running along the side of the Côte d'Or.[29] The N74 (Route Nationale 74) is the famous dividing line.[30] To the north of Nuits St. Georges, the Saône fault is just to the east of the road, and to the south it is just to the west. (Farther south, the road crosses back over the fault around Beaune.)

To the west of the fault, the terroir is based on variations of limestone, ranging from white limestone at the top of the slope to ochre-colored limestone at the bottom. There is also some marl (a mixture of clay and shale). Chardonnay tends to be planted on the soils that are richer in marl, Pinot Noir on the most active limestone. To the east of the fault, the soils are deeper and richer, having filled in when the fault collapsed, and the water table is higher (increasing fertility of the vines).

Two geographical axes impact the wine. Going up the N74 from the Côte de Beaune to the Côte de Nuits, the wines become firmer, less earthy, perhaps even a touch more austere, although

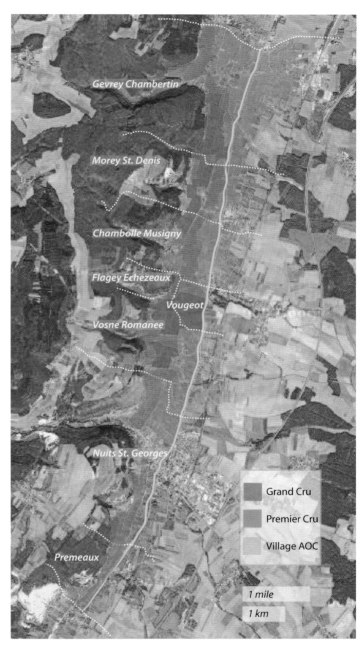

The Côte de Nuits has a line of premier and grand crus along the middle of the slope.

each commune is different. And going across the slope from the N74 at the bottom to the woods at the top, the highest quality is found in the middle. Position on the slope is the main determinant of level in the classification hierarchy, with premier and grand crus occupying the center of the slope.

Vosne Romanée
Damodes
Boudots
Au Cras
La Richemone
Murgers
Chaignots
Vignerondes
Bousselots
Argillas

Nuits St. Georges

Rue de Chaux
Le Procès
Pruliers
Roncière
Poirets
Perrières
Cailles
Les St. Georges
Didiers
Forêts
Corvées
Argilières
Premaux
Clos Arlot
Clos de la Maréchale

Nuits St. Georges AOC
Premier Cru
500m

Vineyards at the very top and bottom are classified for village wines (those across the fault on the other side of the N74 are classified only as regional).

The slope gives good drainage and the best exposure to the sun. The climate in Burgundy historically has been marginal for ripening Pinot Noir. The key to quality in a marginal climate is always which sites ripen best. When the relationships between the village vineyards, premier crus, and grand crus were defined, those in mid-slope had an advantage and became the premier and grand crus. Will this remain true if global warming continues? So far, the rising tide has lifted all boats, but there may come a point when the relationship changes.

Almost all the wines from the Côte de Nuits are red, although in the early nineteenth century, white wines from Clos Vougeot and Le Chambertin were regarded on a par with Le Montrachet.[31] There are only a few whites now. De Vogüé makes a famous Musigny Blanc,[32] and Domaine de la Vougeraie make a white premier cru from the Clos Blanc de Vougeot. There is also a little white Morey St. Denis. Moving away from Chardonnay, Ponsot's Mont St. Luisants stands out as an Aligoté of unusual quality; and Gouges makes a Pinot Blanc from Nuits St. Georges Les Perrières (from a mutant of Pinot Noir that occurred

The appellation of Nuits St. Georges is divided into three parts. Premeaux is at the southern tip (at the beginning of the Côte de Nuits). The rest of the appellation is divided into two parts by the town itself. The 37 premier crus form a band along the middle of the slope, except at the very narrow southern end where they fill the whole width. The premier crus occupy 143 ha; the village AOP has another 175 ha.

The Côte de Nuits is a narrow band of vineyards stretching up the slope from the N74 to the woods at the top.

spontaneously in the vineyard). But with a few exceptions, today the Côte de Nuits is Pinot Noir country.

The emphasis on nuances of terroir sharpens on the Côte de Nuits. In the major communes (Nuits St. Georges, Vosne Romanée/Flagey-Echézeaux, Vougeot, Chambolle Musigny, Morey St. Denis, and Gevrey Chambertin), there are 135 premier crus and 24 grand crus.[33] The grand crus start with La Tâche in Vosne Romanée and extend in a line all the way up to Chambertin and Clos de Bèze. (Corton is the only grand cru for red wine south of Vosne Romanée.) If you are looking for the ultimate expression of Pinot Noir in Burgundy, this is where you will find it; and this is the place to try to define the quality that lifts a wine from premier to grand cru.

At the southern end of the Côte de Nuits, size and variability make it difficult to draw a clear bead on Nuits St. Georges. It used to be said that the most common feature is a certain four-square quality, a lack of the refinement, breed, and tightness that you see farther north. The two major parts of the commune are separated by the gentrified village of Nuits St. Georges itself—quite changed over the past decade. The appellation has something of a

Vosne Romanee AOC

Premier Cru

Grand Cru

Chambolle Musigny

Vougeot
premier crus

Clos Vougeot

Echézeaux   Grands
             Echézeaux

Les Suchots

Richebourg Romanée
           St. Vivant

La Romanée Romanée
           Conti

La Tâche

Vosne
Romanée

Les Malconsorts

Nuits St. Georges

1000 ft

500 m

N74

split personality between heavier wines north of the town and lighter wines to its south.

The best premier cru in the northern part, Les Boudots, is adjacent to Vosne Romanée. The main sweep of premier crus in the southern half starts right out of the town, running down to Les St. Georges, widely recognized as the best premier cru in Nuits St. Georges, and often mentioned as a possible candidate for promotion. (When the grand crus were defined, Pierre Gouges refused to have Les St. Georges considered, on the grounds that this would "create inequalities."[34]) The mixture of clay and limestone along this stretch makes this the best part of Nuits St. Georges. The wines can be rich and structured, but even here they rarely achieve the finesse and silkiness of, say, Vosne Romanée. Perhaps there is too much clay in the soil. At the very southern end in Premeaux, the wines are lighter. Two monopoles, Clos de la Maréchale and Clos Arlot, stand out as the most elegant.

A new generation of winemakers is steadily changing the view of Nuits St. Georges. "The reputation of Nuits St. Georges for rusticity is largely undeserved," says Jean-Nicolas Méo of Méo-Camuzet, although he admits that perhaps the classification is a little too generous with some of the premier crus that still show traditional robustness. A revealing comment about traditional attitudes came from a visit to Domaine Arnoux-Lachaux where Pascal Lachaux comments on his

The central part of the Côte de Nuits, stretching from Vosne Romanée to Vougeot, has the top grand crus of Romanée Conti, La Tâche, Richebourg, and Romanée St. Vivant, as well as the most questionable grand crus, Clos Vougeot and Echézeaux.

premier cru Clos des Corvées Pagets, "This is not typical Nuits St. Georges, it is too elegant." The old generalizations of village character don't always apply any more.

Immediately to the north of Nuits St. Georges, Vosne Romanée is by general acclamation the best village on the Côte de Nuits. It's usually considered together with Flagey-Echézeaux, because, with the exception of the grand crus Echézeaux and Grands Echézeaux, the wines of Flagey-Echézeaux are labeled as Vosne Romanée premier crus.[35] Vosne Romanée is the epitome of refinement. "There are no ordinary wines in Vosne," said a French historian dryly in the eighteenth century.[36] Four of

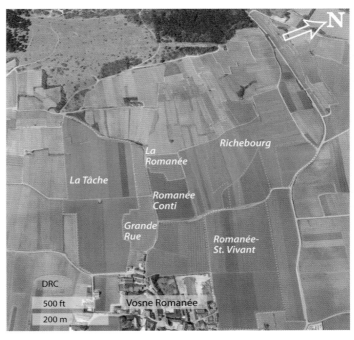

The great grand crus of Vosne Romanée are immediately outside the town. La Tâche and Romanée Conti are monopoles of DRC, which also owns about half of Richebourg and Romanée St. Vivant.

them are monopoles, most famously Romanée Conti and La Tâche, owned by the Domaine de la Romanée Conti; the others are La Romanée (owned by Liger-Belair)[37] and La Grande Rue (owned by François Lamarche, and unusually having been promoted from premier to grand cru in 1992)[38]. The other grand crus are divided among many producers. Richebourg is widely acknowledged to be the best cru after the monopoles, Romanée St. Vivant to be the most elegant, with Grands Echézeaux in third place. The reputations of Richebourg and Romanée St. Vivant are not hurt by the fact that their largest proprietors are the Domaine de la Romanée Conti and Domaine Leroy (generally acknowledged to be the best producers in Burgundy).

The most fabled wine of all, Romanée Conti comes from the middle of the slope, and has the most homogeneous terroir. The measure of greatness is not power, but subtlety and variety, with endless, seamless, layers of flavor. Second by reputation, and somewhat larger, with more variation going up the slope, La Tâche tends to have more body. To the north is Richebourg, with its relatively full style, and below comes the delicate Romanée St. Vivant. If you go up to the hill above the town, you see the most extraordinary panorama of grand crus in Burgundy, but their differences are not at all obvious to the eye.

There are some question marks at the north of Vosne Romanée where Echézeaux and Clos Vougeot are the two largest grand crus. Echézeaux is rather

Richebourg

Romanée St. Vivant

Romanée Conti

La Tâche

N ⇐

The village of Vosne Romanée is at the center of the Côte de Nuits. Seen from the heights to the west (in the foreground), the premier and grand crus are directly above the village.

variable, and many people believe that much of it does not live up to grand cru status.[39] (Echézeaux should not be confused with Grands Echézeaux, a much smaller area of 9 ha, which lies between Echézeaux and Clos Vougeot, and is undoubtedly grand cru.[40])

Clos Vougeot is a single grand cru only because it was physically enclosed by a wall when the monks created the vineyard. In fact, the monks were well aware of differences within the clos, and a sixteenth century map identifies 16 individual *climats* within it. The monks were said in 1831 to make three cuvées whose qualities reflected position on the slope: from the top, the best was kept as the reserve of the abbey, for crowned heads and princes. The second, from the middle, was almost as good and was sold at high price. The third, from the bottom, was somewhat cheaper.[41] In fact, Clos Vougeot extends across the Saône fault, so it is only the upper half that has the characteristic limestone base of the Côte d'Or; the lower part is more like the land that usually lies on the other side of the N74.[42] Attempts to distinguish parts of the clos were beaten off, so in due course it became the biggest discrepancy in the AOC. At its best, Clos Vougeot makes the most overtly generous and fleshy wine of the Côte de Nuits, rich and round. While it is certainly true that the quality of Clos Vougeot is variable, I have to admit that I cannot reliably distinguish wines by their position on the slope in blind tasting.

Clos Vougeot and Echézeaux together total 86 ha, almost a fifth of the 471 total hectares of grand crus on the Côte d'Or. Couple this with the 160 ha of Corton (on the Côte de Beaune), a rather sprawling grand cru with a variety of *climats* of varying quality, and this is not a very impressive start to viewing classification as a guide to the quality of terroir. But it's fair to say that the rest of the grand crus, ranging in size from under 1 ha to almost 20 ha, consistently produce the very finest Burgundy (with the addition of a couple of underclassified premier crus).

To the north lie Chambolle Musigny and Morey St. Denis, the lightest wines of the Côte de Nuits. Chambolle Musigny produces the most elegant wines, with a delicate floral edge, sometimes described as feminine. The pebbly soils are marked by a high proportion of active limestone (which decreases acidity) and a low proportion of clay, making for lightness in the wine.

At the south end of Chambolle Musigny, the grand cru Le Musigny is just west of Clos Vougeot. At the north end, Bonnes Mares is adjacent to the grand crus in Morey St. Denis, where Clos de la Roche usually has the edge over Clos St. Denis. Les Amoureuses, the best premier cru in Chambolle, is often judged to be of grand cru quality; often more expensive than most grand crus, it would very likely be promoted in the unlikely event of a reclassification.[43] All these crus show silky elegance with a sense of precision more than power.

As the largest commune on the Côte d'Or, with vineyards extending from village level to premier and grand crus, Gevrey Chambertin offers fruitful ground for investigating terroir.[44] As a rarity, it includes some vineyards on the "wrong" side of the N74, among which the Clos de la Justice is an exception that can offer wines above the usual village level.

The premier and grand crus fall into two stretches. To the south of Gevrey Chambertin, running almost uninterrupted from the town to the boundary with

Clos Vougeot was at the center of winemaking in Burgundy until it was confiscated during the French Revolution. The walled clos surrounding the château is now broken up into many different holdings. The château is the headquarters of the Confrérie du Tastevin.

Combe aux Moines
Cazetiers
Estournelles
Clos St. Jacques
Gevrey Chambertin
Lavaux

Mazis
Ruchottes

Clos de Bèze

Chambertin

Charmes

Latricières

Mazoyères

Clos de
la Roche

Clos St. Denis

Clos de
Tart

Bonnes Mares

Amoureuses

Musigny

Clos Vougeot

Gevrey Chambertin AOC

Premier Cru

Grand Cru

Morey St. Denis AOC

Chambolle Musigny AOC

2000 ft
500 m

Morey St. Denis, is the lineup of grand crus. At the center, Chambertin and Clos de Bèze occupy the upper edge of the slope. They are flanked by other grand crus both to north and south, and just below on the slope. Some premier crus are adjacent. Then beyond the town itself, running around the edge of the hill to the west, is a sweep of premier crus, including Lavaux St. Jacques, Estournelles St. Jacques, and Clos St. Jacques, with Les Cazetiers and Combe aux Moines to their north.

Differences in exposure may be more important than soils here. A comparison between two of Faiveley's vineyards, Combe aux Moines and Les Cazetiers, is compelling because the plots are contiguous. "The tractor doesn't stop," says Jérôme Flous of Maison Faiveley. Combe aux Moines has a cooler exposure because it angles more to the north than Cazetiers. This difference is accentuated by the fact that Cazetiers extends farther down the slope and so has slightly lower average elevation. Ripening is slightly slower in Combe aux Moines, which harvests two days later than Cazetiers. The

The northernmost part of the Côte de Nuits stretches from Chambolle Musigny to Gevrey Chambertin.

Chambolle Musigny produces the most elegant wines and has grand crus at both ends of the appellation, with the southernmost Le Musigny adjacent to Clos Vougeot, and the northernmost Bonnes Mares adjacent to the grand crus of Morey St. Denis.

Gevrey Chambertin, which is harder-edged, has a set of grand crus in a contiguous group to the south of the town, with the greatest of all, Chambertin and Clos de Bèze, at the center. A group of premier crus lies to the west of the town. It is the only appellation of the Côte d'Or to have extensive vineyards on the eastern side of the N74.

difference is due essentially to sunlight exposure; phenolic ripeness doesn't quite catch up in Combe aux Moines. Yet the impression is not simply that Cazetiers is a riper wine than Combe aux Moines; Cazetiers always has a finer impression, Combe aux Moines seems more four-square.

Clos St. Jacques, the top premier cru of Gevrey Chambertin, provides an unusually clear demonstration of the impact of producers. Most people think that it really should be rated as a grand cru, and indeed, its price is usually at the level of the grand crus.[45] Its rating as a premier cru is a consequence of local politics.[46] At the time of classification in 1935, its owner, the Comte de Moucheron, refused to comply with the procedure and insulted the tribunal.[47] As a result, it became a premier cru, although it has a good slope with perfect southeast exposure. Clos St. Jacques was a monopole until the Moucheron family sold it in 1956, when the present five owners purchased it. Unusually for Burgundy, instead of being subdivided higgledy-piggledy, each owner has a strip running from top to bottom of the Clos. There's quite a bit of variation in soil from top to bottom, but not much from side to side, so each owner has the same diversity of soils. Since their plots are exactly parallel, it's reasonable to associate differences in the wines with differences in viticulture or vinification. The wines range from Fourrier's characteristic elegance, Rousseau's earthiness, Jadot's roundness, Bruno Clair's sturdiness, to Esmonin's sometimes stern representation. Differences result from factors such as harvest dates to the amount of destemming. Here is a powerful demonstration of the effect of the producer on style.

At the very top of the hierarchy, only the grand crus of Gevrey Chambertin, notably Le Chambertin itself and Clos de Bèze, challenge those of Vosne Romanée for leadership. Until the start of the twentieth century, the reputation of Le Chambertin was more or less level pegging with Romanée Conti. One reason why Romanée Conti and La Tâche are now far ahead may be their status as monopoles; under the aegis of the Domaine de la Romanée Conti, their quality has been consistently at the top. Divided among many growers, by contrast, Chambertin's quality is far more variable.

Chambertin and Clos de Bèze have historically been set apart from all the other crus of Gevrey Chambertin, but the distinction between them has not always been clear. Clos de Bèze can be sold under its own name, as Chambertin, or as Chambertin-Clos de Bèze. The name of Chambertin became better known to the point at which few wines were labeled as Clos de Bèze during the eighteenth or nineteenth centuries; almost all were simply described as Chambertin.[48] (Chambertin is supposed to have been Napoleon's favorite wine.) In terms of climate, there is a slight difference between Chambertin and Clos de Bèze, because Chambertin is more exposed to the small valley that divides Gevrey Chambertin from Chambolle Musigny. Cold winds that slide across the upper part may make Le Chambertin cooler than Clos de Bèze,

Chambertin and Clos de Bèze are intimately connected. Wine made in Clos de Bèze can also be labeled as Chambertin, which has been known by its present name since 1276, deriving from Champs de Bertin (the fields of Bertin, an early proprietor). Clos de Bèze takes its name from the Abbaye de Bèze, which was given the vineyard by the Duke of Burgundy in 630.

which is more protected. No one has actually measured any physical difference, but a telling measure is that Eric Rousseau says that Domaine Rousseau always harvests Clos de Bèze earlier than Chambertin.

Comparing vintages, I get the impression that Chambertin has the advantage in the warmer vintages, when its fruits take on a delicious ripeness, but that in cooler vintages the best balance is obtained by Clos de Bèze. I am inclined to the view that there is a continuum of differences all along the stretch of the two appellations, and that the differences you will see in the wines depend on the individual microplots. Yes, terroir and climate are crucial determinants, but no, they are not defined by an arbitrary line between the two appellations.

This is not the end of the Côte de Nuits: beyond Gevrey Chambertin come Fixin and Marsannay, running into the outskirts of Dijon.[49] Marsannay has the only appellation in Burgundy for rosé. "Back in the fifties and sixties, people knew Marsannay for the rosé, and although the image of rosé was poor at the time, people thought of Marsannay rosé as being made more like a red wine. In the last 25 years, Marsannay has gone from rosé into making good red wines. When you taste blind, Marsannay is better than Fixin," says Bruno Clair, whose grandfather was instrumental in creating the AOC for rosé. Marsannay

Reference Wines for Côte de Nuits	
Nuits St. Georges	Henri Gouges
Vosne Romanée	Arnoux-Lachaux
Echézeaux	Mongeard-Mugneret
Clos Vougeot	Lucien Le Moine
Chambolle Musigny	Jean-Marie Fourrier
Morey St. Denis	Domaine Ponsot
Gevrey Chambertin	Armand Rousseau
Fixin	Méo-Camuzet
Marsannay	Bruno Clair

became a village AOC in 1987; previously the wines were simple Bourgogne. There are no premier crus. "The problem with Marsannay is that Dijon is expanding. We are resisting as best we can, the best way is to make top wines," Bruno declares.

The Côte de Nuit's dominance of red wines is shown by ranking the appellations of the Côte d'Or on the basis of price. The grand crus of Vosne Romanée and Gevrey Chambertin fill most of the top twenty places, rounded out by entries from Chambolle Musigny and Morey St. Denis. Two premier crus, Les Amoureuses (Chambolle Musigny) and Clos St. Jacques (Gevrey Chambertin) are generally as well regarded as the grand crus. The top fifty is dominated by the premier crus of Vosne Romanée. The top entries from the Côte de Beaune are the best *climats* of Corton, whose varying reputations intersperse them among the premier crus. Volnay is the only other village to be represented in any number in the top hundred, with several premier crus. The list shows that the classification of grand crus and premier crus does not completely correspond with current reputation.

Reference Wines for Côtes de Nuits Grand Cru	
Chambertin	Armand Rousseau
Clos de Bèze	Bruno Clair
Chapelle Chambertin	Domaine Trapet Père
Charmes Chambertin	Louis Jadot
Griotte Chambertin	Joseph Drouhin
Mazis Chambertin	Maison Faiveley
Ruchottes Chambertin	Georges Roumier
Clos St. Denis	Domaine Dujac
Clos de la Roche	Domaine Ponsot
Bonnes Mares	Jacques Frédéric Mugnier
Le Musigny	Comte de Vogüé

1-10

Romanée-Conti
La Tâche
Musigny
Richebourg
Romanée St. Vivant
Chambertin
Chambertin Clos de Bèze
Griottes Chambertin
Grands Echézeaux
Les Amoureuses, Chambolle Musigny

11-20

Bonnes Mares
Mazis Chambertin
Clos St. Denis
Chapelle Chambertin
Latricières Chambertin
Ruchottes Chambertin
Clos de la Roche
Charmes Chambertin
Echézeaux
Clos St. Jacques, Gevrey Chambertin

21-30

Clos Vougeot
Les Hauts Doix, Chambolle Musigny
Aux Reignots, Vosne Romanée
Les Petits Monts, Vosne Romanée
Les Malconsorts, Vosne Romanée
Les Gruenchers, Chambolle Musigny
Les Suchots, Vosne Romanée
Corton Bressandes
Les Fuées, Chambolle Musigny
Les Sentiers, Chambolle Musigny

31-40

Corton Rognets
Clos des Epenots, Pommard
Les St. Georges, Nuits St. Georges
Les Brûlées, Vosne Romanée
Les Orveaux, Vosne Romanée
Corton Combes
Les Cras, Vougeot
Les Beaux Monts, Vosne Romanée
Corton Clos du Roi
Grèves Vigne De L'Enfant Jésus, Beaune

41-50

Corton Pougets
Le Corton
Les Hautes Maizières, Vosne Romanée
Corton Grèves
Clos de la Perrière, Vougeot
Clos des 60 Ouvrées, Volnay
Les Procès, Nuits St. Georges
Estournelles St. Jacques, Gevrey Chambertin
Les Vaucrains, Nuits St. Georges
Clos des Ducs, Volnay

51-60

Les Cras, Chambolle Musigny
Corton Renardes
Les Cailles, Nuits St. Georges
Clos de Réas, Vosne Romanée
Les Combettes, Gevrey Chambertin
La Petite Chapelle, Gevrey Chambertin
Les Corbeaux, Gevrey Chambertin
Les Baudes, Chambolle Musigny
Corton Maréchaudes
Les Cazetiers, Gevrey Chambertin

61-70

Les Feusselottes, Chambolle Musigny
Clos de la Bousse d'Or, Volnay
Les Boudots, Nuits St. Georges
Aux Murgers, Nuits St. Georges
Les Charmes, Chambolle Musigny
Les Chaumes, Vosne Romanée
Lavaux St. Jacques, Gevrey Chambertin
Clos Fonteney, Gevrey Chambertin
Les Roncières, Nuits St. Georges
Corton Perrières

71-80

La Perrière, Gevrey Chambertin
Les Meurgers, Nuits St. Georges
Corton Clos de la Vigne au Saint
Les Chatelots, Chambolle Musigny
Combe aux Moines, Gevrey Chambertin
Les Millandes, Morey St. Denis
Le Poissenot, Gevrey Chambertin
Les Pruliers, Nuits St. Georges
Combe d'Orveaux, Chambolle Musigny
Petits Vougeot, Vougeot

81-90

Les Damodes, Nuits St. Georges
Clos des Mouches, Beaune
Les Rugiens, Pommard
Les Caillerets, Volnay
Les Jarollières, Pommard
Les Champonnets, Gevrey Chambertin
Bel Air, Gevrey Chambertin
Les Chaboeufs, Nuits St. Georges
Les Perrières, Nuits St. Georges
Les Champeaux, Gevrey Chambertin

91-100

Clos des Chênes, Volnay
Les Chaffots, Morey St. Denis
Les Crots, Nuits St. Georges
Les Chaignots, Nuits St. Georges
Clos de Corvées Pagets, Nuits St. Georges
Clos Sorbè, Morey St. Denis
Clos des Porrets, Nuits St. Georges
Les Taillepieds, Volnay
Aux Beaux Bruns, Chambolle Musigny
Les Grands Epenots, Pommard

The top 100 appellations of the Côte d'Or for red wine are led by grand crus (purple) followed by premier crus (red).[50] Some grand crus should be demoted, and some premier crus should be promoted.

The distinction between the Côte de Nuits and Côte de Beaune is not completely consistent, but as a general rule the Côte de Nuits provides sterner red wines, as much inclined to black fruits as to red fruits, somewhat more generous and rounded, often forceful at premier and grand cru level. Gevrey Chambertin is perhaps the sternest, sometimes with a hard edge when young. Nuits St. Georges ranges from sturdy, almost rustic wines to elegance. Clos Vougeot at its best can be the most generous. There is absolutely no gainsaying Vosne Romanée's unique combination of power and smoothness; but Chambolle Musigny and Morey St. Denis can verge on delicate. This compares with the soft roundness of Corton at its best (yet a thinner quality to Aloxe Corton), the very varied range of Beaune from soft fruits to relatively thin wines, the rustic sturdiness of Pommard, and the crystalline purity of Volnay. With the exception of that taut precision in Volnay, the Côte de Beaune is more likely to offer earthy strawberries than black fruits.

Beaune is the center of the wine trade. Most of the old negociants have their headquarters here, although they have been moving steadily out of the old town to more practical, purpose built, locations on the outskirts. In the center of the old town is the Hospice de Dieu, established as a hospital in the Middle Ages, and funded by wine produced from its own vineyards.[51] One of the highlights of the year in Beaune is an auction at which the latest vintage from the Hospice is sold to local negociants, who then mature the barrels in their own particular styles. At one time these wines were well regarded for their quality, but today the auction is more an occasion to kick off sales of the current vintage than a supply of top-flight wine.

Côte de Beaune

4,752 hectares

20 communal AOPs

325 premier crus

8 grand crus

2.3 million cases

67% red

To the west, the city of Beaune is surrounded by the semicircle of the appellation of Beaune. To the south there is a continuum of vineyards down to the Côte Chalonnaise. To the north is a group of appellations surrounding the grand cru of Corton. The largest grand cru in Burgundy, occupying 160 ha altogether, Corton is somewhat of an anomaly: nominally it is a single grand cru, occupying the upper slopes going up the hill of Corton to the forest at the top, but it is divided into many separate *climats*. It's really their individual names that carry weight. The best, at the top, are worthy of grand cru status: the rest are more doubtful. As for Aloxe Corton, which is immediately to the east of Corton, I do not usually find the reds to have either the structure of the Côte de Nuits or the generosity of the Côte de Beaune.

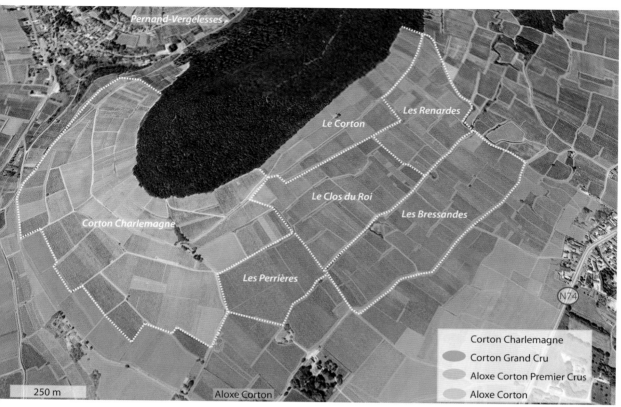

Vineyards wind around the hill of Corton. Corton Charlemagne is on the southwest slopes: some of these can also be used for grand cru Corton. Corton runs down from the top of the eastern flank; the most important of the climats in the grand cru are indicated. Aloxe Corton premier crus are below, and then Aloxe Corton village wines are at the bottom, ending at the N74.

Corton's main claim to fame is the white wine of Corton Charlemagne, which comes from an area on the end of the hill facing southwest. Its name reflects Emperor Charlemagne's ownership of vineyards on the hill; the story goes that the wine originated when he demanded white wine to avoid staining his beard with red. Actually, the proportions of red and white wine from Corton have changed dramatically with time. At the start of the nineteenth century, most Corton was red.[52] The focus on production changed to white during the twentieth century, and today some 72 ha are classified for the white Corton Charlemagne.[53] Some of this area can also be used for red; for example, the climat of Corton-Pougets is contained entirely within Corton Charlemagne. Corton Blanc describes white wine produced elsewhere in the grand cru.

The hill is based on a substratum of limestone, but there is a difference in the topsoil going up the slope, from more iron and pebbles lower down (thought to be better suited to Pinot Noir) to higher clay content at the top. But here as elsewhere, market forces push growers to replant with Chardonnay when vineyards come up for renewal.[54] Going round the hill from Aloxe Corton towards Pernand Vergelesses, there is more flint in the soil, giving more austerity to the white wine (and creating difficulties for black grapes in ripening.) So the terroir is far from homogeneous. Bonneau du Martray has the largest block on the hill, extending from Pernand Vergelesses to Aloxe Corton. "The styles provided by each block are quite distinct," says owner Jean-Charles le Bault de la Morinière. At its best, Corton Charlemagne has a wonderful rich generosity, with a touch of citrus cutting the stone fruits, and sometimes a sense of sternness that recalls the few white wines that are made on the Côte de Nuits. But given the variety of terroirs, there is no single character. The two extremes of styles are represented by the minerality of Bonneau du Martray and the full force opulence of Louis Latour.

Around Corton are what I think of as satellite appellations —Pernand-Vergelesses to the north, Savigny-lès-Beaune to the south, and Chorey-lès-Beaune to the east. They produce both red and white wines, with the best vineyards marked out as premier crus. Less well known than the major appellations along the core of the Côte d'Or, the wines are more straightforward, and can offer good value. Île-des-

Aloxe Corton has the best exposure on the northern part of the Côte de Beaune, with Pernand-Vergelesses facing more to the west, and Savigny-lès-Beaune and Chorey-lès-Beaune at lower elevations.

Vergelesses, at the border with Savigny-lès-Beaune, is generally considered the best of the premier crus of Pernand-Vergelesses. Adjacent to it, Les Vergelesses is considered one of the best premier crus of Savigny-lès-Beaune, so this is a favored patch, extending in fact to Les Lavières just beyond. Immediately to the east, most of the vineyards of Chorey-lès-Beaune are on the relatively flat land on the other side of the N74; the greater content of clay means that the wines here are not so fine, and there are no premier crus. Before Chorey was granted

In the sprawl of premier crus around Beaune, Clos des Mouches stands out as one of the best for both red and white wines.

its appellation in 1970, the wines were sold as Côte de Beaune Villages, and some still are.

The largest appellation on the Côte d'Or, Beaune is hard to pin down. Vineyards stretch from Savigny-lès-Beaune to Pommard. The large size, high number of premier crus, and the fact that they represent three quarters of the appellation, makes for what might kindly be described as variability in quality. (Personally I would demote several of the premier crus, and judging from the low prices they fetch, the market agrees with me.[55]) There is more Pinot Noir than Chardonnay in Beaune, but the whites can be finely structured, sometimes a little tight.

The effects of terroir are shown by the very different characteristics of two of the top premier crus. At the southern boundary of Beaune with Pommard, Clos des Mouches is calcareous. Terraces face from east to southeast and are relatively breezy. Two kilometers to the north, the steep slope of Grèves angles more east; the soil is clay and limestone, shallow with lots of stones and there is often a water deficit. (Grèves is local dialect for stony.) There is a lot of iron in the soil. Clos des Mouches is lighter with more aromatics and finesse, Grèves is sturdier with firmer tannins and structure.

Volnay and Pommard are the southernmost regions for the top red wines, but although they are adjacent, the communes have different styles. Volnay is the epitome of elegance, with precisely delineated red fruit flavors that at their best have a remarkable crystalline quality. Pommard has softer, lusher fruits,

Le Village
1 Clos de la Cave des Ducs
2 Clos de l'Audignac
3 Le Clos de la Chapelle
4 Clos de Château des Ducs
5 Le Village
6 Clos de la Rougeotte
7 Clos de La Bousse d'Or

The best premier crus in Volnay are close to the village. Numbers indicate monopoles in Le Village. Clos des Ducs, Taillepieds, and Champans are other top premier crus.

sometimes considered to be a touch rustic. What is responsible for the difference between the elegance of Volnay and the breadth of Pommard?

Volnay is one of the smaller communes; perhaps that is why there is more consistency to style and quality. It sits on a limestone base, with some variety in the types of limestone, but the base is generally light in color and relatively crumbly. The best plots in Volnay are close to the village. In fact, a premier cru called simply *Le Village* consists of various plots surrounding the village, but you rarely see Le Village on the label because most of these plots are monopoles whose proprietors use their individual names. Other top premier crus are Taillepieds, Champans, Clos des Chênes, and Caillerets.

At the northern boundary, Volnay joins Pommard, where the limestone-based soils have more clay. This is said to give the wines of Pommard their sturdier character. There's also more iron in Pommard, due to ferrous oxide in the soil. Volnay has finer tannins compared to Pommard. Benjamin Leroux, formerly of Comte Armand in Pommard, says that the differences are quite evident when you make the wine. "With Volnay the tannins are extracted slowly and tend to come at the end of fermentation. You don't have to look for extrac-

Many of the top vineyards in Volnay run right into the town, close to the church.

tion in Pommard, it is there straight away, because the tannins come at the beginning."

South of Volnay, the tip of the Côte de Beaune is white wine territory. Characterizing the differences between Meursault, Chassagne Montrachet, and Puligny Montrachet is complicated by the fact that each appellation has a wide variety of producer styles. Conventional wisdom identifies Meursault as soft, nutty, and buttery, while Chassagne Montrachet has a bit more of a citrus edge, and Puligny Montrachet is taut, precise, and mineral. Changes over the past decade or so, especially in Meursault, show that these styles are due only in part to the intrinsic character of each appellation.

Meursault is the largest of the three appellations. Although it has no grand crus, its top premier crus, Les Perrières, Les Genevrières, and Les Charmes, are excellent, with Les Perrières sometimes approaching grand cru quality. Some red wine is produced in Meursault, but the best is a premier cru that is actually labeled as Volnay Santenots. The whites used to be rich rather than mineral, although those of the top producer, Coche-Dury, tend towards a savory minerality. Others have now followed Coche Dury in a more mineral direction, most notably Arnaud Ente and Antoine Jobard. Comtes Lafon makes some of the

Reference Wines for Red Côte de Beaune	
Chorey-lès-Beaune	Tollot-Beaut
Savigny-lès-Beaune	Benjamin Leroux
Pernand-Vergelesses	Rapet Père et Fils, Île des Vergelesses
Corton	Louis Latour, Château Corton Grancey
Aloxe-Corton	Rapet Père et Fils
Beaune	Joseph Drouhin, Clos des Mouches
Pommard	Comte Armand
Volnay	Marquis d'Angerville
Blagny	Robert Ampeau
Saint Romain	Alain Gras
Auxey-Duresses	Comte Armand, premier cru
Santenay	Anne-Marie & Jean-Marc Vincent

longest-lived wines of the appellation, halfway in style between minerality and nuttiness, and his friend Jean-Marc Roulot at Domaine Guy Roulot makes elegant wines. The New Meursault, as I think of it, is as mineral as rich. Is the change to a more mineral focus now the typicity of Meursault, I asked Dominique Lafon. "I think it is typical for the good producers," he holds. At the southwest edge of Meursault is the village of Blagny, whose name appears on Meursault-Blagny premier cru and also in the Hameau de Blagny premier cru of Puligny Montrachet. There's also a Blagny premier cru red.

The typicity of Chassagne Montrachet is usually considered to lie between Meursault and Puligny Montrachet: not as rich as Meursault but not as precise as Puligny. It can be the softest of the three, and sometimes a little diffuse in character. There is more red wine in Chassagne Montrachet than either of the other two appellations; indeed, white wine took over here more recently, as a result of market pressure. The top premier crus are Morgeots (for me always the best), Caillerets, Ruchottes, Chaumées, and La Boudriotte.

Puligny Montrachet is for me the quintessence of white Burgundy: its steely minerality, the precision in the fruits, the sense of backbone—the combination is simply unique. Some of the premier crus are within a hair's breadth of grand cru quality, with Les Pucelles and Le Cailleret sometimes crossing the line. Other top premier crus are Les Demoiselles, Les Combettes, and Folatières. The hierarchy of Puligny is captured at Domaine Leflaive, where the classic style shows in the village wine, intensifies through the premier crus, and then with Les Pucelles or the grand crus adds a Rolls Royce sense of power to that steely finesse. The trend to increasing ripeness at most producers means that many premier crus now show richness before minerality.

Of course, the epitome of white wine is the grand cru Le Montrachet: I am in the camp of those who consider it potentially the greatest white wine in the world (depending of course on the producer). Chevalier Montrachet is usually

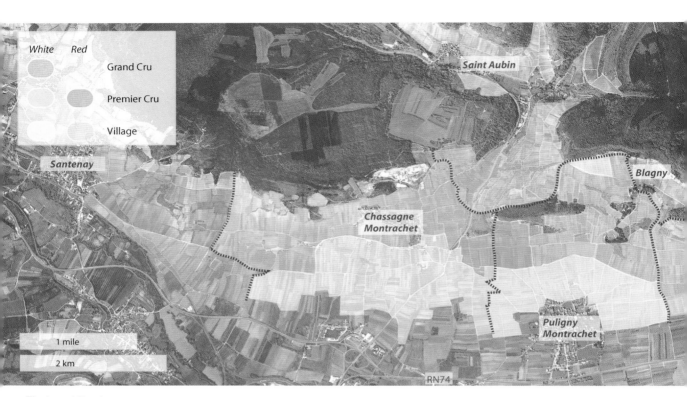

The top white wine appellations lie in a group to the south of Beaune. The line of premier and grand crus continues along the middle and upper slope.

considered second, followed by Bâtard-Montrachet and Bienvenues-Bâtard-Montrachet. Le Montrachet and Bâtard-Montrachet actually are only partly in Puligny Montrachet, with some of each vineyard across the border in Chassagne Montrachet. Criots-Bâtard-Montrachet is solely in Chassagne. The unique quality of these grand crus is that subtly shifting balance of power with finesse. Chardonnays from other sources may have one or the other, but I have yet to experience any other wine with both. In terms of the villages, Puligny Montrachet is clearly the closest in style to the grand crus, especially its top premier crus. In fact, village character may show most clearly at this level, as Le Montrachet itself can be so powerful as to subdue that steely minerality.

Adjacent to the great white wine appellations are the satellite appellations at the southern tip of the Côte de Beaune: Saint Romain, Auxey-Duresses, and Saint Aubin to the west, and Santenay just south of Chassagne Montrachet. These can be good sources for wines in similar style to Chassagne Montrachet, albeit less concentrated and complex, but at considerably lower prices than the more famous communes. The whites of St. Aubin are the best known, while Auxey-Duresses and Saint Romain have become more popular as St. Aubin has increased in price. "The vines in St. Aubin are relatively young because it used to be Pinot Noir, and much was replanted with Chardonnay thirty years ago. The appellation may have the opportunity to improve as the vines get older,"

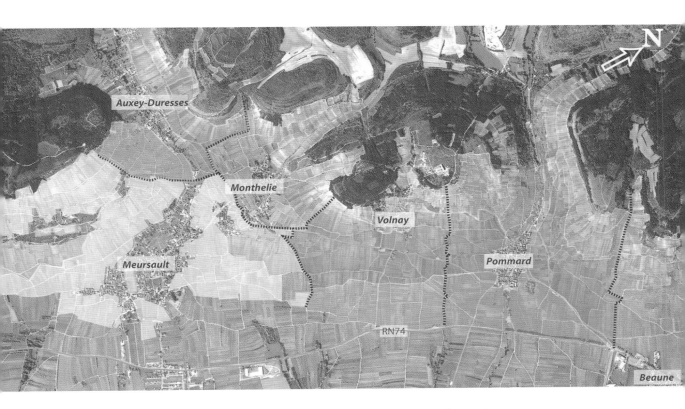

says Damien Colin of Domaine Marc Colin. Chassagne runs almost imperceptibly into Santenay, where vineyards lie along a valley with slopes at all angles.
"Strangely people stop at Chassagne, they don't always come to Santenay,"
says Anne-Marie Vincent in the village. The reds of the satellite appellations
are not usually quite so successful, sometimes failing to reach the roundness
that comes from the top communes, and not showing variations of terroir to the
same extent. The reds of Santenay are the best known, representing a somewhat softer version of Chassagne reds.

The great issue of the day in white Burgundy crosses all appellation
boundaries. This is premature oxidation, so prevalent today that it has become
known by the abbreviation of premox. Before premox became an issue, a village white Burgundy would probably last for six years or so, a premier cru
would not be ready to start for, say, four years, and would last for more than a
decade beyond the vintage, and grand crus would start even more slowly and
last even longer. The problem with premature oxidation first became widely
apparent with the 1996 vintage, when soon after 2000 many wines, even at
premier cru level, began to show signs of oxidation: deepening color, a madeirized nose, and drying out on the palate.

Given significant variability between individual bottles, the immediate reaction was that this was due to a problem with the corks (possibly due to changes

Chevalier Montrachet

Le Montrachet

Bâtard Montrachet

Bienvenues-Bâtard Montrachet

⟹ N

Le Montrachet is in the middle of the white grand crus, with Chevalier above it, and Bâtard and Bienvenues-Bâtard below it.

in the sterilization procedure). It soon became clear that the answer was not straightforward, and a variety of causes was proposed, ranging from changes in viticulture, pressing the juice too clean (because this removes anti-oxidants), too much battonage (stirring up the lees while the wine is in barrique), or reduced use of sulfur at bottling.

More than a decade on, however, no one has pinpointed any single cause, so no white Burgundy of more than three or four years old can be considered safe. This enormously shortens the period for drinking: you have to steer between the Scylla of new oak and the Charybdis of premox. Many wines, especially at the premier or grand cru level, have somewhat evident oak on release, and it takes two or three years for this to calm down; sometimes longer, as in the case of the 2005s, many of which still showed evident new oak in 2013. So not much time is left before premox might set in. My impression is that the problem is worse in the richer vintages (which previously would have been expected to be the more long lived). Fitting with that view, Chablis suffers less than whites from the Côte d'Or.[56] White Burgundy has become a wine that must be enjoyed young.

Dominique Lafon, who has been at the forefront of efforts to fix the problem, believes that premox is a perfect storm of many contributing factors. "What puzzled us was that it was very random. The first thing we thought was

Reference Wines for White Côte de Beaune	
Corton Charlemagne	Bonneau du Martray
Pernand-Vergelesses	Rapet Père et Fils, Clos du Village
Savigny-lès-Beaune	Simon Bize
Beaune	Joseph Drouhin, Clos des Mouches
Meursault	Comtes Lafon
Chassagne Montrachet	Louis Jadot, Clos de la Chapelle
Puligny Montrachet	Domaine Leflaive
Saint Romain	Deux Montille
Auxey-Duresses	Benjamin Leroux
Saint Aubin	Hubert Lamy
Santenay	Anne-Marie & Jean-Marc Vincent
Bourgogne Aligoté	Pierre Morey

that we had cork failures—I think we did—but it was showing the fragility of the wine," he says. He's changed a variety of procedures to make vinification more reductive, and believes the issue has finally been resolved. The underlying problem was that the wines did not have enough resistance to oxidation, so the slightest problem with the cork would allow oxidation. This explains the random occurrence. "Even in the cellars here, one in four bottles of white Beaune from 1999 is oxidized, but the others are absolutely fine," Philippe Drouhin told me in 2010, "so what can it be but the cork?" The cork is certainly a factor, and my own experience is that bottles with unusually tight corks do not seem to show premox problems, but since producers are unwilling to change to screwcaps, the important thing is to ensure that the wines are more resistant to oxidation.

Côte Chalonnaise

The five villages of the Côte Chalonnaise extend for about twenty miles to the immediate south of the Côte d'Or. Viticulture is interspersed with other sorts of agriculture. The wines follow the style of the Côte de Beaune, but the fruits achieve less concentration. There is less use of new oak, and the wines are tighter. Most villages have a large number of premier crus. For the most part, Côte Chalonnaise has its own producers, although some appellations have negociants who have come from the Côte d'Or, the two leading examples being Faiveley in Mercurey and Louis Latour in Montagny.

The Bouzeron AOP is a rare source for Aligoté (the other being the more generic Bourgogne Aligoté). Growers

Bouzeron
60 ha, 26,500 cases, Aligoté

Rully
360 ha, 180,000 cases, 67% red

Mercurey
650 ha, 310,000 cases, 81% red

Givry
270 ha, 140,000 cases, 82% red

Montagny
310 ha, 190,000 cases, white

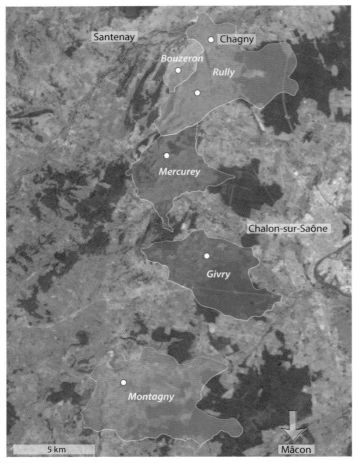

The Côte Chalonnaise has five AOPs.

have to decide whether to label their wines as Bouzeron (without mentioning the grape variety, which might therefore come as a surprise to the uninitiated) or whether to admit the variety but to use the lower appellation label of AOP Bourgogne Aligoté.

Aside from Bouzeron, the objective here is to achieve a level of reliability for Pinot Noir or Chardonnay in a mainstream style. With Côte Chalonnaise you don't get the fat, the richness, the uplift of the Côte d'Or, and this is more of a problem for the reds than the whites. The difference from the Côte d'Or is clear if you compare wines directly from those producers who have vineyards in both areas. Both reds and whites are generally best drunk young while still fresh and charming; it's a bit doubtful how much extra complexity is gained by long aging. The limit for whites is usually about five years after release. Reds are best after three or four years, but will last another three or four.

The largest village, Mercurey, makes the firmest red wines, although they sometimes reveal a slightly hard edge. There is a counterpoise between a superficial rich glycerinic sheen to the fruits and that touch of hardness on the finish. Givry produces mostly red wines in much the same style, perhaps not quite as firm. The reds of Rully are lighter. "For me, Rully always has more elegance, finesse; Mercurey has more depth, it's more robust," says Marie Jacqueson in Rully. Similarly, the relatively rare whites of Mercurey or Givry tend to have less overt fruit compared with Rully.

Montagny is an appellation for white wines only. It has the distinction that all its vineyards were classified as premier cru in 1943, although they were reduced when the appellation was extended in 1989. But this still means that premier cru is a less reliable description in Montagny than elsewhere, although only about half the names are used anyway. Montagny also stands out for the

Reference wines for Côte Chalonnaise	
Bouzeron	Domaine A. & P. Villaine
Givry (red)	François Lumpp, Petit Marole
Mercurey (red)	Paul et Marie Jacqueson, Les Naugues
Mercurey (white)	Château de Chamirey, La Mission
Montagny	Stéphane Aladame, Les Maroques
Rully (red)	Vincent Dureuil-Janthial, Chapitre
Rully (white)	Vincent Dureuil-Janthial, Les Meix Cadot

loss of independent domains and the rise of the cooperative at Buxy, which now accounts for almost three quarters of production.

Aside from Faiveley, the big name in Mercurey is the Château de Chamirey, where a policy of late picking gives unusually ripe wines for the appellation. Rully is dominated by Vincent Dureuil-Janthial, whose wide range of cuvées from premier crus show unusual refinement for Côte Chalonnaise, and an interesting comparison with his wines from the Côte d'Or. The domain of Paul and Marie Jacqueson is a growing concern that offers an opportunity to compare Rully with Mercurey and Bouzeron. The most interesting wines in Montagny come from Stéphane Aladame, who specializes in the premier crus.

The whites are the strongest point of Côte Chalonnaise. At their best they can approach the flavor spectrum of the Côte d'Or, although they rarely achieve the same depth or flavor variety. Reds tend more to show the limitations of the Chalonnaise, but there are definite terroir differences between the appellations.

Chablis stands alone from the rest of Burgundy, both geographically and psychologically. Well to the north, it has the most marginal climate; ripening has traditionally been a problem. It's been the epitome of minerality in white wine, traditionally very different from the fleshiness of the Côte d'Or. Its geology is distinctive, based on the famous Kimmeridgian limestone, a soft mixture of clay and limestone, generally gray in color. This was laid down when the sea retreated in the Jurassic period, leaving a bed of fossils that give the soil its calcareous nature.[57] Kimmeridgian limestone occupies about half of the Chablis region; the rest consists of Portlandian limestone, harder in structure and browner in color.[58]

When the Chablis AOC was defined in 1938, the total vineyard area was only 400 ha, and AOC Chablis vineyards were confined to Kimmeridgian limestone. This

	hectares	cases
Petit Chablis	782	500,000
Chablis	3,256	2 million
40 Premier Crus	776	475,000
7 Grand Crus	103	60,000

175 Producers = 75% production
1 Cooperative = 25% production
(280 growers)

The vineyards of Chablis lie on either side of the valley of the river Serein, which runs through the town.

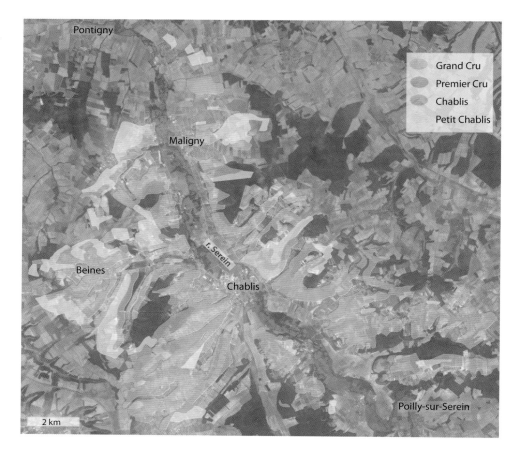

remained true as the AOC expanded to include vineyards in communes around Chablis, but "with the exclusion of parcels not situated on Kimmeridgian soil."[59] Wines produced on the Portlandian limestone never achieved the same quality. But in 1978, when a further expansion occurred, the restriction was dropped.[60] It's hard to better producer William Fèvre's protest at the time: "These areas of woodland and scrub have never had Chardonnay vines in the past. When these bounds are passed, there are no longer any limits."[61]

Chablis comes from both banks of the river Serein, extending away from the town, and has a simple hierarchy with four levels of vineyards. Petit Chablis is a lesser wine made from outlying areas. The most important vineyards are near the town. The premier crus are not quite as numerous as they might seem from the variety of labels, because many have separate names for different areas within them. Just opposite the town on the right bank, there is nominally one grand cru divided into seven *climats*, but it is far easier just to regard this as comprising seven Grand Cru descriptions.

The grand crus occupy a continuous slope, but the land folds and turns so there are changes in exposure and slope, with significant variation in character.

The labels on the image, from left to right: ros, Les Preuses, Vaudésir, Grenouilles, Valmur, Les Clos, Blanchot, Montée de Tonnerre

The minerality of Chablis is at its peak in Les Clos, which is the largest part. Whenever a producer has more than one grand cru, their Les Clos stands out for its reserve when young, which translates into greater longevity. Valmur is usually richer and less mineral; Vaudésir has an intensity that can border on spicy. Les Preuses has more of a perfumed quality; Blanchots can be delicate; and Grenouilles, at the foot of the slope, is firmer; while Bougros is considered to be the slightest. There are three premier crus on the right bank: Fourchaume is just to the north; Montée de Tonnerre, across a deep gully to the south, is usually the best premier cru; and Mont de Milieu is parallel to it farther south.

On the left bank, Chablis is really a series of valleys, fanning out from the town. As there are vineyards on both sides of the valleys, they face in all directions. Usually the premier crus are the most south facing. Montmains and Vaillons, which are the best of the premier crus on the left bank, have similar exposures on parallel hillsides in adjacent valleys, as does Léchet. Usually in Burgundy there's a fine line between premier crus and grand crus, with some premier crus standing out above the others and occasioning argument as to whether they should be promoted to grand cru. In Chablis the argument is more at the other end: there is doubt whether many of the premier crus created in 1978 merit the description.[62]

Because of its cooler climate, Chablis today is thought of as a crisper, more mineral wine than Côte d'Or, but historically the difference was not so obvious. In the fourteenth century, wine from Auxerre (just to the west of Chablis) sold at a higher price than wine from Beaune.[63] Before phylloxera, in fact, Auxerre was close to a monoculture of vines, but it never recovered.[64] Chablis is essentially what remains. Just to the southwest, the tiny AOP of Sauvignon St. Bris is the one place in Burgundy where Sauvignon Blanc is allowed, and adjacent to it lies Irancy AOP, where Pinot Noir is grown. Some Chablis producers also have small vineyards in these appellations. Chablis was very much a minor region until recently, but with around 5,000 ha today, it's comparable to the Côte de Beaune. With this revival has come something of a change in style.

The grand crus form a single continuous line of vineyards with varying slopes and exposures. Premier Cru Montée de Tonnerre lies across a gully at the end of the slope.

"They were all so bad in Chablis twenty years ago. For me, concentration is important, lower yields and riper. But everyone said, we are making Chablis, it's never ripe, the typical Chablis is green. People said, when you make ripe Chablis, it loses its character. But you can't make wine from unripe grapes—all green wines taste the same," says negociant Jean-Marie Guffens, who makes a wide range of Chablis at Verget. Today the rest of Chablis has caught up, and that increase in ripeness is typical of the entire appellation. If effects of global warming on white wine are evident anywhere in Burgundy, it's in Chablis.

The first time I tasted a Chablis from Verget, I was certainly surprised: its density and fatness of structure were quite unusual. It seemed to mark a move in the direction of the Côte d'Or. Jean-Marie's view, of course, would be that instead of surrendering to a traditional view that Chablis is inevitably thin and acid, he was bringing out the true potential of the region. Today this would not be so surprising: in the rich vintages of 2002, 2005, and 2009, many Chablis at premier or grand cru level have moved towards the richer style of the Côte d'Or. (Of course, the whites of the Côte d'Or have also become richer.)

"Global warming has been beneficial for Chablis. My father would have been the happiest of men with the quality of the poorest years we had in the past decade," says Bernard Raveneau of Domaine François Raveneau. Didier Seguier at William Fèvre thinks global warming is a great opportunity, giving better wines that retain acidity and balance, but without losing character. "The typicity of our wine comes from the Kimmeridgian terroir, it's very different (from the Côte d'Or). Warming gives a very interesting maturity today but not sur-maturity."

The big divide in Chablis used to be between producers who do or do not use oak. This is no longer so obvious, perhaps partly because richer vintages have brought some convergence of style. Many producers now use a mixture of maturation in cuve and barrique. Where partial oak is used, the wine may spend only six months in oak before assemblage with the wine from cuve, after which it spends another six months in cuve only. In Chablis, the proportions of cuve and (old) oak are adjusted; in contrast with the Côte d'Or, where the difference between cuvées lies in the proportion of new oak to old oak.

Two producers stand out in the oak camp: François Raveneau and Vincent Dauvissat. But neither uses any new oak. Each house is notable for the subtlety of its style. Is global warming a threat to that subtlety? "No, personally I think the place will adjust. I harvest early, the terroir resets the balance, it's the backbone of the wine," says Vincent Dauvissat. Minerality is always there as a thread running from nose through palate to finish, fruits tend to the citrus spectrum but with hints of stone fruits more evident in warmer vintages, and there's a delicious overtone of anise or liquorice on the finish. Les Clos is the epitome of the style for both producers, always showing a more evident streak of structure, with Valmur placing second for Raveneau, and Les Preuses second for Dauvissat. Montée de Tonnerre is the best of the premier crus for both.

Other producers in the oak camp have their own styles. At Jean-Paul and Benoît Droin, the style is richer, and the various crus have different maturation

Reference Wines for Chablis	
Petit Chablis	Vincent Dauvissat
Chablis	Jean-Claude Bessin
Fourchaume	William Fèvre
Mont de Milieu	Louis Pinson
Montmains	Domaine Laroche
Montée de Tonnerre	Benoit Droin Louis Michel
Vaillons	Christian Moreau
Blanchots	Domaine Laroche
Bougros	William Fèvre
Preuses	Vincent Dauvissat
Vaudésir	Billaud Simon
Valmur	François Raveneau
Les Clos	François Raveneau Vincent Dauvissat

regimes. Stainless steel is used for Chablis AOP, some premier crus, and Blanchots, but Mont de Milieu and Montée de Tonnerre have 25% oak, which increases to 35% for Vaudésir, 40% for Montmains and Valmur, and 50% for Fourchaume and Les Clos. The interesting feature is that there isn't a straight increase going from premier crus to grand crus, as would be usual in the Côte d'Or, but a view that different terroirs have different potentials for handling oak. There is a little new oak here, but less than there used to be, now limited to no more than 10% in the grand crus. Even William Fèvre, who used to overload his top Chablis with new oak, has now backed off significantly.

The arch exponent of the unoaked style is Louis Michel, whose premier and grand crus often achieve a complexity creating the impression in blind tasting that they must have been matured in oak. But the use of barriques stopped forty years ago; since then the wines have been vinified exclusively in stainless steel. In fact, the texture and structure are due to slow fermentation followed by time on the lees (typically 6 months for Chablis, 12 months for premier cru, and 18 months for grand cru). The top wines have an almost granular texture supporting what is perhaps more a sense of steel and stone than overt minerality. They are great wines, although I don't think they have quite the same longevity as the oaked style.

Once you leave the grand crus and top premier crus behind, Chablis is a good deal less interesting. It's certainly worth paying the (relatively) modest premium for a premier cru compared to communal Chablis. Like all Burgundy, the producer's name is of paramount importance, and negociants are definitely well in second place behind the individual growers (Verget and Patrick Piuze being notable exceptions), but it's worth noting that Chablis has one of the better recognized cooperatives in the country, La Chablisienne, which is responsible for around a quarter of all production.

cases white wine	
Mâcon	50,000
Mâcon Villages	1,250,000
Mâcon with village name	850,000
Viré-Clessé	250,000
Saint Véran	430,000
Pouilly-Loché	16,000
Pouilly-Vinzelles	19,000
Pouilly-Fuissé	430,000
Total white	3,000,000
Red	
Mâcon	130,000
Mâcon Villages	80,000

Mâcon stretches from just south of the Côte Chalonnaise to the border with Beaujolais, but very little wine is bottled as Mâcon plain and simple. About 60% of the area is classified as Mâcon Villages, and about 40% of that consists of individual villages whose names can be added after Mâcon, such as Mâcon-Lugny (which accounts for a major part of the individual village wines). Altogether Mâcon Villages accounts for about two thirds of all production. Almost all the wine is white, exclusively from Chardonnay, although there is a little red and rosé (from Gamay) in the Mâcon appellation and from some of the individual villages. Most of the named villages are clustered in the southern half of the appellation, where the town of Mâcon itself is situated.

There are also some individual appellations within the Mâconnais. Viré-Clessé, which was created in 1999 by merging the former village AOCs of Mâcon-Viré and Mâcon-Clessé, is in the center, but the others are located at the southern tip. By far the best known is Pouilly-Fuissé, accompanied by the much smaller satellites of Pouilly-Loché and Pouilly-Vinzelles. Split into two parts, the appellation of St. Véran straddles Pouilly-Fuissé and presents wines that used to be labeled as white Beaujolais.

Mâcon is usually a relatively straightforward wine, vinified and matured in stainless steel. The main difference between the named villages and the general Mâcon Villages appellation is a requirement for slightly greater

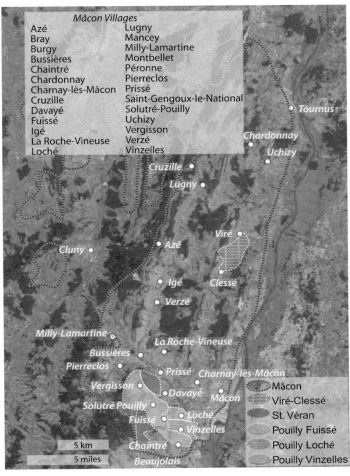

The best-known appellations and villages are clustered in the southern part of the Mâconnais.

ripeness (a named village must achieve at least 11% natural alcohol, compared with 10.5% for Mâcon Villages), but there is no great change in style, and it would be overly ambitious to try to define differences between individual villages. The main importance of the village name is to indicate higher quality. The general style is fruity rather than mineral.

There's a feeling that local interests aren't best served by the predominance of negociants who almost all come from the north. Most Mâcon—around three quarters—is made by negociants; four big negociants from Beaune have around 80% of the negociant market.[65] The largest local negociant is Georges Duboeuf, but his focus is mostly on reds from Beaujolais. Yet there has been significant improvement in the quality of Mâcon at all levels in the past couple of decades, partly driven by growers from the Côte d'Or. Comtes Lafon of Meursault came to Milly-Lamartine in 1999, and Domaine Leflaive purchased

The village of Fuissé is in the heart of the Pouilly appellations, surrounded by vineyards on slopes.

vineyards in Macon-Verzé in 2003. Undoubtedly the most distinctive local negociant is Maison Verget, established by Jean-Marie Guffens in 1990, following the establishment of Guffens-Heynen as a small grower in 1979.

The wines from Guffens-Heynen mark the full potential of the region, and those of Verget show what can be done within practical limitations. "They are completely different," says Jean-Marie. "When you purchase grapes at Verget, you buy an appellation. When you buy Guffens, you buy a spirit. At Verget I work with pre-printed words but at the domain I have a blank page. We have a philosophy at Verget, but at the domain we don't have a philosophy. At the domain there is no leading idea. At Verget the philosophy is to make good wine within appellation rules at a decent price. We try to make wines as personal as possible, admitting the grapes are not grown as I would grow them. The cost price of picking at the domain is higher than the price I pay for the grapes for Verget."

Part of Jean-Marie's success in redefining the region comes from a difference in perspective. "People say no wood for Macon, but a lot for Bâtard Montrachet because it's a great wine. It's stupid, of course. My view is that all wines have to have the same treatment in order to show the terroir. I change

my barrels every five years so there will be no difference between Corton Charlemagne and Mâcon-Vergisson." The Guffens-Heynen wines, from Mâcon-
Pierreclos, St. Véran, and Pouilly-Fuissé, all convey a textured impression of
coming from grander appellations. With a very wide range of cuvées from
Mâcon Villages to Pouilly-Fuissé, Verget's wines offer an unusual opportunity
to see what difference terroir makes in the Mâconnais. (Verget also produces
many cuvées of Chablis and some of Côte d'Or.) Jean-Marie acknowledges
differences, but does not believe they are the only pertinent factor: "Today we
are in terroir-ism—the terroir does everything; no, it doesn't. It's only part. It
would be stupid to say I want the wine to taste only like the terroir, only like
the grapes, only like the vintage, or only like me. The first thing is to make the
wine purely, precisely." So moving from Mâcon to St. Véran to Pouilly-Fuissé,
the Verget wines show increasing fruit concentration and a more subtle range
of flavors, rather than changing in style. It's as clear a view of the region as can
be found.

The great name in the region is Pouilly-Fuissé. "Pouilly-Fuissé used to be a
big brand name in the U.S., and visitors were very upset to come here and find
only a small village," says Frédéric-Marc Burrier of Château de Beauregard. In
fact, there are multiple Pouillys, and in the nineteenth century all the wine was
known simply as Pouilly. When the appellation contrôlée was formed, four of
the villages decided to join Pouilly-Fuissé, but Loché and Vinzelles stayed out,
becoming separate appellations. This may not have been so clever, as Pouilly-
Loché and Pouilly-Vinzelles tend to be regarded now as distinctly second rank
compared to Pouilly-Fuissé.

The general distinction between the Pouilly's and the surrounding appellations is that the Pouilly vineyards are on the slopes, and at the bottom the AOP
changes to Mâcon. So Mâcon-Vinzelles comes from vineyards just below those
of Pouilly-Vinzelles. (Similarly, when Viré-Clessé was created from the best
parcels on the slopes above the villages in the old Mâcon-Viré and Mâcon-
Clessé appellations, the rest became Mâcon Villages.)

Pouilly-Fuissé is far from homogeneous. "There is no typicity in Pouilly-
Fuissé; it all depends on the villages. Chaintré is always fruity, Vergisson is
more mineral," says Jean-Philippe Bret at La Soufrandière in Fuissé. The big
question then becomes whether to blend across the villages or to represent
them in separate cuvées. The trend today is towards defining individual vineyards. "We are working hard to define premier crus. We think it has been really
damaging for Mâcon to be the only area in Burgundy without a hierarchy of
appellations," says Frédéric-Marc Burrier, in his capacity as president of the
growers association. "We were using our best *climats* with an additional indication on the label before the war in exactly the same way as the Côte d'Or,"
he says ruefully, "but when Burgundy introduced the premier cru system, here
they had a letter asking them to classify premier crus, but the president of the

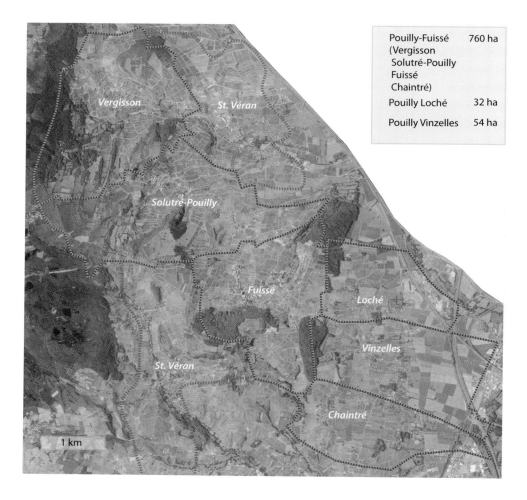

Pouilly-Fuissé consists of four villages; Pouilly Loché and Pouilly Vinzelles are separate appellations.

Pouilly-Fuissé (Vergisson Solutré-Pouilly Fuissé Chaintré)	760 ha
Pouilly Loché	32 ha
Pouilly Vinzelles	54 ha

time did nothing about it. So Mâcon became the only part of Burgundy not to have premier crus and we have been paying for that ever since. We studied the history carefully, and we are asking for about 25 different premier crus, which may amount to around 20% of the appellation." The introduction of a hierarchy will also have the effect of encouraging growers to bottle their own wines, which is perhaps a major (unstated) intention.

Terroirs have been much better defined as part of the preparation for premier crus. Frédéric-Marc maintains that, "The reputation of Pouilly-Fuissé for opulent, rich wines is quite wrong, we have wonderful variety of terroirs, we have all those levels mixed up from different geological periods, we have identified fifty different types of soil and geology. There's a million years' difference between the soils. We can find mineral Pouilly-Fuissé and we can find rich Pouilly-Fuissé from clay all over the appellation."

A tasting at Château de Beauregard illustrates the range of terroir differences in Pouilly-Fuissé. Around ten cuvées from different climats range from precise

The famous rock formation of Solutré looms over the vineyards in the northern part of Pouilly-Fuissé.

and elegant to full bodied. Each is distinctive. And a vertical tasting going back four decades gives a stunning impression of the capacity of Pouilly-Fuissé to age. I would place the wines from seventies in the eighties, and the wines from the eighties in the nineties. These are terrific examples of the potential for aging, achieving a complexity more like what you expect from Meursault than Pouilly-Fuissé.

A move to precision is a common trend at top producers. "What we have at Domaine Ferret is the modern Pouilly-Fuissé, wines that let the grapes speak, and they vary significantly with the terroir. It might be hard to recognize these wines for some who have a stereotypical view of Pouilly-Fuissé with oak covering up the fruits. We are seeing a transparency now that gives a new view of the appellation and the wines," says Audrey Braccini, who took over winemaking at Ferret after Jadot bought the estate.

After tasting through the cuvées of Les Combettes, Le Clos, and Les Brûlées at Château Fuissé, winemaker Antoine Vincent says, "You were asking if there was a single style for Pouilly-Fuissé, here you have all three!" The lightest, Les Combettes, comes from deep soils on limestone, and is aged in old barriques.

Reference Wines for Mâconnais	
Mâcon Villages	Maison Verget
Mâcon-Milly Lamartine	Héritiers de Comtes Lafon
Mâcon-Pierreclos	Guffens-Heynen, Le Chavigne
Mâcon-Verzé	Domaine Leflaive
Viré-Clessé	André Bonhomme, Cuvée Spéciale
St. Véran	Guffens-Heynen, Cuvée Unique
Pouilly-Loché	Bret Brothers
Pouilly-Vinzelles	Domaine la Soufrandière, Les Quarts
Pouilly-Fuissé	Château de Beauregard, Les Charmes
	Château Fuissé, Le Clos
	Domaine Ferret, Le Clos

Just behind the winery, the slope of Le Clos has enough variation to justify older oak for the plots at the top and younger oak for the bottom. Les Brulées comes from the most powerful soils of the domain and uses 100% new oak. So here is a completely Burgundian view: "As I go to more powerful soils I use more oak and more new oak."

By the criterion that there is a difference in character and increase in complexity, not merely an increase in reliable ripeness, there are several *climats* in Pouilly-Fuissé that are worthy of individual recognition. The application for premier crus (which must be approved by INAO) has not had universal agreement in the appellation, although most top growers are in support. Its main effect may be not so much to increase recognition (and prices) for the crus, as to counteract the idea of Pouilly-Fuissé as a relatively homogeneous lower-priced alternative to the Côte d'Or, and to place it on its own pedestal.

Beaujolais Nouveau	3 million cases
Beaujolais	10,000 ha
	55 hl/ha
	2 million cases
	3,000 producers
Beaujolais Villages	6,000 ha
	50 hl/ha
	2 million cases
	1,250 producers
Crus	6,340 ha
	48 hl/ha
	4 million cases
	50-500 producers per Cru

Gamay was common all over Burgundy until the twentieth century, but today is virtually confined to Beaujolais, where the amount of red wine production is about half of Burgundy's total production. The amount of white Beaujolais is insignificant.[66] The relationship between Beaujolais and Burgundy has become rather sensitive, although there is little connection between the wines. A loophole in the regulations permitted the labels Bourgogne Rouge and Bourgogne Blanc to be used for Beaujolais, allowing Bourgogne Rouge to be Gamay,[67] and allowing Beaujolais growers to plant Chardonnay to compete with Bourgogne Blanc. "The Burgundy liner is heading straight for the iceberg of Beaujolais, risking drowning those who paid for the voyage," said a statement issued by the Syndicat des Bourgogne.[68] Responding to this pressure, the rules were changed in 2011 so that only wine from the Beaujolais Crus can be labeled as Bourgogne, but it must say Bourgogne Gamay if it has more than 30% Gamay.[69] The appellation Coteaux Bourguignon, which can be made from Chardonnay or Pinot Noir or Gamay from anywhere in the region, can be used by any red Beaujolais. Half the villages in Beaujolais lost the right to use Bourgogne Blanc for white wine and have to use Beaujolais Blanc, but the others can continue to use Bourgogne Blanc.

Beaujolais falls into three areas. The entire region is entitled to use the description, Beaujolais, but most of the wine labeled as Beaujolais AOP comes from the southern part. The higher level of Beaujolais Villages comes from the northern part. Unlike the Côtes du Rhône, where the Villages AOP consists of islands surrounded by the generic appellation, in Beaujolais the Villages is a large, contiguous area. Within it are the ten crus, each of which is entitled to label its wine solely with the name of the cru.

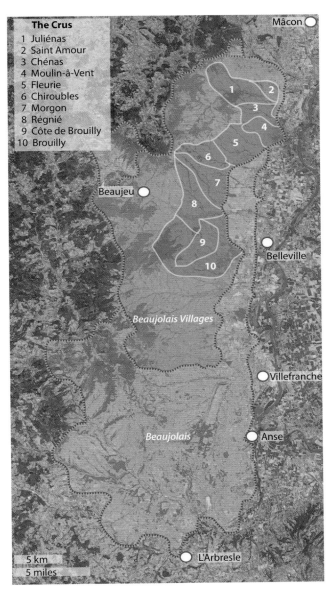

The Crus
1 Juliénas
2 Saint Amour
3 Chénas
4 Moulin-à-Vent
5 Fleurie
6 Chiroubles
7 Morgon
8 Régnié
9 Côte de Brouilly
10 Brouilly

Beaujolais AOP largely occupies the southern part of the area. Beaujolais Villages is the northern part, and the crus are located within the Villages region.

"Classification in Beaujolais is a matter of granite," says Georges Duboeuf.[70] This is the distinction between the areas of Beaujolais and Beaujolais Villages. A band of granite runs between Mâcon and Villefranche, and more or less fills the width of the Beaujolais Villages. The terrain in the Beaujolais AOP to the south is a mix of sedimentary clay and some limestone.

A view of the hills of the Beaujolais from Croix de Rochefort. Courtesy Beaujolais Vignoble.

The only black grape grown in Beaujolais is Gamay, and there is general agreement that it does best on granite. Gamay is not very widely grown—it's also found in the Loire and the Rhône, but much goes into rosé—so there isn't much experience in comparing a variety of terroirs. But I suspect that it's not so much that granite is especially suitable for Gamay (rather than other cépages), but that it brings a tautness needed to counteract a natural tendency to show blowsy fruits. But Gamay should not be heavy: until the past decade or so, chaptalization was something of a problem in giving the wines an artificial weight. "A lot of people in Beaujolais feel that if you don't have 13% alcohol, your wine won't age; people make a connection between alcohol and quality, but I think that's a big mistake," says Louis-Benoît Desvignes in Morgon. Warmer vintages, and an especially good run from 2009 to 2012, mean that lately much more of the alcohol has been natural.

Beaujolais has been in crisis for the past half century. Production of Beaujolais has more than halved since 1999, Beaujolais Villages has fallen almost as much, and the crus have fared only a little better.[71] Gamay is not in favor: over the same period, generic Bourgogne AOP, which is Pinot Noir, decreased slightly, but Bourgogne Passe-Tout-Grains, which includes Gamay, dropped by more than half.[72] Part of the problem is a perception that Beaujolais means low quality. Indeed, a local magazine, *Lyon Mag*, published an interview with oenologist François Mauss in 2002 under the title "Le Beaujolais, c'est de la merde." The producers did the worst possible thing: they sued for libel.[73] They won a decidedly pyrrhic victory; the resulting publicity did nothing to help Beaujolais. (The award was subsequently overturned on appeal.)

Beaujolais production really falls into four categories: independent producers; cooperatives; negociants; and Georges Duboeuf. Although they are the driving force for innovation, independent producers are the smallest part of the mix. About half produce all levels from Beaujolais to crus, a third produce only Beaujolais, and a sixth produce only crus.[74] Cooperatives account for more than a third of production.[75] The negociant scene has been changing as the large negociants in Burgundy, just to the north, have seen value in Beaujolais, and have been acquiring the local houses (and sometimes also land). This may lead to an improvement in quality.

For many the region is synonymous with Georges Duboeuf, who established a negociant business in the Beaujolais in 1964. "My ancestors were vignerons at Chaintré for four centuries. I inherited 4 ha of vineyards at Pouilly-Fuissé, not very large, but I was sure of the quality of my wine and started by selling Pouilly-Fuissé everywhere. People said to me, the Pouilly-Fuissé is very good, but we need a good red. So I started to buy and bottle wine," is how Georges recollects the beginning. Known for his remarkable palate and eye for quality, he now produces a range of Beaujolais across all levels. "Hameau Duboeuf," as his winery at Romanèche-Thorins is now signposted, has become a vast enterprise. By far the largest producer of Beaujolais Nouveau, his firm alone is responsible for a significant part of all Beaujolais production, buying grapes (but no longer wine) from more than 400 growers.[76] Reports variously place Duboeuf's share of all Beaujolais production between 20% and 40%—"Yes, it's something like that," says export manager Romain Teyteau offhandedly when asked for the exact figure. Total production is probably actually around 15-20% of Beaujolais' total of 100 million bottles. While Duboeuf is ineradicably associated with Beaujolais Nouveau, he also produces Beaujolais, Beaujolais Villages, and an extensive series of wines from all the crus, including a substantial number of single vineyard cuvées.

released 3rd Thursday in November
30% of all Beaujolais
50% exported

1982: 3 million cases
1999: 5 million cases
1995: 6 million cases
1982: 6 million cases
1970: 1 million cases

"The most difficult to vinify of all the wines is Beaujolais Nouveau, because it is very fast and depends on technique," says Georges Duboeuf. Beaujolais Nouveau has been at once the resurrection and the downfall of Beaujolais. Beaujolais has always been sold young: called Beaujolais Primeur, through the nineteenth century it was

LES VENDANGES – Un Cuvage en Beaujolais
Départ du vin nouveau

often sold as barrels in which the wine was still fermenting. By the time it reached its destination, it was ready to sell to the consumer! In the twentieth century it was released early in the bistros of nearby Lyon. Today AOP wines cannot be sold until December 15 following the harvest, but an exception is made for "nouveau" wines sold "en primeur." The rule now is that Nouveau wine can be shipped from the second Thursday in November in order to be available worldwide for sale a week later.[77]

Beaujolais Nouveau was about 10% of all production when it first became known by this name in the 1950s.[78] Production of Beaujolais doubled by the 1980s, and Nouveau increased to more than a quarter. At the peak it was significantly more than half of all production, but today it's in decline.[79] Sales are falling worldwide, except for Japan, where the rhythm of the annual ritual remains appealing.[80] In its time, Beaujolais Nouveau was a lifesaver. Sales of Beaujolais were depressed through the 1950s, and the novelty, or perhaps one might say the gimmick, of Beaujolais Nouveau gave a much-needed lift. Beaujolais Nouveau has always been a marketing phenomenon. Races to get the first Beaujolais Nouveau to Paris or to London by unusual means attracted publicity, at its peak involving a hoopla of balloons, parachutes, racing cars, or even supersonic Concord at the end of the century. The slogan *Le Beaujolais Nouveau est Arrivé"* became so effective that it was a rare wine shop that did not have it on a placard in the window on November 15.[81]

Nouveau solved a problem by making something that was acceptable to consumers from vineyards that had not been able to succeed with more conventional wine. But the solution lasted only so long as Beaujolais Nouveau was

One of the more successful recent stunts for presenting Beaujolais Nouveau was a motorcycle cavalcade of chefs through New York led by Franck Duboeuf in November 2008. Courtesy Melanie Young.

in vogue. The more general problem is not really with Beaujolais Nouveau as such, but with collateral damage. Beaujolais Nouveau is certainly different from other wine; fermentation has barely finished when the wine is bottled, and it might more appropriately be called "fermented grape juice" than wine. But it dominates the image of Beaujolais. Fresh, tart, and (sometimes) fruity, with the aromas of fermentation still much in evidence, it needs to be drunk within a few weeks. Most Beaujolais has always been made for early drinking, but Beaujolais Nouveau is the extreme case.

During the 1970s and 1980s, when the phenomenon peaked, Beaujolais Nouveau really pulled the region out of trouble. But its reputation among more serious wine drinkers is terrible. "The Nouveau has destroyed our image. All of Beaujolais is confused with Nouveau," says Jean-Pierre Large, director of Domaine Cheysson in Chiroubles,[82] pointing to the problem that putting "Beaujolais" on the label is tantamount to telling the consumer that quality (and price) must be limited. "The reputation of Beaujolais is very bad because of Beaujolais Nouveau. But Beaujolais and Beaujolais Villages are made in the same way as the crus," says Baptiste Condemine at Domaine des Souchons. The basic problem is that anything with Beaujolais on the label is stamped with the impression created by Beaujolais Nouveau.

With the exception of some top wines from the crus, Beaujolais is made by a method called semi-carbonic maceration. This requires the vats to be filled with whole clusters of berries (so there is no destemming). Fermentation takes place within the berries, releasing carbon dioxide, which maintains an oxygen-free atmosphere. This is carbonic maceration. However, juice is released from

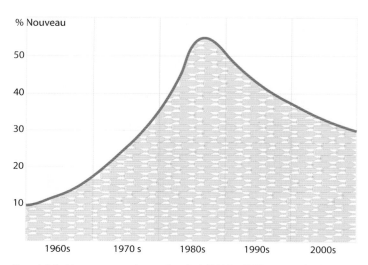

% Nouveau

Beaujolais Nouveau rose from a level of 10% in 1960 to a peak of 55% in 1986 before falling to its present 30% of all Beaujolais.

berries that are broken, and the stems form a network allowing the juice to surround the berries. The juice also ferments (conventionally, catalyzed by yeast), so the overall process is called semi-carbonic maceration. Typically when the process is about half complete, the free juice is run off, the remaining berries are pressed, the free-run and pressed juice are combined, and fermentation is completed just like for any red wine. The minimal exposure of the juice to the skins means that little tannin is extracted, so that simple fruit flavors dominate the wine, which tends to have a bright purple color. The amount of carbonic maceration is determined by the proportion of whole clusters and the length of time before pressing; it is greatest for Nouveau and least for the crus.

The key feature of Beaujolais Nouveau is its immediate fruitiness. Somewhat controversially the style has been enhanced by the use of thermovinification. As used in Beaujolais, this involves heating berries to 55 °C for 8-12 hours and then cooling them down for fermentation. "This is very current here. It increases color and aromatics. It's mostly used for nouveau and a little bit for Beaujolais and Villages. It's especially useful when the quality of the grapes is not so good," explains oenologist Denis Lapalu at Duboeuf. "It's indispensable in a year such as 2012, it's very much a function of the vintage. Without it we would not be able to achieve the quality in some years," adds Georges Duboeuf.

Thermovinification is controversial because it strengthens the impression of fermentation aromatics. "Unfortunately 90% of Beaujolais today is made by thermovinification—it's terrible," says Mathieu Lapierre of Domaine Marcel Lapierre in Morgon. The question is really what you want from Beaujolais Nouveau. It's never going to represent terroir. "In Beaujolais we go from catastrophe to catastrophe. Twenty years ago there were yeasts that made the wine aromatic, hiding the terroir. Today thermovinification is a catastrophe; it's a technique for giving aromas of cassis—but it does it equally for wines from limestone or granite, from Brouilly or Moulin-à-Vent. It does not correspond at all to the idea that the vigneron makes wine to express his vines. It's industrial wine made by technological methods," says Jean-Paul Brun at Domaine des

Terres Dorées. Growers who focus on crus agree. "The difference between crus has disappeared at the negociants and producers who are using thermovinification. Thermovinification started in Beaujolais for handling grapes that had problems, for example, damaged by hail, and allowed you to make decent wine; but at the same time it destroyed the best wine. I don't understand how it's possible to do this within the appellation rules because it destroys the differences between appellations," says Louis-Benoît Desvignes.

Up to half of production from the Beaujolais AOP is Nouveau. Up to a third of Beaujolais Villages is produced as Nouveau, but the crus are not allowed to produce Nouveau. Nouveau is intended for immediate consumption, Beaujolais and Beaujolais Villages should be drunk within a year or so, but some of the crus make wines with ageworthiness.

"You have to dissociate the crus from Beaujolais. They are apart. There are people who drink only the crus and there are people who drink only Beaujolais Nouveau. The crus are distinguished by terroir and vintage, which is different from Nouveau. One speaks of 2009 as a great vintage, 2010 is different, and so on. Moulin-à-Vent has a reputation more like Burgundy," says Georges Duboeuf.

The crus offer a wide range of quality, from wine just above Villages standard, to the top wines of Morgon or Moulin-à-Vent, which may be made by conventional vinification and have aging potential. At their best, these can resemble the Côte d'Or. Not everyone approves of this. "I do not think they are necessarily any better for it," says Clive Coates MW. "Good Beaujolais... is a light red wine, not at all tannic, purple in color, abundantly fruity and not a bit heavy or sweet."[83] Yet Beaujolais is moving in the direction of weightier wines. "It's very important for us to show that Beaujolais can age," says Anthon Collet of the producers' association Inter Beaujolais.[84] The crus are allowed to put the name of the cru alone on the bottle (without mentioning Beaujolais), and often do so to minimize the connection with Beaujolais. While this may be helpful for the crus, of course it denies the rest of the Beaujolais any uplift from the halo of its best wines.

Beaujolais Crus

Cases produced yearly	
Brouilly	850,000
Chénas	180,000
Chiroubles	240,000
Côte de Brouilly	210,000
Fleurie	550,000
Juliénas	380,000
Morgon	730,000
Moulin à Vent	430,000
Régnié	325,000
Saint Amour	200,000

It's a mistake to regard the best crus as ready for drinking upon release. Those from the top producers need at least another year or so. Perhaps in an exceptional year like 2009 the fruits immediately outweigh the structure, but otherwise there can be enough tannin to obscure the fruits. For the best wines

The most famous cru of Beaujolais, Moulin-à-Vent, takes its name from the old windmill.

in a good year, the ideal period may be to enjoy them around five years after the vintage; it is only an exceptional wine—perhaps a top Moulin-à-Vent or Morgon— that is likely to last longer than that. At their best, the top crus can be difficult to distinguish from village wines from the Côte de Beaune.

A move towards a more hierarchical classification is gathering force. Extensive land surveys are taking place in Beaujolais to support the argument for premier crus, with several candidates in Moulin-à-Vent, Fleurie, and Morgon. Already some producers have moved in the direction of recognizing individual vineyards. At Château des Jacques, whose vineyards are just below the famous windmill in Moulin-à-Vent, six individual vineyard cuvées have been added to the general blend (which for years was in any case the best wine of the appellation). In Fleurie the best known sub area is Grille Midi, a large south-facing amphitheatre that is always warm; in Morgon, it is Côte du Py, a hill that rises to 350 m. Individual cuvées are a very recent phenomenon. It's a sign of how things are changing that Louis-Benoît Desvignes recollects, "When I started a special bottling (the Vieilles Vignes from Javernières on the Côte de Py) in 2009, people thought I would lose customers."

There are mixed feelings about the change that premier crus will bring. "In the next five to ten years we will definitely have premier crus. The locomotive is Morgon and Moulin-à-Vent. But it will be both good and bad. People from Burgundy come here to buy land—it's speculation. I'm a peasant, I'm not a financier. The price of land and the wine will increase," Louis-Benoît says. Yet to some extent, an important transition has already taken place with the increasing move toward single vineyard wines. Recognition of premier crus may simply formalize the premium that already is being paid for the best sites.

"Morgon is the oldest cru of Beaujolais. It was the first because it had the history, it's the best. There's lots of schist. There are six *climats*, with Côte de Py the best known. Studies of soils and subsoils have been done to define the areas; there will be premier crus in a few years," says Baptiste Condemine at Domaine des Souchons. But he adds, "Many people know Morgon because they know Marcel Lapierre. I think this is more important for us than the premier crus."

Indeed Marcel Lapierre was at the forefront of a revolution led by the "gang of four."[85] The others were Guy Breton, Jean-Paul Thévenet, and Jean Foillard, all friends from the town of Villié-Morgon. Their impetus came from a winemaker called Jules Chauvet, who introduced them to the notion of picking late for full ripeness, selecting to eliminate rotten berries, using natural yeast, minimizing sulfur dioxide, using slow fermentation at low temperature (the proportion of carbonic maceration varies with producer and vintage), and maturing in barriques. "My father was part of a group that rebelled against the industrial production of Beaujolais," says Mathieu Lapierre, adding, "We try to make natural wines but it's difficult to defend them from the industrial system. We try to master things so as to be as natural as possible, but no one can be superman." It's a measure of his attitude that when asked about global warming, he says, "I'm not sure about that, the real question is why some people in Beaujolais chaptalize; if you reach 12% do you need more alcohol?"

So what is the effect on the wines? A single word describes the difference with the average Beaujolais: structure. This is not to imply that the wines are tough, but behind the fruits is the necessary framework to support development. Lapierre's Morgon can in fact be a little hard in the first year or so, but four years after the magnificent 2009 vintage, it shows tense black fruits with earthy overtones, and a real sense of terroir that might be confused, for example, with Pommard. "Morgon should have an aroma of violets and cherries, with flavors of strawberries and a slightly masculine side," says Mathieu. Morgon is serious wine, often giving a taut impression of its granitic terroir, with the greatest purity of line usually to be found in the putative premier cru of Côte du Py.

"The difference between the crus is the terroir. Brouilly is blue stone, Fleurie is pink granite, and Moulin-à-Vent has manganese. The crus are an element in advancing the reputation of the region," says Georges Duboeuf. A tasting with Georges is an education in Beaujolais. Starting with the Beaujolais Villages, the wine is all about fruit. "This is the side of Beaujolais we all like, very juicy and fruity," he says. "You get fruit and freshness and for another year or two you will be able to enjoy it. What we are looking for in Beaujolais Villages is the pleasure of the moment." The distinction between Beaujolais Villages and the lesser crus is the more direct sense of fruit aromatics in the Villages (reflecting more carbonic maceration).

Turning to the crus, in general the lightest, often barely distinguished from better Beaujolais Villages, are Brouilly (the largest), Regnié, and Saint Amour. Côte de Brouilly is distinct from Brouilly (as its name suggests, it lies on the slopes of Mount Brouilly); and with even more elevation, Chiroubles comes from hillside vineyards often over 300 m. Tasting with Duboeuf, the flavor spectrum of Brouilly and Chiroubles are generally similar, with more weight than the Villages, but less evident aromatics. Then going up the scale of crus, there is more intensity, but not a great change in character. The real difference comes when you reach Morgon, Fleurie, and Moulin-à-Vent. The Morgon is a little tauter, the silky fleshiness of Fleurie is a little softer, and Moulin-à-Vent is quite serious and elegant.

Morgon and Moulin-à-Vent have the most distinctive soils, with manganese prominent in both, and iron in the latter. They often seem more Burgundian as they age. Vineyards in Fleurie close to Morgon or Moulin-à-Vent sometimes take on the more structured quality of those appellations; in the heart of the appellation, the wines are fleshy. The old description was that Fleurie is the queen of Beaujolais, while Moulin-à-Vent is the king. Juliénas, which can be a big, sturdy wine, comes as a surprise, placed in Duboeuf's lineup after the Moulin-à-Vent, and showing a real sense of tightness. The differences as you ascend the hierarchy are more to do with the balance between fruits and acidity, breadth versus tautness, or intensity of concentration, than the flavor spectrum as such.

The tradition in the region is to mature the wine—even the crus—in cement tanks. Slowly wood has been introduced. Château des Jacques in Moulin-à-Vent—always one of the most ageworthy wines—has done this for decades, and the trend has been accentuated since Jadot acquired the estate in 1996. While initially regarded with some scepticism by others, today there is a definite move in this direction, and many producers in the top crus now have at least one cuvée that uses maturation in barriques.

Vinification should be a bigger issue than it is: carbonic maceration has become the new tradition, but actually it's a twentieth century phenomenon. It's clear that it's the lifeblood for Beaujolais Nouveau and probably necessary for Beaujolais and Beaujolais Villages: but is it appropriate for the crus, or do they make better wines by following Burgundian precepts? Carbonic maceration is not a technique that brings out terroir differences, so it's somewhat at odds with a move towards defining a hierarchy of premier crus within the top crus. Of course, no one asks the most fundamental question, which is all but unthinkable: is Gamay the best grape to grow in the Beaujolais?

So what is the real Beaujolais, where is the future of the region? In wines using carbonic maceration to bring out fruits or in wines made more conventionally to balance fruits with structure? Jean-Paul Brun at Domaine des Terres Dorées has had difficulties with his attempts to obtain the AOP agrément for ageworthy wines. He does not use carbonic maceration for any of his wines, not even the Beaujolais. "If you use carbonic maceration it's too short to allow the terroir to express itself. Burgundian vinification for all the wines lasts for 5-6 weeks. A Burgundian vinification has the objective of transmitting the terroir to the wine." If Beaujolais is truly to find a way forward through the classification of premier crus, it's beyond time to stop making difficulties for producers who are making the very wines that should prove the point.

The future is unclear. The practical difficulty is whether there is any alternative for the vineyards that are now producing Beaujolais Nouveau. Needless to say, these are not the best vineyards. Perhaps it's better that they produce Beaujolais Nouveau rather than join the lake of wine to be distilled,[86] but the price is to devalue the reputation of the rest of Beaujolais. "Beaujolais Nouveau is one of the most incredible ideas of the twentieth century. People of my generation don't know that we have crus in Beaujolais—it's crazy," says Louis-Benoît Desvignes. Admittedly the crus vary from wines that are barely distinguishable from Beaujolais Villages to those that might be confused with reds from the Côte de Beaune, but the best are some of the few remaining undiscovered bargains from the region.

Reference Wines for Beaujolais	
Beaujolais	Domaine des Terres Dorées, L'Ancien
Beaujolais Villages	Georges Duboeuf
Brouilly	Jean-Claude Lapalu, Vieilles Vignes
Chénas	Paul-Henri Thillardon
Côte de Brouilly	Domaine des Terres Dorées
Fleurie	Yves Métras, Grille-Midi
Juliénas	Georges Duboeuf, Château des Capitans
Morgon	Marcel Lapierre
Morgon, Côte de Py	Louis et Claude Desvignes
	Jean Foillard
Moulin-à-Vent	Château des Jacques
Regnié	Charly Thévenet, Grain et Granit

Area :	1,845 ha
Production:	1.4 million cases
Producers:	36%
Cooperatives:	24%
Negociants:	40%
Dry white wine	37%
Red wine	26%
Crémant	26%
Vin Jaune	4%
Vin de Paille	1%
Macvin	6%

Jura-Savoie are usually lumped together as those regions which do not fit into Burgundy or the Rhône, but the vineyards are well separated and the connection is slight. The terroirs are different: Jura has rolling hills and Savoie has the grandeur of the mountains. The grape varieties are different. And there is little commonality of style. Savoie is dominated by indigenous varieties, mostly white. The Jura is caught between vinification of the Savagnin grape in an oxidative style producing wine akin to Sherry, contrasted with wines made in the modern style from Savagnin or Chardonnay. The Jura has generally been fairly obscure, with wine made by local producers on a relatively small scale, and not much interest from negociants from elsewhere, but recently there's been a small move into the region by producers from Burgundy.[87]

About fifty miles east of Burgundy, the Jura is separated from the Côte d'Or by the valley of the Saône river. Vineyards in the Jura are more elevated (around 250-400 m), on slopes that face west or southwest. Soils are clay and limestone, with outbreaks of marl (lime-rich mud). There is more clay in the Jura than in Burgundy, because when the massif of the Jura advanced towards Burgundy, clay was pushed up to the surface at the base of the foothills, whereas in Burgundy it remains underground. Cooler than Burgundy, the climate is marginal for wine growing. Côtes de Jura is the general AOP for the whole region; within it the Arbois AOP is far larger than the small AOPs of Château-Chalon (this is the name of the AOP not a producer) and l'Etoile. In addition, there are two AOPs for specific wine styles: Crémant de Jura and Macvin (a sweet vin de liqueur made by adding spirits to stop fermentation at an early point).

In steady decline ever since phylloxera, when there were around 20,000 ha of vineyards, plantings in the Jura have now stabilized at under 2,000 ha, with almost all vineyards in one of the AOPs. Only five grape varieties are allowed in the AOPs: Chardonnay and Savagnin for the whites; and Poulsard, Trousseau, and Pinot Noir for the blacks. The trend is towards increasing production of white wines, which today are about two thirds of production (including sparkling as well as still wines).[88]

Reflecting the symmetry with Burgundy across the Saône valley, Chardonnay is the predominant variety, accounting for about half of all plantings. It is not a newcomer here, having been grown for several centuries under a variety of local names. "People say, oh, now you are making Chardonnay in the Jura, but Chardonnay has been grown here for a very long time—some speak of the fourteenth century," says Stéphane Tissot.[89] Yet in terms of stylistic imperatives, it is Savagnin that makes the running. The local myth is that Savagnin was imported from Tokaji in Hungary in the Middle Ages.[90] In fact, its origins are in the other direction, as it is the same variety as Gewürztraminer in Alsace, yet in the Jura it gives a wine with pronounced savory quality, rather than the floral perfume of Gewürztraminer.[91] Essentially Savagnin is a nonaromatic variant and Gewürztraminer is an aromatic variant of the variety. Savagnin or Chardonnay show a similar savory thread, as do wines blended from the two varieties.

The Jura's claim to fame comes from its oxidative style of wines, almost unique in France. (Similar techniques are used in Gaillac for its *vin de voile*). Traditional winemaking used old barriques, but did not fill them completely or top up to compensate for loss by evaporation. The result is that a layer of yeast, known locally as the *voile* (veil), grows on the surface of the wine. Producers are quick to tell you that the yeasts aren't the same as those involved in the formation of flor on fino Sherry, but the principle is the same, and the results are similar. (Of course, Sherry is fortified but the Jura wines are natural, although evaporation during maturation can increase alcohol to a similar level.) The layer of yeast is thinner in the Jura, and more gray in hue. It protects the maturing wine from becoming oxidized to vinegar, and contributes a distinctive aroma and flavor. The wine has a taut, savory quality with distinct dryness on the finish (because the yeasts consume glycerol). The main aromatic characteristics are the production of acetaldehyde (an oxidized product of ethanol), which gives a faintly nutty character, and sotolon, an aromatic, spicy compound that contributes curry-like notes. In fact, sotolon is also a natural product of the fenugreek plant, whose seeds are used in Madras curry.

The antithesis of the modern trend to fruit-driven wines, the oxidative style is an acquired taste that has been going out of fashion. As a result, most producers now also make wines in a modern, which is to say non-oxidative, style. The most common term used to describe these wines is *ouillé* (from ouillage, meaning topping-up). Wines in the oxidative style are most often described as

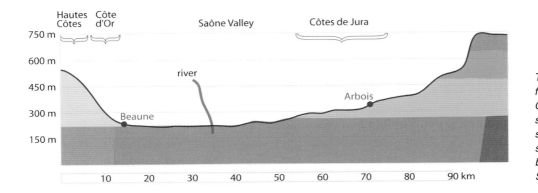

The southeast-facing slope of the Côte d'Or is separated from the southwest-facing slopes of the Jura by the valley of the Saône.

The traditional style in the Jura allows wine to mature in barriques that are not topped up. Yeast grow on the surface of the wine to form a voile (as seen here in a white layer about an inch deep).

traditional or *vinifié sur voile* (or sometimes *typé*). The distinction is a recent development: "The production of wines in the ouillé style at Château-Chalon started only around 1990," says Jean Berthet-Bondet, one of the leading producers. Some old-line producers have eschewed the ouillé style, but it's a sign of the times that Laurent Macle, from one of the most traditional producers in Château-Chalon, produced his first ouillé wine in 2007. It's only four barrels, but a source of argument as Laurent's father does not approve. "He will never be convinced," says Laurent, who believes this may be the true expression of terroir.

"People confuse terroir with the taste of Vin Jaune (vinifié sur voile), but it's the aging that gives the wine its flavor."

The most fascinating aspect of the Jura is a certain sense of convergence between the oxidized and ouillé styles, and between Chardonnay and Savagnin. Even in the ouillé style, Chardonnay sometimes takes on a more savory quality, faintly reminiscent of Savagnin in its oxidized style. Walking in the vineyards, I was convinced I could smell fenugreek on the air. But it's more likely that the presence of both types of wine in the same cellar is responsible. A tasting with Stéphane Tissot at Domaine André et Mireille Tissot provided an interesting comparison. The Traminer and Savagnin cuvées come from the same vines, but the names of the cuvées indicate different types of vinification. Traminer is nonoxidative, but Savagnin has 30 months under voile. Even the first shows some savory influences, but they are much stronger in the second. One seems more like an extreme example of the other, rather than completely different.

Wines in the oxidative style go back at least to the eighteenth century, and the epitome of the style is Vin Jaune, which matures in barrique under a voile for six years.[92] Vin Jaune comes exclusively from Savagnin. For most appellations it is one of several wine styles that can be produced, but Château-Chalon produces only Vin Jaune, and is usually considered to provide its peak expression. (Any other wine produced from vineyards within Château-Chalon must be labeled Côtes de Jura.) "Château-Chalon is the grand cru of Vin Jaune. You don't have the right to produce Château-Chalon every vintage. A commission meets to decide whether to allow the appellation each year," explains Jean-François Bourdy, who has strong views about the roles of the varieties. "The tradition here—for more than fifty years—is that Chardonnay makes the best white wines. Savagnin makes Vin Jaune." Emphasizing the expensive nature of its production, Vin Jaune is sold in an unusual 62 cl. bottle (supposedly to represent what is left after evaporation of a liter of wine from the harvest). Vin Jaune has an intensity that matches a top fino Sherry, but has a slightly different aroma and flavor spectrum, if anything deeper and more savory.

It would be a mistake to regard the difference between the traditional and ouillé styles as a polarizing influence: they are more the extremes of a continuum. Modernism is perhaps

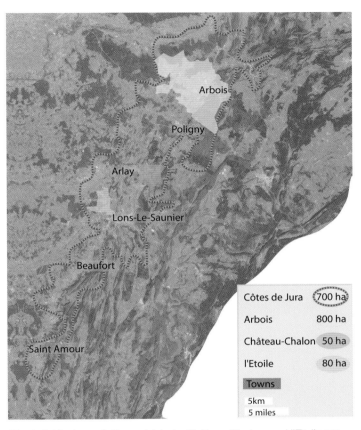

The individual appellations of Arbois, Château-Chalon, and l'Etoile are relatively compact, but the Côtes de Jura extends over 50 miles.

defined by Ganevat, who at the southern tip of the Jura is almost completely devoted to the ouillé style; his Chardonnays show a minerality and freshness reminiscent of Chablis. At the center are producers like Stéphane Tissot, making wines in both styles, but with oxidized wines varying from relatively brief exposure to the full reign of Vin Jaune. Traditional producer Jacques Puffeney makes a Chardonnay in a style that shows herbs and spices of the garrigue with a touch of fenugreek leading into a savory palate, but which is more of a halfway house between traditional and ouillé as it doesn't have the madeirized quality of Vin Jaune. Then of course there is the intensity of Vin Jaune.

The reds in the Jura are less interesting than the whites. They are split between Pinot Noir and the local varieties Poulsard and Trousseau. The main change in the past few decades is an increase in Pinot Noir from almost negligible to around a third of black plantings.[93] (However, Pinot Noir is not a newcomer: in the eighteenth century it was the second most planted variety.[94]) Poulsard (also called Plousard locally) is by far the most important, representing more than three quarters of the black plantings (roughly a quarter of all plant-

Château-Chalon is located at a high point on a plateau overlooking the vineyards of the appellation down below. Soils of blue marl retain heat, and the vineyards are protected from the wind by south-southwest exposure.

ings). Poulsard and Trousseau are somewhat rustic in a light style. Poulsard has such a light, thin skin that it's often taken for rosé. It's relatively rare for Pinot Noir to acquire really enough concentration, although some of the wines from the glorious 2009 vintage could be mistaken for coming from the environs of Beaune. This might be an indication that the Jura would be a good place for Pinot Noir if global warming continues, although of course the presence of more clay and less limestone is problematic in that regard. I'm not sure I see much purpose in blending the varieties: it doesn't give the Poulsard or Trousseau more refinement, nor does it round out the Pinot Noir.

Reference Wines for Jura	
Chardonnay, ouillé	Domaine Ganevat, Les Chalasses
Savagnin, ouillé	Domaine André & Mireille Tissot, Arbois (Traminer)
Chardonnay, traditional	Domaine Jacques Puffeney, Arbois
Savagnin, traditional	Domaine André & Mireille Tissot, Arbois (Savagnin)
Trousseau	Domaine Jacques Puffeney, Les Berangères
Vin Jaune	Domaine Berthet-Bondet, Château-Chalon
Vin de Paille	Domaine Jean Bourdy, Côtes de Jura

The wines of Jacques Puffeney, among the most subtle of the appellation, illustrate the differences between the black varieties. The Pinot Noir is delicate, but with a touch of austerity, somewhat in the direction of a red Sancerre, but tighter. Trousseau has more weight and depth, and although many Trousseau wines from the Jura can seem on the rustic side, Puffeney's Les Bérangères, with its slightly darker color and high alcohol, demonstrates the full potential of the variety for pulling off a richness that Pinot Noir cannot quite achieve in this environment. But Puffeney is recognized as the master of Trousseau.

A significant part of the Jura's production is Crémant, mostly made from Chardonnay, but some black grapes are also used. While there are exceptions, the Crémant is not usually especially interesting, and its main significance may be that it improves the quality of the still wines by using up grapes that are just short of full ripeness.

Even aside from its unique Vin Jaune, the Jura offers an unusual alternative to the monotony of simple fruit-driven wines; traditional or ouillé, Chardonnay or Savagnin, these are some of the more distinctive wines of France.

It's hard to know what to expect of the wines of Savoie. Under the Alps, stretching from Grenoble to Geneva, it's far from obvious that this is a natural area for wine, yet production predates the Romans. Savoie became part of France only in 1860, so its grape varieties and traditions are distinct. Historically vines were planted all the way from the valleys up to around 1,000 m of elevation. At the time of phylloxera, there were about 20,000 hectares of vineyards; since a recovery in the first two decades of the twentieth century, the planted area has been falling steadily, down today to little more than 2,000 ha. Almost all is in Savoie itself, with little left in Haut Savoie (Savoie is the southern half, and Haut Savoie is the northern half, of the former kingdom of Savoy, before it was annexed by France).

The most important vineyards are south of Chambéry, along the gorge of Chambéry or running along the Combe de Savoie, a striking 25-mile long valley bounded by the massive mountains that run on an axis from Chambéry through Aix-les-Bains and Annécy. On the gorge of Chambéry, Les Abymes and Apremont face the vineyards across the Combe de Savoie, where Saint-Jeoire-Prieuré, Chignin, Montmélian, Arbin and Cruet, look towards the mountains.

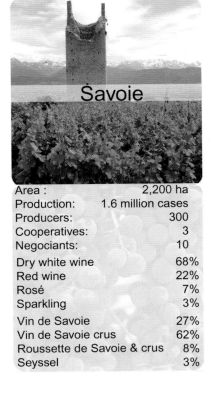

Savoie

Area :	2,200 ha
Production:	1.6 million cases
Producers:	300
Cooperatives:	3
Negociants:	10
Dry white wine	68%
Red wine	22%
Rosé	7%
Sparkling	3%
Vin de Savoie	27%
Vin de Savoie crus	62%
Roussette de Savoie & crus	8%
Seyssel	3%

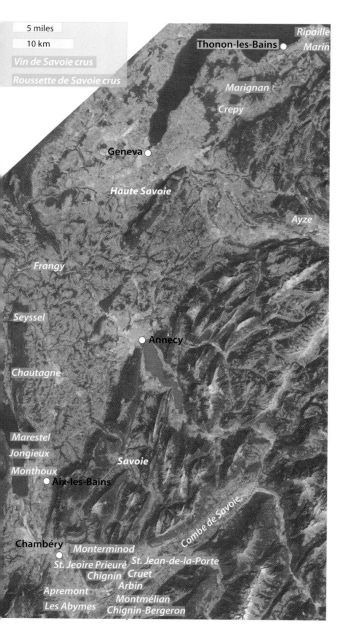

5 miles
10 km
Vin de Savoie crus
Roussette de Savoie crus

Ripaille
Marin
Thonon-les-Bains
Marignan
Crepy
Geneva
Haute Savoie
Ayze
Frangy
Seyssel
Annecy
Chautagne
Marestel
Jongieux
Monthoux
Aix-les-Bains
Savoie
Combe de Savoie
Chambéry
Monterminod
St. Jeoire Prieuré St. Jean-de-la-Porte
Chignin Cruet
Apremont Arbin
Les Abymes Montmélian
Chignin-Bergeron

The wines of Savoie come from three separate areas: the remaining vineyards of Haut Savoie are near Lake Geneva; in the center are vineyards to the north of Aix-les-Bains; and the main group of vineyards is clustered to the south of Chambéry.

Proximity to the mountains, and elevation of vineyards, make this distinctly cool climate territory, comparable to Alsace or the Loire.[95] Most of the wine is white, and falls under the AOPs of Vin de Savoie or Roussette de Savoie (which is monovarietal Roussette from anywhere in the region). In addition to the 90% of production labeled as Vin de Savoie, there are fifteen crus, whose individual names can be appended to the Vin de Savoie AOP,[96] which is really far too many separate appellations. The most important crus in terms of both quantity and reputation are Les Abymes and Apremont. Roussette de Savoie has four crus that can be appended to its name.[97] There is a small amount of production under AOP Seyssel. There's also the IGP Allobrogies, which covers the whole area with a generally similar set of grape varieties. The fact, however, is that the variety, or the blend of varieties, is probably the most important factor in determining style.

Altogether there are 23 grape varieties in Savoie. The main white variety is Jacquère, which accounts for half of all plantings, and is supposed to have been imported into the region in the thirteenth century. It's a late-ripening, productive variety; in fact yields up to 78 hl/ha are allowed for the regional AOP, and between 65-75 hl/ha for the crus. Vins de Savoie are typically blends based on Jacquère; the major blending varieties are Chasselas, Roussanne, and Chardonnay. There are more specific assemblages in some of the crus. Les Abymes must be 80% Jacquère, and Apremont is exclusively Jacquère, as is Chignin; but Chignin-Bergeron is exclusively Roussanne. Crépy is exclusively Chasselas. The second most important white variety, Roussette, also known as Altesse, is mostly vinified as a monovarietal for the AOP

Mont Granier looms over the vineyards of Chignin. Courtesy Savoie-Mont Blanc.

Roussette de Savoie and its crus. Red wine is only a quarter of production, split between Gamay (probably introduced after phylloxera) and Mondeuse, an indigenous variety, with origins related to Syrah. Another indigenous variety called Persan is also found. Mondeuse is especially prominent in the Combe de Savoie, and notably in the crus Arbin and Saint-Jean-de-la-Porte. It gives a slightly astringent, peppery wine, quite tannic.[98]

The best wines can be intriguingly different, and could hardly be more distinct from the modern "international" style, but sometimes lack flavor interest. The nutty notes of Jacquère at its best can be attractive; the Roussanne of Chignin-Bergeron makes a fresher impression. The reds can be a bit rustic. Mondeuse is the most distinctive, but when very young it tends to show a fairly dull flavor spectrum, and it's hard for it to rise above the general level of rusticity, although Louis Magnin's top cuvées can become elegant with age.

Reference Wines for Savoie	
Roussette de Savoie	Domaine du Prieuré Saint Christophe
Vin de Savoie, Arbin	Domain Louis Magnin, Tout un Monde
Chignin-Bergeron	Domaine Louis Magnin, Grand Orgue

Vintages

Burgundy

The most common problem historically in Burgundy is cool or wet weather, especially at time of harvest, but more recently there have also been problems with heat. While there are distinctions between areas, with local conditions giving different results in the Côte de Beaune and Côte de Nuits, and more variation at the northern limit of Chablis, the most important distinction is between red and white wines. There seems to be a trend lately that the best vintages for red wines have resulted in white wines with less acidity and aging potential (a concern increased by the occurrence of premox). Some pairs of vintages, such as 2005/2006 or 2009/2010, have produced a first year that gives superb red wines, but a second year where the whites are crisper and likely to age better. However, uncertainty about the premature oxidation problem means that any white Burgundy more than, say, five years old for village, and eight years for premier or grand cru, is suspect, so notes for older vintages are now really of historical interest only. (Vintage conditions in the Jura generally follow those of Burgundy.)

2013	Cold growing season was difficult, but some improvement in September allowed decent harvest for wines that will be good rather than great.
2012	Erratic conditions led to low yields of both reds and whites, but quality is surprisingly good.
2011	Difficulties in getting to ripeness make this the least successful vintage of the decade to date.
2010	Reds are tighter than the opulent 2009s, with an elegant balance, and potential for good aging.
	Whites show good acidity, mineral in Chablis, crisp on the Côte d'Or; a leaner style than 2009 but with good potential for longevity.
2009	A great year for reds, rich, ripe and opulent, but a lingering question is whether they will have the tannic structure for extended longevity.
	Whites were opulent at first, but unlikely to age long as richness is well ahead of acidity.
2008	Difficult vintage with problems of rain and humidity. Reds show high acidity, whites are on the fresh side.
2007	Growing season was too wet, reds suffered from problems with humidity, the whites are better but on the acid side.
2006	Reds have a tendency towards austerity resulting from cool conditions leading to high acidity.
	The whites of 2006 are leaner than those of 2005, as good acidity has brought a classic crisp minerality.

2005	Reds are on the opulent side but with good tannic structure for long-term development.
	Whites show classic opulence for a warm year, impression of fat when young, but by now the tendency to earlier aging is making most questionable.
2004	Both reds and whites are on the lighter, more acid side, and there are not many of interest today.
2003	Reds tended to be cooked from the outset, and almost all were short-lived.
	The heat was too much for the whites, which tended to be flabby.
2002	Reds are quite rich but well structured, and the best are just right now.
	Whites tended to show opulence but the premature aging of white Burgundy means most are now too old.
2001	Not a bad vintage at the time, although a bit tannic for reds and acid for whites, but not of serious interest today.
2000	Nice enough wines for early drinking, but few survived to the end of the decade.
1999	Generous vintage for reds with good supporting structure; the best are still at their peak.
	Whites showed nice combination of generosity and minerality, but are now too old.
1998	Not very interesting at the time and no longer of interest.
1997	Pleasant wines for short term drinking at the time.
1996	A most frustrating year for reds. Billed as vins de garde, they started with strong tannins, but have never come around. The problem is a punishing bitter medicinal acidity that tarnishes the finish. Some rare grand crus are exceptions where the concentration of fruits comes to the fore.
	This was a lovely vintage for whites at the outset: crisp, mineral, and precise, but it was the first vintage where premox became a major problem, cutting short longevity.
1995	Reds seemed a little tight at first but in retrospect were generous compared with the following vintage in 1996. They developed in a charming, lighter style, rather than opulent.
	Whites showed good concentration and weight, but are too old now.
1994	Autumn rains spoiled the harvest, but whites were better than reds.
1993	Reds gave quite a charming vintage in a lighter style for mid-term consumption, but the whites were less successful due to lack of concentration.
1992	The best wines were picked before rain spoiled the harvest.
1991	A rare vintage where the whites were quite successful, tending to elegance on Côte d'Or, but the reds never quite made it.
1990	A great vintage with good balance of fruit to structure; long-lived for reds.
	A great vintage for the opulent style of white Burgundy.

Beaujolais

With almost all Beaujolais intended for immediate consumption, vintages are usually simply a guide as to whether or not to buy the current release. Even for the crus, little is available on the market beyond the last two or three years, but because there have been some unusually fine years lately, with exceptional potential for aging for the crus, there's more interest than usual. Very few wines are worth keeping more than a decade, however, and recommendations for longevity really apply only to the top crus, Moulin-à-Vent, Morgon, Fleurie, and perhaps Juliénas.

2013	A difficult vintage, with a cold wet start to the season, but good September. Fruits are light and pleasant, but the danger is that they will be overtaken by the acidity.
2012	"2012 is the smallest vintage I have experienced, with hail and rain early, but the weather became sunny from mid August. Harvest started from September 12; the quantity was not there but the quality was definitely there," says Georges Duboeuf.
2011	This is often considered to be as good as 2009, although it hasn't attracted the same attention; but the best wines will age well, as they have good concentration and structure.
2010	Another very good year, which would have been classic if not following 2009. There's a lot of fruit here, although not as opulent as 2009.
2009	"2009 is the best vintage I have known in my life. We had (all the) berries in perfect condition which I have never seen before," says Georges Duboeuf. The top crus will last for several years yet.
2008	A slow, late vintage that called for a lot of selection; wines were relatively short lived.
2007	A nice vintage, small but with good quality.
2006	Rather a mixed vintage, generally with average results.
2005	A very good year, as in Burgundy.
2004	A normal vintage was a relief after the excessive heat of the previous year.

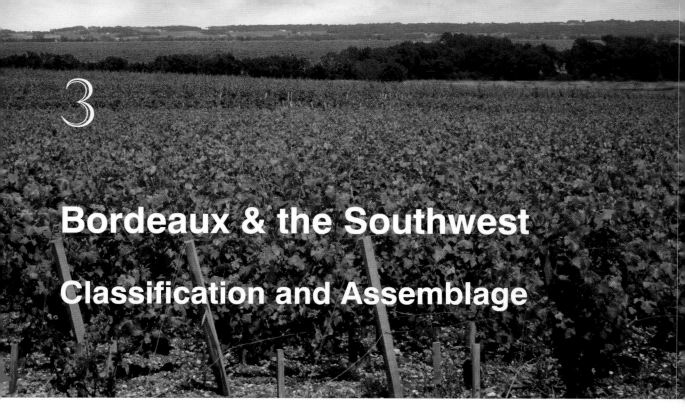

Bordeaux & the Southwest

Classification and Assemblage

Jeremiah was a bullfrog
Was a good friend of mine
Never understood a single word he said,
but he always had some mighty fine wine
(Three Dog Night)

Mighty fine wine somehow seems appropriate for a description of Bordeaux above all else. At its best, Bordeaux is probably the longest-lived wine in the world, the top wines have unmistakable character and backbone, and they have been established as the best of their type for centuries. Bordeaux reflects the history of France itself. Wine production started after the Romans conquered Gaul, but fell into disarray during the dark ages after the collapse of the Roman Empire. It was the English who put Bordeaux on the map as a major wine producer after they took over Aquitaine in 1152. There were ups and downs after Aquitaine was restored to France in 1452. Wines of quality began to be produced during the eighteenth century when the top producers were distinguished, detailed classifications came into effect in the nineteenth century, and Bordeaux reigned supreme during the twentieth century until challenged by competition from the New World. Bordeaux has a reputation for being staid and bound by tradition, but when tradition clashes with the need to preserve market share, commerce wins every time. Today Bordeaux is caught by a dichotomy between the unparalleled success of the top wines and the difficulties, not to say failure, of generic wines.

Bordeaux first became known for its importance as a port, as illustrated by the prominent ships in this map by Munster from 1598.

Bordeaux started as a gateway for distributing wine. When the Romans arrived in 56 B.C.E., it was an important commercial center, but there were no vineyards: the climate was too cool.[1] During the first century C.E., new grape varieties became available that would ripen in more northern climates. Viticulture started in the Dordogne (to the southeast), and then extended towards Bordeaux itself.[2,3] Gaillac claims to be the place where grape growing started in the region.

Viticulture was established around the city of Bordeaux itself, and immediately across the river to the east, by the twelfth century.[4] Vineyards spread out from the city during the next two centuries. Immediately to the south, the Graves was easiest to penetrate. To the north, the Médoc was less attractive terrain, because it was covered in swamps, but vineyards were established in a band running along the Gironde, largely on infertile soils where few other crops could be grown.[5] Viticulture did not become important until the end of the seventeenth century. Increasing in importance, it became close to a monoculture in some parts of the Médoc during the eighteenth century.[6]

As viticulture developed, Bordeaux owed its increasing importance as a wine producer as much to commercial ruthlessness (what's new?) as to superior

quality. Its role as the export center for both local and foreign wines (foreign included the Médoc!) led to the development of a unique system for keeping tight control of distribution. Indeed, Bordeaux's history as a distributor affects the way you buy a bottle of Bordeaux even today. All wines passed through the hands of the negociants. The producer was unimportant (at least to the consumer). The negociants would purchase wines and blend them (often from a variety of sources) to suit the palates of their customers.

The central position of the negociants evolved into an arcane system for distribution called the *Place de Bordeaux*. Almost all châteaux sell their wine only to negociants in Bordeaux, who in turn sell it on to distributors worldwide. This means there are no direct sales from châteaux to retailers, let alone consumers. Few major châteaux bypass the system. One consequence of lack of direct contact with the market can be erratic pricing, which has contributed to Bordeaux's history of boom and bust cycles.

The negociants established their companies on the Quai des Chartrons, close to the port. The change in the Quai des Chartrons today symbolizes changing influence in the market. It's no longer a center of distribution, with negociants established along the waterfront maturing wines in the large caves

The Médoc originally consisted of marshes (marais) with some pastures and woods. The only major marais remaining in the Médoc today is at Bruges, on the northern boundary of Bordeaux.

A view of the Quai des Chartrons around 1907 shows a busy waterfront devoted to transport of wine.

below. Today there are few negociants left on the quay, which is being gentri-fied and converted into a destination for tourists.[7] (The oldest broker in Bordeaux, Tastet & Lawton, one of the few remaining on the quay, is on the corner in the photographs above and opposite.)

Individual producers in Bordeaux are almost all known as châteaux. The use of "château" might be taken to imply a certain grandeur. This is and isn't true. Some of the châteaux in the Médoc are very grand indeed, but for the most part the term is used as a synonym for a producer who makes wine from estate vineyards, without any particular implication as to the size of the prop-erty.

The vast majority of wines from the top areas in Bordeaux are produced by individual châteaux, but there has been a change at the level of generic AOP Bordeaux. Today only about a quarter of generic Bordeaux is sold under the name of a château. About half consists of brands developed by negociants, and a quarter is given over to house brands produced specifically for super-market chains.[8]

Negociant has a dual meaning in Bordeaux. It can describe a trader, who does not produce wine, but essentially is a middleman for selling wines pro-duced by the châteaux. Or it can mean a producer who buys grapes or wine in the old style to produce blends. The largest producers are the negociant arm of Château Mouton Rothschild, which produces Mouton Cadet, and CVBG, who

own several châteaux as well as producing the well-known Dourthe #1 brand. Brands are usually handled in a completely different way from châteaux. Negociants do not own vineyards in order to produce brands; in fact, they directly own less than 5% of the vineyards.[9] Most of the wine for the brands comes from grapes purchased from independent vignerons, often under long-term contract.

After the retrenchment imposed by phylloxera, the area of vineyards stabilized at around 135,000 hectares at the start of the twentieth century. After the second world war, it declined fairly steadily to a minimum just below 100,000 hectares, and then recovered through the 1980s. It now stands at around 120,000 hectares. The steady increase in yields means that Bordeaux has 20% less vineyards than a century ago, but 50% more production.[10] With vintage variation reduced somewhat by modern viticulture, production has been steady for some years at around 60 million cases annually.

In spite of its reputation for sticking to tradition, Bordeaux has actually seen significant change. Its renown over the past two centuries has been based on its red wines, but in terms of overall production, the focus on black varieties is relatively recent. Until the 1960s, plantings of white grape varieties were in the majority. As recently as 1968 they were still 50%, but white wine just wasn't selling, so the Bordelais adjusted. White wine production fell dramatically to a small minority by 1988. Today, Bordeaux produces 90% red wine.

Bordeaux AOPs

	Cases (millions)
Red	
Bordeaux AOP	30
Côtes de Bordeaux	8
Graves	2
Medoc	8
Libournais	6
Dry white	5
Sweet white	1
Total	61

Bordeaux is divided into the left bank and right bank by the Garonne river, which joins the Dordogne river just north of the city to form the Gironde estuary (which gives its name to the local political and administrative unit, the Département de Gironde). The left bank is divided into the Médoc, the peninsula to the north of the city, and the Graves, which extends south from the suburbs of the city. The right bank stands alone, well separated from the city.

Virtually all wine in Bordeaux falls under the Appellation Contrôlée system. Accounting for about half of all production, AOP Bordeaux is the lowest level of the hierarchy. It can come from anywhere in the region, but most of the areas that produce wine under the generic Bordeaux label are on the right bank. At the next level, there are some broad district appellations. Côtes de Bordeaux describes wine coming from broad regions adjacent to the river on the right bank; and Entre-deux-Mers (which literally means "between two seas") describes the region between the Garonne and Dordogne rivers. All of these areas produce both red and white wines.

At the top level, the most important appellations on the right bank are the Libournais, a small cluster of appellations taking their name from the town of Libourne on the Dordogne river (formerly a port used for exporting wine). The best appellations in the Libournais are St. Emilion and Pomerol, surrounded by a group of satellite appellations. They produce only red wine.

Close to the city, Pessac-Léognan is most important part of Graves. The best white wines of Bordeaux come from here, as well as some very fine reds. The rest of Graves extends well to the south. The sweet wine regions around Sauternes lie towards the southern tip of the Graves (with some regions for sweet wine production opposite on the other side of the Garonne).

To the north of Bordeaux, Haut-Médoc describes wines from the southern part of the Médoc, and Médoc describes wines from the Bas-Médoc farther from the city (Bas is not used in the name of the appellation because it is considered to be pejorative). Both can be used only for red wine. (If white wine is made in a red wine appellation, it must be labeled as Bordeaux AOP). Within the Haut-Médoc, communal appellations take the names of the local villages, the important ones along the river being Margaux, St. Julien, Pauillac, and St. Estèphe.

The majority of producers are on the right bank; more than half make wines only of the lowest level appellations, AOP Bordeaux and the Côtes. The left bank altogether has roughly a quarter of the producers. There is a huge price

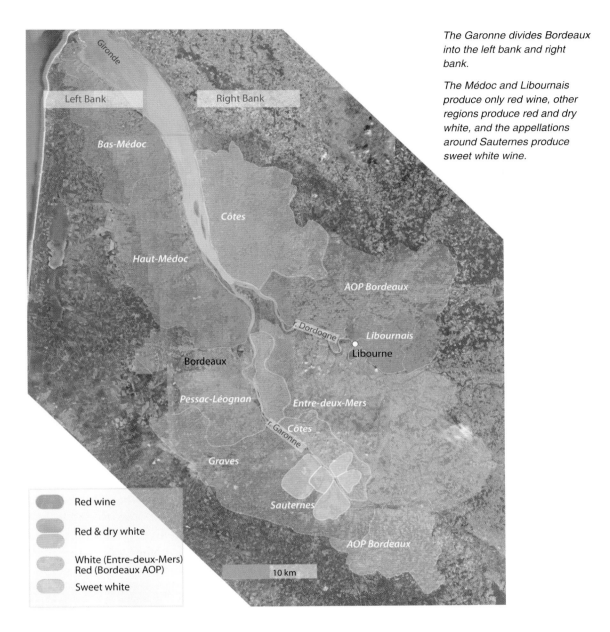

The Garonne divides Bordeaux into the left bank and right bank.

The Médoc and Libournais produce only red wine, other regions produce red and dry white, and the appellations around Sauternes produce sweet white wine.

gap between generic Bordeaux compared with the wines of the Haut-Médoc, Pessac-Léognan, and Libournais, so the latter regions are far more important in terms of revenues.

There is no single prescription for Bordeaux wine. "Bordeaux is huge with a bigger production than the whole of Australia...There is no requirement for it to be homogeneous," says Jonathan Maltus of Château Teyssier. Indeed, there can be wide variation in the proportions of the different grape varieties. Six types of black grapes and six types of white grapes are allowed in Bordeaux,[11] but most black plantings are Cabernet Sauvignon, Merlot, or Cabernet Franc, and almost all white plantings are Sauvignon Blanc or Sémillon.

The appellation rules nominally allow the same grape varieties to be grown anywhere in Bordeaux, but in fact there is a major difference between left bank and right bank. Cabernet Sauvignon and Merlot dominate the left bank, whereas Merlot and Cabernet Franc dominate the right bank. This is a response to the difference in the soils. Gravel-based soils on the left bank create a slighter warmer environment than the cold clay-based soils of the right bank. The result is that Cabernet Sauvignon ripens reliably only on the left bank.

For white wines, it's not so much the geography as the type of wine you want to make that determines the blend. Bordeaux white wines are produced from Sauvignon Blanc and Sémillon, with the former comprising the majority of the blend for dry wines, and the proportions reversed for sweet wines. There is also a little Muscadelle, but its tendency to rusticity has led to a decline.

Although Bordeaux's great reputation was built on wines based on Cabernet Sauvignon, this is really true only of parts of the left bank. If Bordeaux were classified according to the proportion of Cabernet Sauvignon, it would be divided into three parts: Médoc/Pessac-Léognan; Graves; and the right bank. Cabernet Sauvignon is the most important grape in the Médoc peninsula; it's a clear majority of plantings in the major communes, and a bit less in the Haut-Médoc and Médoc AOPs.[12] It's more than half in Pessac-Léognan. Although Graves is usually considered to be part of the left bank—well, of course, it is part of it geographically—in terms of cépages it is half way between the Médoc and the right bank, roughly one third Cabernet Sauvignon to two thirds Merlot. The right bank is three quarters Merlot, with very little Cabernet Sauvignon—where Cabernet is grown it is more often Cabernet Franc. Cabernet Sauvignon is at its lowest in the Libournais, where it is rarely above 10%.

Overall, Merlot is by far the dominant grape variety in Bordeaux, approaching two thirds of all plantings; Cabernet Sauvignon is only a quarter. There has been a steady movement towards Merlot all over Bordeaux during the past half-century. On the left bank, this increases the proportion of Merlot as a minority component;[13] on the right bank it involves a further emphasis on Merlot, which is heading towards monovarietal territory as Cabernet Franc decreases. Other varieties have all but disappeared (there is a small proportion of Petit Verdot in the Médoc, and tiny amounts of Malbec in various vineyards). The increasing proportion of Merlot is a significant factor in the recent change in the style of Bordeaux to be fruitier so that it can be drunk when younger.

The key to understanding the style(s) of Bordeaux is blending. This is a typically pragmatic solution to the problem of growing grapes in a marginal climate (marginal at least for the varieties being grown), by offering some protection against the vagaries of vintage variation. Cabernet Sauvignon does not ripen reliably every year on the left bank, so blending with varieties that ripen more easily offers two advantages: adding riper flavors to the wine than can be obtained with Cabernet Sauvignon alone; and being able to vary the composition of the blend to respond to failures and successes each year. It also allows greater vineyard areas to be cultivated, since Merlot will ripen in spots where Cabernet is not successful.

Each variety contributes its own character to the blend. Wines on the left bank often contain all four varieties. The most powerful, Cabernet Sauvignon, has the most structure in the form of tannins. Its preponderance gives left bank wines their backbone and structure, even a touch of austerity, and is responsible for their longevity. In the context of Bordeaux, the Cabernets can be overwhelming without the softening effect of Merlot, which offers a generous fleshiness to round out the palate. The dominance of Merlot gives right bank wines their generosity, even overt fruitiness. Cabernet Franc on the right bank plays an equivalent role to the left bank's Cabernet Sauvignon, but shows more of a leafy, tobacco quality. As a minor partner, Cabernet Franc adds structure and freshness to lighten up the Merlot. The last variety, Petit Verdot, is usually used in the Médoc only in small quantities, adding a faint spiciness and density that lends interest to the fruit quality of the wine.

Even today, with warmer vintages and better viticulture, there is still significant variation in the proportions of varieties in the blend each year, depending on conditions. Cabernet Sauvignon may do better in a warmer year, but fail to ripen in a cooler year; Merlot may become too ripe in a really warm year, although ripening well in a cooler year. The result is that Cabernet Sauvignon may go from being the dominant variety to less than half the blend from one year to the next in a left bank wine. In an extreme case, Lafite Rothschild was 72% Cabernet Sauvignon in 1992 (just a little under its usual proportion), but there was only 36% Cabernet Sauvignon in 1991.

Vintage character therefore depends not only on overall ripeness, but also on the proportion of each variety that ends up in the blend. (There is less annual variation in the blend on the right bank.) Sometimes they talk about "Cabernet years" or "Merlot years," meaning that one variety was distinctly more successful than the other (this is sometimes caused less by overall temperatures than by the timing of rainfall, which can occur between the harvest dates for Merlot and Cabernet).

Yields in Bordeaux are not such a sensitive issue as they are elsewhere. The range of yield limits is quite small, nominally from 55 hl/ha for generic Bordeaux AOP to 45 hl/ha for the communes of the Médoc. But in fact it's a nonsense. For 2008, the limit for the Haut-Médoc was increased to 55 hl/ha, the same as Bordeaux, and higher than Bordeaux Supérieur which was 53 hl/ha. The communes were even higher yet at 57 hl/ha! "Numbers mean what I say they mean," as Humpty Dumpty might have said. Uniquely for France, there's no relationship between yields and the classification of wines.

A difference in the scale of production between left and right banks has indirect consequences for winemaking. Estates are larger on the left bank, which means they have resources for all the latest equipment, such as machines for optically sorting the berries, or for reverse osmosis or evaporation sous vide to counteract dilution in the must at harvest. All of this contributes to increasing richness in style, showing most directly in the intensity of wines in good vintages, but also in the vast improvement in quality in poor vintages.

	ha	cases
Margaux	1,494	700,000
St. Julien	913	450,000
Pauillac	1,220	600,000
St. Estèphe	1,214	625,000
Listrac	498	300,000
Moulis	596	300,000
Haut-Médoc	4,572	2,400,000
Médoc	5,523	3,000,000
Grand Cru Classé	3,400	2,000,000
Cru Bourgeois	6,000	3,600,000
Cooperatives		1,000,000
Médoc Total	16,029	8,400,000

Driving along the D2 from Bordeaux into the Médoc, the terrain seems unrelentingly flat. The road passes through Margaux, with important châteaux on either side, followed by a break of uncultivated land or pastures, until reaching St. Julien, Pauillac, and St. Estèphe. The highest point in Pauillac is only 30 m; a bit inland, Listrac reaches the dizzy heights of 43 m. You are scarcely conscious of the Gironde, parallel with the road, beyond the vineyards on the right side, although in fact it is the omnipresent influence on climate and terroir.

Today's terrain owes as much to human intervention as to nature. Until the seventeenth century, the area was dominated by palus (wetlands adjacent to the river) and marais (inland marshes). This changed when Henri IV engaged Dutch engineers to drain the marshes in 1599. The work continued over the next two hundred years.[14] The remaining marais are preserved wetlands. The effect on viticulture is mostly indirect: few vineyards are on drained land, but the general lowering of the water table improved the terroir. However, drainage remains an issue. Many of the major châteaux have installed miles of drainage pipes under their vineyards. Better drainage is one reason why gravel terroirs are better than clay, but there can still be problems in a wet season. Bordeaux has a rainy climate, but the issue is not so much total rainfall as the problem of fungal diseases resulting from humidity in the growing season, and rainfall around the time of harvest.

The best vineyards in the Médoc are the most elevated, located on gravel mounds (geological structures that give good drainage). The land slopes down gently to the river. Although the terrain inland looks quite flat to the casual eye, even a small elevation is enough to lift it significantly higher above the water table. The importance of drainage is emphasized by the old Médocian saying, "The best vines can see the river," meaning that the vineyards are located on slopes draining into the Gironde (or sometimes into one of the streams running into it). "It's very easy to spot the best terroir in Pauillac, you don't need to be a

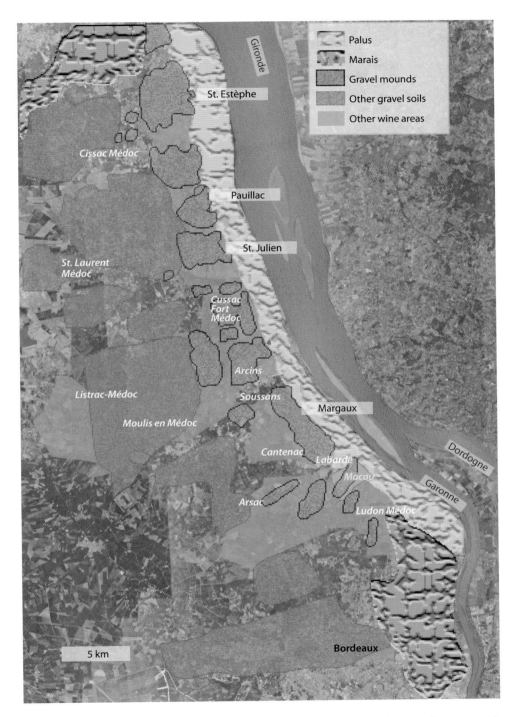

The best vineyards are located on a series of gravel mounds parallel with the Gironde.

Legend:
- Palus
- Marais
- Gravel mounds
- Other gravel soils
- Other wine areas

Gironde

St. Estèphe

Cissac Médoc

Pauillac

St. Julien

St. Laurent Médoc

Cussac Fort Médoc

Arcins

Listrac-Médoc

Soussans

Margaux

Moulis en Médoc

Cantenac

Labarde

Macau

Dordogne

Arsac

Ludon Médoc

Garonne

Bordeaux

5 km

geologist, you just need to be on top of the hill (although hill is a relative term), able to see gravel, and you look ahead and see the river," says Jean-Charles Cazes of Château Lynch Bages.

The Médoc is gravelly with a gentle slope down to the river, as seen in this view from Château Montrose towards the Gironde.

The gravel mounds form a line of outcrops more or less parallel with the river, all the way from Pessac-Léognan to St. Estèphe. A mound is typically 5-6 km long and 1-2 km wide, with topsoil on compact sand, on top of a gravel bed that can range from a few centimeters to 2 or 3 meters in depth.[15] The deeper the better. The gravel mound forces the grapevines to send their roots down deep, in the best cases several meters to the water table, which ensures an even supply of water during the growing season.

In a historical context where the climate was marginal, and Cabernet Sauvignon was the last ripening variety and most marginal of all, yet clearly the most distinguished, inevitably the best terroirs were regarded as those that ripen the Cabernet most reliably. Microclimates are important. Resulting from the combination of soil and proximity to the river, the warmest spots on the left bank are centered on the gravel mounds;[16] this may be what gives the great communes along the Gironde that crucial advantage in maturing Cabernet Sauvignon. Merlot tends to be planted *faute de mieux*, on soils richer in clay where Cabernet would not ripen reliably enough. The clay-rich soils are generally found near the river and then farther inland, confining Cabernet Sauvignon

to a relatively narrow band parallel with the river. "Cabernet
Sauvignon is reserved for the
best terroirs, it's absolutely necessary to have gravel, exposure,
and sun," says Jean Gautreau of
Sociando-Mallet. With one or
two exceptions of notable cases
where Merlot has been planted
on gravel soils (Châteaux Palmer
in Margaux and Pichon Lalande
in Pauillac are the leading examples), the general policy is to
plant Cabernet Sauvignon wher-
ever there is gravel.

Experience at Château Margaux shows the depth of the
distinction between gravel and
clay soils. "We grow Cabernet
Sauvignon in different terroirs

Running along the border of Château Lafite, this jalle (small stream) separates Pauillac (on the left) from St. Estèphe. There are jalles running down to the Gironde all along the Médoc.

here. We are lucky to have the diversity of soils. We grow Cabernet Sauvignon
where it does best, on the gravelly soils, but we also grow it in front of the cellar where there is clay. And the two wines are absolutely different, you would
never believe they are made from the same grape. So the influence of the grape
is much less than the terroir. We have Merlot on both gravels and clay; when
we taste the wines blind we always make a family of the two wines coming
from the same terroir, not from the grapes. So each group represents its terroir,"
maintains Margaux's director, Paul Pontallier.

The traditional view of Bordeaux ascribes distinct characters to each of the
communes. Local attitudes are captured by Jean-Paul Bignot of Château Talbot
in St. Julien: "In St. Julien we like to say that the wines have the elegance of
Margaux and the strength of Pauillac." Certainly Margaux can be the most elegant, sometimes almost delicate, the most feminine they used to say; St. Julien
is the most precise and refined; Pauillac is the most powerful, with a distinct
extra sheen, certainly the most masculine; and St Estèphe is the hardest, even
in some vintages turning towards rustic. This is a simplification, of course, but
the really interesting question is to what extent you can relate these characteristics to the terroirs of the appellations.

Margaux is in some ways the most difficult, because it is the largest and
most disparate. The soils are generally poor, and not very deep, so they warm
up quickly, usually making Margaux the first appellation to harvest. For the
same reason, drought is more of a problem in dry years, which is why Margaux

under-performed in some of the top years for the other communes (notably 1982 and 1990). On the other hand, some low lying parts of Margaux have enough clay that drainage is a problem in wet years. In some ways, the two top châteaux identify two extremes. Sitting on a base of bedrock and gravel, Château Margaux is typically dominated by Cabernet Sauvignon, fine, elegant, and precise. Its neighbor and rival, Château Palmer, unusually has as much Merlot as Cabernet Sauvignon, and conveys a warmer impression. Whether Château Margaux or Château Palmer best represents Margaux is a matter of opinion. Their wines are certainly the richest of the appellation, but there are others at all levels displaying its characteristic finesse. At the southern end, which runs into the Haut-Médoc, the wines are less refined.

Moving north, St. Julien is the smallest appellation, and the most homogenous. Soils are deep gravel: some people feel that the châteaux nearest the river produce the most elegant wines. Actually I'm inclined myself to think that going north along the river, the wines become progressively more powerful, from the tightness of Gruaud Larose or Beychevelle, to the extreme elegance of Ducru Beaucaillou, the precision of Léoville Barton, the roundness of Léoville Poyferré, and the richness of Léoville Lascases, which after all adjoins Château Latour, immediately across the border in Pauillac. St. Julien has no châteaux in the very top level of the classification system (see next section), but the great châteaux along the river have unparalleled refinement.

It would be a fine taster who could always distinguish Léoville Lascases as coming from St. Julien compared with Pichon Lalande as coming from the southern edge of Pauillac. Yet as a rule the wines of Pauillac are the most powerful in the Haut-Médoc. Pauillac is entirely on a gravel mound, but has a slightly higher clay content that increases body in the wine. Pauillac's reputation partly depends on the fact that it has three of the acknowledged top châteaux, with styles ranging from Château Latour's sheer Rolls-Royce power to Lafite Rothschild's supreme elegance, with Mouton Rothschild somewhere in between. The distinction of Pauillac is that it maintains that combination of power and refinement across all levels, from the châteaux considered to be just below the top (Pichon Lalande, Pichon Baron, Lynch Bages, and Pontet Canet) to those representing the mainstream (Grand Puy Lacoste), and even a few small châteaux (although these are slowly being gobbled up by bigger players). There are few ordinary wines in Pauillac.

The town of Pauillac sits at the edge of the Gironde with a partly gentrified waterfront. Between the town and St. Estèphe to the north, it is Rothschild country: the holdings of the two branches of the Rothschild family comprise the majority of vineyards. The company of Baron Philippe de Rothschild owns Châteaux Mouton Rothschild, d'Armailhac, and Clerc Milon; DBR (Domains Barons de Rothschild) owns Châteaux Lafite Rothschild and Duhart Milon. There is more variety in ownership in the southern half of the appellation.

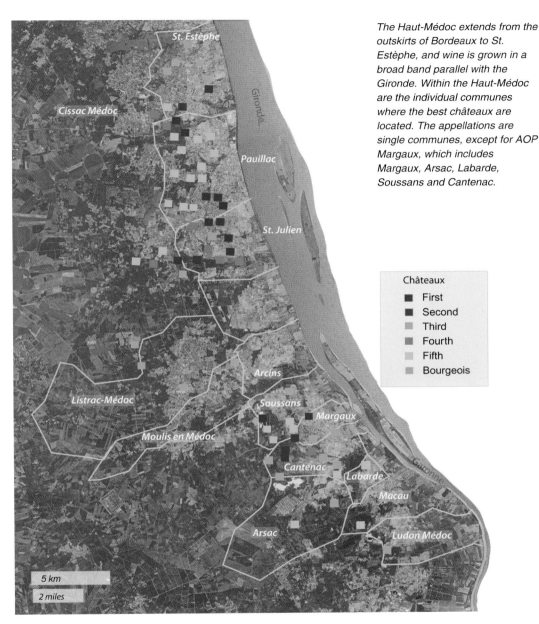

The Haut-Médoc extends from the outskirts of Bordeaux to St. Estèphe, and wine is grown in a broad band parallel with the Gironde. Within the Haut-Médoc are the individual communes where the best châteaux are located. The appellations are single communes, except for AOP Margaux, which includes Margaux, Arsac, Labarde, Soussans and Cantenac.

Châteaux	
■	First
■	Second
■	Third
■	Fourth
■	Fifth
■	Bourgeois

As you cross over the Jalle de Breuil, the small stream that separates Pauillac from St. Estèphe, the land begins to rise, and the vineyards are a little more ele-vated. The best châteaux are close to the river, as farther inland there is significantly more clay; this is responsible for St. Estèphe's reputation for hard-ness or rusticity. The increased clay content means there is more Merlot in St. Estèphe. The extremes of St. Estèphe, and the difficulties of making generaliza-tions, are illustrated by its top two châteaux. With the most exotic appearance in the Médoc resulting from the Indian connections of its first owner, Cos

The Rothschilds own most of the châteaux and vineyards in the northern part of Pauillac.[17]

d'Estournel now makes a wine to match: rich, intense, and more international in style than most. For years at the far extreme of restraint, Château Montrose always made one of the slowest wines to develop, and the longest lived. Any reasonable person would immediately assume this means that Montrose has more Cabernet Sauvignon than Cos d'Estournel; but in fact it's the other way round. No other châteaux in St. Estèphe approach the quality of the two leaders, but there are many smaller reliable châteaux here.

Aligned with the gap between Margaux and St. Julien, but a few kilometers inland, Moulis and Listrac have more of a focus on Merlot, because their distance from the Gironde makes the climate a bit cooler. The distinctive feature here isn't really the appellation name but the Grand Poujeaux plateau, in Moulis, where the best châteaux, Chasse-Spleen and Poujeaux, are located, with terroir that is gravelly like the top communes.

The first thing you ask about most French wines is where the wine comes from: what is its appellation? But Bordeaux is different. The first thing you look at is the name of the château. The place of origin and the quality of the wine are all tied up in this one name. How did this happen?

The key to understanding the relationship of terroir to classification in Bordeaux is that there is no relationship. Or to be more precise, there are two independent classification systems. The appellation system has some connection to terroir, but does not have the same detailed implications for quality as elsewhere in France, because it scarcely has any hierarchy. However, it is true that the best areas are identified by their AOPs: Pessac-Léognan in Graves; Margaux, St. Julien, Pauillac, and St. Estèphe in the Médoc; and Pomerol and St. Emilion on the right bank. Châteaux located in these communes state the AOP on the label.[18] But where there are classification systems defining a hierarchy of quality, it is the châteaux that are classified, and their classification is far more important as an imprimatur of quality than the AOP.

In any case, the large scale of production on the left bank would make it difficult to assign a single classification for the terroir of any individual château. A château's holdings are rarely in a single, contiguous block; often they are interspersed with the plots of other châteaux. And there is significant heterogeneity in the terrain in the Médoc, which can change rapidly over short distances. So usually there is appreciable variation within the vineyards of a single château. Furthermore, a château may produce more than one wine, typically a grand vin (which carries its name) and a second wine, so it's not necessarily straightforward to relate the individual wines to specific terroirs.

Individual châteaux began to fall into a hierarchy during the eighteenth century, as the brokers in Bordeaux established a pricing system. Over a century, châteaux moved slowly up or down the hierarchy, although the top four stayed the same and became separated from the rest.[19] The classification was largely a tool for internal use by the brokers, and it was really just an accident that the order became fixed for perpetuity in 1855, when Emperor Napoleon III organized a Universal Exposition in Paris to provide a showcase for French products. To highlight the wines, the Chamber of Commerce commissioned a wine map of the Gironde. They asked the brokers in Bordeaux to provide a list of the leading châteaux, identified by class and commune, to accompany it.[20] The sole criterion for classification was pricing in prior years.

Classification

61 Grand Cru Classé (1855)
20% production

250 Cru Bourgeois (2010)
30% production

Communes
265 Châteaux; 135 second wines
Haut-Médoc & Bas-Médoc
481 Châteaux; 139 second wines

The Grand Exposition of 1855 at the Palais de l'Industrie in Paris displayed products from all over France. Napoleon III and Empress Eugénie were pictured visiting the exhibition. The arrangements made to include the wines of the Gironde had a permanent effect upon the classification of wines in Bordeaux.

The 1855 classification (as it is now generally known) divided the most important châteaux into five narrowly separated price bands, from Premier Grand Cru Classé (first growths) to Cinquième Grand Cru Classé (fifth growths).[21] The first growths at the top of the hierarchy sold for roughly twice the prices of the fifth growths at the bottom.[22] That gap has now widened enormously, to more than ten fold. The 1855 classification covers 61 châteaux, 60 in the Médoc, plus Château Haut Brion in Pessac-Léognan.[23] The classification was (and is) no more than a snapshot of the brokers' commercial opinions at this particular point in time, but the system has stuck. So unlike other regions in France, Bordeaux classifies producers rather than land. Indeed, the classification has been so successful in establishing the reputations of the châteaux that it was imitated in subsequent classifications in Bordeaux.

The Grand Cru Classés are the smallest group of châteaux in the Médoc, but have by far the most economic importance. They are relatively large estates, with an average vineyard size of 55 ha (135 acres) and an annual production averaging around 300,000 bottles each. Many of them do in fact have a very grand château, although these days they are rarely the homes of the proprietors, and are used more for official entertaining. Although the classed growths have about 20% of the planted vineyards and production in the Haut-Médoc, they account for at least twice that proportion of revenue.

Classification based on price represents nothing more or less than the relative success of each château during the period of assessment. This may depend on the quality of the terroir at that time, but also reflects the quality of viticulture and vinification, not to mention the marketing skills of the owner. A château's vineyards today are not necessarily the same as those it held in 1855, as châteaux can (and often do) change their holdings by trading land. The château is a brand name, and its vineyards can change without affecting its classification. In fact, few classified châteaux have exactly the same vineyards today as in 1855. There are no regulations for the Grand Cru Classés; their status was conferred once and for all by the brokers' list of 1855. This is unique to the left bank of Bordeaux.

The first growths really do have an advantage in terroir, with their key vineyards located on gravel mounds up to 9 meters deep with a relatively low water table.[24] The other leading châteaux also mostly lie along the band of the gravel mounds, but they have more variation in terroir. With the exception of the first growths, there is not really any geological evidence to support a hierarchy among them, or necessarily to distinguish them from other châteaux close by, given the extent and diversity of their vineyards.[25] This is not to decry the importance of terroir, or of making the best matches between grape varieties and individual vineyard parcels, but other factors, including restriction of yield and the assignment of lots between the grand vin and any second wine, are equally important in establishing the brand of each château.

As the 1855 classification has never been revised, it is now wildly out of date: only around half of the châteaux would retain their place in a new classification based on current prices.[26] Yet it continues to have enormous influence. The very existence of the first growths sets a glass ceiling that other châteaux cannot penetrate. Châteaux Latour, Lafite Rothschild, Margaux, and Haut Brion were classed as Premier Grand Cru Classés in 1855; the addition of Mouton Rothschild in 1973 made it the only château ever to be promoted, a tribute to Baron Philippe's political influence, and unlikely to be emulated by anyone else.[27] Classified growths that would not make the cut today have their prices inflated by those magic words "Grand Cru Classé du Médoc en 1855." And the very best of the unclassified châteaux, such as Haut-Marbuzet or Sociando-Mallet, may be kept from achieving yet higher prices by their exclusion. The mythic power of the classification is shown by the resurrection of classified châteaux that became derelict, and all but ceased to produce wine. Lazarus-like, properties such as Desmirail and Ferrières have been reconstituted with new vineyards,[28] gaining instant credibility because the brand is classified.

Except for the first growths, the actual level of classification is now of relatively little significance. Informally, the next group after the first growths are the so-called super-seconds, which include some of the second growths plus others that now perform well above their classification level. At the top, La Mission Haut Brion, Léoville Las Cases, and Palmer price significantly below the first growths, but above the rest of the group, which consists of about six châteaux (Cos d'Estournel, Ducru Beaucaillou, Pichon Lalande, Pichon Baron, Lynch Bages, and Montrose). This is a moving target as other châteaux, such as Léoville Poyferré or Pontet Canet, are rising to join the group. There is a significant price gap between the super-seconds and what remains of the old second growths. After this, there is a more or less continuous distribution of prices for

Château Margaux is known for the grandeur of its tree-lined approach allée. It was bought by André Mentzelop-oulos of the Félix Potin grocer chain in 1977.

the châteaux of the remaining tiers, making it difficult to divide the wines into clear groups.

The Cru Bourgeois classification applies to châteaux that missed out in 1855. The original format in 1932 classified 444 châteaux into the ascending levels of Cru Bourgeois, Cru Bourgeois Supérieur, and Cru Bourgeois Exceptionnel.[29] A revision in 2003 classified 247 châteaux, but was overthrown after challenges from dissatisfied châteaux. Since 2010 there has been a single level of classification for around 250 Cru Bourgeois. In a departure for Bordeaux, the wines are assessed every vintage to determine whether they meet a standard for quality (allowing for vintage conditions),[30] so the number changes slightly each year.[31] "We are not assessing style, everyone is free to define their own style, but we are really concerned with quality. Typicity is really more a matter for the AOC," says Frédérique Dutheiller de Lamothe, Directrice of the Alliance des Crus Bourgeois.[32] So the Cru Bourgeois marque has become more of a stamp of quality each year than a classification of the château.

Châteaux that are not included in the 1855 classification do not necessarily participate in the Cru Bourgeois classification. By any standard, Sociando-Mallet would be well up the list of Grand Cru Classés if there were any re-

classification. However, the château decided not to be included in current classifications because in effect that would stamp the wine at the Cru Bourgeois level: "There are the Grand Cru Classés, there are the Cru Bourgeois, and then there is Sociando-Mallet," they say firmly. Château Gloria, created since the 1940s by acquiring vineyards from Grand Cru Classés, has never belonged to any classification. And several of the châteaux that were originally classified at the top of the hierarchy as Cru Bourgeois Exceptionnel declined to join the new single-level classification.[33]

Château La Tour Carnet in Margaux has black swans swimming in its moat. It is owned by mogul Bernard Magrez.

Today there is a difference in attitudes between the Grand Cru Classés and the Cru Bourgeois. The top Grand Cru Classés are effectively marketed as luxury goods: there is no relationship between cost of production and market price, which has now risen beyond the means of traditional wine lovers. Cru Bourgeois, by contrast, have increased steadily, but less dramatically (and less erratically) in price. Between 2000 and 2009, classed growths roughly tripled in price (more for the first growths) but Cru Bourgeois didn't even double. The Cru Bourgeois have not followed the classed growths into an increasingly lush style with more extraction, perhaps because their terroirs do not support it, but more likely because the economic returns do not justify the costs.

Pichon Baron in Pauillac has a splendid reflecting pool. It is owned by giant insurance company AXA.

There are Cru Bourgeois in all appellations of the Médoc, but roughly 200 are in the Médoc or Haut-Médoc AOPs, leaving few in the top communes. In fact, Cru Bourgeois are somewhat becoming the representation of the best of the Médoc or Haut-Médoc, while Grand Cru Classés represent the communes. All the same, Frédérique Dutheiller de Lamothe says, "The increase in price of cru classés has created a window for us because we are in the same appellations." Indeed, I sometimes wonder whether the top Cru Bourgeois more faithfully represent the tradition of Bordeaux for light, elegant wine that complements food. While they may not be able to compete at tastings with Grand Cru Classés, Cru Bourgeois may offer the last refuge for wine lovers driven out of Bordeaux by the price of the classed growths. Then the question becomes whether to try a Cru Bourgeois or the second wine of a Grand Cru Classé.

Thirty years ago, most châteaux in Bordeaux produced a single wine. Quality would go up and down with the vintage, the blend would vary depending on the success or otherwise of each variety, but basically you would be getting the same wine each year, made from the same vineyards, subject to individual vintage variation. Except for some châteaux that are too small, or whose proprietors object in principle to the concept, most leading châteaux now produce

Cos d'Estournel is famous for its exotic structure. It is owned by Michel Reybier, of the luxury hotel group.

a second wine. (A few have gone in the other direction by creaming off the best of the crop to make a super-cuvée.) Altogether there are around 700 second wines in Bordeaux, divided roughly between left and right banks. They are a bit more common on the left bank, where the larger average size of the châteaux makes it easier to divide production. They also tend to be concentrated in the top communes; on average, up to half of production may go into the second wine, which usually sells for a price under a third of the grand vin.

Before the 1980s, second wines were somewhat of a skeleton in the cupboard, rarely acknowledged directly, often labeled under the name of some other château apparently unconnected with the grand château. But today most châteaux flaunt their second wines, by giving them names that play on the château's name. This creates pressure for quality. "Second wines are second best," was a frequent comment when they were first made by declassifying lots that were not up to the standard of the grand vin. Bruno Eynard at Château Lagrange describes the change in recent years: "The second wine used to be a dumping ground—everything was put in it—but now it's much more an independent brand, and there is selection for it. The second wine of a great year today is better than the grand vin of a minor year previously."

Most second wines now come from a range of sources: inferior plots of land (larger châteaux have almost inevitably accumulated some plots of lesser terroir over the years), production from young vines (which are generally felt to produce wine of lower quality), cépages that were less successful in a given vintage, and use of vin de presse (made by pressing the grapes at the end of fermentation, giving lower quality than the wine made from the juice released earlier). Only a few second wines still come exclusively from lots that are declassified from the grand vin.

The original impetus for second wines was to use declassification of lots to improve the grand vin, so they would increase in proportion in poor vintages,[34] but in the past few vintages they have been approaching 50% of production irrespective of the year. Because total production has increased about 50%, this means that the volume of the grand vin has stayed more or less steady. All the same, almost a quarter of the châteaux now produce more "second" wine than grand vin: sometimes the second wine has been turned into the regular production, with the grand vin effectively becoming a more exclusive cuvée.[35] If the trend continues, second wines may become more typical of left bank production than the grand vins. Second (and third) wines make it clear that blending is no longer simply a matter of protection against the vagaries of climate: it is a tool for directing the style of the wine to be become ageworthy (for the grand vin) or more immediately approachable (for the second wine).

Second wines typically have less exposure to oak than grand vins.[36] On the left bank, they usually have more Merlot than grand vins. This gives them a fruitier, more forward and approachable style, making them ready to drink sooner.[37] This is partly a response to criticism that consumers no longer want to cellar wines for many years until they are ready to drink. Originally, second wines were presented as an insight into the style of the grand vin that was less expensive and could be enjoyed sooner, but now they have become brands in their own right, made with different criteria.

Reference Wines for the Left Bank	
Graves	Clos Floridène
Pessac Léognan	Domaine de Chevalier
Margaux	Rauzan-Ségla
St. Julien	Léoville Barton
Pauillac	Grand Puy Lacoste
St. Estèphe	Cos Labory
Moulis-Listrac	Chasse-Spleen
Haut-Médoc	Sociando-Mallet
Médoc	Potensac
Cru Bourgeois	Sérilhan

The main question is a practical one: how do second wines compare with other wines at the same price level? Do second wines have an advantage because they borrow from the expertise of the grand vin, or are they effectively trading on the reputation of the grand vin, possibly selling at an inflated price without offering any special value?[38] Second wines tend to sell at a price level one or two notches below the grand vin; for example, the second wines of the first growths are usually available at price levels corresponding to the second growths, the second wines of the Deuxième Crus sell with the third or fourth growths, and so on. When I first compared second wines directly with Cru Bourgeois almost ten years ago, the second wines did not come off well; but since then they have become progressively more important, especially when they represent the major production of a château, and today many are fine wines in their own right. But I still doubt whether they represent the château and appellation in the same way as the grand vin.

Immediately south of Bordeaux, the Graves extended directly from the city in medieval times. In the nineteenth century, vineyards were concentrated close to the city in Merignac (where the airport is located today) and Pessac. The vineyards disappeared under the suburban sprawl of Bordeaux: now only a handful of the top estates are left in Pessac, with Haut Brion and Mission Haut Brion surrounded by the city, and the approach to Pape Clément running along a suburban street. Most of the châteaux in Pessac-Léognan are in Léognan or Martillac, a couple of exits down the autoroute from the city.

Graves

Pessac	1,700 ha
	650,000 cases
	80% red
	74 chateaux
	16 Cru Classés
	=20% of production

Graves	3,800 ha
	2 million cases
	67% red
	344 chateaux

No cooperatives

When the appellation of Graves was created in the 1930s, it extended all the way south from Pessac to the sweet wine districts of Sauternes and Barsac (which were excluded from the Graves). In fact, in the first half of the nineteenth century, the vineyards were essentially divided into those in the north around Pessac-Léognan, making dry white and red wine, and those around Sauternes making sweet white wine. In the second half of the century, vineyards expanded south, connecting the two regions, but the southern terroir is not as good.

The Graves is unusual for Bordeaux because white wine has equal billing with red. Graves was classified for red wine production in 1953; the classification system effectively picked out the better châteaux to be described as Cru Classés. The classification was extended to dry white wines in 1959.[39] All the classified châteaux are in the northern part of Graves, which broke away as the new appellation of Pessac-Léognan in 1987. This is

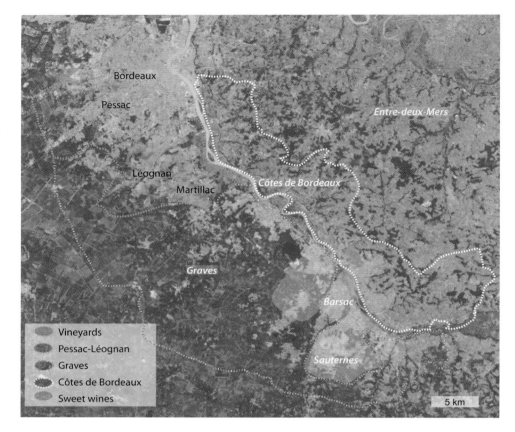

Graves extends south of Bordeaux on the left bank and surrounds Barsac and Sauternes. The northern part of Pessac-Léognan extends right into the suburban sprawl of Bordeaux. The vineyards facing Graves on the right bank are Côtes de Bordeaux.

equivalent in quality to the top communes of the Médoc. Market forces have kept the focus on red wine, which is more than three quarters of production, but this is also the source of Bordeaux's top white wines. However, it's only at the very top level that the reputation of the whites is able to rival the reds.

The gravel mound at Pessac is as profound as those in the Haut-Médoc, but the general mix of varieties in Pessac-Léognan is biased more towards Merlot. Cabernet Sauvignon is just about half of plantings (compared with 60% in the four top communes of the Médoc), and there is also less Cabernet Franc. "There's almost no Cabernet Franc because there is no chalk in the soil," Rémi Edange explains at Domaine de Chevalier. The wines correspondingly can have a slightly softer impression: the classic description for Pessac-Léognan is "cigar box," meaning smoky with a tobacco-like impression on the finish; but these remain distinctly left bank wines, with a pleasing restraint compared to the fleshiness of the right bank. It is probably fair comment that, with the exception of the very top wines, Pessac-Léognan does not age as long as the top communes of the Médoc. Moving south into Graves, there is more clay in the soil, and the style is more amorphous: a cut above most Côtes de Bordeaux, but with few châteaux really standing out.

Haut Brion and Mission Haut Brion are separated by the main road and surrounded by suburban housing.

The Graves classification (really it should now be called the Pessac-Léognan classification) covers a range more or less equivalent to the five levels of Grand Cru Classé in the Médoc. At the very top come Haut Brion and Mission Haut Brion: no dispute about that! Château Haut Brion has made wine since the sixteenth century, and the monks at neighboring Mission Haut Brion were making wine in the seventeenth century. One of the very first to establish a great reputation abroad, Château Haut Brion was the most fashionable wine in London in the late seventeenth century. "I drank a sort of French wine, called Ho Bryan, that hath a good and most particular taste that I never met with," Samuel Pepys famously noted in his diary in 1663. It was the only wine outside the Médoc to be included in the 1855 classification; today its closest rival is Mission Haut Brion, under the same ownership, which makes for some fascinating comparative tastings.

Next comes a group that epitomizes the extremes of style. Château Pape Clément (originating when the Archbishop of Bordeaux became Pope Clément V and gave his private vineyard to the archdiocese), led the way into a more international style when Bernard Magrez started to revive it in 1985. More recently Smith Haut Lafitte has moved in the same direction, and I sometimes

Typical vineyards in Léognan are relatively flat and surrounded by woods. Château Malartic-Lagravière displays typical terrain under the snow of winter. Courtesy Cru Classés Graves.

feel it's difficult to decide which has become more international in any particular year. The classic balance of Haut Bailly is more traditional; it is sumptuous, but always dominated by the structure of Cabernet Sauvignon. It has one of the oldest plots of vines in Bordeaux, dating from the very start of the twentieth century. Unusually for the region, Haut Bailly produces only red wine. Domaine de Chevalier remains for me the most elegant wine, really highlighting the precision of Cabernet Sauvignon. The quartet is more or less equivalent to the second growths of the Médoc. The remaining classified growths run a gamut from third to fifth growths.

What's the problem with white wine? The very top white wines actually price higher than red wines from the same estates: Haut Brion, Laville Haut Brion (the white wine of Mission Haut Brion and since 2009 labeled under the name of La Mission), and Domaine de Chevalier. But others are less successful. The small amount of clay and limestone means there are in fact fewer locations where it's appropriate to plant white grapevines in Pessac-Léognan. The traditional proportions for a white wine are 80% Sauvignon Blanc to 20% Sémillon, with the former contributing those grassy, herbaceous notes, and the latter a waxy fatness. But today there is a good deal more variation, from white wines made exclusively or almost exclusively from Sauvignon Blanc (Smith Haut Lafitte in the lead) with others having more or less equal proportions of the varieties (Haut Brion, Mission Haut Brion, Pape Clément). Recently there's been a move to use some Sauvignon Gris (actually a pink variant of Sauvignon Blanc), which does well on slightly cooler soils.

A white Pessac-Léognan is made much like a white Burgundy, with alcoholic fermentation in the barrel followed by malolactic fermentation. Significant amounts of new oak may be used for the top wines. Varietal character means there tends to be more of a herbaceous bite, less of a buttery impression, but there's that same sense of layers of flavor. Below the top levels, there's a tendency for the wines to seem a little on the thin side, and sometimes lacking in real flavor interest. Moving south to Graves, the low price for white wine and lack of barrel fermentation formed a self-reinforcing cycle until the 1980s when barrel fermentation became common. Where there is more clay and limestone, the soils are actually well suited to white wine, and the best wines today are workmanlike, but, like the reds, cannot really compete with their counterparts in Pessac-Léognan. The tendency in the whites is to make fresh, lively wines, for current drinking.

If it were not for the history of concentrating distribution through the Place de Bordeaux, the Right Bank might well have been defined as a different region from the Left Bank. It shares the same principle of assemblage from more than one variety, but the principal grape is Merlot, and often the only other variety is Cabernet Franc. Its appearance is different, with gently rolling hills rather than the flatness of the Médoc or Graves. Going around the châteaux feels like navigating through a rabbit warren, compared with the linearity of the Médoc. There is more of a contrast between the top wines and the lesser wines than on the Left Bank, as this is the origin of most AOP Bordeaux.

The heart of quality on the right bank is the Libournais. The border between the top appellations, St. Emilion and Pomerol, is all but imperceptible. Pomerol is the epitome of Merlot, as flaunted by its top château, Pétrus, which is effectively a monovarietal. The focus on Merlot brings a general style that is lush, full, and fruity—more so in Pomerol than in St. Emilion, because there is usually less Cabernet Franc in Pomerol, but the difference in style has narrowed a bit in the past decade with the move to increased ripeness. Surrounding these core appellations is a

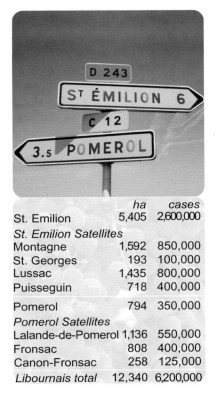

	ha	cases
St. Emilion	5,405	2,600,000
St. Emilion Satellites		
Montagne	1,592	850,000
St. Georges	193	100,000
Lussac	1,435	800,000
Puisseguin	718	400,000
Pomerol	794	350,000
Pomerol Satellites		
Lalande-de-Pomerol	1,136	550,000
Fronsac	808	400,000
Canon-Fronsac	258	125,000
Libournais total	12,340	6,200,000

The town of St. Emilion is on a high point looking out over rolling vineyards.

group of satellites: Fronsac and Canon-Fronsac to the west, Lalande de Pomerol just north of Pomerol, and various subsidiary St. Emilions to the north of St. Emilion, which aim for similar style but have less intensity.

I remember when St. Emilion was a real working town. It was a bit grubby and somewhat dilapidated, but authentic. Now it's a UNESCO site, the number of inhabitants has declined from 8,000 to 2,000, and it's become a tourist site that probably holds the world record for the number of wine shops per mile. It's symbolic of the change occurring on the right bank, which used to be dominated by small family-owned estates but is now succumbing to corporate mergers and acquisitions by the owners of multiple properties, or takeovers by insurance or luxury goods companies. Some châteaux have ceased to exist as they have been incorporated into other, larger properties.

The average size of classified châteaux is 16 ha in St. Emilion, compared with 60 ha for the Grand Cru Classés of the Médoc.[40] By contrast with the many grand châteaux in the Médoc, the buildings are more modest on the right bank. But this is changing. Sharp increases in the value of land have caused many family properties to be sold, not just because of inheritance taxes, but because owners in the family who are not directly involved in wine production want to cash out. The price of top vineyards has reached €2-3 million per hec-

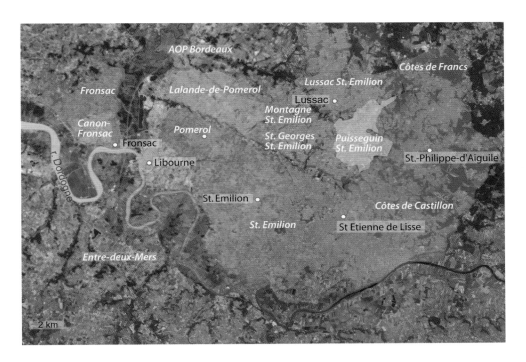

St. Emilion and Pomerol are the heart of the Libournais, ringed by a series of satellite appellations. The appellations to the north are separated from St. Emilion and Pomerol by the stream of the Barbanne. To the south, across the Dordogne, is Entre-deux-Mers.

tare. Flying winemaker Michel Rolland was forced to sell the family estate, Château Bon Pasteur. "It was a family problem—I knew for years that I was going to have to sell the property because my brother wanted to get his share of the money out. It was sad to sell it as it's been in our family since the 1920s."[41] The new owner is an investor from Hong Kong.

As ownership has moved more to rich individuals or corporations, the remaining family owners feel themselves squeezed out. "This is one of the remaining family estates," says Juliette Bécot at Château Beauséjour Bécot. "Family ownership was very common but now it is more and more rare. As a family estate we earn money only from viticulture, but we have to compete with owners who can invest lots of money from other sources." Michel Rolland has a pessimistic view: "No family will be able to save its patrimony."[42]

There's not much official guidance to quality on the right bank, as only St. Emilion has any classification of its châteaux. This did not happen until a full century after the 1855 classification. Classification could have followed the system that had by then been established for the rest of France on the basis of terroir. However, the producers were the driving force, so the châteaux were classified, following the precedent of the left bank. Because INAO was responsible, the classification is nominally part of the AOP system. The criteria for classification are a mélange of price, quality of wine, and terroir, so if a château acquires new vineyards, it may or may not be allowed to use them in the classified wine. This is somewhat shutting the cellar door after the wine has been bottled, as there was never any examination of the terroirs the châteaux had at the outset when the classification was first made.

The first St. Emilion classification was in 1955, with the intention of making regular revisions. In fact, it has been revised four times.[43] The first three revisions made relatively minor changes and were uncontroversial, but the revision in 2006 was thrown out because of legal challenges from châteaux that were demoted. A new St. Emilion classification came into effect finally in 2012. The inclusion of more properties, and the increasing size of the classified properties, has seen the proportion of Grand Cru Classé vineyards increase from 16% in 1996 to 24% in 2012.

Châteaux are divided into three classes. The first group is called "Premier Grand Cru Classé," the same term used for first growths in the Médoc, but is subdivided into two further groups. Originally only two châteaux were classified as the very top level of group A: Ausone and Cheval Blanc. These have always been regarded as generally equivalent to the first growths of the Médoc. Angélus and Pavie have now been promoted into this group. Group B has 14 châteaux in the latest classification. These are roughly equivalent to second growths of the Médoc. A further 63 châteaux are classified just as Grand Cru Classés, nominally equivalent in quality to a range from classified growths of the Médoc to Cru Bourgeois. Actually, these are rather a mixed lot, and some châteaux appear to be included more in recognition of their history than for current quality. In addition, all the producers of St. Emilion (roughly 600 châteaux) can describe themselves as St. Emilion Grand Cru (a term which has little significance except to undermine completely the concept of "Grand Cru"). There is a world of difference between a Grand Cru Classé, which is classified, and a Grand Cru, which has no classification at all.

There is huge variation in terroirs in St. Emilion, to the point at which you wonder how on earth it could have been defined as a single AOC. The answer is that the delineation follows medieval boundaries, with no recognition of the underlying geography. The town of St. Emilion lies at the center of the appellation. Around it is a limestone plateau, where most of the Grand Cru Classés are located. This is called the *calcaire à astéries*, meaning that it's limestone embedded with fossils. Even on the limestone, there is wide variation in the depth of topsoil, but it's the wines from this part of the appellation that define St. Emilion. This is perfect terroir for Cabernet Franc (which was in fact St. Emilion's traditional variety before planting of Merlot was encouraged after phylloxera).[44] The Grand Cru Classés tend to have a little more Cabernet Franc than other wines, although the same trend to an increasing proportion of Merlot has been evident for the past few years as in the Médoc. The cooler clay and limestone soils on the plateau make for later harvests, typically a couple of weeks after the rest of the appellation. Around the limestone plateau, soils are sandy to the west and based on sandstone to the north. To the south, slopes

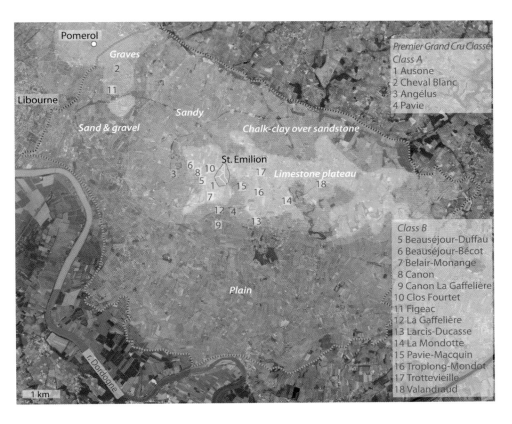

Premier Grand Cru Classé
Class A
1 Ausone
2 Cheval Blanc
3 Angélus
4 Pavie

Class B
5 Beauséjour-Duffau
6 Beauséjour-Bécot
7 Belair-Monange
8 Canon
9 Canon La Gaffelière
10 Clos Fourtet
11 Figeac
12 La Gaffelière
13 Larcis-Ducasse
14 La Mondotte
15 Pavie-Macquin
16 Troplong-Mondot
17 Trottevieille
18 Valandraud

The best terroirs of St. Emilion are the limestone plateau around the town, and the Graves adjacent to Pomerol.

The Premier Grand Cru Classés spread out from the town on the limestone plateau, except for Cheval Blanc and Figeac, which are on the Graves.

with terroir similar to the plateau run down to the plain bordering the Dordogne. Soils are more alluvial here, to the point at which close to the river the classification becomes mere AOP Bordeaux.

The terroir is different in the northwest of the appellation. A gravelly area runs between St. Emilion and Pomerol. There is more Cabernet Franc here, especially at Cheval Blanc where it is usually around half the blend, and there is even some Cabernet Sauvignon at Château Figeac, where the usual blend is one third each of Cabernets Sauvignon and Franc and Merlot. Châteaux just across the border in Pomerol also have more Cabernet Franc.

The Grand Cru Classés show equivalent quality and variation of styles to their counterparts on the Left Bank. I have been struck lately, however, by how similar the styles are for wines at the level of Grand Cru, with a general focus on superficially attractive fruits, a soft palate, and sometimes an impression almost of sweetness on the finish. This may be partly due to common reliance on a small number of oenologues; the days when each proprietor had his own style seem to have passed. "The thing that I find the most unhealthy is the lack of individuality that exists here in Bordeaux. There are around three consultants who appear to drive virtually all of the major Bordeaux players," says Jonathan Maltus of Château Teyssier.

A sign of changing times in St. Emilion, the new winery at Cheval Blanc dwarfs the old château.

The opulent style of St. Emilion became increasingly lush in the last decade of the twentieth century. "St. Emilion in the nineties was the engine for change for fine winemaking," says Jonathan Maltus. This was due to the rise of garage wines, so called because they started as very small scale production, sometimes literally in garages. The principle behind garage wines was to take tiny vineyard plots without particularly distinguished terroir, and to use extreme techniques of viticulture and vinification to produce highly extracted, concentrated wines. There were only about five garage wines when they made their first widespread impact on the market in 1991. Since then, numbers increased fairly steadily until reaching a plateau a few years ago at around 30-40.[45] Garage wines follow the principle of small is beautiful, but perhaps small is expensive would be a more appropriate description: at their peak they were the most expensive wines coming out of St. Emilion.

Garage wines have had an effect out of all proportion to their number and size. There are probably less than 200 ha of vineyards devoted to producing garage wines, generating fewer than 40,000 cases each year in total. This is not much more than the size and annual production of a single Grand Cru Classé of the Médoc. But they have moved the whole market. Initially their innovations were viewed with scorn. "In the early 1990s people in the Médoc were laughing at the garage movement in St. Emilion, but now they have adopted many of the same methods, such as green harvesting," says Stephan von Neipperg at Château Canon la Gaffelière. (Green harvesting consists of pruning off excess berries early in the season to reduce yields).

The phenomenon of garage wines was about as long lived as the wines themselves (with all that extraction they can be attractive when young but tend to fade after a decade), and many of the garagistes have moved on. The trend is typified by two wines. Château Valandraud started in 1991 with only 1,280 bottles, from vines on a relatively sandy plot of land. "I wanted to make a wine that is hedonistic and sexy, soft and chic," says Jean-Luc Thunevin, the self-styled "bad boy" of St. Emilion, who became the first garagiste when he made the first vintage of Château Valandraud (literally) in his garage. Then Valandraud acquired more and better terroirs, and in 2012 became part of the establishment when it was included in the latest classification.

Château La Mondotte, although sharing some of the features of garage wines, comes from a small outstanding plot of 65-year-old vines. It became a separate cuvée because the authorities would not allow it to be included in Canon-La-Gaffelière in the classification of 1996. Subsequently it achieved the reputation of a garage wine. This was the forerunner of a trend for making small cuvées from special plots. "We decided we would bring the single vineyard concept into Bordeaux," says Jonathan Maltus, who produces four special cuvées from different vineyards, pointing out that this is a natural trend for the right bank given the many small vineyards.

Some super-cuvées have been produced by segregating small vineyards of special quality from larger châteaux. Bernard Magrez is somewhat of an expert at this. Sometimes the wines remain as super-cuvées, sometimes they become independent. Magrez-Fombrauge became a separate production after starting as a selection of the best lots at Château Fombrauge. What difference does this make? "I wanted to make it clear that it's the same vines that make the wine each year. The image of a selection is not correct, it gives the impression of taking out the best each year, implying that the château isn't the top wine."

The boundaries have become blurred between garage wines, super-cuvées, and small vineyards with special terroir. There are still some garage wines fitting the original criterion of presenting super-extracted character from terroir of no particular distinction, but they no longer attract the same attention. So are the garage wines finished? "As a phenomenon, that's sure. But not as a niche. But anyway, it's not the phenomenon of garage wines, it's the phenomenon of expensive wines," says Jean-Luc Thunevin.

The latest classification provides a striking validation of the market trend to richer, more powerful, more extracted wines. Ever since the original classification, the perennial contender for promotion to group A has been Château

Vineyards run imperceptibly from St. Emilion into Pomerol as seen by the view at sunset from Cheval Blanc, with the church at Pomerol visible at the right.

Figeac, unusual in St. Emilion for the high content of Cabernet Sauvignon, which gives it more structure and less opulence. But when the first ever promotions to group A were made in 2012, they were of Angélus and Pavie. Château Pavie has been controversial since a famous disagreement between critics as to whether a change in style, after Gérard Pearse bought the château in 1998, was to "a ridiculous wine more reminiscent of a late-harvest Zinfandel" (according to Jancis Robinson MW) or "an off the chart effort...trying to recreate the glories of ancient Bordeaux vintages" (according to Robert Parker). Irrespective of the merits of this wine (the 2003 vintage) the promotion is nothing if not a clear validation of the trend to power. The inclusion in the classification of the former garage wines, Valandraud and La Mondotte, as Premier Grand Cru Classé B, further reinforces the trend.

Completely at the opposite extreme from the gentrified town of St. Emilion, the village of Pomerol is scarcely noticeable: the church is just about the only notable feature. All around are vineyards, mostly with domains housed in small practical buildings. Pétrus was famous for its shabby appearance until some renovations a few years back. Coming from St. Emilion, first you cross the ex-

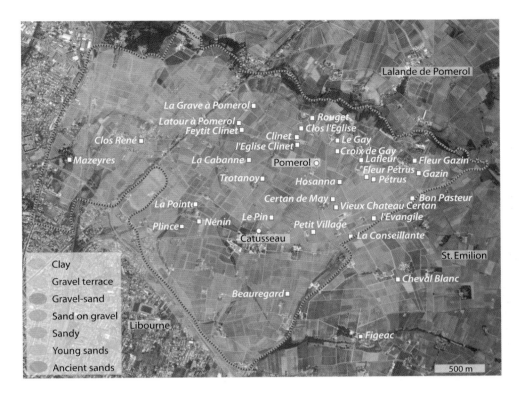

Clay
Gravel terrace
Gravel-sand
Sand on gravel
Sandy
Young sands
Ancient sands

The best châteaux of Pomerol are concentrated on the plateau of gravel terraces in the northeast.

tension of the gravelly area, emerging onto a plateau where the top vineyards are located. This has the oldest soils, and is still relatively gravelly. The most unusual soil is around Château Pétrus, where an area of clay has been pushed up to the surface from lower layers. Named for its protrusion, this is the famous "buttonhole" clay that is thought to give Pétrus its unique character.

Clay in the soil makes a naturally perfect terroir for Merlot, although again Merlot's dominance is relatively recent. It began to increase when replanting was forced by the great winter freeze of 1956. Part of today's increasingly lush style in both Pomerol and St. Emilion is due to the increase in Merlot; since 1983, it has increased in Pomerol from 65-70% to 85% today, and in St. Emilion it has gone from 55-60% to 75% today.

Away from the plateau, the soils are sandier, with varying proportions of gravel: here, to the west and south, the wines are lighter and fruity, but rarely rise to those heights of power and complexity characteristic of the châteaux of the plateau. It's often said of Pomerol that you can taste the iron in the soil. This refers to *casse de fer*, deposits of iron, but there is considerable doubt as to whether and what effect this actually has on the wine.

Pomerol's fame is relatively recent: it was scarcely known outside the region until the second half of the twentieth century. The halo effect of top châteaux is more evident in Pomerol than anywhere else; there is little cheap Pomerol. The

Pomerol produces some of the most expensive wines in the world, but the village contains little besides the church, which is surrounded by some of the best vineyards.

best wines have an openly sensuous style, which is why Pomerol is sometimes called the Burgundy of Bordeaux. This is completely different from the structure and restraint of the Médoc, even in the present era of increased ripeness everywhere.

Moueix is by far the most important proprietor in Pomerol, and recently has turned away from the negociant business to concentrate on the top châteaux. The range of Moueix châteaux encapsulates the variations in Pomerol. At the very peak is Pétrus, now 100% Merlot.[46] Nonetheless it has the structure to age. "The level of tannins is comparable to Château Latour, but the tannins are more approachable, they are Merlot tannins not Cabernet Sauvignon," says Elisabeth Jaubert at Pétrus. Whereas Pétrus is famously on clay, Château Trotanoy is more on gravel, and the wine has a more upright, masculine style. It's still rich and opulent, but the structure can be more overt. La Fleur-Pétrus is relatively light for Pomerol, with a fresher impression than Pétrus or Trotanoy. And then the most recent creation, Château Hosanna (carved out of the breakup of Château Certan-Giraud) is unusual for Moueix, with 30% Cabernet Franc giving the tightest, most elegant style. Yet there is a common thread: that initial impression of opulence.

There are a few garage wines in Pomerol, with Le Pin the most often cited, but actually it's really just a very small vineyard with good terroir. Jacques Thienpont, who acquired Le Pin in 1979, admits Le Pin may have been confused with (and have become a model for) the garage wines, but says, "We knew this was special terroir, wine was always made at the cellar here. It's 100% Merlot, but I don't have the power and richness of Pétrus, Le Pin is more elegant." In fact, given the small size of its vineyards, Pomerol really doesn't have much need of garage wines. The issue with Pomerol is not so much the quality of the top wines, which can scarcely be bettered if you like the very lush, opulent style of fully ripe Merlot-dominated cuvées, but the lower quality of wines that come from the lighter, sandy soils. Without any classification, price is really the only guide.

Pétrus is the most famous property in Pomerol; the buildings used to be shabby but are now quite smart, although still modest in style.

Reference Wines for the Right Bank	
St. Emilion	Canon La Gaffelière
Pomerol	L'Évangile
Lalande de Pomerol	La Fleur de Boüard
St Georges - St. Emilion	Moulin St. Georges
Côtes de Bourg	Fougas Maldoror
Fronsac	Château Fontenil
Côtes de Castillon	Château d'Aiguilhe

Other Right Bank

Côtes de Bordeaux
(Blaye, Cadillac, Castillon, Francs)
(Côtes de Bourg)
12,600 ha
6 million cases (red)
200,000 cases (white)
1,400 producers
9 cooperatives = 17% of harvest
Entre-deux-Mers
7,400 ha
1 million cases (white)
2 million cases (red Bordeaux AOP)
250 producers
40 cooperatives = 70% of harvest

Going north from St. Emilion and Pomerol across the Barbanne stream, you come to the various satellite appellations. Here the soils are clay-limestone, similar to St. Emilion itself (and distinctly better than the soils on the plain of St. Emilion to the south). The result is an inconsistency: although there are few wines in the satellites that really reach the heights, many are at least as good as the so-called Grand Cru St. Emilions coming from the plain.

The St. Emilion satellites (parts of which used to be included in St. Emilion itself) are slightly cooler than St. Emilion, as a result of greater distance from the Dordogne. They are not very well distinguished from one another.

Lalande de Pomerol has more varied soils, with quite a bit of gravel, changing from clay in the east to sand in the west. The wines here are solid rather than refined.

There is no useful distinction to be made between Fronsac and the smaller area of Canon-Fronsac embedded within it (supposedly of higher quality). The wines of Fronsac were well regarded in the eighteenth century, but today are not at all well known. The style is Merlot-based, but less refined than Pomerol.

Côtes de Bordeaux is a new, and not completely coherent, concept. As elsewhere in France, "Côtes" indicates an area that rises above the generic AOP, but without really establishing its own distinctive character. In the case of Bordeaux, there used to be five separate Côtes: Bourg, Blaye, Cadillac, Castillon, and Francs. This was a significant part of the confusion created by the excessive number of AOCs in Bordeaux, so it was decided to merge them into a single Côtes. As Côtes de Bourg did not agree, it remained independent, but the other four are now known as the Côtes de Bordeaux, although each individual area may append its own name. The Côtes are relatively important in terms of quantity, accounting for about 14% of Bordeaux's production, but the individual areas are quite separate. Bourg and Blaye are well to the north, Francs and Castillon are to the east of Libourne, and Cadillac is a tiny area adjacent to the Garonne better known for sweet wine.

At the northern extremity of the right bank, Blaye and Bourg are relatively cool climates. Vineyards run up to the Gironde. Yet there is a surprising amount of Cabernet Sauvignon, and this area is the last holdout for Malbec in Bordeaux. There's also a little white wine labeled as Premières Côtes de Blaye. The best wines come from Bourg, notably from Châteaux Roc Des Cambes (clearly *hors de classe*) and Fougas Maldoror, but these are strong exceptions.

Immediately to the east of St. Emilion, Côtes de Castillon produces only red wine from the usual right bank blend. Some producers from St. Emilion have established outposts here, looking for vineyards with good terroir at more reasonable prices. Oenologist Stéphane Derenoncourt (at Domaine de l'A), and Stephan von Neipperg from Canon La Gaffelière (at Château d'Aiguilhe) are the top examples. The best wines are equivalent to St. Emilion. "Castillon is an extension of the limestone plateau of St. Emilion, and it's a bit cooler here. The difference between the appellations for me is the price. In St. Emilion you have a market price that lets you make sacrifices with lower yields. Castillon can make wines that will compete with St. Emilion (although not with the top Grand Cru Classés). We can make a wine here that reflects its terroir, much better than the plain of St. Emilion. The aging potential is similar to St. Emilion," says Stéphane Derenoncourt. But Castillon's obscurity is an impediment. "The problem is economic. Even in France, Castillon is totally unknown. More than half the wines of Castillon are declassified to Bordeaux because it is easier for the negociants to sell. We are victims of the appellation."

"Entre-deux-Mers does not have a specific terroir: its characteristics come from assemblage from diverse terroirs, often varying from one parcel to the next," says the producers' organization. This is a major source for white wine just one notch above the generic Bordeaux AOP; but the reds are labeled as Bordeaux AOP. Following the translation of the name as "between two seas," "between" is a good description for the wines. There is little that really stands out here. Cooperatives are unusually important, given the economic difficulties of lesser regions of Bordeaux.

Sauternes

There is little quite so disgusting on a grapevine as the appearance of a bunch of rotten grapes. Yet this is the basis for making Sauternes. Noble Rot, which gives sweet wines such as Sauternes their delicious piquant, honeyed quality, happens when the fungus Botrytis cinerea forms a mold on the surface of the grape. If the skin actually breaks, noble rot turns to gray rot, and the wine is ruined by unpleasant aromas and flavors of mold and mushrooms. So very special conditions are required to start the rot but then to stop it from getting out of hand.

Perhaps not surprisingly, given the discrepancy between appearance of the grapes and taste of the wine, it is somewhat unclear when Sauternes began to make sweet wine. There are some fanciful stories, a favorite being that the Marquis de Lur Saluces, owner of Château d'Yquem,

Sauternes & Barsac
1 Premier Cru Superieur
11 Premier Crus
14 Deuxième Crus
166 other châteaux

	hectares	bottles
Sauternes	1,669	4,300,000
Barsac	594	1,600,000
Cadillac	215	730,000
Loupiac	400	1,750,000
Cérons	63	200,000

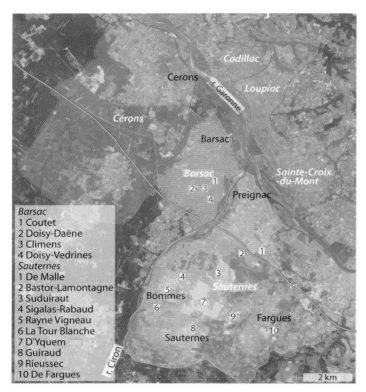

Barsac
1 Coutet
2 Doisy-Daëne
3 Climens
4 Doisy-Vedrines
Sauternes
1 De Malle
2 Bastor-Lamontagne
3 Suduiraut
4 Sigalas-Rabaud
5 Rayne Vigneau
6 La Tour Blanche
7 D'Yquem
8 Guiraud
9 Rieussec
10 De Fargues

Sauternes, Barsac, and Cérons lie on the left bank at the southern tip of Graves. Ste. Croix du Mont, Loupiac, and Cadillac face them across the Garonne. The Ciron river runs between Barsac and Sauternes and empties into the Garonne.

was away on a trip in 1847 and left instructions that the harvest should wait for his return; because he was delayed, the grapes developed noble rot—but the wine was delicious. In fact, however, it seems that the origins of sweet wine in Sauternes go back to the period of Dutch dominance of Bordeaux in the seventeenth century, when they encouraged production of white wines with residual sugar. Although these were the most highly priced white wines of Bordeaux, we do not know whether botrytis was involved. By the eighteenth century there was probably conscious use of botrytized grapes, although this may not have been publicly acknowledged for fear of scaring the clientele.

At the southern tip of Graves, the climate creates perfect conditions for botrytis, where the cool Ciron tributary runs between Sauternes and Barsac, shaded by overhanging trees until it empties out into the warmer Garonne river. The Ciron is only a few meters wide at the junction, so there is something of the effect of a jet stream of cold water hitting the Garonne. Autumn mists created by the humidity sweep across from the junction of the rivers to the vineyards, persisting until burned off by the morning sun.[47] The alternation of damp mornings and dry afternoons (which let the surface of the grape dry out) is perfect for generating botrytis.[48] On the right bank across the river, conditions are similar, but not so reliable.

By the nineteenth century, the fame of the region was well established, and the 1855 classification also included the sweet wine producers of Sauternes and Barsac (no distinction was made between them at the time), dividing them into three tiers, with Château d'Yquem at their head as Premier Cru Supérieur, and the others as Premier Cru Classés and Deuxième Cru Classés.

Barsac and Sauternes are far and away the best appellations for producing dessert wines. Sauternes is larger and better known; indeed wine produced in

Morning mist rises up from the rivers, creating the conditions for noble rot in the vineyards. Courtesy Matthew Bywater.

Barsac can also be labeled as Sauternes. It would be a fine taster who could systematically tell the difference, but there is more clay in the soil in Barsac, and a substratum of limestone; because the Ciron washed away the gravel from Barsac eons ago, the soils are shallower. All this partly explains why the wines of Barsac tend to be a little lighter in body than those of Sauternes, which tend to be more powerful. But the main feature here is not the soil: it is the climate.

Immediately to the north of Barsac is the lesser area of Cérons, and across the river are the appellations of Cadillac, Loupiac, and Ste. Croix de Mont. Wines are also made from the same grape varieties in the region of Bergerac to the southeast, including the appellation of Monbazillac, but most do not achieve the same concentration. (Emphasizing the difference between the requirements for producing sweet versus dry wine, the vineyards in Monbazillac tend to face north, where fogs develop best, as opposed to facing south to catch the sun.)

Botrytis is capricious, usually attacking the grapes really effectively only three or so times per decade. Of course, the moist, humid conditions that are ideal for botrytis are anathema to producing quality red wine, so the great vintages for dessert wines do not usually coincide with those for reds. In the first

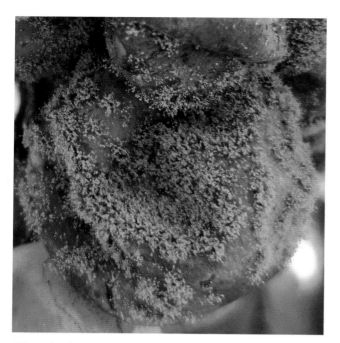

A botrytized grape has a layer of fungus on the surface.

decade of this century, some vintages stand out for one or the other. 2000 was a great red wine vintage but mediocre for Sauternes. 2001 was decent for reds but superb for Sauternes. 2007 was average for reds but very good for Sauternes. 2005 was the one vintage that was top notch for both red and sweet white wines.

Any vendange tardive (late harvest) has a desiccating effect, because the grapes dry out with the prolonged hang time. They are said to be *passerillé*. Botrytis infection enhances this effect. The fungus breaks down the wax on the surface of the grape, making the skin more permeable so that moisture can escape. As the grape shrivels, the juice inside becomes more and more concentrated. By the time the grapes are harvested, they may be less than half of their original weight, with sugar concentration increased by a third. Because botrytis develops on individual grapes within a bunch, multiple passes through the vineyard (*tries*) are necessary to select grapes one by one as the season ends.

The fungus does much more than concentrate the grapes. It consumes a major part of the tartaric and malic acids, but generates some acetic acid, giving that delicious piquancy to the wine. Botrytis also increases the level of glycerol. Botrytis destroys esters and terpenes, so that grape varietal character is reduced. But the wine gains more complexity from the fungal additions than it loses.[49] The characteristic honeyed taste of botrytized wine is due to fungal production of a compound called sotolon. Sotolon is produced by a series of chemical conversions from an amino acid, and it's not unique to botrytis, but is also produced by the so-called flor yeasts that grow on top of barrels of Sherry or Vin Jaune. At higher concentrations, its taste can change from honey to curry. The combination of high sugar concentration, increased acetic acid, glycerol, and sotolon give botrytized wines a common sweet, piquant, viscous, honeyed impression.

Sweet wines in Bordeaux typically reverse the proportions of grape varieties used in dry white wine, with 80% coming from Sémillon and 20% from Sauvignon Blanc. Sémillon is particularly susceptible to botrytis, and its thin skin allows the fungus to penetrate more easily. It's said to give a musky quality to the wine. Sauvignon Blanc adds high acidity and that counterpoise of faint

herbaceousness. A third variety that's less in favor these days, Muscadelle, is susceptible to botrytis, and brings a grapey quality, but it's difficult to grow and has a more rustic character.

The viscosity of the must makes it difficult to press and ferment botrytized grapes. Pressing can take hours, and fermentation can last weeks. "The preferred juice is the one that is difficult to extract, it is the opposite of the red wine, where the natural juice is the best," explains Alexandre Lur Saluces. Curiously chaptalization is legal in Sauternes (although it should not be) as are methods of cryo-extraction (basically freezing the grapes to remove some of the water content as ice), but the top Sauternes avoid such artifice.

What do you do if botrytis does not develop? You can make a sweet wine simply from late harvest grapes, more passerillé than botrytized; indeed, this is not uncommon. Barring that, you can try to make a dry white wine, but there are two practical impediments. By the time you know whether or not there will be good passerillage or botrytis, it's too late to harvest the grapes for conventional vinification; and the vineyards in the Sauternes area are generally planted in the 80:20 Sémillon: Sauvignon ratio that's suitable for dessert wines rather than 20:80 ratio that would be used for a dry white Graves.

Château Yquem is the only Premier Cru Supérieur in Sauternes. Grapes are harvested well into autumn, with up to 10 or more passes through the vineyard.

Reference Wines for Sweet Bordeaux	
Sauternes	Château Rieussec
	Château Suduiraut
Barsac	Château Climens
	Château Coutet

"Some say that Sauternes is in crisis, but that depends on the quality of the Sauternes," says Alexandre Lur Saluces from Château d'Yquem, who now makes wine at another old family property, Château de Fargues. Nonetheless, a worldwide decline in interest in sweet wines has put some pressure on Sauternes. Some châteaux now regularly make some dry white wine as a hedge against harvest conditions. The first, and most famous, is Y (pronounced Ygrec) of Château d'Yquem, produced since 1959. Several other châteaux have followed, and slowly the white wines have become an objective in their own right. One impediment has been that Sauternes and Barsac must label dry white wines as Bordeaux AOP. "We are in the middle of Graves and this is just a French stupidity. It goes back to a fight in the thirties," explains Pierre Montégut at Château Suduiraut, but there is a proposal on the table to allow the Graves AOP to be used. However, the special feature of the area is the occurrence of morning fog, so it's not really evident that a switch to dry wines will yield quality equivalent to producing sweet wines here.

Today's styles of white Bordeaux offer more variety than the traditional blend of 80% Sauvignon Blanc, 20% Sémillon, with dry wines varying from monovarietal Sauvignon Blanc to those dominated by Sémillon. But white wine remains a bit player, except for Pessac-Léognan. The best dry whites from the Sauternes area are good, but quantities are rather small. Some interesting whites are now coming from châteaux in the Médoc, and even St. Emilion, but except for the long established Pavillon Blanc at Margaux, quantities are usually too small to have much impact on the market. When you taste a really good white Bordeaux, with subtle oak influence, richness from the Sémillon, and crispness from the Sauvignon Blanc, you are inclined to wonder what would happen if Chardonnay was allowed: well, it is permitted under the label of IGP Pays de l'Atlantique, but economic considerations are against trying to make really high quality wine in the IGP. But it would be interesting...

Reference Wines for White Bordeaux	
Entre-deux-Mers	Château Marjosse
Graves	Clos Floridène
Pessac-Léognan	Domaine de Chevalier
Médoc	Pavillon Blanc de Margaux (Bordeaux AOP)
Libournais	Clos Nardian (Bordeaux AOP)

The combination of Cabernet Sauvignon with Merlot is so successful that it is known worldwide as "the Bordeaux Blend." It is imitated all over the New World, where Cabernet Sauvignon has become the most widely planted black variety. What Bordeaux has given to the world is the concept that the austerity of Cabernet Sauvignon and fleshiness of Merlot make a perfect blend. (With the New World focus on varietal labeling, much production is labeled as Cabernet Sauvignon, but it often contains a proportion of Merlot.) Of course, the Bordeaux Blend is somewhat simplistic as a view of Bordeaux, as blends dominated by Merlot with Cabernet Franc are in fact its main production.

The Bordeaux Blend

Médoc
52% Cabernet Sauvignon
40% Merlot

Graves
31% Cabernet Sauvignon
61% Merlot

Libournais
10% Cabernet Sauvignon
74% Merlot

What blend is best for Bordeaux in the era of global warming? "We have benefited from global warming, but we benefit far more with Cabernet Sauvignon than with Merlot. With Merlot we are far closer to the drawback than the benefits, especially on the right bank," says Philippe Blanc of Château Beychevelle. Indeed, a series of increasingly warm vintages began to pose the question of whether it was becoming *too* hot for Merlot on the right bank. "The future of Bordeaux is Cabernet Sauvignon, forget the right bank," says David Launay of Château Gruaud Larose. "There's a noblesse to Cabernet Sauvignon, you know, it has everything, freshness, purity of line, fruit, and when we have ripe Cabernet Sauvignon it's at 13% (compared to Merlot at 14%)," says Frédéric Engerer at Château Latour.

Alcohol is higher on the right bank because Merlot develops more sugar than Cabernet Sauvignon at ripeness. Increasing alcohol levels may bring a halt to the trend to increase Merlot. "Global warming obliges us to reduce the proportion of Merlot, it's not a matter of over ripeness in the Merlot, but the alcohol level is too high. The replacement is intended to maintain the character of the wine. Merlot was always planted historically because Cabernet Sauvignon wasn't so successful," says Didier Cuvelier at Château Léoville Poyferré.

Bordeaux has definitely changed. "We are not producing wines that are too tannic (like 1975 or 1986) or unripe (like 1997)," says Jean-Guillaume Prats, formerly of Cos d'Estournel. "The big change in Bordeaux is that now we can have maturity in Cabernet Sauvignon," says Jean Merlaut of Château Gruaud-Larose. There's really no comparison between the wines of (say) the seventies and those of today in terms of quality and enjoyability when young. The unresolved question is whether they will be so delicious after thirty years (and whether anyone cares about this any more).

Harvesting grapes at greater ripeness brings higher alcohol, softer tannins, and lower acidity. Acidity has been declining at roughly 10% per decade; it is now only about two thirds of the level of the 1970s. The average alcohol level in Bordeaux has increased steadily from a range of 12-12.5% thirty years ago (including a per cent or more due to chaptalization) to a range of 14% or more today. Not everyone feels it's necessary to go to these levels to get ripeness. "The Barton wines have never been over 13% and you can make good wine at 12%," says Anthony Barton. But this is a minority position.

The trend to higher alcohol is a significant factor in the move to a more powerful "international" style at some châteaux, and has been especially marked in the past decade. Personally, I believe this represents a decline in elegance—if you go back to older Bordeaux at lower alcohol levels, you can see what we have lost. One oenologue of the old school said to me, "In a vrai [true] Bordeaux you have no alcohol perception—if you feel alcohol it is not a true Bordeaux."

The 1982 vintage is often taken as the demarcation line between the old and new styles of Bordeaux. Before 1982, the general character of the left bank tended towards herbaceous. This is not necessarily pejorative: top vintages would show a delicious catch of herbaceousness to cut the fruits; but herbaceousness could certainly get out of hand in weaker vintages. This was regarded as the typicity of Cabernet Sauvignon. From 1982, fruit became the driving force, and herbaceous became a term that producers would regard as insulting. Enabled by warmer vintages, the transition was part of a worldwide trend to harvest later, using the criterion of phenolic ripeness instead of sugar level. One driving force was competition from the New World, where Cabernet Sauvignon varietal wines showed intense black fruit character.

The move to a more intense style can be very successful commercially: wines with high extraction and alcohol have won acclaim from critics (especially in the United States). They do well at comparative tastings, when they make it more difficult to appreciate less intense (but more subtle) wines. Because it reflects a consensus on emphasizing ripeness above all else, this "international" style can reduce sense of place. The question is hotly debated as to how far this trend can go before wines in the new style of Bordeaux lose their character and traditional age worthiness. (Cooler vintages that do not conform are now sometimes called "classic" to contrast with the new style.) "Consumers prefer wines that are rounder, but Bordeaux has a different typicity, there are years when we can produce wines that are round and agreeable, but not every year," is how Bernard Magrez (who owns châteaux on both left and right banks) describes the situation.

When the 1982 vintage was released, traditionalists argued that its low acidity meant the wines would never have the staying power to develop with age. This turned out to be pessimistic: although the wines were amazingly approachable when young, they continued to develop. Somewhere around twenty years of age, as the luscious fruit concentration began to fall off, they showed something of a reversion to type, with a fine herbaceousness cutting the fruits. Finally they were recognizable in the tradition of Bordeaux!

Other warm vintages since then have made 1982 look quite restrained: 1990 and 2005 stand out as representatives of the new style, marked by dense fruit concentration and increasing alcohol levels. But any thoughts that global warming has brought an era of nothing but good vintages has been set to rest by the roller coaster of the past few years. The trend of warmer, richer vintages that started in 1982 came to its culmination in 2009 and 2010, when the problem was controlling high alcohol levels. Then the climate deteriorated steadily for the next three years, until the cold, wet vintage of 2013 brought a return to chaptalization with a vengeance.

Certainly the top years since 1982 have produced delicious wines: I think it is an open question whether they will revert to type in the same way as 1982. The controversy as to whether the 1982 vintage would age was all but reprised with 2009, which achieved a reputation en primeur for atypically lush wines, high in alcohol and low in acid: a great vintage but pushing the envelope even further towards the international style. But with the record of 1982 in mind, we can perhaps assess them more thoughtfully. The general impression of the vintage is certainly ripe. There is scarcely a taste of herbaceousness in any of the wines. But they are not over-ripe. With a handful of exceptions of overtly international wines, all fall within the parameters of traditional Bordeaux: fruits supported by good acidity, a tendency towards the savory rather than the forcefully fruity, some tannic support showing its bones on the finish. Bordeaux has a surprising capacity to recover its character from warmer vintages and to retain its traditional freshness.

It's a difficult question whether Bordeaux is losing its character by succumbing to a more international style. In every commune there are châteaux that now seem to have embraced the trend, and there are those that have remained more restrained. Cos d'Estournel is flashy whereas Montrose remains reserved, if no longer really showing the full austerity of St. Estèphe; Lagrange and Léoville Poyferré are ripe in the modern idiom, whereas Léoville Barton retains the classic precision of St. Julien; Lascombes and La Tour Carnet are powerful for Margaux, where Rauzan-Ségla or Rauzan-Gassies are lighter; Pape Clément and Smith Haut Lafite in Pessac-Léognan offer full force fruits compared to Domaine de Chevalier's elegant precision. In all these cases, the wines that have moved more in the international direction have increased their standing in the marketplace. It's a one way street to modernism: in many cases, it's the reaction of a new proprietor to the decline of the past.

The clash between traditionalists and modernists is less pronounced in Bordeaux than elsewhere, because there is almost universal agreement on the

Pétrus
Le Pin
Château Ausone
Château Lafite Rothschild
Château Latour
Château Lafleur
Château Cheval Blanc
Château Margaux
Château Mouton Rothschild
Château Haut Brion

1-10

Château Angélus
Château Pavie
La Mondotte
Carruades de Lafite
Château La Mission Haut Brion
Chapelle D'Ausone
Les Forts de Latour
Château de Valandraud
Château Palmer
Château Lafleur Pétrus

11-20

Château L'Église Clinet
Château Bellevue Mondotte
Château Léoville Lascases
Le Petit Mouton
Château Trotanoy
Château Le Tertre Rôteboeuf
Petit Cheval
Vieux Château Certan
Château l'Évangile
Château Ducru Beaucaillou

21-30

Château Cos d'Estournel
Château Gracia
Hosanna
Pavillon Rouge du Château Margaux
Château Pavie-Decesse
Château Pichon Lalande
Château Lynch Bages
Château La Conseillante
Château Magrez Fombrauge
Château Pichon Baron

30-40

Château Montrose
Château Pape Clément
Château Figeac
Château Pontet-Canet
Le Dôme
Château Clinet
Clos Fourtet
Château Beychevelle
Château Le Gay
Château Léoville-Poyferré

41-50

Château Péby-Faugères
Château Duhart Milon Rothschild
Château Troplong Mondot
Château la Fleur de Gay
Château Lascombes
Château Smith Haut Lafitte
Château Pavie Macquin
Clos l'Église
Château Léoville-Barton
Château Calon Ségur

51-60

Château Canon La Gaffelière
Château Canon
Château Haut Bailly
Château Gazin
Château La Gomerie
Château Rauzan-Ségla
Château Clerc Milon
Château Certan de May
Alter Ego de Palmer
Château Trottevieille

61-70

Château d'Issan
Château Malescot-Saint-Exupéry
Château Latour à Pomerol
Château Beausejour Duffau
Château Clos de Sarpe
Château La Gaffelière
Château Petit Village
Château Gruaud Larose
Château Magdelaine
Château Bon Pasteur

71-80

Château Branaire Ducru
Château Boyd Cantenac
Le Carillon de L'Angélus
Château Grand Puy Lacoste
Domaine de Chevalier
Château Monbousquet
Château La Lagune
Château Saint Pierre
Château Talbot
Château Cantenac Brown

81-90

Château Lafleur-Gazin
Château Beauséjour-Bécot
Château Larcis Ducasse
Château Giscours
Château Kirwan
Château Roc de Cambes
Château d'Armailhac
Château Durfort Vivens
Château les Carmes-Haut-Brion
Château Lagrange

91-100

The top 100 red wines of Bordeaux classified by price include 50 from the right bank (purple) and 50 from the left bank (red). There are 8 second wines and 6 garage wines.[51]

desirability of producing wine that is ready to drink sooner. It used to be said that if Bordeaux was enjoyable to drink when it was young, it would not have the capacity to age well. That is no longer true. While the red wines of Bordeaux have more tannin than ever before,[50] the combination of warmer vintages and better tannin management means the tannins are riper than they used be. Top vintages have enough tannin to age, but the tannins are subsumed by the concentration of fruits, so the wines can be drunk much sooner. In some ways this is a pity, because the full complexity of the wine will not show until at least a decade has passed to allow further flavor development. The basic difference from the past is that today the potential of the wine is hidden by the fruit, whereas previously it was hidden by the tannins. Lighter vintages tend to show their tannins more obviously when young.

The balance between the Left Bank and the Right Bank has shifted since 1982. For about a century, the 1855 classification was very much the public face of Bordeaux, placing the emphasis almost exclusively on the Médoc. But today's list of the top hundred wines in Bordeaux (judged by price) is split between left and right banks. Pomerol and St. Emilion have been better poised to satisfy the modern craving for rich, intense, ripe if not over-ripe, wines. The rise of the right bank is shown by the way its wines dominate the top fifty.

The Southwest is a real grab bag of regions, including everything between Bordeaux and the Languedoc. The wide variety of terroirs and climatic variation result in many different wine styles. There is a concentration of indigenous varieties that are grown nowhere else; indeed, there may be more unusual varieties here than in the rest of France combined. Clive Coates MW divides the region into two areas: Bordeaux satellites; and the far Southwest (near the Pyrenees), which is a good way to look at it.

If there's one single word that describes the dominant character of the red wines of the entire Southwest, it is: tannin. This reflects the character of Malbec, once a dominant grape in Bordeaux, and today grown only in the area immediately to its southeast, and Tannat, the most important black grape of the Pyrenees. Both have a natural tendency to very high tannins.

Dry white wine has been something of a struggle, and the best known whites are the sweet wines. In the Bordeaux satellites, these come from the same varieties as Bordeaux, with an emphasis on complexity coming from botrytis. In the Pyrenees, they come from the more aromatic varieties of Petit and Gros Manseng, with passerillage (desiccation on the vine) as the means of achieving concentration.

Bergerac	9,580 ha
Buzet	1,900 ha
Cahors	4,300 ha
Gaillac	3,000 ha
Monbazillac	1,800 ha
Pecharmant	385 ha
Saussignac	70 ha

red
Malbec, Merlot, Cabernet Franc
white
Sauvignon Blanc, Sémillon

The production of sweet wines all over the southwest makes the point that this is a hot climate extending into autumn. It's not always obvious that the dry reds, dry whites, and sweet whites come from the same areas, because different appellation names may be used for each style (sometimes Sec is used to distinguish dry wine), but the fact is that this is a region with a Continental climate inclining to strong temperature transitions. The reds are powerful; the traditional varieties stand up to the heat well, but the key to red winemaking in the southwest is taming the powerful tannins.

The winegrowing regions of the Dordogne are just to the southeast of Bordeaux; in fact winegrowing here preceded Bordeaux. The mix of varieties is similar. Bergerac (for dry wines) and Monbazillac (for sweet wines) are the best known appellations. The distinction between these regions and Bordeaux was not always so clear. When the zone for the wines of Bordeaux was first specified in 1909, it included many communes in the Dordogne and in Lot-et-Garonne.[52] Protests from Bordeaux caused the region to be limited strictly to the department of the Gironde, so Bergerac and Monbazillac had to develop their own identity.

Bergerac and Monbazillac cover the same geographical area, but the wine is called Bergerac if it is red, Bergerac Sec if it is dry white, and Monbazillac if

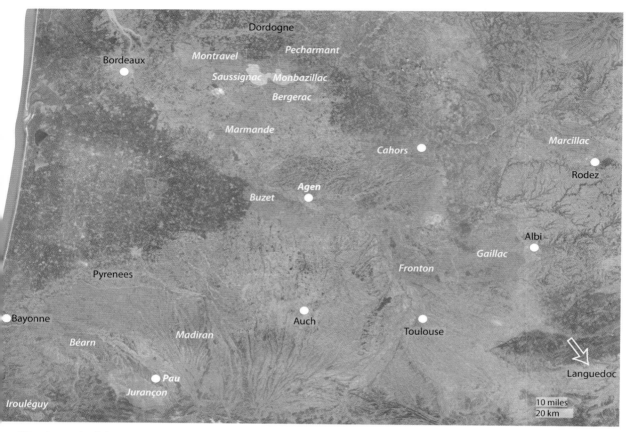

The vineyards of the Southwest extend from Bordeaux at the north, and to the Pyrenees at the south. To the southeast is the Languedoc.

it is sweet. Although reds are often based on Merlot, they don't have the generosity of the right bank of Bordeaux, but convey a slightly harder, sometimes more rustic impression. There's quite a bit of Cabernet Sauvignon and Malbec; Cabernet Franc is less evident. As they age, the reds often develop notes of truffles to contrast with the fruits. It can be difficult to get the right balance between softening the wines (at risk of losing character) and keeping so much tannin that aging is required (which may not be so appropriate for Bergerac as for Bordeaux).

The red is undergoing a bit of an identity crisis. Attempts at modernization lead to soft almost furry tannins, but the rustic character remains in the background. In terms of comparison with Bordeaux, the best wines are closest in style to the Côtes de Castillon. In an attempt to improve quality, a higher level appellation called Côtes de Bergerac has been introduced, with yields limited to 50 hl/ha compared to 60 hl/ha for Bergerac, and chaptalization is forbidden. But it's only 4% of the production of Bergerac. There's some talk about calling it Grand Cru instead of Côtes. Côtes de Bergerac is also used for moelleux (medium sweet) white wines (fully sweet liquoreux remain Monbazillac).

Bergerac Sec tends to show a perfumed quality, with stone fruits of apricots and peaches rather than citrus, turning in a more savory direction than you find with white Bordeaux. Varieties for the sweet wines are similar to Sauternes, with Sémillon as the driving force, but there tends to be somewhat more Muscadelle in Monbazillac, which may contribute to a more perfumed note. There is often less botrytis, with a mixture of some botrytized berries, some passerillé, and some very mature berries. Monbazillac in the hands of an average producer can appear to be a poor man's Sauternes. But from a top producer, such as Tirecul La Gravière, it displays its own character, more savory, with herbal overtones running to anise providing a counterpoise to the sweetness. Aromas of truffles are common on the sweet wines, and intensify after a few years. The very best wines come into their own after a decade and continue to develop for another decade or so. A new label, SGN, has been introduced for the top Monbazillacs: it requires 17% potential alcohol (compared with 14% for Monbazillac), maturation for 18 months, and chaptalization is forbidden. Essentially this will be a wine based on full botrytis.

Moving another fifty miles west and a bit south, imagine a triangle with Cahors at the apex, and Fronton and Gaillac at its base to the south. Malbec, once a dominant grape in Bordeaux but no longer much grown there, is a major variety in Cahors. Fronton is probably the only place in France that grows the Negrette grape. Gaillac, a very old established area for wine production, is the last place growing Len de l'El, Mauzac, and Ondenc.

Vineyards in Cahors occupy something of an oval around the river Lot, with the town of Cahors at one end. The most important producers are concentrated around the town of Vire-sur-Lot. There are vineyards on the flat and on a series of terraces running up to the woods. The terraces are the defining geographical feature, representing different geological ages and soil types. Producers' views vary as to whether to reflect different terraces in different cuvées, as at Clos Triguedina or Cosse Maisonneuve, or whether to try for more complexity by blending, as at Château de Cèdre.

Malbec is not so overwhelming as in the days when the wine was known as the "black wine of Cahors," but must still comprise at least 70% of the blend in Cahors. The rest is usually Merlot. But the top wines of the top producers are often 100% Malbec. Catherine Maisonneuve makes four different Malbecs from different positions on the slope. Why are they 100% Malbec? "Merlot has been here only for 60 years; they authorized Merlot because they had planted Malbec in the 1960s that was too productive, but it's the Malbec that expresses the terroir," she says.

The same effect of increasingly refined character going up the slope is seen here and in the Trilogie of wines from successive terraces at Clos Triguedina, where Jean-Luc Baldès explains: "Malbec can bring finesse and elegance, it does not need to be massive, it can be fresh and mineral. Our problem is that

Most vineyards in the Cahors appellation are located in the plain along the river (upper). Terraces dating from different geological eras rise up to the south as seen in a cross-section view (lower).

The second terrace is clay on top of calcareous subsoil, giving fruitiness. The third terrace has clay with round pebbles and calcareous subsoils, giving richness. The fourth terrace is clay on hard limestone, giving finesse and elegance.

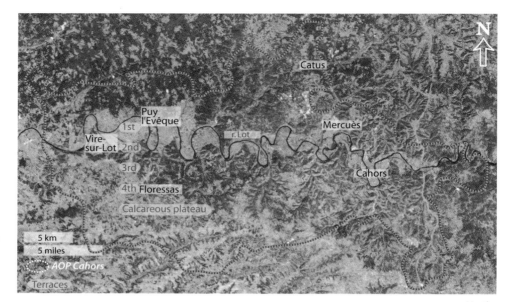

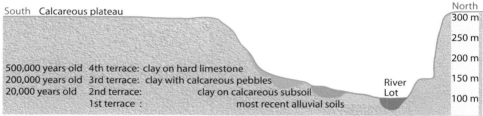

the image of Cahors in the 1980s was for a rather rustic wine. The success of Argentina opened the door to making another style of wine. Our objective is to show the refinement and elegance of Malbec."

At its best, Malbec can indeed be quite refined, without either the overt fleshiness of Merlot or the bare bones structure of Cabernet. The problem is that the best examples are wines where, even if the tannins are fine, they are still quite present when young. There are now second wines made in a more fruity and approachable style, but in my opinion, even if Cahors is no longer the impenetrable black wine of the past, it still always needs at least five years after the vintage before you can see the fruits clearly and enjoy them. It is just the DNA of Malbec in this region.

Moving south and east towards Albi, Gaillac supports its claim to be one of the oldest sites for wine production in France by pointing to the existence of wild grapevines in the Grésigne forest near the river Tarn.[53] Wine was made here during the Roman era, all but destroyed by the Moors during their occupation in the Middle Ages, and then revived by the monks, led by the Abbaye of Saint Michel, which developed a thriving export trade. The development of Gaillac and surrounding regions was impeded by the protectionism of the Bordelais, and it wasn't until the eve of the French Revolution that the wines of Gaillac could be sold freely.

Gaillac has an unusually wide range of grape varieties. In reds, the principal varieties include Duras and Fer Servadou (also known as Braucol or Verdot), which are traditional varieties going back more than a century, and Syrah (introduced more recently): Gamay used to be allowed but has now been eliminated. All the Bordeaux varieties are permitted. Malbec, Tannat, and Negrette are also found. The traditional white varieties are Mauzac (both blanc and rosé), the curiously named l'En de l'El (a contraction from le-Loin-de-l'Oeil), Ondenc, and then the usual suspects from Bordeaux.

The debate in Gaillac as to whether the appellation should preserve the old varieties or represent the new has been won by the modernists. The authorities in Gaillac seem especially determined to stamp out individuality among their producers, yet have no clear idea of what Gaillac should represent. It's a very curious view the appellation

Wild grapevines grow in the forest of Grésigne. Courtesy IFV Sud-Ouest.[54]

Reference Wines for the Southwest	
Bergerac	Vignoble des Verdots
Bergerac Sec	Domaine l'Ancienne Cure
Cahors	Clos Triguedina
Gaillac	Domaine Plageoles
	Causse Marines
Monbazillac	Tirecul La Gravière

has of itself, that wines made from varieties as different as Braucol, Duras, or Syrah can be labeled as Gaillac; styles as different as dry white, semi-sweet white, and a vin de voile (an oxidized style grown under a layer of flor) can be labeled as Gaillac; even a sparkling wine made from the Mauzac grape: but varieties that were grown here two centuries ago aren't allowed, and producers who make low-sulfur wines are thrown out of the appellation because of supposed notes of oxidation.

So top producers, such as Plageoles, Patrice Lescarret at Causse Marines, and Michel Issaly, who have reintroduced some of the really old varieties, have to label the wines as Vins de France because the cépages aren't allowed in the appellation. Their rediscovery is due largely to Robert Plageoles, who recollects, "One day I realized, that's our heritage. It was a grand adventure to restart, to find the old varieties, but it was a long road, very lonely at first." Black grape varieties include Prunelart, Mauzac Noir, and Verdanel; whites include various subvarieties of Mauzac.

Tasting the old varieties leaves me with mixed feelings. They are definitely different from the international style, but they don't always offer enough distinctive flavor interest. Certainly it's easier to make wine to the general taste from the more common varieties. "My wines are completely atypical. No one would recognize them as Gaillac because there are very few vignerons left who work with authentic varieties. They are all using Merlot, Syrah, and Gamay. We are losing the appellation with the most distinctive set of varieties," says Michel Issaly.

The most authentic taste of Gaillac perhaps comes from the Vin de Voile, which is distinctive in tending to show more overt fruits than you see with either the Jura or Sherry. Some producers bottle it as a vintage (after seven years under the voile), some make multi-vintage blends, and Patrice Lescarret has a solera. "Vin de voile is different, it's the true history, wine like this gives the true impression of Gaillac. I believe this is the best wine you can make in Gaillac," says Michel Issaly.

Béarn	217 ha
Irouléguy	225 ha
Jurançon	950 ha
Madiran	1,300 ha
Pacherenc	235 ha

red
Tannat
white
Petit Manseng, Gros Manseng

Considered part of the Southwest, but completely different from the area between Bergerac and Cahors, the vineyards close to the Pyrenees show the influence of the Basque country. Madiran is famous for the strong Tannat grape that is the backbone of its red wine. Jurançon makes dry and sweet white wine from the Gros and Petit Manseng varieties. Irouléguy's vineyards are close to the border with Spain, just up against the Pyrenees, and also grow Tannat and the Mansengs.

Madiran is among the most powerful wines of France. Tannat is the traditional grape, although the proportion that is required or allowed has kept changing since the appellation was created. The last iteration specified between 40% and 80%,[55] with Cabernet Sauvignon, Cabernet Franc, and Fer Servadou as the other varieties (none exactly known for softness). However, whether formally allowed or not, the top wines are often 100% Tannat.

The problem is that it's Scylla and Charybdis between becoming round, soft, jammy, and losing character, as against displaying the nature of Tannat, which inevitably means showing tannins. It's not just that the strong tannins take years to soften, but just as much that the fruit flavor spectrum tends to be monolithic: it takes about a decade before flavor variety develops. The high praise given to wines such as the prestige cuvées of Château Montus during their youth reflects potential for what will happen in another twenty years, more than present drinking pleasure. It's quite difficult to judge Madiran when it's young.

Tannat is a darkly colored, thick-skinned variety (inset). A small plot at Château Barréjat has pre-phylloxera vines, planted in pairs in the old style.

There are different opinions on how best to tame the tannins. Introduced by Patrick Ducournau in 1990, a popular approach is micro-oxygenation, which involves exposing the wine to a stream of tiny oxygen bubbles. This softens the tannins (technically it causes them to polymerize sooner), making the wine more approachable. However, the most important producer in Madiran, Alain Brumont (of Châteaux Bouscassé and Montus), is scathing about the technique "I have nothing to do with it," he says, "I buy new barrels and that provides quite sufficient oxygenation." Tannat needs oak to soften it. The problem with Tannat is that it's not very aromatic, and can lack freshness (which is why Cabernet is often included in the lower level cuvées). The appellation white wine that's produced in the region goes under the name of Pacherenc-du-Vic-Bilh (labeled Sec when it's dry), mostly from Petit and Gros Manseng, with some Petit Corbu.

The terraced vineyards at the Jardins des Babylone are typical of Jurançon.

The great name for white wine in the region, however, is Jurançon. This originated as an exclusively sweet wine, in the category called *moelleux*, which comes from late harvested grapes (as opposed to even sweeter *liquoreux* wines, which usually come from botrytized grapes). It can come from Petit or Gros Manseng, but the former is by far the finer, and dominates the top cuvées. It's about a quarter of all plantings. Petit Manseng is very susceptible to passerillage. In fact the grapes look pretty much as shriveled as botrytized grapes although there is no botrytis. More recently, Jurançon Sec has been introduced as a category for dry white wine, and has been increasing in importance; currently it's about a third of all production. Usually the Sec is vinified in stainless steel, while the Jurançon is matured in old barriques. Independent producers represent about a third of production; the rest goes through the coop.[56]

Style in Jurançon is determined by date of harvest, with grapes for dry wines usually harvested around September, grapes for the moelleux in October-November, and grapes for some super-concentrated cuvées as late as December.[57] Some exceptional dry wines are harvested at the same time as the moelleux, in order to get a riper fruit spectrum, and they tend to have rather high alcohol, becoming quite spicy and spirity. The sweet wines tend to show

Grapes for making Jurançon are left on the vine into late autumn or winter and become desiccated by passerillage. Courtesy Domaine Cauhapé.

apricot fruits and stewed apples, sometimes with a perfumed edge. As the sweet wines move to later harvest they become more concentrated in aroma and flavor, but do not usually seem particularly sweeter. They tend to develop aromas of truffles after about three years, providing a savory counterpoise to the piquant sweet fruits.

The terrain in Jurançon is spectacular. Driving around, you find yourself going up and down hills, across the tops of valleys on one track roads, and periodically you see vineyards, usually on steep slopes, sometimes ingeniously terraced. There isn't much sense of an exclusive focus on viticulture, as fields of other crops appear in the valleys. "Visitors to Jurançon say they don't understand, they can't see vines: that's because suitable locations for vineyards are restricted by the lie of the land," explains Pierre Coulomb at Domaine Guirardel. "Most of the properties are very small, and polyculture is common."

The Southwest as a whole—both Bordeaux Satellites and Pyrenees—offers a distinctive difference from the rest of France, with neither the edginess coming from marginal climates, nor the full force ripeness of the south. Whether strong reds or sweet whites, the wines tend to be powerful and characterful.

Reference Wines for Pyrenees	
Madiran	Château Montus
Jurançon Sec	Domaine Cauhapé
Jurançon	Domaine Guirardel
Irouléguy	Herri Mina

Vintages

Since the trend to warmer vintages started in 1982, there has been a zigzag between years producing increasingly riper conditions and reversion to the old "classic" conditions. The vintages of 1990 and 2000 might be considered directly in the line of 1982; 2005 was richer yet, and then 2009 was the richest vintage of all; 2010 is in the same line, but more structured without really becoming classic. (This is to ignore real heatwaves, such as the "canicule" of 2003, which went far beyond the bounds). Lesser years are much better than they used to be: whereas 1984 and 1987, and then 1991 and 1997 were all but write-offs, 2007, 2008, and 2011 are decent.

The Modern Era in Bordeaux (since 1982)	
2013	Cool Spring made for a very slow start to season with uneven flowering, leading to late harvest at the start of October. Acidity is high, fruits are light and more often in the red spectrum; these are wines to enjoy young before the fruits fade. Just over half the usual size, this was the smallest harvest since 1991.
2012	"Lovely restaurant wine" is the phrase that appears most often in my tasting notes of this vintage. It's generally described as a Merlot year, but in spite of rains in the Médoc in September, there are many wines that will be elegant in the mid term. Graves is relatively soft, so is St. Emilion, but Pomerol is more structured than usual. Whites are often described as excelling, but I find them good rather than great.
2011	Saved from disaster by fine conditions in September, but uneven. On the right bank, St. Emilion tends to cover up the problems with an edge of apparent sweetness, but the wines won't last; Pomerol is more even, but superficial. On the left bank, Margaux is extremely variable, St. Julien is rather tight, Pauillac stands out for its consistency, and Pessac-Léognan has managed to retain typicity. Not a very generous vintage, drink before it goes flat.
2010	The vintage is as ripe as 2009, but acidity and tannins are higher, giving a more classic impression. The conventional description is that this is more classic and will be longer lived, but I am not so certain the fruits will outlive the tannins and acidity into really old age. On both left and right banks the wines tend to elegance rather than power.
2009	Reputed to be so rich as to break tradition, but in fact showing surprising freshness on release. Ripe, round, and attractive already: very possibly longer lived than general commentary would suggest, but probably not destined to be a very old vintage in classic tradition.
2008	Rain at the beginning and end of the season was the problem this year. There's variation from dilute impressions to more classic wines, but these are wines for the short term.
2007	Wines are lighter, due to cool and wet conditions, and for short term consumption.

2006	The wines of the left bank tend to be a little flat, with slightly hard tannins, and not quite enough fruit, resulting from alternating hot and cold periods during the growing season. Wines of the right bank lack their usual richness.
2005	A great year with perfect conditions following the precedent of 1982. Certainly a vintage in the modern idiom, but without the excesses that were to come in 2009 and 2010. The wines should mature to elegance and finesse.
2004	A classic restaurant vintage: well balanced wines for mid term drinking, now at, or sometimes passing, their peak.
2003	The year of the canicule. Don't believe the propaganda that acidity suddenly corrected itself and the wines came into balance: they tend to be clumsy and over-extracted; even the first growths did not escape.
2002	The vintage is usually described as classic, but does not really have the concentration to pull off the style.
2001	A nice well balanced vintage at the outset, perhaps similar to 2004 in style, but with a bit less concentration, and higher acidity and more evident tannins, so now moving past its peak.
2000	Another in the series of vintages following the model of 1982, but with some of the wines surprisingly tiring at this point. The best may mature in a classic direction.
1999	Lighter wines, with the best superficially attractive, but nothing profound. On balance probably just a bit better than 1998, although this may vary.
1998	One of those vintages with a distinct difference between left and right banks. The left bank suffered from a combination of high tannins with dilution resulting from rain. The right bank is good.
1997	A large crop with problems of dilution and lack of ripeness; not of interest today.
1996	Seemingly a great classic vintage of vins de garde with high acidity and tannins. As it matures, herbaceousness is overtaking the fruits, making this a distinct throwback.
1995	Another generally dry year with good concentration, fine on both Left and Right Banks; in the modern idiom, but still going strong.
1994	Overrated (because of the previous three years); wines were rich and agreeable at first, but in any case are not now of interest.
1993	An improvement from the previous years but no longer of interest.
1992	A poor vintage now of little interest, with wines diluted by rainfall.
1991	The first (and worst) of four uninteresting years.
1990	The better of a pair of back to back promising vintages. An excellent growing season and good harvest conditions led to well balanced wines. On paper, very similar to 1989, but the wines today show an undeniable increase in finesse over 1989, perhaps because harvest was later in 1990.

1989	Initially this seemed a vintage along the lines of 1982, with warm conditions giving ripe wines. The best wines have developed in a delicious direction, but too many seem powerful rather than elegant.
1988	More inclined to power than elegance, slow to come around, with the best wines having classic structure, although others may seem a little clumsy.
1987	A poor vintage now of little interest.
1986	Often described as a classic vintage, meaning good tannic structure, so better on the left bank than the right bank.
1985	A delicious, forward vintage, often described as charming, and equally good on left and right banks.
1984	A poor vintage now of little interest.
1983	A very good vintage, although not up to 1982, except in Margaux where conditions had been too dry in 1982. For a while, the 1983s in Margaux pulled ahead of 1982, but now 1982 is universally better.
1982	The great vintage that started the modern era. Initially fruit-forward and accessible, then closing up in the late nineties, and from year 2000 reverting to type with a touch of herbaceous often balancing the fruits. The best wines are still splendid and classic.

	Older Vintages Still of Interest
1975	An object lesson in vintages of the century. Billed as producing vins de garde that would take a long time to come around, but would be classic in time. But the tannins outlived the fruits and almost none ever came around.
1970	Initially richer than 1966, but fruits fading in the past decade to leave an austere tannic impression.
1966	Universally good on the left bank, where a dry September led to wines that were at first austere but later turned elegant. The best wines still show great finesse (but there are not many left).
1964	On the left bank great wines were made by those who picked before the Autumn rains (Latour is a standout, equivalent to 1966), but the others were ruined. A very good year on the right bank where rain was not a problem. Fading now by comparison with 1966.
1962	This would have been considered a great vintage if not so overshadowed by 1961. The top wines are still interesting.
1961	Second only to 1945, with crop size reduced, and the wines concentrated by Spring frost. Very much a Cabernet year, so the wines still to drink are from the left bank. Mouton and Latour remain terrific.
1959	A lovely vintage, fine and elegant, with Château Margaux still displaying the elegance of the vintage,
1945	In spite of terrible conditions in viticulture at the end of the war, the best year of the century. The top wines lasted fifty years before beginning to fade. Some can still be enjoyed although past their peaks.

Champagne and Crémant

Méthode Champenoise

I saw her today at a reception
a glass of wine in her hand
(Rolling Stones)

Take regions where wine production is marginal and full ripeness occurs only occasionally. Most struggle to survive. But the genius of Champagne is to turn weakness into strength by requiring the wine to be acidic and bland as a neutral base for introducing bubbles, with a touch of sweetness to counteract the acidity. The reason why almost all potentially competitive regions have failed to produce anything matching Champagne is that they can actually make reasonable wine: they are simply not marginal enough. You might think that as sparkling wines are far more manipulated than still wines, Champagne would be easier to imitate, but in fact very few alternatives are really competitive in terms of character and quality. Champagne has progressively pushed all other aperitifs into relative insignificance. That glass of wine in her hand at the reception was very likely Champagne.

The same method is used to produce all quality sparkling wine: performing a second fermentation in the bottle to trap the carbon dioxide that is released *in situ*. This is called *Méthode Champenoise*, but the term means far more than merely a method for making sparkling wine. The fact that it is banned from use by anyone but the Champagne producers tells you a great deal about their commercial ruthlessness in enforcing their market position. The only term that is allowed for wine made elsewhere by the same methods as in Champagne is *Méthode Traditionelle*.

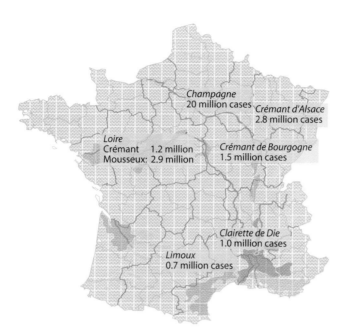

Champagne
20 million cases
Crémant d'Alsace
2.8 million cases

Loire
Crémant   1.2 million
Mousseux: 2.9 million

Crémant de Bourgogne
1.5 million cases

Clairette de Die
1.0 million cases

Limoux
0.7 million cases

Sparkling wine production is concentrated in the North. Outside of Champagne, it is divided between Crémant (made by Méthode Champenoise) and Mousseux (which has lower pressure and is not made by Méthode Champenoise).

Champagne is the most important (and best) sparkling wine produced in France. Sparkling wine is about 5% of all French wine production, and Champagne accounts for about two thirds of the 30 million cases produced each year in France. Champagne is the only region where sparkling wine is the main product; elsewhere, it is distinctly second-best to still wine. The next quality level is Crémant, made in the same way as Champagne, but coming from other areas. This accounts for about 20% of sparkling wine. It is no surprise that it also comes mostly from cool northern regions: Alsace, the Loire, and Burgundy.[1] Grape varieties depend on the region of origin. The Loire also produces a lot of sparkling wine in the lower category of Mousseux, made by second fermentation in bulk. In the south, some regions produce alternative types of sparkling wine. The traditional wines of Clairette de Die and Blanquette de Limoux are made by bottling the wine before the first fermentation has finished, so the pressure is much lower. This was probably the very first method used to make sparkling wine.

Fermentation to convert sugar into alcohol releases huge volumes of carbon dioxide. There is still controversy about the origin of the idea that you could make sparkling wine by trapping that gas in the bottle. Although Dom Pérignon is often given credit for introducing the second fermentation, in fact his career as cellar master at the Abbey of Hautvillers was devoted to trying to stop adventitious fermentation that was occurring in bottled wine and causing the bottles to explode. At the time, the major production of the region was still a conventional mix of dry red and white wine. Sparkling wine was first made in Champagne in 1695,[2] but it was not until around 1720 (just after Dom Pérignon's era) that it became fashionable,[3] stronger bottles became available that could contain the pressure, and Champagne became the premier sparkling wine.[4] (Today pressure is not usually a problem, but some Champagne houses make visitors wear protective glasses when visiting the caves, just in case a bottle explodes, and every so often you do see a hole in a stack of bottles where one has in fact burst.)

The principle of Méthode Champenoise is that the first fermentation —which occurs in exactly the same way as fermentation for any other wine—continues to completion, generating a still base wine with low alcohol (10.5-11%). Then a solution called the *liqueur de tirage* containing wine, sugar, and yeast is added, and the bottle is sealed with a crown cap. A second fermentation takes place, bringing alcohol up another per cent or so, and releasing enough carbon dioxide to create the required pressure of 5-6 atmospheres in the bottle.[5] The discovery of sparkling wine was almost certainly an accident resulting from adulteration of the wine with sugar, molasses, and spices, which led to an adventitious second fermentation. The process was pretty hit and miss until methods were developed for measuring sugar levels (from 1846). When Louis Pasteur discovered a decade later that yeast is responsible for fermentation, it became possible to add yeast together with a precise amount of sugar.

Poor Dom Pérignon! He spent most of his career trying to eliminate the bubbles that were spoiling the still wines of the Champagne region, but is remembered as the person who created Champagne. He is credited with developing techniques for producing white wine from black grapes, harvesting under cool conditions to preserve freshness, and introducing the idea of blending wines from different areas to make a more complex wine.

The second fermentation leaves a sediment of dead yeast cells. The method of dealing with this goes back to Madame Clicquot Ponsardin's disgust with the mess at the bottom of the bottle. The eponymous Veuve Clicquot had taken control of the Champagne house in 1805, and the story goes that she was infuriated by the sediment. Simply turning the bottles upside down did not work because particles continued to stick to the sides. Experimenting at home, she cut holes in her kitchen table to hold the bottles, and discovered that the sediment would collect in the neck if they were kept inverted and periodically rotated. It was later discovered that the process works best if the bottles start at an angle of 45°. *Remuage* (riddling in English) became a regular part of production, using a *pupître*, which consists of two boards hinged to form an inverted V; each board contains 60 holes cut at 45°. The bottles are rotated very gradually so that after a period of some weeks they come to a full vertical position.

Moët et Chandon
Remuage

Phot. Em. Choque, Imp.-Edit., Epernay

At the start of the twentieth century, Champagne house cellars were full of pupîtres for riddling.

The romantic view of Champagne production is that a skilled remueur (or riddler) can turn several hundred bottles a day, adjusting the angle by tiny increments. Almost all tours of caves in Champagne take you past rows of pupîtres, but the fact is that today the process is largely mechanized. A machine called the gyropalette is used for virtually all Méthode Champenoise production. Holding bottles in a crate, it follows a program for rotating them en masse until they are vertical. It takes days, compared with weeks for conventional riddling. Less romantic, but more practical—and more economical.[6]

How does the quality compare? "It's absolutely clear gyropalettes give better results than riddling by hand. I did not want to believe it, but the inventor of the machine visited and gave me a machine to test. After 6 months I looked and I could not see a difference between gyropalettes and hand riddling. So I took sample bottles to a lab to measure turbidity, and the machine was doing a better job. I decided I must not be nostalgic, I should take the best of modern technology," says Bruno Paillard, whose modern facility on the outskirts of Reims is full of gyropalettes. "Gyropalettes have the advantage of being able to go from absolutely horizontal to absolutely vertical. Quality depends on how you use the machine: you can rush the process through in as little as four days, or spend a week to get it perfect."

Once the sediment has collected in the neck it has to be disgorged. This is the most amazing part of the process. The necks of the inverted bottles are dipped into a refrigerated bath. The sediment in the neck becomes frozen. The bottle is turned upright, the cap is taken off, and voila!—the internal pressure ejects the sediment. *Dégorgement à la glace,* to give the process its full name, was invented in the late nineteenth century. The original concept is the basis for more automated machinery today.

Most riddling in Champagne or elsewhere is now performed by gyropalettes.

After the second fermentation, the wine should be completely dry, but the natural high acidity of Champagne generally needs to be counteracted by some sweetness. The style of Champagne is determined by a topping-up process that follows disgorgement. A small amount of wine is added to compensate for material that was lost when the sediment was ejected. This is done by using a solution called the *liqueur d'expédition*, also called the *dosage*, which consists of sugar dissolved in wine. Then a new cork is put on.

Champagnes (and other sparkling wines) are labeled according to the amount of sugar in the dosage. A wine without any added sugar is called Brut Natur or sometimes Zero Dosage. A wine with less than 6 g/l of sugar can be called Extra Brut, while Brut (by far the most common label) can have from 0 to 12 g/l.[7] In addition, there are various levels of sweetness in the Sec category.[8]

The machine for dégorgement à la glace was invented in 1884 (left). Modern equipment uses the same principle, but is completely automated (right).

However, the perception of sweetness depends a great deal on the balance between the level of sugar and the acidity (sweetness is less evident at high acidity, or put another way, a wine with higher acidity may require higher dosage).

Méthode Champenoise is the highest quality method for making sparkling wine because the second fermentation that generates the bubbles occurs in the very bottle that you will open. There's a slight exception for very small bottles (splits) and for bottles larger than magnums, where riddling and disgorgement may not be practical: the Champagne is produced in a normal bottle, but is then transferred into smaller or larger bottles. This *transvasage* involves emptying the bottles into a vat, which is then used to fill the smaller or larger bottles, but although all this is done under pressure, it's difficult to avoid some loss of gas. Bottles and magnums are therefore the way to enjoy sparkling wine under optimal conditions.

The unique characteristic of sparkling wine is its mousse—the fine froth of bubbles that forms on the surface when it is poured. Once the initial rush has died down, the bubbles help to propel aromas out of the glass, contribute to the sense of acidity, and give the wine its characteristic prickle. One mark of quality is the size of the bubble: the smaller the better, as this gives an impression of finer texture. There are more than 20 million bubbles in every bottle, and they are not just for show.

Champagne's beginnings as a wine-producing region were not propitious. The word "Champagne" was used in the fourteenth century to describe the poor area around Reims used for pasture and growing cereals.[9] Until the sixteenth century, the wines of the region were lumped together with those produced around Paris as "wines of France." By 1600, the wines of Reims and Epernay had their own identity and were known by the sobriquet "Champagne."[10] The areas considered to produce the best wines were the Montagne de Reims (devoted to red wines) and Aÿ (specializing in white wines).[11] Like Burgundy, the best areas were defined by the monks: in the twelfth and thirteenth centuries, the Abbaye of Saint-Nicaise in Reims went on a buying spree of top vineyards.[12]

Champagne	
Remuage	1816
Dosage	1846
First Brut Champagne	1876
Echelle des Crus	1895
Federation of Syndicats	1904
Marne v. l'Aube Riots	1911
Expansion of vineyards	1927
AOC defined	1936
Gyropalette	1975
Expansion of vineyards	2020?

Although sparkling wine was being produced by the early eighteenth century, it was a long time before it became the major product of the region. Until the nineteenth century, the wine was light (9-10% alcohol) and not highly sparkling (1.5-2 atmospheres).[13] At the start of the nineteenth century, cheap red wine was 90% of production, and by 1850 it was still almost three quarters.[14] A dramatic transition took place in the twentieth century, when cheap wine production collapsed in the period before the first world war. This left sparkling wine as the major product.

Sparkling wine was originally produced from black grapes. Lack of color was made possible by the development at the start of the eighteenth century of methods for gentle pressing that allowed juice to be obtained by running it straight off with minimal skin contact.[15] Before then, most Champagne was probably rosé. This was one of Dom Pérignon's accomplishments. It's uncertain exactly what grape varieties were used in Dom Pérignon's time, but Pinot Noir and Pinot Gris, known locally as Fromenteau, were major varieties.[16] Juice from white grapes began to be included only in the second half of the eighteenth century, first becoming common in the region around Avize, which became known as the Côte des Blancs.[17] Before phylloxera arrived, no less than 80 different grape varieties were growing in the Champagne region.[18] The replanting caused by phylloxera focused on the varieties that are dominant today.

When the first appellation rules were defined in 1919, Champagne was limited to seven varieties. Only three of them are important now: one white variety, Chardonnay, and two black varieties, Pinot Noir and Pinot Meunier. The other varieties remain legal, but today are grown only in tiny quantities. The main change in the varieties from the nineteenth century is the disappear-

Gentle pressing is achieved in Champagne by the traditional basket press, in which the lid comes down onto the mass of grapes, and the juice comes out between the wooden slats. Courtesy CIVC.

ance of Pinot Gris.[19] Most Champagne is made from a blend of varieties, but a Blanc de Blancs comes exclusively from Chardonnay, and a Blanc de Noirs comes exclusively from black varieties (usually only Pinot Noir).[20]

All Champagne, even a Blanc de Noirs, should be a pale golden color. Except, of course, for rosé. This can be a bit of a trick: most rosé Champagne is made simply by adding a little red wine to the base wine. This is illegal as a means of producing rosé for all wines in the E.U. except for Champagne; and, indeed, proposals to legalize it for still wine production led to a great outcry about loss of quality. The method of production means that rosé Champagne does not necessary come from black grapes; because the color is provided by a small percentage of red wine, the rest can include Chardonnay.

Where exactly Champagne comes from is not quite as simple a question as it might appear. Defining the area of Champagne has always been controversial. The heart of the region is focused in the Département of the Marne, between Reims and Epernay, a little less than a hundred miles to the east and north of Paris. But 50 miles to the south, beyond the city of Troyes, is the region of the Aube, where the vineyards were regarded historically as belonging to Champagne. In fact, the Aube is closer to Chablis than it is to Reims. The justification for its inclusion was basically that this allows Champagne to cover the entire administrative region of Champagne-Ardennes, as defined after the Revolution.[21] So the Aube was included for administrative convenience, whereas geography might have made it equally logical for it to be part of Burgundy.

Tension between the Marne and the Aube came to a head in 1907 when a commission established to define the limits of Champagne excluded the Aube. In 1911, as the rules came into effect, riots culminated in some of the major Champagne houses being sacked.[22] The Aube remained excluded until the limits of Champagne were redefined in 1927.[23] The conflict at this time was that the Aube had a large amount of Gamay, which was considered unsuitable for Champagne. However, the Aube was readmitted to Champagne on condition that the Gamay would be removed over the next twenty years. (In fact it was well into the 1950s before all the Gamay was gone.)

Everywhere wine is produced in France, the winemaker is the key person. (Even though sometimes in Bordeaux one is driven to think about the marketing manager…) But in Champagne, the master blender is king: the wine is a neutral basis for him to work his skill. The crucial fact is that Champagne is all about blending, by assemblage from different years, different locations, and different grape varieties.

The vast majority of Champagne is nonvintage, meaning that wines from recent years are blended before the second fermentation. Each Champagne house prides itself upon maintaining consistency of style by blending, and it's the nonvintage Champagne that best displays its skill. As many as 30-40 different cuvées,

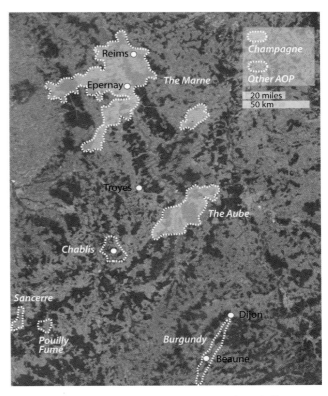

The vineyards of Champagne are the most northern in France. The major vineyards extend from Reims and Epernay, but Champagne also includes the Aube, which is farther south.

coming from different parts of the region, will be included in the blend; possibly only the blending of perfumes has the same complexity. A major factor in maintaining quality and consistency is the use of reserve wines. Some producers establish reserve wines by setting aside part of each vintage to be kept (under inert conditions) for later use, some keep their reserves as a blend of older vintages, and some maintain what is called a perpetual blend, replenished each year by adding wine from the latest vintage to replace what is withdrawn.[24]

A typical nonvintage Champagne probably contains up to three quarters of wine from the most recent vintage, a fair proportion from the previous couple of vintages, and smaller amounts of reserve wine from older vintages. The proportion and age of the reserve is often a measure of quality.[25] Reserve wines aren't necessarily any better in quality than the current vintage; the significance is more that their different characters provide the basis for blending.

Using reserve wines evens out vintage variation, and crucially allows sub par vintages to be absorbed. But the disadvantage is that you do not see the maximum quality in nonvintage wines when vintages are good. Ann de Keyser

Champagne Ayala was one of the Maisons sacked in the riots of 1911. The stock and the building were destroyed. Ayala unusually had an insurance policy and was rebuilt (but the insurance company was bankrupted).

at Nicolas Feuillatte is quite honest about it: "Reserve wines may be used to increase or decrease quality depending on the current vintage." As Dominic Demarville, chef de cave of Veuve Clicquot, explains, using all the wine in a good year would cause quality to be compromised in lesser vintages because of the lack of high quality reserve wines. "It's a delicate balance," he says. Because of small volume, Krug decided not to release a vintage in 2012. "We are keeping the 2012 wines for creating (nonvintage) Grand Cuvée over the next 15 years," explains Eric Lebel, Krug's chef de cave.

Most producers accept the model of "blend, baby, blend," but a handful go another way. "The concept of nonvintage, of being completely consistent, began to frustrate us," says Jean-Hervé Chiquet at Champagne Jacquesson. "In 1998 we were still making a classic blend, we were working on the 1997, and it was very good but it would be impossible to reproduce in another year. So we made another blend. But afterwards we realized that we'd made a wine that wasn't as good. So we decided we should make the best wine (each year) and we identified it by the number of the cuvée." Now each numbered release consists of an assemblage from a base year supplemented by the assemblages from the previous two years. There's more sense of variation between releases, without going to the extremes of representing a single vintage. Some other producers, such as Pierre Moncuit, make what are effectively undeclared vintages by not using any reserve wine.

Vintage Champagne typically is made only three or four times a decade as and when there are vintages above average. Here variation is expected to reflect the character of the year, as seen through the prism of house style. Vintage Champagnes are also blended, of course, but the blend is only between vineyard sources and grape varieties. Whereas nonvintage Champagne is intended for consumption soon after release, vintage Champagne is intended to support some aging in the bottle.

Another significant feature of vintage Champagne is that it spends longer before disgorgement. The rules require nonvintage Champagne to rest on its lees for 15 months before it is disgorged; for vintage Champagne the period is increased to three years. Many producers age their wines—especially prestige cuvées—for longer than the minimum. The process of aging is completely different before and after disgorgement. While the wine is on the lees, it is in a reductive environment (effectively oxygen is excluded) and it picks up flavor and richness due to the process of *autolysis*, as the dead yeast cells break down to release material that protects the wine against oxidation and aging, giving a fresh flavor. After disgorgement, the environment is oxidative, and the major factor influencing development is a process called the Maillard reaction, which involves interaction between sugar and amino acids that were released by autolysis. This is the reaction that gives Champagne those biscuity notes of toast and brioche as it ages. As a rough working rule, the longer a Champagne has spent before disgorgement, the longer it will continue to age interestingly after disgorgement. But the basic moral is that if you like your Champagne in a relatively fresh style, you should drink it soon after disgorgement, whereas if you prefer some toast and brioche, you should wait, perhaps a year for a nonvintage Champagne and three years for a vintage.

Aside from a small proportion consisting only of Chardonnay (Blanc de Blancs) or only of Pinot Noir (Blanc de Noirs), most nonvintage Champagne is a blend of all three grape varieties. Chardonnay and Pinot Noir are held in distinctly higher esteem than Pinot Meunier, but Pinot Meunier has the practical advantage that it flowers later than Pinot Noir, so it is less susceptible to Spring frosts. "Pinot Meunier is the most rustic cépage in Champagne, but it's the only one that resists difficult conditions," says Rodolphe Peters of Champagne Pierre Peters. The warming trend has made this less of a factor, and the proportion of Pinot Meunier has been declining: it was the most important variety in the vineyards in the 1950s, when it was

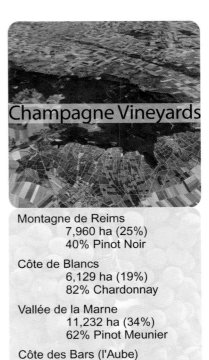

Champagne Vineyards

Montagne de Reims
7,960 ha (25%)
40% Pinot Noir

Côte de Blancs
6,129 ha (19%)
82% Chardonnay

Vallée de la Marne
11,232 ha (34%)
62% Pinot Meunier

Côte des Bars (l'Aube)
6,817 ha (21%)
87% Pinot Noir

The terroir throughout Champagne is based on chalk. Courtesy CIVC.

45% of all plantings, but today it is only 32%. Pinot Noir is now the most widely planted variety at 39%, and Chardonnay is 29%.[26]

A variant of Pinot Noir, Pinot Meunier takes its name from the white flour-like appearance of the underneath of its leaves (Meunier is French for miller). The problem with Pinot Meunier is that flavor can be a bit rustic: you see this most clearly in those rare still red wines that are made as varietals.[27] It brings more forward fruits and aromas, which are felt to help the wine when it is young: perfect for nonvintage Champagne. "We do consider Pinot Meunier as essential in the blend. It's all a matter of selecting the terroir and using the proper proportion in the blend. On average we have a third of each cépage. It's true that Pinot Meunier will mature a little quicker than Pinot Noir or Chardonnay and won't last as long, but it helps create more harmony and balance," says Jean-Marc Lallier-Deutz at Champagne Deutz. But it tends to bring an element of coarseness with aging, which is why it is often excluded from vintage Champagne.

The classic regions for producing Champagne are to the south and west of the city of Reims, and account for three quarters of the vineyards. The key to

Miles of caves have been hollowed out from the chalk underneath the Champagne houses. Courtesy CIVC.

understanding the terroir of Champagne is chalk: the best vineyards have thin topsoil on a subsoil of chalk beds. The limestone is friable, and acts like a sponge to absorb the rain. The most pronounced outcrops of chalk are found in the Montagne de Reims and the Côte des Blancs, with a small stretch also running along the river in the Vallée de la Marne. The chalk is evident in occasional cliff faces, and more dramatically in the caves that have been excavated under Reims and Epernay, where there are a couple of hundred of kilometers of underground galleries. Pinot Noir and Chardonnay are concentrated on the chalk outcrops. Going farther south, there's a disjoint when you go all the way down to the Aube, where the wines become somewhat heavier. The subsoil here is mostly a Kimmeridgian clay, which is more like Chablis and Sancerre than the vineyards in the Marne.

The differences between the three major areas extending out from Reims have more to do with the lie of the land and climatic exposure than soil. The forest of the Montagne de Reims separates Reims from Epernay, and around its circumference to the east are the vineyards named after it. Vineyards are on the slopes running down from the forest. Historically this area was well regarded

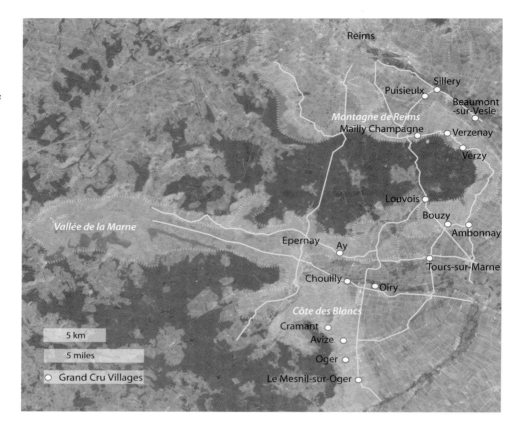

for red wine, and today it produces the most full-bodied sparkling wines, and has a high concentration of Pinot Noir. Lying just to the south of Epernay, the Côte des Blancs has east-facing slopes that are protected from the wind and from Spring frosts, allowing the vines to mature slowly. It concentrates on Chardonnay and is known for its finesse. The Vallée de la Marne runs along the river to the west. There is a high concentration of Pinot Meunier because its later bud break and earlier ripening makes it more resistant to the frosts typically associated with the valley. To the east of Epernay, a focus on Pinot Noir places Aÿ with the Montagne of Reims. The view that blending from all three areas gives the best quality and complexity goes back to Dom Pérignon.

Because Champagne is usually blended, you rarely see sources indicated, but in fact Champagne has a classification system for vineyards dating from the end of the nineteenth century. This is the *échelle des crus*, which gives every single village a rating from 80% to 100%. Villages classified at 100% are called grand crus, and villages rated between 90% and 99% are premier crus. Until a few years ago, the rating determined the price paid for grapes from each village: whatever base price was set for the vintage would be pro-rated according to the village's position on the scale.

To preserve freshness, Champagne grapes are usually pressed close to the vineyard in local press houses; then the juice is transported to the winery.

Out of the 319 villages, 17 are classified as grand crus, and 43 are classified as premier crus. The crus are mostly located in the Montagne de Reims or Côte des Blancs, with a couple on the eastern edge of the Vallée de la Marne. The grand crus represent 13% of the area, and the premier crus represent 19%. It's an indication of how the grape varieties are regarded that Pinot Meunier cannot be given grand cru status. There is a rather small amount of Pinot Meunier in premier cru villages.[28] (Pinot Meunier is in fact about half of all plantings outside the premier and grand crus.) A Champagne can be labeled as grand cru if all the grapes come from vineyards anywhere within the grand cru villages.

The major problem with the échelle des crus is that the whole village is classified at the same level. Imagine if all Vosne Romanée was classified at the same level: no Romanée Conti, no premier crus, no separate village wine, all just one level. The price paid for grapes in Champagne historically did not depend on the quality of the individual grapes or even of the individual vineyard, but simply on the rating of the village. Today there is more discrimination. "The pricing of the grapes is not linked to classification any more, it's a free market, we have private contracts with growers, with prices that are linked to the prices indicated by the CIVC. Everything is handled by parcel," explains Jean-Marc Lallier-Deutz. As Hervé Deschamps, cellarmaster at Perrier-Jouët, says, "There are 180 tanks for base wine from 70 villages for our nonvintage. It's very important to understand that each tank is different. If you have twenty tanks for one village they are all different, they are not the same. They differ in the

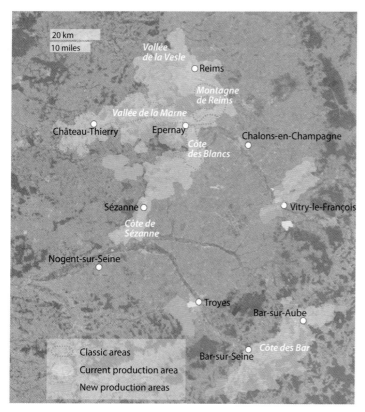

20 km
10 miles

Vallée de la Vesle

Reims

Montagne de Reims

Vallée de la Marne

Château-Thierry   Epernay

Côte des Blancs

Chalons-en-Champagne

Sézanne   Vitry-le-François

Côte de Sézanne

Nogent-sur-Seine

Troyes

Bar-sur-Aube

Classic areas   Côte des Bar
Current production area   Bar-sur-Seine
New production areas

The present Champagne production zone has 319 communes extending over 300,000 ha, and includes 33,000 ha of vineyards. Proposed new production areas include 40 extra communes, but vineyards have not yet been classified.

slopes, the grapes, the time of harvest." There can be wide variations in terroir between vineyards within the same village (or in the efforts of individual growers), and it's certainly not true that all grand cru vineyards are better than all premier cru vineyards. The present classification is a blunt tool indeed.

The current controversy in Champagne concerns the expansion of the vineyards. Champagne is bursting at the seams. Under pressure to increase production, in 2003 the producers asked INAO to reclassify the area, this of course being a euphemism for increasing the approved area, which has re-opened the controversy about where Champagne should really be made. Champagne has contracted and expanded according to the rhythm of the day. Just before phylloxera, there were 60,000 hectares of vineyards; by 1919 there were only 12,000 ha. When the zone for production of Champagne was defined by the law of 1927, 40,000 hectares of vineyards were included in 407 villages. Responding to a decline in the market, this was reduced to 34,000 ha in 302 villages in 1951. Only 11,000 ha were used for Champagne production in the 1950s, but since then the vineyards have expanded steadily to fill the entire allotted area of the AOC. Today there are just over 33,000 ha.

Over a three year period, INAO reviewed the areas where grapes can be grown and wine can be made. A leak to the press revealed that the proposal was to include 40 new villages and to remove two existing villages. Detailed examination of vineyards in these villages is still continuing, and no one knows yet exactly which plots will be included in the Champagne AOP. It won't be until around 2017 or thereabouts that the first new vineyards are actually planted, and so it will be 2020 or later before their grapes are included in Champagne.[29] The rationale for the reclassification is that there was much less knowledge about conditions for viti-culture when the original limits were defined, and historical accidents influenced the outcome—such as the mayor of a village seeing no point in being included in the AOC. (When the vineyards were classified in 1927, grain, dairy, and cattle farming were more profitable than Champagne, and many landowners were aristocrats who were not interested in wine production.) Most of the new areas lie close to or within the existing areas, the two outstanding exceptions being a large expansion around Troyes and also just below Château-Thierry.

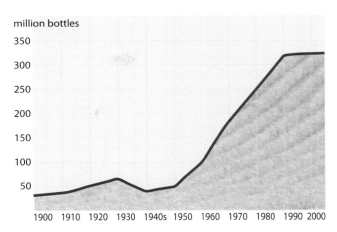

Champagne production doubled in the first half of the twentieth century, and in the second half increased almost ten fold.[30]

The question is whether this is more than a ploy to increase production at the expense of quality. The precedents are not good: most expansions of the vineyards of classic wine regions have been associated with dilution of character. There seems to be some skepticism about the potential new villages at top producers. Will you buy grapes from the new villages, I asked Jean-Pierre Mareigner, cellar master at Champagne Gosset? "No—perhaps in a hundred years, but not now. We work essentially with grand cru and premier cru in the traditional villages. The new areas will be unplanted land which hasn't had vines before; we look for the typicity of established vines." Understanding the character of the vineyard is the main issue. "When we taste for assemblage we have a long history of the parcel, but if we work with wine from vines that are only a few years old, we have no history to guide us," explains Jean-Marc Lallier-Deutz. The view is more positive at the largest Champagne houses, which feel more need for a wider supply of grapes in order to expand.

The major controversy in Champagne should be the extraordinary yields, but almost no one ever mentions this. The exponential growth in Champagne production in the past fifty years has partly been due to an increase in the vineyard area, but equally due to a tripling of the yields.[31] Yields are calculated in an unusual way in Champagne. Elsewhere in France, the limits are in terms of the amount of wine that can be produced from a given area, as hectoliters per hectare. But in Champagne they are calculated as the kilograms of grapes harvested per hectare. This is a moving target, set each year with a primary agenda that regards market demand as a more significant factor than quality of grapes. A great deal of misinformation is put out in an attempt to make yields appear lower than they really are. They are usually actually around 14,000 kg/hl,[32] but with a restriction that only some of the harvest can be used for producing wine for current consumption; the rest, however, can be used to make reserve wines for future use.[33] While this may serve its purpose for manipulating supply and demand, in terms of quality it's the total yield that matters. Converting to a more conventional measure, 14,000 kg/hl corresponds to a whopping 89 hl/ha, equivalent to table wine, and about double the usual limit for quality wine.[34] The only relief is that pressing is divided into two stages: the first pressing, called the cuvée, is used by most producers, and a second, smaller pressing, called the taille is usually not used.[35]

The Champenoise defend their extraordinary yields by arguing that they need to make a neutral base wine: as they are not looking for the same level of ripeness or flavor development that would be appropriate for a still wine, higher yields are in order. This may be true up to a point, but I have my doubts whether it extends all the way to the dizzy heights of 89 hl/ha. Because Champagne is extensively blended, it's hard to directly assess the effects of lower yields. Occasionally you get a chance to taste a Vieilles Vignes Champagne, where the vines are old enough that yields are significantly reduced. Comparing Moncuit's 2004 Vieilles Vignes with the regular vintage bottling, there is distinctly more concentration on the palate, to the point at which you can see what would be gained if only they would reduce yields in Champagne. I think it's very probable that if harvests were limited to, say, 10,000 kg/ha, there'd be a noticeable all-round improvement in quality. Of course, whether the consumer would want to pay for this is another matter.

Champagne Styles	
Nonvintage	94%
Vintage	6%
Extra-Brut	0.5%
Brut	97%
Sweet styles	2.5%
Rosé	9%
Prestige Cuvées	4%

Champagne today tastes richer than it did ten or twenty years ago; superficially you might think an impression of more softness and even sweetness represents an increase in dosage, but actually it's the other way round; dosage has been declining to compensate for the extra ripeness of the grapes. (Although the grapes harvested in Champagne would be regarded as seriously unripe by the standards of still wine production in, for example, Burgundy.) The fact that chaptalization is still often needed indicates that the region remains marginal for wine production. This is a major factor in its success. If they reach a point in Champagne at which chaptalization is no longer necessary, they will be on the verge of succumbing to the same problem as their would-be rivals where adequate ripeness prevents success. (Should this happen, the long history of Anglo-French rivalry comes to the fore in suggesting southern England as a possible location for future Champagne production.)

Champagne was sweet until the last part of the nineteenth century, and very sweet at that, with anything from two to five times the sugar level of a sweet champagne today. The impetus for reducing sugar came from British wine merchants, who found that Champagne was not competitive with other sweet wines, but that in relatively dry form, it could be sold to accompany food or (later) as an aperitif.[36] As Charles Perrier (son of the founder of Perrier-Jouët) said in 1846, "Today the English do not like Champagne too sweet. Most know that the use of high sugar levels is almost always to mask a lack of quality." The effect of sugar remains an interesting question even today, when by far the most common style of Champagne is Brut.

Dosage is not a simple issue: it's more about balancing acidity than creating a perception of sweetness. In fact, three factors go into determining the balance of the wine: the acidity of the grapes at harvest; whether malolactic fermentation is performed; and how much sugar is included in the dosage.

The perception among producers is that global warming has produced higher potential alcohol and lower acidity at harvest. This is certainly the trend, but the actual change measured by the CIVC is still quite small.[37] Perhaps the producers have been compensating for climate change by harvesting relatively earlier. It's a prime objective in Champagne to harvest early enough to retain high acidity in the grapes. "We used to harvest in October and we were caught between lack of maturity and development of botrytis. Now we harvest in September, the days are longer, there are fewer disease problems, and we get perfectly ripe berries. We can harvest up to 11% alcohol, so chaptalization is often still necessary," says Rodolphe Peters.

The major stylistic issue after alcoholic fermentation is whether to perform malolactic fermentation (MLF). This reduces acidity (by converting the sharp malic acid to the softer lactic acid), but it also makes wine generally creamier. The old school of thought was that malolactic fermentation was more appropriate for nonvintage champagne, but that retaining higher acidity was better for the ageability of vintage. That seems to have been replaced by a view that malolactic fermentation generally produces a better balanced wine, and it has become the rule rather than the exception, with less distinction made between nonvintage and vintage. "It reduces sharpness of the acid and gives better lines to the wine, a final touch on the finish of minerality, salt, citrus, between zest and fruit," says Rodolphe Peters. "If you block MLF you'd better be sure to have good storage because the wine will need to be kept longer before release," says Jean-Marc Lallier-Deutz. It may also need more dosage. "Without dosage malic acid can be very aggressive," says cellarmaster Hervé Deschamps at Perrier-Jouët. Most Champagne houses today have a general policy, either to perform or to block malolactic fermentation (the majority perform it).

While it's true that excess dosage can be a means to cover up other problems, producers refute any simplistic idea that less dosage is always better. "Dosage is not to give sweetness, but to keep the same taste and to reduce acidity, it's the last touch of the chef to increase flavor," is how Hervé Deschamps describes his approach. "If you believe you can use dosage to counter natural austerity, it doesn't work. If you add high dosage you get an artificial sucrosité at the end," says Jean-Hervé Chiquet at Jacquesson. Viewing dosage as part of the means by which consistency of style is maintained across vintages, most producers have reduced it over the past ten or twenty years in response to their sense that the grapes are riper.

Dosage is not necessarily fixed for a cuvée, but may be different for subsequent disgorgements of the same wine. Because a wine gains in richness with time on the lees, later disgorgements may have less dosage than earlier disgorgements. Jean-Marc Lallier-Deutz explains the approach at Deutz: "We dose on the basis of tasting. But Classic starts with 9.5 to 10 g/l when we begin disgorging, and later disgorgement will go down to 9 g/l, and then with the new cuvée back up." There is more to maintaining consistency than simply getting the blend right. Deutz cellarmaster Michel Davesne adds, "Over thirty years the dosage has gone down, we have reduced it because there is less acidity. And I think the consumer prefers a lower dosage." Dominique Garreta confirms the trend at Taittinger: "Globally over the range dosage is 9 g/l, decreased from 11-12 g/l a few years ago. We changed dosage because the grapes have changed." Vintage Champagne tends to have lower dosage than nonvintage, because it comes from riper years.

The Brut classification covers a multitude of sins: anything from 0 to 12 g/l dosage. Extra Brut can be used to describe wines below 6 g/l, but is not necessarily always used, because for some cuvées around the limit, the producer wants to maintain flexibility to go over or under the limit depending on annual conditions. Producers also think some consumers react against the name of Extra Brut, so there is now a surprising amount of Brut Champagne that is below 6 g/l dosage. "We use 4.5 g/l dosage in the vintage wines. The wines are still labeled Brut, but we are asking ourselves if we should change the label to Extra Brut," Charles Philipponnat says, describing his policy of having reduced dosage since he took over at Philipponnat.

There is also something of a trend to produce Brut Nature, or Zero Dosage, as the current fashion calls it, with absolutely no additional sugar. This is controversial. Champagne Ayala, after it was acquired by the Bollinger family in 2005, decided to distinguish itself with a move to low dosage. Zero dosage wine has a tendency to austerity, but the best zero dosage champagnes are not merely the same wine as the Brut without dosage. Some producers distinguish the zero dosage by giving longer time on the lees to pick up some richness to compensate for the lack of dosage; at Ayala the zero dosage has an extra year before disgorgement. Some producers make zero dosage wine specifically from parcels that achieve greater ripeness.

"The trend for zero dosage is nothing new to us," says Anne-Laure Domenichini at Laurent-Perrier. "Veuve Laurent Perrier created the first non dosage champagne—Grand Vin Sans Sucre—around 1881, at the request of British customers. It was withdrawn around the first world war as it wasn't to the taste of the French. Bernard de Nonancourt reintroduced it in 1988 when nouvelle cuisine started the trend for sauces without cream. He called it the naked Champagne." Today the Ultra Brut comes from an equal blend of Pinot Noir and Chardonnay chosen for high ripeness and low acidity; in fact, it's not made in years that aren't sufficiently ripe. Indeed, I am not sure I would peg this as zero dosage in a blind tasting, because the fruits are so ripe. "This is not the nonvintage with no dosage, but is its own wine," Anne-Laure emphasizes.

But there are skeptics. "It's very amusing to disgorge a wine and drink it in the Nature style, but zero dosage is a bit like a chair with three legs—it's missing something. An Extra Brut is always more interesting than a Nature—it brings out the fruits better. Zero dosage usually has 1 g/l sugar anyway because it's made by using indigenous yeast and they never ferment absolutely dry," says Rodolphe Peters. And it may not be so simple as deciding to go for the zero style at disgorgement. "I believe zero dosage champagne is a global project, meaning that it starts in the vineyard when you select your grapes with the idea that there won't be any dosage. There are in fact very few champagne houses that respect this concern. There are few really great zero dosage champagnes," says Dominique Garreta at Taittinger. A side issue is that, because the aging of Champagne depends on sugar (for the Maillard reaction), there's a question as to whether zero dosage wines will have aging capacity.

My own opinion is that you see the purity of fruits more directly with zero dosage; but this means they need to be absolutely top quality. Otherwise the acidity can be somewhat brutal. A direct comparison of zero dosage with Brut at Philipponnat (the same wine with a few months difference in disgorgement) shows that that the zero dosage is less generous, less broad, but more precise. The main point is that the difference is not just a matter of the sweetness level, but the whole flavor spectrum is shifted from stone to citrus. Generally, I would be more inclined to have zero dosage with a meal and Brut or Extra Brut as an aperitif. I often prefer Extra Brut to Brut, because going into the Brut range tends to muddy impressions. But there are really no rules: there are Brut Champagnes at the level of, say, 9 g/l dosage which appear drier on the palate than some Extra Bruts. It's all in the balance: dosage is a key tool in compensating for vintage variation.

The objectives in producing nonvintage Champagne are somewhat opposed to those for vintage: nonvintage champagne relies upon an assemblage that evens out vintage variation, whereas vintage champagne is intended at least in part to highlight the character of the vintage. Because vintage Champagne is produced only in the most successful years, the grapes are likely to be riper at the outset. A longer period before disgorgement increases richness; and the tendency to exclude Pinot Meunier increases refinement. So a vintage Champagne should be finer, more precise, and it should show more complexity because it can be aged longer than nonvintage. Indeed, one of the criteria for making a vintage Champagne is that it should have aging potential. But maintaining house style is still a paramount concern: vintage variation is allowed to go only so far.

The issue of disgorgement dates is a hot topic in Champagne. With nonvintage Champagne, production is a more or less continuous process, and there is an assumption that the wine is disgorged, and the dosage is adjusted, so that it is ready to drink when released: for practical purposes this means within a year or so of purchase.

With vintage Champagne, the date of disgorgement becomes a significant issue. A vintage Champagne will usually become available between four and five years after the vintage, but it will not necessarily all be disgorged at that point: some may be kept back to be disgorged later. It will gain increased complexity from longer time in the bottle before disgorgement, but the aromas and flavors are different from those developing after disgorgement. There may be a huge difference in flavor between a Dom Pérignon 1990 disgorged in 1996 and one disgorged in 2006. Some people prize vintage Champagne for the character it develops when it ages after disgorgement, but others believe it is most interesting for the increased richness that happens with a delay before disgorgement.

The view in Champagne is increasingly coming around to the position that the wine is best enjoyed soon after disgorgement. This was the logic behind the creation of Bollinger's R.D. cuvée: R.D. stands for recently disgorged:[38] a great vintage is kept on the lees for a protracted period—the current release is the 1999. Other houses have followed suit. The same principle lies behind Dom Pérignon's Oenothèque series: you could have purchased the 1996 Dom Pérignon when it was first released in the early 2000s; but today the same wine, held for an additional decade before disgorgement, has been re-released as the Oenothèque 1996.[39] Which you like better depends on whether you prefer mature or fresh flavors.

It's controversial in Champagne whether disgorgement dates should be stated on the bottle. In the case of nonvintage, this would protect the consumer against bottles that have been left for too long in the distribution chain. (The same issue arises with other quality wines that don't have a vintage, such as Sherry). With vintage wines, because they may be disgorged at different times after the vintage, and because there's more of a tendency to age them before consumption, it's more a matter of indicating style.

Some Champagne houses now indicate disgorgement dates on the back label. Bruno Paillard was the first, but until recently was followed by relatively few others. "I started putting disgorgement dates on bottles in 1983; for more than twenty years I was the only one to do it," Bruno says. Why did you do this, I asked? "Like everyone I saw variations in bottles with no explanation. You could guess but you should have the information." Some houses, such as Krug and Taittinger, are putting codes on the back label that can be scanned by a smart phone to give the date of disgorgement as well as other information. Some houses are moving more towards a code that can be read by the trade, but not necessarily by the consumer.

The objections to giving information about disgorgement are ostensibly that it may be misleading. "It's not very relevant because the pattern of aging after disgorgement is very different for each wine. If we put dates on, some consumers will look at the label and say, it's three years, it's too old; others might say it's too young," explains Jean-Pierre Mareigner, cellarmaster at Gosset. Even the trade isn't completely trusted. "There is a risk that distributors will just sell the youngest wine and the oldest will accumulate in the chain," says Hervé Deschamps at Perrier Jouët. At Taittinger, Dominique Garreta is forthright about the issue: "For us it's a nonsense to put a disgorgement date on the label for several reasons. Putting a date on anything you eat or drink means an expiration date for the consumer, so this would lead to a total misunderstanding. And for us disgorgement date is not an indication; there could be the same disgorgement date on two quite different blends. Let's be honest, most of the brands that print disgorgement dates don't age very well." Personally I think Bruno's position is irrefutable, but it seems likely that it will be some time yet before dosage information becomes widely available, although there is a definite trend towards more openness, including stating the assemblage (base wine and reserve wine vintages and proportions) and dosage.

It is both a strength and a weakness that Champagne has only a single appellation. It gives instant recognition to anything that says Champagne on the label, but it makes it more difficult to distinguish wines that come from particular areas. The only official distinctions are the marks of premier or grand cru (very general) and the styles (Blanc de Blancs and Blanc de Noirs). Insofar as there is any emphasis on terroir in Champagne, it focuses on the superiority of grand cru and premier cru vineyards. The échelle des crus may have become irrelevant, but "the most common question I am asked is whether the grapes come from grand cru or premier cru villages," says Jean-Marc Lallier-Deutz.

Producers are quite conscious of the differences between villages, but this is more in the context of using them to increase complexity and balance the blend than to represent the differences in individual cuvées. Le Mesnil-sur-Oger is famous for its austerity; Oger for its opulence. It's a reasonable question whether and how differences between individual villages might be reflected in

Krug's Clos du Mesnil is one of the most famous single vineyards. The 1.8 ha clos is nestled under the village of Mesnil-sur-Oger, protected by walls dating from 1698.

finished Champagne given the extent of manipulation during production. There are relatively few Champagnes representing individual villages through which the question might be examined, and it's probably fair to say that there is little chance of individual villages developing reputations for particular styles, equivalent to communes in Burgundy, for example, because the style of the individual house is more important.

But some insights into the potential for single vineyard Champagnes come from exceptional producers who make a point of them. At the head of this rather small group is Champagne Jacques Selosse. A person of strong opinions, Anselme Selosse takes his marching orders from Burgundy, where he learned oenology. "When I saw Romanée Conti, it was a revelation. The vines come from selection massale and are the same as with the other slopes. The exposure is the same. The water is the same. So it must be the soil." First he divides his vineyards into those with less than 15% incline and those with more, as this determines types of soils, especially how much clay accumulates at the bottom of the slope. This leads to four "topographic" nonvintage cuvées (two Blanc de Blancs and two rosé).

The emphasis here is on differences: differences between vintages and differences between places. For vintage wines, "I prefer that each wine should be different. I do not want the wine to be the same every year... And there is a false idea that the vintage ends when the vigneron decides to harvest, but conditions after are different too—which is why malo is left to happen or not happen," he says. Bottlings from individual lieu-dits are nonvintage: "The objective is to display terroir rather than vintage." They are made as a blend of several recent vintages, which may develop into something equivalent to a Perpetual Reserve. They make the rare point that even after the involved process of making Champagne, terroir can show: Les Carelles from Mesnil has a very fine impression of the minerality of the village, whereas Sous le Mont from Mareuil has a more powerful linear impression. Anselme sees the differences as resulting from the minerals in the soil: more magnesium at Mareuil makes the limestone harder, and the wine sterner.

Dosage is very low or zero to allow the terroir to express itself in the Selosse single vineyard wines, and this is part of a general movement. There's a correlation between low dosage and production of single vineyard wines: producers who want to show origins often feel that lower dosage is important. "We want to have Champagne that really tastes of where it comes from, that's why we make single vineyard Champagnes. The aim is to make dosage invisible, we want to taste the wine, the most we ever use is 3-4 g/l" says Sophie Larmandier of Larmandier-Bernier.

Anselme Selosse defies conventional wisdom in another respect: oak. Generally, there is little oak in Champagne. Base wines are made and held in stainless steel until the second fermentation is started in bottle. Krug and Bollinger are unusual in fermenting in (old) barriques; they feel this adds richness and depth to the wine, and makes for longer aging. More recently there's been a move towards maturing wines in barriques after fermentation, but generally this is only for special cuvées. At Selosse, the base wine is both fermented and aged in oak, with about 15% new barriques. The wines tend to seem more mature, reflecting the generally oxidative style of winemaking, but are not oaky in any conventional sense, allowing the lieu-dits to show their differences. Anselme can pull this off successfully because of the sheer quality of his wines, but it might be problematic at another producer.

There is some skepticism about single vineyard wines, not so much as to whether they reflect significant differences, but as to whether they make the most complex wines. "Elegance is more difficult to obtain than concentration. Our top parcel is like Puligny for still wine, but for balance it needs to be blended. That's the key about single vineyards. It's not necessarily the case that a plot making a wonderful still wine will by itself make the most complex Champagne," says Didier Gimonnet, explaining why he has been resisting calls to make a single vineyard wine from the parcel. Gimonnet has in fact just pro-

Wine for some prestige Champagnes is vinified in oak. Quantities can be very small: a few barriques account for the entire production of Bollinger Vieilles Vignes Françaises.

duced its first single village wines, a break with the past when the blend was always between grand cru for structure and premier cru for freshness. There's a concern about the effects of taking out the best wines. "Because people wanted to produce great quantities they blended more, so everything became more the same—and the growers are reacting against that, they want to express authenticity. But it's less complex, the best balance comes from blending. Of course there are exceptions but it's very rare. And of course the more you take off the best terroirs the more you decrease the quality of your blend. That's why philosophically I'm against single vineyard wines," Didier explains.

If nonvintage, vintage, and single vineyards all represent different types of Champagne, rosé is a further distinct style. It is the most recent innovation in Champagne, in a sense a reversal of the success in eliminating color in the eighteenth century. It owes its origin to the introduction of the style by a handful of houses around forty years ago. The idea was to introduce a style that was more expensive than nonvintage Brut but less than the prestige cuvées. Production has increased sharply in the past few years.[40]

My complaint with many rosés is that the red wine seems to stand aside. It softens and rounds out the Champagne without adding any character or really integrating into the wine. As this is a Champagne and not a still wine, you are not looking for overt red fruit character; indeed that would detract from the sense of Champagne, but surely there should be something of that sense of the elegance and precision of fine Pinot Noir coming from the structure of the wine, perhaps a slightly fuller impression of a Blanc de Noirs. Of course, you might think that a rosé should be made from black grapes, but because the color can come from adding a small proportion of red wine, any grape variety can be used for the major part. The rosé character should add something, but too often in Champagne it dampens down the flavor profile. The reason may partly be that addition of red wine reduces the sense of liveliness.

Many Champagne producers regard rosé not exactly as a frivolity, but as something they produce because fashion has created a demand, rather than because the wine offers something distinctively interesting. Bollinger, one of the most serious Champagne houses, introduced its rosé only very recently, having mostly eschewed the style. On the other hand, Billecart-Salmon is best known for its rosés, but they have an unusual elegance and character. "It's a secret," says cellarmaster François Domi when asked what's special about Billecart's rosés, but later he relents and explains that it's the quality and character of the red wine. When asked about the total production of rosé, he says that's *really* secret, but admits that it's somewhat more than is usual at most Champagne houses. "We search for a rosé Champagne but not a Champagne rosé," is how François puts it. "In the rosé we balance the power of Pinot Noir with the Chardonnay. We look for elegance and delicacy, it should be discrete and not too heavy. Red wine is about 10%. The color of the red wine is obtained before fermentation. There shouldn't be too much tannin, enough to stabilize the color but not more. If the red

Most Champagnes are produced exclusively in stainless steel. Quantities for major brands can be very large. The tank halls at Nicolas Feuillatte are among the largest in Champagne.

isn't good, you cannot make rosé; if the red isn't good enough there won't be a vintage rosé. If you served this in black glasses, it would be important not to be able to tell, the rosé should have the aroma and taste of Champagne not red wine." Here the rosé indeed has the delicacy and elegance of top Champagne.

Another house that is well known for its rosé is Laurent-Perrier, one of the leaders in introducing rosé in 1968. The Laurent-Perrier rosé comes exclusively from Pinot Noir, mostly from Grand Cru; it is a *rosé saignée*, in which the color comes directly from maceration of up to 72 hours, and not from adding red wine. It gives a sense of structure you don't get with a *rosé d'assemblage* (made by blending). You get an impression of the earthy quality of Pinot Noir here, almost a faint tannic texture. Any difference between rosé saignée and rosé d'assemblage may be partly intrinsic, but choice of technique may also reflect a difference in objectives, and that may in part be why saignée rosés sometimes seem to be more structured.

At the peak of Champagne, there are the special cuvées. What makes them special? Well, first, of course, since we are in Champagne, the price: anything from double the price of a regular Champagne to ten times or more. Technically they usually represent long disgorgements, longer than three years and up to ten years. With the notable exception of Krug, they almost always exclude Pinot Meunier. They rarely represent single vineyards, so the principle of assemblage remains intact. Anywhere else you would look to old vines or reduced yields as an important part of the special character, but those features are rarely mentioned in Champagne. What makes the grapes special remains somewhat undefined. And the style of a special cuvée does not necessarily bear a close relationship to other cuvées from the same producer. Most prestige cuvées are vintage, but there is something of a recent trend to make special nonvintage cuvées at a price level going into the vintage range. Prestige cuvees usually come from grand and premier crus, but the brand name is more important to the consumer than the source of grapes. Of course, it is generally true of Champagne that reputation of the brand is emphasized over vintage or source.

The best known special cuvées, if only because they are the most widely available, are Moët's Dom Pérignon and Roederer's Cristal. These are really brands in themselves.[41] Most large houses now have an equivalent high-end cuvée. And then there are the houses that produce nothing but special cuvées: Krug and Salon, which interestingly take quite different approaches to top quality. Neither is independent any longer. Krug was family owned until the house was sold to LVMH in 1999, although Henri Krug continued to run it. Today the family feeling has been replaced by a more corporate atmosphere, but the wines remain extraordinary. The Grand Cuvée is a Brut nonvintage that outshines most vintage Champagnes, and unusually for this level includes Pinot Meunier; the range continues with rosé, vintage, and two single vineyard wines, the Clos du Mesnil (Blanc de Blancs) and Clos d'Ambonnay (Blanc de Noirs). Salon is a smaller operation, acquired by Laurent-Perrier in 1988, now run in conjunction with its neighbor Champagne Delamotte, and still focusing on a Blanc de Blancs produced from Mesnil-sur-Oger only in top vintages (37 times in the twentieth century, five years so far in the twenty-first). The objectives of its founder were to produce a vin de garde; he thought Le Mesnil had the appropriate austerity, and this remains one of the tightest and longest lived Champagnes.

Many of the characteristics of Champagne are intrinsic to its production: assemblage is a means to compensate for the vicissitudes of vintage variation in a marginal climate. But some are an indirect consequence of the organization of Champagne, in particular an extraordinary dichotomy between grape growing and wine production. The leading Champagne houses produce two thirds of all Champagne, accounting for three quarters of its value, and 80% of all exports. But they own only 3,000 ha out of the 33,000 ha in Champagne; the other 30,000 ha are owned by some 15,000 growers.[42] And individual vineyard holdings tend to be very small; those 33,000 ha are broken up into 276,000 individual parcels.[43]

Because the major Champagne houses own relatively few vineyards, they must buy most of their grapes. Roederer and Bollinger, in the exceptional situation of owning enough vineyards to supply most of their grapes, are much envied by other producers. Power in the inevitable clashes between growers and producers oscillates according to the state of the economy. When times are good, the growers have the whip hand, and it's dangerous for producers to turn away grapes, even if quality is not up to their standard. When times are bad, the growers may be squeezed on price. This makes for a tug of war when the CIVC decides on the yield limits each year: the growers need to maximize returns, but the houses will not want more than they believe is supported by the current market. The situation reduces interest in single vineyard wines: when parcels are tiny, and the producer may not even own them, it is hard to commit to a single vineyard cuvée.

It's a common impression that Champagne is all grand Maisons, with snazzy tasting rooms where degustations are conducted by PR people. This is certainly true of the producers on the Avenue de Champagne in Epernay, where the Maisons are very grand indeed, or in the center of Reims, for example. But although this may account for the majority of Champagne production, it's a small proportion of the number of houses, many of which are (relatively) small. Going out into the villages to visit smaller houses, you get quite a different impression of passionate producers, often very conscious of their family history, and somewhat akin to Burgundy in their general attitude; this is where most of the driving force comes from for recognizing terroirs in individual cuvées.

Champagne production has become steadily more concentrated in the hands of a small number of owners. The bigger fish are continuing to gobble

Growers and Houses

NM (Houses)
66% of market
349 houses

RM (Growers)
16% of market
1,900 growers

RC (Coops for growers)
9% of market
2,750 growers

CM (Coops)
8% of market
43 cooperatives
(13,000 growers)

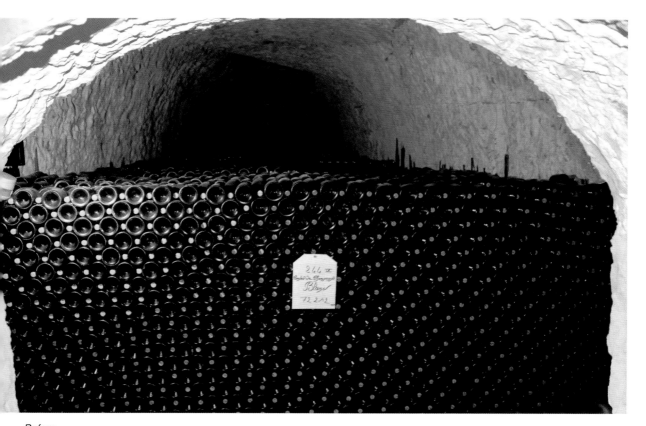

Before disgorgement, Champagne is stored flat. Thin layers of wood are usually included every few rows, which gave rise to the name "sur latte."

up the smaller ones at a fairly steady pace. Well over half of all production comes from five major groups[44] and another quarter from a small number of large houses. These are the Grand Marques. (Grand Marque was defined by a group of major houses who formed an association,[45] later disbanded, but now is more loosely used to indicate major houses with significant international representation.[46]) Grand Marque carries no implication of quality.[47] As large producers, the Grand Marques rely on a mix of grapes from their own vineyards and purchases from growers (in most cases a majority of the latter); they are the leading houses in the group that is described as Négociant-Manipulants, indicated by NM on the label.

Every bottle of Champagne carries a mark on the label indicating the character of the producer (but it is very discrete). At the other extreme from NM is the Récoltant-Manipulant, indicated by RM on the label. This describes a grower who vinifies wine only from estate grapes. These are the so-called Boutique or Grower Champagnes. They are relatively small, with holdings typically ranging up to about 30 ha. Indeed, any size increase is limited by the fact that it's all but impossible to buy vineyards, and of course purchasing grapes would mean a change in character. In fact, the only way to obtain vineyards is to buy a Champagne house that owns them. LVMH have been playing this game with some success. They purchased Pommery in 1991, and then sold it to Vranken in 2002, but without its 300 ha of vineyards, which were kept in the LVMH portfolio. Even more swiftly, LVMH purchased Montaudon in 2008 and then sold it in 2010 to the Champagne Alliance cooperative—but without its vineyards or contracts to purchase grapes. "For some years there has been a war for grapes in Champagne. There is a gigantic super power. Unfortunately the panzer divisions of M. Arnault [LVMH] have won the war," a smaller producer comments.

The oldest bottles still awaiting disgorgement at Salon come from the great 1928 vintage.

I don't want to indulge in a naive critique of large houses, but there is generally a certain skepticism about production of Champagne on such a vast scale. On the one hand, the large houses do maintain a remarkable consistency in spite of the scale of production, but on the other, the question is what the wine represents: place, vintage, or production process? By contrast, a grower's vineyards are usually concentrated in one area of Champagne, which helps to bring character to the wine. Where there is a house style, it owes more to the taste of the grower than to the perceptions of the marketing department. I'd be inclined to say that grower Champagnes are usually more interesting—even if you don't always entirely like the choices that have been made.

CM describes a cave coopérative, producing wine from grapes harvested by its members. Nicolas Feuillatte is the most prominent example, developed in 1987 as its marque by the Centre Viticole federation of cooperatives. An impressive facility, with all the latest equipment, this is the very model of a modern cooperative, and one of the most successful in France. Champagne Jacquart (which now also owns Montaudon) was acquired in 1998 as its principal marque by Alliance Champagne, another major cooperative group. Although coops have become progressively less important in France as a whole, and generally are of lower importance in more prestigious areas, Champagne is an exception in which they retain a major (even a growing) place, accounting today for more than a third of the harvest.[48] This is another consequence of the system in which there are many growers with parcels that are too small to justify producing finished wine. Finished Champagne sold from cooperatives falls into two categories.[49] About half is sold under the cooperative label, and is marked CM. The other half goes under the RC category, which indicates a grower who sticks his own label on wine produced by a cooperative to which he belongs. This is unlikely to be of high quality. "Out of 5,000 growers, 4,000 make the same wine at a cooperative under a different label; only 1,000 are really independent," says Bruno Paillard.

What you do not want to see on a label is ND, which stands for Négociant-Distributeur. This means the finished wine (bubbles and all) was produced by someone else, and was simply purchased by the final owner, who disgorged it and put his own label on it. This is known pejoratively as the trade *sur latte*. Reports that it had been banned as of 2004 appear to have been exaggerated, as producers say today that it is perfectly legal. Some restrictions have been introduced, including a requirement that the label says *distribué par* rather than *elaboré par*, but it is a rare consumer who might spot this on a bottle. The deceptive thing is that a major house may sell both its own wine and sur latte wine under the same label, and you would really have to look at the small print to see whether it's their own wine or something they picked up in the market to bulk out sales. Is this fraudulent or is it fraudulent? I have been unable to find producers who will admit to the practice, but there is something of a feeling among producers that it serves a useful purpose in establishing market prices.

Reference Wines for Champagne	
Zero Dosage	Ayala
	Laurent-Perrier
Extra Brut	Jacquesson
	Larmandier Bernier
Brut	Bollinger
	Bruno Paillard
	Deutz
Blanc de Blancs	Pierre Gimonnet
	Pierre Peters, L'Esprit
	De Sousa
	Ruinart
	Tarlant
Blanc de Noirs	Egly Ouriet
	Philipponnat
Rosé	Billecart-Salmon
	Laurent-Perrier

The distinction between Champagne and Crémant is no longer a matter of method of production, but simply comes down to place of origin (and the grape varieties that are allowed in each place). The formal classification of sparkling wines in France is determined by the pressure of carbon dioxide in the bottle, the method of production, and, of course, the place of origin. Originally the pressure was a major distinction, with Champagne above 5 bars (usually it is around 6 bars), Crémant above 3 bars, and Pétillant between 2.5 and 1 bar. Mousseux is a general term that describes all sparkling wine with a pressure of more than 3 atmospheres of carbon dioxide, but it carries the implication that the wine did not achieve the higher status of Crémant.

Crémant is made by Méthode Champenoise: by performing the second fermentation in the bottle. Today it is usually technically similar to Champagne, with the same pressure.[50] The original areas for Crémant were Burgundy and the Loire. Most of the other Crémant appellations were created after 1985, in a quid pro quo that allowed additional regions to use the term Crémant in return for abandoning Méthode Champenoise as a description, so Crémant now states Méthode Traditionelle. Like Champagne, the major regions for Crémant production have cool climates, but the grape varieties tend to be more exotic. This can be a problem, as the aromatics may clash with the neutrality that is required from the base wine.

Crémant de Bourgogne would be the obvious challenger since it comes from the same grapes as Champagne, but the fact is that sparkling wine in Burgundy is very much an also-ran, made mostly from grapes that simply aren't good enough to make still wine. Something of the same problem is found in the Loire, where grapes are selected for dry, sweet, or sparkling wines depending on vintage conditions, and much sparkling wine is used to absorb grapes that didn't quite make it. The other problem in the Loire is that the aromatics of Chenin Blanc do not fit gracefully into the spectrum of sparkling wine. The flavor profile is flatter than Champagne. The Loire is the largest producer of sparkling wine after Champagne, with 2-3 times more Mousseux than Crémant.

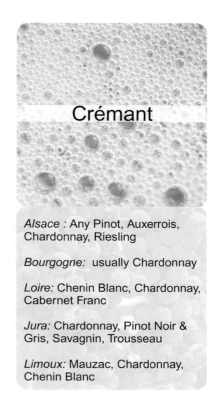

Crémant

Alsace : Any Pinot, Auxerrois, Chardonnay, Riesling

Bourgogne: usually Chardonnay

Loire: Chenin Blanc, Chardonnay, Cabernet Franc

Jura: Chardonnay, Pinot Noir & Gris, Savagnin, Trousseau

Limoux: Mauzac, Chardonnay, Chenin Blanc

Crémant usually has the same pressure as Champagne and forms a similar mousse when poured. Courtesy Cave de Lugny.

Reference Wines for Crémant & Pétillant	
Crémant de Bourgogne	Domaine de la Vougeraie
Crémant d'Alsace	Albert Boxler
Crémant de Loire	Château de l'Eperonnière
Crémant de Jura	André et Mireille Tissot, Indigène
Blanquette & Crémant de Limoux	Domaine Antech
Saumur Mousseux	Thierry Germain, Bulles de Roche
Anjou Pétillant	Domaine Richou
Touraine Pétillant	François Pinon
Vin de France	Couly-Dutheil (Chinon)

Vouvray makes both Crémant and Pétillant. Although Pétillant is sometimes disdained as having less fizz, purists consider that it shows off the character of Chenin better, because varietal character is less obvious under a full mousse. "I make a Pétillant (not a method traditionelle) because I don't like too much pressure," says François Pinon in Vouvray. Purists also feel that Pétillant is harder to produce, as it shows up any problems with the grapes more directly.

Limoux is another place where the tradition is for Pétillant. Blanquette de Limoux is one of the last holdouts for the Méthode Ancestrale, in which wine is bottled before the first fermentation has completed, creating a low pressure of bubbles. The traditional grape here is Mauzac, and at its best this gives a light sparkling wine with an impression of apples, but it can tend to be a bit sour or bitter. Moving into the modern era, there is now a Crémant de Limoux, which includes Chardonnay and Chenin Blanc as well as Mauzac; this is smoother and creamier than Blanquette.

Alsace is the largest producer of Crémant, which can come from Riesling, any of the Pinots, Auxerrois, and Chardonnay, although by and large Riesling is too valuable to include. So the varietal composition can be more similar to Champagne than you might expect. In spite of the similarity of climate, however, the Crémant tends to have a softer, more perfumed impression. A rosé can come only from Pinot Noir (whatever would happen if they introduced such a regulation in Champagne…)

Champagne's unique advantage lies in picking grapes very early specifically with sparkling wine in mind; elsewhere they would not really be considered ripe. It's conceivable that other regions in the cool north could make high quality sparkling wine, but so far they have failed to use varieties sufficiently challenged by marginal conditions. (The problem outside of France is often that the region is not sufficiently marginal: as a rough rule of thumb, if you can make good still wine, conditions may not be marginal enough to make the highest quality sparkling wine.) So Champagne reigns supreme.

Vintages

There are no official figures for how many houses produce a vintage Champagne each year, but global warming has seen a trend for vintage Champagnes to be produced more often—five or six or even more times per decade at the present. One measure of the year is whether the great prestige cuvées—Dom Pérignon, Cristal, Salon, Krug—are made. Totaling the number released each year gives a rough rating of vintages as 1 to 4 star. By that measure there was universal enthusiasm for 2002, 1996, 1995, and 1990, and minimal enthusiasm for 2005, 2003, 2001, and 1994. Remember that it's about five years before a vintage is released and can be assessed in bottle. Because vintage Champagne is intended for aging, and some wines are re-released as late disgorgements many years later, older vintages are of more than usual interest.

There is unlikely to be much vintage Champagne for 2009-2011, which means that the current release for most houses is 2008. This is reckoned to be best for wines based on Pinot Noir, with elegant acidity and concentration. The best year of the decade was 2002, which is regarded as exceptional right across the range. The 2004 vintage is somewhat in the same style, but not quite as intense. Before that, 1996 was the exceptional vintage of the mid nineties, although the decade started with the outstanding 1990.

Although the purpose of nonvintage Champagne is to absorb vintage variation, the vintage of the base wine does have some effect, and some Champagne houses now indicate it on the back label. Even nonvintage Champagne is likely to be a little deeper and richer when the base vintage is a great year.

		DP	CL	SN	KG
2013	Flowering problems reduced crop size of Chardonnay more than Pinot. Rescued by Indian summer and very late harvest. Good acidity means vintage wines may have longevity. Not as good as 2012.	-	-	-	-
2012	The growing season was poor, starting with frosts, and continuing with wet conditions. But August was warm and September was dry, enabling many grapes to be picked around 11% potential alcohol. All varieties did equally well and there will be some good vintage Champagnes.	*			
2011	An average year with high yields and some problems with maturity.				
2010	Very variable, little vintage wine. Rot reduced the size of the crop.				
				continued	

		DP	CL	SN	KG
2009	Variable with few vintage wines. There is a tendency for the wines to be a little too heavy.		*		
2008	Generally a vintage year, faute de mieux. Good but not remarkable.			*	*
2007	Chardonnays are considered to have done best so some nice Blanc de Blancs. Generally a light year.		*	*	
2006	Generally disappointing year.			*	*
2005	A bit on the warm side. Overall an average year but quite a few vintage wines.		*		
2004	A very good year, similar style, but not quite as good as 2002; generally better than 2005 with more vintage wines.	*	*	*	
2003	Too hot to achieve the elegance and acidity needed for longevity.	*			
2002	Regarded as the top year of the century so far, equally successful for Chardonnay and Pinot Noir.	*	*	*	*
2001	Universally unsuccessful due to very high rainfall.				
2000	Above average with many vintage wines. Soft and attractive, but not long-lived.	*	*		*
1999	A workmanlike year above average, but acidity is on the low side, so for consumption relatively soon.	*	*	*	
1998	Just a little better than 1997, softer and more elegant. Attractive when young but not for long aging.	*			*
1997	A decent year but overshadowed by 1996.		*	*	
1996	The best vintage of the decade after 1990, with a wonderful combination of refreshing acidity and ripeness that has enabled the wines to age very well indeed. The only criticism might be that some are a little austere.	*	*	*	*
1995	The first really good vintage year since 1990. A top vintage for the Chardonnays of the Côte des Blancs.	*	*	*	*
1994	Rain was a problem in all vintages between 1990 and 1995, but this was the worst.		*		
1993	Less ripe than the previous year at the time, but those vintage wines that were made have lasted as well as the 1992s.	*	*		
1992	A passable year felt to be the only one really suitable for vintage between 1990 and 1995.	*			*
1991	Generally a disappointing year with only the occasional vintage wines.				
1990	One of the great vintages of the century, combining ripeness with good acidity. This is a classic.	*	*	*	*

5

Alsace

Varietal Territory

Strawberries, cherries, and an angel's kiss in spring
My summer wine is really made from all these things
(Nancy Sinatra)

Alsace must surely have the most picturesque villages and vineyards in France. Driving along the Route des Vins from Strasbourg to Colmar, you pass through an endless series of wonderfully preserved medieval villages. This is quite surprising considering that the region has changed hands several times in wars between France and Germany. Germanic influence has impacted wine production, from the types of grape varieties to the mix of dry and sweet styles. It is no accident that Alsace is the only region in France where the focus is as much on grape varieties as appellations. Its history has also had a significant effect on aspirations to quality (or lack thereof).

You are always conscious of the Vosges mountains. Vineyards extend eastward from the lower slopes of the mountains. Most of the best vineyards are on the middle slopes between 200 and 350 m, which are a degree or so warmer than the land above or below.[1] From the relatively narrow band of vineyards, the land opens out to the east on to a plain extending to the Rhine (which however is too far away to have any direct influence on the climate). The Vosges mountains are the dominant climatic influence. "Bad weather stops on the Vosges," they claim locally. Because rainfall is absorbed by the Vosges, Alsace had the driest vineyards in all France.[2]

*Bad weather stops
on the Vosges.*

The cool climate has historically forced a concentration on white grape varieties. Today the most important varieties are Riesling and Gewürztraminer, each with about 20% of plantings; Pinot Gris is a little lower at 15%. Fifty years ago, the most important variety was the nondescript Sylvaner, which is now disappearing from view, together with the even more characterless Chasselas.[3] The other big difference is that the trend of global warming has led Pinot Noir to increase from insignificant amounts to about 10% of plantings. Total plantings have increased from 12,000 ha in 1982 to just over 15,000 ha today.

Virtually all approved vineyards in Alsace are Appellation Contrôlée.[4] Unusually for France, the AOP is organized in terms of varietals rather than regions, and almost all wines are labeled with the name of a single grape variety. This means the wine is a monovarietal, except for Pinot Blanc. Nominally Pinot Blanc is the most commonly produced variety in Alsace, but because of a historical mix-up, wines can be called Pinot Blanc when they contain Auxerrois, a much inferior variety. Roughly two thirds of the grapevines that were classified as Pinot Blanc are really Auxerrois, so many wines labeled as Pinot Blanc actually contain a majority of Auxerrois.[5]

The Gentil category comes from blending varieties, but it's always an entry-level wine. Besides the still wines, there is a good deal of sparkling wine, labeled under its own AOP as Crémant d'Alsace. Most often based on Pinot

Blanc and Auxerrois, it is about a quarter of all production.[6] (However, it may be significant that none of the producers I visited in Alsace thought it was worth including Crémant in what were often very long tastings.)

Grown since the fifteenth century, Riesling is an old variety in Alsace. Gewürztraminer and Muscat date from a century later.[7] Pinot Gris was probably first grown in Alsace in the seventeenth century: it used to be called Tokay d'Alsace, reflecting the (improbable) legend that it was brought from Hungary, but European Community rules now ban use of this name because of supposed confusion with Tokaji.

Alsace's reputation for quality wines is a feature of the past half century. The wines used to be regarded as low quality, mass production—what the French call vins de comptoir. One story dates this reputation from the period when Alsace came under German control following the war of 1870, and production was used to

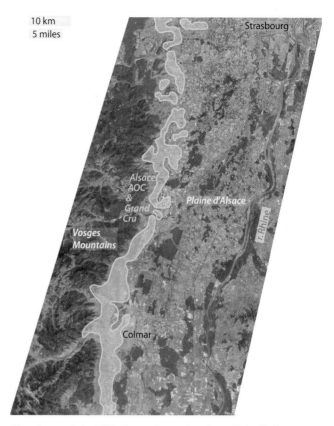

The vineyards in AOP Alsace form a band parallel with the Vosges mountains running from Strasbourg to south of Colmar. To the east of the vineyards, the Plaine d'Alsace extends for about 20 km to the Rhine.

improve German wines. But in fact, Alsace had 65,000 hectares of vineyards (five times today's plantings!) mostly given over to high-yielding, low quality grape varieties when the war started.[8] Nor did production habits change when Alsace became French again after the First World War.[9] Quality varieties began a slow takeover after the AOP finally came into full effect in 1962, but it was not until 1980 that the last low-grade varieties were legally excluded.

In spite of the move to quality, Alsace has been undergoing an identity crisis for years. There is a great difference between the cheap wines produced by most negociants or cooperatives and the quality wines produced by independent growers (and by some producers who have vineyards but also buy grapes). A major problem is that yields are far too high; while good producers will be well below the legal limits, there is no obligation. There is no agreement on style, so that wines that are not specifically identified as late harvest may in fact range from absolutely bone-dry to off-dry or even relatively sweet. All of this is a consequence of the looseness of regulations and the classification system.

Yields have been reduced only slowly from the bad old days, from a maximum of 120 hl/ha in 1974, to 96 hl/ha in 1982, to 80 hl/ha today. Limiting yields for individual varieties (as opposed to total production in the vineyard) became the rule only in 1999 (until then, the average for any vineyard/grower had to conform to the limit, but one variety could be above and another below it). Maximum yields are much higher than allowed elsewhere in France; only Champagne is higher.[11] Yield limits are the same for all grape varieties. It is obvious that quality would be improved by restricting yields, but "the large negociants and cooperatives are against it," explains Céline Meyer of Domaine Josmeyer. Independent growers are in a small minority.[12]

The appellation system in Alsace is unique in France. There are only two levels of appellation for still wines: AOP Alsace, and AOP Alsace Grand Cru (the grand cru is named on the label). The 52 grand crus were created over a protracted period: Schlossberg was the first in 1975, then a large group followed in 1983, and another group in 1992.[13] They cover 7% of the vineyard area and account for 5% of production, as yields are lower (originally 70 hl/ha but reduced to 55 hl/ha in 2001). Terroirs vary widely. The common feature is elevation: all are on the slopes of the Vosges, sometimes quite steep, often rising up sharply from a town. Grand crus are restricted to Riesling, Gewürztraminer, Pinot Gris, and Muscat (actually there is very little of the last).[14] (Other varieties, such as Pinot Noir, can be planted, but cannot be labeled as Grand Cru.)

There are special regulations for sweet dessert wines. Wines from berries with more than a certain sugar level can be labeled as Vendange Tardive (late harvest), and may have some botrytis. At higher sugar levels, Selection des Grains Nobles comes exclusively from botrytized grapes. Both VT and SGN are restricted to the same four varieties as the grand crus.

The best grape varieties of Alsace are distinctly aromatic. The lesser varieties of Chasselas and Sylvaner make pleasant wines for summer quaffing but rarely have much interest. Occasionally you find an old vines cuvée, where lowered yields have brought some character; usually this takes the form of more savory, herbal impressions: interesting in their own way for showing a different potential of the variety, but not rising to the level of the noble varieties.

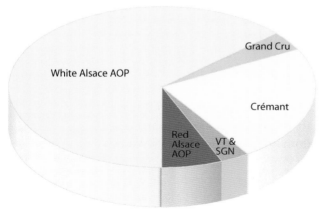

The great majority of Alsace production is white Alsace AOP. Crémant is the second major category. Red Alsace has become significant. Grand Cru and VT/SGN remain small categories.[10]

Pinot Blanc might make an interesting wine, but as it is usually mostly Auxerrois, it tends to lack flavor interest. In fact, I am not sure I have encountered a single Pinot Blanc in Alsace that was made exclusively from the named variety. I did find some monovarietal Auxerrois, with vieilles vignes cuvées from Josmeyer and Paul Blanck really demonstrating an unusual level of character.

Chardonnay is permitted in Alsace for the sparkling Crémant, but not for still wine. "Few people can see the difference between an Auxerrois vine and a Chardonnay; quite a few growers use some Chardonnay in their still Pinot Blanc blends, but would never admit doing it. It always goes officially into the Crémant," says Olivier Humbrecht MW of Zind-Humbrecht. So the composition and quality of "Pinot Blanc" are rather unpredictable. "Chardonnay was not admitted in the AOC category, mostly for political reasons, I think, not quality," says Olivier, whose "Zind" cuvée (a Vin de France) gives a good indication of what Chardonnay can achieve in Alsace. Coming from the top Windsbuhl vineyard, it shows the character of terroir as much as the variety.

Muscat can in principle be intensely grapey, but is a mixed bag in Alsace as there are plantings of both Muscat Blanc à Petit Grains (high quality) and Muscat Ottonel (much lower quality)[15]. Alsace's quality wines therefore come from Pinot Gris, Gewürztraminer, and Riesling.

Pinot Gris reaches its full height of expression in Alsace; certainly it bears no resemblance at all to Pinot Grigio, the expression of the same variety in Italy. It's grown scarcely anywhere else in France. Although it is a color variant of Pinot Noir, with skin of varying color, it is vinified as a white wine and its aromatic profile is different. I wouldn't go so far as to call its character blowsy, but it has relatively low acidity, and with some rare exceptions, tends to have broad, soft flavors, sometimes with an oily texture, showing stone fruits tending to apricots; but it can also move in a more savory direction, sometimes veering towards suggestions of mushrooms.

The big issue with Pinot Gris is that it really reaches ripeness only at high alcohol levels, so usually fermentation stops before completion, leaving some residual sugar.[16] "It's complicated to make a dry Pinot Gris," is the way Céline Meyer at Domaine Josmeyer puts it. Residual sugar may be fairly minimal for wines labeled as Alsace AOP, but most grand cru Pinot Gris is perceptibly sweet. It also makes a fine late harvest wine, where those notes of mushrooms, accentuated by botrytis, can add complexity to the sweet apricot fruits.

Gewürz is German for spice, but Gewürztraminer is usually more perfumed than spicy. It is by far the most aromatic variety of Alsace, with a typical scent of roses on the nose; lychee fruits are characteristic on the palate.[17] The classic description of Gewürztraminer is that it smells sweet but tastes dry, although this is not really true in Alsace. Those aromas of roses can turn quite phenolic on the finish and give a drying impression, but usually there is enough residual sugar to show perceptible sweetness. Even with some residual sugar, the alco-

Vinification traditionally takes place in foudres.

hol level is often quite high. Gewürztraminer is a mainstay of the late harvest wines, with peaches and apricots joining lychees in Vendange Tardive, and botrytized flavors hiding the usual perfume at the level of Selection de Grains Nobles.

Riesling is the glory of Alsace, appearing in all styles from completely dry to totally botrytized. None of the other varieties can compete with its purity of flavors. When completely dry it can be steely and mineral, sometimes even saline. Fruits remain in the citrus spectrum, sometimes overlaid by a characteristic touch of petrol (which develops earlier here than it does in Germany). Riesling offers producers more of a choice in determining style, because it ripens at lower alcohol levels than Pinot Gris or Gewürztraminer. Because Riesling ripens more slowly, it is less prominent among the late harvest styles than Pinot Gris or Gewürztraminer.

Virtually all high quality wine in Alsace is monovarietal. Marcel Deiss is probably the only producer who blends his top wines. When I asked Jean-Michel Deiss if he uses all seven varieties of Alsace he said, "Yes, all thirteen varieties!" There are the principal varieties such as Riesling (more than half of his plantings), then some secondary varieties (about a third), and finally, less than 10%, there are some old varieties that he is trying to preserve from disappearing. Jean-Michel is quick to point out that he does not produce his wines by assemblage, the mixing of wines made from different varieties, but each is a single wine produced from grapes of different varieties intermingled in the vineyard. "I don't make wines to express the cépage but to express the terroir," he says. He believes that to express terroir you need to grow varieties together. But this is distinctly a minority view.

Reference Wines for Dry White Alsace	
Chardonnay (Vin de France)	Zind-Humbrecht, Zind
Sylvaner	Paul Blanck, Vieilles Vignes
Auxerrois	Josmeyer, "H" Vieilles Vignes
Pinot Blanc	Marc Tempé, Zellenberg
Muscat	Domaine Ostertag, Fronholz Domaine Weinbach
Pinot Gris	Bott-Geyl Josmeyer, La Fromenteau Louis Sipp, Trottacker
Gewürztraminer	Paul Blanck Bott-Geyl Louis Sipp
Riesling	Valentin Zusslin, Liebenberg Meyer Fonné, Pfoeller Marc Tempé, Grafenreben Louis Sipp, Hagel Domaine Josmeyer, Le Kottabe Domaine Paul Blanck, Rosenbourg

Because the emphasis in Alsace is on aromatic varieties, there is no malolactic fermentation, which would introduce creamy notes clashing with varietal character (as well as reducing acidity in Pinot Gris and Gewürztraminer, which are already low acid varieties). So alcoholic fermentation is followed directly by a period of maturation. Fermentation in the traditional foudres is still used for top wines, but these days most wines are fermented in temperature-controlled stainless steel. Maturation usually lasts a few months for entry level wines; top wines are most often bottled just before the next harvest. "In Burgundy they talk about négociant-éleveurs but they don't exist in Alsace because we don't have élevage," says Marc Tempé, who is one of the few producers to break with tradition and use extended élevage in barriques. With rare exceptions, protracted maturation is not part of the style in Alsace.

The only black grape permitted in Alsace is Pinot Noir. Until recently, this was very definitely an also-ran, with most of the wines showing a resemblance to rosé. Global warming has changed things: producers are now taking red wine seriously. Have you always made Pinot Noir, I asked Etienne Sipp of Domaine Louis Sipp. "Yes but not in the present way. There is a big change, people are rethinking Pinot Noir, they plant it in good places, they produce more concentrated wine." It's a sign how things have changed that at Hugel, who were probably first to make Pinot Noir in a Burgundian way when they started in 1977, winemaker Johnny Hugel said "If you force me to make Pinot Noir, I'll make vinegar," but today Marc Hugel makes very fine Pinot Noir.

Grand Crus in Alsace are often the most elevated sites near each village. Kitterlé rises up steeply immediately above the town of Guebwiller

"The idea is not to copy Burgundy, but the Pinot comes from the most calcareous places in the vineyards. We want to produce something silky and elegant in Pinot Noir," says Jean-Christophe Bott of Domaine Bott-Geyl. The style in Alsace usually more resembles Côte de Beaune than Côte de Nuits, and tends to be soft, smooth, and earthy. The reds sometimes seem to show an aromatic spectrum relating to the fact that Alsace focuses on aromatic white varieties. The best wines tend to come from calcareous areas of grand crus. Typically they are ready about five or six years after the vintage, but will hold as long again. The warming trend has definitely created a new opportunity for Alsace. "With the climate change, we probably now have the same climate in Alsace that Burgundy had twenty years ago," says Etienne Hugel. It's an interesting question as to whether this will be recognized by allowing Pinot Noir to be included in the grand cru classification.

With only two categories, Alsace AOP and Alsace Grand Cru, the appellation system in Alsace is one of the least informative in France. Grand Crus were controversial when they were introduced, and they remain controversial today. The lack of any hierarchy in the initial classification system—all AOP wines were originally described simply as Vins d'Alsace—led to the establishment of a committee in the 1970s to consider the promotion of the best vineyards to

Reference Wines for Pinot Noir	
Burlenberg	Marcel Deiss
Les Neveux (lieu-dit Pflostig)	Maison Hugel
"V" (Vorbourg grand cru)	René Muré
"M" (Mambourg grand cru)	Marc Tempé
"W" (Clos des Capucins)	Domaine Weinbach
Bollenberg Harmonie	Valentin Zusslin

higher status. But the results were so controversial that several of the most important producers refuse to use the system. The basic problem was that in order to get the system approved, too many grand crus were created, and many of them are much too large. The first one set the pattern. The hill of Schlossberg lies between the great château of Kaysersberg and the town of Kintzheim, avowedly including some of the best terroir in Alsace. The original committee recommended it should include a total area of about 25 ha, but as finally approved it consists of about 80 ha: politics triumphed over geology.

It is no coincidence that most of the villages on the Route des Vins have a single grand cru associated with them. Each village proposed its best vineyards for grand cru status, and some sort of liberté, égalité, fraternité resulted, with most villages getting one, and only one, grand cru. Often enough, it's the steepest hill near the village. It's fair to say that the grand crus do include most of the best sites in Alsace, but the political nature of the process makes the label unreliable as an indication of the very best quality. "Johnny Hugel (who chaired the first committee) wanted to define the best of the best, but his peers didn't understand that there would be problems years later if you expanded the grand crus," says Marc Hugel. The Hugels believe that the whole concept has been devalued, and so far have refused to use the names of grand crus.

"There are too many grand crus in Alsace, and the size of some of them is just too big. Also the yields in grand crus are too high. More than half of grand cru juice goes to cooperatives, who have no idea what to do with it, so you can find grand cru wines in supermarkets at (low) prices that are simply criminal," says Hubert Trimbach. The most notable example of a wine from a top site that does not state the grand cru on the label is in fact Trimbach's Clos Ste. Hune, widely acknowledged to be one of the best, in fact probably the best, Riesling from Alsace, which comes from a 1.6 ha vineyard in the Rosacker Grand Cru. As Hubert points out dryly, "Clos Ste. Hune and even Frédéric Emile (another top cuvée from Trimbach) are better known than any grand cru." But by the time you add up the top wines from Trimbach, Hugel (the major owner of the grand crus Sporen and Schoenenbourg), and Léon Beyer (another top producer who does not use the grand cru system), a significant proportion of grand crus have been deprived of recognition.

Grand Cru Schoenenbourg rises up immediately outside the town walls of Riquewihr.

"It's not the number of grand crus that's the issue but the delimitation. Some of the tops and bottoms of hills should perhaps be premier cru," says Felix Meyer at Meyer-Fonné. Premier cru is the name of the game in Alsace today, with a proposal at INAO to create a more hierarchical appellation structure, including premier crus and perhaps village wines. This development is already widely anticipated, with many producers labeling single vineyard wines with the names of lieu-dits that they hope will become premier crus; some producers are labeling wines from plots around each village with its name. But this will not eliminate a surreal element in the present system. "Some premier cru wines may sell at higher prices than some grand cru wines," says Céline Meyer at Domaine Josmeyer, recognizing that lieu-dits are being used to indicate wines of higher quality, whereas grand crus remain extremely variable. Could any grand crus be demoted? "No, there is no willingness to open the grand cru box. The system is not perfect but it exists. It's much more important to organize a classification of the intermediate levels," says Etienne Sipp at Domaine Louis Sipp.

With probably several hundred lieu-dits being proposed for promotion, it's a legitimate concern whether the system will become so complicated as to confuse the consumer. In any case, nothing seems likely to happen soon—producers are talking in terms of the next ten years or so. I am afraid that the system will lack credibility unless the variability of the grand crus is taken in hand at the same time. But it seems likely that the most that will happen is more precise definition of which specific varieties are allowed in each grand

Grand Cru Sommerberg is just outside Niedermorschwihr.

cru. This may bring a recognition of the significant advances made with red wine by adding Pinot Noir to the permitted list for some grand crus.

Grand crus are better known for extra richness and (sometimes) for higher quality than for specific aspects of terroir. Yet there is a wide range of terroirs, including granite, volcanic, sandstone, marl, and calcareous. Among the granite grand crus, Brand is taut, Furstentum is delicate, Schlossberg gives precision, and Sommerberg has grip. The calcareous terroir of Osterberg is upright. The marl of Geisberg and Sporen tends to opulence, and in Hengst to power. Rosacker's muschelkalk gives tension. But few grand crus have really achieved reputations in their own right, perhaps because many are associated with a single wine from a particular producer, rather than from several producers. "It's important that a lieu-dit or premier cru should be represented by multiple producers so it doesn't just have one style," says Jean-Christophe Bott.

The warming climate has resulted in a trend to leaving some residual sugar in the wine. Indeed, sugar is the word that cannot speak its name in Alsace. Wine production is bedeviled by the issue of sweetness, and the major single factor that has held Alsace back from better success in the market is probably the unpredictable level of sweetness in its wines. "When I started 35 years ago, almost all wines had less than 3 grams residual sugar. Now most wines have more. I think there is a relation between the fact that Alsace has placed itself with sweet wines and the fact that prices have stayed low. One problem is that every other region has regulations for alcohol levels and sweetness but Alsace does not," says Marc Hugel. "Our image as a dry-wine region is at risk," says Etienne Hugel.

There are two conflicting trends in Alsace today. One is a demand for dry wines to go with food; younger producers especially are trying to make wines in a drier style than their parents. The other is that sugar levels at harvest have been pushed up by warmer vintages to a point at which producers feel that alcohol would be too high if fermentation went to completion, and that it's better to have lower alcohol by leaving a little residual sugar. Even producers who consider that sweetness is a problem concede that there are benefits. "I would say that in Alsace global warming has increased enormously the quality of the wine, even if it has brought the problem of residual sugar," Marc Hugel allows. Sometimes there are suspicions that producers are stopping fermentation to make the wines more crowd-pleasing, but Jean Boxler at Domaine Albert Boxler says that, "We have more problems in continuing fermentation than in stopping it at a specific sweetness."

Some producers believe that wine should always be dry. "Our wine is bone-dry and therefore suitable to accompany food," says Hubert Trimbach. Other notable houses in this camp are Hugel and Josmeyer. But what is dry? A wine will always taste dry if it has less than 4 g/l residual sugar (this is the usual limit for calling a wine dry in most regions), but it may taste virtually dry if it has high enough acidity, even if it is over 4 g/l residual sugar.

Achieving a dry balance is more problematic with Pinot Gris and Gewürztraminer than with Riesling. Statistically speaking, if you select a Riesling from Alsace from an unknown producer you have a good chance of it being dry or almost dry, but Pinot Gris or Gewurztraminer will almost always be at least a little sweet. This is partly because these varieties reach phenolic ripeness only at higher sugar levels, and partly because they have lower acidity that makes any residual sugar more obvious.

Reference Wines for Alsace Grand Cru Riesling	
Brand	Josmeyer
Eichberg	"R" de Beyer
Furstentum	Paul Blanck
Geisberg	Trimbach
Hengst	Josmeyer
Kirchberg de Ribeauvillé	Louis Sipp
Kitterlé	Domaine Schlumberger
Mandelberg	Bott-Geyl
Muenchberg	Domaine Ostertag
Osterberg	Louis Sipp
Pfersigberg	Léon Beyer, Comtes d'Eguisheim
Pfingstberg	Valentin Zusslin
Rangen	Zind-Humbrecht
Rosacker	Trimbach, Clos St. Hune
Schlossberg	Domaine Weinbach, Cuvée St. Catherine
Schoenenbourg	Hugel, Jubilee
Sommerberg	Paul Blanck
Wineck-Schlossberg	Meyer-Fonné
Vorbourg	René Muré, Clos St. Landelin
Geisberg/Osterberg	Trimbach, Frédéric Emile

The issue of sweetness is tied up with the grand cru system, because the grand crus were defined at a time when getting to ripeness was problematic. So they are the sites that achieve greatest ripeness, often south-facing hillsides. An outdated regulation requires potential alcohol to reach 10% at harvest, but today it's more of a problem to restrain alcohol. In a typical vintage when the grand crus were defined, the distinction might have been that a grand cru reached an acceptable level of alcohol naturally, whereas an AOC Alsace vineyard needed chaptalization. So the wines would have the same (dry) style, but the grand cru would display the extra character that goes with greater ripeness. In the present era of warmer vintages, however, the appellation vineyard may reach an acceptable level of potential alcohol, and the grand cru may rise above it. This explains why at many producers the entry level wine is always fermented to dryness, but the grand crus show some residual sugar.

The argument is basically that something has to give: either alcohol will be too high or there will be residual sugar. This might not be so much of an issue if the style was consistent for any given producer and stayed the same between vintages. Vintage variation is a problem when a wine is dry in one vintage and sweet in another. And it's equally confusing when a producer changes style from AOC Alsace to grand cru. "The problem is not with the entry level, it's more with the grand crus, where the Riesling may be picked at 14% potential alcohol. It's more difficult to achieve dry Riesling and we can find grand crus with 7-8 g/l sugar or more; it's totally stupid for the grand crus to have residual sugar," says Pierre Trimbach. In my view, this is spot on as a criticism, because it is impossible to appreciate the difference between an appellation Riesling and a grand cru Riesling if the first is dry and the second is sweet. I should admit to a prejudice here that you can't really appreciate nuances of terroir when the palate is muddied by residual sugar. So at some producers, the most interesting wines are the middle of the range, because the basic wines are too simple, but the grand crus are too sweet.

Even the most committed producers admit that it's mostly impossible (and maybe undesirable) to get completely dry Pinot Gris or Gewürztraminer from grand crus. "Pinot Gris ripens very rapidly. Sometimes you say you harvest in the morning and it's dry, you harvest in the afternoon and it's sweet," says Etienne Sipp. "Gewurztraminer will reach 13-14% when Riesling gets to 11%," Marc Hugel says, conceding, "It's better to have 14% alcohol and 7 g/l sugar than 15% alcohol and bone dry." And Céline Meyer at Domaine Josmeyer points out that "If Gewurztraminer is completely dry it's not agreeable because it's too bitter." So the consensus is that, faute de mieux, Gewürztraminer (and Pinot Gris) are going to have some sugar. "I prefer to make dry wines and for Riesling it's easy to be dry, but with the grand crus for Pinot Gris and Gewurztraminer we cannot produce dry wines. To follow what the terroir has to give you, the wine would not be balanced if you picked early enough to make dry

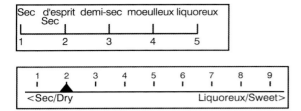

Two scales coming into common use on Alsace back labels rate sweetness by 5 or 9 points. The first three points usually indicate dry, off-dry, and medium sweet.

wine," says Jean-Christophe Bott. But he adds ruefully, "Of course the market is looking for dry wine." The best you can do with Pinot Gris and Gewürztraminer is usually to produce a wine that tastes very nearly dry.

Alongside the issue of sugar, is the question of botrytis. While botrytis is desirable in late harvest wines, producers differ on whether they welcome it in dry (or nearly dry) wines, but it's not uncommon, especially at the grand cru level, to have a small proportion of botrytized grapes. Indeed, at Meyer Fonné, Felix Meyer only makes SGN where there's enough botrytis not to deprive the grand cru: "In most years there's 15% or so in the grand cru Gewürztraminer, and I don't want to take that out, it's part of the character," he says. At Domaine Paul Blanck, Frédéric Blanck takes a different view: "I don't want to see botrytis in the classic (entry-level) range because it changes the flavor of everything. Botrytis is perfect in late harvest but has nothing to do with grand cru because you can get concentration without it, and we want to see the purity." You can make delicious wine with or without botrytis; it's really a matter of whether you regard it as a feature of terroir or as a complication.

One of the biggest problems for the consumer has been the failure to come to terms with sugar levels: unless a wine is Vendange Tardive or SGN, there is no official way to know whether it is dry or off-dry. Producers have finally realized that this is a major impediment in the marketplace, and many have introduced a scale of sweetness on the back label. Etienne Hugel is against the idea because "it means we have lost the battle," and it's fair to say that it may help to resolve uncertainty, but at the cost of reinforcing the image that wine from Alsace is not reliably dry. However, it is no more than a partial solution, because information on the back label is not evident on, for example, a restaurant wine list; and furthermore the scale is neither consistent nor objective. Some producers use a 5 point scale, some use a 9 point scale.

Actually, I do not think either scale has much significance beyond the first three points, because once a wine is sweet, it is sweet, and it would be a rare person who would choose it on the basis of just how sweet. The critical point is whether a wine tastes bone dry, or what I call ambiguously dry (when you don't think it's bone dry, but can't quite taste sweetness), or distinctly off-dry. Aside from that, the problem is that right at the most sensitive point of the scale, the difference between bone-dry and off-dry, most producers are assigning #1 or #2 on the basis of taste. This is a mistake because sensitivities differ: indeed, when I've questioned whether a particular wine should really be #1, producers sometimes say that the number depends on who is making the as-

Reference Wines for Pinot Gris and Gewürztraminer Grand Cru and Late Harvest	
Pinot Gris	
Grand Cru	Josmeyer, Brand
Vendange Tardive	Marc Kreydenweiss, Muenchberg Zind-Humbrecht, Clos Windsbuhl
SGN	Bott-Geyl, Sonnenglanz
Gewürztraminer	
Grand Cru	Trimbach, Cuvée des Seigneurs de Ribeaupierre
Vendange Tardive	Marc Tempé, Mambourg Domaine Weinbach, Furstentum
SGN	Meyer-Fonné, Sporen

signment that day. "The problem is that everyone has their own system, when I see what's on the label sometimes I'm astonished," says Marc Hugel. None of this is going to work until producers accept that there is an international standard for bone-dry wine: less than 4 g/l of residual sugar. The best solution of all, of course, would be for Alsace to have a formal AOP of Alsace Sec that appears on the front label for wine that is unambiguously dry. If even in Champagne they have started to put dosage levels on the label, why can't they put the level of residual sugar on the label in Alsace?

For all of the problems with sugar confusing the palate of supposedly dry wines, there is no argument about the quality of the sweet wines of Alsace. Vendange Tardive and Selection de Grains Nobles dessert wines have been classified separately in Alsace since 1984. Even here the classification refers to the sugar level at time of harvest rather than to residual sugar after fermentation; however, given the sugar levels at harvest, VT and SGN wines are always sweet. Chaptalization cannot be used for VT or SGN wines; in fact, the regulations for their production are among the strictest in France for dessert wines. Their reputation is as high as for any sweet wine anywhere, but they represent only an average 1-2% of production, with amounts fluctuating widely from year to year according to vintage conditions.

"We cannot compete on price or varietal name. We are on steep slopes, we have high labor costs. Let's try to put our terroir into the bottle," says Etienne Sipp, expressing his view of the future for Alsace. The region has one of the great varieties in Riesling, which I think is possibly the most versatile white variety of all. There is a series of different terroirs at grand cru level where Riesling shows all the nuances of its range of expression as a dry wine. Pinot Gris and Gewürztraminer can show real varietal character in Alsace. The late harvest wines can achieve great purity and interest extending beyond mere sweetness. It is a shame that uncertainty about wine styles, and failure to be strict enough about yields and to take the classification system in hand, have prevented the region from establishing the reputation it deserves.

Vintages

Historically Alsace has alternated between good vintages and poor vintages, but the recent global warming trend has produced a run of good vintages, albeit with different characters. There's a marked difference between 2007 or 2009, which are both overtly rich, and 2010, which has high acidity, for example, providing a style for every taste.

2013	Rain at harvest meant that early pickers did best, so the wines tend to be light and fresh. This is a vintage for early drinking.
2012	Warm August and cool September gave good results, with a classic balance of fruit to acidity. It was especially successful for Pinot Noir.
2011	Decent but not great vintage, generally giving a fresh, fruity style; not much in the way of late harvest wines. Dry wines should be drunk early.
2010	Very high acidity caused many wines to take time to come around. Riesling can still be piercing, but the best wines are fresh and pure with classic minerality, and should have longevity. There are few late harvest wines.
2009	Precocious vintage in rich style, with powerful Rieslings and opulent Pinot Gris and Gewürztraminer. Alcohol is high for dry wines.
2008	Generally cool season saved by Indian summer; the style is often restrained, and some wines were slow to open. Not as good as 2007 or 2009.
2007	Regarded as a great vintage all round, rich with even Riesling tending to opulence rather than minerality. Possibly the richest since 1997, with some great botrytized wines.
2006	A variable year, with rather heterogeneous results resulting from difficulties with getting to ripeness, but good acidity for Rieslings.
2005	Not such a good year in Alsace as elsewhere in France, with some problems reaching ripeness; grand crus are the most reliable.
2004	High yields resulted in lack of concentration. Rieslings performed best. There are few late harvest wines.
2003	The great heat of this vintage produced wines that matured early, although some of the reds have been very fine.
2002	Difficult year because of alternating hot and cold conditions, but the best wines had good structure and acidity, and sufficient ripeness.
2001	Poor and late start to season, recovery in August, then problems in September, but wines were harvested in October Indian summer, giving some exceptionally fine late harvest wines.
2000	An early start was followed by a favorable growing season, but there were heavy rains in October. Dry wines are good, if not outstanding, and there are even some late harvest wines.

6

The Loire

Cool Climate Varieties

A bottle of white, a bottle of red
Perhaps a bottle of rosé instead
(Billy Joel)

"Loire producers are thought of as traditionally making white wine, but now there is some red wine," says François Robin of the producers' organization, Inter-Loire, but this is an understatement as production today splits more equally between red, white, and rosé. The emphasis is on cool climate varieties, as the Loire is at the northern limit for viticulture; in fact, it is only due to the ameliorating influence of the river that wine can be made at all in the region.

The longest river in France, the Loire rises in the Massif Central, and runs more or less north to Sancerre, where it turns west. No longer navigable, it meanders through the wine regions for about 400 km (250 miles) before it empties out into the Atlantic. The Loire is divided into four general regions for wine production: the Nantais near the coast, Anjou centered on Angers, Touraine centered on Tours, and the Centre around Sancerre. All styles of wine are found in the Loire as a whole, but going from west to east, the Nantais is dominated by dry white, the largest production in Anjou is rosé, the bulk of Touraine is red, and the Centre (the general name of the eastern vineyards) focuses on dry whites. The sweet whites of Anjou and Touraine have a great reputation, although production volume is small.

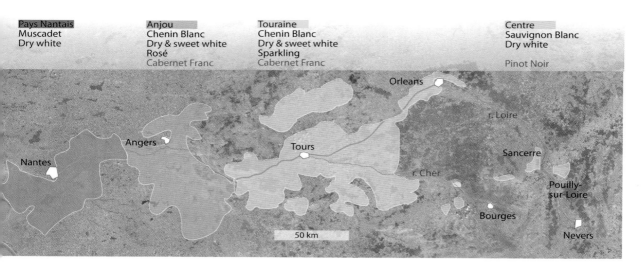

Pays Nantais	Anjou	Touraine	Centre
Muscadet	Chenin Blanc	Chenin Blanc	Sauvignon Blanc
Dry white	Dry & sweet white	Dry & sweet white	Dry white
	Rosé	Sparkling	
	Cabernet Franc	Cabernet Franc	Pinot Noir

Extending for several hundred kilometers, the Loire contains four distinct wine-producing regions.

The wine regions of the Loire are near the river or its tributaries. Legend holds that vines were being cultivated on the banks of the Loire before the Roman invasion of Gaul. Whether or not this is true, there are detailed descriptions of winegrowing by the sixth century, and by the Middle Ages the forests along the river were being cleared to plant vineyards. Planting was confined to the area immediately around the rivers, not because this was the most appropriate terroir, but because it made it possible to transport the wine to market. During the twelfth to fifteenth centuries the wines were drunk at the Royal Court in the Loire and exported to England.[1] The style of the wines at this time is unknown.

Before the phylloxera epidemic in the nineteenth century, there were about 160,000 ha of vines along the Loire. Now there are about 50,000 ha in the four regions devoted to AOP wines and another 20,000 in IGP. The regional description of IGP Val de Loire covers the whole area and accounts for almost all the IGP wine (this used to be the Vin de Pays du Jardin de la France). Vineyards lie mostly on the south side of the river. Although the region is protected from climatic extremes, its cool climate ensures good acidity for the whites. Ripening can be a problem for the reds.

Each of the four regions of the Loire has its own character and focus. The white wines are mostly varietal-based, with the variety changing from west to east: Muscadet in the Nantais, Chenin Blanc in Anjou and Touraine, and Sauvignon Blanc in Sancerre or Pouilly Fumé. With such diversity of varieties, you might not expect to see much universality of style, but the cool climate is reflected in the common features of crisp, fresh fruits for both reds and whites.

Almost half the production of the Loire today is dry white wine. Muscadet is more than half of the total white. Melon de Bourgogne is the formal name for the principal variety of Muscadet, reflecting its origins in Burgundy.[2] (Like Gamay, its planting was frequently banned in Burgundy itself). Today it is more often just called Muscadet. The most planted white grape in the Loire, Muscadet accounts for almost all production in the Nantais.

In Anjou and Touraine, production is more or less evenly divided between red, rosé, and white (including still and sparkling). White and sparkling wines are dominated by Chenin Blanc; the oldest white grape of the region, it probably originated in the Loire.[4] Chenin Blanc is made in a complete range of styles, from dry to sweet, and from still to sparkling. The relative proportions of still and sparkling wine depend on the weather. In better vintages, more still wine is made; in less successful vintages, more is turned into sparkling wine. Production of sweet wines also depends greatly on vintage, in particular on whether a good growing season extends long enough into the autumn to favor late harvest.

Rosé dominates the production of Anjou. The largest single category is the slightly sweet Cabernet d'Anjou, which usually comes mostly from Cabernet Franc. Rosé can be made in most of the appellations of Anjou and Touraine, but no individual area is considered a quality leader. Production of the generic Rosé d'Anjou, which can be made anywhere in the region, has declined.

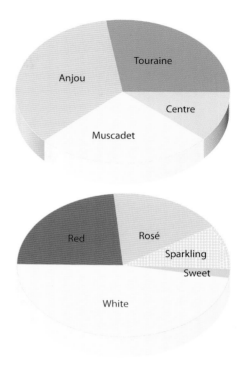

The major production of the Loire is split between Muscadet, Anjou, and Touraine, with less in the Centre. Almost half is dry white, and most of the rest is red or rosé.[3]

Red wine is most important in Touraine (where it is about half of all production), but the red wine areas extend over the border into Anjou. There is a blur in focus between the regions, as the red wines are more similar than different. Cabernet Franc is the major black grape of both Anjou and Touraine, and most wines are pure varietals. A small amount of Cabernet Sauvignon is also grown (less than 10% of the amount of Cabernet Franc), but is limited to a small proportion, or even disallowed, in some appellations.

The grape varieties that were grown historically are unknown, but curiously the first references appear to be to black varieties. The oldest was probably the variety called Pineau d'Aunis; not much is left today.[5] Cabernet Franc made its way from Bordeaux to the Loire; in 1635, "Cardinal Richelieu sent several thousands of the best vine of Bordeaux to the Abbé Breton in Chinon."[6] Still known as Breton or Petit Breton in the Loire, this was Cabernet Franc.[7]

It's back to white wine at the eastern end of the Loire wine regions, where Sauvignon Blanc dominates Sancerre and the other appellations of the Centre (so called because the area is central in France). Sauvignon Blanc probably

Grapes are still grown at Saumur castle (left), and have been harvested since at least the start of the fifteenth century (right).[10]

originated in the Loire, and may be an offspring of Savagnin, the white grape of the Jura.

Although white wine is dominant in the Centre, red wine has old origins here. Legend holds that the monks at the Augustine monastery of Saint Satur (adjacent to Sancerre, on the Loire river) were making red wine in the twelfth century,[8] and folklore rates red wine of equal importance to white in the region in the period before phylloxera.[9] Replanting after phylloxera concentrated on the grape varieties that were easiest to grow, which is when Sauvignon Blanc became predominant, but recently Pinot Noir has been making a comeback in Sancerre.

All over the Loire, the style of the white wine has been modernized by a move to greater ripeness. Muscadet now shows a tendency to emphasize fruits rather than minerality. In Anjou and Touraine, Chenin Blanc has lost its characteristic "wet wool" in favor of more direct fruits. In Sancerre and Pouilly Fumé, Sauvignon Blanc is less aggressive, with its former grassy or even herbaceous flavors replaced by citrus fruits, sometimes merging with stone fruits. Perhaps it's a little harsh to say that there's a tendency to reduce intensity in favor of amorphous fruit flavors, but it might be fair to say that there's a certain sense of convergence among entry-level wines, and in order to see real regional and varietal character it's necessary to seek out specific cuvées.

A significant change is an emerging focus by producers all over the Loire on expressing single cépages through a variety of terroirs. Traditionally most producers used to make an assemblage for a single wine, or possibly a couple of cuvées, from their various plots. Voicing a common view, "At first I worked to select lots and assemble them, but things have advanced, today there is much more focus on terroir," François Pinon says in Vouvray. In each region the top producers now often offer several cuvées, each representing a different terroir.

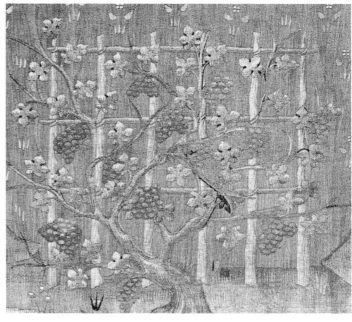

One point to be made is the sheer value of the top dry white or red wines from the Loire. It

Grapevines were grown on a trellis as early as the fourteenth century in Anjou, as seen in this depiction in the Apocalypse Tapestry of Angers of 1373.

would be hard to find a white Burgundy or red Bordeaux of equivalent quality at the same price level.[11] With the modernization of style in the past decade, these can be wines with significant interest as well as an attractive price. The top sweet wines are priced more highly.

Winegrowers in Muscadet have a sense that the region is in free fall. "The vineyards of the Nantais are passing through an unprecedented crisis," starts a recent book on the region.[12] In year 2000, 17,500 ha of vineyards included 14,000 ha of AOC. Ten years later, the total AOC area had decreased to 9,000 ha.[13] The number of producers has fallen as wine production has simply become uneconomic, especially after a frost destroyed a large part of the crop in 2008. Today there are about 600 producers left. The value of vineyards has been dropping steadily; in 2000 it was about the same as the average for the Loire, but since then the value has more than halved.[14] An incidental benefit has been a move towards quality. "It's a good thing that vineyards have been reduced, it's let us concentrate on the better terroirs," says Marie-Luce

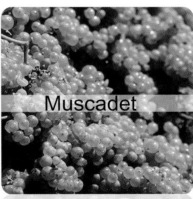

Muscadet

Muscadet AOP	2,400 ha
Muscadet Sèvre et Maine	6,250 ha
M Coteaux de la Loire	150 ha
M Côtes de Grandlieu	300 ha
Gros Plant (VDQS)	600 ha

Production
5 million cases
(70% Sèvre et Maine)
(50% sur lies)

600 producers	(23%)
4 cooperatives	(7%)
13 negociants	(70%)

Métaireau of Domaine du Grand Mouton. "13,000 ha is too much," says André-Michel Brégeon. "It's necessary to select the best terroirs and to create village appellations with a new hierarchy."

The myth about the origins of Muscadet is that Melon de Bourgogne was imported into the Nantais in the early eighteenth century, when growers were looking for a grape variety to replace the black varieties that had been killed by frost in the great winter freeze of 1709. But in fact Melon was already an abundant variety a century earlier.[15] At all events, by the eighteenth century, the Nantais had switched to white wine production.[16] During this period, much of the wine was exported by Dutch traders from the port of Nantes after distillation into eau de vie; the thin, acid wines of the region were ideal for this purpose.[17] Another grape giving good results was Folle Blanche, today one of the principal varieties for brandy production in Cognac and Armagnac. It's known in the Loire as Gros Plant because of the large size of its grapes. This became the most widely planted variety.

When phylloxera struck, plantings were two thirds Gros Plant. During the twentieth century, the balance shifted to producing white wine for drinking, and Muscadet (Melon) increased to become the vast majority.[18] Gros Plant was a VDQS (a level below AOC) until 2011, but became an IGP when the rules changed.[19] Production has dropped steadily to less than ten per cent of Muscadet. No producers now focus specifically on Gros Plant; those remaining are Muscadet producers who also grow some Gros Plant.

The alternative to producing Muscadet is to plant other varieties under the IGP Val de Loire. The firm of Lieubeau is a leader, with one quarter of their total 80 ha planted to IGP, mostly for Chardonnay and Sauvignon Blanc. Prices are similar to entry-level Muscadet, but because yields are higher, the IGP is more profitable. Is the IGP more modern? "Muscadet is drunk by old fashioned people," says François Lieubeau. "If you say Val de Loire Chardonnay or Sauvignon Blanc, it's very effective, but that's not the case for Muscadet, it's hard to be competitive."

There are three major appellations: Muscadet (including a hierarchy of sub appellations), Gros Plant Nantais, and Coteaux d'Ancenis (an area at the eastern edge that runs into Anjou). Muscadet describes the entire area where Melon de Bourgogne is produced, but is divided into regional appellations. The most important AOP is Muscadet Sèvre et Maine, which has about 80% of the total plantings. (Sèvre and Maine are the two major rivers that run through the region; they are tributaries joining the Loire at Nantes.) To the west is Muscadet Côtes de Grandlieu and to the northeast is Muscadet Coteaux de la Loire (which includes the Coteaux d'Ancenis).[20] But the most important determinant of quality is a feature of production called *sur lie*. This describes the tradition of keeping the wine on the lees through the winter, and then bottling directly in the spring. The wine gains additional flavor and texture from its contact with

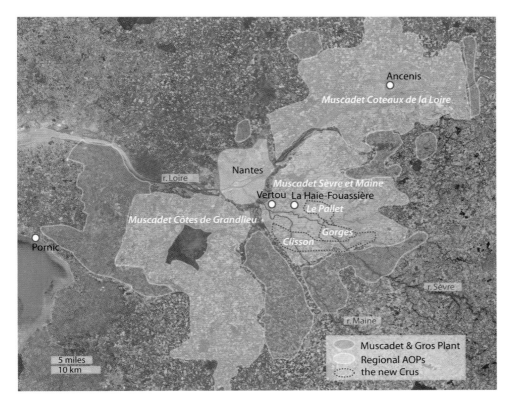

The Muscadet region forms a semi circle around Nantes and is divided into regional appellations.

Le Pallet, Gorges, and Clisson are the first three Cru Communaux.[21]

the lees; sometimes just a faint touch of spritzen from carbon dioxide remains at the time of bottling.

The attempt to lift Muscadet out of the doldrums focuses on the introduction of Crus Communaux (Communal Crus): anywhere else these would probably simply be called premier crus. They identify the best terroirs in Muscadet Sèvre et Maine, and have higher standards for vinification. The first three were approved in 2011, another four are expected to be approved soon, and two more are still being studied. Yields are lower in the crus,[22] and the wine spends longer on the lees: in fact, it will not carry the description sur lie, because this requires Muscadet to be bottled by the November of the year after the vintage.[23] The extension of lees contact beyond this period makes for more intense wines (and also means there will not be any spritzen remaining at bottling). Definition of the crus is partly a recognition of existing practices. "The great variety of subsoils in Muscadet has been little known; we are working to define the geography, which is the basis for the crus. But for a number of years the vignerons have been treating wines from different terroirs separately," explains François Robin. In fact, the names of the crus have been used on labels for some years, often appearing more prominently than "Muscadet."

The intention is to emphasize variety. "Historically Muscadet was very well known but considered always to have the single characteristic of freshness. It's

Muscadet has expanses of vineyards overlooked by small villages, with the church spires often visible on the horizon.

difficult today to make people understand that it's not just one homogeneous wine, but comes from a diversity of terroirs, and has evolved in quality to a range extending from the regional wines to the communal crus. Our job is to explain to people that Muscadet is no longer just a single wine, but that it can age well. We would like people to forget their past impressions of Muscadet and be surprised by the crus. We want to put an 's' on Muscadet and make it plural," says François Robin. "Sometimes people say, 'this is good but it's not Muscadet'," he adds.

My own experience has been that the crus show more intensity of flavor, but generally follow the same stylistic imperatives as Muscadet Sèvre et Maine. Applied to wines coming from better terroirs, lower yields and longer periods for maturation (typically eighteen months on the lees) definitely pay off in superior quality, but I would say that the style is not very different. What you get with Muscadet where there has been extensive lees aging is a sense of structure, showing as a sort of granular texture to the palate. When the wine has been aged in stainless steel, this offers a counterpoise against its natural freshness. When barriques are used, they are usually old enough for the wood influence to be simply oxidative rather than to add any oak flavors, and there may be a softer impression, even extending to a faint sensation of nuttiness (especially when lees aging has been very long). Usually Muscadet AOPs are aged in stainless steel, but the crus tend to be aged in old barriques.

Muscadet passed through a period when producers went to extremes of vinification in order to try to develop character, such as using new oak or performing malolactic fermentation. This has mostly died out now. The examples of wines that might follow the description of "good but not Muscadet" tend to use such techniques. These wines can be interesting, but blur the focus, and sometimes I feel they are not what I look for in Muscadet, especially when new oak is used. My own view is that the wines develop more interest as the result of lees aging than they do from exposure to new oak; I do not really think the grape variety is fat enough to support the oak. Perhaps I am falling into François Robin's trap of regarding Muscadet as a homogeneous wine; certainly wines with long lees aging make his point about the potential of Muscadet for producing wine that is interesting as it ages.

A major, and controversial, determinant of style is battonage—stirring up the wine while it is on the lees.[24] Producers use more battonage if they are looking for a more powerful style, and less battonage if they are looking for elegance. The combination of longer lees aging and battonage adds stone fruit flavors to the citrus fruits. The wine can become quite complex, but not everyone wants to see the increased richness. "We want the wine to be natural and fresh; battonage introduces richness, which is very nice, but is not our style here," says Marie-Luce Métaireau, explaining why Domaine du Grand Mouton does not use battonage.

Muscadet is responding to the market in two partly contradictory ways. At the generic level, there has been a change of style, emphasizing fruit and aromatics; these wines are direct in flavor but well made, often with an initial slightly perfumed or aromatic impression, which persists through the palate. I have never really considered Muscadet as an aromatic variety, but in these wines, you see phenolics as much as flavor. They remain quite acidic and low in alcohol, but otherwise fit the image of a modern wine better than a traditional Muscadet. They can be somewhat interdenominational, and although they retain acidity, I do not think they will complement oysters in the same way as a more saline or savory traditional Muscadet. The problem here is lack of typicity: nothing distinguishes these wines, except perhaps price, from the competition.

The other direction is to emphasize differences in terroir. Muscadet has quite varied terroirs, mostly derived from types of metamorphic rocks. The most common are gneiss, orthogneiss, and granite, but serpentine, amphibolite, and gabbro (a type of basalt) are also found. The crus epitomize the variation: Clisson has a mix of pebbles and granite, Gorge extends across the river Sèvre with soils from gabbro to clay and quartz, Le Pallet is a warm spot (harvest is usually

The crus (and proposed crus) have different geologies. Different types of granite are dominant in Clisson and Château-Thébaud; gabbro is dominant in Gorges and Mouzillon-Tillière (also known as Rubis de la Sanguèze as rubis is the local name for gabbro); schist features in Goulaine (with mica in both granite and gneiss); there is gneiss with some orthogneiss in Monnières Saint Fiacre; and Le Pallet has various soil types.

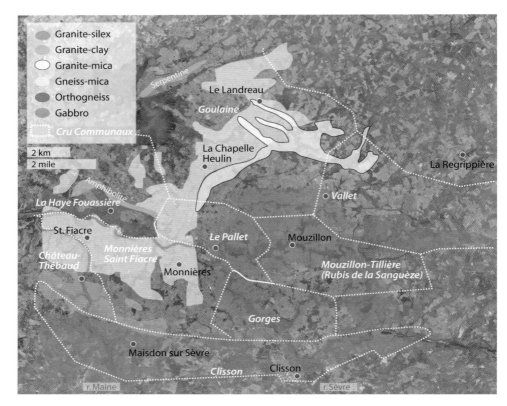

early here) with gneiss and gabbro, and Château-Thébaud is based on granite. Moving away from the tradition of making an assemblage to get regularity in the wine, top producers now tend to make cuvées from parcels to emphasize terroir. "I think we have 20-30 producers who are looking for terroir in their wines. I think this is the richness of Muscadet, the future is to make different wines," says Marie Chartier-Luneau at Domaine Luneau-Papin, where eight different cuvées, distinguished by terroir and vine age, offer interesting interplays of savory notes against a background of fruits that changes with the terroir and the age of the vines.

The most brilliant demonstration of terroir came from a tasting at Domaine de l'Ecu, where Guy Bossard was a pioneer in expressing terroir in Muscadet. "At first we looked for complexity by assemblage and I continue to do that; but the best tasters in my clientele are looking for a personality, an expression of the terroir. I started with my father, we always vinified each parcel separately, and the assemblage was done at bottling. We started to bottle the separate terroirs around 1970," he says. "The cépage is the same, the vintage is the same, the work in the vines is the same, the work to make the wine is the same, so if we see differences in the wines it must be the terroir." The emphasis on terroir extends to labeling the wines simply by the types of terroir: Gneiss, Or-

A steep cliff rising up from the Maine river shows the typical granite terroir with thin topsoil of Château-Thébaud.

thogneiss, and Granite. The wines become progressively more precise, mineral, and savory, and a little weightier, moving along the terroirs.

Variations on granite became clear from a tasting at Domaine de la Pépière, where Marc Olivier and Rémi Branger are regarded as among the leaders in modern Muscadet. "We were making wine from two different parcels of granite, one at Château Thébaud and one just north of it, and we only understood the differences we were finding in the wines when we saw the geological map [which was prepared as part of the development of the crus]. The granite of Clisson is more siliceous, which captures heat better. Château-Thébaud is mostly granite, but it is a specific type, and has more clay," explains Rémi.

Although the crus certainly have distinctive terroirs, there is enough heterogeneity within each cru that it's not obvious at this point whether they will develop distinctive styles related to terroir, or whether the variety of approaches from different producers will mean that there is no single typicity for any one cru. The crus offer the logical extension of the tendency towards longer lees aging for the best wines; as well as showing more intensity and character than simple Muscadet Sèvre et Maine, they also have significantly greater aging potential. They tend to become more mineral as they age. I'm inclined to the view that their importance comes more from providing an easy way to identify the best wines than for specific characters associated with individual crus.

The traditional view of Muscadet is that it should be drunk right away, while it is fresh.[25] However, minerality begins to show around two years of age. "Few people know this aspect of Muscadet because they drink the wine soon after the vintage," says Patrick Macé, winemaker at Chéreau Carré. Focusing on youthfulness definitely gives a mistaken view of the better cuvées or crus, where it takes at least four or five years for the increasing complexity with age to develop. Marie-Luce Métaireau at Domaine du Grand Mouton recollects that in the fifties and sixties, her father used to say that Muscadet would age well, but when he took old Muscadet to wine fairs in the area, people did not want to taste it. "It's only in the past 15 years or so that people have accepted the idea of older vintages from Muscadet," she says. The most impressive demonstration of aging came from a tasting at Domaine Luneau-Papin, where young wines show a nice sense of restrained minerality, and become more savory and herbal with age. The top wines have significant potential for aging; the oldest I tasted were almost fifteen years old, and still lively.

So will the crus rescue Muscadet? They account for only a tiny proportion of the vineyards. "The crus are not made in sufficient quantity to resolve the *crise*, but we think they will be a locomotive; people will see Muscadet in a more positive light," says François Robin. "The Crus are a very good thing because it's important to have wines like that to make people understand that Muscadet is not just for drinking with oysters," says Rémi Branger. Marie Chartier-Luneau takes the broad view that crus may lead to a greater sense of identity. "Winegrowers are peasants who are used to working alone; we have to change and work with our neighbors. The importance of the Cru Communaux may be as much for getting the producers to work together as to identify the wine to the consumer," she says. The most negative opinion comes from Guy Bossard, who thinks the regulations do not go far enough. "The idea is interesting, but the regulations are not strict enough. You cannot make grand crus with industrial methods. They have not required manual harvest. You need to use natural yeasts," he believes. The issue of harvesting may be a critical point. "To harvest by machine you have to make a higher trellis and you lose the typicity of the wine. Muscadet should be trimmed low and the grapes sheltered under the umbrella of the large leaves," says Marie-Luce Métaireau.

But only a relatively small proportion of Muscadet is made by independent growers. More than two thirds is produced by negociants. "There used to be about twenty negociant houses in the Nantais but the larger negociants have purchased most of them and now most Muscadet is made by only two or three negociants," says François Robin. The problem here is the lack of local commitment: Muscadet becomes just one possible source for supply of cheap white wine. Muscadet Sèvre et Maine sur lie bottled by a grower committed to quality can be fresh and attractive—perhaps not a competitor to Sancerre or Chablis, but nonetheless a refreshing accompaniment to sea food. Many of the negociants' wines are somewhat characterless. "The big negociants who sell in bulk have spoiled everything. The wine is made without any passion, all sorts of treatments are used," says Guy Bossard. The only good side to this is increased pressure for growers to bottle their own wine. "Negociants are less interested in Muscadet; they prefer to buy wines from Spain and the south of France, and this is pushing growers who want to stay in business to produce their own wine," says Marie Chartier-Luneau. "For whatever reason, there's never been much interest in cooperatives, so it's either sell to a negociant or do it all yourself," she adds.

I might not go so far as François Robin, who says that, "In a blind tasting you would find the Crus Communaux to be more like Burgundy than Muscadet," but the Burgundian model certainly holds insofar as there are interesting differences between terroirs that accentuate with age. One great advantage of Muscadet is that it is possibly the only region in France that does not have problems with increasing alcohol. This may partly be due to a propensity to harvest early. Elsewhere in France, the growing season has been lengthened by postponing harvest to get riper berries. But in Muscadet, they are not following the trend; they are more concerned about maintaining freshness as the important criterion. In any case, it's fair to say that there is no risk of alcohol obscuring the terroir. The crus are definitely the way forward, but it remains to be seen whether they (and equivalent cuvées) can have enough impact on the market to change the general perspective of Muscadet.

Reference Wines for Pays Nantais	
Muscadet Sèvre et Maine	Domaine de l'Ecu, Granite
	Domaine Pierre Luneau-Papin, L de l'Or
	Domaine du Grand Mouton, Cuvée #1
Muscadet Sèvre et Maine (with MLF and oak)	Château de la Fruitière, M de la Fruitière
Gorges	André-Michel Brégeon
Le Pallet	Vignerons de Pallet
Clisson	Domaine de la Pépière
Château-Thébaud	Domaine de la Pépière
Monnières St. Fiacre	Domaine La Haute Févrie
Goulaine	Domaine Pierre Luneau-Papin, Excelsior
Gros Plant de Nantais (Folle Blanche)	Domaine Pierre Luneau-Papin

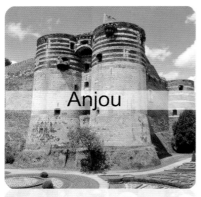

Dry white
    1,250 ha   625,000 cases
Red
    3,800 ha 2.3 million cases
Rosé
    7,400 ha 4.7 million cases
Sparkling
    1,700 ha 1.2 million cases
Sweet
    1,900 ha   550,000 cases
Total
  16,400 ha 9.4 million cases

Anjou has the best known appellations in the Loire for dry wines, both red and white, and for sweet (white) dessert wines, although in each category there is a counterpart in Touraine. The most important appellation for red wine is Saumur-Champigny, made exclusively from Cabernet Franc: just to the east are Bourgueil and Chinon in Touraine. The top dry white wines of Anjou come from the small area of Savennières, just outside Angers; the closest competitor in Touraine would be a dry wine from Vouvray. Production is really tiny in the top appellations for sweet wines, Chaume, Quarts de Chaume, and Bonnezeaux, and here the top sweet wines from Vouvray are effective rivals for the crown in the Loire.

Anjou's greatest production by far is rosé. Produced anywhere in Anjou, Cabernet d'Anjou is a slightly sweet rosé,[26] made almost entirely from Cabernet Franc (although Cabernet Sauvignon is also allowed). Rosé d'Anjou is not quite as sweet,[27] and can come from any of several black grape varieties.[28] (So can Rosé de Loire, which is dry).[29] After the rosés, the next most important single appellation in terms of quantity is Saumur Mousseux, the sparkling wine from the large area of Saumur (made from Chenin Blanc, Chardonnay, and Cabernet Franc). Although red comes after rosé in total production, it is divided among many appellations.

All white wine in Anjou and Touraine comes exclusively from Chenin Blanc. Sometimes called Pineau de la Loire locally, it may have originated in Anjou in the ninth century, subsequently migrating to Touraine in the fifteenth.[30] The big issue with Chenin Blanc is always the yield. At low yields, the wine can have character, but at high yields it is completely bland. It has natural high acidity.

"Chenin is more civilized today, we look for more fruit now," as Jacques Couly of Couly-Dutheil says. The traditional description for the white wines of Anjou and Touraine used to be "wet dog," "wet straw," or "wet wool," according to your predilections, all reflecting a somewhat humid impression of the variety. Perhaps this resulted from incompletely ripe grapes, but it is no longer appropriate. Today I often get a flavor spectrum for Chenin Blanc between cereal and nutty, with a savory, almost earthy edge, accompanied by fruits ranging from citrus to stone, sometimes with a hint of apples. (As Chenin Blanc rarely undergoes malolactic fermentation, there is often enough malic acid to create a faint impression of apples). Some people see quince in the wine. I asked Evelyne de Pontbriand of Domaine du Closel whether she thinks this

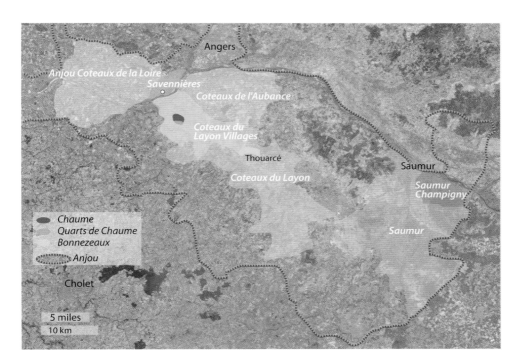

Chaume
Quarts de Chaume
Bonnezeaux
Anjou

5 miles
10 km

The Anjou region is defined by the Anjou Villages AOP. The western part contains appellations devoted principally to white wine, including the small AOPs for the top sweet wines (see key). Savennières is the top AOP for dry white wine. The eastern part of the region around Saumur produces reds as well as whites. Saumur-Champigny is exclusively red.

change simply reflects a greater degree of maturity in Chenin Blanc. "Well, harvesting later is one important change, but the move to more natural wine-making, including using native yeasts and using less sulfur is important," she believes. "But a major factor was that the wine had to be bottled at the latest by the following June, because the cellars are above ground. Being able to bottle later (because of air conditioning) has a big effect. So does the use of barriques, which are made possible because now we can do extended élevage in temperature controlled cellars. So there are multiple factors."

Anjou white wines tend to show direct fruit flavors, usually in the direction of citrus, sometimes accompanied by a fugitive whiff of exotic fruits. High acidity is common, but necessary to keep the flavor spectrum lively. There can be a touch of superficial richness, which increases further by the time you reach Vouvray and Montlouis in Touraine. This may be partly due to the change in terroir from schist in Anjou to chalk in Touraine, but is probably more a stylistic choice, with a tendency to leave a little residual sugar in the wine in Vouvray.

Savennières brings out the savory side of Chenin Blanc. Consisting of three hills facing south-southwest towards the river, Savennières makes the best dry white wines of the Loire (although historically it was known for its sweet or semi-sweet wines). It declined to only 46 planted hectares in 1977, but revived in the 1980s as growers from neighboring sweet wine appellations became interested in producing dry Savennières. Today's wines from Savennières are typically fresh when young, then close up for some years, and finally mature

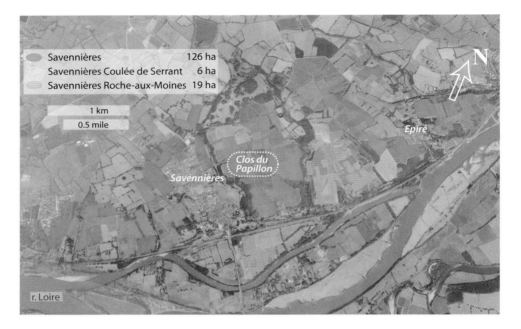

Savennières is a small appellation immediately north of the Loire. Coulée de Serrant and Roche-aux-Moines are separate appellations within it. Clos du Papillon is one of the most important vineyards.

gracefully as the longest lived dry wines of the region. Due to a protected microclimate, Savennières has less rain than Touraine, so the grapes ripen more reliably, and alcohol levels are a little higher. The Savennières AOC was restricted to dry wines until the rules were changed in 1996 to allow sweet wines, but the overwhelming proportion remains dry. You might say that the whites of Chinon and Saumur give a more modern impression than those of Savennières, with more overt fruit—but for that very reason, less typicity of the variety. Savennières tends more to the mineral side.

Savennières is a small appellation, yet carved out within it are two further tiny appellations, Savennières Coulée de Serrant and Savennières Roches-aux-Moines. Curiously these are not premier crus of Savennières, but actually named as independent appellations. This raises the question of what about Coulée de Serrant and Roche-aux-Moines is distinctively different from Savennières? Assessment is complicated by the fact that Coulée de Serrant is a monopole, owned exclusively by Nicolas Joly of Château Roche aux Moines. It's difficult to determine whether the character of a vineyard is due to unique terroir or to winemaking when there is only a single owner.

"Life is a permanent fight against time," Nicolas said as he rushed in for our meeting at Château Roche aux Moines. The weather had suddenly turned sunny after three weeks of rain, and there was no wind, so he had been out in the vineyard organizing the workers to take advantage of the break in the weather to spray sulfur to protect the vines against fungal infections. "We can protect the vines for the next month by spraying now," he explains. "The sulfur

we are spreading this morning comes from a mine. It is a natural product as opposed to coming from the petrochemical industry," he adds. Committed to the biodynamic approach, he has had a widespread influence on viticulture, as well as locally influencing style in Savennières.

"Often Savennières is too shallow; it would be improved by more maturity. My belief is that a bit of maturity is part of the taste. We harvest four times over three weeks, looking to get the grapes at each round at the same point of maturity. I don't look for late harvests, but I do wait for maturity," Nicolas says. This results in a powerful savory flavor spectrum, often accentuated by a touch of botrytis resulting from the late harvest; sometimes there is a little residual sugar.

Botrytis is desirable in sweet white wine (where it increases concentration and brings a delicious honeyed piquancy), it is ruinous in red wine (where the flavors clash), and in dry white wine... it is unusual. For most styles of white wine, especially those where freshness is the main criterion, botrytis is considered undesirable, but Savennières is one of the rare places where you find botrytis in dry wine. It tends to be confined to top sites, where late harvest is

The famous Coulée de Serrant is in the foreground; behind it is the Clos des Moines, with the Château de la Roche aux Moines at the far end of the vineyard. The Loire runs parallel on the left.

possible. As Charles Sydney, a broker in the Loire, comments, "Given Chenin's tendency to be acidic, it is essential to wait until the grape reaches full phenolic maturity before harvesting... A harvest with no rot is very unlikely to be ripe."[31] The tendency seems to be to harvest early for freshness in entry-level wines, but to harvest later for more complexity in top wines. Other examples of dry wines relying on late harvest are Baumard's Trie Spéciale, a selection of more mature berries, sometimes but not necessarily botrytized, and Domaine du Closel's Clos du Papillon. In Savennières, botrytis is an exception, but in Savennières Roches-aux-Moines, it is more common, since the eight producers seem to have a general policy of later harvest.

Nicolas Joly makes wine in all three appellations and the style of late harvest definitely trumps appellation differences, at least to the extent that the wines unmistakably come from a single producer. Yet Coulée de Serrant is more intense than the Savennières Roche-aux-Moins (Clos de la Bergerie), which is more intense than the Savennières (Le Vieux Clos). While this validates the appellation hierarchy, it bypasses the question of whether there is a difference in *character* or just an increased potential for achieving higher ripeness. Claude Papon at Château Pierre Bise also produces Savennières in a mature style, and his Roche-aux-Moines and Savennières Clos de Coulaine are variations on a theme, with Roche-aux-Moines fruitier, but Coulaine in fact more interestingly savory. The producer seems more important than the appellation in determining overall style.

So is there a typical style for Chenin Blanc? The tradition used to be to avoid exposure to oak or malolactic fermentation, giving a decidedly crisp wine. Today maturation in oak is more common. At Château de Fesles, winemaker Gilles Bigot uses a mixture of oak and acacia. "Acacia gives a fruitier and more aromatic impression; it does not give such a woody impression as oak," he explains. Barriques have become common for the top wines, although the proportion of new wood is usually limited. When new barriques are used, most often there is no MLF, so you do not get the pronounced aromas of vanillin and butter that are often associated with combining new oak with MLF. New oak without malolactic fermentation gives an impression more akin to walking into a first year barrel cellar: lots of smoky impressions and that faint sense of fresh-cut oak. While this can be appealing in itself, it isn't necessarily something that melds well with Chenin Blanc. I have had only a few examples of Chenin exposed to large proportions of new oak, and I believe it is usually a mistake.

The "new" typicity of Chenin avoids those humid notes that used to be associated with the variety, but has a slightly savory edge, accentuated by late harvest when there are botrytized grapes. The general tendency in Savennières is becoming quite Burgundian: maturing the entry level wine in cuve, the intermediate wine in old barriques, and perhaps using young barriques, and more extended time on the lees, for the top wine. Some producers have become laissez-faire about malolactic fermentation, which means there can be a change of style from year to year. All this marks a significant change in the past ten or twenty years. "When I was young, Savennières was always semi-dry, and we changed the style at the end of the 1960s. We never used to age on the lees; that started in 2000. And then we introduced a little MLF. The new generation try to make wine like Burgundy, but we don't have the same soils or cépages. As a result of changes we drink the entry-level wine younger—in the first two years—but the top wines last longer," says Luc Bizard at Château d'Epiré.

For the most part, the whites of Saumur tend to be nondescript, but there's an exception at Brézé, a small area just to the south of Saumur, surrounded by the red wine appellation of Saumur-Champigny. The most famous dry white wine in Anjou used to come from here. The wines of the Château de Brézé are reputed to have been common in the royal courts of Europe in the fifteenth century, to the point at which they later became known as Chenin de Brézé. An elevated site, sitting on a hill of tuffeau (local limestone), Brézé is dominated by the Château de Brézé, and when the AOC of Saumur-Champigny was established in 1957, its owner, Comte de Colbert, demanded that Brézé should have its own AOC because its terroir was so superior. Because of the poor quality of the wines—"an entire century of relatively terrible wines from one of the best sites in the Loire," is one description—the demand was refused, and M. le Comte then declined to be included in Saumur-Champigny. As a result, the red wines as well as the whites are classified only as Saumur. Today's best white wine from Brézé is no doubt Clos Rougeard's, with great purity of fruits showcasing the typical cereal/savory notes of Chenin Blanc, and a steely minerality that makes you think of Puligny Montrachet. The Château de Brézé itself is being renovated, and together with the efforts of other producers such as Domaine Guiberteau, we may see Brézé restored as a significant vineyard site.

Reference Wines for dry white Anjou	
Savennières	Domaine Baumard, Clos du Papillon
	Domaine du Closel, Clos du Papillon
	Château d'Epiré, Cuvée Spéciale
Savennières Coulée de Serrant	Château Roche aux Moines
Savennières Roches-aux-Moines	Château Pierre Bise
Saumur	Domaine des Roches Neuves, L'Insolite
Anjou	Philippe Delesvaux, Cuvée Authentique
	Domaine Richou, Les Rogeries
	Domaine Eric Morgat, Litus
Vin de France	La Sansonnière, Les Fourchades

Coteaux du Layon
    1,400 ha   400,000 cases
Coteaux du Layon Villages
    300 ha   90,000 cases
Bonnezeaux
    90 ha   22,000 cases
Chaume
    70 ha   17,000 cases
Quarts de Chaume
    50 ha   5,000 cases

Facing Savennières on the south side of the Loire, the focus turns to sweet wines. The area of the Coteaux du Layon, where the best sweet wines are made, is defined by the river Layon, a tributary that runs into the Loire just to the west of Savennières. It has to be said that most Coteaux du Layon wines are rather ordinary, often only just above off-dry sweetness,[32] but the top areas, Quarts de Chaume, Bonnezeaux, and Chaume, are the glory of sweet wine in Anjou: in good years when levels of botrytis are high, they can rival Sauternes. But the reputation of the area has suffered from recent controversies, first about the descriptions of the appellations, and then about what techniques should be permitted.

Coteaux du Layon is the generic description for the entire area, but there is a higher level of Coteaux du Layon Villages for six villages that are allowed to append their name to the label.[33] Chaume used to be one of these villages; recognized as the best of them, it had more restrictive requirements, including lower yields, but was somewhat overshadowed, by Quarts de Chaume, the best appellation for sweet wine in Anjou.[34]

When INAO decided in 2003 that Chaume merited a promotion above the category of Coteaux du Layon Villages, and proposed to call it Chaume Premier Cru des Coteaux du Layon, there was a furious objection by the producers of Quarts de Chaume, who felt that the natural hierarchy was being revised. INAO then proposed to call the appellation simply Chaume, but that was not acceptable to the Quarts de Chaume producers either. They went to court, and won a ruling in 2009 that returned Chaume to its old description of Coteaux du Layon Chaume. This led to an agreement that Quarts de Chaume should be described as a grand cru, allowing Chaume to be described as premier cru. The new descriptions came into effect for the 2010 vintage. Curiously, Bonnezeaux, which is usually regarded as almost the equal of Quarts de Chaume, is not given grand or premier cru status (nor is Savennières, as there are no crus for dry white wines).

"Making great sweet wines in the Loire is risky," admits Gilles Bigot at Château de Fesles. This is true everywhere that sweet wine is made, of course, and the reputations of sweet wine appellations really depend on how reliably they develop botrytis. The advantage of the region is that mist rises from the Layon river in Autumn mornings, is trapped by the rolling hills on either side of the river, and then blows off in the afternoons. This allows botrytis to develop, but prevents it from turning to rot.

Quarts de Chaume is situated close to the Layon river; in fact it touches the river at some points. Its great reputation stems from the fact that it's the most susceptible area to botrytis. The hill of Chaume, which lies between the village of Chaume and the river, protects the vineyards from wind, helping to sustain more botrytis. Farther away from the river, Chaume does not usually achieve as much botrytis concentration. When conditions are right, Chenin Blanc is a great grape for making sweet wine. Those herbal or even vegetal characteristics that producers have struggled to control in dry wines by obtaining greater ripeness provide the necessary counterpoise to lift the sweet wine above mere sweetness into complexity. And natural high acidity helps to keep the wine refreshing instead of cloying.

Botrytis develops unevenly in the bunch. Some berries have only speckles of botrytis while others are completely desiccated. This requires berries to be picked individually in successive passes through the vineyard.

All the same, the style of the top wines can change dramatically from year to year, depending on the level of botrytis. The recent year with most botrytis was 2010, but then 2011 was too dry for botrytis. When this happens the sweet wines are made by *passerillage*, effectively a desiccation of the grapes. This concentrates sugar, but does not give the delicious piquancy resulting from the growth of the botrytis fungus on the skin of the grapes.

For Quarts de Chaume Grand Cru, yields must be below 20 hl/ha and grapes can be harvested only if they have more than 298 g/l sugar, equivalent to potential alcohol of 18%.[35] This means that grapes are required to have so much sugar that after fermentation comes to an end, at least 85 g/l residual sugar should remain, but in a good vintage there will be a lot more. Claude Papin, president of the Syndicat Quarts de Chaume, says that, "The typicity of Quarts de Chaume should come from the terroir and climate of each vintage and not from wine-making techniques." This refers to the controversy as to

Mist rises over the Quarts de Chaume in the morning, but blows off in the afternoon, creating ideal conditions for development of botrytis. Courtesy Domaine Baumard.

whether techniques should be allowed to increase concentration during vinification.

The technique in question is called cryo-extraction. It mimics a feature of making ice wine, when berries are allowed to hang on the vine into the winter, until it becomes cold enough for them to freeze. They are harvested at night in the frozen state, and pressed immediately, while still frozen. Ice crystals that have formed within the berries effectively remove some of the water, which increases the concentration of the must. Large berries are more susceptible, because they have more water. Cryo-extraction creates a similar situation artificially by putting very mature berries into a freezer for a few hours before they are pressed.

Should cryo-extraction be used to make a wine such as Quarts de Chaume, I asked Florent Baumard, who has one of the largest holdings in the appellation, and is embroiled in controversy about his use of the technique. "First we should talk about cryo-selection not cryo-extraction, cryo-extraction is an improper term. We select grapes in the vineyard, but the berries are very delicate and easily ruined, when you try to remove individual berries (that you don't want) you can damage the others. [So we put] the berries into cold chambers for several hours below freezing temperature, and when you press, the juice comes from the more mature berries. This is a supplementary selection, not a concentration." Yet the question remains: is the wine as good when concentration is increased by cryo-extraction compared to botrytis or passerillage (desiccation) in the vineyard?

Florent's main objection is that people should not tell him how to make good wine. (Welcome to France!) "People say that cryo-selection abolishes the expression of terroir, but these wines—13 vintages of Quarts de Chaume—are all completely different. Contrary to views that it's not authentic, cryo-selection magnifies the terroir. I don't want to be pushed into Vin de Table, because I am an ambassador for the region. I have used this since 1987 and have never hidden what I am doing." It's a fair point that Baumard's Quarts de Chaume, irrespective of whether and to what extent cryo-extraction was used in any year, is one of the great wines of the appellation. But it's also a fair point that the technique bypasses the expectations of the consumer who is paying a hefty premium for Quarts de Chaume based on the fact that it's extremely expensive to select berries individually by successive passes through the vineyard.

In any case it seems reasonable for regulations supported by the vast majority of producers in the appellation to exclude the technique (which will be banned in the grand cru from the 2020 vintage). What is surprising, however, is that while there is controversy about Baumard's use of cryo-extraction, there's no general criticism of the fact that chaptalization is allowed in Coteaux du Layon (it is no longer permitted in Quarts de Chaume). For a dry wine, chaptalization changes the character indirectly, because all the added sugar is converted to alcohol. For a sweet wine, however, chaptalization must mean that the added sugar ends up directly sweetening the wine. The effect is just the same as adding sugar to the completed wine (which would be illegal). The better producers don't use chaptalization, of course, but the reputation of the appellation is undermined by the practice, and it's hard to see how any sweet wine appellation can have credibility when chaptalization is allowed.

Reference Wines for sweet Anjou	
Coteaux du Layon	Domaine Philippe Delesvaux
Coteaux du Layon Villages	Domaine Vincent Ogereau, Harmonie
Coteaux du Layon Chaume	Château Soucherie
Quarts de Chaume	Domaine Baumard
	Château Pierre Bise
Bonnezeaux	Château de Fesles

Touraine

Touraine	4,325 ha
Vouvray	2,200 ha
Montlouis	370 ha
Chinon	2,350 ha
Bourgueil	1,350 ha
St. Nicolas de Bourgueil	1,075 ha
total	*13,150 ha*

Production

Red	3.8 million cases
Rosé	400,000 cases
White	2.1 million cases
Sparkling	1.5 million cases

Moving from Anjou to Touraine, the balance shifts to red wines, which come from the western edge of Touraine. The rest of Touraine is devoted to white wines, ranging from dry to sweet. The heart of production for quality white wine is the single appellation of Vouvray, north of the Loire just to the east of Tours, together with Montlouis across the river to the south. Because Vouvray is at the limit between Atlantic and Continental influences, where winds from the sea and winds from inland meet, vintage has a particularly strong effect. There's huge variation as to whether still wine is made (in the better vintages) or whether it's converted into a sparkling wine (in less successful years). The choice of style may not be made until September. With the recent warming trend, sparkling wine production has decreased, and the proportion of sweet and semi-sweet among the still wines has increased. A generation ago a minority of harvests gave sweet wines; now it is a majority. Harvesting has moved two weeks earlier since 2000, and botrytis occurs more often, especially when there is an Indian summer into October. Now the problem can be lack of acidity whereas previously it was lack of alcohol.

The wide range of styles with regards to sweetness makes it difficult to define typical character for Vouvray. Producers mostly do not specialize: wine styles are determined more by vintage conditions than by choice. A tasting at even a small producer is a protracted affair, because all producers make wines at all sweetness levels: there's usually sec (dry) and demi-sec (off-dry), and when conditions permit, moelleux (sweet) and liquoreux (very sweet), in increasing order of sweetness. "We are just at a point of balance here, one talks of the Loire as the northern limit for grape growing. So there can be great differences depending on vintage. This is why Vouvray varies so much that it is the one appellation of France where all styles of wine are possible," says François Pinon. This has its advantages, however; when I asked François if he had a problem with alcohol levels being pushed up by global warming, the answer was simple. "Not at all, if that happens I make a demi-sec." His general view is that, "Chenin is not an aromatic variety, it is very versatile, a chameleon, and its character depends on the terroir and vintage. In 2011 we made mostly Pétillant, in 2003 mostly moelleux. Our philosophy is to get the best berries possible, but Nature decides..."

Personally, I am inclined to find the most interest in the wines at both ends of the spectrum. The dry wines can show Chenin Blanc character, although it can be partly obscured by the tendency to leave just a little residual sugar

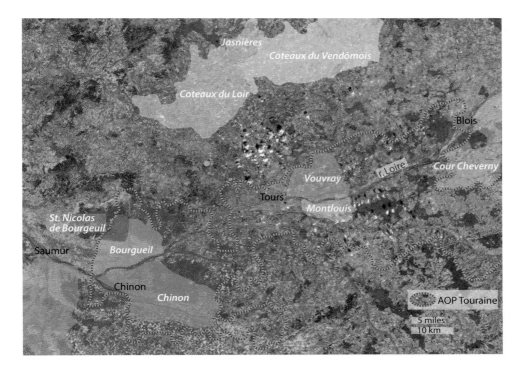

The vineyards of Touraine stretch from Chinon to Blois. The regions adjacent to Anjou at the western edge focus on reds; the rest of the region focuses on whites. The generic AOP Touraine includes geographical subdivisions of Touraine-Azay-le-Rideau, Touraine-Amboise, and Touraine-Mesland. Other appellations lie to the north.

(wines can be labeled dry even if they have more than the usual limit of 4 g/l residual sugar under an exception that applies when acidity is high enough). When you quiz producers or sommeliers in the region as to whether a wine is dry, the usual euphemism is to say, "Well, it's fruity." Versatile but unpredictable might be a fair summary of style in Vouvray. "How dry is the sec?" I asked Anthony Hwang, the new proprietor at Domaine Huët. "It depends from year to year. If acidity is high, fermentation is stopped sooner; the objective is to taste dry." At the other extreme, where wines have sweetness at the high end of the moelleux range or into liquoreux, intense concentration can also bring out Chenin Blanc typicity in the style of dessert wine: sweet, honeyed (if there has been botrytis), nutty, often with strong acidity.

The producers of Vouvray mostly don't seem to believe in truly dry wines: the informal retention of the sec-tendre category may indicate where their heart lies. This has more sugar than qualifies for sec, but not enough to be demi-sec (what the Germans would call halbtrocken or half-dry). However, it is not legal to use sec-tendre on the label. My main complaint about the intermediate levels of sugar is that when the wines are young, the sweetness tends to obscure the character of the grape and give a somewhat one dimensional impression. For me the line is crossed into losing typicity around the transition to demi-sec.

With that tendency towards residual sugar even in the nominally dry wines you might think Vouvray would be the perfect white wine for the Coca Cola generation. There seems to be an attitude here (somewhat akin to the old

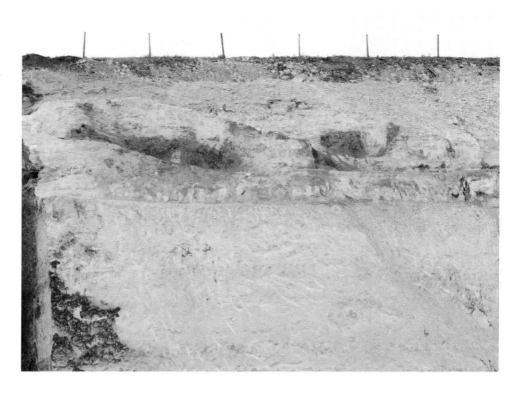

attitude in Germany before the trocken trend swept through Riesling) that a little sugar is needed to bring out flavor and to counteract intrinsic bitterness in Chenin Blanc. My main concern about Vouvray is that there isn't always enough flavor concentration to stand up to the sugar (until you get to the very sweet). As the sweetness category is often not indicated on the label for wines that are sec or demi-sec, the only safe attitude is to assume a Vouvray is likely to be off-dry unless there is specific information to the contrary.

Character for me shows most clearly in the sec and moelleux categories, but you do have to taste them at the right point in development to see this most clearly. "You see the purity of the terroir straight away with the dry wines, but you have to wait to see it with sweet wines," Anthony Hwang believes. "Chenin Blanc takes at least five years to show its typicity. The more concentration of sugar you have, the longer you have to wait. A sec will show after 3 years, a demi-sec after 5 years, a moelleux after 5-10 years, and the very sweet wines only after ten years. The sugar hides the expression of the variety," says Bernard Fouquet of Domaine des Aubuisières.

Vouvray runs for 20 kilometers along the north bank of the Loire. The best vineyards are the premier coteaux, immediately beyond the alluvial soil along the river, and around the town of Vouvray, but the appellation extends well inland. The soil type is known locally as perruches, a greenish clay containing

large flinty pebbles. This is considered to give the most
delicate, even austere, wines.
Beyond, on the plateau, the soils
have more clay over the typical
tufa rock, a soft yellow limestone, that is characteristic of the
area, but there is significant heterogeneity.

The character of Vouvray, or
perhaps one should say the
characters of Vouvray, are captured by Domaine Huët, one of
the oldest, and certainly the
most famous, producer. The
domain holds three of Vouvray's

Les Bournais on the edge of the Loire in Montlouis has a few rows of
ungrafted vines. Courtesy François Chidaine.

most important vineyards and makes wines at all levels of sweetness from each
of them. So here is an opportunity to compare the effects of terroir and sweetness. Le Haut Lieu is one of the highest points on the plateau just above the
town, facing south towards the town. It has heavy clay soil over the tufa rock.
Just below, Le Mont has the classic perruches soil. Overlooking the church in
Vouvray, and dating from the eighth century, Clos du Bourg is the oldest vineyard in the appellation. This has the shallowest soil, only a meter deep, directly
above the tufa rock.

The dry wines offer a striking demonstration of the effect of terroir on
Chenin Blanc: character goes from forward and supple at Le Haut Lieu, to
broad and rich at Le Bourg, and tight and backward at Le Mont (always the last
vineyard to be picked). The reputation of the domain was made with its sweet
wines, especially at the moelleux level. But their very nature, the extra concentration and flavors produced by passerillage or even more by botrytis, make it
more difficult to see terroir; at this level the reputations of the individual vineyards come more from their propensity to allow the necessary ripening and
development than from direct effects of terroir on flavor development as such.

Across the river, the terroir is more homogeneous in Montlouis. The appellation forms a small triangle lying between the Loire and Cher rivers. Although
there are some soils of perruches, they contain less schist than in Vouvray,
making the wines of Montlouis softer. Montlouis makes the same range of
wines as Vouvray, from sec to moelleux. With vineyards running down to the
river in Montlouis, you might expect more focus on botrytis, but the problem
here is that it's not usually hot enough; so if there is rot it is not necessarily noble, and botrytized wine is less common than in Vouvray. Whenever it is
possible to compare Vouvray and Montlouis directly from the same producer,

The top vineyards of Vouvray are on the slopes just above the town, overlooking the church.

the difference shows most clearly in the moelleux wines, where Vouvray has more intensity than the Montlouis.

Even with the increase in the proportion of still wines resulting from warmer vintages, more than half of Vouvray's production remains in sparkling wine. (Sparkling wine production originated in the first world war as a result of the opportunity created by shortage of Champagne.) Production today includes two styles: Crémant (Méthode Champenoise) and Pétillant, which has lower pressure (see Chapter 4).

The northernmost vineyards in the west of France are about 50 kilometers north of the city of Tours, centered on the Loir river (with no "e" at the end, this runs parallel with the Loire). The terroir has the usual base of tufa, but it's cooler here than in the appellations in the center of Touraine. This is an area that was devoted to Pineau d'Aunis from around the ninth century, and the Coteaux du Loir is effectively the last remaining place where it is still grown in France. In better vintages it makes a red wine, but in poorer vintages may be used for rosé. The best of the three northern appellations is Jasnières, where there are some fine, almost delicate, white wines from Chenin Blanc. Most are dry or demi-sec, but there are moelleux wines in good vintages. Comparing the

Reference Wines for white Touraine	
Vouvray (sec)	François Pinon
Vouvray (demi-sec)	Vincent Carême, Tendre
Vouvray (moelleux)	Domaine Huët, Clos du Bourg
Vouvray (liquoreux)	Domaine Huët, Cuvée Constance
Montlouis (sec)	François Chidaine, Les Bournais
Jasnières (sec)	Domaine Bellivière, Calligramme
Chinon	Bernard Baudry, La Croix Boisée
	Charles Joguet, Clos de la Plante Martin

relationship to the most famous vineyards of Germany, Jacqueline Friedrich says, "If Rheingau is Savennières then Jasnières is Mosel".

There is some Chardonnay in Touraine, as AOP Touraine allows Chardonnay to be used but not to be stated on the label, although monovarietal Sauvignon Blanc can be named on the label. An unnamed Touraine AOP Blanc may therefore be Chardonnay rather than Sauvignon, although strictly speaking the proportion of Chardonnay is supposed to be limited to 20%. There is in fact some monovarietal Chardonnay, but when it is presented for approval, the producer describes it as a blend, another example of the tricks producers are forced to play to survive in the system.[36]

Widely planted in Anjou and Touraine, Cabernet Franc is the most important black grape of the Loire. A major part of it goes to make Cabernet d'Anjou, which although named for the variety, is in fact a rosé, not a red wine. Both the rosé and the red can also include Cabernet Sauvignon, although this is not common. In addition, there is some Gamay, which is used for Anjou Gamay and for Touraine red and rosé.[37]

The appellations for red wine are adjacent at the border between Anjou and Touraine. The burning question is whether each appellation has a distinct character. "The difference with the other (red wine) appellations is that Chinon has more diversity. Typicity really depends on the soils," says winemaker Kevin Fontaine at Domaine Charles Joguet in Chinon. "There are really two styles: the fruity ones where the fruit overpowers the wine; and the others that are more vins de garde where the tannins are more evident and drive the structure." At Château Hureau, Philippe Vatan agrees. "Chinon is larger so there is greater variety of terroirs. The character of Saumur-Champigny is that the tannins are sterner. But there is more resemblance

Cabernet Franc

Saumur
        570 ha   340,000 cases
Saumur-Champigny
        1,465 ha   900,000 cases
Chinon
        2,050 ha   1,100,000 cases
Bourgueil
        1,300 ha   740,000 cases
St. Nicolas de Bourgueil
        1,050 ha   675,000 cases

The top regions for Cabernet Franc lie at the border between Anjou and Touraine, with Saumur and Saumur-Champigny of Anjou adjacent to St. Nicolas de Bourgueil, Bourgueil, and Chinon of Touraine.

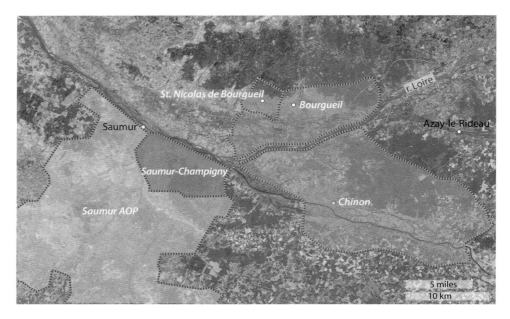

between Saumur-Champigny and Chinon made in the same style than among the wines of either individual appellation." Across the river, Yannick Amirault has vineyards in both Bourgueil and St. Nicolas de Bourgueil. "There's large diversity in terroir and no single typicity for either appellation. You can find the same types of soil in St. Nicolas or Bourgueil. St. Nicolas has a reputation for lighter wines but that's due to yields and the policies of the individual vignerons. In a blind tasting you cannot tell the difference between St. Nicolas, Bourgueil, and Chinon," he says.

Chinon is divided into roughly three parts: the plain, the coteaux (slopes), and the plateau. Along the river Vienne towards the southern border, only some of the plain, where the terroir is generally sandy, is considered appropriate for AOP wine. Extending up the slopes of the coteaux going north, the best terroirs are often calcareous, forming a line more or less parallel with the river Vienne to its north. This is where most of the famous single-vineyard Cabernet Francs originate. Then up above lies the plateau, where the soils are sand and silt, based on subsoils of sand and clay with some flint.

While there may be some stereotypes for the appellations, in reality each appellation offers a range of styles. The general tendency is to lighten up the wines, and at entry level the wines tend to follow a similar style: Cabernet Franc is not a variety to make overtly fruity wine, but relatively speaking, the wines are light, fruity, fresh, and approachable for drinking in the short term. But top producers are increasingly focusing on demonstrating the effects of terroir. Sometimes this is achieved by cuvées from single vineyards with different terroirs, sometimes by assemblage from several small plots all with the same

sort of terroir. The old idea of assemblage from lots that come from plots with different, complementary, properties is no longer fashionable.

Some producers make a range of wines from entry level up to top cuvées. The difficulty here is distinguishing between them, as there is no system to indicate the underlying character of the terroir. In Burgundy, you know at once that a Bourgogne will be a producer's simplest wine, and a very different affair from a premier or grand cru. In the appellations of Anjou and Touraine, there is nothing to distinguish the cuvées except the producer's individual names. Sometimes these may represent a generic wine, sometimes an assemblage from plots, sometimes a single vineyard. But seeing a wine in isolation—for example on a restaurant list where there is no external guide to quality—it can be impossible to place in the hierarchy.

There's almost as much Cabernet Franc in the Loire as in Bordeaux, but the difference is that in Bordeaux it is almost always part of a blend, whereas in the Loire it is most often vinified as a monovarietal. So it's really these Loire reds that offer the best opportunity to see the varietal character of Cabernet Franc. But different producers have very different ideas on how this should be achieved.

"The Loire doesn't really have a tradition of barriques; people have used all sorts of wood and other containers in the past," says Jacques Couly, of Couly-Dutheil, the most famous producer of Cabernet Franc in Chinon. "My father and grandfather matured the wine in large casks. We asked whether we should go back to tonneaux (900 liters) or use barriques. I tried wines in tonneaux and I wasn't very enthusiastic—and they are not very practical. So barriques came in." But after the 2000 vintage, Jacques decided that the wines were not as round and ripe as they should have been. Under the influence of his son, Arnaud, yields were reduced and grapes were picked later to increase ripeness;

Chinon has a variety of terroirs. From left to right these soil samples show: alluvial soil near the river; gravel from the plain; clay and yellow limestone from the slopes; clay and white limestone; highly calcareous soils; sand and limestone from the plateau (two examples). Courtesy Domaine Bernard Baudry.

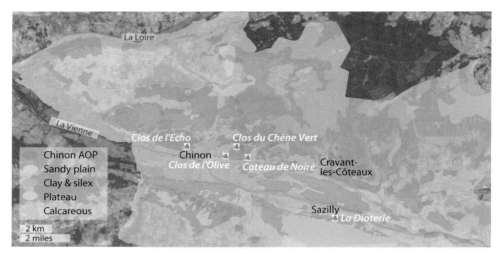

but equally important, in 2003 they threw away the 400 barriques and started to mature the wines in stainless steel.

"Since Arnaud came in, we have done more work on the vineyards and the berries arrive in a much more mature state. So we asked, if the grapes are really good, are barriques needed to achieve roundness? It was a series of choices, from tonneau to barriques to the modern. There is an attitude in France that to make a grand vin you need to mature in barriques. But it's stupid to judge one wine by another. We shouldn't imitate what is happening elsewhere. The Loire is a region; we should ask, is wood the right route? The idea is to put the fruit of Cabernet Franc first; we are the sole region in France to make wine solely from Cabernet Franc, why mask the flavors with wood? Everything now goes into stainless steel. This complicates things and means there must be more work in the vineyards because steel is pitiless in revealing the true character of the wine. It requires the Cabernet Franc to be completely mature."

The immediate question is whether the wines have the same aging potential. Judged by the two most famous wines, Clos de l'Olive and Clos de l'Echo, there is increased purity of fruits without any loss of complexity. "Clos de l'Olive is a true clos in the Burgundian style," says Jacques Couly. Only 5 ha, it is enclosed by walls, and was acquired by René Couly in 1951. The south-facing slope still has some hundred-year-old vines. The Clos de l'Echo is somewhat larger, around 13 ha, and has a variety of exposures, ranging from a flat plateau, farthest from the town, to quite a steep slope running down to the walls of the castle at the bottom.[38]

Given a variety of terroirs and exposure in Clos de l'Echo, "The wine is an assemblage in Bordeaux style," says Jacques Couly. Two wines are made from Clos de l'Echo. The major cuvée follows the new lines at Couly-Dutheil of élevage in stainless steel. Pure fruits meld into mineral and earthy impressions with a touch of tobacco: the epitome of Cabernet Franc. The Crescendo cuvée

Clos de l'Echo is
the only vineyard in
the town of Chinon,
and runs down from
a plateau to the
castle.

comes from some of the oldest parts of the vineyard, close to the château, and is matured exclusively in new barriques. Crescendo is very good, an example of fully ripe Cabernet Franc, but the oak obscures the typicity of the variety. "You might ask, is this Chinon? The French have a single idea in their head," says Jacques Couly. "If a young vigneron made this, it might be refused the agrément. This is idiotic. Chinon used barriques long before." But I am with the dissenters, at least to the extent of asking: if you can show the sheer purity of Cabernet Franc in cuve, what is gained by adding lashings of new oak?

The producer most committed to new oak is probably Philippe Alliet, who treats Chinon like Bordeaux, with extended maturation in mostly new barriques for his top wine, Coteau de Noiré. It's fair to say this is controversial: some regard the wine as preserving the tradition of claret, others believe Chinon should offer a more fruit-driven impression of Cabernet Franc. The other great producer of Cabernet Franc in Chinon, Charles Joguet, pursues a traditional Burgundian policy of increasing oak exposure with the quality of the terroir. In fact, it was Charles Joguet who first introduced the idea of making cuvées from different terroirs when he came back to Sazilly from art studies in Paris in 1959. At that time, most Chinon was sold in bulk. "People thought he was crazy, he was an artist with odd ideas," says Anne-Charlotte Genet, whose family came into the winery in 1995 when Charles decided he wanted to return to art. The entry level cuvée is matured in cuve, but the top Clos du Chêne Vert spends 12-15 months in barriques of one to three years' age. Here there's a clear increase in complexity going up the hierarchy, with that elegant purity of Cabernet Franc most evident in the top cuvées. Coming from a variety of terroirs, the Joguet wines demonstrate the increase in complexity and weight with the progression from sand to gravel to limestone.

Cabernet Franc can certainly make vins de garde in the Loire, nowhere better demonstrated than by Yannick Amirault in Bourgueil and St. Nicolas de Bourgueil. Once again there is a palpable increase in weight going from sand to limestone; all the wines here are relatively stern, but these are the most Cabernet Franc-ish wines in the appellations. Always vinified in wood, these wines bring out the more reserved side of Cabernet Franc.

Saumur-Champigny has the greatest reputation for Cabernet Franc in the Loire, and I am far from alone in regarding Clos Rougeard as its top producer, indeed as the greatest producer of red wine in the Loire. The wines are made by brothers Nady and Charlie Foucault, who are famous for their reserve, but the three red cuvées of the domain absolutely shine out. Their U.S. importer, Joe Dressner, quotes Charles Joguet as saying: "There are two suns. One shines outside for everybody. The second shines in the Foucaults' cellar." Actually, the cellar consists of a rabbit warren of very cold, old caves carved out of the rock under the house. Intensity of Cabernet Franc increases through the three cuvées, the domain wine, Le Poyeux, and Le Bourg (from a single hectare behind the house on the main street in Chacé).

The major characteristic of the house style is the sheer purity of fruits. There is a wonderfully seamless, smooth edge to the Cabernet Franc; you feel you are tasting the unalloyed purity of the variety. The underlying structure is so refined it is hard to see directly. Precisely delineated fruits are supported by a very fine underlying granular texture, with a sheen on the surface. Hints of stone and tobacco show on the finish. All the cuvées offer an unmistakable impression of pure Cabernet Franc, with a smooth generosity to each wine that, in terms of comparison with Bordeaux, might be regarded as more right bank than left bank. The reds are by far the best known, but the white (Le Brézé) is also very fine: concentrated, mineral, and savory.

There are other fine red wines in Saumur-Champigny and Chinon, but it is fair to say that nothing else I tasted on a recent visit to the region left me with that impression of seamless purity. I asked the Foucaults what is responsible for the difference at Clos Rougeard. "We had a chance, our parents never used herbicide; they were the only people in the appellation not to do so in the 1960s and 1970s. The other vignerons mocked us because we had weeds among the vines. And in the 1980s we were the only ones to mature our harvest in barriques; most people only used cuves," says Nady Foucault. The difference is so marked, it's hard to believe that is all there is to it! When pushed, all Nady would add was that they have kept the winemaking practices of their parents and grandparents. But with all due respect, I would be astonished if the wines were this fine two generations ago.

The Foucaults are conscious of the fact that their wines are different. "For thirty years we have been the only ones to respect the lieu-dits and to distinguish our wines by the Burgundian philosophy of climats... This was lost after the second world war when mechanization resulted in the destruction of the walls. Just as Beaujolais abandoned its climats with Beaujolais Nouveau, so Saumur-Champigny became a light, fresh, fruity wine... However, there's a tradition of vins de garde coming from the extraordinary diversity of terroir in Saumur and Saumur-Champigny, and at Chinon and Bourgueil also. Our grandparents distinguished their lieu-dits, and we have done the same, even if today INAO recommends against it... Bourg has always had a famous ability to age, and it would be scandalous to make a light wine to drink immediately," is Nady's general philosophy."[39]

With some rare exceptions, such as Clos Rougeard, I do not think the red wines of Anjou benefit from long aging. Certainly the better wines of Saumur-Champigny, Bourgueil, and Chinon need at least a couple of years after release for the tannins to soften and for the fruits to show: to drink them upon release may be to miss their complexity. But although producers will say, "They can age for ten or fifteen years, no problem," I suspect most are at their best around five to six years after release, and any increasing development with age may be offset by a decline in a fruit density. I would be inclined to drink the top wines between five and ten years after the vintage.

The Loire is pretty far north to grow Cabernet Franc. Even in Bordeaux, father south, ripening is not assured every year, and it's often a problem in the Loire (except perhaps for the Foucaults!) This raises the question: why not blend with another, softer, earlier-ripening variety, as they do, for example with Merlot in St. Emilion? In terms of varieties historically grown in the Loire, no other quality black variety is available; and of course the possibilities have now been set in stone by AOP rules. But in any case, although to do so might make a more reliable wine in most years, you would not get to see that wonderful purity of Cabernet Franc in the top years.

Reference Wines for Loire Cabernet Franc	
Saumur-Champigny	Clos Rougeard, Les Poyeux
Bourgueil	Catherine & Pierre Breton, Franc de Pied
St. Nicolas de Bourgueil	Yannick Amirault, Les Malgagnes
Chinon	Couly-Dutheil, Clos de l'Echo
	Charles Joguet, Clos du Chêne Vert

Sancerre	2,900 ha
Pouilly Fumé	1,250 ha
Menetou-Salon	500 ha
Quincy	260 ha
Reuilly	210 ha
Coteaux de Giennois	200 ha
Chateaumeillant	100 ha
total	5,400 ha
White:	2.8 million cases
Red :	340,000 cases
Rosé :	160,000 cases

281 growers, 390 producers,
33 negociants, 5 cooperatives

"Our white is one of the great wines of the world, with purity, finesse, and fruit. We have excellent terroir for Sauvignon Blanc. We have to keep our heads straight, not to be influenced by other regions of the world, and to keep the typicity that made our wines successful." That's the view from Catherine Corbeau-Mellot at Joseph Mellot in Sancerre. "Purity, finesse, and fruit" is a fair enough way to describe the best wines of Sancerre today; certainly this is a long way from the wines of twenty or thirty years ago that were often quite herbaceous and punishingly acid. "Cat's pee" was the most common description for Sauvignon Blanc at this period. This was the consequence of failing to get the grapes ripe, but since then the view of Sauvignon Blanc has bifurcated. Its fame as a variety in New Zealand comes from pushing expression of Sauvignon's sharp, grassy tang: offset by ripe citrus fruits, this makes an attractive wine with bright, not to say aggressive, contrasts. Sancerre has taken another route, producing a more restrained wine, where the fruit spectrum tends to citrus, sometimes with grassy overtones, sometimes melding into stone fruits of peaches and apricots (but rarely into exotic fruits, such as the passion fruit often found in New Zealand). When I asked winemakers in Sancerre if they had been influenced by New Zealand's success with the variety, all denied any direct effect, but agreed that the modern consumer wants to see more fruit. Their view of the appropriate fruit, you might say, is more traditional than it is in New Zealand.

Loire Centre is the smallest part of the Loire in terms of vineyard area, and its individual appellations are relatively well separated. The vast majority of production in the region is monovarietal Sauvignon Blanc. In fact, Sancerre and Pouilly Fumé dominated the world supply of Sauvignon Blanc until New Zealand's rise to fame. By far the best known appellation in Loire Centre, Sancerre is the largest, extending over six communes, while Pouilly Fumé has about half the vineyard area on the other side of the river. The tiny area of Menetou-Salon is just to the west of Sancerre; Quincy and Reuilly are farther west. Sancerre has the most dramatic terrain, with really steep hills, whereas the vineyards between Reuilly and Menetou-Salon lie on rolling hills.

In the early nineteenth century, Sancerre produced mostly red wine.[40] But Sauvignon Blanc has been planted in the area since the sixteenth century, and was used for producing white wine together with Pinot Gris and Chasselas. Sauvignon Blanc fell out of favor and was replaced by Chasselas (an overproductive, characterless variety), and then came back again after the phyllox-

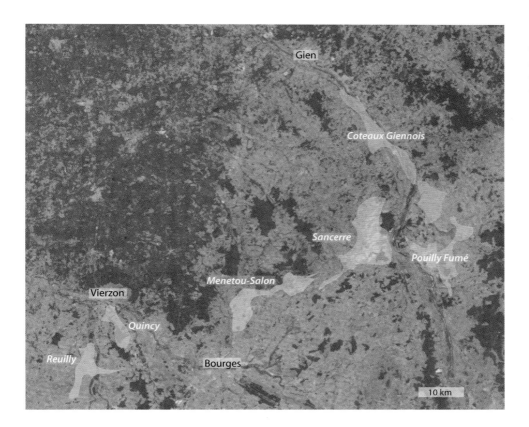

The major
appellations of
Loire Centre extend
over 100 km on an
east-west axis.

era epidemic.[41] But the reputation of the region for quality white wine is more recent. Before Appellation Contrôlée regulations put a stop to such shenanigans in 1936, much of the white wine was sent to Champagne to augment the local product; when this stopped, the Sancerre vineyards declined, until by 1960 there were only 600 ha.[42] Today plantings are up to about 2,500 ha, with 80% of the production being dry white wine from Sauvignon Blanc.[43]

The Centre is actually at the eastern edge of the Loire, but its name reflects the fact that it is central with regards to other vineyards in France. It is at a dividing point. (In terms of political units, Sancerre is part of the Loire while Pouilly-sur-Loire will appear on your GPS under Burgundy. In fact, Sancerre was more or less the western edge of the old Duchy of Burgundy in the Middle Ages.) To the west, the vineyards of Touraine are the Centre's immediate neighbor. Only a little farther in the other direction, to the east, are the vineyards of Burgundy. Chablis and Champagne are to the northeast: Paris is more or less directly north. The Loire Centre's geographical allegiance is connected more with Burgundy and Champagne to its east than with the rest of the Loire to the west; in fact, the same soil type runs from Loire Centre through Chablis to Champagne.

A band of
Kimmeridgian
terroir runs for 150
miles from the most
eastern vineyards
of the Loire,
through Chablis, to
the vineyards of the
Aube.

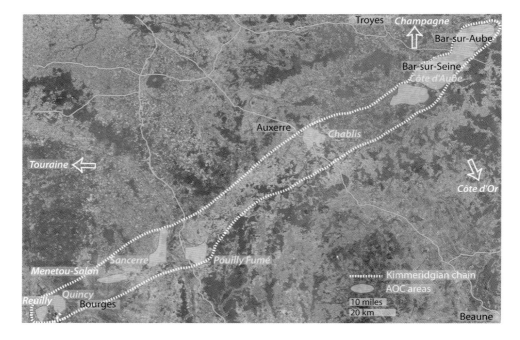

This is Kimmeridgian marl, a limestone with clay formed by marine deposits many millions of years ago. (Occasionally large marine fossils turn up in the
vineyards.) The wine-producing areas are geological islands in what geologist
James Wilson called the Kimmeridgian Chain.[44] It's most famous in Chablis,
but similar terroir is found in Sancerre, and to a lesser extent in the other appellations of Loire Centre. Champagne, of course, is also famous for its chalk
deposits, and the northern end of the Kimmeridgian chain extends into the
vineyards of the Aube, a southern outpost of the Champagne region. It's remarkable that these three parts of the Kimmeridgian chain produce such
different wines: Sauvignon Blanc, Chablis, and Champagne. If appellations
were defined by geology, the Kimmeridgian Chain would be a single appellation (although it would show some climatic differences from one end to the
other). The similarities along the Kimmeridgian chain are emphasized by the
wines of St. Bris, a small area near Chablis that is Burgundy's outpost for producing Sauvignon Blanc. Its relationship to Sancerre makes you realize that the
focus on Chardonnay in one place and on Sauvignon Blanc in the other is as
much due to historical accident as geological imperatives.

Sancerre is the most complex of the appellations of the Centre geologically,
but the same principal three kinds of terroir are found throughout the region.
The Kimmeridgian soils are called Terres Blanches locally, describing their
white appearance. They are common in Pouilly Fumé, prominent in Sancerre,
and peter out in Quincy and Reuilly. Caillottes describes the small pebbles that
cover the lower slopes of hills, and which consist of Portlandian or Oxfordian

The calcareous soils of Sancerre appear white in winter.

limestone (a bit harder in structure). Silex is a completely different type, essentially flint with varying amounts of clay.

A major fault running through Sancerre is the dividing line between terroirs. Most of the limestone is to the west of the fault; most of the flint is to the east, where it's a strong influence in Pouilly Fumé, but it's not a hard and fast rule. The big question is what difference this makes to the style of the wine, and whether there is a consistent typicity for each appellation.

"The Central Loire train's engine is Sancerre. The coaches are, by order of recognition, Pouilly, Menetou-Salon, Quincy and Reuilly," says Claude Lafond of Reuilly. Although Pouilly Fumé may be almost as well as known as Sancerre, it's fair to say that the others are less well established. Until recently it was difficult to make direct comparisons, because producers were entirely local, but now there's something of a move for producers to make wines from more than one appellation. "Menetou-Salon is being bought up by foreigners from Sancerre," one producer goes so far as to say.

Where it's possible to make comparisons, Reuilly, Quincy, and Menetou-Salon tend to be lighter weight; I would not say the fruits are necessarily less ripe, but they seem less intense. The terrain at Reuilly is sandier and less cal-

The three major terroirs are Terres Blanches (Kimmeridgian limestone with some clay), Caillottes (small pebbles of Portlandian limestone), and Silex (small pebbles of flint). Terre Blanches is most common around Chavignol, Caillottes around Bué, and Silex to the east of Sancerre and in Pouilly Fumé, but all three terroirs are found in all areas.

careous, giving white wines with more freshness and less intensity; Menetou-Salon has more heterogeneity (including a rare patch of silex), and Paul-Henry Pellé sees the wines as elegant but not as "large" as Sancerre. The reds also tend to be a little tighter than those of Sancerre, but much depends on conditions of cultivation. "We're right at the limit of ripeness," says Paul-Henry.

When you ask producers what difference they see between Sancerre and Pouilly Fumé, there is usually agreement that there's a difference, but little consensus as to how to describe it. Freshness and minerality are the qualities always mentioned for both appellations. Personally, I've usually found Pouilly Fumé to be a little rounder, a little less aggressive. This may be because of the higher proportion of flint in its vineyards. "It keeps warm during the day, and at night it can be two or three degrees warmer than limestone, so the berries reach ripeness sooner. And drainage is better," says Frédéric Jacquet at Joseph Mellot. But if this is historically true, the difference has been narrowed by the move to greater ripeness. In any case, today's focus on expressing individual terroirs means that the difference between limestone and flint may be more important than the difference between Sancerre and Pouilly Fumé.

Is there any single typicity for Sancerre? "Only that it is Sauvignon," says Stéphane Riffault at Domaine Claude Riffaut. "Each vigneron has his own manner of working and his own typicity." Variation is enhanced by the move towards making wines from single vineyards, which represents a real change in attitude. Sancerre used to be made by assemblage from different terroirs. Many producers still make an entry level cuvée based on assemblage; this is pretty much a necessity for any significant volume of production. But now the best vineyards are often singled out for individual cuvées, supplemented by cuvées that merge lots from parcels sharing similar terroir. The idea that a cuvée should represent a specific terroir is a real reversal from the old objective of gaining complexity by blending between different areas.

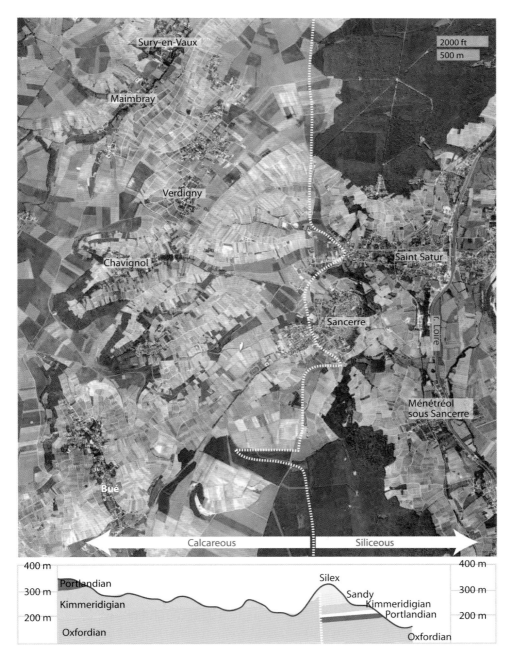

Sancerre vineyards are mostly to the west of the geological fault (dotted white line) that separates calcareous soils from the siliceous soils on the eastern side (map at top). A cross section through a line running from Chavignol to Sancerre (bottom) shows that Portlandian soils are found on the hilltops, Kimmeridgian soils on the slopes, and Oxfordian soils at the bottom. The structure is different to the east of the fault line.

The villages of Sancerre AOP are Sury-en-Vaux, Maimbray, Verdigny, Chavignol, Bué, and Sancerre.

Sancerre made an early decision to focus on the single name of the appellation, so the six individual villages within the AOP are not allowed to attach their names to the label. Yet producers think of their wines in terms of the villages; and wine lists at local restaurants, for example, usually divide the wines according to village. The names of individual sites are a guide to quality and

The hilltop town of Sancerre dominates the local vineyards.

style. The top vineyards are located in Chavignol and Bué. In Chavignol, the best is Les Monts Damnés, followed by La Grande Côte and Le Cul de Beaujeu. In Bué, the best is Le Chêne Marchand—"Whenever a winemaker has Chêne Marchand, it is always the most complex wine in his cellar," says Clément Pinard—followed by Grande (and Petite) Chemarin. Bué's soils have more compact chalk, and less marl and clay, than Chavignol, so tend to finesse and precision, sometimes almost perfumed, whereas Chavignol tends to more powerful expression. There's general consensus on which vineyards are superior, but a tacit agreement that it would be too divisive to try to achieve any formal classification of Crus. "The difficulties and arguments about classification in St. Emilion are a warning about trying to make a classification," says Gilles Crochet of Domaine Lucien Crochet.

Chavignol is famous for its goat cheese, the Crottin de Chavignol, which is supposed to be a perfect match for the wine. However, the locals chuckle when you ask, where are the goats? On the tops of the hills, they say at first. When you point out that the hills are now covered with vineyards right up to the summits, they admit there are no longer any goats in Chavignol: the vine-

yards proved sufficiently profitable that the goats were completely displaced during the eighties. The goats are now in Cosne-sur-Loire, a few miles away, but the AOP remains Crottin de Chavignol. But does it still make a perfect match with Sancerre? The pairing was based on a period when the wine was grassy and herbaceous, with its punishing acidity a match for the sharp tang of the cheese. Is the desertion of the goats a metaphor for the change in style of Sancerre, which with sweet citrus and stone fruits is perhaps no longer any more a match for the cheese than the goats are for the town.

The change in the view of varietal typicity has come with the move to picking later. "In the seventies, people harvested early, they were scared of rain and rot, now with globalization we are obliged to harvest at greater maturity. But it should not go too far, it would be ridiculous if all the wines tasted of mango," says Gilles Crochet. The time of harvest is really critical. "The window of harvest for Sauvignon Blanc is just four days for each block: you have to be in that time if you want to display varietal character," says Jean-Laurent Vacheron. Typicity disappears at over-ripeness in the same way that it's harder to see at under-ripeness.

Mont Damnés, one of the most famous vineyards of Sancerre, rises up steeply immediately behind the village of Chavignol.

Goats were still being kept at Chavignol in the 1970s, but now have been completely displaced by vineyards. (The AOC of Crottin de Chavignol was created in 1976, just before the goats began to disappear. Now they are mostly in Cosne-sur-Loire, a few miles to the north. The cuverie of Henri Bourgeois now stands where the goats used to roam.)

Emphasis on terroir is common now. Yet producer style, especially the decision on time of harvest, has an equally large effect, creating an almost-Burgundian situation in which each producer expresses differences between terroirs in terms of his own style. This may take the form, for example, of a shift in the balance between citrus (emphasized by less ripe sites) and stone fruits (showing up as fruit becomes riper). Alphonse Mellot (père) explains the effect: "The change in flavor comes from the increased fruit maturity. When Sancerre becomes really ripe it loses more tartaric acid than malic acid, and it's the tartaric that gives the citrus impression."

The appellations of the Loire Centre now offer a complete gamut of Sauvignon Blanc flavors. Herbaceousness and cat's pee are rare, but wines in the traditional mode may still show grassy aromas and sweaty overtones. In the mid range, fruits become sweet citrus, ranging from lemon and grapefruit to a delicious touch of lime. Stone fruits begin to creep in for the producers who pick later, with apricots and peaches adding to the flavor spectrum. Gilles Crochet says that you know what style of wine you will get from the color of the grapes at harvest. "The aromatic complexity of Sauvignon Blanc depends on the color of the skin, which indicates which precursors are present. If it's green it has the precursors for grassy or herbaceous aromatics; if it's yellow the precursors give peach and pear; gold gives mangos and passion fruit."

The transition between terroirs shows at Domaine Vacheron from the steely minerality of silex at Les Romains, to the tight citrus of north-facing limestone at Guigne-Chèvres, to the breadth of lime with stone fruits from the clay-limestone at Chambrates, to stone fruits with apricots from very steep, south-facing limestone at Le Paradis. At one extreme of ripeness, François Cotat is usually one of the last to pick in Chavignol. His Caillottes is perfumed with finesse, Monts Damnés shows mature citrus and gooseberries, Cul de Beaujeu is more open with some apricots flavors, and La Grande Côte has hints of peaches and cream. The terroirs seem to be expressed in nuances of ripeness. Details differ for each producer, but the principle is the same.

The general tendency in Sancerre is to use stainless steel for the basic cuvées, and old oak for the more advanced cuvées, but it may be just as important how long the wine spends on the lees before it is bottled. Tasting in Spring 2014, I saw a great difference depending on which vintage was the current wine at each producer. This was not so much because of the difference between the years, or even the extra age of an older vintage, but the result of the time the wine spends on the lees before bottling. When the current vintage was 2013 it had spent only four months on the lees, whereas when it was 2012 it had spent up to a year before release. The difference was like night and day.

There are top wines matured in either stainless steel or old oak, but to my mind the use of new oak is usually a mistake: when there is sufficient fruit concentration, this can certainly make nice wine, but in the case of Sauvignon Blanc it obscures terroir differences. Sauvignon Blanc may not reflect terroir as obviously as, say, Riesling, but the move towards single vineyard wines in Sancerre highlights the interest of different sites.

Sauvignon Blanc is prized for its freshness and usually consumed young, while it is fresh, delicious, and primary. Many of the single vineyard wines need a little more time: about five years after the vintage is often the perfect point to capture full expression. Sauvignon Blanc will develop further, but with a change of character. A typical aging pattern for top wines is to develop notes of truffles and exotic fruits after about a decade. This is a different style: not everyone will like it, and certainly some wines come off with more subtlety than others, as it can be overpowering.

Sancerre's reputation for crisp, mineral, whites far outshadows the reds (and rosés), but there has been enormous progress in the past two decades with Pinot Noir. The reds used to have a similar reputation to the whites: rather thin and acidic; but today's reds are different. Some wines follow the old tradition of Sancerre, showing light fruits of red cherries with good freshness, and just enough tannin to hold the wine for current drinking. Others have moved in the direction of Burgundy, with dense fruits, often showing precision and good delineation of flavors. The best will easily age for a decade. Producers are quick to say that they are not trying to make Burgundy but Sancerre, but in a blind tasting I would not be surprised if the best wines were confused with the more elegant appellations of the Côte d'Or.

"The consumer desires that red Sancerre is fresh, that it represents the character of the Loire. It's a wine of Spring and Autumn," says Jean-Marie

Bourgeois. With this as the stylistic objective, you might think that the wines would not age, but a vertical tasting going back twenty years at Bourgeois shows quite the opposite, with the wines moving in the same savory direction as Burgundy as they age. The cherry fruits of youth become more tertiary, flavors broaden out, and you think about comparisons with the Côte de Beaune.

One sign of the change in emphasis comes from Alphonse Mellot, where a few years back Alphonse fils persuaded his reluctant father to introduce Pinot Noir. Today Alphonse père expresses admiration for his son's foresight, and says forthrightly, "It's difficult to make really good Pinot Noir. If you don't want to reduce your yields to make a top Pinot Noir, you should make a rosé. You can make very nice rosé from Pinot Noir at 80 hl/ha." Tasting through the cuvées, he compares the reds from different vineyards with various parcels of Vosne Romanée. Producing several red cuvées, Alphonse Mellot has taken the lead in Sancerre in demonstrating that Pinot Noir is just as expressive of terroir here as it is in Burgundy. At Vincent Pinard, Clément Pinard shows that Pinot Noir is robust enough to be vinified vendange entière (with the stems). Most of the Pinot Noir in Sancerre is planted on Kimmeridgian terroirs, but Domaine Vacheron is different in focusing its Belle Dame cuvée on siliceous terroir. This brings an elegant, taut quality to the fore, and when you taste the wine, Volnay comes to mind. The last word on the subject goes to Pascal Reverdy: "The image of red Sancerre is the clairet [light red wine], but it's really not true any more."

Reference Wines for Loire Centre	
Reuilly	Claude Lafond, Le Clos des Messieurs
Quincy	Jean-Michel Sorbe
Menetou-Salon	Henry Pellé, Vignes de Ratier
	Philippe Gilbert, Les Renardières
Pouilly Fumé	Didier Dagueneau, Blanc de Fumé
	Jonathan Didier Pabiot, Aubaine
Sancerre	Alphonse Mellot, Les Romains
	Domaine Vacheron, Les Romains
	Henri Bourgeois, Monts Damnés
	Lucien Crochet, Le Chêne
	François Cotat, Cul de Beaujeu
Sancerre (rosé)	Vincent Pinard
	Pascal & Nicolas Reverdy
Sancerre (red)	Alphonse Mellot, En Grand Champs
	Domaine Vacheron, La Belle Dame
	Henri Bourgeois, La Bourgeoise

Muscadet

2012 was very good in Muscadet, although not in much of the Loire because Muscadet harvested early, just before the rains that spoiled the harvest elsewhere (Muscadet is always the first region to harvest). In Muscadet, Spring was precocious and then cold weather blocked development; there was very small production but nice quality as September gave good maturity. 2011 was complicated by a risk of rot that forced producers to harvest early: alcohol levels are low. "In 2011 it was essential to have manual harvest—the machine harvested grapes were terrible. This is why people say that 2011 was a bad vintage and it got such a poor reputation. But it wasn't so hard if you were able to select your grapes," says Marie Chartier-Luneau. 2010 and 2009 were the recent great vintages: 2009 is the richer, but the risk is that its ripeness makes the wine too rich and fat to be a classic representation of Muscadet. 2008 had a freeze that destroyed a major part of the crop, 2007 was very good, 2006 was average, 2005 was good, 2004 was delicate, 2003 was less affected by the heat wave than elsewhere in France, and 2002 was good.

Anjou and Touraine

The big distinction is between dry wines and sweet wines, in particular whether the weather is good enough after the end of the season for botrytis to occur. 2012 was a very difficult year for all wines because of rain: there was almost no sweet wine, and most whites were dry. "In 2012 we were forced to harvest before the rain. We made only three dry wines, one Sec from each property," says Hugo Hwang at Domaine Huët. Conditions were the opposite in 2011, which was too dry for much botrytis: most sweet wines are passerillé, but the dry wines are quite good.

(continued)

	2013	2012	2011	2010	2009	2008	2007	2006	2005	2004	2003	2002	2001
Muscadet		***		***	**	*	**		**	*	*	***	**
Anjou/Touraine white			**	***	**		**		**	*	*		
Anjou sweet white			*	***	***		**		***		**		
Anjou/Touraine red			*	**	***		**		***	*	**	**	*
Centre		**	*	**	**		*		***		*	***	*

The previous years, 2010 and 2009 offer an interesting contrast. As typified by Savennières, but in the Loire generally, 2009 was a rounder year that has more extract and less minerality, generally rich (although not as much as 2005 or 2003). If you really want to see the typicity of Chenin Blanc, it is clearer in 2010. For sweet wines, 2010 offered good development of botrytis. "2009 was a glorious year; every producer was able to decide what they wanted to produce," says Hugo Hwang. For the reds, the extra heat of 2009 produced a richness that is not so obvious in 2010, but Yannick Amirault in Bourgueil says, "The 2010 was for me the great vintage, better than 2009. 2010 is perhaps less gourmand but it has good acidity." At Couly-Dutheil, Jacques Couly says that, "2010 is an aristocratic vintage, but 2009 has richness."

2008 was a difficult year and many wines have vegetal aromas. Although there were sweet wines produced in 2008, they suffer from the same vegetal impression as the dry wines. 2007 was a powerful vintage, perhaps too much so, for dry wines, but made rich sweet wines and ripe red wines. Previously 2005 and 2003 were the richest vintages.

Sancerre & Pouilly Fumé

The 2013 vintage was surprisingly good in the Centre, given difficulties all across France; the wines are lively and fresh. "We were very worried about 2013 but pleasantly surprised at fermentation. The wines have come out well," says Nathalie Lafond. Rain was the difficulty in 2012 but the wines have retained good fruit and freshness. In the end, this is a rich vintage; producers are especially pleased with their Pinot Noirs. "2012 is one of the best vintages for Pinot Noir, it is really ripe, but it is not heavy, it's fresh and elegant," says Clément Pinard.

The precocious vintage of 2011 has given wines with less obvious fruit than 2012 that are attractive in the short to mid term. The difference between 2010 and 2009 is the same as elsewhere: 2010 is more classic, leaner and fresher, while 2009 tends to opulence. Cool wet conditions of 2008 produced wines with high acidity, often developing rapidly; 2007 started in similar fashion but was rescued by a good autumn.

Rain at harvest in 2006 spoiled many wines, and any left are probably now too old. 2005 was an excellent vintage; only the best whites are still interesting, but the reds are just coming into their own. 2004 was too rainy, and 2003 was too hot. 2002 was a classic vintage; the whites have now turned from freshness to truffles, but the top reds are just about right.

The Rhône

From the Côtes to the Heights

I got red blood, and I got blood red wine

Which I bring you, when the snow is heavy on the ground

(Rolling Stones)

The powerful red wines of the Rhône are definitely wines to enjoy in the winter. Viticulture most likely started in the warm climate of the Mediterranean coast when grapevines were brought from Greece to Massilia (now Marseilles) around 600 B.C.E. The importance of wine production increased after the Romans took over Gaul in the first century B.C.E. By the first century C.E., wine production had expanded north as far as Vienne, the capital of mid-Gaul, under the influence of the Allobroges tribe, who were admired by the Romans for their skill in producing a wine called vinum picatum.[1] Under the Romans, wine production became increasingly sophisticated, with the best known wines coming from Marseilles, Vienne, and Narbonne.

The river Rhône flows south from Lake Geneva across Savoie, before turning west to Lyon, from where it flows more or less directly south for two hundred miles before debouching into the Mediterranean near Marseilles. Wine is produced all along the Rhône, from below Lyon to the south of Avignon. Production divides naturally into two regions, the Northern Rhône and Southern Rhône, which are about as distant and distinct from one another as they are from Beaujolais to their north. There is a gap of about 30 miles be-

The importance of winemaking in the Rhône in the Roman era is indicated by the inclusion of several panels devoted to viticulture and vinification in a mosaic showing the agricultural calendar in the third century C.E., discovered in a Roman villa near Vienne. These included treading the grapes (left), operating a wine press (center), and producing amphorae for storage (right).[2]

tween the regions. The major difference between north and south is driven by climate: the Northern Rhône is only a little warmer than Burgundy, but the Southern Rhône distinctly belongs to the warm south. It's a measure of the difference that chaptalization is allowed in the Northern Rhône, but is forbidden in the south. The grape varieties in the north and south are different, but both are definitely red wine country: white wine production is only about 10%. The difference is eloquently put by Ralph Garcin at Maison Jaboulet: "For me the Rhône is ying and yang, it has two heads, Syrah and Grenache, the people are different, there is the north and there is the south."

Although the skinny band of the Northern Rhône extends for more than fifty miles, and the Southern Rhône encompasses a much wider area, spreading far beyond both banks of the river, each region is relatively homogeneous so far as vintage conditions go. It would be unusual to see vintage reports distinguishing one part of the Northern Rhône from another, or one part of the Southern Rhône from another, but conditions can be different between the north and south, with either one distinctly more successful than the other in any particular year.

The Rhône is a rift valley, created when the Mediterranean flooded the area that collapsed between the Massif Central and the Alps after their collision about forty million years ago. To the west, the terrain is based on metamorphic rocks, created by heat; to the east, the rocks are sedimentary, deposited by the floods. The vineyards of the Northern Rhône are on the edge of granitic terrain that stretches all the way across the Massif Central. As the river dug down deeper into the valley it created steep hills on either side, which are at their most dramatic on the west bank. Terraced vineyards were constructed along the river by the Romans. The vineyards of the Southern Rhône are on a base of sedimentary rocks of various types, spread across plains and slopes.

The organization of the two parts of the Rhône is quite different. The North has a series of individual appellations running along the river. Virtually all the wine is vinified under one of these eight AOPs. The Northern Rhône is dwarfed by the South, which occupies a much larger area, and also has a more hierarchical organization. The Côtes du Rhône AOP occupies a vast area in the center of the South; it is the second largest AOP in France (after generic Bordeaux AOP). Surrounding the Côtes du Rhône is a series of regional AOPs, similar in style but lesser in quality. Within the Southern Rhône are individual appellations that are known as "Crus" in the region. The best known of the eight Crus is Châteauneuf-du-Pape, the oldest and most distinguished appellation of the South. The other Crus produce wines that are similar in character, but usually less refined. In addition to dry red and white wines, there's also production of rosé and fortified sweet wines.

Altogether, the appellations of the North account for 4% of production, and their counterparts in the South for another 8%. The Côtes du Rhône accounts for roughly two thirds, and the regional AOPs account for about 20%. Putting the difference in size between the Northern and Southern Rhône into another perspective, the total area of all the vineyards of the northern appellations is about the same as the area of the single major appellation of Châteauneuf-du-Pape in the south.

Besides AOP production, wine is produced under the broad rubric of the IGP Méditerranée (or the departmental IGPs within it), which covers a wide swatch of the Rhône and Provence: most of it comes from the Ardèche (to the west of the Rhône) and the Vaucluse (stretching southeast from Avignon into Provence).

The river Rhône is the dividing line between metamorphic or volcanic rocks (to the west) and sedimentary rocks (to the east). Soils are sedimentary except as indicated. Vineyards of the Northern Rhône are north of Valence; vineyards of the Southern Rhône are south of Montélimar.

Northern Rhône

Area :	3,365 ha
Syrah :	2,775 ha
Marsanne:	350 ha
Viognier:	175 ha
Roussanne:	50 ha
Red :	1.2 million cases
White:	200,000 cases

A single grape variety dominates the varietal reputation of the Northern Rhône for red wine: Syrah is the sole black grape throughout the region. For whites, Viognier is the only grape variety in Condrieu and Château-Grillet, the white wine appellations at the north of the region. It is vinified as a monovarietal wine. The principal white grape changes for the appellations farther south to Marsanne, which is often blended with Roussanne, a related variety, but monovarietals of either variety are also made.

Many imaginative ideas about Syrah's origins (the best perhaps being that it came from Shiraz in Persia) were disposed of by the discovery that it resulted from a (spontaneous) cross between the varieties Dureza and Mondeuse.[3] Dureza comes from the Ardèche (the area to the west of the Rhône), and Mondeuse comes from Savoie (towards the Alps to the east). This suggests that Syrah originated at the intersection, which is to say in the Northern Rhône. Syrah's relationships with other varieties suggest this happened within the last few hundred years.[4] But Syrah today may not be exactly the same as Syrah a century or so ago. Until the nineteenth century, the traditional black varieties were called Serine in Côte Rôtie and Petite Sirrah in Hermitage; they were recognized as being the same variety only in 1846.[5] These old cultivars now represent less than 10% of plantings: since the 1970s they have been replaced by modern clones—with mixed results, as the new clones generally have larger berries and are more productive.

There's some disagreement as to whether Serine is merely local patois for Syrah in Côte Rôtie, or whether it represents a distinct sub-cultivar, but Pierre Gaillard is quite clear about it. "When I started in the 1980s, we had two different types of Syrah. One with round berries gave more alcohol and tannins; but Serine had more ovoid berries. When they started to make the selection with clones, most of the Serine had virus, so the clones mostly came from Hermitage (with the round berries). But now we have some clones from Serine and people are planting them. Serine gives a bit less structure but more complexity in the aromas and flavors." Guillaume Clusel at Domaine Clusel-Roch, who has been involved in a project to perpetuate the old vines from Côte Rôtie, says that, "The clones are more aromatic straight away, and sweeter. Serine is more restrained at first, but more complex later." It's really impossible to say whether any special quality of Serine comes from older vines or a difference in the sub-cultivar, or from lower yields or its unusual pruning system,[6] and it will be interesting to see what style comes from the new clones.

One unusual feature of red wine production in the Rhône has been the inclusion of white grapes in red wine. Plantings of black and white grapevines were historically intermingled, and the grapes were fermented together.[7] The practice was more common in the Northern Rhône, where regulations still say that up to 15% or 20% white grapes can be included.[8] In Côte-Rôtie, Viognier can be used; in Hermitage, Crozes-Hermitages, and St. Joseph, the permitted white varieties are Marsanne and Roussanne. The practice is not common today, but it is still followed by a few top growers, most notably Guigal for some Côte Rôties. "I am convinced that the Viognier brings an interesting aromatic complexity and some fatness, but it is belief only," Philippe Guigal explains. The inclusion (or not) of Viognier in Côte Rôtie today often seems to be as much a matter of history as philosophy. When there are white grapes intermingled with red, producers are happy to include them, but when they replant, it's most often just with Syrah. There's little dissent from the view that a small amount of Viognier can add aromatic complexity, but no strong belief either that it's necessary.

The situation is a bit different outside of Côte Rôtie because of the change in the white grape varieties, and because there is the option of making white wine from them. "Côte Rôtie is different because Viognier is an aromatic grape. For Hermitage it is different, Marsanne and Roussanne were useful to soften the tannins," says Jean-Louis Chave. But he believes the extent of the practice was determined more by market forces. "In Hermitage it's possible to include up to 15% white (in the red). But it doesn't make sense. It was more because demand was more for red so you could increase red production (by including the white grapes) but 15% is way too much." Winemaker Jacques Grange of Delas Frères agrees. "Including white grapes with the reds is a mistake. It's a historical agrément. Often they could not sell the whites so they were allowed to put them in the red, but there is no oenological reason. So here all our reds are 100% Syrah," he says. Better tannin management today means that it's not necessary to soften the tannins of the black grapes, and the white wines are selling well, so almost all the reds of Hermitage, Crozes-Hermitage, and St. Joseph are now 100% Syrah. In the Southern Rhône, the white grape Clairette is occasionally used to increase acidity and lower alcohol in red wines.

The vineyards of the Northern Rhône run along the steep hillsides of the river valley, which make mechanization impossible. The need to work vineyards manually was largely responsible for their decline in the twentieth century. Costs were so much higher than elsewhere that production from the slopes was not competitive. "Except for Hermitage, the vineyards were mostly abandoned in the 1970s, and the few vines that were left were old but mostly not in good condition," recollects Pierre Gaillard. "The wines of this region have character—whether we like it or not—and it was only in the late 1980s

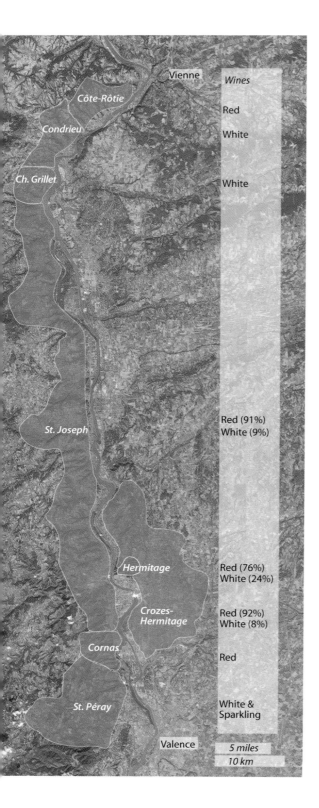

Vienne

Wines

Côte-Rôtie

Red

Condrieu

White

Ch. Grillet

White

St. Joseph

Red (91%)
White (9%)

Hermitage

Red (76%)
White (24%)

Crozes-
Hermitage

Red (92%)
White (8%)

Cornas

Red

St. Péray

White &
Sparkling

Valence

5 miles
10 km

that people became prepared to pay for it. Ironically it was the introduction of herbicides that made it possible to work the terraces," he says.

There's a lot of interest now in the area in moving to organic viticulture. The big difficulty is working the soil. "There's no mechanization. This area was saved by herbicides. Now it's a challenge to get off the herbicides," says Alberic Mazoyer at Domaine Alain Voge. The soils are poor enough that allowing unrestricted cover crops creates too much competition for the vines. But weed control by manual means is backbreaking on the steep terraces—and expensive. "It takes 1000 hours to work a hectare here. We are in France—you can imagine the cost per hour!" says Alberic. Yet the majority of the producers I visited recently are now partially or fully organic.

Most of the wine-growing regions are classified as AOP; six of the eight appellations lie on the western side of the river, with only Hermitage and Crozes-Hermitage on the eastern side. Some outlying areas (often on adjoining flat land) are classified as IGP Collines Rhodaniennes. The best appellations for red wines are Côte Rôtie, near Vienne, and Hermitage, at a turn in the river a bit north of Valence. Indeed, these are the most prestigious appellations in the entire Rhône. The reds of Crozes-Hermitage, St. Joseph, and Cornas are not as fine. Syrah is grown in all appellations except Condrieu, Château-Grillet, and St. Péray, which make only white wine. The change in white varieties going south means there's a stylistic difference between Condrieu or Château Grillet and the white wines of the other appellations. Cornas produces only red wine.

The northern Rhône is a skinny band of vineyards running along the river for fifty miles from Vienne to Valence.

One word describes the terroir of the best sites in the Northern Rhône: granite. Depending on the minerals that were present when granite was formed as the rocks cooled, it can have many different colors, as seen in Côte Rôtie. Although Côte Rôtie means "roasted slope," the appellation is really more a series of slopes, rising up from the river. The best vineyards are on the slopes opposite the town of Ampuis, where the two most celebrated lieu-dits of the Côte Rôtie take their names from the colors of the minerals. Just above Ampuis, the rocks are a mixture of muscovite (white mica) and biotite (black mica), which together give the brown impression that led to the name Côte Brune. Just south of the town, there is white-colored gneiss, which gave rise to the name Côte Blonde. Going on south, the terroir is pure granite. But this should not be taken to mean impenetrable: in fact, the granite is quite friable, and if you hit one of the rocks lying on the surface, it usually breaks up into smaller pieces quite easily. This is not easy terrain to work: many of the hills have very steep inclines, and viticulture is possible only when vineyards are terraced. Sometimes there needs to be one terrace per row of vines. The vines grow as individual bushes.

	ha	bottles
Seyssuel	30	150,000
Cote Rotie	242	1,250,000
Hermitage	136	500,000
Condrieu	133	625.000
Ch. Grillet	4	18,000

Although today Côte Rôtie has a reputation to match Hermitage, the other great name in the Northern Rhône, it was much less well known until recently. During the nineteenth century, Côte Rôtie used to sell at around half the price of Hermitage, but after the second world war, it was being sold off for pennies.[9] Vineyard plantings have gone up and down, from 420 ha in 1907, to 72 ha in 1973, and back up to 242 ha today.[10] Much of the revival is due to the halo effect of Marcel Guigal's series of splendid single vineyard bottlings starting in the 1970s. Until then, most wine was handled by negociants or sold off in bulk; little Côte Rôtie was bottled by growers.

There is more variation in terroir here than in the more compact hill of Hermitage. The plateau at the top of Côte Rôtie is the least distinguished terroir. The ravine of Reynaud is the dividing line between Côte Brune and Côte Blonde. Strictly speaking, Côte Brune and Côte Blonde originated as merely two of the 73 lieu-dits on the Côte Rôtie, but the terms have become widely used to distinguish the northern and southern parts of the appellation. The general difference in terroirs between north and south is that Côte Brune has harder rocks, with more schist, and iron–rich soils, giving the typically taut, structured quality of volcanic terrain. Côte Blonde has more friable granite, and the wine tends to be fine and elegant, with less evident tannic structure. This soil extends into Condrieu.

Côte Rôtie offers the most rounded expression of Syrah in the Rhône. Usually it is softer than Hermitage, although generalizing is difficult given the difference between Côte Brune and Côte Blonde, and variations in winemaking, extending from destemming to inclusion of Viognier. The tradition in the Rhône has been to blend from different terroirs in order to increase complexity. Sometimes, of course, it's a matter of necessity: a producer may have many small lots in different locations. As Pierre Gaillard comments, "You have to do vinification terroir by terroir because of differing maturities. The tradition in Côte Rôtie is to make a blend of Côte Brune and Côte Blonde. There are economic arguments to make small and rare lots, but if you are going to stay in the appellation system, it is best to follow the traditions of the vineyards."

The game changer was Guigal's introduction of single vineyard wines that attracted wide critical acclaim. In addition to the focus on terroir, Guigal also introduced a new style, with long maturation in new oak. La Mouline, La Turque, and La Landonne are splendid wines that stand on their own merits, but it is fair to say that the character is definitely powerful compared to the more delicate, sometimes almost perfumed, wines that traditionalists regard as typical of Côte Rôtie. However, critics might remember that Côte Rôtie was in desperate straits before Guigal spurred its revival.

There's no clear consensus on the use of new oak, although Guigal definitely started a trend. "I don't think old versus new oak is a debate now, although it used to be. I am the first to say new oak can be good or bad for wine," Philippe Guigal says. "We have a single variety—Syrah—and it can be very powerful. By using new oak we have oxidation, which affects the structure of the wines. I cannot change the quantity of tannins, but by doing long aging, for 36-42 months for the Côte Rôties, I can change the quality of the tannins. The wines will show as more subtle and soft when young—and they will age for more than ten years. Using new oak barrels, it's not the aromas that are essential, it's the work on the tannins, making the wine ready to drink." Philippe makes his point with a selection of single vineyard wines from recent vintages:

The steep slope of Côte Rôtie requires terraces every few rows, and vines are grown as individual bushes. Courtesy Inter-Rhône, Christophe Grilhé.

certainly all are powerful and spicy, but tannins are tamed by the fruits, and new oak is not overwhelming. There is also an homage to tradition here in the form of the Brune et Blonde cuvée (a blend from the different areas of Côte Rô-tie) and the Château d'Ampuis (a selection of the best lots from various terroirs).

The tradition of making a single wine by blending different parts of Côte Rô-tie has given way to a focus on expressing differences. Most producers now have multiple cuvées. Sometimes the distinction is terroir, sometimes it is vine age, sometimes it is just selection. Styles vary from perfumed, lacy, and elegant, to powerful and spicy, but the common feature should be a certain smooth-ness. There's almost always a definite step up in quality when Côte Rôtie comes from a lieu-dit; of course, the effect may really be more the other way round, that is, the interest of the regular bottling has been reduced by removing the best lots. I wonder if that is why recently I have had more Côte Rôties that have disappointed me by lacking that traditional plushness.

Before moving on south from Côte Rôtie, we need to make a detour farther up the Rhône, to Seyssuel, north of Vienne. Known as Saxeolum during the Roman era, Seyssuel may have been the source of the wines of Vienne that enjoyed a high reputation during the Middle Ages. Olivier de Serres, in his de-finitive book of 1600, compared them to Côte Rôtie. Subsequently the

The heart of Côte Rôtie is above the town of Ampuis. Slopes rise up steeply from the Rhône.

vineyards had their ups and downs, but 120 ha were being cultivated in 1820. Destroyed by phylloxera at the end of the nineteenth century, the Seyssuel vineyards fell into disarray, and were revived only at the instigation of Pierre Gaillard, who in 1996 persuaded Yves Cuilleron and François Villard to join him in recreating the old vineyards. Under the name of Vins de Vienne, they replanted vineyards and started to produce wines, naming the cuvées for the wines from the area that were famous in the Roman era.

The vineyards are on the east bank of the Rhône, at a point where the river is at its narrowest. The terroir is similar to the Côte Brune, based on schist; when they planted Seyssuel, they had to use a bulldozer and ripper to break up the ground. However, whereas Côte Rôtie faces southeast, on the opposite side of the river Seyssuel faces more southwest. It's better protected from the wind, which is stronger at Côte Rôtie. In addition to Vins de Vienne, each of the three founders has taken one hectare of vines to make their own wine. Now other vignerons have also established vineyards in the area, and Seyssuel counts more than a dozen producers today, with 30-40 ha of vineyards. (Supposedly the few vignerons still working at Seyssuel were asked if they wanted to be included in Côte Rôtie when the appellation was created, but they declined. So Seyssuel falls under the IGP of Collines Rhodaniennes.)

I have been impressed with the wines of Seyssuel. The reds are pure Syrah (there are also some whites from Viognier). They show a refined quality, at least as fine as Côte Rôtie; perhaps, if you are looking for a distinction, a little less round and more precise. They have an unobtrusive structure and a tendency towards silkiness. In each pairwise comparison of wines from the same producer, the wine from Seyssuel seems at least as complex aromatically as the Côte Rôtie, and I sometimes find the texture to be finer.

Returning to the main drag of the Northern Rhône, Côte Blonde runs into Condrieu, where only white wine is produced. Wine has been produced at Condrieu since the Roman era, and in the Middle Ages it was shipped down the river to the popes in Avignon. Little is known about its character then, but it seems to have had a good

Individual vines are densely planted. Each has a supporting pyramid.

reputation. However, by the end of the 1960s, Condrieu, together with its tiny neighbor, Château-Grillet, had what amounted to the last few hectares of Viognier in the world.[11] A revival started in the 1980s,[12] and today Condrieu has 140 ha planted out of a potential area of 262 ha.[13] The AOP turned back towards quality when its size was reduced by about a third in 1986 by excluding all terrain above 300 m elevation. Now there are also significant plantings of Viognier elsewhere in the Rhône and in Languedoc.[14]

A strongly aromatic variety, Viognier can be perfumed and floral, even musky.[15] With relatively low acidity and high alcohol, it is best drunk young. There are enormous quality differences between a top Condrieu with intense aromas and palate, and lesser versions, where the perfume may outrun the fruits; in short Viognier is a variety that needs concentrated fruits to give good balance against its perfumed background. Viognier made from inferior clones that give high yields of less aromatic fruit (of which a good number were planted when its popularity revived) can be clumsy. It can be vinified in a variety of styles from fresh and clean to heavily oaked; this makes it difficult to get a bead on any consistent style for Condrieu.

The main stylistic factors influenced by winemaking are whether to perform malolactic fermentation and whether and what type of oak to use. "Viognier

The old château of the archbishop at Seyssuel is now surrounded by the restored vineyards, planted with the same pyramidal pruning as Côte Rôtie.

has a character of flowers, but flowers and vegetal are very close, and if you don't do the MLF they can be a bit green and vegetal. We pick the Viognier very ripe, and there is very little malic acid, so the MLF doesn't change the acidity very much, but it makes the wine more stable," says Pierre Gaillard. "We use barriques instead of tank because it brings just the right level of oxidation. I did trials with stainless steel but we just got reduction." Another modernist, Yves Cuilleron, also believes in oak. "In the nineteenth century Condrieu was vinified in new oak. Today we use a bit less than 20% except for the vins de garde." He believes that Condrieu's potential for aging is underestimated. "Condrieu has a reputation for (lack of) aging that I think is wrong. Amateurs like the aroma of the young wine, but for me it's a wine with minerality that can age, although of course it changes, and the aromatic complexity becomes different."

Known for the elegance of his wines, René Rostaing has strong views on the subject. "Oak destroys the typicity of Viognier. In France we make wine with grapes, not oak. I'm the adversary of new oak. The source of oak is not important—it's only an instrument. When I am President of the French Republic, new oak will be forbidden in Condrieu." My own view is that Viognier loses its character if too much new oak is used, and for me, too much means any detectable sensation of new oak, because it clashes with the natural aromatics of the grape.

Château-Grillet is an enclave surrounded by Condrieu. Even given its high reputation, it's unclear why this single vineyard should have been picked out as a separate AOP (rather than perhaps being marked as a "Cru" of Condrieu). The answer lies in the politics of the period. "This appellation is located in the heart of the geographical area of the AOP Condrieu. Its history is closely linked to that of Condrieu, however it differs because it has been the property of bourgeoisie from Lyon. This domain has been owned by the Neyret-Gachet family since 1820," is all the justification that appears in the original declaration of the AOP. The mystery is deepened by the description of the wine: "Aromatic white wine is marked by fruits of peach and apricot. Acidity is present but discreet compared to the richness," which is fair enough—but exactly the same words are used to describe Condrieu.

This tiny appellation of 3.5 ha remained in the Neyret-Gachet family until it was sold to François Pinault (of Château Latour) in 2011. The wine has always been rare and expensive, and although like Condrieu it is made exclusively from Viognier, it has been considered quite distinct: wine that should not be drunk young, but should have at least a decade's age. Because it is a monopole, it's impossible to say whether its character is intrinsic to the terroir or depends on specific features of viticulture and vinification. Perhaps connected with the expansion of the vineyard from the original planted area of 1.7 ha to the current area of 3.5 ha during the 1970s and 1980s, the style was considered to be tired by the 1980s. In 2004, Denis Dubourdieu, who was largely responsible for resurrecting white wine production in Bordeaux, was brought in as a consultant. Since then the style has become fresher, but the big question of the moment is what other changes M. Pinault will introduce, and whether he will be able to restore the reputation of this former legend.

Maps usually show a linear progression of appellations down the Rhône: Côte Rôtie - Condrieu - Château-Grillet - St. Joseph, which is how the appellations started, but today there is some overlap because the appellations have been extended. Condrieu was originally three villages at the northern end, but has been extended farther south by four villages. And today St. Joseph is so extended that its northern part overlaps with the southern part of Condrieu: from Chavanay to Limony, growers may plant Viognier to make Condrieu, Syrah to make St. Joseph red, or Marsanne and Roussanne to make St. Joseph white. "In the same village you may have Marsanne to make St. Joseph and Viognier to make Condrieu. The grapes decide the appellation. It's totally crazy," says Jean-Louis Chave, whose family has been making wine in St. Joseph for centuries. This is a unique situation in France. How does it equate with the view that terroir is all-important?

The Condrieu AOP includes 7 villages extending from Condrieu itself to Limony. The three northern villages (Condrieu, Vérin, and St. Michel-sur-Rhône) were included in the original appellation in 1940. The four southern villages were added later and also form the northern part of the St. Joseph AOP.

The wines from the northern part of the Condrieu appellation are richer, bringing out the floral, sometimes exotic, quality of Viognier, with pears, apricots, and honey. In the southern villages, the style is tighter and more mineral. There is also a range from fully dry to sweet wines, going all the way to late harvest, so in short, there is no easy generalization about style. If you really want to see the typicity of Viognier, however, stick to dry wines or to the just off-dry. Aging is a mixed bag: those early, floral, aromatics disappear, and you have to wait for something else to replace them. Its aromatics make Viognier a wine that to my mind can be difficult to match with food: it's a splendid aperitif, although on the richer side. It's sometimes claimed to be good with foods that are difficult to match with other white wines, such as asparagus and artichoke.

Overlapping with Condrieu, St. Joseph extends 40 miles down the Rhône, where at its southern end it faces Hermitage and Crozes-Hermitage. Hermitage has always been the great name in the Rhône, although its role has changed. Ever since the eighteenth century, Hermitage was regularly sold to negociants in Bordeaux or Burgundy to strengthen their wines. During the nineteenth century, as much as 80% of the production of Hermitage was bought by the Bordeaux wine trade.[16] And it was by no means the lesser wines of Hermitage that were sent up to Bordeaux. "The first growths are sent to Bordeaux to be mixed with the clarets which are made up for the English market, and only the second growths are sold in the trade as Hermitage," according to a popular report in 1874.[17] The practice was so common that it gave rise to a verb; to "Hermitager" meant strengthening the wines of Bordeaux (or Burgundy) with stronger wines from the Rhône.

This had to stop after new regulations came into effect at the start of the twentieth century, but the wine continued to be sold in bulk. The white wine had a higher reputation than the red; in fact, negociants were compelled to buy the red in order to obtain the white.[18] Things more or less collapsed after the first world war, with a large part of production moving from small growers to a cooperative, and only four negociants handling the wines. Most of the wine was sold to negociants until the revival of the 1970s. By then, the appellation was almost fully planted.[19] Today about three quarters of production is red.

Because Hermitage is a single hill, its geography restricts the size of the appellation to about 135 ha. It consists of a granitic outcrop, an anomaly that is virtually the only granite on the east side of the river, created when the river changed its course long ago to flow to the west instead of to the east side of the hill. The hill rises directly up steeply above the town of Tain l'Hermitage (originally called Tain until it was renamed to reflect the glory of the wine), with houses extending right up to its base. Retaining walls are used to hold in the topsoil. Southern exposure is an important feature, protecting the vineyards from the north wind and giving

Looking north along the Rhône, the hill of Hermitage stands out for its southern exposure. The northern part of Crozes-Hermitage is also hilly. St. Joseph is on the west side of the river.

good sunlight. "Like the Pinot Noir in Burgundy, we're at the northern extreme of the Syrah's ripening here at Hermitage," according to Jean-Louis Chave, one of the top producers.[20]

There is some variation in terroir around the hill. Granite at the western end changes to stones resulting from glacial deposits at the eastern side. Running round the hill are a series of *climats*, each with its own characteristics. The top climats are the granite-driven sites at the west: Les Bessards, Le Méal, and l'Hermite. If Hermitage was part of Burgundy, many or all of the lieu-dits would be bottled as separate wines, but the tradition here has been more towards blending. Jean-Louis Chave, who is widely acknowledged as the master of blending, explains why Hermitage is different from Burgundy: "What was local in 1936 when the AOP was created? For sure, what was local in Burgundy was to have Crus. In 1936 they thought about having Crus here, but what was local here was to blend wine from different sites to make the Hermitage. It's not like in Burgundy where there are small differences reflected between the Crus, here there is a very big difference from granite to loess—so at the end the question is: what is Hermitage? For sure, you can make wine from Les Bessards or other plots, but they are not Hermitage, they are Bessards etc."

This remains a lively argument in Hermitage. Philippe Guigal sees a difference with Côte Rôtie. "On the heritage, I think it is important to make people realize that, like Burgundy, we have one of the most important precision of terroirs in Côte Rôtie. Many people have followed the example of vineyard bottlings. But also look at Hermitage. Chapoutier says the real Hermitage is a bottling of individual terroirs, but Chave believes that it is a blend. In Côte Rôtie, I like the idea of single vineyards very much. Although there is a difference between south and north, in a blind tasting you end up by saying, this is Côte Rôtie. But for me Hermitage is a melting pot." Following this line of thought, Guigal's top Hermitage is a blend from very old vines, coming from the Grippat vineyards that they purchased a few years ago. The Ex Voto red Hermitage comes from 60-year-old vines from four climats; the white comes from the oldest vines of Les Murets, planted around 1910-1920, together with some from L'Hermite. White Hermitage can be long lived. Philippe says of the white Ex Voto that, "I believe like Chave that we will probably drink our reds before our whites; this should last for twenty years."

If there is any single definition of the character of Hermitage, it is probably Chave's cuvée, with its backbone coming from Les Bessards. "Every year we ask the same question: 'What should Hermitage be like given the conditions of that particular year?'" says Jean-Louis.[21] I wondered whether the parallel here might be more with Bordeaux, where all wines are blended and the blend depends on the year, than with Burgundy? "No, the parallel would be more Burgundy, because Bordeaux blends different grapes and they often blend early to find the balance. We are more like Burgundy, everything is vinified separately and at the end we blend." So Jean-Louis feels that blending terroirs is quite different from blending cépages.

Assessing the effect of terroir is difficult in Hermitage, because relatively few producers make separate cuvées. But a barrel tasting at Chave is an education in terroirs. The striking differences immediately make Jean-Louis's point about the extent of terroir differences compared to Burgundy. The most tannic wine for most producers usually comes from Les Bessards, which is the backbone of several important Hermitage bottlings. At Chave, it's the most concentrated, tannic, and tight: for me, this is the barrel sample that most directly fits my image of Hermitage. Just to the east of Les Bessards, turning from southwest to pure south-facing, lies Le Méal, where small stones near the surface mean it is always hotter than Les Bessards. Less granite brings a less austere, fuller, fruitier, impression. Chave's sample gives a great impression of refinement. L'Hermite is above Les Bessards and Le Méal; soils vary more here, and it is

planted with a mix of white as well as red grapes. Chave's barrel is less concentrated than Les Bessards, but smoother and more refined. At the very top of the hill, Les Grandes Vignes does not ripen as reliably as l'Hermite, Le Méal, and Les Bessards below it. Farther round the hill, at the northern limit, Rocoule is quite structured, but aromatic; Péléat just below is softer and rounder; and Beaume farther west is more animal. "You have to balance the character of the vintage: in a soft year you need more backbone; in a year that gives tight wine, the flesh is more important. In a cool year Le Méal will be more important in the blend than Les Bessards, in a warm year it will be the other way round. What is important is the balance at the end," Jean-Louis says.[22]

Another important blended wine, which for many years defined Hermitage, is Jaboulet's La Chapelle. The name comes from the chapel that stands on Jaboulet's part of Les Bessards (reputedly constructed by the Chevalier de Sterimberg, the original hermit in the thirteenth century). "What made Hermitage famous fifty years ago was La Chapelle, but it's a commercial name, not a vineyard, and it was 1,500 bottles; in a small place like Hermitage, this was a big quantity, and it was only possible because of blending," Jean-Louis explains. The blend was heavily based on the large holding of Le Méal that Louis Jaboulet built up over three decades starting in the 1950s.[23]

La Chapelle was one of the great wines of Hermitage through the 1960s, and the 1961 is legendary, but it seems to me that concentration declined through the nineties. Part of the problem may have been a great increase in quantity—9,000 cases by year 2000—but production of La Chapelle has been decreased since 2001 with the introduction of a second wine, La Petite Chapelle. Quality began to recover after Jaboulet was sold in 2006 to the Frey family (who own Château La Lagune in the Médoc). "La Chapelle had to be-

The hill of Hermitage (seen from across the river) rises up immediately behind the town of Tain l'Hermitage, folding round a turn in the river.

come what it used to be. When we took over, we decided to keep Petite Chapelle and make it more fruit-driven, more approachable young. It's a second wine, but it's not a simple declassification—sometimes some lots are shared between the wines," explains Ralph Garcin at Jaboulet.

Ownership of Hermitage is quite concentrated, with two thirds held by the large firms of Chapoutier, Jaboulet, and Delas, or bottled by the cooperative. With 26 ha of Hermitage, as well as a further 5 ha that are leased, Chapoutier controls almost a quarter of the Hermitage hill. The major production is under a brand name, Monier de la Sizeranne, but Chapoutier also produce one of the few examples of a vineyard series, comprising Les Greffieux, Le Méal, L'Hermite, and Le Pavillon.[24] Here is a direct reflection of the reputation of each plot in the ascending price of the series (Le Pavillon comes from Les Bessards).[25] The step up in quality from Monier de la Sizeranne to the vineyard plots is striking. On the one hand, it makes you wish there were more examples where expression of terroir could be represented; on the other, it makes the point that even on the fabled hill, some plots of Hermitage are less equal than others. However, relatively few of the more than twenty producers of Hermitage produce individual vineyard wines.[26]

Since its revival, Hermitage has never been particularly cheap, but the top single vineyard bottlings have increased in price disproportionately relative to communal Hermitage. One incidental complication in trying to understand the characteristics of each *climat* is that the special vineyard bottlings usually come from the oldest vines in the plot.[27] The problem in forming a view of the typicity of Hermitage is that the major volume of blended wines no longer has its former intensity, and there are few (among which Chave is at the top and La Chapelle hopefully will resume its position there) with the sheer quality to compete with the single vineyard bottlings.

Red Hermitage can be stern when young, but very long-lived, developing savory flavors resembling Bordeaux after ten or twenty years. That was a fair assessment until the recent warming trend. Since then there has been something of a move here as everywhere else to wines that are more attractive when young, displaying forward, primary fruits. With regards to producing wines that are easier to drink, I realize it's damned if you do, and damned if you don't, but I do wonder whether Hermitage should ever be easy and approachable? Syrah as a grape certainly has the potential to produce extremely lush wines; the more dramatic and forceful examples of Australian Shiraz (the New World name for Syrah) can be quite overwhelming in their powerful aromatics of black fruits. But "we can't make Shiraz and they (Australians) can't make Northern Rhône Syrah, it's just impossible. They are completely different wines made from the same grape," says Ralph Garcin. The classic description of red Hermitage was always "pepper," associated with something short of what would today be regarded as real ripeness. This is rare now, as the expression of Syrah in Hermitage has moved more in the direction of black plums. Yet most wines still retain good freshness.

The southern exposure, hillside slopes, and granitic soil explain Hermitage's unique quality. Crozes-Hermitage is much larger, at about 1,500 ha, and spread out in a semi-circle, with the hill of Hermitage at the bull's eye. Only a rather small proportion of Crozes-Hermitage is produced by domains actually in the appellation. More than half comes from small growers who send their grapes to the cooperative at Tain l'Hermitage, another cooperative accounts for a further 10%, and many of the remaining vineyards are owned by the large negociants (Chapoutier, Jaboulet, and Delas). Probably less than 20% actually comes from producers whose focus is on Crozes-Hermitage.

	ha	bottles
Crozes-Hermitage	1,514	8 million
St. Joseph	1,211	5 million
Cornas	131	525,000
St. Peray	73	250,000

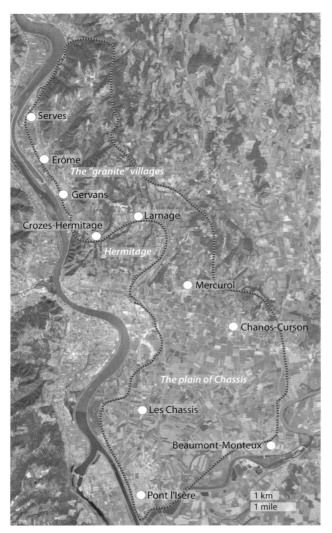

The northern part of Crozes-Hermitage produces more structured wines from the four granite villages along the river; the southern part produces more fruit-forward wines from the plain of Chassis.

Like many other appellations in the Northern Rhône, Crozes-Hermitage started as a small area immediately around the village, just north of Hermitage. As it became successful, it expanded into the surrounding areas. Crozes-Hermitage is now the largest appellation in the Northern Rhône, but it's fair to say that quality is more or less proportional to distance from the original village. There's a split personality between the northern and southern parts of the appellation. The steep hillside vineyards based on granite hills to the north give taut wines, whereas the southern plain of Chassis gives wines that are simpler and fruitier. None of this, however, is of much relevance to the consumer, since so far as the label is concerned, Crozes-Hermitage is Crozes-Hermitage. The producer's name is the more important guide.

It's hard to find growers who emphasize expression of local terroir. Philippe Belle is an exception—he even has examples of the soils from different terroirs in his tasting room—and his cuvées highlight the characteristics of each terroir. Coming from pebbly terroir on the plain of Chassis, Les Pierelles has the most forward fruits—"Everything is destemmed, because we want fruit," says Philippe— but the structural underpinning brings some character and shows that the plain doesn't have to be as simple as it often is. The grapes for Cuvée Louis Belle (from white clay terroir around the winery in Larnage) and Roche Pierre (granitic terroir) are partially destemmed "Because these are vins de terroir." Moving into more granitic terroir there is an increasingly taut edge to the fruits. Crozes-Hermitage is never going to compete with Hermitage—for one thing, most of the best growers produce both wines so Crozes will always be second—but the "granite" villages in the north deserve more overt recognition.

The focus in Hermitage and Crozes-Hermitage is on Syrah, which is planted on the best granite terroirs; the white grapes of Marsanne and Roussanne are planted elsewhere *faute de mieux*. Roussanne is usually reckoned to be the finer grape, but is difficult to grow. Marsanne is the more widely grown; it does not do especially well on granite soils, but does better on the other soil types, such as clay and chalk.[28] Often blended together, Marsanne and Roussanne make a dry wine with savory and herbal aromas and a nutty (sometimes bitter) taste. The overall impression is aromatic and a little perfumed, with a dry finish that emphasizes the perfume. Marsanne (and Marsanne-Roussanne blends) tend to be dumb at first, often needing three or so years for flavor to emerge. One objective of winemaking is to control the (potential) bitter taste.

The chief exponent of Marsanne is Chapoutier, who makes a 100% varietal Hermitage. "The structure is the bitterness," says Michel Chapoutier, "Marsanne is the only grape variety that can live a long time without much acidity."[29] "The bitterness is a mark of Marsanne: I call our whites, tannic white wines," says Alberic Mazoyer at Domaine Alain Voge. Guigal also makes a pure varietal, while Chave includes 15% or so Roussanne. The most important blended white wine in Hermitage is Jaboulet's Chevalier de Sterimberg, with about a third Roussanne. White Hermitage is usually reckoned to be at its best after about ten years. The problem with whites from Crozes-Hermitage is that there is often not enough fruit concentration to compensate for the low acidity.

Across the river from Hermitage, the southern part of St. Joseph surrounds the town of Tournon-sur-Rhône. Originally this *was* the appellation in 1971, consisting of 97 ha in the villages immediately to the north and south of Tournon (from St.-Jean-de-Muzols to Mauves). Then it was expanded dramatically. "In the early 1990s, I saw the appellation of St. Joseph slipping away from its original values, due to quick over-expansion," says Jean-Louis Chave,[30] who lately has been replanting the vineyards that his family first cultivated in 1481. That is quite a mild statement considering the extent of the expansion into land that used to be only Côtes du Rhône. St. Joseph grew to 540 ha in 1989; today it is 1,200 ha. This is the old phenomenon of *fureur de planting*, historically leading to a boom and bust cycle. The local Syndicat has finally taken the situation in hand and proposes to remove unsuitable vineyards from the appellation—but only starting in 2021![31]

With the appellation extending for 40 miles along the river, it is not surprising that there is a difference between the northern and southern parts. "In St. .Joseph there are years that are better in the south versus the north, but the soils are relatively homogeneous," says Yves Cuilleron. The differences are in exposure and elevation, and a warmer climate in the south. Quality has been erratic, with one significant factor being that many vineyards are so recently planted.[32] "The main difficulty in St. Joseph is that we have two poles," says Philippe Guigal, "Although Guigal is in the north, our St. Joseph is all from the

The expansion of St. Joseph created an AOP with the most variability in the Northern Rhône. Vineyards run for 40 miles along the Rhône, extending inland from near the river to slopes with varying exposure. Courtesy Inter-Rhone, Christophe Grilhé.

south." The original St. Joseph consisted of five valleys where the rivers created hills facing south or southeast. In the expanded appellation, the vineyards tend to face east: "It's not very logical, exposure should have been a criterion in defining the appellation," says Claire Darnaud McKerrow at Delas Frères.

The best wines come from established vineyards in the heart of the old appellation, known locally as the "berceau" [cradle] of St. Joseph. They are often in fact better than the average Hermitage (and priced accordingly), such as Chapoutier's Les Granits (both red and white), Delas's L'Epine, and Guigal's Vigne de l'Hospice. The last is especially interesting, coming from a hillside directly across the river from Hermitage. This is the other part of what was originally one massive granite outcrop, before the river cut through, leaving 20% on the west bank, with the other 80% forming the hill of Hermitage on the east bank. If the river had not switched from one side of the hill to the other, l'Hospice would be part of the same block as Hermitage.

It's an interesting question whether to choose St. Joseph or Crozes Hermitage when faced with a choice from unknown producers. The general advice from producers is that St. Joseph is a less risky bet. "Between St. Joseph and Crozes Hermitage, St. Joseph is safer, it is more traditional. The difference is due to the fact that most of Crozes Hermitage is on the plain of Chassis, whereas most of St. Joseph is a slope," says Jacques Grange of Delas Frères.

The village of
Cornas is below the
vineyards on the
hills.

The next village down the river, Cornas often has more character, but exactly what is that character? With only just over a hundred hectares of vineyards, and production exclusively of reds, Cornas has a much sharper focus than St. Joseph. A small area almost at the south of the Northern Rhône, it is protected by hills just to the north that make the main climatic factor the warm wind from the south; Cornas usually ripens a week earlier than Hermitage. Green oaks and junipers mark the point of transition in Cornas to Mediterranean vegetation. Cornas is an exception to the usual rule that vintages are homogeneous in the Northern Rhône; it can do better than other appellations in poor years.

Certainly there have been ups and downs in viticulture; there was a decline in the planted area, which fell to just over 50 ha in 1970, before rising steadily. The terraced vineyards start at the village (just above the Rhône at 110 m elevation), rising up on hills that go up to about 420 m. Like Burgundy, the feeling is that the best sites are in the middle of the slope, although there are some exceptions. "There's a big difference with altitude: more wind at the top, more water and humidity at the bottom, and an average 2 °C temperature drop from bottom to top. There's very different hydric stress between the bottom and the top: pruning continues at the bottom after it has stopped at the top. Harvest can be three weeks later at the top than the bottom," says Cyril Courvoisier, viticulturalist at Jean-Luc Colombo.

The warmer trend of recent years allows viticulture higher up the slope. "With climate change now it's possible to cultivate vineyards there. When Colombo planted land higher up in Cornas people said he was crazy, that the grapes would not ripen," Cyril recollects. But now the trend has been taken to

Cornas is an appellation of 125 ha centered on the village.

extremes. There is concern that recent expansion right on to the top of the hills may adversely affect the typicity of Cornas. A good breeze in center slope can be a gale from the north at the exposed summit. Standing in a vineyard at one point on the summit where the wind was absolutely howling, it was hard to believe that it would be possible for the vines to get through flowering, let along develop ripe berries. "When the appellation was defined, we did not expect people to go up there and plant," says Olivier Clape of Domaine Auguste Clape. The big question is really whether the reputation of Cornas can withstand the expansion into unsuitable terroirs.

Rustic is no longer a fair description of Cornas, but the wines remain sturdier than those of Hermitage or Côte Rôtie; certainly they tend to be well structured (which is why Cornas is often tasted last in comparisons). I often get high-toned aromatics in Cornas, taking the form of pyridines (sometimes showing as truffles), but I haven't so far identified any common origin for this feature. "We don't want to impress with the concentration. We are in Cornas, it's difficult to make rosé (meaning that the fruits inevitably have a certain weight and toughness). We want purity of fruits and freshness," says Alberic Mazoyer at Domaine Alain Voge. Even at traditionalist Auguste Clape, whose wines for me define the tradition of the appellation, there is now a more approachable young vines' bottling (aptly called Renaissance). There is absolutely no sign of new oak in the Clape cellars, and the traditional cuvée certainly needs time; about ten years would be right. At the other extreme, Jean-Luc Colombo was regarded as a young Turk when he introduced new oak into Cornas, about twenty years ago. "When my parents were criticized for making more sophisticated wine, people would say, this wine is not typical," Laure Colombo comments, but I would say that Colombo has won the argument: the more modern style is now found throughout the appellation. Although Colombo's wine may have a little more new oak than most, it is not obtrusive.

Immediately to the south of Cornas, St. Péray (the southernmost appellation in the Northern Rhône), is a bit of an oddity: production is exclusively white, from Marsanne and Roussanne,[33] but this includes a proportion of sparkling

The steeply terraced vineyards on the slopes of Cornas overlook the village and the valley beyond.

wine. Production of sparkling wine started in the early nineteenth century, and the wine was quite well known at that time, but today it's mostly consumed locally, and little is exported. Certainly Marsanne and Roussanne are not obvious varieties from which to make sparkling wine, and today its production is dwindling (probably down to less than 15% of total). Indeed, total production in St. Péray is very small, and even the dry white wine remains the least well known of the Northern Rhône. In fact, St. Péray was in danger of extinction a few years back, when the local growers went to Jaboulet and Chapoutier and asked for help; by buying grapes and producing an appellation wine, the negociants rescued the appellation. The problem with St. Péray, however, is a certain lack of character compared with its northern neighbors: the wines can be pleasant in a soft, direct way, but they rarely take on much character.

A single black variety, Syrah, is grown all along the Northern Rhône, yet the character of each appellation (or at least of the traditional heart of each appellation) is quite different. Even allowing for the fact that Côte Rôtie can include Viognier, that Hermitage, Crozes Hermitage, or St. Joseph can include Marsanne and Roussanne, and that Cornas is exclusively Syrah, this is a clear enough demonstration of the effect of terroir. Until the modern era, there may have been local differences in the cultivars of Syrah, but today the widespread introduction of clones means that growers all over the Northern Rhône are likely to be using the same plant material[34] (except for those who are skeptical about the character of the clones and prefer to perpetuate the heritage of their vineyards by selection massale). Jean-Louis Chave has a typically strong view on this. "The main clones of Syrah were selected in the eighties, and the aim at that time was to have more ripeness. We have at least 1%, sometimes 1.5%, less alcohol with our plants coming from selection massale than with clones. And with the very old vines we don't get to this crazy level of sugar. The old vines are less perfect than the clones, which all look the same, ripen the same way—and give the same wine at the end."

Most of the appellations of the Northern Rhône have now expanded well beyond their initial focus. The only exceptions are Hermitage (limited by the hill) and St. Péray (limited by lack of interest). It's taking the concept of the appellation to breaking point when it includes totally different areas, such as the granitic northern half of Crozes Hermitage and the alluvial southern plain. "We should have two appellations, Crozes and Crozes Hermitage," one producer told me (he asked not to be quoted by name!). If there were two such appellations, they would almost certainly have rather different reputations. Similarly the "berceau" of St. Joseph is of distinctly more interest than the new parts of the appellation. "It would be right for St. Joseph to accept that there are different levels, and to have Crus," says Jean-Louis Chave. Confusion about typicity probably prevents the best parts of the appellation from casting a halo over the weaker parts; indeed, the relationship may be the other way round, with the weaker parts of the appellation preventing recognition of the better villages.

While global warming has been pushing up alcohol levels everywhere, in some cases threatening to overwhelm the traditional style, it seems to have had less effect in the Northern Rhône. Most wines stay in a range between 13% and 13.5%, and retain their traditional freshness. The difference from the past is that all the alcohol is natural. "In the north thirty years ago we used to chaptalize every year, now not at all," says Laure Colombo. Philippe Guigal thinks global warming has been a benefit so far. "Lots of people talk about global warming. I'm very concerned about Châteauneuf-du-Pape with 16% alcohol. I prefer to have more Mourvèdre and to keep alcohol lower. In the Northern Rhône I have a strange answer: I prefer the situation today. Thirty years ago we were harvesting in late September and chaptalizing every year. In the past we always harvested during or past the equinox when it often rains. Now with global warming we often harvest just before the strong rains of the equinox."

"The advantage of granite is that even in warm years the grapes do not become cooked," says Jean-Louis Chave. Excluding the unprecedented heat of 2003, the most testing vintage recently was 2009, which has produced unusually ripe wines, more popular with the public than 2010, which was more typical. "2009 is more of a consumer vintage; 2010 is more of a winemaker vintage that really reflects the appellations," says Olivier Clape. If 2009 were the limit of the trend, everything would be fair set for the Northern Rhône. Only a minority of the wines from recent vintages have enough alcohol to disturb me, but if conditions become even warmer, there is a risk that higher alcohol and lower acidity will change the style.

Two tiny appellations at the very southern tip of the southern Rhône, Brézème and St. Julian en Saint Alban, offer surprisingly cool climate impressions of both northern and southern varieties. During the nineteenth century, Brézème had a reputation equal to Hermitage, but it never recovered from phylloxera. "The traditional style of Brézème—if you can say that because there was only one grower left by the 1950s-1960s—is to be light. Now some growers are going for a bigger style—we have 6 growers and half are traditional and half are going for late harvest and extraction," says Eric Texier, who has contributed to the recent revival. The climate is relatively cool, resulting from winds coming off the hills to the vineyards halfway down the slopes of limestone terroir: "Especially for whites, Brézème is one of the places in the northern Rhône where naturally you get good acidity and low alcohol with ripeness." Brézème has the traditional northern varieties, Syrah and Viognier, as well as southern varieties. St. Julian en Saint Alban also has some Grenache; in fact it's the northernmost planting of Grenache in France. The wines of both appellations give cool climate impressions.

	Reference Wines for the Northern Rhône
Côte Rôtie	Maison Guigal, Château d'Ampuis
	René Rostaing, Côte Blonde
	Clusel-Roch, Grandes Places
Hermitage	Jean-Louis Chave (red and white)
	Jaboulet, La Chapelle (red), Chevalier Sterimberg (white)
	Michel Ferraton (red and white)
Crozes Hermitage	Maison Belle, Roche Pierre (red), Roche Blanche (white)
St. Joseph	Yves Cuilleron, Les Serines (red), Le Lombard (white)
	Delas Frères, L'Epine
	André Perret
Cornas	Auguste Clape
	Jean-Luc Colombo, Les Ruchots
Condrieu	Yves Cuilleron, Les Chaillots
	Clusel-Roch, Verchery
	Pierre Gaillard, Fleurs d'Automne (late harvest)
Seyssuel	Vins de Vienne, Sotanum

Côtes du Rhône

45,000 hectares
5,200 producers
70 cooperatives
20 negociants

Côtes du Rhone : 19 million cases
Côtes du Rhone Villages: 4 million
18 individual villages: 1.5 million

Major black grapes: Grenache,
Syrah, Mourvèdre, Carignan,
Cinsault, Counoise

Major white grapes: Bourboulenc,
Clairette Blanche, Grenache Blanc,
Marsanne, Roussanne

The southern Rhône is where the transition occurs to lush, fruit-driven wines. The bulk of the vineyards of the southern Rhône lie between Montélimar and Avignon, spreading out on both sides of the river. The south has a more Mediterranean climate than the northern Rhône, with more sunshine and less rainfall. The valley widens out and there is a variety of terrains, including alluvial deposits, sandy areas, and limestone. The major quality grape is Grenache, bringing a richer, sweeter, more alcoholic style, but not usually long-lived.

The Southern Rhône focuses on blended wines. Grenache became increasingly dominant in the last part of the twentieth century, until backing off after the millennium, perhaps due to the impact of warmer vintages. The biggest change is an increase in Syrah from virtually nothing in the 1960s to 20% of the blend today. The trend is to wines that producers call GSM, shorthand for Grenache-Syrah-Mourvèdre, which now total three quarters of production. Plantings of Carignan have been declining and it no longer has much significance. Cinsault has also been diminishing, and is now around the same level as Mourvèdre. It's often regarded as a quality grape, but I'm inclined to regard it as neutral, not having very much effect on quality either way. Red is by the far the greatest part of production. Rosé comes next, largely from Grenache. The whites rarely reach the same level of interest as the reds. Most are made from Grenache Blanc and Clairette, neither really a high quality variety. Some white wines have Roussanne or Viognier.

The Côtes du Rhône extends across the entire Southern Rhône. The name is actually an old description for wine from the area. The town of Roquemaure claims to be the origin of the Côtes du Rhône. Originally a walled village close to the river, Roquemaure has been producing wine at least since the seventeenth century, and was one of the villages on the west bank of the Rhône whose wine was included in "La Côte du Rhône," as defined in 1737 with a regulation that the barrels should have C.D.R stamped on them.

Whether or not Roquemaure was indeed the birthplace of the Côtes du Rhône, a century later it was where the destruction of winegrowing in France started. Faced with an epidemic of the fungal disease oïdium, a wine merchant and grower called M. Borty imported 112 grapevines of various types from America in the belief that they would resist oïdium. Planted in 1862 in the 2 ha of the *clos* behind his house, indeed they flourished. Unfortunately, some were infected with the louse phylloxera.

Although the imported American grapevines were resistant to phylloxera, the indigenous French grapevines were extremely susceptible, and by 1866 vines were dying as phylloxera spread to neighboring vineyards. Within a few years every grapevine in France had to be replaced by one grafted onto resistant (American) rootstocks. (M. Borty's house is still standing at the scene of the crime, but the garden behind appears to have been partly built over, and in any case no longer has grapevines.[35]) Today the vines of Roquemaure are partly classified as Côtes du Rhône (some are in AOP Lirac) and partly as IGP.

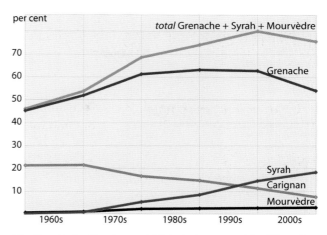

Plantings in the Vaucluse, which includes most of the Côtes du Rhône, show increasing focus on a few varieties.

Surrounding the Côtes du Rhône are a series of regional appellations, which together account for around 8 million cases of production each year. The principles of production are similar to the Côtes du Rhône, focusing on improving the wine by specifying a minimum level of Grenache, but regulations are less stringent, and yields are higher, than in the Côtes du Rhône. Producing pleasant, but generally undistinguished, country wines, they are a direct demonstration of the expansion of the appellation system to a point at which AOP becomes a questionable concept. The best known are Ventoux (formerly the Côtes du Ventoux) and Grignan-les-Adhémar (formerly Coteaux du Tricastin, but with a recent name change to remove any connection to the nuclear power station at Tricastin).

Reflecting its position in the appellation hierarchy, Côtes du Rhône has a different commercial organization from the Northern Rhône or indeed from the better known appellations in the south. The vast majority of Côtes du Rhône follows a model in which growers sell grapes to a cooperative or negociant who produces the wine. Close to two thirds of Côtes du Rhône wines are made by cooperatives.[36] A significant part of the rest is made by negociants; the negociants of the north—Guigal, Chapoutier, and Jaboulet—all have substantial production of Côtes du Rhône, as do negociants from the south, such as Perrin (who started at Château Beaucastel in Châteauneuf-du-Pape). Only a relatively small part of production comes from growers who make wine themselves. And many of the best wines come from small producers whose primary focus is wine from a smaller appellation, but who also have vineyards in the Côtes du Rhône. In fact, it's fascinating to see how far the style of the higher level appellation carries into the Côtes du Rhône in cases where a producer has vineyards

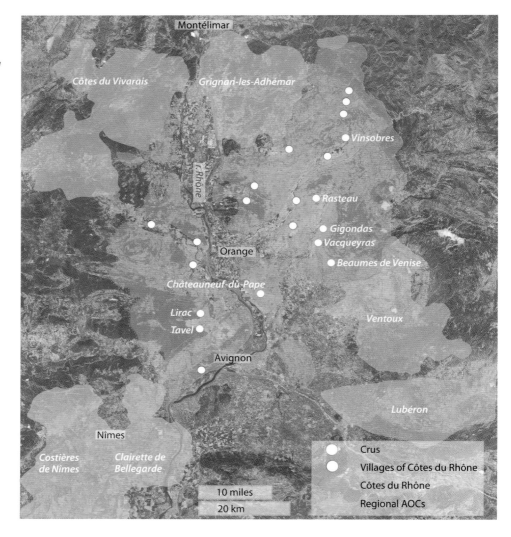

*The Côtes du Rhône
occupy most of the
southern Rhône.
They are surrounded
by other regional
appellations. Within
them are the
individual villages of
the Côtes du Rhône
Villages and the
"Crus" (individual
appellations).*

in both. Some of the best Côtes du Rhône come from producers in Château-neuf-du-Pape, for example. There are few producers whose reputation has been built on the Côtes du Rhône as such.

A superior level of wine, the Côtes du Rhône Villages, was created in 1953. Today it occupies about a quarter of the area of the Côtes du Rhône, and pro-duces roughly 4 million bottles per year. About half of the village areas are allowed to label the wine with the name of the individual village.[37] The main differentiating factor in the quality of the village wine is that Grenache must be at least 50% (compared to 40% for Côtes du Rhône), and Syrah and Mourvèdre must together be at least another 20%. Yields become progressively lower go-ing from Côtes du Rhône to Côtes du Rhône Villages, to the individual villages.[38] And wine from the Villages tends to be made by conventional vinification, whereas there is a more of a tendency in Côtes du Rhône to use carbonic maceration, the technique pioneered in Beaujolais to produce a simple, forward, fruity wine.

Some of the villages have been promoted out of the Côtes du Rhône Villages to become appellations in their own right. The first was Gigondas in 1971, followed by Vacqueyras in 1990, and most recently Vinsobres in 2007. Some of the historical changes in status can be quite confusing. Beaumes de Venise has been an AOP for sweet, fortified white wine made from the Muscat grape since 1945. But it was also part of the Côtes du Rhône Villages for red wine production, and became a named village in 1978. Then in 2005 Beaumes de Venise became an appellation for red wine production. Rasteau has a similar history: it was an appellation for sweet fortified wines, and dry reds were sold as Côtes du Rhône Villages. In 1996 it became a named village, and in 2010 obtained an appellation for red wine. The detailed characterizations and changes in status seem positively theological (very appropriate for an area that once hosted the Papacy).

Before the promotion of villages from the Côtes du Rhône, there was only a small number of individual appellations, formally known as the "Crus" of the Côtes du Rhône, each with its own rules and regulations.[39] The first, and by far the best known, is Châteauneuf-du-Pape. Indeed, Châteauneuf-du-Pape was there at the very creation of the AOC system. Following it came Lirac and Tavel, and for a long time these were the only three independent appellations in the Southern Rhône. Most of the appellations in the Southern Rhône allow production of red, rosé, or white wine (although red wine is always in a strong majority), but in addition to the (former) specific vin doux appellations of Rasteau and Beaumes de Venise, Tavel is another exception, this time solely for rosé.

The mix of grape varieties is similar across the Southern Rhône; the only really significant difference between appellations is just how strongly Grenache dominates. So what is responsible for differences in character—terroir? climate? historical accidents? I suppose it's a throwback that alcohol level increases along the hierarchy of appellations or cuvées: in 2010, Côtes du Rhone (including Villages and named villages) averaged 14.2%, Gigondas was 14.5%, Châteauneuf-du-Pape was 14.7%, and the Châteauneuf-du-Pape special cuvées were 14.9%. This goes back to the time when there was a struggle to reach ripeness, which was taken as a marker for quality. But while more alcohol may have been better then, it is a problem today.

The dividing line in expectations of quality comes when the label has an individual place name. "People call the villages of the Côtes du Rhone Villages by name as though they were Crus. They think the big difference comes between the Côtes du Rhône and Côtes du Rhône Villages on the one hand, versus the individual village names and the Crus on the other. The villages with names and the crus are very close today," says Christian Voeux, who makes wine at Château La Nerthe in Châteauneuf-du-Pape and also at his Domaine d'Amauve in Séguret. This view is certainly reinforced when you look at the labels: the village name is the most prominent feature whether the wine is from a named village or a cru, and you would have to look carefully at the small type underneath to determine the difference.

How important are the differences between places? "There's a range of vineyards in Séguret, Sablet, and Gigondas from the Coteaux to the high slopes, but differences among the wines are due less to the terroir than to the style of each producer," says Christian, although the villages have different (and better) exposures than the plain of the Côtes du Rhône as a whole. In horizontal tastings of the Côtes du Rhône, it seems to me that there is usually a step up in quality, showing as greater concentration, going from Côtes du Rhône to Côtes du Rhône Villages. I do not actually sense any further increase moving on to the named villages, nor do I see any specific characteristics that consistently distinguish one village from another (perhaps Sablet gives the finest impression). There are negociant wines that seem well made but uninteresting (you feel you might be able to pick out the wines of the big negociants in a blind tasting for their squeaky clean impression), wines from independent producers that are aimed at the market for immediate gratification on the basis of simple, forward, fruits, and wines that are more "serious" with enough structure to improve for a year or so. Perhaps there are more in the last category when the village is named, but the producer's name needs to be the guide here. At all events, the issue in choosing a Côtes du Rhône is style and quality, rather than expression of terroir. What happens when we move on to the "Crus"?

Châteauneuf-du-Pape

Area : 3,164 ha
Production: 1 million cases

Producers :   320
Cooperatives : 1 (7% of production)
Bottling: 55% producers
                       45% negociants
Black grapes:
Grenache, Syrah, Mourvèdre,
Cinsault, Vaccarese, Cournoise,
Picardan, Terret Noir, Muscardin
White grapes: Bourboulenc,
Picpoul, Clairette, Roussane,
Grenache Blanc

There is little dispute that the best red wines of the Southern Rhône come from Châteauneuf-du-Pape, which has produced wine for centuries. During the Middle Ages, most inhabitants of the town owned vines, with 200-300 ha under cultivation.[40] During the eighteenth and nineteenth centuries there was a steady increase in viticulture, until phylloxera struck.

Châteauneuf-du-Pape has always been blended from many grape varieties, but the varieties have changed over time. The major variety in the eighteenth century may have been Terret Noir, which is possibly the variety referred to in 1706 as "le bon plant du Languedoc." At this period, there was none of today's predominant variety, Grenache, which originated in Spain under the name of Garnacha. Grenache first became common in Roussillon, and then was introduced into the Vaucluse (the Département of Châteauneuf-du-Pape) in the 1820s. The result was "a more generous, full-bodied wine with a deeper color, but less elegance."

At first, the trend to richer wines was resisted in Châteauneuf-du-Pape. After phylloxera, when Joseph Duclos led the replanting at Château La Nerthe, he recommended a maximum of 20% of Grenache and Cinsault (and a minimum of 10% of white grapes).[41] By the late 1930s, Baron Le Roy de Boiseaumarié of Château Fortia, who was instrumental in making Châteauneuf-du-Pape one of the first appellation contrôlées (in 1936), was denouncing producers who had made their wines rich and heavy with Grenache. There's a reasonable case for saying that today the best Grenache-based wines in the world come from Châteauneuf-du-Pape, although there are some regions in Spain that might challenge the claim. "Châteauneuf is a marriage between the worst soil in the world and Grenache," says Daniel Brunier of Domaine du Vieux Télégraphe.

The impetus for planting Grenache, however, may have been only partly connected with the character of Châteauneuf-du-Pape. Through the 1920s, growers in Châteauneuf-du-Pape were encouraged to produce Grenache because they got twice the price for selling it to "improve" Burgundy than they could get for other varieties.[42] Presumably the Grenache went into Châteauneuf-du-Pape after the AOP regulations stopped it being exported to Burgundy in the 1930s. Grenache became so dominant in the southern Rhône in the 1960s that INAO advised growers to "cool the ardor of the Grenache" by planting Cinsault[43]—pretty terrible advice that, when accepted, led to dilution in the wine. Reducing Grenache was not a bad idea, but Cinsault was not the right substitute. A move away from Grenache reduced the overall proportion in Châteauneuf-du-Pape to 79% by 1991; today it has fallen further to around 72%.[44]

The regulations for the AOP limit the grape varieties that can be grown, but not their proportions. It's usually said that thirteen varieties are permitted, but actually the total is fourteen because Grenache (Noir) and Grenache Blanc are counted as one variety.[45] The total includes nine black varieties and five white varieties.[46] However, almost all production (more than 90%) is red. Most Châteauneuf-du-Pape is blended, although it is now rare for all of the permitted varieties to be used; Château Beaucastel and Domaine de Beaurenard are holdouts that insist on including at least a small amount of every variety, but their styles are very different, with Beaurenard much more driven by Grenache.

After Grenache became the predominant grape variety, fashions changed regarding other varieties. After the debacle with Cinsault, Syrah became popular in the 1970s; today it is the second most planted variety, although it still amounts to only 11%. Mourvèdre is next at 7%. Cinsault is reduced today to a mere 2.5%. So a typical red Châteauneuf is full bodied, with forward fruits

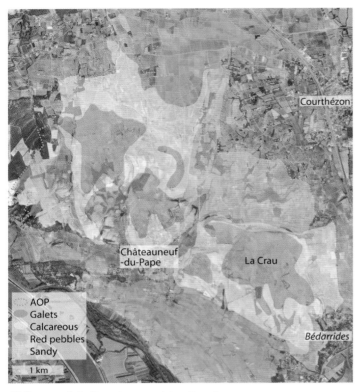

Châteauneuf-du-Pape has a variety of terroirs.

coming from the predominant Grenache component. Syrah brings structure and aromatics; Mourvèdre brings strong tannins. The proportions of Cinsault, Counoise, Vaccarèse, and Muscardin have been decreasing, and the other varieties are hardly used at all. For practical purposes, the average red Châteauneuf today is a blend of up to three quarters Grenache supported by Syrah and Mourvèdre, that is, a more or less classic GSM wine.

For the whites, Grenache Blanc and Clairette tend to be the dominant components, with lesser amounts of Roussanne and Bourboulenc. The only one of these varieties with any pretensions to quality is Roussanne, and it achieves its heights in the Vieilles Vignes monovarietal Roussanne bottling from Château Beaucastel. Yet there are always exceptions: although Château Rayas is most famous by far for its red wine, the white, coming from Grenache Blanc and Clairette, offers a wonderful savory representation of the garrigue.

The tradition in Châteauneuf is to blend both grape varieties and terroirs. Terroir is an interesting issue, as the size of the appellation means there are several different sectors. Soils range from calcareous in the west, to sandy in the east, and to rocky in the south. Both to south and north, there are red soils, with iron-rich rocks and pebbles. The best known terroir consists of the famous *galets roulants*, rolling pebbles, most prominent on the plateau of La Crau in the southeast, but also found in the northwest. Their well-rounded shape reflects their origin in having been deposited by the Rhône. The special quality of this terroir is often attributed to the fact that the galets absorb heat by day and reflect it back up at the vines at night. Now this is a curious contrast with the common view in most wine regions that diurnal variation is helpful because a cooling-off at night allows the vines a necessary respite from the heat of the day, and helps to retain acidity. Perhaps a more important attribute of the galets is that they form a barrier to evaporation, and therefore help to retain moisture in the soil in this dry climate.

The galets (round stones) of Châteauneuf-du-Pape cover vineyards in the eastern part.

It's curious that producers will discuss the characteristics of the various terroirs with regards to their effects on the character of the wine, including the advantages to be gained by an assemblage of lots from different terroirs, but I have never heard a producer express the idea that different grape varieties should be matched to the terroirs in Châteauneuf-du-Pape. Yet this is the very first concern about terroir everywhere else in France: Cabernet Sauvignon is planted on gravel, while Merlot is planted on clay in Bordeaux; Pinot Noir is planted on calcareous soils, but Sauvignon Blanc on siliceous soils in Sancerre; and Syrah is planted on granite, but white varieties on more calcareous soils in the Northern Rhône. Châteauneuf producers are pragmatic about grape varieties, adjusting the mix in accordance with their stylistic preferences, but there appears to be no concentration of any specific variety on any specific terroir. If there's any distinction, it is simply in choosing whether black or white varieties are the most appropriate for a plot.

Châteauneuf producers divide their wines into two categories. The first group is "traditional"; the second group is described as the special cuvées, or just the "cuvées". "Traditional" refers to the way the wine was assembled, and doesn't necessarily carry any stylistic implication. Sometimes the "traditional" wine is in the old style of Châteauneuf, but sometimes it's a more modern take. "For traditional cuvées, the tendency is to make a blend from different terroirs; single terroirs are processed separately only for the special cuvées," explains Michel Blanc of the producers' association. "Châteauneuf-du-Pape is a blend, it's interesting to make a vinification of a special terroir for a special case, but it should not become a majority of production," he believes. Some of the special cuvées come from old vines (these are often very old, going back to the first replanting after phylloxera).

The traditional position was expressed by Sophie Armenier at Domaine de Marcoux when I asked her view of special cuvées. "I don't believe in them. Well, everyone can do what they want, of course. I think that the strength of Châteauneuf is diversity, the different results coming from the cépages and the terroir, and if I made cuvées from each sector, one year the south would be good, another year a different area. The most interesting wine is made by assemblage." Of course, it's an open question what effect it will have on the regular Châteauneuf-du-Pape to put the best selections into special cuvées. With more than a hundred producers now offering special cuvées,[47] so that today they amount to almost 10% of production, can the remaining 90% of Châteauneuf-du-Pape withstand the loss?

Relatively few wines show the thick, jammy character that might have been associated with Châteauneuf a decade or more ago. Many wines are strongly fruit-driven, but a surprising number are more structured, and show refined palates with some tautness to the tannins and underlying structure. A tendency towards high-toned aromatics, however, is common with warmer vintages. My general impression is that Châteauneuf would be a more interesting wine—and a better match for food—if producers pulled back a bit further on the Grenache.

The cuvées tend to be more powerful. You reach a point at which it's difficult to distinguish them: one cult wine at this level looks much like another, irrespective of origin, irrespective of cépage. Part of the extra concentration of the special cuvées is because many come from low-yielding old vines, so they tend to be Grenache, as this is the predominant variety in really old vines. I am not atall sure that cuvées of 100% Grenache are the best way to go for the region. I would say Châteauneuf is quite aromatic enough without needing to go any further in the direction of über-Châteauneufs. Admitting that the special cuvées are impressive in terms of power and intensity, I might prefer a traditional Châteauneuf for dinner, especially if it is in the more elegant (modern) style. And along with greater concentration, the cuvées tend to have more alcohol.

There's also a tendency with some of the special cuvées to use new oak barriques. The tradition in Châteauneuf is to mature red wine in foudres—very large wooden casks, usually of old oak. Demi-muids (600 liter) casks, are also

used. The high ratio of volume to surface area reduces exposure to oxygen; foudres are favored because Grenache is an oxidative variety, prone to spoil if exposed to too much oxygen. Some producers use barriques to mature Syrah (and sometimes Mourvèdre), because these varieties need more exposure to oxygen to counter their natural reductive tendencies. "Barriques are interesting for people who make Syrah and Mourvèdre separately, but we do assemblage first, so the wine is 70% Grenache when it's maturing," says Didier Negron, explaining why Domaine Roger Sabon uses the larger containers.

If any single factor is most responsible for changing the character of Châteauneuf-du-Pape, it's been the introduction of special cuvées, but if producers agree on one thing, it's that Châteauneuf has flexibility. "We have the possibility in Châteauneuf-du-Pape with 13 varieties for each vigneron to develop his own style. There are no rules. Some go for 100% Grenache, others like to make an assemblage. The large variety of styles is very important for Châteauneuf-du-Pape," says Christian Voeux at Château La Nerthe, where they make the Cuvée des Cadettes only in years when they feel selecting the best lots won't harm the traditional bottling.

One of the holdouts for tradition is Domaine du Vieux Télégraphe, where Daniel Brunier has gone in the opposite direction, improving the quality of his

The "red soils" south of Châteauneuf-du-Pape consist of ferruginous pebbles. Vines are pruned as individual bushes to withstand high winds

The traditional foudres—wooden casks of around 4,500 liters—are stacked along the sides of the cellar at Château Beaucastel. There are some 225 liter barriques in the center.

regular cuvée by producing a second wine (Télégramme) from declassified lots. "I think the special cuvées did a lot for Châteauneuf-du-Pape," he says. "I mean a lot positive and a lot negative. The problem is that today people think a special cuvée has to be more: more tannin, more wood, it's terrible. It brings a lot because they tend to attract, they turn the light on Châteauneuf-du-Pape, that was good, but a negative point for me is that they tend to push the people to make wine for someone else, not for themselves. I am convinced that people who make fruit bombs do not serve this wine to their family."

With alcohol levels often pushed up near 15% by the warming trend, you have to worry about what global warming means for Châteauneuf-du-Pape. "Today it is helping to make superb wines. Since 1999 the quality of our wines has increased. But if it continues for another 20 years we may have a problem, but there are cépages we do not use very much, like Counoise that do not develop high alcohol, so we could use more of them," says Christian Voeux. So far so good. "The biggest effect of global warming is that we harvest earlier," says Daniel Brunier. "My concern with global warming is not the temperature, it is that if we don't have rain, then there will be a problem. Soil that needs to be irrigated is not called a terroir; it's just a soil, it has no interest for us."

Michel Chapoutier created a furor when he raised the issue of trying to deal with increasing alcohol: "The southern Rhône is too warm for Syrah. Of course we don't want to reduce the alcohol by physical means. If you use reverse osmosis to reduce the alcohol, you sacrifice some of the aromas. When you physically concentrate the grape must, you concentrate everything—including less desirable aspects. So how about simply adding back the water lost by evaporation? If you harvest on the basis of the ripeness of tannins in Grenache you risk having wines at 15.5 or 16% alcohol at least. We experimented and found that adding water did actually result in better wines. Wines with 17% alcohol just don't make sense. Lots of winemakers do it [adding water], and I think we should make it legal and bring it out in the open. It's the future of wine. We can't make Châteauneuf with 16% alcohol. We must have the courage to defend this point of view."[48]

Increasing alcohol levels may be part of the reason for a recent move away from Grenache towards Syrah and Mourvèdre. Grenache's tendency to high alcohol is enhanced when the growing season is shortened by higher temperatures. "Today we are convinced that Grenache is ripe only when it is very ripe—the Grenache *really* needs to be ripe to get concentration," says Daniel Brunier. The trend towards Syrah has been strong, but may have run its course. "There were a lot of plantings of Syrah in the 1980s-1990s, but now this has stopped, because more than 15-20% in the blend changes the wine too much," says Michel Blanc.[49] "Our objective here is the same as elsewhere, to have the same alcoholic and phenolic maturity; perhaps we should have more Mourvèdre," he says. Indeed there's a move to Mourvèdre, but it's still only a small proportion of plantings. "In the past thirty years we have increased Mourvèdre; originally it was only 5%. But it's not so easy, you have to decide to pull out some vines. We wanted to have more definition of tannins and potential for aging. The Mourvèdre can be black and dense compared with Grenache, which is too nice, too round," says Daniel Brunier.

The great advocate for Mourvèdre has always been Château Beaucastel: in fact, with 30% in the blend (and double that in the special cuvée Hommage à Jacques Perrin), they have by far the most of any producer in Châteauneuf-du-Pape. They also have by far the least Grenache of any producer (the same proportion as the Mourvèdre). Syrah and Counoise are the other important varieties. Château Beaucastel was quite controversial through the 1980s and 1990s because of the presence of Brett in its wine. (Brett is caused by the spoilage yeast Brettanomyces and gives an earthy, leathery note to the wine; the problem is that while a small amount can add complexity, it's erratic, and can easily reach a level at which it spoils the wine.) Personally I'm somewhat inclined to wonder whether the fruits of Châteauneuf-du-Pape aren't so overpowering, that a touch of something to take off the edge is helpful in achieving complexity. They believe at Beaucastel that people may have confused Brett with the natural animal quality of Mourvèdre; but all the same, in the late nineties they renovated the cellars to eliminate Brett. Whether because of this cleanup or for other reasons I can't say, but I wasn't entirely sure I recognized the current vintages of Beaucastel when I visited recently: they were far more overtly fruit-driven than the wines I remember from the last two decades of the twentieth century. Perhaps this is just the modern trend, but for whatever reason, the wines of today seem to have come more into the mainstream (meaning fruit-driven) of Châteauneuf-du-Pape. I can't help but feel slightly regretful about this, although anyone who feels that any Brett is an unacceptable contamination of the purity of fruits will disagree with me.

Showing that there is an infinite variety of ways to make great wine, another renowned producer, Château Rayas, makes its Châteauneuf-du-Pape exclusively from Grenache. Château Rayas has always been an odd man out, with eccentric proprietors who marched only to the beat of their own drum. I still have in my cellar an old vintage of Rayas with a label that says "Premier Grand Cru," a term that is very definitely not legal in Châteauneuf-du-Pape. On a recent visit, Château Rayas lived up to its reputation for having dilapidated cellars. The "Château" is a utilitarian building on a small hill, in a slightly obscure location that is not so easy to find. Several rough holes have been knocked in the concrete floor that separates the two storeys, presumably to allow pipes to be run through. Aside from the fermentation cuves, everything is old wood, very old wood in fact, in various sizes from barriques or tonneaux to larger containers. I asked Emmanuel Reynaud, the proprietor, if he ever uses any new oak. "Why would I want to do that," he said with a look of amazement. "I make wine," he added as a further (self-evident) explanation.

Rayas has several individual vineyards, each surrounded by the local forest. Next to the Château is the "Coeur" vineyard. The terroir is sandy and a slight elevation relative to the surrounding countryside ensures breezes that give freshness. The other major plots are the Couchant (to the west) and the Levant (to the east). All the plantings are Grenache. A little to the north is the Pignan area, used to produce a second wine. The vines date back about 70 years, and are replaced individually as necessary; there is never any wholesale replanting. Emmanuel is not especially forthcoming about his techniques, so I was not really able to establish his opinion on how these features contribute to Rayas's ability to retain freshness so well.

Barrel samples provide an unusual opportunity to directly compare different expressions of Grenache. Coeur is silky, refined and sophisticated rather than fleshy. Le Couchant is warmer and nuttier (more typically Grenache, you might say), rounder and richer, with a faint sweet impression on the finish. Le Levant is sterner: I felt this might provide the backbone for the blend. I could see these components combining to offer freshness, fruits, and structure, but the whole is undoubtedly greater than the sum of the parts in the magic that is Rayas.

High alcohol levels remain my main concern about Châteauneuf-du-Pape today. The wines have always tended to be alcoholic, easily achieving 12.5-13% alcohol in mid twentieth century. A level of 13.5% towards the end of the century was part of the richness of the style. But today it is usually higher. In fact, "I think it's difficult to make a good Châteauneuf under 14.5% alcohol," says Sophie Armenier at Domaine de Marcoux. Producers have a variety of views about the current trend. "For us the alcohol content is the same since the beginning. When you get to 15.5% alcohol but you have no taste of alcohol, you have minerality and saltiness—it's magic," says Daniel Brunier. "The increase in alcohol is difficult to manage because it's just coming from the sun," says Michel Blanc at the Fédération. "You have to choose between alcohol and maturity. It's a matter of one or two days. If you are a day too late, the alcohol is a per cent higher," says Fabrice Brunel at Les Cailloux. The consensus, insofar as there is one, is that so far the situation has been manageable; but it will be difficult if the trend continues. I think this is optimistic: when alcohol exceeds 15%, it has (in my opinion) gone over the top. Even if it's not an overt presence on the palate when tasting, it's fatiguing when you try to drink a bottle. It's unclear how far a move away from Grenache might help without involving a significant change in style. But the situation may be more serious in other appellations, where there tends to be less fruit concentration to balance the alcohol.

Gigondas :	red (99%)
	rosé (1%)
Vacqueyras :	red (96%)
	white (3%)
	rosé (1%)
Vinsobres :	red
Rasteau :	sweet (25%)
	red (75%)
Beaumes de Venise	Muscat (34%)
	red (66%)
Lirac :	red (83%)
	white (8%)
	rosé (9%)
Tavel :	rosé

The most striking geological formation in the entire Southern Rhône is undoubtedly the Dentelles de Montmirail, a massive rock structure with a distinctly toothy appearance. The stark rocks loom over the village of Gigondas, and form the center of a semi circle of appellations: Gigondas, Vacqueyras, and Beaumes de Venise. Aside from Châteauneuf-du-Pape, these are the best known appellations on the east side of the river. They share the generally protective influence of the Dentelles, but the most direct effect is on Gigondas, where vineyards actually extend up the slopes of the mountain. The big difference in the region is not so much between appellations as between the plain and the slopes.

Gigondas is a very old area for wine —there's evidence of production in Roman times. Production was more or less halted by phylloxera, and the predominant crop became olives for the first half of the twentieth century. The great freeze of 1956 killed most of the olive trees, and then planting turned back to grapevines.[50] The focus was heavily on Grenache, typically more than 90%, and the wine was known as the poor man's Châteauneuf-du-Pape.

Gigondas had been part of the Côtes du Rhône when the appellation was created, and from 1951 was allowed to include the village name on the label; as early as 1954, it began to agitate for its own appellation, but was rejected.

When it was finally approved in 1971, Gigondas became the fourth independent appellation in the region.[51] The range of grape varieties was widened; current regulations limit Grenache to 80% and require a minimum of 15% of Syrah and/or Mourvèdre. The other varieties of the Côtes du Rhône, except Carignan, are also permitted. The most significant change was the inclusion of Syrah, which is regarded as introducing a more supple quality into wines that had been too hard.[52] Aside from one per cent of rosé, all production is red. Oak is not a big factor here: most vinification is in large cement cuves, with very large old oak foudres as the alternative. The cooperative remains a significant force, although there has been the usual move towards estate bottling. When the wine was almost exclusively Grenache, it was never considered to have much aging potential—the usual advice was not to decant because it might oxidize in the decanter—but today there is more potential, although it remains true that most wines are best consumed within about five years.

Gigondas has by far the greatest variation of terroir in the region. Vineyards extend from the surrounding plain, on to slopes near the village, and up the Dentelles approaching the summit. Extending from the village to the west, soils are rocky; on the Dentelles they are calcareous. It is quite a bit cooler on the Dentelles, and harvest can be as much as two weeks later. Soils are infertile, and yields are low (averaging only 32 hl/ha).[53]

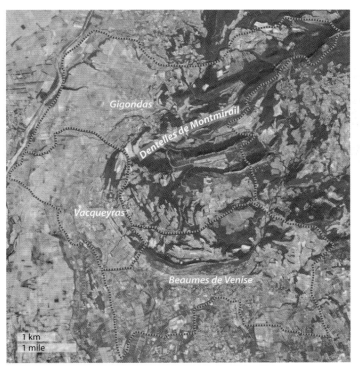

The appellations of Gigondas, Vacqueyras, and Beaumes de Venise form an arc around the Dentelles de Montmirail.

How do you see the difference between Gigondas and Vacqueyras, I asked Jean-Michel Vache at Clos des Cazaux in Vacqueyras. "We are lucky because our Gigondas is high on the mountain and very stony, our Vacqueyras is more sandy. Because the terroirs are so very different, we don't have to create a difference," he says. I received a similar answer from Thierry Faravel at La Bouissière in Gigondas. "That's a difficult question, they are adjacent. It's easy for us because our Gigondas comes from the Dentelles, but on the plain there's only a stream separating the two. For us the Gigondas is finer, more mineral: the Vacqueyras is more rustic. For producers with vineyards in the plain, there is not much difference."

The peak of the Dentelles is around 400 m; the slope declines steeply past the village at 280 m, then has a strong gradient going down to the main road at the west at around 200 m, and declines more gradually to the western boundary of the appellation at around 120 m. Taking the main road to define the boundary between the plateau to the west and the slopes to the east, probably around half of the vineyards are on the plateau (or garrigue as it is more euphemistically called in Gigondas), and half on the slopes, with half of the latter really well into the Dentelles on steeply terraced vineyards. "The three terroirs here are very different, but many people blend, so the discovery of terroir in

The highest vineyards in Gigondas are terraced on the steep slopes of the Dentelles. This vineyard is at 350 m altitude.

the wines is limited. Harvest on the plateau is generally around 20-25 September, in the village at 30 September, and in the mountains around 10 October," says Louis Barruol of Château de Saint Cosme.

The best wines of Gigondas tend to be special cuvées, often from old vines. These often come from near the village, as it was the first area to be planted. "I have been through years of experiments to find exceptional soils. The geologic diversity at Saint Cosme makes me manage my estate like a Burgundy estate," says Louis Barruol. "I finished with three lieux-dits which have consistent and complex expression of the soil they come from. They are more or less old vines: from 50 to 130 years old. Many lieux-dits were not interesting enough to be released."

A mainstream Gigondas, if we can use that term, can be robust, although it's likely to be smoother than it would have been a decade ago. By comparison, Châteauneuf-du-Pape has an extra sheen, another layer of sophistication. Gigondas solely from the plateau would be closer to Vacqueyras, with a more rustic impression. Yet Gigondas is really focused on Grenache, whereas Vacqueyras is turning to Syrah as an ameliorating influence. "Gigondas typicity comes from the highest vineyards in the region plus the northwest exposure," says Yves Gras at Domaine Santa Duc. "In Vacqueyras they are developing

Syrah, but Gigondas should focus on Grenache and Mourvèdre because they are at the northern limits." Syrah could well be a way forward (although at present the proportion is restricted by rules in both appellations). I tasted one wine in Vacqueyras where Syrah was the majority variety; albeit of dubious legality, this was the best wine I tasted from the appellation.

The problem of rising alcohol is exacerbated by the tendency of Grenache to build up sugar. But appellation rules all over the southern Rhône require Grenache to be the dominant grape. Is the commitment to Grenache going to be a problem for Côtes du Rhône generally? "It *is* a problem, not it will be. It's getting close to a nightmare now. We have to get rid of Grenache, but the main trouble is that we are an AOP. Either we stay in the AOP and make undrinkable wine or we leave and make table wine," says Jean-Michel Vache. He is investigating some of the other varieties from Châteauneuf-du-Pape, and also increasing production of whites, especially Clairette, which is a low alcohol variety that still gives only around 13% in the present climate. The problem with that, it seems to me, is that it's difficult to base a really interesting, flavorful wine on Clairette (but not impossible as witnessed by Château Rayas).

The plateau at the west of Gigondas extends south to Vacqueyras and north to Cairanne, which is the oldest of the named villages in the Côtes du Rhône, but curiously has never been promoted to appellation status. Why isn't Cairanne a Cru? I asked Laurent Brusset in Cairanne. "It's a question of the people at the head of the appellation. In Gigondas there was a strong force with Gabriel Meffre. We had no one like that in Cairanne. The cooperative [much more important in Cairanne than in Gigondas] was run well but wasn't interested in becoming a Cru." In 1985, his father and other producers assembled a dossier to submit to INAO to apply for promotion, but it never went anywhere. Since 2008 they've been organizing again. "I think Cairanne will become a Cru because we have some young vignerons who are very motivated," Laurent says. My own sense is that with relatively homogeneous terroir, extending from garrigue to an alluvial plain, Cairanne is one of the best villages in the Côtes du Rhône.

On the southeastern slopes of the Dentelles, only a dirt track separates Gigondas from Beaumes de Venise, but the appellations could scarcely be more different. Beaumes de Venise is known for vin doux naturel, a sweet, fortified, dessert-style wine made from Muscat.[54] With its intensely grapey character, the wine has a distinctly perfumed quality that blends well with its sweet finish, but flavors tend to be straightforward rather than complex. This is about a third of production in the appellation; the majority is the usual red GSM (labeled with the appellation name since 2005).

Farther to the north, Rasteau was originally an AOP only for its sweet, fortified wine, in this case made as red, white, or rosé, mostly from Grenache (Noir or Blanc). Since 2009, the AOP has also applied to dry red wine. In fact, the

The Dentelles loom over vineyards on the plain below the village of Gigondas.

quantity of fortified wine is very small (only 5% of total production). Both sweet and dry red wines often seem to lack refinement, however.

The other significant exception from red wine is Tavel, just north of Avignon on the west side of the river. Tavel produces only rosé, with Grenache and Cinsault as the main grapes. These are probably among the most powerful rosés of France, with a color that sometimes seems more like a light red wine (see Chapter 8).

Avignon forms the peak of a triangle, with the southern Rhône to its north, Provence to its east, and Languedoc to its west. Within thirty miles to the west is the old Roman city of Nîmes, center of the AOP Costières de Nîmes, a segue to the Languedoc. Costières de Nîmes became an AOC in the Languedoc region when it was promoted from VDQS in 1986, but in 1998 the producers requested that it should be attached to the Rhône wine region to reflect the true character of the wines. INAO approved the move to the Rhône in 2004.

So what is the typicity of Costières de Nîmes, I asked Chantale Comte at Château de la Tuilerie? "It's a good question, but I'm not sure there is a typicity," she says. "It's very variable. Anyway, it's not a feminine wine." There is more red wine than white, and there are complicated rules governing the blend.[55] A combination of north-facing exposures, the effects of the mistral in winter, and the climatic influence of the sea in summer, reduces temperatures by 2-3 degrees, giving good acidity and enabling the whites to maintain freshness. The reds to my mind seem to be somewhat along the lines of Côtes du Rhône, at all events more resembling the rusticity of the south than the elegance of the northern Rhône.

The tradition in the Rhône has always been for blending. The focus of the north on Syrah as its sole black variety meant that blending was directed to-

Reference Wines for Southern Rhône	
Châteauneuf-du-Pape (both red and white)	Château Rayas
	Château Beaucastel
	Château La Nerthe
	Domaine du Vieux Télégraphe
Châteauneuf-du-Pape (cuvées)	Domaine Les Cailloux, Cuvée Centenaire
	Domaine Henri Bonneau, Marie Beurrier
	Domaine Roger Sabon, Secret des Sabon
	Domaine Pierre Usseglio, Cuvée de Mon Aïeul
Gigondas	Domaine Les Pallières
	Château de Saint Cosme
Vacqueyras	Domaine le Clos des Cazaux
Rasteau (red)	Domaine de Beaurenard
Cairanne	Domaine Brusset
Sablet	Domaine Bertrand Stehelin
Séguret	Domaine de l'Amauve
Côtes du Rhône	Domaine Paul Autard
	Domaine Santa-Duc
Côtes du Rhône Villages	Château Sixtine
Lubéron	Château des Tourettes
Ventoux	La Martinelle
Costières de Nîmes	Château de la Tuilerie
Beaumes de Venise (VDN)	Domaine de Durban

wards combining lots from parcels with complementary terroirs. In the south, with less emphasis on terroir, blending focuses more on assemblage of different grape varieties. But in the past decade or so, there has been increasing emphasis on producing multiple cuvées. In the north, they tend to represent single vineyards. In the south, cuvées tend to focus on selection, often of old vines, which pushes them towards more Grenache. But the lack of any consistent focus creates potential for confusion. When a producer has multiple cuvées from a single appellation, each with a name intended to make it stand out from the crowd, the issue becomes how to resolve the significance of the name. Even in the Côtes du Rhône, most wines now have brand names. With the exception of the climats of Hermitage and the most famous individual terroirs of Côte Rôtie, every producer uses different names: unless you are intimately familiar with the wines of that producer, it's impossible to know whether a name is a lieu-dit, an old vines selection, a special assemblage, or a brand name for some other selection. Even if it works for the producer, is it good for the region as a whole? Uncertainty is the enemy of sales.

The first decade of the 2000s has shown extremes from the universal heat wave of 2003 to the floods of 2002 or high rainfall of 2008. The best recent vintages are 2009 or 2010 (depending on personal stylistic preferences), followed by 2005. "2010 had a beautiful balance; 2009 was more powerful and attracted more attention, but the press always talks about extremes," says Alberic Mazoyer at Domaine Alain Voge. "2009 will be an easily understood vintage of liquid pleasure, 2010 is a more serious vintage," says Philippe Guigal.

2013	Good, but not great year in north, with an unusually late harvest compensating for difficulties during the growing season.
	The south was hit by a problem with flowering of Grenache, so reduced quantities mean wines are lighter in style (but more refreshing) than usual.
2012	Michel Chapoutier describes the north as "pure classicism," which means elegant fruits retaining freshness.
	Aside from intermittent rain, conditions were good in the south, much better than 2011, ripe but not over-ripe.
2011	Warm but not especially sunny in Northern Rhône; good but not as classic as 2010 or as ripe as 2009, with some dilution resulting from rain in September.
	A large vintage, more straightforward with a fruity quality in Southern Rhône. Good but not comparable with 2010 or 2009.
2010	Classic vintage in north, textbook Syrah, fresh with good tension, widely regarded as having perfect balance and offering longevity.
	In the south, 2010 is seen as the best vintage since 1990 because of its balance, ripeness and freshness. Aging potential is higher than usual.
2009	The vintage in the north received widespread acclaim for its sheer ripeness: the wines are very appealing.
	Vintage was a little too warm in some parts of the south and gave big wines with more tannins, classic in the sense of being robust and solid.
2008	Vintage was spoiled in both north and south by high rainfall in the summer. Some top cuvées were not produced.
2007	Late start to the season was followed by cool conditions, but the vintage was rescued by a warm September: overall good rather than great in the north.
	Wet Spring, but then high winds helped keep a generally fresh impression to this warm year, which is regarded as a top one in the south.
2006	Warm September rescued the vintage from a mixed August and this is considered a good vintage in the north, for drinking before the 2005s.
	A decent vintage but not considered as good in the south as in the north. Best wines have finesse but some are light.
2005	Considered the best year since 1990 in both north and south, giving wines with concentration and real longevity.
2004	Not many wines of interest today surviving in either north or south.
2003	Too hot everywhere: north better than south, but both questionable today.
2002	Poor all over southern France because of extensive floods.

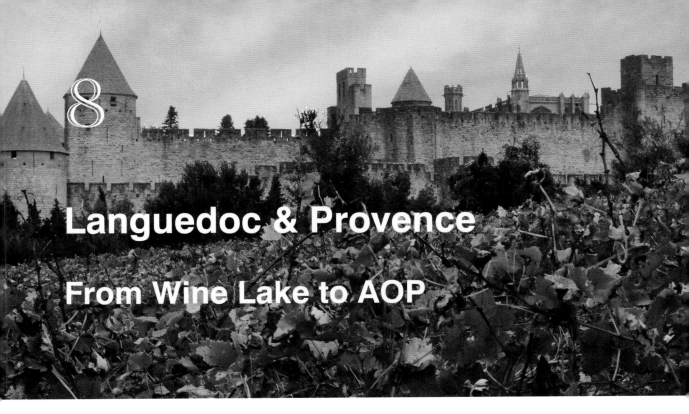

Languedoc & Provence

From Wine Lake to AOP

Red, red wine
Goes to my head...
Red, red wine
Stay close to me
(UB40)

If the Languedoc were an independent country, it would be in fifth place in the world for wine production (more or less equal with Argentina and after the United States). It accounts for one third of all wine production in France. To give it its full name, Languedoc-Roussillon is a vast area, stretching around the Mediterranean from near the Rhône to the Pyrenees at the west. (Roussillon is the southernmost part adjacent to Spain). To say that the history of wine production is chequered would be kind. Together with Provence, immediately to its east, the region used to be known as the Midi, famous for providing the major bulk of Europe's wine lake, a vast quantity of characterless wine from high-yielding varieties. But things are different today. Overall production has decreased sharply, production of Vin de Table has been reduced to a small proportion, and although production remains predominantly IGP, there are some AOPs establishing good reputations. Most of the wine is red.

Rich is the word that comes most immediately to mind to describe the style. The warm climate makes this a fertile area for growing grapes, but until recently, quantity ruled over quality. At the start of the nineteenth century, the focus was on producing wine for distillation; the Languedoc made about 40% of all spirits in France.[1] After the railway connected Montpellier to Paris in

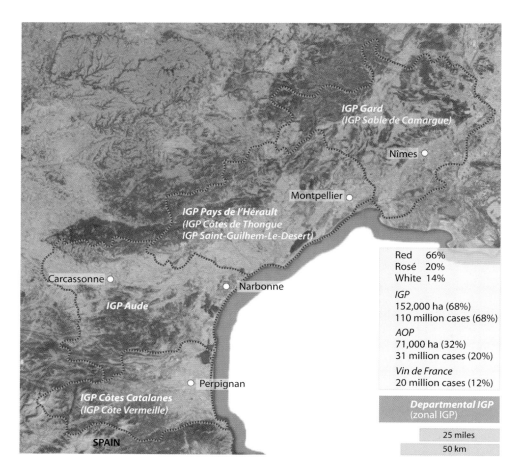

Languedoc-Roussillon stretches from Nîmes to the Spanish border.

The IGP d'Oc covers the whole area, and includes four departmental IGPs.

IGP Côtes Catalanes corresponds to Roussillon; IGP Aude and IGP Pays d'Hérault are the heart of Languedoc; and IGP Gard extends from the Languedoc into the Rhône.

Some of the better known zonal IGPs are named in parentheses.

Red   66%
Rosé   20%
White   14%

IGP
152,000 ha (68%)
110 million cases (68%)

AOP
71,000 ha (32%)
31 million cases (20%)

Vin de France
20 million cases (12%)

Departmental IGP
(zonal IGP)

25 miles
50 km

1845, producers switched to making cheap table wine that could be sent to the industrial cities in the north.[2] Phylloxera wiped out the vineyards here as elsewhere—there were riots in Montpellier in 1907 to protest cheap imports of wine from Algeria—but by the second decade of the twentieth century, recovery was under way. Production still focused on price; wine was produced as cheaply as possible, often blended with foreign imports, and sold in bulk.[3] Almost all was Vin de Table, and as the demand for plonk declined, this surplus became the largest single contributor to Europe's wine lake. At its peak around 1970, Languedoc-Roussillon had 450,000 hectares of vineyards.

Economic difficulties, combined with incentives to abandon production, led to a substantial decline in vineyard areas. Over the past forty years, production has declined by about half. In fact, subsidies for pulling up vineyards became a significant part of the income of the Languedoc. Today there are about 220,000 hectares of vineyards. The number of growers has declined, and in spite of a move by the more enterprising to bottle their own wine, the cooperatives are more important here than anywhere else in France. Of the 700 cooperatives in

3. RIVESALTES. — Pays de Joffre. Gare de Rivesaltes
Remplissage des wagons-réservoirs (vin alias pinard)

Wine being loaded for transport from Rivesaltes by rail in "wagons tonneaux." The station opened in 1858. The railway led to the development of the Midi as the source of bulk wine for the north.

France, around 500 are in the Languedoc, where the struggle of the past twenty years has been to improve quality.[4] Overall, 72% of production goes through coops.[5]

The decline in production has been accompanied by a move to quality. The major change has come in the collapse of Vin de Table production, now only about 10% of its peak, and alone responsible for most of the decline in the category in France.[6] Even so, almost half of France's remaining Vin de Table (now named Vin de France) still comes from the Languedoc. IGP has increased about three fold; the Languedoc is now far and way France's most important producer of wine at the IGP level. Of course, the change is partly cosmetic: the vast increase in IGP has come from vineyards that used to be Vin de Table.

Accounting for more than three quarters of production, the IGP Pays d'Oc covers the whole region, and is the prominent face of the Languedoc. Within the generic IGP are four Départemental IGPs: IGP de Gard, IGP Pays d'Hérault, IGP d'Aude, and IGP Côtes Catalanes (the last represents the Pyrénées-Oriental département, effectively equivalent to Roussillon). There are also many zonal IGPs, varying from single communes to broader swatches of the area, but almost none has established any typicity or made any particular reputation. Many grape varieties are allowed in the IGPs, and wines can be monovarietal, blended from two varieties, or blended from multiple varieties. Under the old system, there was an attempt to identify a better class of Vin de Pays with the introduction of the Grand d'Oc classification in 2001, intended for no more than a percent of the wines, but this seems to have died with the transition to

Even Vieilles Vignes Carignan produces large bunches.

IGP. It was in any case controversial whether the additional classification fitted with the concept of Vin de Pays.

For several decades the Languedoc was plagued by the characterless wines produced by the infamous trio of Carignan, Cinsault, and Aramon; today these are only a quarter of the black varieties.[7] A major drive to improve quality a few years back focused on "cépage amelioration," the replacement of poor quality varieties with better ones. Its success is indicated by the fact that Syrah (introduced relatively recently) and Grenache (a traditional variety of the region) overtook Carignan as the most planted varieties in 2009. In fact, there is now more Syrah and Grenache in Languedoc-Roussillon than in the Rhône. The newcomer Merlot is the last of the big four. Cabernet Sauvignon is in a distant fifth place. White varieties are less than a quarter of all plantings, with Chardonnay and Sauvignon Blanc now the leading varieties.

In spite of its evident deficiencies—most notably the tendency to over produce—Carignan remains a major variety. Its history is not encouraging: "Carignan was introduced from Spain and was planted everywhere to make Vin de Table. It eliminated all the traditional cépages," says Jean Orliac at Domaine de l'Hortus. Reality is recognized in the AOP rules by allowing it to be included, but often restricting the maximum proportion. Carignan's tendency to show bitterness without fruitiness is sometimes counteracted by using carbonic maceration (similar to Beaujolais), but the result does not show much typicity. My general marker for a wine made from Carignan, or containing a large proportion of it, is a certain flatness, a lack of liveliness, on the palate.

But because almost no one is planting Carignan any more, what's left tends to be old vines. Some committed producers regard the old Carignan as the glory of the Languedoc. "Carignan is the great classic vine of the Languedoc, it's the Pinot Noir of the Languedoc. Why doesn't it have a better reputation? It's been a victim of its success. It's been planted everywhere, and because it's a productive variety, people have made wine at very high yields. But at low yields it is perfectly adapted to the terroir," says Rémy Pédréno at Roc L'Anglade. My own view is that vines have to be a century old before the wine comes into an elegant balance that lets the fruit become the dominant note. Granted that the fruit profile of Carignan will always be flatter compared with the exuberance of Grenache or the freshness of Syrah, you can certainly find some Vieilles Vignes Carignans that are elegant, smooth, and seamless.

Most IGP wines carry varietal labels; in fact, the Languedoc is the largest source of varietal-labeled wines in France. The order of importance of varietal-labeled wines looks quite different from tradition: Merlot, Cabernet Sauvignon, Syrah, and Chardonnay scarcely existed in the region twenty years ago. By contrast, the AOPs are blended wines, and carry identification only of origin. The generic Languedoc AOP requires a minimum 50% of the GSM trio (Grenache, Syrah, and Mourvèdre) for red or rosé (which in effect means Syrah and Grenache as there is relatively little Mourvèdre). Each individual AOP has its variations on this theme. Chardonnay and Sauvignon Blanc are not allowed in white AOPs; the use of Viognier is restricted, so it also tends to be found only in the IGPs. Because all of the AOPs in Languedoc require wines to be blended from at least two or three grape varieties, producers who want to make mono-varietal wines, even from traditional varieties, are forced to declassify them to IGP or even to Vin de France.

It's a major distinction between the IGPs and the AOPs that international varieties are grown in the IGPs, whereas they are mostly not allowed in the AOPs. This means there tends to be a difference in character as well as quality between AOP and IGP, with the AOP more traditional, and the IGP more

Reference Wines for Vieilles Vignes Carignan	
Faugères	Château de La Liquière, Nos Racines
IGP Hauterive (Corbières region)	Château La Baronne, Pièce de Roche
IGP du Mont Baudile (Hérault)	Domaine d'Aupilhac, Le Carignan
IGP Côtes Catalanes (Roussillon)	Domaine Olivier Pithon, Le Pilou
IGP Côtes Catalanes (Roussillon)	Domaine du Mas Amiel, Val de Nuits
IGP Côtes Catalanes (Roussillon)	Domaine Roc Des Anges, Vignes Centenaires Carignan
Vin de France (Corbières region)	Domaine Ledogar, La Mariole
Vin de France (Saint Christol)	Terre Inconnue, Cuvée Léonie

"international" in the choice of varieties. "In the Midi you can cultivate all the cépages, although their characters may be different from elsewhere. It's really a matter of deciding what type of wine you want to provide," says Serge Martin-Pierrat at Château les Hospitaliers. There is continuing debate as to whether concentrating on making wines from the traditional varieties in the AOPs, or producing international varieties in the IGPs, is the best way forward. There's some criticism of INAO for its insistence on maintaining the original Southern varieties as the exclusive basis for AOP wines.

Modernism elsewhere in France tends to imply a move towards a more "international" style, usually meaning greater extraction to make more powerful wines. In the Languedoc, it has almost the opposite meaning; a move away from the old, heavy, extracted alcoholic styles to finer, more elegant wines (although there will always be alcohol in Languedoc). Innovation at the top level does not so much take the direction of trying new varieties, but more on moving in a more refined direction with the varieties (Grenache, Carignan, Cinsault, and more recently Syrah) that were previously known for producing powerful alcoholic wines. Ageworthiness is becoming an issue. "People have forgotten that wines of the south can age—it's a pity. You can forget about the wine for 8-10 years and then drink it. But people think they need to drink the wines of the south straight away," says Frédéric Pourtalié at Domaine de Montcalmès.

Languedoc AOPs

There is definite progress, with excess production diminishing, and plantings of better varieties increasing, but no clear regional leader has emerged. With its (relatively) reliably hot climate, Languedoc-Roussillon better resembles the wine-producing regions of the New World than any other part of France. Today you meet many thoughtful, intelligent winemakers in Languedoc who are rethinking what they can do with the region, the very antithesis of the old view of the Midi as a bulk producer of rustic wines. Many are young winemakers for whom one attraction is that the Languedoc is one of the last places where they can still afford to buy vineyards.

AOP regions make up a third of the area, and AOP production has been reasonably constant at just under a quarter of all volume for several years, but there are continuing changes in the organization of the AOPs. The region was divided into different appellations in the early 1980s, and since then a significant part of the effort to improve wine production in the Languedoc has focused on developing a hierarchy.

	cases
Languedoc	4,400,000
Corbières	6,200,000
Cabardès	200,000
Faugères	770,000
Limoux	900,000
Malepère	220,200
Minervois	1,700,000
Minervois-Lavinière	77,000
Muscats du Languedoc	420,000
Saint Chinian	1,400,000

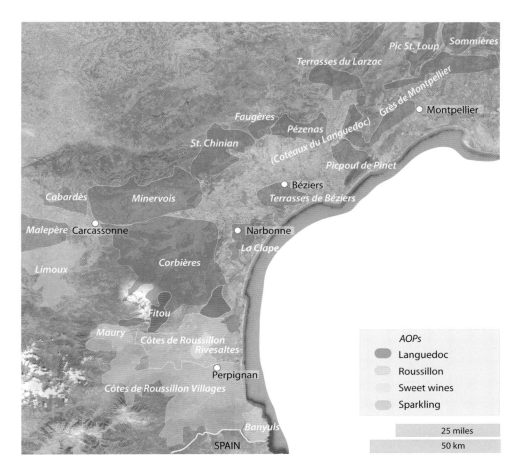

The AOPs of Languedoc-Roussillon extend from Montpellier (west of the Rhône) to the Spanish border.

Insofar as there is any geographical integrity within such a large region, it falls into three parts. The area from Montpellier to Narbonne used to be covered by a catch-all AOC called Coteaux du Languedoc. This has been replaced by the regional Languedoc AOP, which essentially includes *all* of the AOP areas, all the way from Montpellier to the Spanish border.[8] The stated objective is to "define the typical characteristics of the Languedoc region and grapes," but the creation of such a broad appellation seems retrogressive, since it's really impossible for it to have any coherence. Most of the wines in the Languedoc AOP are the same wines that used to be labeled as Coteaux du Languedoc, but there are some from additional areas, and others from within sub-regional AOPs that for one reason or another do not fit the requirements of their particular AOP.

The best parts of the old Coteaux du Languedoc are the new appellations of Pic St. Loup and Terrasses du Larzac. The soil is poor, the sun is hot in summer, there can be dramatic rainstorms off the mountains, and the cold wind from the north dries everything out. Spreading out from the base of Mont Hortus, Pic St.

Loup is a plateau surrounded by calcareous cliffs. The AOP of Terrasses de Larzac takes its name from the protective mountains to the north. Cool air coming down from the Larzac plateau creates a microclimate with very high diurnal variation, up to 20 degrees, the highest in Languedoc: "That's what preserves acidity and gives the elegance," says Frédéric Pourtalié at Domaine de Montcalmès. Vineyards are at elevations from 80 m to 200 m on the slopes of two valleys. A tasting of Grenache barrel samples from different terraces in the eastern part of the appellation shows a range from a jammy impression where there are galets (large pebbles), to broad flavors from the calcareous terroir at the base of the slope, to more mineral overtones from vineyards at higher altitude. The wines can be more restrained here (relatively speaking). A little farther west and at lower elevation in Jonquières, Mas Cal Demoura divides its vineyards into those with more clay (planted with black varieties) and the more pebbly and calcareous (planted with white varieties). "Terrasses de Larzac has a balance between traditional generosity of Languedoc with an additional liveliness and freshness," says Vincent Goumard at Cal Demoura. There's enough variation across the AOP to find places that are suitable for each grape variety.

The heart of the Languedoc is a large semicircle of AOPs radiating around Narbonne—the producers' organization likes to talk about the amphitheater of AOPs. Languedoc now includes around thirty AOPs,[9] but the core AOPs are Faugères, St. Chinian, Minervois, Fitou, and Corbières (this last being about the size of all the others combined). The reputations of the appellations really pertain to their red wines: some of them in fact allow only red wine, with the whites labeled simply as Languedoc. INAO refused to allow the Languedoc to have grand crus, but has allowed crus to be delineated within some of the appellations: these are Minervois La Livinière, Corbières Boutenac, St. Chinian Berlou, and St. Chinian Roquebrun.

There is a certain scepticism among producers about the usefulness of a detailed hierarchical classification. "Languedoc is a vast region. It's very heterogeneous. What matters is the quality of the work, rather than the label or the AOP. There are really only twenty or so domains of interest, in my opinion. For me the appellation has no importance, it's the work on the terroir that counts," says Paul Lignères at Château La Baronne in Corbières. There's a feeling that the process has been rushed. "For me arriving at a cru means a high quality, it must really be better. But it takes time to do that. We haven't got the microclimates that Burgundy has. With a young appellation you can't divide into crus in only thirty years, it takes time to know the terroir," says Jean-François Orosquette at Château La Grave in Minervois. Nearby at Château La Tour Boisée, Jean-Louis Poudou believes the process is too political. "You can't decree a cru just like that—it's an INAO-esque method that irritates me. There are producers who are increasing the quality of the Languedoc. The organization of crus, for example in the Coteaux du Languedoc, is more of an administrative

Calcareous cliffs loom over the vineyards of Pic St. Loup.

matter: it's all a political issue. The two appellations that genuinely have independence are St. Chinian and Faugères. There are really only two Crus—La Livinière and Boutenac," he says.

The name "Midi" somehow conjures up an impression of a vast plain of vines, but actually much of the Languedoc is distinctly mountainous. From Pic St. Loup, north of Montpellier, to La Clape just inland from Narbonne, massive calcareous cliffs overlook the vineyards. While it may be difficult to pinpoint characteristics of each area, there are both widespread and local differences. As a rough measure, Syrah is more dominant in the north and Carignan is more dominant in the west, but the common focus across the region on GSM (Grenache-Syrah-Mourvèdre) blends with or without Carignan means that differences between appellations should be due principally to terroir or climatic variations rather than varieties. So how distinctive are the appellations: was the effort in distinguishing them really justified, and are the crus really distinct in character and quality?

Some of the appellations are relatively homogeneous with regards to soil types, while others vary quite extensively, so there is no simple rule. While there are some differences in temperatures and rainfall, depending on prox-

*Faugères has thin
topsoil based on a
deep layer of schist.*

Faugères has thin topsoil based on a deep layer of schist.

imity to cliffs, elevation of vineyards, and exposure to maritime influence, the fact is that the Languedoc is a warm, dry climate prone to make powerful wines. Skillful winemaking is key in restraining the reds and keeping freshness in the whites: the producer is the most important variable.

Faugères was reportedly denied cru status because a large proportion of its production is vinified by the cooperative and sold at prices that are felt to be too low for a cru, but it was considered one of the more promising appellations when the AOCs were first established. The day I visited Faugères was autumnal, a week or so after the harvest. The road to Faugères climbs up steadily for miles, and by the time we arrived, the vineyards on the slopes were shrouded in a mist so thick you could scarcely see from vine to vine. Faugères seemed to be floating in the clouds. Terroir is based on very friable grey schist, typically 6-7 m deep. It's relatively homogeneous, divided between grey and violet schist. How is this reflected in the wine?

A tasting at Jean-Michel Alquier, one of the leading producers, showed wines in a variety of styles: fresh and light for La Première, the GSM entry level wine from the base of the slope; fruity with a touch of piquancy for Maison Jaune, a Grenache-dominated wine from the middle of the slope; and massive black fruits for Le Bastide, a Syrah-dominated wine from the top of the hill, developing very slowly indeed over a decade. The distinguishing feature isn't merely the producer, but winemaking choices along the way. "There was a period when everyone used new wood and the wines tended to taste the same, but now we have taken a step back," explains Jean-Michel.

There's a similar philosophy and range at Château de La Liquière. "At the start of the 2000s, people were trying to make wines that were very powerful. In Languedoc it's very easy to make wines that are very powerful. But public taste began to change and vignerons realized that great concentration reduces expression of terroir. People started to use less aggressive methods, including short maceration," says winemaker François Vidal. The entry level wine, Les Amandiers, classified as Languedoc, comes from the vines at lower elevation, while Cistus, the top Faugères, comes from vines higher up. "It's generally true—for both reds and whites—that more complexity and elegance, length and finesse, come from vines at high altitudes," says François. So in this sense the top wines are wines of altitude.

Adjacent to Faugères, Saint Chinian is sometimes said to make harder wines than Faugères. It is divided in two by the rivers Orb and Vernazobre. To the north, the vein of schist extends from Faugères, mixed with subsoil of grès (gravelly marl, a sort of muddy limestone). The vineyards in this part of the appellation are on the hills, whereas those in the south are on the plain below, where the soil is calcareous with clay. There's a view that wines coming from schist are more mineral, whereas those from the clay-chalk soils of the south are firmer. The two crus, Berlou and Roquebrun, occupy scattered areas in the north, with soils marked by schist, and an interesting difference in their grape varieties: Roquebrun must have less than 30% Carignan, whereas Berlou has a minimum of 30% Carignan. A series of cuvées from different terroirs produced by Jean-François Izarn at Borie La Vitarèle shows more obvious structure in Les Schistes, coming from terroir like Faugères, and more rounded, forceful fruits, in Les Crès, coming from terroir with round galet pebbles that resembles Châteauneuf-du-Pape.

A relatively large area to the east of the ancient city of Carcassonne, Minervois has different terroirs. Soil types, elevations, and climatic exposure are quite varied, including the characteristic grès, as well as calcareous soils, schists, marble, and large pebbles. This makes it hard to get a bead on typicity. In the north of the appellation, the cru of La Lavinière has 200 ha of vineyards; this represents only some 5% of Minervois, and is restricted to red wines at slightly lower yields than Minervois. Even in this restricted area, there is significant heterogeneity, a sort of recapitulation in miniature of the entire area of Minervois. The tendency in Minervois is to make cuvées from different terroirs, giving interesting variety, but making it difficult to define any single character for the appellation. At the northeast corner of Minervois, Saint-Jean-de-Minervois is a small appellation focused on vin doux naturel.

Corbières is hilly and rugged. Courtesy Jean-Luc Raby.

If Minervois is heterogeneous, then Corbières, adjacent and much larger, can verge on incoherence. A major part of production goes to negociants or cooperatives (where the giant Val d'Orbieu cooperative is predominant). The result is that only a small proportion of Corbières is actually bottled by growers. Corbières-Boutenac is the cru, characterized by a good proportion of very old Carignan vines (often dating back more than a century). Here the proportion of Syrah is limited to 30%, so if there is anywhere that will make the case for Carignan, this is it. Carved out of the southern end of Corbières, Fitou consists of two completely separated areas. It's not obvious why it's a separate appellation as opposed to a cru of Corbières.

It may be difficult for the outsider to obtain a clear bead on Corbières, but the AOP has a firm view of its typicity, or rather, of what isn't its typicity. A producer of natural wines, Domaine Ledogar has a mix of wines in the AOP and Vin de France. "All my parcels are in Corbières-Boutenac, I present my wines for approval because I was born here, but some do not conform. Why? Because I don't add yeast, I don't add tannins, I don't acidify... so my wines don't conform! They are true wines of terroir" says Xavier Ledogar. "And because Corbières must be a blend, I don't present my monocépages." La Mariole is a cuvée from century-old Carignan; precise and refined, it is the very model of a modern Languedoc. Tout Nature is a classic blend showing the broader flavors of what you might call old Languedoc, but that did not get approval to be labeled as Corbières. So here are two of the best wines of the appellation, respectively representing more modern and traditional styles, which in fact are labeled as Vin de France without any indication that they come from Corbières!

To the east of Corbières, La Clape is a relatively small AOP, but somewhat varied. Inland, it seems more like the appellations at the northern extremes of Languedoc: massive calcareous cliffs loom over the area. This is the driest part of Languedoc—it rains less then forty days per year—but the climate is softened by the humidity resulting from proximity to the sea. By the coast vineyards run down almost to the water. Styles vary across the appellation.

At the western boundary of Languedoc, the appellations are a little different. Just north of Carcassonne, the small appellations of Malepère and Cabardès have just enough exposure to the Atlantic climate to be allowed to include the Bordelais varieties (Merlot, Cabernet Sauvignon, and Cabernet Franc), not to mention Malbec and Fer Servadou, as well as Syrah and Grenache. The best wines here are based on combinations of Syrah and Cabernet Sauvignon. Just to the south is Limoux, where the focus is on sparkling wines, with the traditional Blanquette now giving way to the more modern Crémant.

Reference Wines for Red Languedoc	
(Coteaux du) Languedoc	Prieuré St. Jean de Bébian
	Domaine Peyre Rose, Clos Léone
Corbières	Domaine Ledogar, Tout Natur (Vin de France)
Faugères	Jean-Michel Alquier, La Maison Jaune
	Château de La Liquière, Cistus
La Clape	Château De Pech Redon, Centaurée
Languedoc-Montpeyroux	Domaine d'Aupilhac
Languedoc-Pézenas	Domaine les Aurelles, Solen
Minervois	Château La Tour Boisée, Marie-Claude
Pic St. Loup	Domaine de L'Hortus, Grand Cuvée
	Clos Marie, Metairies du Clos
Saint Chinian	Borie La Vitarèle, Les Crès
Terrasses du Larzac	Mas Cal Demoura, Feu Sacré
	Mas Jullien, Carlan
IGP de Gard	Roc d'Anglade
IGP Pays d'Hérault	Mas de Daumas Gassac
	Domaine de la Grange des Pères
	Domaine d'Aupilhac, Les Plôs de Baumes

IGPs: d'Oc & Herault

IGP d'Oc	million cases
Production :	65.0
Varietals :	55.0
Merlot :	16.5
Cabernet Sauvignon :	11.0
Chardonnay :	6.7
Syrah :	4.7
Sauvignon Blanc :	3.8
Grenache :	1.3
Viognier :	1.1

The label of IGP d'Oc is by far and away the single largest category of wine in France, accounting for two thirds of all IGP production and 90% of all varietal-labeled wines. It represents a third of all vineyards in the Languedoc. Altogether 56 varieties are authorized in IGP d'Oc, but two thirds of production is represented by varietal wines coming from only five international varieties. Brands from large negociants (and cooperatives) are a significant proportion of production.

Within the four departments included in the region, the Hérault is the most important, essentially providing the engine of the Languedoc. With more than 90,000 hectares of plantings (three quarters in IGP), its vineyards make it the second most important department in France for wine production. (The Gironde is first, with just over 100,000 ha in Bordeaux.) The Hérault accounts for more than a third of wine produced in the Languedoc, and after the catch-all IGP d'Oc, the IGP Pays d'Hérault is the best known of the region's IGPs.

The Hérault is also home to some of the top wines of the Languedoc; denied AOP status because they do not conform to the rules for varietal blending, these are simply labeled as IGP Pays d'Hérault. Just to the west of Montpellier, Aniane is home to two of the producers, Mas de Daumas Gassac and Domaine de la Grange des Pères, who completely defied tradition in the area when they created their wines.

The pioneer for Cabernet Sauvignon in the Languedoc was Mas de Daumas Gassac, where winemaking began in 1972 as the result of an accidental encounter. Aimé Guibert had bought a house and land at Aniane, near Montpellier, as a country residence. The family was considering what sort of agricultural use they might find for the land when a family friend, the famous geographer Henri Enjalbert, remarked during a visit that the terroir reminded him of Burgundy's Côte d'Or and would make a remarkable vineyard. Aniane is a special place, not only for its red glacial soils, but also for the protected microclimate in the Gassac Valley, where cool night winds give greater diurnal variation than elsewhere in the vicinity.

The Guiberts were not much impressed with the local grape varieties. They did not feel that the climate was right for Pinot Noir, and as Bordeaux drinkers they naturally gravitated towards Cabernet Sauvignon. As Aimé recounts, "I consulted all the great oracles in Languedoc, asking them, 'How do you make great wine?' And these great professionals invariably answered, 'If it were possible to make great wine in Languedoc, we would already know about it.' They

made fun of me."[10] But by 1978, Emile Peynaud, the doyen of Bordeaux oe-
nologists, became an advisor, and Mas de Daumas Gassac produced its first
vintage, a blend based on Cabernet Sauvignon.

The blend has changed over the years, but has generally consisted of
around 80% Cabernet Sauvignon with the remainder coming from a wide
range of varieties, some Bordelais, others more exotic: initially they were
mostly Malbec, Tannat, Merlot, and Syrah; by 1990 they were described as
Cabernet Franc, Syrah and Merlot; and today the label just says "several other
varieties." One reason for adjusting the blend may have been to calm down the
tannins, as some criticism had been expressed of rustic tannins, and current
winemaker Samuel Guibert says freely that the wines could be tough and tight
for the first few years. In the mid nineties, the young wines started to show
more elegance and finesse, he says, probably as a result of increasing vine age.

The avowed intention is to produce a "grand cru" of the Languedoc, but
these are not always obvious wines to characterize in the context of Cabernet
Sauvignon. "We don't make a Cabernet wine; we make Daumas Gassac. The
wine is no more typical of Bordeaux than it is of Languedoc," Samuel says.
Perhaps the character of the wine depends on whether Atlantic or Mediterranean influences predominate during the vintage. I find something of a split,
with some vintages tending more towards the savory, which I see as Atlantic
influence, while others are softer and less obviously structured, which is more
what you might expect of the Mediterranean. The differences for me really amplify with age, and were typified by the 1982 and 1983 vintages, the former
tending more towards classic savory characteristics of Bordeaux, the latter
more towards the soft, perfumed quality of the south. Cabernet is more obvious
in the Atlantic vintages; it can be more difficult to perceive in some Mediterranean vintages. Today's wines may be more elegant, with notes of the garrigue
cutting the black fruits of the palate, but perhaps they are not so long lived as
those from the eighties.

At Daumas Gassac they tried the traditional local varieties of Carignan,
Grenache, and Syrah for a while, but eventually pulled them out because they
seemed to over-produce and lack finesse in this terroir. Almost adjacent, however, is the Domaine de la Grange des Pères, where the philosophy is almost
the antithesis, but the wines are equally interesting. Laurent Vaillé established
Grange des Pères soon after Daumas Gassac; his first vintage was 1982. It's not
especially easy to make an appointment with Laurent who is nothing if not
reticent, but the rendezvous, if successful, takes place in the working cave,
where samples can be tasted from barriques. The wine is a blend of roughly
equal proportions of Syrah and Mourvèdre with a minor component of 20%
Cabernet Sauvignon. Minor, but essential. "Grange des Pères should have a
southern character, but with freshness, and that's what the Cabernet Sauvignon
brings," Laurent says.

Vineyards at Mas de Daumas Gassac are individual parcels surrounded by woods and trees. Courtesy Mas de Daumas Gassac.

Vineyards at Mas de Daumas Gassac are individual parcels surrounded by woods and trees. Courtesy Mas de Daumas Gassac.

The Cabernet is planted in the coolest spots, and is always the last variety to harvest. Syrah is planted quite close by, and ripens reliably to make a rich, deep component of the wine. The Mourvèdre is planted a few kilometers away on a hot, south-facing terroir. Tasting barrel samples, you can see what each variety brings to the blend. All are rich and powerful with a good level of tannins, the Syrah full of rich, deep black fruits, the Mourvèdre distinctly spicy, and the Cabernet herbal and fresh. It's not so much the acidity of the Cabernet as such, but the tightness of its structure that freshens the blend. Without it, the wine would have more of that jammy fruit character of warm climates. So here the Cabernet in effect is playing a moderating role on the forceful fruit character of the other varieties: almost exactly the opposite of the role it plays elsewhere as a "cépage ameliorateur" in strengthening weak varieties. The wines can be quite aromatic when young, but have long aging potential; the 1994 seemed at the midpoint of its development in 2012 and should be good at least for another decade.

Because Cabernet Sauvignon was not permitted under local AOP rules, the first vintages at Mas de Daumas Gassac were labeled as Vin de Table. Subsequently the wines were labeled as IGP Pays d'Hérault, as are those of Grange des Pères, which also is excluded from the AOP because of its content of Cabernet Sauvignon. It's difficult to over-estimate the revolutionary extent of the concept of planting Cabernet Sauvignon at the time, as there was virtually none in the south of France prior to the 1980s. Domaine de Trévallon in Provence had been the first in 1973, when Eloi Dürrbach produced his 50:50 blend of Cabernet Sauvignon with Syrah.

These three domains produce some of the best known "grand vins" in the south, but they are typical neither of the AOPs nor of the IGPs. Did they lead the way for the subsequent wave of plantings that brought Cabernet Sauvignon and Syrah to prominence in the IGPs of the Languedoc? Not really. Most of the IGP wines originated from an impetus to compete in the market for wines that represent varieties rather than place; this is a completely different level. Varieties and styles were chosen more with an eye on New World competitors than by looking at existing wines and styles. The best wines of the south essentially represent themselves; but as they are sui generis, they have set few precedents and created little in the way of a halo for others in the region.

Moving from Languedoc to Roussillon, the scene changes. Here the region is divided essentially into two large AOPs, Côtes de Roussillon, and Côtes de Roussillon Villages (with several villages now distinguished by the right to add their name to the label).[11] The best known AOPs in the region, Maury, Banyuls, and Rivesaltes, are known for their sweet dessert wines. The climate makes this natural—Roussillon is the hottest and driest Département in France—and the classic sweet wine is the Vin Doux Naturel (VDN), lightly fortified by stopping fermentation by adding distilled spirits (the method is similar to the production of Port but uses less spirits). A third of production in Roussillon is devoted to this style, and the region provides the vast majority of fortified wine produced in France.[12]

	cases
AOP Vin Doux Naturel	2,500,000
AOP dry wines	3,500,000
IGP	4,700,000
Vin de France	1,000,000

AOPs (sweet wine)
Banyuls, Maury, Rivesaltes
AOPs (dry wine)
Côtes de Roussillon (& Villages)
Collioure, Maury Sec
IGP
Côtes Catalanes

Until the eighteenth century, sweet wines were made by the technique of passerillage—allowing the berries to stay on the vine long enough to become desiccated. This produces such high sugar levels that there is still residual sugar when fermentation stops, usually around 14% alcohol. The development of distilleries in the eighteenth century allowed passerillage to be replaced by mutage, when fermentation is stopped by adding spirits.[13] Today the production of vin doux naturel in the AOPs is limited to growers of Muscat, Grenache, Macabeo, and Malvoisie. The grapes must have a natural richness with a sugar level of at least 252 g/l (equivalent to 14.5% alcohol), and 5-15% alcohol is added to block fermentation around two thirds of the way through,

The sweet fortified wines of Roussillon are traditionally matured at Mas Amiel for a year in glass bonbons outside, before transfer to foudres for extended aging.

leaving a sweet wine. However, with the fashion for sweet wines in worldwide decline, the production of VDN has been falling for decades.

Roussillon is still making the painful transition from providing the bulk wines of the Midi towards the higher quality required today. The construction of the railway to Paris in the mid nineteenth century gave a great boost to the region: production increased ten fold in two decades.[14] Phylloxera crushed the region at the end of the century, but after replanting, production was even greater (largely because grafted vines gave double the yields). Total production was around 27 million cases when France entered the European Community, roughly half being Vin de Table.[15] Production today is under half this level, with table wine reduced to about 10%. Even in the past decade, the area of vineyards for table wine has dropped from 40,000 ha to 27,000 ha. A major part of the decline is due to Carignan being pulled out, leaving Grenache as the most important black variety. Relatively new to the area, Syrah is now in second place.

The distinctive features of the wines of Roussillon go back to Roman times, when Muscat was the main grape variety, and wines were made in an oxidized style (today known as rancio).[16] The Muscat appears to have been the finest subvariety, Muscat à Petit Grains; the less refined Muscat of Alexandria (which is also grown as a table grape) was imported later from Spain.[17] In black varieties, Mourvèdre and Grenache have been established since the Middle Ages, with Grenache being used for sweet dessert wines. Roussillon's reputation for dry red wines historically has been that they are the strongest in the south.

A distinction is made between Muscat and other varieties used for sweet wines, as indicated by the use of Muscat in certain appellation names. The Muscat grape is a natural for hot climates, and there are appellations devoted to it scattered all over Languedoc: Muscat de Lunel, Muscat de Mireval, Muscat de Frontignan, and Muscat de Saint Jean de Minervois, all make sweet fortified wines. In Roussillon, where fortified wines are more dominant, Muscat de Rivesaltes is distinguished from Rivesaltes and Maury, where the main varieties are Grenache and Macabeo. The appellation system becomes complicated here, as there are different AOPs for dry wines and sweet wines. In effect, the Rivesaltes AOP for fortified wines more or less overlaps the Côtes de Roussillon and Côtes de Roussillon Villages AOPs for dry wines, and the Banyuls AOP for sweet wines overlaps the Collioure AOP for dry wine. Maury is a rare AOP that now has both dry and sweet wines.

The traditional oxidized styles are made in both vintage and nonvintage (the latter usually coming from a blend of two or three vintages). The key determinant of style is how long the wine ages before it is bottled. In the traditional oxidative style, the wines undergo aging for up to fifteen or twenty years in large wood casks. They can achieve a lovely concentration, but admittedly the oxidized style is an acquired taste. Today it is being partly replaced by wines made in a more modern idiom, using a nonoxidative approach. To avoid confusion, different names are used for the different styles.

Reference Wines for Roussillon	
Dry Red	
IGP Côtes Catalanes	Domaine Gauby
	Olivier Pithon, Le Clot
Collioure	Domaine De La Rectorie, La Montagne
Côtes du Roussillon Villages	Domaine Gauby, Coume Gineste
Sweet	
Banyuls	Domaine de la Rectorie, Cuvée Thérèse Reig
Maury VDN (modern)	Mas Amiel, Vintage
Maury VDN (oxidized)	Mas Amiel, Classique
Muscat de Rivesaltes	Domaine Cazes

Vineyards of Banyuls extend to the coast.

Just north of Perpignan, Rivesaltes is divided into three colors: ambré, tuilé, and grenat. The first two are oxidized styles: ambré is essentially white, coming from Grenache, Macabeo, Malvoisie, and Muscat, while tuilé is red and excludes Muscat. Hors d'âge indicates ambré or tuilé wines that have had at least five years of élevage under oxidative conditions. Rancio may be added to the label for wines made by traditional oxidative methods. Grenat comes only from Grenache and is made exclusively by reductive methods.

The southernmost AOP in France, Banyuls is the flag carrier for sweet wines. It is divided into three types. The traditional Banyuls is an oxidized style; the Rimage style is a more recent introduction requiring aging for twelve months in an airtight environment. Banyuls Grand Cru is distinguished not by terroir, but by vintage (only the best) and aging (a minimum of 30 months in oak). All types of Grenache (black, gray, and white) are allowed, but Banyuls must have more than 50% Grenache Noir, and Banyuls Grand Cru must have more than 75%.

The same vineyards can be used to make the sweet wines of Banyuls or the dry red wines of Collioure, but there are practical problems in making the tran-

Inland the vineyards of Banyuls are on steep, convoluted hills.

sition from sweet to dry wines. The vineyards that are most suitable for achieving very high ripeness to provide berries for making sweet wines may not necessarily be appropriate for harvesting earlier to make dry wines. "Plots are transitioned to dry wine because they have the right quality—they face north or east—and acquire the appropriate phenolic maturity," explains Jean-Marie Piqué at Mas Amiel.

Banyuls has some of the most striking vineyards in the region. Small vineyards are nestled into the steep hills, and access is difficult. There are amazingly convoluted folds of the hills, with channels for water run-off. The terroir is based on schist, which is evident everywhere. Differences between vineyards are due mostly to exposure and altitude (rising up to 400 m from sea level). "The tendency in reds is towards dry wine in Collioure. Oxidized styles (for Banyuls) are declining," says Jean-Emmanuel Parcé at Domaine de la Rectorie in Banyuls. Another sign of the times is that the focus here is as much on whites and rosé as on reds. An interesting comparison between two cuvées that come from the same Grenache grapes, the dry Collioure l'Oriental and the Banyuls VDN Cuvée Thérèse Reig, shows the first to be an elegant dry wine, very much the style of the south in a modern take; but the Banyuls expresses sweet round black fruits that make you think that perhaps here is the real typicity of Grenache.

It's been possible to make dry as well as sweet wine in Maury since 2011, and the change at Mas Amiel is a sign of the times. Forty years ago, all production was of sweet wines in an oxidized style. Today half of production is dry wine, and a third of that is white (there was no white as recently as ten years ago). The best selling wine in the sweet styles is modern (non oxidized) vintage. This is a sea change in the region.

Southern Whites

AOPs for white wine
(Coteaux du) Languedoc
Clairette du Languedoc
Corbières
Faugères
Minervois
Picpoul de Pinet
Saint Chinian
Collioure
Côtes du Roussillon

White wine is very much a minor preoccupation in the Languedoc; overall it is less than 15% of production. It's allowed in only a few of the AOPs. The blended white wines of those AOPs are confined entirely to traditional varieties.[18] In addition, there are two AOPs for varietal wines, Clairette du Languedoc and Picpoul de Pinet. For whites made from traditional southern varieties, but coming from appellations that allow only red wine, Coteaux du Languedoc (now Languedoc) has become the AOP of choice. The break between the AOPs and the IGPs is even more striking for white wine than for red, as the two major white varieties in Languedoc as a whole are Chardonnay and Sauvignon Blanc. Banned from all the AOPs, together they are 40% of all white plantings,[19] and dominate the white IGP wines as varietal labels.

I'm not convinced that either Chardonnay or Sauvignon Blanc makes interesting wines in the south, but another import from the north, Chenin Blanc, makes some of the most interesting whites. "Chenin Blanc was introduced under the aegis of INAO about twenty years ago to get livelier white wines," explains Vincent Goumard at Mas Cal Demoura. "Because we are in France, there was a tasting after ten years. And the character was rejected as atypical. All the vignerons who took part decided to keep their Chenin, but were forced into the IGP." Vincent's white is IGP Pays d'Hérault, and he adds that, "Of course we have to find calcareous soil to magnify its character. I hope we'll have a white AOP in Larzac; it's a good terroir, and it's a pity but it probably won't happen for another twenty years." A little farther north, Rémy Pédréno at Roc d'Anglade achieves a steely minerality with an IGP de Gard that's a blend of Chenin Blanc with Chardonnay.

The dominant white varieties in the AOPs of the region are Grenache Blanc and Clairette, both somewhat nondescript. There's a tendency to apply more modern techniques to update the style. "Originally the white wines were like all the others of the Languedoc—heavy. Our objective was to have a dry wine with more minerality. It's done with vinification following Burgundy: fermentation in new barriques followed by élevage with battonage," explains Alain Asselin at Domaine du Puech Haut. But is this enough? The problem with the whites of the south, to my mind, is a sort of amorphous aromatic quality, phenolics without flavor, that takes over the palate. One rare example of a white from a quality variety suited to the region is the monovarietal Roussanne from Domaine Les Aurelles. But yields are so low you can see why this might not generally be a viable option. Another example is Prieuré St. Jean de Bébian's white, a blend based on Roussanne, which has moved in recent years from a very ripe to a fresher style.

Indeed, freshness is the key. This makes it all the more remarkable that some of the most interesting whites come from Roussillon. Pushing up against the Spanish border, Roussillon is as hot and dry as it gets in France, but the trend is towards refinement. "In ten years there has been a revolution here. The cooperatives have advanced from the old wines of extraction and alcohol—there are many producers now who make whites based on freshness and balance. Gérard Gauby was the initiator of all this," says Olivier Pithon, whose winery is right in the center of the small town of Calce, a few miles northwest of Perpignan. Gauby's wines are remarkable by any measure.

"The profundity of wine does not come from alcohol," Gérard believes. Gauby's wines are notable for their moderate alcohol: around 12.5-13%. Why and how are alcohol levels so much lower here than elsewhere? "I don't use herbicides or pesticides: it's all natural. Phenolic maturity arrives before alcoholic maturity. People say you need 14 or 15 degrees to get Grenache ripe; that's completely mad." Whether or not it's as simple as organic viticulture and early picking, the fact is that the wines, both red and white, are fully ripe yet always retain freshness. The Vieilles Vignes white comes from a blend based on Macabeo and Grenache Blanc, with vines aged from fifty to a hundred years. The top white wine is Coume Gineste, an equal mix of Grenache Blanc and Gris, from terroir based on pure schist. "This is a wine for those who don't understand minerality; after tasting this they will understand minerality,"

Reference Wines for White Languedoc-Roussillon		
		Main Variety
IGP Pays d'Hérault	Mas Cal Demoura, Paroles de Pierres	Chenin Blanc
IGP de Gard	Roc D'Anglade	Chenin Blanc
IGP Côtes Catalanes	Domaine Gauby, Coume Gineste	Grenache Blanc
Coteaux du Languedoc	Domaine les Aurelles, Aurel	Roussanne
	Prieuré St. Jean de Bébian	Roussanne

Gérard says. There's also an orange wine (white wine made with red wine methods), La Roque, entirely from Muscat. "This is the oldest variety in the world and we are working it like the Greeks and Romans. We have rediscovered Muscat," Gerard claims. I left Domaine Gauby wondering, as I always do, why other producers can't get the same level of flavor variety and interest without going to extremes. Gauby's reds are as brilliant as his whites, offering a fresh impression of Côtes de Roussillon that few others can match.

Côtes de Provence	19,330 ha
Coteaux Varois	1,800 ha
Coteaux d'Aix	3,800 ha
Bandol	1,770 ha

Rosé :	87%
Red :	9%
Blanc :	4%

Producers : 540 (15% of all wine)
Cooperatives: 60 (67% of all wine)
Negociants : 40

Today Provence is all but synonymous with rosé. This is both old and new. The wine in Roman times was a *vin clair*, made by immediate pressing with no maceration. This style remained dominant until the thirteenth century. It was a wine of aristocrats, whereas vin rouge was heavier and given to the workers. "When classes reversed after the Revolution, color also reversed. Red became dominant and rosé remained in (only) two regions: Provence and the Loire," explains François Millo of the CIVP. With much of its wine consumed locally,[20] Provence has adapted to the demands of visitors, and the real impact of rosé dates from the transition to summer tourism in the 1930s. "But it wasn't until the sixties or seventies that quality really began to increase," François admits.

Extending around the Mediterranean from Nice to beyond Marseilles, Provence is divided into rather large AOPs, somewhat hard to distinguish in terms of character. The catch-all AOP of the Côtes de Provence by far and away dominates production, with three quarters of all wine from Provence. A deluge of rosé, much of it extremely inexpensive, sometimes makes it hard to take Provence seriously as a producer of wines of interest. At the least, you could say there's a Mediterranean easiness to the wines, with the vast majority appropriate for summer quaffing.

Efforts to improve the reputation of Provence include dividing the Côtes de Provence into subregions. The subregions are rather wide areas, and are defined essentially on the basis of soil types, as there is little variation in climate. But these differences are not represented with much consistency in the style of rosé wines, and producers generally seem skeptical about the significance of subregional descriptions. Possibly this might become useful in marketing to indicate higher quality wines, but at least for the moment, the names don't have much resonance for consumers. Trendsetter Château d'Esclans is within the new subregional AOP of Côtes de Provence Fréjus, but the wines are la-

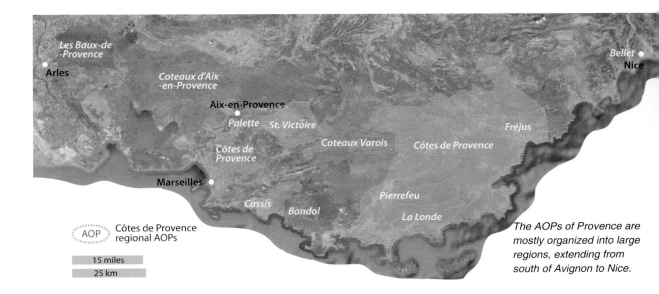

The AOPs of Provence are mostly organized into large regions, extending from south of Avignon to Nice.

beled simply as Côtes de Provence. "If they had called it St. Tropez, I would have used the name," says owner Sasha Lichine.

Emphasizing the importance of rosé, the only classification system in Provence defines Cru Classés for the rosés. Exactly a hundred years after the famous 1855 classification of Bordeaux, this followed the same principles: classifying producers on the basis of wines, rather than terroir. There were 18 producers in the original classification, but it's now so seriously out of date that it's not even particularly valuable as a marketing tool. Almost all of the classi-fied producers remain among the best regarded, but there would be at least as many again in any updated classification.

But is it possible to build a high reputation for the region solely on rosé? Some producers are trying to move towards production of reds to make more impact. "We are producing a lot of red and white, at Château St. Roseline we produce 55% rosé, 30% red, and 15% white. We want to produce red. To be recognized by journalists, to be famous, you have to produce red," explains proprietor Aurélie Bertin Taillaud. All the same, rosé has made strides. "For a long time rosé was not considered a real wine, but in the past ten years the quality has improved a lot and now it's considered to have the same quality as the reds and whites," she says.

The problem with the whites is that the traditional varieties do not give very interesting wines. The main varieties are Italian: Ugni Blanc (the local name for Trebbiano) and Rolle (the local name for Vermentino) have a tendency to pro-duce soft wines without much character.[21] It's true in Provence as in Languedoc that a move towards more "northern" white grape varieties brings

Vineyards in Provence extend from the Mediterranean (above) to Mont St. Victoire (facing page). Courtesy François Millo.

more interest than the often interdenominational aromatics and phenolic impression of the indigenous varieties. One of the successes is the Blanc de Blancs that Clos Mireille (part of Domaines Ott at La Londe-les-Maures) makes from Sémillon with a small proportion of Vermentino.

That focus on "traditional" southern varieties has driven some producers out of the appellation system. You can understand why they might not want to allow Chardonnay into the system, but they must be mad to ban Roussanne from the Baux de Provence AOP. One of the most interesting whites of the south is La Carrée, a 100% Roussanne that Henri Milan produces from a half hectare in his vineyards near Aix-en-Provence. It has a hard-to-describe mix of herbs and nuts, tarragon and spices, accompanied by savory impressions of the garrigue, and is rich, almost fat, on the palate. There is a generally savory trend among Milan's whites, with other cuvées comprising blends from multiple varieties, but treated unconventionally. "I decided to plant different vines in the same place (as rows of individual varieties), it is more harmonious. The grapes are picked and cofermented together," Henri explains. The wines from Domaine Milan used to be in the AOP system, but now they are all labeled simply as Vin de France! They demonstrate a potential for making interesting wines

with a complexity that is rarely achieved in Provence—but you have to be prepared to think out of the box.

The best reds come from some specific small areas or from exceptional producers who buck the local system. In terms of showing individuality, Henri Milan, Domaine de Trévallon, and Domaine Richeaume all make interesting red wines. The Milan reds are mostly blends of Grenache and Syrah, but always show good structure from the Syrah to counterpoise the fleshiness of the Grenache. They also include a monovarietal Merlot, picked early to achieve a remarkable degree of elegance.

Also near Aix-en-Provence, Trévallon uses a less conventional blend of equal proportions of Cabernet Sauvignon and Syrah in its (relatively) cool microclimate. Cabernet Sauvignon can be austere, but Syrah softens it (without acquiring the jammy notes of the southern Rhône). The wine started out as an appellation contrôlée, in the Coteaux des Baux en Provence, but in 1993 the rules for red wine in the appellation were changed to exclude more than 20% of Cabernet Sauvignon. INAO even demanded also that Grenache should be included. As this was not acceptable, Trévallon became a Vin de Pays des Bouches du Rhône. It is a long lived wine—usually it does not open up for ten years, says Antoine Dürbach—and as it ages, Cabernet recedes and it tends to show its Syrah element more strongly. I would be inclined to say the wine has something of the aromatics of the south combined with the texture of Bordeaux.

A little farther east, just under Mont Sainte Victoire, Domaine Richeaume is on the site of an old Roman villa. There's a monovarietal Cabernet Sauvignon, and blends of Cabernet Sauvignon with Syrah or Grenache. The Cabernet-Syrah blend, Columelle, is a good compromise between the varieties: Syrah aromatics with that structure of Cabernet underneath. Again this shows the potential for making an interesting wine, but these sui generis exceptions prove the rule that there's not a whole lot of interesting red under the Provence label. Although the Richeaume wines were initially labeled as Côtes de Provence, now they are either IGP Bouches du Rhône or simply Vin de France.

Exceptions come from some small AOPs, Palette and Bandol. Just outside Aix-en-Provence, Palette, which has only 42 ha, is really a story of two producers, Château Simone and Henri Bonnaud. The reds are based on Grenache, as elsewhere in Provence, but with a good measure also of that much sterner grape, Mourvèdre. The style follows the southern Rhône, but with less intensity. The whites and rosés are less easily distinguished from those of the surrounding Côtes de Provence.

Two other small specialized appellations are at opposite ends of Provence. A few miles to the west of Marseille, Cassis is a small fishing port surrounded by 200 ha of vineyards. Its twelve producers concentrate on white wine, with Marsanne as the predominant variety in the blend. However, the style tends to be somewhat nondescript.

Perched on precipitous hillsides on the western side of Nice, Bellet's 50 ha are divided among ten producers. Barely visible, small vineyard plots are nestled on the hillsides, with all the producers on the single road running around the mountain at an elevation of 200-300 m. Italian influence is evident. Vermentino is the main grape for the whites, but can be blended with Chardonnay and other varieties. The reds are based on Folle Noir, a highly productive vari-

Reference Wines for Red and White Provence	
Bandol	Domaine Tempier
	Château de Pibarnon
Baux de Provence (VdF)	Henri Milan
Côtes de Provence (white)	Clos Mireille
Bellet (white)	Clos St. Vincent
Palette	Château Simone
Corsica (VdF)	Comte Abbatucci

ety, that isn't grown much anywhere but Bellet;[22] they include smaller amounts of Braquet, and of course the ubiquitous Cinsault and Grenache. The rosés are based on Braquet (somewhat perfumed, another local variety), either as mono-varietals or blends with the other black varieties. The reds tend to rusticity, the rosés don't really distinguish themselves from the rest of Provence, but the whites can have a good combination of freshness and aromaticity; they are more interesting, although unfortunately of academic interest only, unless you happen to be in Provence where almost all the wine is sold.

The major exception from those soft fruits of the south is a complete antithesis: Bandol, where the reds (and rosés) are based on that austere variety, Mourvèdre. Bandol is one of the oldest areas for wine production in France, dating from before the fifth century B.C.E. when the Phoenicians arrived in Provence. By the Middle Ages, regulations had been passed to protect the quality of Bandol.[23] Mourvèdre was probably brought from Spain in the sixteenth century; by the eighteenth century it was established as the dominant quality grape in Bandol. It makes a powerful red wine that was suited to its consumption by visitors who came to Provence in the winter. However, after tourism switched to the summer, producers turned to making rosé, and Mourvèdre was often replaced by the more productive Aramon and Alicante. A revival started when Lucien Peyraud of Domaine Tempier persuaded others to follow him in replanting Mourvèdre in the 1940s.

Today the appellation rules require red or rosé Bandol to be more than half Mourvèdre, with an upper limit of 95%. Grenache and Cinsault are the other major black grapes; Carignan and Syrah are also allowed (up to a 20% limit). Mourvèdre is a stubborn variety with very low yields; the limit for the appellation is 40 hl/ha, and that is not always achieved. The vines must be at least eight years old for Mourvèdre to be used for red wine; after four years it can be used for rosé. While Bandol is famous for its red wine, history seems to be repeating itself at least insofar as there is a move towards rosé, which is now more than half of production. White wine production remains almost negligible, but is based on Clairette (with a minimum of 50% in the blend).

Bandol

Red :	2.4 million bottles	(40%)
Rosé :	3.3 million bottles	(55%)
White :	300,000 bottles	(5%)
53 producers		(50%)
3 cooperatives		(50%)

Red and Rosé
50-95% Mourvèdre
plus Grenache and Cinsault
(and <20% Syrah + Carignan)

Mourvèdre forms small berries and has powerful tannins with low acidity. One of the latest-ripening grapes in France, Mourvèdre requires very sunny conditions. Vineyards extend for a few miles inland, bordered by a ring of hills, usually facing south towards the ocean. Most of the area consists of clay-

The major grape of Bandol, Mourvèdre tends to grow upright.

limestone soils, with a high siliceous content; there are some occasional out-crops of calcareous rocks. Vineyards are often on hilly slopes, terraced by the stone walls known as the restanques of Bandol. The climate is rather arid.

Bandol is an amphitheater; from everywhere in the vineyards you can see the ring of surrounding hills; the Mediterranean forms the southern boundary. The microclimate has a lot to do with the character of the wine. It might be an exaggeration to say there are two Bandols, but there is certainly a striking dif-ference between the geography of vineyards in the hills—high enough up that with the right exposure you can see over the Mediterranean—and those on the plain running down to the sea.

Bandol is never going to be an easy wine: Mourvèdre always brings too much tannic structure for that. Even the rosé often has a slight impression of austerity. But modernization is evident in the mastery of tannins in today's wines. Mourvèdre has a tendency to reduction, which can introduce leathery, animal aromas, but these are scarcely evident in Bandol now: increased ripe-ness means they have been replaced by dense damson fruits supported by fine-grained tannins. Refinement has replaced rusticity.

The move towards rosé in recent years is not necessarily bad for the reds. When I asked Eric de St. Victor of leading Château Pibarnon how Bandol has changed, he felt that, "One of the main changes has been the production of more rosé, and keeping the best Mourvèdre for red wine. So the move to rosé

has improved the quality of the red; some of the Mourvèdre was probably too hard. For the red you need small grapes and good ripening, for the rosé the grapes can be larger and less ripe." Bandol's advantage is that "Mourvèdre is planted in the warmest south-facing spots. Bandol is more or less the northern limit for Mourvèdre; the microclimate is just hot enough to ripen it. Mourvèdre gives a good balance, our wines are usually 13.5-13.8%, we are not looking for muscular or international wines." The change in Bandol from a tougher to more supple style is partly due to better viticulture and vinification, aided by global warming, and partly represents changing values. "The wine has changed together with the food; there used to be a cuisine of sauces, you needed tannins to stand up to the cream, but now there is juice, and the match with wine is different." Eric adds ruefully that, "It's very difficult to evolve the wine, you feel if you extract less you will make less great wine, it's difficult to trust the terroir and make wine that is less extracted."

Bandol is making the same transition as other areas from a focus on assemblage to interest in single vineyards. The pioneer here again was Domaine Tempier, whose cuvées from La Migoua, Tourtine, and Cabassaou, starting in

Running a few miles inland, vineyards in Bandol are hilly and may have sufficient altitude to overlook the Mediterranean.

1969, define the peak of Bandol. Here as elsewhere, it is noticeable that ascending the vineyard scale correlates with an increased proportion of Mourvèdre, up to the limit of 95% allowed by the appellation.

Not everyone agrees with the move to single vineyards: Eric Boissieux at Château Vannières is sticking with one wine, but he wishes it could be 100% Mourvèdre. "5% of Grenache, what difference does that make, it's idiotic. It doesn't make any difference in the red, with the rosé perhaps it's different," he says. He doesn't think Bandol has changed so much as consumers have changed. "It's not in Bandol's character to make a supple wine and I don't think people are looking for that. Is Bandol a little difficult to drink when young? Perhaps. But that's why we like it... Consumers have become accustomed to structured wines now—thirty years ago the structure of Bandol was shocking."

Yes, Bandol mostly remains well structured, but better tannin management makes it much more supple (and finer) than it used to be. Some wines are now made with the intention of being more approachable, where the tannins are positively soft and wines are ready to drink very quickly—but I agree with Eric to the extent that, for me, these are not what Bandol is about. Yet for all that Bandol has lightened up, I still find many wines are not really ready until they have had several years (at least four or five) to age in the bottle. It's not so much that the tannins are aggressive as that the sheer density of Mourvèdre requires time to allow flavor variety to develop.

Corsica

Area: 5,800 ha

(48% AOP, 47% IGP, 5% VdF)

AOP : 1.3 million cases

IGP : 2.1 million cases

Vin de France: 200,000 cases

Red 32%; Rosé 48%; White 20%

Producers: 106 (AOP), 8 (IGP)

Cooperatives: 8 (96 growers)
                70% of production

The history of wine in Corsica owes more to Italian tradition than French, as it was governed by the Republic of Genoa until the island came under French control in 1769. Accordingly, the main red grape of the island is Nielluccio, which is the local name for Sangiovese (the major grape of Tuscany). Unlike Tuscany, however, where Sangiovese is often vinified as a monovarietal, in Corsica it is usually blended, its main partner being Sciacarello, which originated as another Tuscan variety (Mammolo, now little grown in Tuscany).[24] Other varieties planted for red and rosé include the obscure Barbarossa and the ubiquitous Grenache.[25] The whites are mostly based on Vermentino, here known by its Italian name (rather than the French Rolle), and often made as a monovarietal. The island has roughly 6,000 ha of vineyards, cultivated by more than a hundred independent wine producers, with another hundred growers sending grapes to one of the cooperatives.

Vineyards in Corsica are typically at elevations on hills near the coast. Courtesy Vins de Corse.

Vineyard locations reflect the mountainous terrain. Most are on coastal hills, running more or less round the island, with an average elevation around 300 m. The climate is warm and dry. Production is split between AOP and the IGP Île de Beauté. The catch-all AOP for the island is Vin de Corse (accounting for almost half the wine produced on the island), but in addition there are eight sub-regional AOPs, the most important being Patrimonio (the first to be granted AOP status) and Ajaccio. The regional AOP requires red and rosé to be at least half Nielluccio, Sciacarello, and Grenache in total, but Patrimonio requires at least 90% to be Nielluccio for reds (75% for rosé), and Ajaccio marks a point of difference by requiring at least 40% Sciacarello.

A significant proportion of the IGP wines carry varietal labels, including the traditional varieties (Nielluccio or Sciacarello for the reds or Vermentino for the whites) or international varieties such as Cabernet Sauvignon or Merlot. You might think that the hot climate would make for heavy wines, but the reds of top producers are quite light and fresh, with a tendency to show cherry-like fruits, and the whites are often relatively savory, and fresh.

In spite of the effort put into defining 9 AOPs and the IGP, the best known wines from Corsica are not in the AOP system. With roots going back to the French Revolution, when Comte Abbatucci was one of Napoleon's generals, Domaine Abbatucci is Corsica's most important producer. Both the entry level wines (which used to be AOP Ajaccio) and the flagship wines in the Cuvée Collection are Vins de France. The Collection is focused on rescuing indigenous varieties—Carcajolu Neru, Montaneccia, Morescono, Morescola, and Aleatico joining Nielluccio and Sciacarello for the reds, with Carcajolu Biancu, Paga Debbiti, Riminese, Rossola Brandica, Biancone for the whites. These are beyond the remit of either AOP or IGP, but have a character that is hard to find in the other wines of Corsica. Altogether there are eighteen varieties, which were collected from old abandoned vineyards in the 1960s and planted in a single plot of granite terroir on the Abbatucci estate. Other producers, including notably Clos Canarelli, also make cuvées from old varieties, most commonly white from Biancu Gentile and red from Carcajolu Neru.

AOP	32 million cases
IGP	32 million cases
Vin de France	9 million cases

AOP rosé	million cases	percent of region
Provence	14	87%
Loire	6	19%
Rhone	5	15%
Bordeaux	4	7%
Languedoc	2	9%

Is rosé a white wine with a little color, a side-product of producing red wine, or a mixture of red and white wine? It can in effect be any of these, depending on how it is produced.

With one notable exception, rosé is made from black grapes, by giving the juice minimal exposure to the skin that provides the color. The exception is Champagne (and other sparkling wine), where a little red wine (typically about 10%) is mixed with the white base wine to produce the rosé color. Mixing red and white wines is illegal for production of still rosé wines.

A key factor in producing rosé is how long the juice spends in contact with the skins. Contact occurs right at the beginning, and after that, vinification is essentially the same as for white wine. Rosé production is usually divided into three types: direct pressing, macération pelliculaire, and saignée, although in fact there is really a continuum of possibilities.

Direct pressing means that the grapes are pressed immediately. Essentially the juice is in contact with the skins only while the crushed grapes are being drained. At its extreme, this produces the so-called vin gris, which is a very pale pink indeed. This is made only from grape varieties with light skins. Macération pelliculaire means that the crushed grapes are held in the press for a while before the juice is drained off to be fermented. Color and tannins are extracted into the juice in proportion to duration of time in the press. Color can vary from quite light to relatively dark.

Saignée isn't exactly controversial, but it's not really intended for the production of rosé. When you are making red wine and the juice isn't as concentrated as you would have liked—perhaps it rained just before harvest—you can strengthen the wine by running off some of the juice right at the beginning. This reduces the amount of juice that is left in contact with the skins, and means there will be greater extraction when the red wine is made. The grapes have not been pressed, and the run-off juice has only brief contact with the skins (usually a few hours); it is light enough to ferment into a rosé. In terms of duration of contact, saignée is usually somewhere between direct pressing and maceration. The difficulty with this approach is that the grapes will have been harvested with the intention of making red wine, which typically means they will be riper and have less acidity than is really ideal for making rosé. So the wine can be a little heavy.

"Saignée is not true rosé," says François Millo of the Provence Wine Council. "[It's] a bad way of making rosé. The wine is more of an afterthought, very few people in Provence use it."[26] François sees this as one of the major distinctions between rosé in Provence and elsewhere. "In Provence we make 87% rosé, so the decisions about vinification are made with rosé in mind, whereas in regions where rosé is 20%, all the decisions are focused towards red wine production. If you grow varieties in order to make powerful red wines, you cannot make a good rosé."

Rosé was regarded with some disdain until relatively recently. Roselyne Gavoty, one of Provence's leading producers of rosé, believes the situation has changed. "The image of rosé has evolved, and people have learned to appreciate it. Thirty years ago, it wasn't even regarded as wine. Today it's Provence that captures its essence."[28] Provence is certainly France's largest producer of rosé by far, and it's the only region where rosé is the most important type of wine. Elsewhere, the Rhône shares with Provence a reliance on Grenache as the principal grape in rosé, as does Languedoc to a lesser degree. Farther north, in the Loire and Bordeaux, rosés are usually based on Cabernet Franc.

No grape variety is dedicated exclusively to rosé: all are better known for their red wines. Do the same characteristics show in rosé? And do rosés reflect their place of origin or is the method of production paramount? It's a fair question whether rosés are more like one another or more like the other wines from their regions.

As a class, rosés are short lived. The little tannin that is extracted along with the color is not enough to offer the protection for aging that you get with red wine, but it may be enough to unbalance the wine after only two or three years. A key feature of rosé is that it

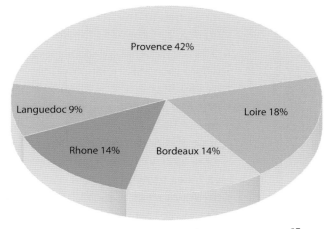

Almost half of France's AOP rosé is produced in Provence.[27]

needs freshness to offset that tannin and keep it lively. For that reason, malolac-tic fermentation is usually blocked to maintain acidity.[29] Rosé is usually fermented and matured in neutral containers such as stainless steel; but in the search for character, some producers are now trying maturation in oak (al-though new wood is almost always a mistake). "The character of rosé of Provence is elegance, it becomes too massive in barrique," says Jean-Pierre Fayard of Château Sainte-Marguerite.

"Rosé is more technological than red; vinification needs to be very precise," explains François Millo. The dilemma with rosé is that showing varietal charac-ter too clearly can be at odds with the requisite light freshness. But if there's no varietal character, what distinguishes one rosé from any other? It's a fine judg-ment to give a rosé enough fruit concentration to overcome tannic bitterness, but not enough to become sickly with red berry fruits. Although the rosés of Provence are always dry, I find a sense of sweetness coming from the red berry fruits to be disconcerting in some wines. The tendency to show phenolics at lower quality levels may reflect lack of fruit concentration, or put the other way round, the phenolics that come from skin contact are hidden when there is suf-ficient fruit concentration. It's not that much different from the need for fruit to balance tannin in red wine.

I divide rosés into two general types: those where the dominant influence is soft red berry fruits; and those that are more savory. The first group are fine as an aperitif but perhaps not lively enough for a meal; the second class are more suitable to accompany food. There's a move in Provence towards what are called premium rosés, defined by higher price, and usually reflecting a more savory trend. "We need to broaden the range of rosé. Ten or twenty years ago, there was only one rosé. It's absolutely crucial rosé should mature, that there should be rosés and not a rosé. There must be haut de gamme [top of the line] and très haut de gamme. We need a category of rosé de garde, which will last for several years," says François Millo. There's a sense that changes in cuisine, in particular the introduction of more international influences into food in France, has changed the convention that courses need to be accompanied spe-cifically by white or red wine, and has opened up possibilities for food pairings where rosé may be appropriate.

How far terroir is reflected in rosé is an interesting question given the fact that rosés have a much narrower range of expression than whites or reds, be-cause the grapes are harvested relatively early and are pressed very lightly. I have an impression that the rosés of Provence coming from gravel or schist ter-roirs tend to have a more savory quality, but that may reflect the choice of varieties grown on these soils, and/or the fact that they may be a basis for the premium rosés. Generally it's difficult to see direct connection with grape vari-ety, except for the rosés of Bandol, where the high concentration of Mourvèdre brings a more austere character. "Bandol rosé is more reserved, it's suitable for

a meal, Côtes de Provence is more perfumed and floral, more of an aperitif," says Eric Boissieux of Château Vannières in Bandol.

"Terroir plays a role, yes, but for rosé technology plays a more important role. It's easy to make rosé, but hard to make good rosé," says Sasha Lichine, whose Whispering Angel has taken over a major part of the export market for Provence rosé. "I thought there was really an opportunity in Provence," he says, explaining that he looked at many properties before settling on Château d'Esclans. "The terroir is excellent, and the vines are old," Sasha adds. Since purchasing the property in 2006, he has roughly doubled the size of the vineyards. Right from the start, four cuvées were produced. Whispering Angel comes largely from purchased grapes, but the château wine and two super-premium cuvées, Les Clans and Garrus, come only from estate grapes.

So what makes the difference between the cuvées: terroir? yields? grape varieties? vinification? All the wines start out in the same way. Temperature is brought down to about 8 °C with dry ice, the wine goes into closed presses under nitrogen, and as soon as juice comes out it is tasted and assigned to one of the four cuvées. The wines come 90% from free-run juice, with the rest from pressing, so there is essentially no maceration. "The cold system is the key," Sasha explains. "What used to happen in Provence was that people were pick-

Night harvests are common in Provence to maintain freshness for rosé. This requires mechanical harvesting. Courtesy Domaine Ste. Lucie & Domaine des Diables.

ing too early and then macerating to get the color out. We manage to pick a bit later and riper."

All the wines are dominated by Grenache, but there's a small change in other varieties going up the ladder. Whispering Angel also includes Cinsault, Syrah, Mourvèdre, and a very small amount of Vermentino. "We exclude Syrah as much as possible because it tends to give a candy taste," Sasha says, "and there's more Vermentino moving up the ladder, it brings creaminess, and we get rid of all the other varieties."[30] There's also a change in vinification: Whispering Angel spends a short period in cuve, Château d'Esclans spends six months in cuve and wood, and Les Clans and Garrus spend ten months maturing in an equal mixture of cuves and old demi-muids (600 liter casks) with frequent battonage.

Yield is less of an issue with rosé than with other wines. The top wines do tend to come from the older vines—Garrus comes from the oldest vines of Grenache and Vermentino—so the yields tend to be a bit lower, but the basic criterion is to select lots with appropriate character at the very start. "For the first vintage of Garrus we just creamed off the best three barrels, and then for Les Clans we creamed off again," Sasha recollects. And is there a difference in style? "Totally. As you go up the ladder, the wine fills your mouth more, you should not necessarily taste the wood, the wine should keep its freshness, and by Garrus you should get tiny tannins." My own description for the change in style would be that the wines become progressively less overtly fruity and more savory, to the point at which I would prefer the first wine as an aperitif and the last one to accompany a meal. Even the colors are different: all are very pale, but Whispering Angel shows a pink hue, whereas Château D'Esclans and the others are more salmon. The change in style along the range is a striking demonstration that rosé is not necessarily just rosé, but that it can have distinctive character and (to some extent) ageworthiness. No single factor is solely responsible, but selection and winemaking are relatively more important than terroir.

"They are not competitive because the wines are sweet," says Eric Dufavet of the CIVP, when asked how the rosés of the Loire compare with Provence. Indeed, Cabernet d'Anjou (which must come from Cabernet Franc and/or Cabernet Sauvignon) must have more than 10 g/l residual sugar; Cabernet de Saumur is up to 10 g/l. (You might think this was somewhat of a waste of Cabernet Sauvignon or Cabernet Franc.) Rosé d'Anjou, which comes from a wider spectrum of grapes, often including a fair amount of Grolleau, has at least 7 g/l of sugar. Together these three appellations account for three quarters of Loire rosé. The residual sugar results from stopping fermentation before completion, so alcohol levels are usually low (around 11.5%). The perceptible sweetness makes it hard to get any sense of varietal typicity. Three quarters of the sweet rosés are handled by negociants; there is little artisanal production.[31] The largest production of dry rosé goes under the broadest appellation, Rosé de Loire.[32]

After Provence, Tavel is probably the best known rosé of France, but the first thing you notice about Tavel is the exact opposite of Provence: just how dark it is. A little to the southwest of Châteauneuf-du-Pape on the other side of the Rhône, Tavel is unique in the French appellation system as an AOP reserved for rosé alone. It was one of the handful of villages entitled to the description of Côte du Rhône in the eighteenth century. During the following century, Tavel followed the national trend towards producing wines that were increasingly darker in color. However, by the time the appellation was created, in 1935, the wine had been characterized as having "a clear ruby red tinged with gold."[33] In the modern era, this became transmogrified into rosé.

Rosés vary widely in color. Those of Provence (left) are among the lightest in France, while those of Tavel (right) are the darkest.

Vinification in Tavel starts with a cold maceration of up to 48 hours; whether you call this rosé or a light red wine is a matter of opinion, but at all events the color comes directly from maceration. At this point, the grapes are pressed in a pneumatic press; typically the free-run juice and the press wine are then vinified separately. Fermentation is usually at low temperature to retain aromatics; malolactic fermentation is usually blocked in order to retain acidity. The wine is matured in cuve for about six months. It's ready to drink when bottled. As everywhere else in the Southern Rhône, a variety of cépages are used, but Grenache is dominant, giving a generally soft character to the wine, with more of a direct red berry impression than other rosés. Tavel rosé is unmistakably a wine of the south.

Skin maceration also brings more tannin to the wine, so Tavel can lack that natural freshness of a lighter rosé. Certainly the rosés from Tavel make a more powerful impression than those from other areas. Historically Tavel has been a great name for rosé in France, but a danger lies with increasing alcohol levels in the Grenache—high alcohol really does conflict with the style of rosé—and the alternatives of introducing other varieties such as Syrah or Mourvèdre tend to make the wine even more powerful.

Grenache is probably the grape most commonly used to make rosé. In the south, it's often blended with Cinsault (generally rather broad in its profile, if not rustic) and Syrah (more sense of precision and liveliness if the grapes are harvested soon enough). The blend has more pizzazz than rosé made from Grenache alone. Moving north, a significant amount of rosé is made from Gamay, often with the same sense of recent fermentation that comes with Beaujolais. The sternest rosés are made from Mourvèdre in the south (where

Reference Wines for Rosé	
Côtes de Provence	Château d'Esclans
	Château Ste Roseline, La Chapelle de Ste. Roseline
	Clos Mireille (Domaines Ott)
Baux de Provence	Domaine Hauvette
Bandol	Château Pibarnon
Coteaux du Languedoc	Château de La Liquière
	Domaine d'Aupilhac
Tavel	Château d'Aqueria
	Domaine de La Mordorée
Sancerre	Domaine Vacheron
	Domaine Vincent Pinard
	Domaine Claude Riffaut
Menetou-Salon	Domaine Philippe Gilbert
Reuilly	Domaine Claude Lafond, Cuvée André
Anjou	Domaine Richou (L'R Osé)
Marsannay	Bruno Clair
Bergerac	Domaine l'Ancienne Cure

Bandol can verge on the austere) and from Cabernet Franc in the north (excluding the sweet Cabernet d'Anjou or Cabernet de Saumur).

Perhaps the most elegant rosés are made from Pinot Noir in Sancerre: fresh and precise, they are usually in the camp that's modeled on white wine, and inclined to savory development. "For me, when you taste a rosé of Sancerre with your eyes closed, it's identical to white wine. It has aromatic freshness, it's the opposite of a rosé de Provence," is how Pascal Reverdy describes it. Sancerre rosés can be almost lacy in their impression when young. Actually one of the best rosés I have had from Pinot Noir came from Burgundy: in problematic years, Domaine des Lambrays makes a rosé from less ripe grapes that are selected out on the sorting table. Less ripe or not, the sheer fruit quality of the grand cru Clos des Lambrays comes right through, with a savory character. A more regular source for rosés of Pinot Noir is Marsannay, which is the only appellation in Burgundy for rosé.

Grape character does come out in rosé, although not as clearly as in red wine: Grenache-based rosés are softer and rounder, Gamay has that sense of immediacy, demanding to be drunk right away, the Cabernets are crisp if sugar is not an issue, and Pinot Noir is refined. Irrespective of origin or variety, however, rosé is for current consumption: in that sense, the style of vinification trumps everything else.

Vintages

You might think that vintage variation would be less important in Languedoc-Roussillon as it is the driest and warmest region of France, but even if the summers produce a relatively reliable amount of heat, variations in rainfall from drought to floods, especially at the beginning or end of the season, make for significant variation. However, relatively few wines are made with aging in mind. (Given that most production in Provence is of rosé intended to be enjoyed within the year, there is no vintage chart for Provence.)

2013	Producers feel the vintage was better than elsewhere in France. After a wet Spring and late start to summer, poor flowering reduced yields; but summer continued into September, and a late harvest gave quality grapes.
2012	The vintage can best be described as problematic, with difficulties ranging from drought to mildew during the season, followed by uneven ripening at the end.
2011	Rain restored quantities to normal after three drier years, but there are problems with rot in some places.
2010	This was a standard year: dry conditions gave good quality, if low quantities.
2009	The vintage was as good here as virtually everywhere else in France, with wines achieving high concentration.
2008	Drought created problems in the summer, especially difficult for whites, but reds have good concentration.
2007	Summer was unusually cool, with more cloud cover than usual, so getting to ripeness was the problem.
2006	This is a decent vintage without any special distinguishing characteristic that would make for interesting aging.
2005	This was a good year, and would have rivaled the classic regions elsewhere, but there was some rain at harvest.
2004	This is the most "typical" vintage of the decade, with reliable conditions everywhere in the region and no particular problems.
2003	The year of the heatwave was no easier in Languedoc than anywhere else, and many wines just went over the top.
2002	This was a cloudy summer and the disastrous floods in the Rhône extended into the eastern part of the region.
2001	A hot dry year made for difficult conditions until it rained in September, but this was too late to help those who picked early.
2000	Floods were a problem in November 1999, but after that conditions were good, and the wines are generally good quality.

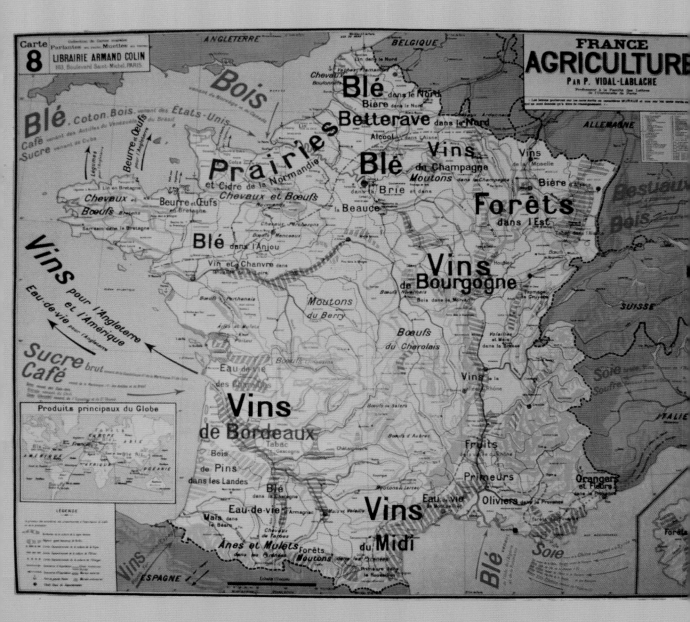

A school map of agriculture in France in the 1880s shows the importance of wine and its export.

9

The Challenge to France

Causes and Consequences

Non, je ne regrette rien
(Edith Piaf)

"Today, the Barbarians are at our gates: Australia, New Zealand, the United States, Chile, Argentina, South Africa," stated a report by the French Ministry of Agriculture in 2001. "Until recent years, wine was with us. We were the center, the unavoidable reference point."[1] A more personal point of view came from Aimé Guibert of Mas de Daumas Gassac, when he was leading the fight to stop Mondavi of Napa Valley from investing in the Languedoc: "Every bottle of American and Australian wine that lands in Europe is a bomb targeted at the heart of our rich European culture."[2]

The competition is so poignant because France sowed the seeds of competition by exporting its best cépages. The grape varieties that have swept the New World all come from France. Cabernet Sauvignon is the most widely planted black variety in the New World. Forgotten varieties of Bordeaux dominate South America: Malbec in Argentina and Carmenère in Chile. Syrah became Shiraz in Australia. Chardonnay is the most successful white variety in the world, with a range extending from quasi-Burgundian to completely different styles. New Zealand has made its reputation with Sauvignon Blanc.

Just before phylloxera devastated winegrowing in Europe at the end of the nineteenth century, France was the clear market leader with almost 40% of world production. (Most of the rest came from Italy and Spain.) France remained the most important producer as Europe recovered from phylloxera.

France's share of world wine production continues to decrease.

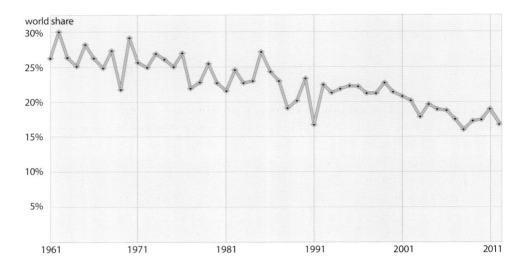

World wine production remained Eurocentric, but other countries took greater shares; by the second world war, France's part was down to about a third.

Since then, its share has continued to fall, along with other European countries, especially as the challenge from the New World has developed over the past two or three decades. Today France has about 17% of world production, and has fallen to third place (behind Italy and Spain) for exports. Against a background of declining consumption at home, and more competition in export markets, there is no easy way out.

France remains the world's most important wine producer. Its leadership is under constant challenge, but it still has more grapevines than any other country,[3] its total production is first or second in the world (in some years it is just edged out by Italy), and in terms of fine wine production it is nonpareil, with Burgundy, Bordeaux and Sauternes, and Champagne, famous as reference points worldwide, just to name the most obvious. Yet viticulture in France has been in continuous decline since the second half of the twentieth century. In the past fifty years, the area of vines has almost halved, and the number of producers has been reduced to a tenth. Even since 1995, the number of producers has halved.

The overall decline underscores a movement towards more professionalism—it's the smallest producers and growers who are being forced out—and towards higher quality wine. "The only good solution for French wines," said Laurent Gosset, when he owned Château de la Grille in the Loire, "is to look for excellence. Producing standard wine is too expensive and difficult in France. France cannot compete in producing everyday wines. France must produce vins de terroir [wines of origin] and not vins de cépage [varietals], and must not try to produce wines as cheaply as other countries, with which we cannot compete anyway."[4]

Climates are more reliable in the countries of the Barbarians (although climate change has produced increasing variation in recent years). Uninhibited by history, grape varieties have been planted where they perform best (and changed rapidly when occasion demands). Regulation of grape growing and wine production is far less stringent, and varietal wines have evolved their own styles, independent of the origins of the varieties in France. Burgundy remains nonpareil for Pinot Noir, although new styles are emerging in New Zealand and Oregon. Bordeaux is still the essential reference point for Cabernet Sauvignon blends, but is challenged by the sheer power of ripe Cabernet Sauvignons from the United States and Southern Hemisphere. Shiraz from Australia and Sauvignon Blanc from New Zealand are quite different from the expressions of the same varieties in the Rhône or Sancerre, and in some markets have become the defining style for the variety. Consumers worldwide have embraced the New World's identification of wines by grape variety.

Competition has had an effect on France, as seen by efforts everywhere to produce more "international" wines. Results have to be judged region by region, but it is fair to say that no region in France is immune from the challenge. France may have created the competition by disseminating its grape varieties throughout the world, but the influence has become reciprocal: the question now is how France responds to alternative definitions of the grape varieties that it had long taken for its own. What does France need to do to remain competitive, if not to continue to provide the unavoidable reference point? How does it balance its love of tradition with the need to compete?

Who owns the commanding heights of the wine economy in France? There is an enormous divide between the scale of the industrial and the artisanal, whether the comparison is between small producers and large brand owners in Languedoc, or between growers and Champagne houses at the northern ex-

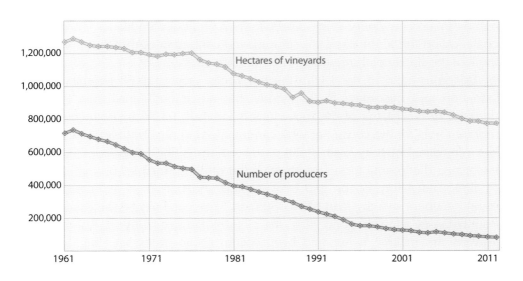

Vineyard area is declining and the number of producers is falling.[5]

tremities. It's received wisdom that negociants operate on a large scale and tend to make wine to the lowest common denominator; cooperatives are somewhat limited by their ability to control quality; but small vignerons have the freedom to aim for distinction.

Yet size is not necessarily the enemy of quality. Among classic regions, Burgundy, and to a lesser extent the Rhône, show the least division between growers and producers, as there are many leading grower-negociants who both own vineyards and make wine from purchased grapes. Two of the most successful wine-producing regions in France, Bordeaux and Champagne, demonstrate that large producers can be at the forefront of quality.

Bordeaux is the prime case where big battalions provide the driving force. The situation is highlighted by the change in ownership of the Grand Cru Classés of the Médoc. Historically these were never more than marginally profitable, and there was a constant stream of proprietors who had made their fortunes elsewhere, and then sought prestige from owning a Bordeaux château. A rich businessman would buy a château in decline, make investments to restore quality, and the cycle would repeat as he ran out of money or lost interest. Half of the Grand Cru Classés have changed hands in the past fifty years.[6] The major trend over this period is that the purchasers are now split between rich individuals and large corporations (although sometimes it can be difficult to tell the difference).

The situation of the châteaux that have remained in the same family hands is equally significant. "In the seventies, yields were so low we almost went bankrupt," says Jean-Charles Cazes of Château Lynch Bages. But today the Cazes family is on the list of the top fifty fortunes made in wine.[7] The big difference in today's list of rich owners— and we're talking serious money here, with rich meaning a fortune in excess of $200 million—is that there are just as many who made that fortune in wine as those who came into wine with money made elsewhere. Wine has become a profitable endeavor. The newest châteaux on the Right Bank are such magnificent edifices that they make you think of the stately pleasure domes of Kubla Khan.

This goes hand in hand with the top wines ceasing to be objects of consumption and becoming luxury goods that are traded more than they are drunk. The cult status of the top wines is fantastic for their producers and a problem only for the consumer who cannot afford to pay for them. Elsewhere it is a very different story, with small producers struggling to survive. (This is an interesting dichotomy for a country founded on the principles of fraternité and égalité). The nature of the gap between top and bottom is expressed in his usual trenchant style by Jean-Marie Guffens. "You can't say Vosne Romanée or Pouilly-Fuissé all make good wine, there is still plenty of rubbish. But the good growers are making better and better wine. I sometimes say that the good growers have tripled in the top appellations, they have gone from 1% to 3%...

But I don't think the €4 Bordeaux you buy in the supermarket is any better than it used to be twenty years ago."

Considering the history and economic importance of wine production in France, producers labor under an extraordinary handicap: almost unrelenting hostility from the government. One official report placed wine in the same category as heroin and cocaine (very dangerous). The Loi Evin, which regulates all media content featuring wine, is clear evidence that the lunatics are running the asylum. Advertising is all but impossible, and there have been proposals to ban all mention of wine in the press and on the internet. (What happened to free speech?) A magazine has been prosecuted and fined for reviewing Champagne releases before Christmas.

There's a real sense of bitterness among producers about the fanaticism and success of the anti-alcohol movement. "I don't understand how the anti-alcohol lobby, which is rather small, managed to get the politicians to pass laws that are destroying wine production. Two years ago they almost passed a law making it illegal to taste at domains. But politicians like wine and food!" says Pierre Coulomb at Domaine Guirardel in Jurançon. "They are supported by the government," Stephan von Neipperg said with resignation when I expressed surprise at the situation. In the economic wreck that is France today, vignerons may be the last people left in the country, because they can't move the vineyards. Well, they can invest overseas, who knows where that will lead...

Supposing that wine production in France is allowed to continue, what path should it follow? Everywhere in the world of wine, there is a continuing debate between tradition and modernity. But it is a bit different in France: I don't think I have met a single vigneron who would admit to being modern. When I told producers my book was about the wines of modern France, many were quizzical, and asked if you could truly put "France" and "modern" in the same sentence. And many made an immediate disclaimer, "I am not the most modern vigneron," says Marc Tempé of Zellenberg in Alsace. Yet he started his own domain in 1993: "We had a clean page," he says. But he has an interesting view of the current situation. "What is modernity?" he asks, then answering his question: "Everything now is insecticides, herbicides, and tractors. The great difficulty is that all the teaching since the sixties favors productivity using industrial and chemical techniques."

This is a common view among artisan producers: modernity means mass production using industrial methods, and you are a traditionalist if you reject them. Perhaps this is why no one wants to admit they are a modernist in France: the important thing is to redefine tradition so that your wine fits in. I had an interesting disagreement about modernity with Christophe Perrot-Minot, who makes clean, bright, flavorful wines that, for me, express the quintessence of modern Burgundy. When I asked whether he regards himself as a modernist, he was almost insulted. "For me this is traditional, not modern. It's not that I'm looking for drinking young, I'm looking for balance, and they will age well. For me, a modern wine is made by thermoregulation and long cold maceration. Wines that are too tannic, I call them rustic, not modern or traditional." Personally, I see modernity in terms of fruit-forward approachability (I could say instant gratification if I wanted to be pejorative), but Christophe sees what I call traditional as rustic, and his own wines as traditional because they have elegant tannins and will age.

Jean-Luc Thunevin typically has his own view of modernism. "The theme of your book seems curious to me because even the classics are modern now," he comments. "I give you an example," he continues: "Le Pin: is it a modern wine or a classic? It's not a garage wine but it inspired me." Then another example: "It's not so easy to find a classic wine: Léoville Barton? But it's also a modern wine." Then a little more argumentative: "The image of modern wine is new oak. But then Mouton 1947 was a modern wine. Everyone made a modern wine in 1982—and in 1961." In the best French tradition, Jean-Luc asks himself a question: what is the philosophy of modernity? "The success of modernity is to be able to have a product that pleases the clients," he concludes. "What's a wine that's a has-been? It's one that doesn't please the clients." I argue that Valandraud was a modern wine that altered the paradigm by introducing changes that many others followed, first in St. Emilion and then elsewhere. Jean-Luc agrees at least that he sparked a change. "I was the first garagiste. We protected the fruits, took precautions against oxidation, introduced green harvest, leaf pulling. Everyone does it now." When will this become tradition?

The very concept of modernism is viewed with suspicion. Jean-Luc Colombo all but created a scandal when he introduced new oak into Cornas thirty years ago. When I asked his daughter Laure whether she regards her father as a modernist, she responded with a question: "What is tradition—is it twenty years or fifty years or a hundred years?"—a fair point as Jean-Luc's approach now has been widely followed. Mounir Saouma, at micro-negociant Lucien Le Moine in Beaune, sees the "young tradition" as the last thirty or forty years, and the "old tradition" as the preceding period. He views the essential difference as the level of intervention. "So I saw the need for a place where we would make wine in the old tradition. There was a window for a policy of 'I don't do.' Many people were saying 'I do so and so.' The objective was to be as classic as possible. I don't like the word old-fashioned, it's pretentious. Hundreds of years ago there was a simple way of making wine: if it's red, put it in a tank, push down the cap, press, wait, bottle. I tried experiments in making wine very simply, putting it in tank and leaving it." Today Mounir makes his wines pretty much that way, and they have a wonderful bright elegance, very pure and precise. I would call them modern by comparison with the muddier flavor profiles of the past.

Just as history is written by the victors, wine styles are determined by fashion. If the current style were for light wines with a faint prickle of carbon dioxide, today's densely extracted wines with concentrated flavors would seem rustic. This is not so far fetched: two hundred years ago, lightly colored clairet was favored over dark-colored rouge in Bordeaux or Burgundy. Typicity is a moving target. So are attempts to recreate "authentic wines" not so much a matter of authenticity as sentiment? Certainly there's a reason why some indigenous varieties have disappeared: they do not make very interesting wines.

The attempts of the authorities in the Languedoc to suppress traditional varieties (which were introduced to make bulk wine) are double edged. They have led to a significant improvement in quality, but some appellations behave like the mullahs of wine, enforcing political correctness in the form of the same style on everyone. This is where attempts at modernity have lost sight of the heritage. The authorities should stop persecuting natural wine producers, and should allow them to succeed or fail in the marketplace on the basis of their quality (or lack thereof). Jean-Marie Bourgeois, of Domaine Henri Bourgeois, which has roughly equal holdings in Sancerre and in Marlborough, New Zealand, feels that the system in France discourages independence. "In the New World, the producer is responsible for the quality of his product. In France the responsibility has shifted to the appellation, people accept less responsibility for their own product."

If an appellation is to stand for anything, it isn't unreasonable to demand that its wines should share some common features. The question is where to draw the line between ensuring quality and suppressing innovation. Too often the regulations are defined for the benefit of the larger players, often negociants whose interests may not be the same as the smaller growers. And while sometimes regulations try to increase quality, for example by minimizing the proportion of inferior grape varieties, or by preventing cheap fixes such as immersing oak cubes in the wine instead of putting the wine in barrels, at other times they ignore quality: allowing chaptalization of wines that are sweet is no different in effect from simply sweetening the wine by adding sugar. The rules should focus on quality rather than uniformity.

The case for defining wine in France by appellations (rather than varietals) is captured by Jean Orliac at Domaine de l'Hortus in the Languedoc: "We have a savoir faire that's adapted to each region. Our experience and knowledge of terroirs is unique. The passion is always there—of course there are problems—but overall it's an intelligent approach, the dynamism of the viticulture of terroir. Wine in France is not just the product of terroir, it is the product of a thousand years of knowledge and experience. The position of vins de terroir is unquestionable. We have expensive costs like any developed country and of course we cannot compete at the lowest levels. But for the vins d'appellation, the production is unique, there we have the history."

The emphasis on place of origin has endless consequences. At premium levels, except for the best known wines, consumers are becoming accustomed to following the model of the New World and identifying wines by varietal name before place of origin. They may not know that wines from a particular appellation come from a specific variety. This can place appellations under a competitive disadvantage, especially the lesser known. At lower price levels, it's difficult to produce brands on a scale to match the New World, because most AOP or IGP regions are not large enough. Crossing the geographical border means that the wine can only be labeled as Vin de France, which marks it as coming from the lowest level of classification.

The view of terroir über alles makes the appellation a sacrosanct concept in wine production in France. In many cases, the driving force to create an appellation was a consortium of producers who found common ground in a well defined area. Success sometimes brings expansion, and a fair number of appellations have been devalued by expanding into unsuitable terroirs, such as St. Joseph, now stretching far to the north and south of the historic area, or Crozes-Hermitage across the Rhône, now merging the Plain de Chassis with the original granitic villages. If an appellation means anything, it should be confined to an area of reasonably homogeneous terroirs. The attempt to bring wine production in France into the modern world by reducing production of Vin de Table has led to a misguided fervor for promoting unsuitable areas into the AOP system, contradicting the very basis of the system.

Not all appellations have true terroir. It's almost a golden rule that Côtes or Coteaux are poor imitations of the "real" appellations that they adjoin. They are too often cumbersome amalgamations of various secondary terroirs living off the name of the great appellation nearby. If there's no distinctive terroir or character, should an area be an AOP? It would do a great deal for the bloated appellation system if these regions were demoted to something less than AOP. (This is the exact opposite of the last proposal at INAO, to promote the best AOCs into super-AOCs, but it recognizes the same principle that there is far too great a distance between the best and the worst in the system.) I hate to suggest another layer of complexity, but all the same…

The increasing focus on single vineyard wines leads many producers to make multiple cuvées from a single appellation. Here there is far too much room for confusion. Under the appellation, a wine can have a name that may be a specific lieu-dit, meaning that it comes from a specific place; or the label may just have a made-up brand name. Should brand names be distinct from lieu-dits, I asked Joseph Burrier at Château Beauregard, who is immersed in the attempt to define crus in Pouilly-Fuissé. "This is a very big issue, we are looking at that. But it's a free market, it's a pure nightmare—and Vieilles Vignes—it's an issue everywhere." I like the solution that has been adopted by the Bret brothers at La Soufrandière in Pouilly-Vinzelles. "All names on the labels are *climats*, except that if it's a selection, it states cuvée," explains Jean-Philippe Bret. What could be simpler? A name without qualification must be a specific place of origin; anything else must be preceded by a qualifier such as "cuvée".

"Mis en bouteille en Château (or Domaine)" is a powerful statement that a producer is completely responsible for a wine. The words "château" or "domaine" can be used on a label only for estate-bottled wine. Yet that's almost irrelevant compared with the extension of branding in which Bordeaux châteaux use their names for wines that aren't even from the appellation. Many Grand Cru Classés of the Médoc, to take the leading example, extend the marque of the Grand Cru from their second wine (from the estate) to a communal wine or even to wine from a neighboring appellation (typically the Haut-Médoc or even Bordeaux). The concept of brand extension is spreading into the right bank: one château adds purchased grapes to the estate grapes for its second wine. Doesn't this devalue the concept of the château? Will there be rosés and sparkling wines next? But if they introduced proper regulations, what would they do about Mouton Cadet, which now has only the most tenuous of connections with Mouton Rothschild where it all started…

What makes French wine unique? "Because it's not too much. And it's also the aging potential (sometimes)," says Etienne Sipp of Domaine Louis Sipp in Alsace. "Not too much" is (or perhaps was) the key: increasing ripeness and alcohol may threaten the ability to remain fresh and lively. France is scarcely immune from the general modern trend for elegance to give way to power. Perhaps it's no coincidence that the regions where the wines of France remain most unmistakably French are more or less north of the line of chaptalization. Yet the corollary of making wine in marginal conditions is that, while the top wines may be unsurpassed, the lesser wines may struggle to reach ripeness. South of the line of chaptalization, things are more regular, and the wines are richer, more extracted, and more alcoholic: the corollary is that their origin is less immediately identifiable and they are more open to competition from the New World. The best have a lightness of being that is atypical for the region.

There is (in my view) little to match the top French wines. While there are many individual examples of great wines in other countries, there are few places elsewhere in the world that equal the top regions of France for the sheer concentration of great wines. Perhaps trying to capture the essence of French wine is trying to define the indefinable, given the breadth of styles from cool to warm climates, and the variety of approaches from making a different blend each year to expressing a unique terroir with a single variety. But the best wines do have a certain sense of restraint; rather than trying to extract everything that can be extracted, they stop short so that you can see the complexity of flavors. We can only hope that in the era of global warming it remains possible to retain a sense of place together with the impression that a great vintage is a triumph of the struggle against marginal conditions.

VINS DE FRANCE

SANTÉ
GAIETÉ
ESPÉRANCE

Commissioned by the government in 1937, this poster reflects an era when France believed wine represented health, gaiety, and hope.

Vineyard Profiles

Symbols

- Town
- AOP (if different from town)
- IGP
- Red   Rosé   White   Sweet   Reference wines
- **2** Second wine
- **G** Grower-producer
- **N** Negociant (or purchases grapes)
- Cooperative
- Lutte raisonnée (sustainable viticulture)
- Organic
- Biodynamic
- Tastings/visits possible
- By appointment only
- No visits
- Sales at producer
- No direct sales

ha = estate vineyards; bottles = annual production

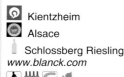

Eguisheim

Alsace

Les Ecaillers Riesling

www.leonbeyer.fr

20 ha; 700,000 bottles

Domaine Léon Beyer

This is one of the most traditional houses in Alsace—"Viticulteurs de Père en Fils depuis 1580"—formally founded in 1867. Vineyards, including an additional 40 ha that the Beyers work but do not own, are in the vicinity of Eguisheim. All of Alsace's varieties are represented, although Sylvaner is not being replanted. Beyer takes pride in making wines to accompany food, which means that everything is vinified bone dry (except for Vendange Tardive or SGN). "Typical and classic Alsace wines are, and always have been, dry, fresh and light." Vinification is in very old foudres, and the wine spends eight months on the lees, but vintages are often released somewhat later than other producers. Marc Beyer says that, "The style of the house has not changed in the past fifty years, except that yields have decreased so concentration has increased." The dry wines fall into three ranges: Classic, Reserves, and Grandes Cuvées. As Marc Beyer is one of the strongest critics of the grand cru system, Beyer's own names are used for the Grandes Cuvées, although the Riesling Les Ecaillers comes from the grand cru Pfersigberg, and the Riesling R de Beyer is from grand cru Eichberg. The top wines carry the label Comte d'Eguisheim, and are made only in the best years. They include Pinot Gris and Gewürztraminer, as well as Riesling, again from grand cru vineyards. They age well: the Riesling 2000 was vibrant and lively in 2014. Beyer also produces several Eaux de Vies.

Kientzheim

Alsace

Schlossberg Riesling

www.blanck.com

36 ha; 230,000 bottles

Domaine Paul Blanck

"My grandfather Paul established the domain in the 1920s, but we are the nineteenth generation of growers in the village, although there's nothing special about that," says Philippe Blanck, who runs the domain today with his cousin Frédéric, the winemaker. Vineyards are local: "The idea is to work the vineyards around the valley of Kaysersberg, it's interesting because we have many different types of soil here," Philippe explains. The range of dry wines is divided between the Classic Cuvées and Vins de Terroir. About 60% of production, the Classic Cuvées include all the varietals, and are vinified dry, or almost dry, in stainless steel, and bottled under screwcap. The Vins de Terroir come from lieu-dits or grand crus. After fermentation in stainless steel, they mature for twelve months in foudres. Here the natural richness is expressed by allowing some residual sugar. "The people who buy the Vins de Terroir know the wines so they aren't confused by varying sweetness," Philippe says. The style tends generally to richness, even at the Classic level, where there is often a buttery undercurrent. The range includes an impressive array of seven grand crus, with six in Riesling, and three each in Pinot Gris or Gewürztraminer. Riesling varies from the delicacy of Furstentum to the richness of Wineck-Schlossberg, and the sheer grip of Sommerberg. Pinot Gris and Gewürztraminer show great character, often with a lovely savory or herbal counterpoise to the typical sweetness.

Domaine Bott-Geyl

Located in a back street of Beblenheim, surrounded by suburban housing, the building is much larger than it appears from the outside, as a new three storey warehouse-like gravity-feed winery was constructed three years ago on top of the old caves. Vinification is in a mix of stainless steel and old foudres; most cuvées have some of each. The key to the style here is that fermentation is very slow, lasting several months, so the wines are bottled in the summer following the vintage, as by then there has been ample extraction. Jean-Christophe Bott doesn't have a set idea about style: "Each vintage imprints its character," he says. Although he tries to pick early, he believes the balance may differ with the vintage, so the wines are not necessarily dry. Christophe's aim of producing dry wines is usually achieved with Riesling, but balance in Pinot Gris and Gewürztraminer generally requires some residual sugar. The wines are divided into Vins d'Assemblage (blends of varieties), Vins de Fruits (Les Eléments: Riesling, Muscat, Pinot Gris, and Gewürztraminer), and the Vins de Terroir (lieu-dits and grand crus); and then of course the sweet wines. By the time you reach the vins de terroir, most of the wines do in fact have a touch of residual sugar. The style here often has a delicious sweet-sour balance, with savory impressions counterpoised with the fruits. It's always measured, so that Pinot Gris and Gewürztraminer show their character without overwhelming.

Beblenheim
Alsace
Grafenreben Riesling
www.bott-geyl.com

22 ha; 85,000 bottles

Domaine Albert Boxler

Discretely located in the main street of the town (no sign is evident in the street, but when you go round the back the winery and the family house are organized around a charming courtyard in typical Alsace style), the domain is just under the grand cru of Sommerberg. This is very much a family domain; I tasted with Jean Boxler in the house, with children playing in the next room. Boxlers have been here since the seventeenth century, but the domain was created by Albert Boxler in 1946 when he started to bottle his own wine. His grandson Jean has been making the wine since 1996. Most of the 30 individual vineyard parcels are in the immediate neighborhood, including several that are used to make different cuvées from Sommerberg. All of the cépages are grown here, but the focus is on Riesling, which is 40% of plantings. Everything is vinified as whole cluster, and there's a tendency to vinify the sweet wines in stainless steel and the dry wines in oak, but it doesn't always exactly work out. The Riesling is usually dry, but the Pinot Gris is usually demi-sec. Jean is not a fanatic about dryness and believes that the overall balance is more important. A pleasing sense of restraint characterizes all Albert Boxler's wines. Contrasting with the natural acidity there is a common warm softness. A consistent style runs across cépages, intensifying in Riesling, and then from Alsace to Grand Cru to Vieilles Vignes Grand Cru. Even the Crémant shows precision.

Niedermorschwihr
Alsace
Brand, Riesling

14 ha; 60,000 bottles

 Bergheim

 Alsace

Rotenberg Riesling
www.marceldeiss.com

27 ha; 135,000 bottles

Domaine Marcel Deiss

My last discussion with Jean-Michel Deiss had a surreal air. I found him doing the pigeage, physically immersed in a cuve of Pinot Noir, in the old way. I had to perch on top of a ladder leaning against the vat to talk with the disembodied head of Jean-Michel as he wallowed in the must. Jean-Michel has the air of a fanatic. "Cépage is a nonsense, it's a modern concept. It's impossible to make a great wine from a single cépage," he says. But he is a fanatic for making wine true to what he sees as the ancient tradition of Alsace: from more than one variety rather than from a single cépage. He is quick to point out that he does not produce his wines by assemblage, the mixing of wines made from different varieties, but each wine is produced from grapes of different varieties that are intermingled (complanté) in the vineyard. Indeed, floating in the must of the Pinot Noir were several bunches of white grapes. Production here offers both conventional and unconventional wines. The wines are grouped as Vins de Fruits (the usual varieties of Alsace, vinified as single varietals); Vins de Terroirs (wines from specific vineyards, including grand crus: whites consist of various varieties intermingled, and reds consist of Pinot Noir with small amounts of other varieties); and Vins de Temps, which are late harvest wines. Jean-Michel's son Matthieu has been responsible for winemaking since 2008, but Jean-Michel remains in charge, and the philosophy remains as idiosyncratic as ever.

 Riquewihr

Alsace

Jubilee Riesling

Les Neveux Jubilee
www.hugel.com

30 ha; 1,200,000 bottles

Maison Hugel & Fils

Maison Hugel dates from the seventeenth century and is run by brothers Marc and Étienne and their cousin Jean-Philippe (the twelfth generation since the house was founded in 1639). The winery occupies a picturesque rabbit warren of buildings in the old town of Riquewihr. Hugel is one of the larger negociant-growers, with estate vineyards providing about a quarter of its grapes. There are five lines of wines. Classic (entry level, from purchased grapes), Tradition (mid range, with stricter selection of purchased grapes), and Jubilee (the top cuvées, coming only from estate vineyards) are always fermented dry. This is something Étienne feels strongly about: "It's a very serious problem that affects the whole image of Alsace, with wines being made in sweet styles," he says. Only the late harvest wines, Vendange Tardive and SGN, are sweet. Hugel produces all of the varieties of Alsace, and was a pioneer in introducing Pinot Noir as a serious red wine. Hugel are well known for their rejection of the grand cru system—"The grand cru classification is meaningless as an indication of quality," says Étienne—so their wines are labeled only as Alsace, although Marc admits, "More than half of our vineyards are in grand crus, and in the best parcels at that, so it's absolutely surreal not to have grand cru on the label." The Jubilee Riesling comes from grand cru Schoenberg, and the Gewürztraminer from Sporen, and they are in fact the defining wines for these appellations.

Domaine Josmeyer

"We make dry white wines to go with food," says Céline Meyer, who runs Domaine Josmeyer together with her sister Isabelle. Created in 1854 by Alois Meyer and transferred down the generations, the domain is located in charming buildings around a courtyard in typical Alsace style, on the main street. Vineyards are mostly local, but spread out over many small parcels, about 80 in all. Vinification is traditional, with everything matured in old foudres. The focus here is classic: after a quick excursion into Pinot Blanc and Auxerrois (including the Pinot Auxerrois "K" cuvée which comes exclusively from old Auxerrois vines), tasting focuses on Riesling, Pinot Gris, and Gewürztraminer. Going up the range of Rieslings, flavors turn from petrol (in Le Kottabe from the plain) to citrus (in Les Pierrets from the slopes) to stone fruits (in grand crus Brand and Hengst), and the wines become increasingly reserved. These are not wines for instant gratification, but need time for full flavor variety to emerge. In spite of the commitment to dry style, alcohol levels are moderate. Brand Riesling is upright and Hengst is more powerful. A similar transition is seen with Pinot Gris, from the classic Fromenteau (Alsace AOP) to Brand and then Hengst: these are as dry as Pinot Gris gets, increasing in richness and power along the range. For Gewürztraminer, Les Folastries is almost dry, and the grand crus are a bit richer. The style brings out varietal character, muddied as little as possible by sugar.

JOSMEYER
ALSACE

PINOT GRIS
GRAND CRU HENGST

🔘 Wintzenheim
⚫ Alsace
🍾 Les Pierrets, Riesling
www.josmeyer.com
25 ha; 200,000 bottles

Domaine Marc Kreydenweiss

Located towards the northern tip of the vineyards, the Kreydenweiss domain was established in the seventeenth century, has been bottling wines since the mid nineteenth century, and includes vineyards that belonged to the Abbaye of Andlau before the French Revolution. The tasting room is located in a charming old house in the village. Marc Kreydenweiss has been running the domain since he took over in 1971 at the age of 23. He was one of the first in Alsace to adopt biodynamic viticulture, and in 1984 decided to focus on single vineyard wines; most of the dozen cuvées come from named plots, culminating in three grand crus. The Kreydenweiss operation has expanded beyond Alsace, first by purchasing the Perrières domain near Nîmes in 1999, and then by extending a negociant activity to Châteauneuf-du-Pape. In fact, more wine is now made in the south than at the original estate in Andlau. In Alsace there are also brandies made from Riesling, Pinot Gris, and Gewürztraminer, as well as eux-de-vie Mirabelle. An unusual feature of vinification here is that malolactic fermentation is encouraged, but this does not seem to detract from the freshness of the wines. The grand cru Rieslings have a penetrating minerality, and the lieu-dit wines follow the same style with less intensity. Pinot Gris often has savory overtones to balance the residual sweetness. Purity is the mark of the house, enhanced by low yields (around 40 hl/ha).

ALSACE GRAND CRU
2003

Le Moine
MŒNCHBERG PINOT GRIS
APPELLATION ALSACE GRAND CRU CONTROLÉE

MARC KREYDENWEISS

🔘 Andlau
⚫ Alsace
🍾 Wiebelsberg Riesling
www.kreydenweiss.com

14 ha; 70,000 bottles

Alsace

Wettolsheim

Alsace

Furstentum Pinot Gris
www.albertmann.com

21 ha; 120,000 bottles

Domaine Albert Mann

The Mann and Barthelmé families have been making wine in Wettol-sheim since the seventeenth century. The domain is named for Albert Mann (who started bottling his own wine in 1947), and whose grand-daughter, Marie-Claire, is married to Maurice Barthelmé; since 1989 the domain has included both families' vineyards, and is run today by Maurice together with his brother Jacky and their wives. Divided into almost a hundred different plots, the vineyards include five grand crus that represent about a third of the total. There are about 35 cuvées. Entry-level wines have been bottled under screwcap since 2004; everything else remains under cork. Vinification and aging is in stainless steel, and the wines are bottled relatively early to maintain freshness, except for some cuvées matured in barrique (a Pinot Blanc "élevée en barrique" and the reds). The domain is known for its hands-off approach. "We don't do oenology or make technical wine," says Maurice. The entry-level line, including most of the cépages, is intended to be fruity and approachable; they are mostly off-dry. Rieslings from the lieu-dits and grand crus vary from dry to overtly sweet; Pinot Gris is off-dry or sweet, and Gewürztraminer is always sweet. The style is relatively rich and powerful. There's an unusual emphasis on Pinot Noir, with no less than four single vineyard cuvées: Clos de la Faille and Les Saintes Claires from lieu-dits, and Grand P and Grand H from the Pfersigberg and Hengst grand crus.

Katzenthal

Alsace

Pfoeller Riesling
www.meyer-fonne.com

15 ha; 85,000 bottles

Meyer Fonné Vins

With a spectacular view from his living room window of the fortress on top of the hill of the Wineck-Schlossberg grand cru, Felix Meyer is right under the vineyards. The Meyer family have been in Katzenthal since 1732; Felix's great grandfather created the domain. The family house is at one end of the courtyard; at the other end are the winery buildings, where everything has been modernized. Felix has been in charge since 1992. He expanded the estate from an initial 6 ha, and now there are vineyards all around the local area, including several grand crus. Riesling and Pinot Blanc are the most important, but all the varieties are made except Sylvaner. There are usually 22-30 cuvées depending on whether there is VT and SGN. The focus is on terroir. "I'm very interested in terroir and passionate about it, we work on five grand crus and three lieu-dits, and this goes back twenty years so it's not something new," Felix says. The first level of wines, Alsace AOP and some Katzenthal village cuvées, are always vinified to dryness, and bottled in the Spring to preserve freshness. The lieu-dits and grand crus usually have a minimal touch of residual sugar, and are bottled just before the next harvest. Felix tries to be consistent. "Each cuvée has a single style, I don't want a cuvée to be sweet one year and dry another year," he says. The Rieslings are quite textured at lower levels and have a tendency to power at the grand cru level. Pinot Gris and Gewürztraminer tend to be quite forceful.

Domaine René Muré

This family domain has been producing wine since the seventeenth century. Véronique and Thomas Muré, the twelfth generation, work with their father René. In addition to estate vineyards, they buy grapes from growers under long term contract for around another 30 ha. The winery is just south of Rouffach, overlooked by grand cru Vorbourg, which includes the Clos St. Landelin, a monopole that is a lieu-dit at the southern tip purchased by René Muré in 1935. Wines are divided into those under the René Muré label and those under the Clos St. Landelin label, which include grand crus around Rouffach. Vinification is in old foudres (some more than a century old, but with internal temperature control). The wines spend 15 months on the lees. The Clos St. Landelin wines are organic. There are all the varieties, with a full range from dry to vendange tardive and SGN, but the Rieslings and Pinot Noirs are the signature wines here. Crémant and brandy are produced as well as still wine. Pinot Noir is about 10% of production, and has increased in proportion with the recent run of warm vintages (a return to the past as Rouffach was known for red wines in the Middle Ages). "Clos St. Landelin, it's paradise for Pinot Noir," says René. Wines under the René Muré label are intended for consumption relatively soon, but those under the St. Landelin label should have longevity of one to two decades. Riesling is intense and racy; Pinot Noir is earthy and spicy.

Rouffach

Alsace

Riesling Clos St. Landelin

"V" (Vorbourg)

www.mure.com

25 ha; 150,000 bottles

Domaine Ostertag

This domain was created by André's father in 1966, but he abruptly handed over the winemaking in 1980 to André when he was only twenty. There's more freedom to innovate here than in a domain bound by a long history. Behind the unassuming front on a back street in Epfig is a charming courtyard, surrounded by winery buildings. André essentially works the domain alone, using only estate grapes from his 75 individual vineyard plots. "This is crucial because the major part of quality comes from the work in the vineyards," André says. There are three series of wines: the basic series are AOP Alsace, there are some grand crus, and then there are the Vendange Tardive or SGNs. Except for the latter and for the Gewürztraminer, all the wines are dry. The Pinot Blanc is matured in barrique and (unusually for Alsace) goes through malolactic fermentation. In fact, the grand crus are sometimes refused the *agrément* on grounds of lack of typicity (because of exposure to new oak), and a compromise has been reached in which the name of the grand cru is put on the back label rather than stated on the front. About 7-8% of production is Pinot Noir, which also is matured in barriques rather than the traditional foudres. There is 100% destemming to make the wine as soft as possible, and délestage (a procedure in which the must is racked off and pumped back) is used rather than punch-down. The village wine uses one third oak and is bottled in July.

Epfig

Alsace

Muenchberg, Pinot Gris

domaine-ostertag.fr

14 ha; 100,000 bottles

Alsace

 Guebwiller

Alsace

Kitterlé, Pinot Gris
www.domaines-schlumberger.com

130 ha; 750,000 bottles

Domaine Schlumberger

Schlumberger's vineyards are in a long contiguous block running along the hillside (really more like a mountain slope) parallel with the town of Guebwiller, which nestles under the mountain. Vineyards are mostly at elevations of 250-350 m. To visit the vineyards, Séverine Schlumberger drives you up from the town in a Landrover. As the road goes up from the town, it narrows into little more than a muddy path running along a ledge between successive terraces of vineyards, with a sheer drop to the vineyards below. At one point it becomes so narrow that you are asked to get out and walk ahead while the car inches along behind, rather than risk everyone in the Landrover. It's around this point, Séverine says with a wicked grin, that they usually ask clients if they'd like to complete the order form. Established with Nicolas Schlumberger's purchase of 20 ha in 1810, today Schlumberger is one of the larger landholders in Alsace, with half of the holdings in the four grand crus around Guebwiller. "We don't believe in following fashions, which come and go, but make very much the same mix of varieties and styles as traditionally," Séverine says. Vinification is in foudres of very old oak. The wines are divided into Les Princes Abbés (with all seven of the varieties), the Grand Crus (with Riesling, Pinot Gris, and Gewürztraminer), and Les Collections (Vendange Tardive or SGN dessert wines). All wines come exclusively from the estate, and are very reliable.

Colmar

Alsace

Rangen, Clos St. Théobald
Riesling

16 ha; 120,000 bottles

Domaine Schoffit

The domain has an obscure location at the end of a tiny road through a housing estate close to the autoroute on the eastern edge of Colmar, yet there is a constant stream of visitors to the tasting room. Vineyards extend from Colmar to the south. The most important are in grand cru Rangen (well to the south at the end of the grand crus). There are all the cépages of Alsace, with a majority of Riesling. Depending on the year, there are 20-30 cuvées. Fermentation is allowed to proceed until it stops naturally, which usually leaves around 6 g/l residual sugar for Riesling, 7 g/l for Pinot Blanc, 12 g/l for Pinot Gris, and 30 g/l for Gewürztraminer. In the introductory range, Tradition, the wines taste drier than in the Caroline range, which is richer. Cuvée Alexandre is used for wines that are sweet but not labeled as Vendange Tardive. Wines from lieu-dit Harth have more concentration than AOP Alsace, and grand cru Sommerberg (only available in small amounts for old clients) increases in complexity; the top of the range is Rangen and the wines from the Clos St. Théobald monopole within it. For Riesling, Sommerberg showcases tense acidity and Rangen brings out delicacy. The Gewurztraminers are unusually subtle at levels ranging from sweet through VT to SGN. Vendange Tardive for both Pinot Gris and Gewurztraminer shows its character more as texture and flavor variety than overt sweetness; lovely if you want the flavor spectrum without too much sweetness.

Maison Louis Sipp

In charge of this family domain since 1996, Etienne Sipp has a thoughtful, quasi-academic approach, perhaps explained by his Ph.D. in mineral science. Created after the first world war, the domain has been located right in the center of picturesque Ribeauvillé since 1933. Today production comes exclusively from estate grapes, "From the historical part of the vineyards on the slopes," Etienne says. "Our vineyards are concentrated in a radius of 3-4 km," he adds, explaining that this is an area within a fractal field that is exceptionally diverse in its soil types. "Geology and climate are very specific here, which is why we can produce a high diversity of wines. The only negative is that the wines do not open quickly; they age well but need some time to open." Under a yellow label, the entry level range is divided into young wines and Nature'S wines, the latter being organic; the Reserve Personelle wines have longer aging before release. There are five single vineyards and two grand crus in the cuvées from specific terroirs, as well, of course, as late harvest. Purity of style allow vintage influence to show directly, as illustrated by a vertical of Riesling from Osterberg: 2010 is steely citrus, austere and needing time; 2009 is soft pleasure, with a smile of sweetness on the stewed citrus; 2008 is all delicate citrus; 2007 is more reserved; 2004 is quite floral. Pinot Gris and Gewürztraminer are more forward, and here the reserved style can translate into delicacy.

Ribeauvillé

Alsace

Osterberg Riesling

www.sipp.com

40 ha; 350,000 bottles

Marc Tempé

Located in an old house in the square in Zellenberg, the domain looks like it might go back eons, but in fact was started by Anne-Marie and Marc Tempé in 1993 when they obtained vineyards from their parents, who were retiring as members of the cooperative. "We asked ourselves what we should do with 7 ha, we had a clean slate, we weren't obliged to follow the history of our parents and grandparents. It was obvious to me that I should make wine as I wanted," says Marc. The domain remains small and hands-on: Marc came back from the vineyards on his tractor for our tasting. The clean slate has led to a distinctive style in which the wines have long élevage in barriques. "My aim is to make a dry wine because it goes best with food. Fermentation is never stopped here because the wine stays two years in cave with no intervention. It will find an equilibrium even if sometimes there is residual sugar," explains Marc. So some of the wines have a minimal level of sugar, just at the level of detection, but perfectly integrated. The wines are flavorful, with Rieslings generally soft but delicate, yet conveying a definite sense of silky texture. Pinot Gris shows its character with a herbal texture, and Gewürztraminer conveys an unusual sense of varietal character without becoming overwhelming. The Vendange Tardive or SGN Gewürztraminer is a knockout for its delicacy. In fact, if a single word describes the domain it's that delicacy of character running through the range.

Zellenberg

Alsace

Grafenreben Riesling

www.marctempe.fr

8 ha; 40,000 bottles

Maison Trimbach

One of the most important houses in Alsace, Trimbach remains a hands-on family business. "I can still drive a fork lift when needed," says Pierre Trimbach. Trimbach's heart is in Riesling, which is more than half of production. Riesling is always completely dry, and Pinot Gris and Gewürztraminer are vinified as dry as balance will allow. The winery on the main road through Ribeauvillé has a quaint appearance—Trimbach goes back to 1626—but wine production is entirely modern. Trimbach owns enough vineyards to supply about a third of its grapes. The Trimbachs do not believe in the grand cru system, although the wines for their top Rieslings come from grand cru terroir, Frédéric Emile from 6 ha in Geisberg and Osterberg, and Clos St. Hune from 1.67 ha in Rosacker. Recently, they have in fact introduced the first grand cru, a Geisberg Riesling. Yellow labels identify the Classic and Réserve lines. Gold labels indicate the terroir wines, which include Frédéric Emile Riesling, Réserve Personelle Pinot Gris, and Seigneurs de Ribeaupierre Gewürztraminer. White labels are the very peak, including Clos St. Hune and the Vendange Tardive and SGN. The style of Riesling is mineral, saline, bordering on austerity; going up the hierarchy, increasing time is needed for development, a couple of years for Réserve, five years for Geisberg, eight for Frédéric Emile, and at least a dozen for Clos St. Hune, which is widely acknowledged as one of the top Rieslings of Alsace.

Ribeauvillé

Alsace

Frédéric Emile Riesling

www.maison-trimbach.fr

45 ha; 1,300,000 bottles

Domaine Weinbach

This matriarchal domain makes some of the most precise and elegant wines in Alsace. It really doesn't matter if the variety is Riesling, Gewürztraminer or Pinot Noir: there is always that precise delineation of flavors. The name on the label says Domaine Weinbach, but the wall surrounding the Clos de Capucines at the heart of the vineyard (underneath the hill of grand cru Schlossberg) says Domaine Faller on one side and Le Weinbach (the name of the lieu-dit) on the other. The domain was acquired in 1898 by the Faller brothers, inherited by Théo Faller, and since 1979 run by his wife, Colette, and her daughters Catherine and Laurence. All the varieties are produced, and the wines are vinified dry with some notable exceptions. Where else do you find such elegant Muscat or refined Gewürztraminer, let alone the granular Pinot Gris and the steely Rieslings? The Rieslings are certainly the top of the line, from cuvée Théo (from the Clos des Capucines), Schlossberg, Cuvée Sainte Catherine (from the oldest parcels at the foot of Schlossberg), and Sainte Catherine l'Inédit, which comes from the best parcels in Schlossberg in the best years, and is the exception that often has a touch of residual sugar. There's a similar range of Pinot Gris and Gewürztraminer, and a brilliant Pinot Noir. 2014 was a sad year for the domain because Laurence, the talented young winemaker, died unexpectedly in May, followed later by Colette. Catherine and her family continue.

Kientzheim

Alsace

Riesling Schlossberg, Cuvée St. Catherine

www.domaineweinbach.com

30 ha; 120,000 bottles

Alsace

Domaine Zind Humbrecht

Created in 1959 with the marriage of Léonard Humbrecht to Geneviève Zind, this domain has become one of the best regarded in Alsace under the leadership of their son Olivier, who took over in 1989. Humbrechts have been making wine here since the seventeenth century. The domain moved to a stylish new building in the Herrenberg vineyard in 1992. Zind-Humbrecht was a pioneer in biodynamic viticulture and in reducing yields, typically now around 30-40 hl/ha. One consequence is increased richness, which is allowed to show itself by levels of residual sugar that vary with the vintage; the domain was one of the first (in 2001) to indicate the level of sweetness by marking it on the label against a five point scale. Most wines are bottled as lieu-dits, so there are around 30 cuvées altogether. The best known are perhaps Clos Windsbuhl (close to the Rosacker grand cru) and Clos Saint Urbain (a monopole within the Rangen grand cru). The only generic wines are Zind (a Chardonnay-Auxerrois blend from Windsbuhl labeled as Vin de France), Pinot Blanc, Riesling, and Muscat. The Calcaire cuvées come from calcareous terroirs. Then there are 7 Rieslings from lieu-dits or grand crus, 4 Pinot Gris, and 4 Gewürztraminers as well as the vendange tardive and SGN. The hands-off approach makes it hard to find a single description for the style, but it tends to a rich and powerful expression of each variety. Olivier is sceptical about Pinot Noir, so the emphasis remains on whites.

Turckheim
Alsace
Herrenweg de Turckheim Riesling
www.zindhumbrecht.fr
40 ha; 200,000 bottles

Domaine Valentin Zusslin

Jean-Paul and his sister Marie are the thirteenth generation to run this family domain since the Zusslins moved from Switzerland three centuries ago to settle in Orschwihr, where there are now several producers called Zusslin in the Grand'Rue. There's a huge genealogical chart of the Zusslins on the wall of the tasting room. Riesling is the most important variety, but unusually Pinot Noir is close behind. The main three cuvées are the Rieslings from Bollenberg (a lieu-dit), Clos Liebenberg (a monopole close to grand cru Pfingstberg), and Pfingstberg. Rieslings are pressed slowly for 10-12 hours, settled, and fermented in foudres. The style is racy, a very pure and precise expression of the variety, with savory overtones increasing from Bollenberg to Clos Liebenberg to Pfingstberg. A vertical of Pfingstberg similarly shows savory elements increasing with age and beginning to turn tertiary after ten years. The Bollenberg Harmonie Pinot Noir (Harmonie is the best plot for reds in Bollenberg) offers smooth red fruits supported by silky tannins and lovely aromatics. It's destemmed, vinified in wooden cuves, and matured in barriques with 50% new oak. The impression is softer and more aromatic than Burgundy, but very fine. About five years after the vintage is the right time to start the reds. In some years there is a vendange tardive Riesling from Pfingstberg, which is extraordinarily subtle; in fact, subtle is the one word that sums up the domain.

Orschwihr
Alsace
Clos Liebenberg Riesling
Bollenberg Harmonie
www.zusslin.com
16 ha; 90,000 bottles

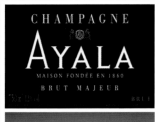

🜨 Aÿ
◉ Champagne
🍾 Brut Majeur
www.champagne-ayala.fr
▣ ⚒ G N
1 ha; 700,000 bottles

Champagne Ayala

Founded in 1860 by Edmond de Ayala (of Spanish descent) when he obtained the Château de Aÿ and vineyards as dowry, the house of Ayala was one of the original Grand Marques. Known for its (relatively) drier style, in its heyday in the 1920s Ayala was producing a million bottles annually. By late twentieth century, its reputation had slipped; in 2001 it was purchased by the Frey Group, who then sold it in 2005 to the Bollinger family (but Frey kept the old stock and the vineyards). There has been considerable investment, including a new cuverie. "Today there is a young team, the youngest in Champagne," they say proudly. Run independently, Ayala is being repositioned as a Chardonnay-driven brand. Wines that do not correspond to this style have been dropped, and the line focuses on the Majeur nonvintage (Brut, Rosé, and Natur), the Blanc de Blancs vintage, and the Perle d'Ayala prestige cuvée. Nonvintage is typically 40% Chardonnay, 40% Pinot Noir, and 20% Pinot Meunier; Perle d'Ayala is 80% Chardonnay to 20% Pinot Noir. Returning to Ayala's roots, dosage is always low, the highest being 7 g/l in the brut and rosé. The house has made something of a stir with its zero dosage (the Majeur Natur). House style is crisp and sassy, emphasizing clean lines and purity of fruits, showing at its peak in the Brut Nature and Blanc de Blancs; the Brut Majeur is light and elegant, the rosé is delicate, and Perle d'Ayala is rounder and fuller.

🜨 Mareuil-sur-Ay
◉ Champagne
🍾 Brut Rosé
www.champagne-billecart.fr
▣ ⚒ G N
50 ha; 2,000,000 bottles

Champagne Billecart Salmon

Presently in the seventh generation under François Roland Billecart, the family sold a minority interest (45%) to the Frey Group in 2005. The house was founded in 1818 by two families who had been in the village since the sixteenth century. The original vineyards were lost in 1925, but later partly restored; today estate grapes provide about a quarter of the supply, which comes from all over the region. Cellar master François Domi uses prolonged fermentation at low temperature with the philosophy that, "We are not looking for expression, we are looking for discretion." There is no set policy about malolactic fermentation, which depends on the acidity of the year. A small proportion of the vintage Champagne is vinified in old fûts. "There are no rules" is the most frequent expression here, "Everything depends on the year." The range includes nine cuvées, extending from the nonvintage Extra Brut, Brut, Blanc de Blancs, and Rosé to the vintage, the named vintage cuvées, Nicolas François and Elisabeth Salmon (rosé), and the single vineyard Clos Saint Hilaire. In addition, the range has now been widened by the Vintage line (intended to make vintage wine more accessible) and the Sous Bois (using barriques to achieve broader flavors). The fame of the Maison is based on the elegance of its rosés. The Brut Rosé vintage adds an integrated smoothness to the flavor spectrum of the Brut nonvintage, and the Elisabeth Salmon vintage offers seamless layers of flavor.

Champagne Bollinger

Still controlled by the original family, Bollinger is the most important of the Champagne houses remaining in private hands. It is the most traditional of houses, but that is not to say stultified. It is known for using barriques (3,000 of them) for vinification, using corks rather than crown caps for the first bottling, and storing Reserve wines in magnums. All this contributes to a recognizable intensity of style. An exceptionally high proportion of grapes (almost three quarters) come from Bollinger's own vineyards. Until recently there was no rosé, because it was not regarded as serious enough, but the house succumbed to market pressure and introduced one in 2008. The nonvintage is called the Special Cuvée, and the vintage has been called Grand Année since 2004. The Vieilles Vignes Françaises is a Blanc de Noirs from two small plots of ungrafted vines behind the Maison. Pinot Noir is the dominant grape, more than 60% in the Special Cuvée and Grand Année. Bollinger are sceptical about Pinot Meunier; cellarmaster Gilles Descôtes says, "It is more rustic and does not age as well. This does not matter for nonvintage (where it is limited to 15%), but is an issue for vintage." Bollinger introduced the idea of re-releasing old vintages by holding them on the lees for several extra years until disgorgement, as indicated in the name of the prestige R.D. cuvée (Recently Disgorged). Whether nonvintage or vintage, the style is dry, toasty, muscular, and suitable as a match for food rather than an aperitif.

Aÿ
Champagne
La Grand Année
www.champagne-bollinger.com

164 ha; 2,500,000 bottles

Champagne Deutz

Founded in 1838, Deutz remained under family control until it was sold in 1983 to the Rouzard family who own Roederer. Estate vineyards account for about 20% of supply, and the rest comes from vineyards within a 30 km radius of the Maison. "We concentrate at Deutz in developing a strong purity, finesse, and elegance—no wood barrels, no fermentation in wood," says Jean-Marc Lallier-Deutz. To maintain freshness, reserve wines come from the past couple of years, and form a high proportion of the Brut Classic, which accounts for around 90% of production. Malolactic fermentation is routine, and dosage is usually around 9 g/l. "The Deutz style is already clean and mineral; with less dosage or no MLF, the wines would be too aggressive, too austere," explains Jean-Marc. The hallmark of the house style for me is a certain sense of texture on the palate, suggestive of long time on the lees, which counterpoises the typical freshness. This shows clearly in the Brut Classic, and is accompanied by just a touch more density and power in the vintage Blanc de Blancs. It becomes a backdrop to a style that is more delicate and precise in the Armour de Deutz (a Blanc de Blancs); and then with the richness of the spectacular William Deutz the texture is superficially less obvious because of sheer fruit concentration. The vintage rosé is elegant, showing the refinement and purity of Pinot Noir (until 2006 it was 100% Pinot Noir; since then a little Chardonnay has been included).

Aÿ
Champagne
Brut Classic
www.champagne-deutz.com

42 ha; 2,000,000 bottles

Champagne

Urville

Champagne

Carte d'Or

www.champagne-drappier.com

56 ha; 1,500,000 bottles

Champagne Drappier

This house has an unusual location, well to the south of the main Champagne regions, in the Aube; southeast of Troyes, it's closer to Chablis than to Reims. Surrounded by apartment buildings in Urville, Drappier is the most important Champagne house in the Aube, although it also has cellars in Reims. The southern location results in a dominance of Pinot Noir. In fact, Drappier led the region in replanting Pinot Noir in the 1930s. Founded in 1808, this family house is now in its eighth generation, led by Michel Drappier. The estate vineyards are all around Urville, but there is an equal area of vineyards under contract throughout the rest of the Champagne region. Wines are mostly fermented in stainless steel, everything goes through malolactic, but barriques are used for partial maturation of the top cuvées. The regular Brut cuvée, the Carte d'Or, is 80% Pinot Noir; however, it is fresh and lively, with a touch of salinity on the palate bringing it close to Blanc de Blancs in style. The commitment to Pinot goes so far as to include 5% Pinot Blanc in the Blanc de Blancs. A focus on low dosage sees an unusual rosé that is a 100% Pinot Noir produced by saignée with zero dosage, and this trend is combined with an emphasis on low sulfur in a Blanc de Noirs Brut Natur that is bottled with no sulfur. The vintage Grande Sendrée is 55% Pinot Noir to 45% Chardonnay. There is a cuvée of forgotten white varieties (still legal but rare) called Quattuor.

Ambonnay

Champagne

Blanc de Noirs

12 ha; 100,000 bottles

Champagne Egly Ouriet

Founded in Ambonnay in 1930, this boutique house focuses on black varieties and today is run by Francis Egly, the fourth generation, who is known for being difficult to contact, if not actually reclusive. "That's Francis," others growers say, when you comment on his idiosyncratic manner. Most of the vineyards (8 ha) are in Ambonnay; all are grand cru except for a 2 ha plot of premier cru Pinot Meunier in Vrigny. The emphasis in the vineyards is on controlling yields, with a strong green harvest, so yields are about half of the typical level for Champagne. This results in greater levels of ripeness. Wines are fermented and matured on the lees in a mixture of oak barriques and tanks; there is no fixed policy about malolactic fermentation; and aging after the second fermentation is longer than usual, typically almost four years for the Brut Tradition. The ripeness of the grapes allows dosage to be kept low, typically less than 3 g/l (although the wines are labeled Brut). Three quarters of plantings are Pinot Noir. The plot of old (40 year) Pinot Meunier in Vrigny is used for an unusual monovarietal cuvée, Les Vignes de Vrigny. This is an interesting wine, but less refined than the Blanc de Noirs or the Brut Tradition (70% Pinot Noir and 30% Chardonnay). Dominated by Pinot Noir, the house style is relatively weighty and oxidative, developing classic toast and brioche fairly soon after disgorgement. Egly-Ouriet is also known for producing a still red Pinot Noir from Ambonnay.

Champagne Pierre Gimonnet et Fils

Gimonnets have been in the village of Cuis since at least 1720, but it was Didier Gimonnet's grandfather who created the Maison after he began to vinify his own wine in the 1920s. He had a variety of crops, and sold white wine to the bistros, as well as a few bottles of Champagne; and he kept cows until 1959. "It was my father who gave a real identity to our wine when he began to vinify parcel by parcel in stainless steel, and to make rational blends," says Didier, who runs the domain today with his brother Olivier. "We are engineering graduates and for us everything must be rational," he adds. The focus here is on Blanc de Blancs, with different cuvées representing assemblages of parcels in different proportions. The house philosophy is to blend grand crus for structure with premier crus for freshness. The two nonvintage cuvées are the Cuis premier cru, which plays on delicacy, and the Oger grand cru, which is fuller than the usual Gimonnet style. Responding to market demand, there is also a Rosé des Blancs, which is 90% Chardonnay. Gastronome is a lighter vintage style. Fleuron is the principal vintage wine. Oenophile is a zero dosage version of the same wine (it's labeled Extra Brut). Special Club is a Vieilles Vignes bottling, and shows increased purity and precision. Except for Oenophile, all the wines have low dosage, usually 6.5 g/l. The house style tends to freshness and lightness, with filigree acidity: airy and delicate is how Didier describes it.

 Cuis

Champagne

Cuis Premier Cru
www.champagne-gimonnet.com

28 ha; 250,000 bottles

Champagne Gosset

The oldest house in Champagne, Gosset was established in Aÿ in 1584, when Pierre Gosset started producing red wine. For much of the twentieth century, it produced champagne for sale by other brands. In 1994 it was sold to the owners of Cognac Frapin, and in 2009 they purchased Château Malakoff from Laurent Perrier for the new headquarters in Epernay. The underground caves are vast, with 2 km of galleries that can store 2.5 million bottles. Owning virtually no vineyards, Gosset purchases grapes from about 200 growers, cultivating 120 ha all over the region. The house style emphasizes freshness. "We are one of the few houses that avoid MLF, we want to keep the freshness, the acidity, so the Gosset signature is to avoid malo. Until ten years ago we used oak, but never for the first fermentation. We were storing wines in oak to get more richness and roundness. But then the wines had sufficient richness, so we stopped using oak. Using oak doesn't really correspond to the Gosset style," says export manager Philippe Manfredini. The style shows clearly on the Blanc de Blancs, and is softened by the broader flavors of the Grande Réserve. In addition to the Grande Millésime vintage, the prestige vintage cuvée, Celebris, has evident depth to nose and palate, cut by that trademark citric freshness. Rosé is unusually important at Gosset—it is at least 10% of production—but the style here is slightly different, a touch broader and more rustic without that characteristic freshness.

 Aÿ

Champagne

Grande Reserve
www.champagne-gosset.com

1 ha; 1,200,000 bottles

Champagne

Champagne Charles Heidsieck

Relationships between the various Heidsieck Champagne houses have changed over time. Charles Heidsieck was the last of the three to be established, in 1851: the houses that later became known as Piper-Heidsieck and Heidsieck Monopole had been founded at the end of the previous century. Founder Charles Camille Heidsieck broke away from his family to start Charles Heidsieck as a negociant business. Today Charles Heidsieck and Piper-Heidsieck are owned by EPI, the holding company of the Descours family (owners of various clothing brands), who purchased them from Rémy-Cointreau in 2011. (Heidsieck Monopole is part of the Vranken group.) The same team is responsible for winemaking at Charles Heidsieck and Piper-Heidsieck, but Charles Heidsieck has the greater reputation, while Piper-Heidsieck has the greater volume. Charles Heidsieck has a flamboyant history, going back to when Charles Camille became known as "Champagne Charlie" during a stay in the United States, when he was imprisoned during the Civil War on suspicion of being a spy. The prestige cuvée was named for him until the name was changed after 1985 to Blanc de Millènaires. The Brut Réserve, which has equal proportions of all three grape varieties and is more than three quarters of production, is a very solid Champagne, with dosage of 11 g/l making it soft and broad. There is also a nonvintage rosé, and both vintage Brut and rosé.

 Reims
 Champagne
 Brut Réserve
www.charlesheidsieck.com

65 ha; 1,000,000 bottles

Champagne Henriot

The commercial history of this house is intricately linked with the ups and downs of Champagne. The family came to Champagne in 1640, and founded the house in 1808; it has remained in their hands, but with many changes of direction. The founder's grandson, Ernest, was involved in founding Charles Heidsieck (Charles was his brother-in-law). Under Joseph Henriot, who took over in 1962, Henriot actually purchased Charles Heidsieck in 1976 and sold it in 1985. At the same time, Joseph sold most of the 125 ha of Henriot estate vineyards to Veuve Clicquot, which he then ran until 1994, when he returned to rescue Henriot. Then Henriot expanded by purchasing Bouchard Père in Beaune, followed by William Fèvre in Chablis. Joseph's son, Stanislas, ran Henriot from 1999 until 2010, when he was replaced by his brother, Thomas. Reduced to 35 ha of vineyards, without much in the way of grand crus, Henriot now buys 70% of its grapes. Vinification is exclusively in stainless steel, malolactic is usually performed, and a small proportion of reserve wines is kept as a perpetual reserve. Dosage is usually in the upper part of the Brut range, around 9-10 g/l. Until recently, Henriot did not use Pinot Meunier, but now includes some in its Brut Souverain and Rosé. Quality has revived in the present decade, and the style tends to be dense, with even the Brut Souverain more suitable to accompany a meal than to drink as an aperitif.

 Reims
 Champagne
 Blanc de Blancs
www.champagne-henriot.com

35 ha; 1,500,000 bottles

Champagne Jacquesson

Founded in 1798 in Châlons-sur-Marne, Jacquesson was a large producer by the mid nineteenth century, then collapsed and had a chequered history through several owners. Jean Chiquet was a grower in Dizy when he bought it in 1974. Production was transferred to the family property, where there's a charming house and courtyard on one side of the main road, and very large cellars on the other side. "I joined in 1977 and spent ten years negotiating with my father to change things," recollects Jean-Hervé Chiquet, who together with his brother, has transformed Jacquesson into a quality boutique. Providing three quarters of the grapes, estate vineyards focus on premier and grand crus; volume has been reduced to improve quality. The Chiquet brothers reject the conventional wisdom of Champagne. "Our idea is the opposite of the nonvintage concept, we don't care about consistency, we want to make the best wine we can without hiding the base vintage," says Jean-Hervé. So a wine is made each year with the current vintage as base, and the previous two years as reserve; it's identified with a number (#738 has base year 2010). Dosage is always minimal—virtually everything is Extra Brut—and the style is crisp, mineral, and saline. "If we are making the best wine we can, we cannot also make a general vintage," explains Jean-Hervé, but there are small cuvées of vintage wines from single vineyards in Dizy, Ay, and Avize. Flavorful would be a fair description of the style.

 Dizy
 Champagne
Cuvée #737
www.champagnejacquesson.com

36 ha; 270,000 bottles

Champagne Krug

The first time I visited Krug, a tour and tasting was followed by a leisurely lunch at a bistro in Reims with Henri Krug. The house was already owned by LVMH, but it still felt like a small family business. On my most recent visit, it felt like part of an international conglomerate. A professional hostess conducted a tour and tasting, and a winemaker was full of corporate caution in discussing Krug's policies. In spite of the change in atmosphere, however, the Champagne remains every bit as good, the only change perhaps being that the corporate environment has resulted in brand extension into more expensive special cuvées. The characteristic features of Krug's production have been maintained, in particular the unusual emphasis on Pinot Meunier, and the use of old oak casks to ferment the wine. Wine is then transferred to stainless steel. MLF is neither encouraged nor discouraged. Emphasis on blending is on identifying the character of individual lots: "You cannot say there is a specific proportion of a variety, we never speak of varieties, this is a nonsense," says winemaker Julie Cavil. Usually Krug is in fact driven by Pinot Noir, but occasionally Chardonnay is more successful and predominates. The nonvintage Grande Cuvée is more than 85% of production. There are two single vineyard wines, Clos de Mesnil (Blanc de Blancs) and now also Clos d'Ambonnay (Blanc de Noirs). The Krug collection comes from re-releases, not necessarily from later disgorgement.

 Reims
Champagne
Grande Cuvée
www.krug.com

20 ha; 500,000 bottles

Champagne

Aÿ

Champagne

Blanc de Blancs

www.champagne-lallier.fr

12 ha; 400,000 bottles

Champagne Lallier

A mid-sized house, Lallier prides itself on using only Pinot Noir and Chardonnay from premier and grand cru vineyards. (In fact, it's mostly grand cru, premier cru being used only for the rosé.) The 43 parcels of estate vineyards are on the slopes around Aÿ, and provide a quarter of the grapes; the rest come from the Côte des Blancs and Montagne de Reims. Although the Lallier family has been long established in Aÿ, the history of the house is not very old: the brand as such started in 1996 when René James Lallier purchased a winery in the center of Aÿ, in fact constructing a facility on top of eighteenth century cellars. Then in 2004, he sold Champagne Lallier to winemaker Francis Tribaut (himself fourth generation in Aÿ). Expansion has caused production to be moved to a new facility in Oger. Fermentation is in stainless steel, and malolactic is only partial in order to preserve freshness. There are only six cuvées; except for the Blanc de Blancs, all are dominated by Pinot Noir. Matured for 48 months before release, the Grande Réserve is 65% Pinot Noir to 35% Chardonnay and shows a stone fruit spectrum, with hints of exotic fruits and impressive density. The Blanc de Blancs has a very clean pure fruit expression, with a precision of focus and clarity of fruits that is the mark of the house style, followed also by the zero dosage and vintage cuvées. Dosage is low for all cuvées, except for the cuvée Grand Dosage, which is sweet.

Vertus

Champagne

Terre de Vertus

www.larmandier.fr

16 ha; 130,000 bottles

Champagne Larmandier-Bernier

The emphasis here is on terroir. The Maison has an unlikely location near a semi-industrial estate on the outskirts of Vertus, at the southern end of the Côte des Blancs, but inside the gates is a modern facility surrounded by a charming garden. Producing wine only from their own vineyards on the Côte des Blancs, Pierre and Sophie Larmandier try to represent their vineyards by biodynamic viticulture, vinifying the wine in wood, and keeping it on the full lees in wood until bottling. Wood of various sizes is used, matched to the terroir. "The more powerful wines, like Cramant, go into barriques, and the more delicate, like Vertus, into foudres," Sophie Larmandier explains. Two concrete eggs are used for the rosé de saignée (mostly Pinot Noir), which has three days of maceration. The biodynamic approach is all-inclusive. "Yeast is part of the terroir," Sophie explains, "We are trying to develop our own yeast for the second fermentation." All the cuvées are extra brut or zero dosage in order to focus on terroir. Latitude is an extra brut, and Longitude is a premier cru extra brut, showing a savory palate with a mineral finish; in vintage, Terre de Vertus is a zero dosage premier cru exhibiting saline delicacy when young, softening with age. There are also wines from Avize and a Vieilles Vignes from Cramant, which stands out as the richest wine in the range. There's a distinctive character here, with an authenticity far from the manipulated quality of many Champagnes.

Groupe Laurent-Perrier

"Brut dosage, reliance on Chardonnay, vinification in stainless steel to maintain freshness—we were the first to abandon barriques—it is the root of our style of lightness and elegance that made Laurent Perrier an ambassador for contemporary champagne, that is, for an aperitif wine," says Anne-Laure Domenichini. Laurent-Perrier was founded in 1812, and was in dire straits by 1939, when it was sold to the de Nonancourts. After the war, Bernard de Nonancourt established the principles on which the Maison is still run today by the third generation. One of the five largest houses, it is a public company, however, and expanded significantly by taking over Château Malakoff in 2004: it also owns Salon-Delamotte and de Castellane. The winery is located in an extensive estate on the main road through Tours-sur-Marne (east of Aÿ, away from the other major houses). Estate vineyards provide 11% of the grapes, the rest coming from 1,200 growers. With 50% Chardonnay and 11 g/l dosage, the Brut is a very mainstream aperitif. I find the Ultra Brut, an equal blend of the ripest Chardonnay and Pinot Noir, relaunched in 1981, to be a step up in refinement: more precise rather than particularly drier in its impression. The rosé ("launched in 1968 when rosé was considered a froufrou") is famous as a saignée, conveying an unusual sense of structure. Grand Siècle (created in 1959) is a prestige cuvée blended from three vintages that were declared by Laurent Perrier.

 Tours-sur-Marne
 Champagne
 Ultra Brut
www.laurent-perrier.fr

150 ha; 7,000,000 bottles

Champagne

Champagne Moët et Chandon (& Dom Pérignon)

A flagship of LVMH, Moët & Chandon is by far the largest house in Champagne, with almost 1,200 ha of estate vineyards, and an annual production of 30 million bottles (ten per cent of all Champagne). The style cannot honestly be said to be extraordinary, but of course Moët also produces the famed Dom Pérignon brand, perhaps the best known prestige cuvée in Champagne, and an altogether different quality level. Production of Dom Pérignon is around 5-6 million bottles (which alone would place it among the top Champagne houses by size). It was first made as a late disgorgement of Moët Champagne, from the fabled 1921 vintage (in 1936), but since 1947 has been produced separately. Dom Pérignon is first released a minimum of 8 years after the vintage; subsequently there are two Oenothèque (late disgorgement) releases, P2 after a minimum of 12 years, and P3 after a minimum of 18 years. The initial releases have an impressive ability to age; the original release of 1996 is still drinking well today, although of course it is not as fresh as the Oenothèque disgorged in 2008. Since 1959 there has also been a rosé cuvée. The assemblage contains only Pinot Noir and Chardonnay, with up to 60% of either, depending on vintage. Vineyard sources are grand crus from Moët's holdings, with some premier cru from around the abbey at Hautvillers, which Moët now owns. Dom Pérignon is created in more years than you might expect, with seven vintages in the 1990s.

 Épernay
 Champagne
www.moet.com

1190 ha; 30,000,000 bottles

Champagne Pierre Moncuit

The third generation runs this family domain, divided between 15 ha on the Côte des Blancs and 5 ha at Sézanne. All wines are Blanc de Blancs, except for a rosé. There are three nonvintage cuvées, a Brut (Hughes à Coulmet), the prestige Brut (Pierre Moncuit-Delos), and a rosé grand cru. For vintage wines, there is a Brut and an Extra Brut (or sometimes a non dosé); and a Vieilles Vignes is made occasionally. Except for the Extra Brut, dosage is always around 7-8 g/l. Vinification is in stainless steel, and malolactic fermentation always occurs. The style here makes few concessions, even to vintage: nonvintage cuvées actually come from a single recent vintage (in 2013 the cuvées I tasted at the Maison all came from 2010). This unusual policy started when Pierre Moncuit decided he wanted to capture the spirit of each year. Vintage-dated wines are reserved for exceptional years. Although there will be more variation in the nonvintage cuvées than usual in Champagne, the style generally tends towards the austere, highlighting purity of fruits, which can be aggressive in some vintages. The moderate dosage only just cuts the acidity, and even the Brut gives somewhat of the drier impression of an Extra Brut. Fruits are pure and clean but not overly generous. These are wines that may need extra time in bottle to show at their best. When the Moncuits are asked to define house style, the answer is rather bland: "To maintain continuity of style, without any change from the past."

 Le Mesnil-sur-Oger

Champagne

Pierre Moncuit-Delos
www.pierre-moncuit.fr

20 ha; 180,000 bottles

Champagne Nicolas Feuillatte

Reflecting the unusual importance of cooperatives in Champagne, Nicolas Feuillatte is probably the most prestigious of France's cooperatives. (There really was a Nicolas Feuillatte, and he sold his brand to the Centre Viticole in 1987.) Feuillatte's annual production of almost 10 million bottles places it as one of the largest Champagne houses, third in worldwide sales, behind Moët & Chandon and Veuve Clicquot. It represents 82 of the 140 cooperatives in the Champagne region, with 1,000 growers covering 2,250 ha (about 7% of the vineyards), including holdings in grand and premier crus. Production facilities are on an industrial scale (the plant occupies 11 ha, with 15 individual tank halls), employing a highly automated vinification process. Malolactic fermentation occurs for all cuvées, and the nonvintage wines are aged for three years before disgorgement. The range includes almost 20 cuvées. The regular Brut cuvées are not especially interesting (but the same might be said about most of the major brands). However, Nicolas Feuillatte goes head to head with the major brands in developing prestige cuvées (the Palme d'Or Brut and rosé cuvées come from grand crus), and a series of single vineyard vintage wines (from Mesnil, Cramant, Verzy, and Chouilly). For a cooperative, this is a dynamic venture, and there isn't a whole lot to distinguish its quality from standard major brands, except perhaps slightly more reasonable prices. The style tends to freshness.

Reims

Champagne

Blanc de Blancs
www.nicolas-feuillatte.com

0 ha; 10,000,000 bottles

Champagne Bruno Paillard

Bruno Paillard had worked with his father as a grape broker for six years when he decided to found his own house in 1981. "I tried to persuade my father, but he thought I was crazy," he recollects. "The idea was to take the north face road, to make the best quality wines for restaurants." The winery is a striking modern building of glass and steel on the outskirts of Reims. "It was difficult—and expensive—to acquire vineyards," Bruno says, but estate vineyards now provide more than half the grapes; the rest comes from 60 growers. The style here is airy and delicate. "I like tension and vibrancy, and that's why people sometimes find the wines a little austere at first; perhaps I should not say austere, but they are discrete and open slowly, they need a little more time." Vinification uses a mix of stainless steel and barriques. Aging on the lees more than doubles the legally required period, and there is a delay before release as Bruno feels strongly that disgorgement is a trauma to the wine. The Brut is a classic blend with almost half Pinot Noir; the rosé uses a mix of short and long maceration (and has a little Chardonnay for freshness); and the Blanc de Blancs has a slightly lower atmospheric pressure to enhance its finesse. Dosage has been lowered steadily and now is typically 6 g/l for nonvintage; vintage wines are slightly lower at 5 g/l. Both vintage and nonvintage show great fruit purity with a silky finish.

 Reims

 Champagne

Première Cuvée, rosé

www.champagnebrunopaillard.com

32 ha; 450,000 bottles

Champagne Perrier-Jouët

Founded in 1811, Perrier-Jouët has rather grand quarters on the Avenue de Champagne in Epernay, just across the street from Château Perrier, built by the family in 1854. In 2005 Perrier-Jouët became part of Pernod Ricard (who also own Mumms). Perrier-Jouët (or P-J as it's known in the trade) has around 10 km of galleries in its extensive underground caves, which can store 10 million bottles. About a third of the grapes are supplied by estate vineyards, with half on the Côte des Blancs, giving strong emphasis to Chardonnay; this contributes to a more feminine style, says cellar master Hervé Deschamps. Perrier-Jouët makes only Brut Champagne. Dosage is usually 8-10 g/l, depending on the year. "We don't change the dosage, low dosage is a fashion," Hervé says. Vinification is in stainless steel, and all wines go through malolactic fermentation. "Malo opens the wine, when fermentation was in oak we did not use MLF, but kept the wine longer before shipping," says Hervé. Nonvintage spends three years before disgorgement, and vintage spends six years. The house style is clear and elegant; you might say Perrier-Jouët is the archetypal aperitif champagne. A characteristic cleanness of line, a very fine floral impression, runs from the Grand Brut nonvintage through the Belle Époque vintage wines, showing elegance and delicacy rather than power. The Belle Époque Blanc de Blancs adds silkiness, while the rosé is softened, but that characteristic clarity runs throughout.

 Épernay

Champagne

Grand Brut

www.perrier-jouet.com

65 ha; 2,500,000 bottles

Champagne

Le Mesnil-sur-Oger

Champagne

Cuvée de Réserve
www.champagne-peters.com

20 ha; 170,000 bottles

Champagne Pierre Peters

Now into the sixth generation, this family domain produces Champagne only from estate grapes. Production started with still wine; the first Champagne was a demi-sec, called Veuve Peters, in 1919. The Pierre Peters label was introduced in 1944. The premises in Mesnil-sur-Oger look like a private residence, but behind and underneath is a modern cellar. Vineyards are almost exclusively Chardonnay on the Côte des Blancs, three quarters in Grand Cru villages. The objective is to bring out fruit: grapes are harvested for freshness, the wine goes through malolactic fermentation, and dosage for the nonvintage Brut is only 6-7 g/l. There is an Extra Brut with dosage of 2 g/l. Vintage wines have 4-5 g/l dosage. "I use stainless steel to safeguard the pure character of the wine. Dosage for me is a means of compensating between cool and warm years to maintain consistency in the nonvintage. The vintage is different, it shows the style of the year," says Rodolphe Peters. Kept in tulip-shaped cement cuves designed to maximize contact with the lees, the reserve goes back a long way. "I assemble all my wines into one reserve, it's a reserve perpetuelle that has almost 15 years." The style extends from the relatively straightforward Brut to the precision of the Extra Brut (in fact an undeclared vintage); the same variation is reprised in the vintage wines, with breadth to L'Esprit, the general vintage wine, but a wonderful tight precision to Les Chétillons, a single vineyard wine from Mesnil-sur-Oger.

Mareuil-sur-Ay

Champagne

Royale Réserve Brut
www.champagnephilipponnat.com

17 ha; 600,000 bottles

Champagne Philipponnat

The Philipponnats were growers and merchants at Aÿ in the sixteenth century, but the house was officially founded in 1910 in Mareuil-sur-Aÿ. The family sold the house in the seventies, its reputation declined during the nineties, and in 1997 it became part of the Lanson-BCC group. Charles Philipponnat, grandson of one of the founders, came from Moët to run it in 2000. "We haven't really changed the style, we've made it more precise," Charles says, but that's understating the effect of the first change he made, to drop dosage for nonvintage (Royale Réserve) from 12 g/l to 8 g/l. For vintage, "We use 4.5 g/l dosage in every vintage (called cuvée 1522), so if there are differences in perception they reflect vintage character." All of the cuvées except the Grand Blanc (a Blanc de Blancs) have a majority of Pinot Noir. Fermentation and maturation use a mix of stainless steel and barriques. The top wine is the Clos des Goisses, which comes from a narrow strip of land rising up steeply from the river Aÿ just along the road from the Maison. This achieves an unusual degree of ripeness, and (perhaps uniquely in Champagne) is made in virtually every vintage; it has the same blend as 1522, two thirds Pinot Noir and one third Chardonnay. The style of the house is full and powerful, showing the dominance of Pinot Noir, but there's a refreshing catch of citrus at the end, reflecting the use of only partial malolactic fermentation.

Champagne Pol Roger

The most famous consumer of Pol Roger was Winston Churchill, for whom the prestige cuvée was named in 1975. (He once described Pol Roger's Maison as "the world's most drinkable address.") One of the Grand Marques, founded in 1849, this is still a family-run company, with an impressively massive headquarters on the Avenue de Champagne in Epernay. A buying spree has increased estate vineyards to provide just over half of supply. Pol Roger has always been a popular Champagne in the U.K., which remains its major export market. The cellars are completely modernized, with vinification in stainless steel, and the wine goes through malolactic fermentation. The house attributes its extra-tiny bubbles and finesse to the fact that the caves at Pol Roger are unusually deep and cold, so everything takes longer. The White Foil cuvée was introduced in 1955 with a back label "Reserved for Great Britain." Dosage on the White Foil (now officially called the Extra Cuvée de Reserve) was reduced in 2010 to 9-10 g/l, and the wine now lives up better to the house's aspiration for freshness. The Pure cuvée has zero dosage (although labeled Extra Brut), and the Rich cuvée is a 35 g/l demi-sec. All of these are blended from equal proportions of each of the three grape varieties. Vintages wines include Brut, Brut Rosé, and Blanc de Blancs. Cuvée Sir Winston Churchill is dominated by Pinot Noir to achieve a rich, full-bodied style in keeping with its name.

Épernay
Champagne
Blanc de Blancs
www.polroger.com

90 ha; 1,600,000 bottles

Champagne Louis Roederer

Roederer describes itself as one of the last independent family-run Champagne houses, but this is a little deceptive as it is now quite a wine conglomerate: it created Roederer Estate in California, purchased Champagne Deutz (which continues to be run independently), and also owns Château Pichon Lalande in Pauillac, Domaines Ott in Provence, Delas Frères in the Rhône, and Ramos Pinto Port in Portugal. Louis Roederer, who inherited the company from his uncle in 1833, focused on purchasing vineyards, and today the estate vineyards supply two thirds of the grapes, an unusually high proportion in Champagne. The house is famous for its prestige cuvée, Cristal, which was created (as a sweet blend) for Tsar Alexander II; the name reflects the fact that it was bottled in clear crystal. It became Roederer's commercial prestige cuvée after the first world war, and remains one of the best known ultra-prestige cuvées. The style is elegant and precise, almost tight when young. The nonvintage Brut Premier is a blend of 40% Pinot Noir, 40% Chardonnay, and 20% Pinot Meunier; dosage has been reduced to 9 g/l from 12 g/l a decade ago. The vintage Brut and Rosé both have 70% Pinot Noir to 30% Chardonnay, and there is also a Brut Nature. A proportion of the wine is fermented in large oak vats (about 5% for nonvintage, 30% for vintage, 100% for Cristal). Malolactic is partial for nonvintage and vintage, but blocked for Brut Nature and Cristal. The style is very consistent.

Reims
Champagne
Brut Premier
www.champagne-roederer.com

214 ha; 3,000,000 bottles

Champagne

Champagne Ruinart

In 1735, Nicolas Ruinart moved from the textile trade to selling "wine with bubbles." One of the Grand Marques, the house remained independent until it was taken over by Moët in 1962; today it is part of LVMH. Ruinart's focus is on freshness and Chardonnay. "Chardonnay for us is everything," says winemaker Amelie Chatin. "Freshness is the golden thread of the house." To preserve freshness, the nonvintage cuvées use only young reserve wines; typically a nonvintage includes 25% of wines from the previous two years to supplement the 75% from the current vintage. "To achieve our signature freshness we have a reductive winemaking process. For crushing we use a pneumatic press, not the traditional basket press. And there is no wood, everything is fermented and matured in stainless steel. Fermentation is at low temperature to maintain aromatics. Every stage is important, including our special shaped bottle, which has a narrow neck to admit less oxygen." The main focus of vintage wine is the Dom Ruinart Blanc de Blancs; there is a vintage rosé, but it is 80% Chardonnay. The style of the Ruinart Blanc de Blancs is quite deep. Indeed, I find more of the crisp brightness of Chardonnay in the "R" de Ruinart Brut than in the nonvintage Blanc de Blancs, which is deeper and nuttier. The vintage Blanc de Blancs follows the same profile as the nonvintage, but with greater intensity, showing a complex creaminess that deepens to caramel and toffee with age.

Reims
Champagne
Blanc de Blancs
www.ruinart.com
17 ha; 1,700,000 bottles

Champagne Salon

The most unusual house in Champagne, Salon has only one wine, a vintage Blanc de Blancs coming exclusively from Le Mesnil, made in 43 vintages since the house was founded in 1911. Eugène Aimé Salon came from Champagne, but he made a fortune in furs before establishing Champagne Salon. "Even the locals didn't understand what he was doing: using a single cépage to make only a vintage," says Audrey Campos of Salon. After M. Salon died in 1943, the house remained in family hands for twenty years until it was sold to Pernod-Ricard, who sold it on to Laurent-Perrier in 1989. Today it is run in association with Delamotte, which is next door: "You cannot speak of one without the other." When Salon is not made, the grapes are used by Delamotte. Salon did not buy vineyards; a 1 ha vineyard behind the house, known as the garden, is the only one owned by the house. Grapes come from 10 ha of 19 parcels, all in mid-slope, owned by various proprietors, but mostly worked by Laurent-Perrier. (The only change has been that Clos de Mesnil was part of Salon until it was purchased by Krug in 1979.) Vinification switched from large oak vats to stainless steel in 1995, and malolactic is always blocked. With dosage of only 5 g/l, and around ten years before disgorgement, the style shows restrained minerality when young, but with an infinitely refined sense of tension. Needing twenty years to reach its peak, this is surely the most precise Champagne of all.

Le Mesnil-sur-Oger
Champagne
www.salondelamotte.com
10 ha; 60,000 bottles

Champagne Jacques Selosse

This house has a reputation for marching to the beat of a different drum. Jacques Selosse was a baker who bought land in Avize in 1949, and sold the fruit to Lanson. In the 1960s he started bottling his own Champagne, and his son Anselme went to Burgundy to learn oenology. When Anselme started making the wine—"1974 was my first vintage, not one to make a millésime"—he began following a Burgundian model, focusing on parcels (or groups of parcels given that the vineyards are divided into 47 different plots). Most of the vineyards are grand cru, with 4 ha in Avize; there is some premier cru in Mareuil. Burgundian methods extend to vinification in fûts (with 15% new oak) using barriques of 228 liter and larger casks of 400 liter. The Selosse wines have sometimes been criticized for showing too much oak, but for me it seems that the oak is not so much obvious directly as indirectly, in the increased richness and more oxidative style. Certainly these are powerful wines, more suited for a meal than an aperitif. The style shows wide breadth of flavor and a strong body, sometimes with a trademark touch of minerality or salinity on the finish. These are wines that make a statement. The focus is on terroir, and bottlings from individual lieu-dits started in 2003; today there are six nonvintage lieu-dit cuvées, three Blanc de Blancs and three Blanc de Noirs, as well as vintage wines. Expanding a bit, Anselme has now opened a hotel and restaurant at the Maison.

Avize

Champagne

Version Originale

www.selosse-lesavises.com

8 ha; 60,000 bottles

Champagne De Sousa

This small house has a distinctive style. The family arrived when Erik de Sousa's great grandfather came from Portugal during the first world war. Erik's parents created the marque, and Erik took over in 1986, making wine in two cuveries on either side of the main square in Avize. Estate vineyards have increased from the original 3 ha, and now include two vineyards in Aÿ and Ambonnay, bringing Pinot Noir to complement the Chardonnay of the Côte des Blancs. There are 7-8 nonvintage cuvées as well as vintage wines: "We take care that each cuvée has a specific character whether it's cépage, terroir, or use of wood," Erik explains. Brut Tradition comes from vines that aren't grand cru, while Brut Reserve is Chardonnay from grand crus. Both are vinified in cuve. Cuvée 3A is a blend from Avize, Aÿ, and Ambonnay, poised between Chardonnay and Pinot Noir. Cuvée des Caudalies nonvintage is a Blanc de Blancs from old vines, vinified in wood. Cuvée des Caudalies vintage is vinified in wood with 15% new oak, and the Le Mesnil cuvée comes from the oldest vines. Umami is a vintage made once so far, in 2009, when conditions fulfilled Erik's aim, conceived after a visit to Japan, of representing umami in a wine. Two rosés come in a presentation box, one from assemblage, one from saignée. The style develops from fruity for the Brut, mineral for Blanc de Blancs, powerful for Caudalies, and quite savory for Umami and vintage Caudalies. These are wines of character.

Avize

Champagne

Brut Reserve

www.champagnedesousa.com

13 ha; 100,000 bottles

Champagne

Champagne Taittinger

The largest family-owned house in Champagne, Taittinger has headquarters in Reims, with a stylish reception area, a cinema for showing movies about the house, and all the other accoutrements of a Grand Maison. It stands on the site of the Abbey of St. Nicaise, which was destroyed in the Revolution. The caves underneath go back to the monks, dating from the thirteenth century (with a lower level of even older caves dating from the fourth century). There are 4 km of cellars at this site—which is used for producing prestige cuvées—and in the center of Reims is another even larger site, more mechanized, with another 10 km of cellars. It's difficult to define house style here, given a wide range of cuvées, every one apparently designed to fit a different niche. The Brut Réserve and Rosé are mainstream. The premium cuvée Prélude has a level of refinement and tension, while the vintage is broader and more opulent, although both have equal proportions of Pinot Noir and Chardonnay coming from grand and premier cru sites. "With the vintage we are looking for the specificity of the harvest, but also something with more roundness and aromatics, more of a match for food," says Director Dominique Garreta. The flagship Comtes de Champagne is fine and precise, the quintessence of the Blanc de Blancs style. And then there is Nocturne, a Sec champagne designed for nightclubs, in purple packaging that might glow in the dark. The various cuvées are interestingly different.

 Reims
Champagne
Cuvée Prelude
www.taittinger.com
 N
290 ha; 3,000,000 bottles

Champagne Tarlant

Dating from 1687, this is an old family domain, presently run by Benoît Tarlant and his sister Mélanie, with its own vineyard holdings in 55 separate parcels in the Vallée de la Marne, mostly on the south side of the river. It was necessary to replant after the second world war, so the vines date from 1946 to the 1970s. There's an emphasis on single vineyards, with wine from each plot vinified separately. "Terroir is more determinative than cépage," Benoît says. "The final tasting for assemblage is blind, with little attention paid to variety." About 60% is fermented in barriques, and reserve wines are aged in wood. There is no malolactic fermentation. As well as the usual varieties, Benoît has planted some of the old varieties: Pinot Blanc, Petit Meslier, and Arbanne. In addition to the range of nonvintage and vintage wines, there are some special cuvées. La Vigne d'Or comes from Pinot Meunier in a single plot. "When I made the first Blanc de Meunier, in 1999," Benoît says, "it was considered to be pushing the limits, but now there are several others." There's also a plot of ungrafted Chardonnay on (relatively) sandy soil, which makes the special cuvée Vigne d'Antan (a Blanc de Blancs whose name means, vines of yesterday). There is little or no dosage; most cuvées are Extra Brut, so the house style is crisp and precise. In the past decade, Benoît has moved steadily towards zero dosage. The vintage wines age well, with the Vigne d'Antan 2000 showing at its peak in 2013.

Oeuilly
Champagne
Blanc de Noirs
www.tarlant.com
G
14 ha; 100,000 bottles

Champagne Veuve Clicquot

Introduced in 1873, Veuve Clicquot's vivid yellow label is one of the most effective marketing images in Champagne, immediately identifying one of the largest and most successful Champagne houses. Founded in 1772, Veuve Clicquot's history is bound up with the history of Champagne, since, after taking over in 1805, it was the eponymous Veuve Clicquot who invented the pupître for riddling in 1816. Veuve Clicquot is the second largest house in Champagne (behind Moët), with estate vineyards providing about 40% of the grape supply, and since 1987 has been part of LVMH. The criticism, of course, is that volume prevents it from scaling the heights, but it's an achievement in itself to keep consistency at this level. With a majority of Pinot Noir in all the cuvées, the style of the Brut is relatively full, the vintage is definitely more refined, and the prestige cuvée (La Grande Dame) has real weight. The nonvintage yellow label is by far the most important cuvée, and cellarmaster Dominique Demarville says that Clicquot will be "declaring fewer vintages than we did in the past and ageing the reserve wines a bit further to add complexity," with the intention of improving quality. Veuve Clicquot are not believers in zero dosage—the wine needs to be protected with some sugar, they say—and dosage is usually moderate, between 7 g/l and 10 g/l. Very occasional re-releases from late disgorgement go under the name of Cave Privée.

Reims
Champagne
www.veuve-clicquot.com
393 ha; 14,000,000 bottles

Champagne Vilmart et Cie

Known for its extensive use of wood and full-bodied style, Vilmart is a boutique house located in the northern part of the Montagne de Reims. Vineyards are relatively compact, with 12 separate plots, almost all in the village of Rilly-La-Montagne (and therefore premier cru). Vilmart was established in 1872, but really came to fame (or to notoriety at the time) about forty years ago when it began to ferment and mature the base wines in wood. (This seems to have started by accident when there was a shortage of vats.) Today foudres are used for the nonvintage, and barriques or demi-muids for the vintage wines, comprising a mix of new wood with one-year and two-year. The wine stays in the wood for ten months. Since 1989, Vilmart has been run by René Champs, the fifth generation of the family. The basic nonvintage cuvée (not exported to the U.S.) is called the Grande Réserve and is 70% Pinot Noir to 30% Chardonnay; the rosé, Cuvée Rubis, is 90% Pinot Noir. All the other cuvées are dominated by Chardonnay. There is no Pinot Meunier. The Grand Cellier nonvintage has 70% Chardonnay to 30% Pinot Noir. The vintage wines, Grand Cellier and Coeur de Cuvée, have about 80% Chardonnay. Coeur de Cuvée comes from the oldest vines (about 60 years) and is made almost every year. Malolactic fermentation is blocked for all cuvées, but the impression on the palate shows stone fruits more than citrus. Dosage is well into the brut range, usually 7-11 g/l.

Rilly-La-Montagne
Champagne
Grand Cellier
www.champagnevilmart.fr
11 ha; 130,000 bottles

Champagne

 Gorges

 Muscadet Sèvre et Maine

Gorges

7 ha; 35,000 bottles

André-Michel Brégeon

Committed to making wines for aging, André-Michel Brégeon believes that the route forward for Muscadet involves focusing on a smaller overall appellation area with a hierarchy of the best terroirs. He was involved in establishing the Gorges Cru, for which his wine is regarded as a flagship, coming from the classic terroir of gabbro (a basalt-like rock). His Muscadet Sèvre et Maine also comes from gabbro terroir. After working on the family domain, he established his own estate in 1975 with just 3 ha; he inherited some additional vines from his father in 1989. Viticulture involves minimal treatment of the vines. Vinification is as natural as possible: grapes go straight into the press, the must is only partially clarified, fermentation is by natural yeasts, and the domain is known for keeping wines on the lees for much longer than usual, up to seven years, in glass-lined cuves underground. The white label Muscadet Sèvre et Maine is aged on the lees for between 18 months and 89 months, depending on the vintage. The yellow label usually has 89 months aging. The Gorges cuvée comes from 2 ha of vines with more than 50 years of age, located on a plot near the river Sèvre where there is clay on top of the gabbro. There's also a small plot of Gros Plant du Pays Nantais. The style emphasizes purity of fruits, and the wines have definite age worthiness. Although André-Michel retired in 2011, his protégé Frédéric Lailler has taken over, so production of these characterful wines should continue.

Saint Fiacre-Sur-Maine

Muscadet Sèvre et Maine

Château de l'Oiselinière, Le Clos

www.chereau-carre.fr

100 ha; 700,000 bottles

Domaine Chéreau Carré

An old family in the region, Chéreau Carré expanded in the 1960s-1970s. Today it is one of the larger independent producers of Muscadet, with four separate properties: Château de Chasseloir, Château l'Oiselinière, Château de la Chesnaie, and Domaine du Bois Bruley. All production is sur lie. There is manual harvesting, 48 hours maceration, and vinification with natural yeast: the general concern is to preserve fruit as long as possible. Wine is kept on the lees with battonage every two weeks for six months for the Cuvée Classique, longer for special cuvées, up to 15 months. Stainless steel is used except for a special cuvée that is vinified entirely in barriques of new oak (labeled as *vinifié en fûts de chêne neufs*). Château de Chasseloir is the most important holding, with most vines more than 40 years old, and a small parcel of 100-year-old vines that makes the Comte Leloup Cuvée des Ceps Centenaires. The original vines were planted on rootstocks, but since then have been propagated by marcottage (sticking shoots in the ground to form new roots). The other old vines bottling is Le Clos du Château l'Oiselinière from terroir of orthogneiss. At the other extreme, there is a bottling from young vines called La Griffe Bernard Chéreau. The style here varies with the cuvée, from straightforward with the basic Muscadet Sèvre et Maine of each property, to the greater structure of the old vines bottlings, and the somewhat overwhelming oak of the cuvée in new wood.

Domaine de L'Ecu

"He's a vrai de vrai," someone who knows the wine scene well in the Loire said when they heard I was visiting Guy Bossard at Domaine de l'Ecu, which I suppose is as good a way as any of saying that Guy is the real thing. Indeed he is... Guy makes proper wines with a tendency towards the savory rather than the aromatic. Even the Cuvée Classique, the general assemblage from young vines (young here means less than 35 years), shows minerality. The domain has vineyards on three terroirs, gneiss, orthogneiss, and granite, which are the basis for individual cuvées from older vines (40-45 years). The style is precise, mineral and stony, offering insights into the typicity of the variety and its response to terroir. All wines are matured in cuves in the traditional way, bringing out the purity of fruits, with minimal intervention, including very low sulfur. The Cuvée Classique stays on the lees for 10 months, the three terroir bottlings for 15-18 months. The domain was one of the first to take up biodynamic viticulture. The latest cuvée is the Taurus bottling, which is matured in old fûts (barriques in some years). The inspiration for Taurus came from Guy's partner, Fred Niger, who came into the domain two years ago. You would expect nothing less than a top result from Guy Brossard, but somehow I have the feeling that his heart isn't in this in the same way as in the terroir-driven series. There is also a sparkling wine, La Divina, made from an assemblage of several varieties.

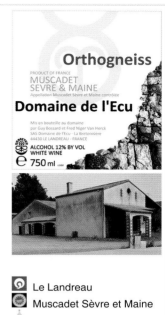

Le Landreau

Muscadet Sèvre et Maine

Granite

www.domaine-ecu.com

25 ha; 110,000 bottles

Domaine de La Fruitière

"We may have seven generations of winemakers, but in fact my father did everything," says François Lieubeau. "Two generations ago my grandfather had 7 ha." Today there are 60 ha spread over four properties in Muscadet, and another 20 ha for IGP. In Muscadet the properties are Château de la Bourdinière (granite), Château de la Placelière (granite), Château de l'Aulnaye (gneiss in Château-Thébaud), and Domaine de la Fruitière. One of the largest producers in the region, Lieubeau was one of the first to plant Chardonnay, responding to demand from export markets. "We have very good terroir in the Pays Nantais and Chardonnay is well adapted to it," says François. The Chardonnay and IGP Sauvignon Blanc sell at around the same price as the entry-level Muscadet. Wines are all aged in cuve, using glass lined underground tanks (traditional here) or stainless steel. The style shows significant variation from the entry level wines to the cuvées or crus. Entry level wines are made in a fruit-forward, crowd-pleasing style, whether Muscadet or varietal-labeled IGP Val de Loire. The more advanced wines split between a fairly traditional Prestige cuvée from Château de la Bourdinière or the Château Thébaud Cru from Château de l'Aulnaye, and the more "international" M de la Fruitière, which exceptionally uses both oak and malolactic fermentation. There is clearly a conscious attempt to pay some attention to the demands of the market.

Château Thébaud

Muscadet Sèvre et Maine

Château de la Bourdinière, Prestige

www.lieubeau.com

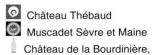

80 ha; 500,000 bottles

Loire: Muscadet

⊚ Saint Fiacre-Sur-Maine

◉ Muscadet Sèvre et Maine

▯ Muscadet Sèvre et Maine,
Vieilles Vignes
www.gadaispereetfils.fr

▨ ⛫ G ⬥
52 ha; 360,000 bottles

Domaine Gadais Père et Fils

Christophe Gadais is the fifth generation of winemakers in the family; after a stint in Sancerre, he took over the domain in 1994. Vineyards are in the commune of St. Fiacre, where they are divided into 120 small parcels. "We are in the heart of the appellation and there are five cuvées; each comes from a different set of parcels," Christophe says. A good sense of structure runs through the wines, which are solid representations of Muscadet. Except for the simple Muscadet, Emotions, which comes from young vines near Vertou, all the wines are sur lie. Even the entry level Domaine de La Tourmaline has a savory sense of structure rather than simple aromatics. The Vieilles Vignes (from a vineyard originally planted in 1929) shows a definite texture coming from the lees, and the Les Perrières monopole (from a parcel planted by Christophe's father in the 1950s, but produced as a separate cuvée for the first time in 2009) is matured half in oak to give a broader style. Gadais is one of the few producers in Muscadet who have tried screwcaps (principally for export). Does this change the wine? "I don't know, but it depends what you expect of aging, do you want the wine to change its taste?" Christophe says. The wines will remain labeled as Muscadet Sèvre et Maine, as the name of the Cru covering Gadais's vineyards is Monnières St. Fiacre. "The name of the cru is too complicated and difficult to explain, I'm not going to use it," is Christophe's view.

⊚ Maisdon-sur-Sèvre

◉ Muscadet Sèvre et Maine

▯ Grand Mouton
www.muscadet-grandmouton.com

▨ ⚒ G
30 ha

Domaine du Grand Mouton

Grand Mouton is located on a rise in the middle of the region between the rivers Sèvre and Maine. The winery is surrounded by a parcel of 23 ha and there are a further 7 ha in two other villages. Terroir is mostly gneiss with various kinds of mica. The oldest vines go back to 1937, when Grand Mouton was planted. Most vines are now around 40 years old. There are 3-4 cuvées depending on the year. Petit Mouton is the young vines cuvée (although young vines here might be Vieilles Vignes elsewhere); Grand Mouton is the major bottling. MLM comes from a small plot established in 1933 on the other side of the village, just above the river. Cuvée #1 comes from the oldest vines in Grand Mouton, planted in 1937 at the foot of the hill; it is made only in the best vintages. Wines spend 7-9 months on the lees. The general style here brings freshness to the forefront, although the wines become perceptibly more powerful as you move from the first cuvées to MLM and then to Cuvée #1. The style can be quite reserved when young, with flavor variety broadening out around three years after the vintage. The wines usually show a fine structure. They do not like high alcohol here. "It's one of our aims to start the harvest as soon as possible; usually we are the earliest to start in Muscadet. Sometimes there is a cuvée called 10.5, named for the (low) percent of alcohol. It's difficult to get grapes ripe enough at 10.5% but we like to do it when we can," says Marie-Luce Métaireau.

Domaine La Haute Févrie

Located in the village of Maisdon-sur-Sèvre, the domain has a beautiful house and garden with a practical cellar underneath. Claude Branger now works with his son Sébastien, who represents the fourth generation. Vineyards are in several parcels, spread out all around the village, mostly in plots of 3-4 ha. Viticulture is mostly lutte raisonnée, although 9 ha have been converted to organic. There are several cuvées of Muscadet (all but one are sur lie), defined by terroir or the age of the vines. The domain wine comes from 35-year-old vines; Moulin de la Gustais is from 50-year-old vines; and Cuvée Excellence is from 50- to 80-year-old vines first planted in 1922. There are also cuvées from specific terroirs: Gras Moutons (from an area of amphibolite between the rivers Sèvre and Maine) and the Cru Monnières St. Fiacre. All of these are vinified and matured in cuve, but there is one further cuvée, Clos Joubert, produced in small amounts, using a mixture of acacia and oak barriques. There are also sparkling and late harvest wines. The entry-level cuvées spend 6-8 months on the lees, the top cuvées spend 15-16 months, and the crus spend 21 months. The style here is very round for Muscadet. Young wines can verge on spicy, with earthy hints of sweet tobacco, which become accentuated as the wine ages. This richer style of Muscadet shows potential for aging, as I have had wines of more than a decade's age (back to 1999) that still remain lively.

🔾 Maisdon-sur-Sèvre
◉ Muscadet Sèvre et Maine
🍾 Cuvée Excellence
www.lahautefevrie.com
21 ha; 70,000 bottles

Domaines Landron

Joseph Landron's father started with his brother in 1945 with a couple of hectares. He expanded the estate and formed a group of vignerons to sell wine direct. Joseph joined in 1979 and expanded the business further. Today there are two domains, Le Château de la Carizière and Domaine de la Louvetrie. When his father retired, he started to reduce yields. "The aim is to make a natural wine. I was reacting against the situation with yields that were too high, chaptalization, etc.," he says. After an accident that poisoned some vines, Joseph moved to organic and then biodynamic viticulture. Today there are six cuvées, and also a sparkling wine and a tiny production of Vin de France. Vinification by terroir started with one exceptional parcel, but since 1982 everything has been vinified by parcel. Three cuvées are based on terroirs reflecting different types of soils: quartz, orthogneiss, amphibolite; one cuvée is an assemblage. Cuvée Tradition comes from clay soils, and is treated differently. "This is the only cuvée that I allow myself to vinify in oak," Jo says. With an eye for modern marketing, the name of Jo Landron is more important than the names of the individual domains. The wines give an impression of being well balanced for immediate consumption, although one or two older wines showed better aging potential than might be suggested by current vintages. A common sense of restraint on the nose translates into an impression of delicacy on the palate; acidity and fruits are rarely aggressive.

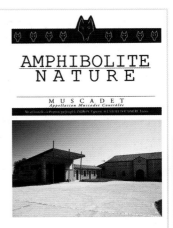

🔾 La Haie Fouassière
◉ Muscadet Sèvre et Maine
🍾 Domaine de la Louvetrie
www.domaines-landron.com
50 ha; 300,000 bottles

Loire: Muscadet

Domaine Pierre Luneau-Papin

"Ah, that will be a long visit," they said at other domains when they heard I was visiting Luneau-Papin. Indeed it was. Marie Chartier-Luneau, Pierre Papin's daughter-in-law, bubbles over with contagious enthusiasm, not merely for the domain but also for the appellation. She makes a fine ambassador for Muscadet. Created in 1990, the domain took its name from the marriage of Monique Luneau to Pierre Papin (both from old winegrowing families). The domain has 35 ha and leases another 15 ha, in many small parcels. The focus is on terroir, with eight cuvées from Muscadet distinguished by different terroirs and vine age. Vinification is similar for all. "Everything is done in cuve. We have no oak, no barriques, no MLF, no chaptalization. Yields vary from 25-45 hl/ha depending on the age of the vines. Time spent on the lees is the only variable aside from the terroir. There is battonage in the spring after harvest, but otherwise we close the tank and wait until bottling," says Pierre-Marie Luneau. The cuvées include: Pierre de la Grange, from mica-schist; Clos des Allées, from 50-year old vines on mica-schist near the winery; Les Pierres Blanche, from 55-year-old vines on gneiss near Chapelle-Heulin; "L" d'Or, from 35-year-old vines on granite; Terre de Pierre, from 35-year-old vines on serpentine rock; and the top cuvée, Excelsior, from 80-year old vines on mica-schist in the area of the Goulaine Cru, which is given three years on the lees. The wines are splendid examples of modern Muscadet.

Le Landreau
Muscadet Sèvre et Maine
Muscadet Sèvre et Maine, L d'Or
www.domaineluneaupapin.com
35 ha; 220,000 bottles

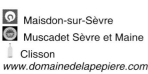

Domaine de La Pépière

This widely acclaimed domain was started in 1984 by Marc Olivier and Remi Branger with 8 ha. Today it has 30 ha of Muscadet and 5 ha for making IGP Val de Loire red. The winery is a ramshackle looking group of buildings in the woods just outside Maisdon-sur-Sèvre. Cuvées are based on terroir. Gras Mouton comes from gneiss and spend 7 months on the lees; Clos des Briords comes from 60-year-old vines on granite similar to Château-Thébaud, and spends 7 months on the lees. Clos Cormerais comes from vines planted after 1927, on east-facing clay-silex, and is the only cuvée matured in wood (in a mixture of oak and acacia barriques: "We're not looking for the taste of oak, just for oxygen exposure," Rémi says). Clisson spends 24 months on the lees; Château-Thébaud Clos des Morins spends 30 months on the lees; and Cuvée #3 stands for three years in the cuve. There's battonage more or less once a year. The house style shows finesse. There's a refinement and elegance to the cuvées from Muscadet Sèvre et Maine, with the same style taken to greater intensity by the wines from the Crus and Cuvée #3 (an assemblage from Clisson and Château-Thébaud that provides a perfect compromise between the two Crus and makes a strong case for blending). As refined as Muscadet comes, the wines have a precision of fruits that is unusual for the appellation, and a definite sense of ageworthiness. They are among the top wines of Muscadet.

Maisdon-sur-Sèvre
Muscadet Sèvre et Maine
Clisson
www.domainedelapepiere.com
35 ha; 200,000 bottles

Domaine Patrick Baudouin

Patrick Baudouin started out as a Maoist with revolutionary intentions and has strong views on the appellation system and the true character of Loire wines. The domain was founded in 1920 by his great grandparents, and he returned to Anjou in 1990 to take it over. His original intention was to make sweet wines in the Coteaux du Layon. One early experience was that some wines stopped fermentation at only 9% alcohol. "For me this was evidence that one should not care about alcoholic strength, what matters is to have good botrytis and to select the berries carefully." Compelled by vintage conditions, Patrick made his first dry wine in 2000, and in 2001 started regular production of dry wines. Today the domain has 10 ha of Chenin Blanc and 3 ha of Cabernet Franc; the main holdings are in Quarts de Chaume. "My belief is that my dry wines should be true dry wines at 13% or 14% without botrytis," he now says. Vinification uses old barriques and demi-muids. Patrick divides his wines into 'vins de fruit' and 'vins de terroir.' There's a small negociant business (Patrick Baudouin Vins) that produces Anjou Rouge and Blanc, but the main interest comes with the domain wines from specific parcels. The dry wines are Anjou Blanc and more recently a Savennières under the negociant label (a hectare for the estate was planted in Savennières in 2009); the reds are Anjou Rouge. Patrick remains best known for his sweet wines from Coteaux du Layon and Quarts de Chaume.

Chaudefonds-sur-Layon
Coteaux du Layon
Coteaux du Layon, Les Buandières
www.patrick-baudouin-layon.com

15 ha; 45,000 bottles

Domaine Baumard

This is one of the leading domains of the region for both dry and sweet wines, created by Florent Baumard's father, although the family have been winegrowers for generations. The estate has 50 ha, with 35 ha in production. The top dry wine comes from Savennières, where Baumard owns half of the famous Clos du Papillon; it displays the savory minerality that characterizes Chenin Blanc at its best. There is also the Trie Spéciale, a Savennières AOP produced only in some years by successive harvests: often it has some botrytis. Baumard's style tends to richness, especially as you progress from Savennières AOP to the Clos du Papillon to the Trie Spéciale. These are very fine wines. However, the domain is best known for its sweet wines. From the Coteaux du Layon, Carte d'Or is a selection from many parcels, Clos de Sainte Catherine comes from a specific north-facing schist terroir, and cuvée Le Payon represents selection from the same parcels as Carte d'Or but at the same quality level as Sainte Catherine. The top sweet wine comes from the Quarts de Chaume and is a peak example of the botrytized style; although there is controversy about Baumard's use of cryoextraction, the wine speaks for itself: concentrated, delicious, honeyed, and long. In addition to the white wines, Baumard produces Anjou red, rosé, and Crémant, and also Vin de France, including the Vert de l'Or that is a play on the name of Verdelho, a grape variety from Madeira that used to be grown in the Loire.

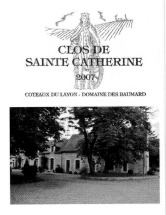

Rochefort-sur-Loire
Coteaux du Layon
Quarts de Chaume
Savennières, Clos du Papillon
www.baumard.fr

35 ha; 180,000 bottles

Loire: Anjou

Domaine du Closel

The rather grand château is located right in the town square. "This is a typical property for Anjou of the nineteenth century, with a château and park leading to the vineyard," says Evelyne de Pontbriand. One of the largest properties in Savennières, the domain notably owns half of the Clos du Papillon. A change to a richer style occurred in the early 2000s, with ripeness assessed by phenolic rather than alcoholic maturity. Three cuvées from Savennières are harvested at different times to produce different effects. La Jalousie is harvested from the youngest vines when the berries are still yellow, to give direct, forward fruits. Les Caillardières comes from the top of the hill and is harvested when the berries are a little browner to produce a fuller result; the wine has more obvious Chenin typicity. Clos du Papillon is harvested last with very ripe berries, which may even include some botrytis. The first two are matured in cuve, the Papillon in 2- to 3-year-old barriques. The domain was certified organic in 2006, and is biodynamic today. House style varies because the vintage is allowed to express itself—MLF may or may not occur, although usually it does not—but the common thread is a sheen of glycerin through which come the characteristic cereal, nuts, and savory notes of Chenin Blanc. Depending on vintage, wines may vary from precise as in 2010 to the broader impression of 2009. Like proprietor Evelyne de Pontbriand, they are always elegant.

 Savennières
Savennières, Clos du Papillon
www.savennieres-closel.com
16 ha; 50,000 bottles

Domaine Delesvaux

The domain lies between the Loire and Layon valleys and specializes in sweet wines from the Coteaux du Layon, but there are also dry white wines under the Anjou appellation and varietal Cabernet Franc (Le Roc) and Cabernet Sauvignon (La Montée de l'Epine). Catherine and Philippe Delesvaux have been making wine here since 1978. Three quarters of plantings are Chenin Blanc. Vinification is natural, with no added yeasts or chaptalization, very little sulfur, and maturation in old barriques with battonage when necessary. The three cuvées of Coteaux du Layon are distinguished by levels of botrytis as well as by terroir: fully botrytized, half botrytized and half passerillé, and passerillé (the latest harvest of all). The top botrytized wine is labeled SGN (selection de grains nobles). The two Anjou Blancs make an interesting comparison. They come from two 1 ha plots within the Coteaux du Layon; this could in principle make either dry or sweet wine, but presently the vines are cultivated to make dry wine (although the wine may be sec or sec-tendre depending on the vintage). Feuille d'Or comes from vines grafted on rootstocks in the conventional way, while Cuvée Authentique comes from a plot of ungrafted vines across the road (planted in 2000 on previously uncultivated land. The ungrafted vines give yields of 6 hl/ha at best, whereas the plot on rootstocks gives yields of 15-20 hl/ha. While Feuille d'Or is very good, Cuvée Authentique lifts Chenin Blanc to a new level of intensity.

Saint Aubin de Luigné
Coteaux du Layon
Anjou, Feuille d'Or

11 ha; 30,000 bottles

Château d'Epiré

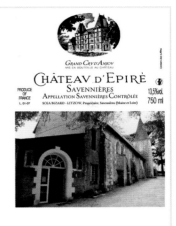

The winery is located in the old church of Epiré, just across from the rather splendid nineteenth century château (which is no longer part of the vineyard estate). Luc Bizard inherited the vineyards, where the largest parcel, Le Parc, located just behind the château, was planted in 1969. Terroir is mostly schist, but quite heterogeneous. Viticulture is conventional, but yields have been going down. "Yields are usually 35-45 hl/ha; 25 years ago they were 45-50 hl/ha. I reduced yields to make richer wine, but now we are on the other side, the wines can be too rich and alcoholic," Luc says. There are three principal dry cuvées and (depending on the vintage) sometimes wines in sweet styles (usually moelleux). There is no single style here because the three dry cuvées are all quite different. The mainstream Savennières is the Château d'Epiré, fermented and matured in cuve. Cuvée Spéciale comes from a 1 ha parcel with an unusual terroir of black stones, just south of the Château. This is fermented and matured in old barriques. Made since 2000, Hu-Boyau comes from the oldest part of the vineyard, and is barrel fermented with complete MLF; there are 7-8 barrels (one of which is new). "Here we make a wine for the international taste," Luc explains. The richness overwhelms the typicity of Chenin Blanc (which to my palate shows more clearly on the Cuvée Special). There's also an entry-level wine with a touch of residual sugar (Cuvée E) and an Anjou red.

Savennières
Savennières, Cuvée Spéciale
www.chateau-epire.com
11 ha; 45,000 bottles

Château de Fesles

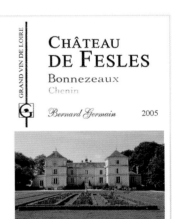

The château is an impressive building set in lovely grounds, surrounded by vineyards. Château de Fesles was bought by the major negociant Les Grands Chais de France in 2008, and the sparkling new cuves of stainless steel show that there has obviously been much investment. 35 ha of the holdings are immediately around the château, which is on the edge of Bonnezeaux, where they own 14 ha (schist terroir, all planted with Chenin Blanc), which makes Château de Fesles the largest owner of Bonnezeaux. The château is on a high point so there are constant winds, which prolong the growing season. In addition to Chenin Blanc on the slopes, Cabernet Franc and Cabernet Sauvignon are planted on the gravel plateau for Anjou red, and there is also some Grolleau and Gamay for the Anjou rosé. The style is workmanlike. The bottlings from Anjou are all good examples of the various styles; the rosé d'Anjou is more to my palate than the Cabernet d'Anjou; the whites show Chenin character and the reds show Cabernet Franc character. The highlight here is of course the Bonnezeaux. "We make one cuvée of Bonnezeaux, which is the best we can make. Basically the Bonnezeaux is a selection and anything that does not make the cut is declassified to Coteaux du Layon," says winemaker Gilles Bigot. In 2012 there was no Bonnezeaux, as it was all declassified to Coteaux du Layon, but the 2010 is far and away the best example of Bonnezeaux in recent years.

Thouarcé
Coteaux du Layon
Bonnezeaux
www.fesles.com
55 ha; 270,000 bottles

Loire: Anjou

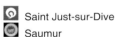

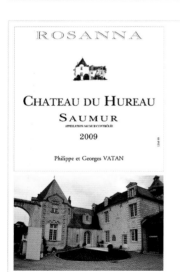

Saint Just-sur-Dive

Saumur

Saumur Blanc, Domaine
www.domaineguiberteau.fr

10 ha; 45,000 bottles

Domaine Guiberteau

Founded at the start of the twentieth century, the domain was greatly extended in 1954 by the purchase of 7 ha on the famous hill of Brézé just south of Saumur. However, the vineyards were leased out in 1976 when no one in the family wanted to take over the estate. It was revived in 1996 when Romain Guiberteau decided to take back the leases and manage the domain. His first vintage was guided by Dani Foucault of Clos Rougeard; since then Romain has increasingly put his stamp on the domain. Divided between Chenin Blanc and Cabernet Franc, plantings include vines up to eighty years old. Besides Brézé, there are smaller vineyards (a hectare each) nearby at Bizet and Montreil-Bellay. There are four white wines and three reds. The influence of Clos Rougeard shows in the purity of style. Le Domaine is the introductory wine in both red and white, coming from younger vines and matured without oak exposure since 2009. Then in whites there are Clos de Guichaux (a blend from the youngest vines in Bizay and Brézé), Brézé (a blend from two parcels of 50-year-old vines on clay-limestone terroir, matured in a mix of new, one-year, and two-year barriques), and Clos des Carmes (from a recently replanted plot in a clos dating from the eleventh century that's considered to have the best terroir in Brézé). The two single vineyard reds are Les Motelles (from a 1 ha plot of sandier soil at Montreil-Bellay) and Les Arboises (from a small south-facing parcel on the hill of Brézé).

Dampierre-sur-Loire

Saumur

Saumur-Champigny, Four
à Chaux
www.domaine-hureau.fr

20 ha; 120,000 bottles

Château de Hureau

Located at the edge of the Saumur-Champigny appellation, close to the Loire, the château itself dates from the eighteenth century, with an impressive octagonal tower, but has thirteenth century caves carved out from the underlying tufa rock. The focus is on red wines, exclusively Cabernet Franc, but there is also a dry white (matured in a single foudre), and in exceptional years a liquoreux. About 3 ha of vineyards are in a flat parcel above the Château, but the rest are broken up into many small parcels in Dampierre. The subsoil here is tufa, with variations in the top soil showing a typical mix of clay and calcareous for the region. Most (90%) plantings are Cabernet Franc. The style brings out minerality and showcases purity of fruit. The red cuvées come from different terroirs, and vary in their balance of overt fruit to structure. Fours à Chaux is perhaps the most direct (coming from sand and tufa, which gives a fine structure), Lisagathe is the purest (from just above the Château, where 60-year-old vines grow on clay soil), and Les Fevettes (from deeper soils) shows the broadest flavor spectrum. Proprietor Philippe Vatan, who took over in 1987, says about Les Fevettes, "I call this my Bordeaux cuvée, because it takes five or six years to open out." Philippe says that increased purity and precision resulted from the conversion to organic viticulture together with the élevage in foudres (since 2006). Precision shows in the white also.

Domaine Eric Morgat

Eric Morgat did not go far when he left the family domain, Château de Breuil in the Coteaux du Layon. Crossing the Loire, he established his domain in Savennières. Making a fresh start, vineyards were planted on land that had been uncultivated or long since abandoned. His major vineyard is L'Enclos, 2.9 ha on schist and volcanic rocks in the sector of Beaupréau, planted in several stages since 1995. More recently he has planted another 1.5 ha on the steep slope of La Pierre Bécherelle. (A special tractor is required to work the slope.) He also rents a small plot in Roche aux Moines (so far the wine has been blended into L'Enclos, which remains his sole cuvée from Savennières), and he retained a hectare in the vineyards of Château de Breuil in Beaulieu-sur-Layon when the property was sold in 2006 (this is the Litus cuvée, under the Anjou AOP). Eric's initial vintages were labeled as Domaine de la Monnaie (from the original address of the domain), but since 2002 have been labeled as Domaine Éric Morgat. The style has changed a bit, as botrytized grapes are now excluded (although the intention is to go for full maturity) and malolactic fermentation is no longer encouraged. Vinification and élevage are in 400 liter barrels (with up to 20% new wood), and battonage is used, giving a rich modern style. Sometimes there has been a touch of residual sugar, but in principle the wines are dry. There's a definite impression of purity of fruits against that rich background.

Savennières
Savennières, L'Enclos
www.ericmorgat.com

6 ha; 16,000 bottles

Domaine Vincent Ogereau

Vincent is the fourth generation at this family domain, established in the 1890s. Vincent took over in 1989—"Being a vigneron always attracted me, as a child I never thought of anything else," he says—and his son Emmanuel is now helping him. The largest holding (8 ha) is Coteaux du Layon Villages, then there are 2 ha in Savennières, and more in Anjou and Anjou Villages. "We are best known for our Coteaux du Layon. Ogereau may be a small producer but we have the whole range, from rosé to white to red and sweet white, and that is typical of production in the Loire. We have clients who want to buy a range of wines," says Emmanuel. The mark of the house is to bring out the expression of each variety. Chenin Blanc has a characteristic dry quality in the Savennières, but is given a powerful representation in the Coteaux du Layon, which begins to approach Bonnezeaux. The top wines are the Clos des Bonnes Blanches in Coteaux du Layon St. Lambert, Clos le Grand Beaupréau in Savennières, and Côte de la Houssaye in Anjou-Villages. This last is unusual: a varietal Cabernet Sauvignon. The Ogereaus believe in Cabernet Sauvignon. "We like the extra freshness that comes from Cabernet Sauvignon compared with Cabernet Franc," says Emmanuel. The main difficulty is not so much getting ripeness as avoiding botrytis. In some years the Cabernet Sauvignon goes into the rosé instead of making a red wine.

Saint Lambert du Lattay
Coteaux du Layon
Coteaux du Layon, Harmonie
www.domaineogereau.com

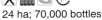

24 ha; 70,000 bottles

Loire: Anjou

 Anjou

 Quarts de Chaume

Coteaux du Layon

Savennières, Clos de Coulaine

55 ha; 120,000 bottles

Château Pierre-Bise

Château Pierre-Bise is a sixteenth century property on a ridge above the river Layon. The domain started when Pierre Papin purchased the château in 1959 together with 9 ha of vines in Beaulieu-sur-Layon. Claude Papin took over from his father in 1974, and the domain has now grown significantly (partly with vineyards that came with Claude's marriage). It now includes vineyards in three distinct parts of Savennières on the other side of the river. The domain is famous for its sweet Quarts de Chaume and Coteaux du Layon, but the range extends to the (usually dry) three expressions of Savennières; each is considered a definitive representation of its terroir. The vines of Clos de Coulaine are the youngest; at Grand Beaupréau older vines have roots descending into schist or phtanite; and at Roche aux Moines there is more heterogeneity with a partly volcanic terroir. Claude believes that Savennières offers the most complex expression of Chenin: "The variety is a veritable sponge for absorbing terroir," he says. Working the soils here is minimal, as Claude believes that breaking up the surface does more harm than good. Style varies with the vintage, as MLF may or may not occur, and there may or may not be residual sugar (Clos de Coulaine was 'doux' in 2003 but is usually dry). The dry whites have a savory quality, enhanced by the inclusion of some botrytized grapes, which Claude believes enhances the expression of terroir. There are also Anjou reds and rosé.

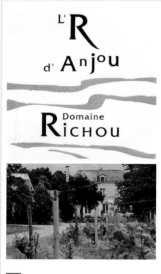

Mozé-sur-Louet

Coteaux de l'Aubance

Anjou, Les Rogeries

www.domainerichou.fr

30 ha; 130,000 bottles

Domaine Richou

This family domain is divided into 9 parcels, run by third generation Didier Richou together with his brother. The domain had 42 ha, but Didier got rid of 12 ha he did not like. The winery is just off the main road through Mozé-sur-Louet, in the southeastern corner of the Aubance of Anjou. Most of the wines are under the Anjou label, but there are also dry Savennières and sweet Coteaux de l'Aubance. The domain is located in a band of grey schist that runs northwest to southeast across the region, but each of Richou's parcels is different. There are small bands of volcanic terroir, and many small areas with different geologies. Cuvées represent terroirs from schist to volcanic. The wines here are workmanlike, solid representations of their appellations. There is a full range including red, dry and sweet white, rosé, and sparkling. The most interesting wines are those that break out of the mold, such as the Anjou Villages Brissac which is an equal assemblage of Cabernet Franc with Cabernet Sauvignon (from an unusually warm schist terroir that lets the Cabernet Sauvignon ripen), or the L'R Osé, a rosé (from 90% Cabernet Franc and 10% Cabernet Sauvignon) that is not labeled as Cabernet d'Anjou because it is almost dry. Sweet wines depend on the year, with regular production of La Sélection and Les Violettes (passerillé or botrytized depending on conditions), but Les 3 Demoiselles is produced only in top years.

Château Roche Aux Moines

Nicolas Joly, one of the most famous proponents of biodynamic viticulture, produces three wines at this old domain (supposedly first planted by Cistercian monks). The most famous is Coulée de Serrant (which has its own appellation), but there is also a Savennières, Le Vieux Clos (labeled as Clos Sacré for the United States), from the adjacent vineyard, and Clos de la Bergerie (from Savennières Roche-aux-Moines). "What makes the authenticity of Coulée de Serrant?" Nicolas asks. "Vines have been here for 900 years. The long history comes in the bottle. The two kinds of terroir—slate and chalk—bring two different types of Chenin. I really feel that Coulée, which has always been a good wine, has improved in the past five years. It has deep roots in the diversity of the geology." All the Joly wines show the same powerful style resulting from very late harvest, often so late that there is some botrytis. Sometimes there is a touch of residual sugar. Wines are matured in cuve. "I would be ashamed to put the taste of wood in my wine. It would mean I do not trust my wine enough. We put wine in the cellar in October and we do nothing until we take it out in April," Nicolas says. The wines have been criticized for their high alcohol, often pushing 15%, and I think this is a fair point. The savory intensity and flavor variety are impressive, and the wine has little in common with the pallid offerings of Chenin Blanc often found in the region, but alcohol at 15% can be fatiguing.

Savennières
Coulée de Serrant
www.coulee-de-serrant.com
15 ha; 32,000 bottles

Domaine des Roches Neuves

Thierry Germain is the six generation of winemakers from Bordeaux but he left Bordeaux in 1991 and bought this old domain in 1996. There was a single tiny building when he started, but this has now been extended into a modern warehouse. He makes 6 red cuvées and 3 whites. Thierry is passionate about terroir and biodynamics; the domain has been biodynamic since 2000. Thierry has a fine reputation for his reds from Saumur-Champigny (which constitute 90% of his production), but I liked his whites just as much, if not more (including a sparkling wine made without dosage). The whites display an unusual precision for Chenin Blanc, with the fine fruits edged by minerality. They need time, not because they are austere, but to let the potential complexity emerge. The reds also point in a mineral direction, and although Thierry's aim is to avoid excess tannin and bring out floral qualities, they can be quite stern and flat when young; here time is needed for the structure to resolve. "I detest Cabernet Franc with tannins that are too powerful. I look for floral notes," Thierry says. "I am against new oak; it always has a tendency to destroy the floral character. I want to express the diversity in the soil." His cuvées come from different terroirs (varying from sandy to calcareous), sometimes from patches of old vines that he has rescued, and he has taken the search for authenticity to the extent of planting a small plot of Cabernet Franc on sandy soil with vines on their own roots.

Varrains
Saumur-Champigny
Saumur-Champigny, La Marginale
Saumur, L'Insolite
www.rochesneuves.com

28 ha; 120,000 bottles

Loire: Anjou

Clos Rougeard

The unassuming appearance of Clos Rougeard belies its reputation as the best red wine of the Loire. Located in a residential street in Chacé, there is no nameplate or even street number to distinguish the domain. Inside, the house is to one side, and across a courtyard is the entrance to the winery, with a rabbit warren of old caves underneath, carved out of the rock and very cold. The domain has 9.5 ha of Cabernet Franc and 1 ha of Chenin Blanc. The three cuvées of Cabernet Franc are the domain wine (an assemblage of many parcels), Les Poyeux, and Le Bourg: the white comes from Brézé. Les Poyeux is a 3 ha plot of 40-year-old vines with soils varying from clay-silex to clay-calcareous. Le Bourg has 70-year-old vines on clay-calcareous terroir (located behind the house), with 1 ha in two parcels. Usually the reds spend 24 months in barrique, Le Bourg in new barrels, Les Poyeux in older oak. The domain wine is elegant and pure, Les Poyeux is the crystalline essence of Cabernet Franc, and Le Bourg is tighter with higher acidity and tannins, and needs more time. With 20% new oak, Le Brézé offers a wonderfully savory impression of Chenin Blanc. As for methods, "We are very traditional, we are making wine exactly like our parents and grandparents," Nady Foucault says. Vines are maintained by selection massale. There's no chaptalization, no collage, no filtration, no racking (for reds: sometimes there is battonage for whites). The wines are at their best around ten years after the vintage.

⦿ Chacé

◉ Saumur-Champigny

🍶 Saumur-Champigny, Les Poyeux

🍶 Saumur, Le Brézé

◎ ⚒ Ⓖ ◿
10 ha; 22,000 bottles

Ferme de La Sansonnière

Mark Angeli has run this small domain for more than twenty years, and has an influence out of proportion to its size. He is committed to biodynamic viticulture, and together with Virginie Joly organizes an organic fair every July: "The purpose is to say that what is normal is organic," he says. He's had problems with the *agrément* for the AOC, with arguments when he started to make dry white wines (because the general style was sweet at the time) or about the color of his rosés. So now his wines are labeled as Vin de France. The style here is towards flavor. Because winemaking attempts to be as natural as possible, and fermentation is very protracted, the wines are not necessarily completely dry. This can be a problem in maintaining consistency of style. There are three white wines, a sweet rosé, and a red from Grolleau. All the wines except the rosé are matured in old wood. Of the whites, La Lune is a blend from several different plots, in fact covering twelve different terroirs. It's never completely dry and usually ends up with 4-5 g/l residual sugar. Les Fourchades comes from a vineyard just across the road from the winery. Les Blanderies Vieilles Vignes comes from 76-year-old vines and is the most savory of the whites. Mark sums up his approach by saying, "I'm very annoyed when people say that a winegrower is an artist—there is no artistry in this job. We have to take decisions that are very important, we are artisans but not artists. Most important is when to harvest."

⦿ Thouarcé

◉ Anjou

🍶 Vin de France, Les Fourchades

◫ ⚒ Ⓖ ◿
7 ha; 15,000 bottles

Château Soucherie

Château Soucherie was originally a farm owned by the Duke of Brissac, and the Château was built as a leisure house. Sold to the Tijou family between the wars, it was bought by its present owners in 2007, who put in place a new, young team. The property is on a high point, running down to the river, with 22 ha of the vineyards immediately around. All the vineyards are on schist, although the type of schist varies, facing south, and protected from the north wind. There is a wide range of wines. Most plantings are Chenin Blanc, for the Coteaux du Layon and Anjou Blanc. The top wines come from 4 ha in Chaume and 2 ha in Savennières (the Clos des Perrières). There is no MLF for the whites. Cabernet Franc is grown on the slopes for the Anjou reds, and there is also some Grolleau. The house style is quite delicate and concerned to preserve freshness, which is why they want no botrytis in the dry white wines. (Botrytis develops rapidly here because the vineyards are close to the river. Handpicking is essential to exclude botrytized grapes from the dry whites.) "For us the schist is really tremendous for the dry and sweet white wines, but for Cabernet Franc schist is not an easy expression, the finish is always a little tannic, we are looking for fruit to balance the tannins in Anjou Rouge, and for more structure and a velvety quality for the Cru; but always with the freshness that for us is typical of the Loire valley," says marketing manager Florence de Barmon.

Beaulieu-sur-Layon
Coteaux du Layon
Coteaux du Layon, Chaume
www.domaine-de-la-soucherie.fr

28 ha; 100,000 bottles

Château de Villeneuve

The magnificent eighteenth century château stands on a plateau above the Loire, looking over the cliff to the river beyond. Vineyards run back from the château, which was purchased in 1969 by Jean-Pierre Chevallier's parents. Jean-Pierre took over in 1982, and has moved into organic viticulture, with the introduction of cover crops to control fertility. "But sometimes the cover crops can impede maturity of the grapes," he says. As well as four cuvées of Saumur-Champigny, there are two white Saumurs. Cabernet Franc has cold soak of 5-6 days, and remains in wooden tronconique cuves for a month at temperatures below 23 degrees; élevage is in 500 liter casks varying from new to 3 years old. Sulfur levels are kept low. Besides the château bottling, there are cuvées from two lieu-dits, Le Clos immediately around the château and the 1.5 ha Clos de la Bienboire, and also a Vieilles Vignes assemblage from three parcels. The old vines are used for selection massale to replant the other vineyards. The style here is quite solid: these are well made wines in which you see the characteristics of the Chenin Blanc and Cabernet Franc varieties in Saumur and Saumur-Champigny. The cuvées are not quite as distinctive as I would have liked. "You can keep the cuvées of Saumur-Champigny for 15 or 20 years, it's not a problem, but generally we drink immediately after bottling when they still have fermentation and other volatile aromas, or we wait three or four years," says Jean-Pierre.

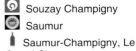
Souzay Champigny
Saumur
Saumur-Champigny, Le Grand Clos
www.chateau-de-villeneuve.com

25 ha; 140,000 bottles

Loire: Anjou

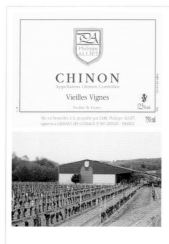

Domaine Philippe Alliet

As a devotée of Bordeaux, Philippe Alliet sets out to produce long-lived wines aged in barriques (which are sourced from Bordeaux). The domain was established in 1985 with 8 ha of inherited vines (located in the lesser known area of Briançon, where the wines tend to be lighter). Since then it has expanded, and there are now four major cuvées, all from Chinon. There's an entry-level wine called Tradition. The major production is the Vieilles Vignes cuvée, which is sometimes said to resemble claret more than typical Chinon. The most recently acquired vineyard, l'Huisserie, effectively gives a young vines cuvée, which is matured in demi-muids. Philippe's most famous holding is Coteau de Noiré, a steep south-facing slope with very calcareous terroir that he planted in 1996. This is in the best known part of the appellation, between Chinon itself (still within sight of the Château) and Cravant-les-Côteaux. Coteau de Noiré is produced in Bordelais style: long fermentation in cuve, malolactic fermentation in barrels, and élevage from 12-18 months in barriques with 80% new oak. This is a controversial domain: some believe that these wines demonstrate the (usually unrealized) potential of Chinon; the counter criticism is that Chinon does not give sufficient fruit concentration to handle such an extended oak regime. Philippe's response is to ask, "What is a typical Chinon? No one knows. In any case, not dilute wine with a nose of green pepper."

 Cravant Les Côteaux
Chinon

17 ha; 70,000 bottles

Domaine Yannick Amirault

The domain is located in an unassuming house opposite the vineyard, but at the rear is a practical, modern winery. The domain started in 1936; since Yannick took over in 1989 he has more or less doubled the size. "But now it is going to stop," he says. There are 25 separate parcels, with 13 ha in Bourgueil and 7 ha in St. Nicolas de Bourgueil. "The particularity of the domain is that all the wines are vinified in wood, varying from barriques to large casks," Yannick says. "The potential for aging is the most important thing." The style is somewhat stern, showing quite strong tannins, the fruits tend to be earthy, and there is a stony sense to the finish. This theme runs through all the wines, from the lightest entry level to those that Yannick regards as his Crus. The style is towards vins de garde, but I sometimes worry whether the fruits are generous enough to support really long aging. The entry level wine, La Coudraye, which comes from sandy soil around the winery, is the lightest; Les Malgagnes comes from calcareous terroir and has more generosity; Les Quartiers comes from 60-year old vines on white limestone, and Le Grand Clos comes from 50-year old vines on a mix of soils including silex. There is increasing weight going up the hierarchy. In addition to the reds, there is also a rosé. "Usually rosés have some residual sugar but I want to make a dry rosé," says Yannick. "It is my white wine." The wines represent a definite philosophy. "There is a place for wines with strong personality."

Bourgueil
St. Nicolas de Bourgueil,
Les Malgagnes
www.yannickamirault.fr

19 ha; 90,000 bottles

Domaine des Aubuisières

The winery occupies a warehouse in a back street of Vouvray—access was blocked by a huge truck loading wine for Majestic in England when I visited—but inside at the back is a neat tasting room seemingly carved out of the rock face. "I'm the first generation," says Bernard Fouquet when asked about the history of the domain. He started in 1982 with 5 ha; today 50% of the vineyards are on clay-calcareous soils and 50% are on clay-silex soils. "I have different cuvées, of course, that reflect the terroirs," he says. Four come from the calcareous terroirs (Le Marigny, Le Bouchet, Le Plan de Jean, Le Clos de L'Auberdière), and three from silex (Les Girardières, Les Perruches, Les Chairs Salées). Some of the dry wines and the demi-sec are matured in cuve, but the sweeter wines are matured in wood. "You do not see the minerality if you vinify in cuve, you need to use wood; the cuve emphasizes aromatics," Bernard explains. He believes the wines require time to show complexity—the sweeter the wine, the longer it takes to show its character—and is concerned that most are drunk too early. "People drink the wines far too young. I am sure that all the 2009 and 2010, I have sold have already been consumed. It is a great pity, but people won't wait any more." There is an extensive range here, from dry through demi-sec to liquoreux, all Vouvray AOP. The style of the domain shows best at the moelleux level, with the maturation in wood bringing an attractive smokiness to the finish.

 Vouvray

Vouvray Moelleux, Plan de Jean

www.vouvrayfouquet.com

30 ha; 180,000 bottles

Domaine Bernard Baudry

The domain was created in 1975, but there was a long prior history of winegrowing in the family. Mathieu Baudry joined his father in 2000. The property is on the main road just outside Cravant Les Côteaux; the courtyard leads to an old house, but a modern winery has been built in a warehouse behind. The estate is 98% Cabernet Franc and 2% Chenin Blanc. The vineyards are dispersed around the valley, coteaux, and plateau. Most of the vines are in Cravant but some are in Chinon. There are five red cuvées and two white, each representing a different terroir from estate vineyards. "We work in the spirit of Burgundy, with the same cépage but different terroirs. It is not an obligation of the appellation, it's a personal choice," says Mathieu. "Our aim is to get transparency of terroir in the wine." There is a pretty good correlation between terroir and wine style here, with the sandy soils of the domain Chinon producing light fresh wine, a more gravelly texture emerging from pebbly soil of Les Grezeaux, a somewhat more chalky impression as you move into limestone of Clos Guillot, and then full force fruits as the soil becomes full clay-limestone at La Croix Boisée. The reds become steadily rounder and riper as the limestone increases. Within Clos Guillot there is a small patch of vines planted on their own roots. La Croix Boisée represents two wines, red and white, with the white coming from the most calcareous terroir.

 Cravant Les Côteaux

Chinon

Chinon, La Croix Boisée

www.chinon.com/vignoble/bernard-baudry

30 ha; 130,000 bottles

Loire: Touraine

L'homme
Jasnières
Jasnières, Calligramme
www.belliviere.com
15 ha; 43,000 bottles

Domaine de Bellivière

Jasnières is decidedly off the beaten track, well to the north of the Loire. But here Eric Nicolas has made a name not only for his Jasnières (Chenin Blanc) but also for his cuvées from Pineau d'Aunis, an old red variety of the Loire that is now quite rare (although it remains the principle red variety for Coteaux du Loir. The domain started in 1995 with 3.5 ha in Coteaux du Loir. Today the vineyards are divided between Jasnières and Coteaux du Loir, mostly planted with Chenin Blanc. Vineyards are perpetuated by selection massale, and there are experiments in planting vines at very high density. White wines are vinified and matured in 1- to 3-year-old barrels; there is no MLF or battonage. Rosés are vinified in old barrels, and reds are vinified in open top vats followed by maturation in barrique (with very little new wood). The 4 ha of Pineau make two Coteaux du Loir red wines: the Rouge-Gorge cuvée comes from young vines; l'Hommage à Louis Derré comes from hundred-year-old vines. Depending on the vintage, there may also be some rosé (which may include a little Grolleau), labeled as Vin de France, in varying styles of sweetness. The white wines include both dry and sweet styles from both Jasnières and Coteaux du Loir. The Jasnières include Les Rosiers (from young vines), Calligramme (from old vines)—these may vary from dry to off-dry styles depending on the vintage—and the sweet wines, Discours de Tuf and Elixir de Tuf from selections of botrytized grapes.

Beaumont-en-Véron
Chinon
Bourgueil, Les Galichets
www.domainebreton.net
11 ha; 80,000 bottles

Domaine Catherine et Pierre Breton

The first time I visited the Bretons, I went to a charming old property in the middle of the vineyards. The house and old cave are still used for visits by tourists (and for élevage) but the main facility for fermentation and handling moved to a warehouse on an industrial estate in 2012. It's not glamorous, but it's practical. "Moving wasn't to expand, it was just to have more room to work. We were surprised to realize that we had managed to fit everything in before," Catherine says. There's a wide range of wines, with an emphasis on natural production. Sulfur use is minimized, and sulfur is not used before bottling. There is one completely sulfur-free wine (d'Ivresse) where sulfite is not used even on the grapes. The house style is for a certain finesse (the entry-level wines are of course simpler), but after that there is real refinement—and at moderate alcohol. Why don't you have a problem with increasing alcohol, I asked? "But we do. In 1998 we were getting 10.5-11% alcohol—we never chaptalized but chaptalization was common in the Loire. We have probably gained 1% alcohol. Alcohol hit 13% only in 2003." Production is about two thirds Bourgueil to a third Chinon. There is also some Vouvray and IGP. The most interesting reds come from Bourgueil, where there is a fascinating opportunity to compare the conventional bottling from Les Galichets with a small plot of Franc de Pied (vines on their own roots), which is the epitome of refinement.

Vincent Carême

Vincent Carême took over the vines of his parents and established this domain in 1999 after working in Muscadet, Alsace, and South Africa to gain experience. He's now considered to be one of the leading vignerons of the new generation. There is a small cellar in a back street of Vernou (well, they are all back streets in Vernou). Vineyards are all on the première côte in Vouvray, the first slope that runs up from the town, except for a tiny parcel that is used for production of Vin de France. The vineyards were converted to organic between 2007 and 2010. There are two sparkling wines and six still wines (including moelleux and liquoreux cuvées that are made only in some years). The Brut is made by méthode traditionelle, while a second sparkling wine is made by méthode ancestrale. The Sec and Tendre cuvées come from the same vineyard; Tendre is a demi-sec with 20 g/l of residual sugar. Two cuvées (usually dry) come from single parcels: Peu Monier comes from clay-silex, and Le Clos from pure limestone (usually it is sec but in 2008 it made a demi-sec). Everything here is always matured in barriques of old oak. Any residual sugar is a consequence of fermentation stopping naturally. There is sometimes partial malolactic fermentation. The house style tends to be quite powerful and fruity with a texture on the palate coming from the extended maturation in wood. There is good flavor concentration and the impression of richness is accentuated by the relatively high alcohol.

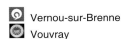 Vernou-sur-Brenne

 Vouvray

Vouvray Sec, Peu Morier
vincentcareme.fr

14 ha; 45,000 bottles

Domaine Champalou

The domain was created in 1995 by Catherine and Didier Champalou. Catherine is the eleventh generation of a winemaking family, but did not inherit the familial domain because she was a girl. But she is attached to her roots. Didier isn't from the region, but after going to oenology school decided to settle on Vouvray because he liked the idea of being able to produce a range of wines from one cépage. The cave is built into the hillside, with an old section at the back, but is mostly a modern concrete facility built in 2004. From 1.8 ha initially, the domain has grown to have vineyards in 47 separate parcels in 3 of the 8 communes of Vouvray. "At the start it was easy to buy vineyards because no one wanted them. An old vigneron would say, 'I'm retiring,' and would be glad to hand his vines on," Catherine recollects. Every parcel is vinified separately. There is assemblage for 4-6 different cuvées (moelleux and liquoreux are not made every year). At lower sweetness levels, neither sec nor demi-sec is indicated on the label. "People know that Fondraux is our demi-sec," Catherine says. The style of the wines is distinctly modern, although it goes in two directions. The dry whites either show the freshness of stainless steel vinification or they go to the extreme of barrel fermentation in new barriques, with quite overwhelming oak in the Le Portail cuvée. Why did you create this, I asked? "Because of you the journalists. This was basically to make a more international wine."

 Vouvray

Vouvray, Les Fondraux
www.champalou.com

20 ha; 120,000 bottles

Loire:Touraine

⊙ Soings-en-Sologne

◉ Touraine

🍾 Touraine, Sauvignon Blanc
Le Vinifera
www.henry-marionnet.com

👤 🏭 G 🍃
60 ha; 400,000 bottles

Domaine de La Charmoise

This family domain is run today by Henry Marionnet and his son Jean-Sébastien. Located on the eastern edge of Touraine, the wines are AOP Touraine. The estate lies on a high point between the Loire and Cher rivers, and has the classic "perruches" soil of clay, flint and gravel. Just over half the plantings are Gamay; most of the rest are Sauvignon Blanc. The unique feature of the domain is a focus on ungrafted vines, which form the basis for the Vinifera cuvées, including Chenin Blanc, Sauvignon Blanc, Gamay, and Malbec. These come from 6 ha of vineyards planted relatively recently, but the Provignage cuvée comes from a small plot of pre-phylloxera vines of Romorantin. Another throwback is the Cépages Oubliés, which comes from an old clone of Gamay, the Gamay de Bouze, which has colored juice, and was relatively common until it was banned by INAO. The Premières Vendanges cuvée is bottled without sulfur. Vinified in stainless steel in completely modern cellars (there is no oak here), the style focuses on purity of fruit—"The ideal is to make wine without interference," Jean-Sébastien says. To my mind, the cuvées from the ungrafted vines definitely have a sheen of extra purity, and provide splendid examples of each variety. There is usually some carbonic maceration for the Gamay. The reds are often compared favorably with Beaujolais, and the whites with Sancerre. The top wine among the regular cuvées is the M de Marionnet, a Sauvignon Blanc.

⊙ Restigné

◉ Bourgueil

🍷 Bourgueil, Busardières
www.domainedelachevalerie.fr

👤 🏭 G 🍇
38 ha; 120,000 bottles

Domaine de La Chevalerie

The Caslot family founded this domain in 1640, and today it is run by the thirteenth and fourteenth generations, Pierre Caslot and his children Emmanuel and Stéphanie. The house sits on one of Touraine's largest cellars, excavated during the eleventh and thirteenth centuries to provide stone to construct the village of Restigné; the caves actually cover a hectare. It's one of the most picturesque wine sites of the region, but the wines are completely serious. Extending all around the house, 24 ha of vineyards are divided into six blocks with soils varying from sandy to clay. Grapes from another area to the north are sold off to negociants. The wines are exclusively Cabernet Franc under the Bourgueil AOP. The focus is on what the Caslots call Cuvées Parcellaires, coming from single vineyards. There's one from each of the six blocks. The lightest is Peu Muleau from relatively sandy soils; this is intended for early drinking. Galichets tends to be the most fruity, and Busardières the leanest. The most structured is the eponymous Chevalerie from the vineyard immediately around the house, where the vines are the oldest on the property (around seventy years). There are also blends to produce wines with particular characters, ranging from Bonn'Heure (light and straightforward for immediate drinking) to the Vin de Garde cuvée that was produced to characterize the 2005 vintage. All grapes are destemmed, and wines are matured in demi-muids.

François Chidaine

François Chidaine is somewhat of a mover and shaker in Montlouis, where he has a wine shop (La Cave Insolite) in the main street that offers tastings of his wines and an excellent selection of bottles from the region and elsewhere. François founded the domain 25 years ago with 3 ha, and he also owns a domain in Spain (his wife is Spanish). Today the domain consists of many small parcels, totaling 10 ha in Vouvray, 20 ha in Montlouis, and 7 ha in Touraine. There is a complete range from dry to fully sweet still wines and also sparkling wines. The wines offer a rare opportunity to compare those of Montlouis and Vouvray directly. The dry wines are not necessarily completely dry, and Chidaine does not mark sec or demi-sec on the label as the objective is to look for balance in which the sugar is not intended to be a noticeable feature. The view here is that anything up to 6-7 g/l residual sugar is effectively dry: "There is always a roundness," they say at the domain. The best dry white comes from Le Bournais in Montlouis, where there is a small patch of ungrafted vines whose lower yield gives a wine with distinctly more intensity and character (and a price to match). There is one moelleux each from Vouvray and Montlouis, and a liquoreux is made in exceptional vintages. The difference in terroirs shows most clearly at the moelleux level, where the Vouvray has a similar flavor spectrum but distinctly more intensity than the Montlouis.

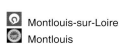

Montlouis-sur-Loire
Montlouis
Montlouis, Les Bournais
www.francois-chidaine.com

37 ha; 150,000 bottles

Maison Couly-Dutheil

Founded in 1921, Couly-Dutheil is one of the largest producers in Chinon. A modern winery on multiple storeys allows gravity operation; underneath are miles of old caves. There are extensive vineyard holdings (almost all Cabernet Franc in Chinon), but grapes are also purchased from other growers to round out the line. Long recognized as the top red wine producer in Chinon, Couly-Dutheil went through a sticky patch in the late nineties. Third generation Jacques Couly runs the domain today, together with his son Arnaud, after a family dispute that led other members of the family to leave in the mid 2000s. Arnaud, who started in 2000 after experience in the United States, introduced a policy of picking later to increase ripeness, and in 2003 stopped using barriques in favor of stainless steel. The entry level wine, Les Gravières, comes from gravel terroir near the Vienne river. "The object here is to have fruits that are easy to drink," says Jacques Couly. Baronnie Madeleine, from the middle of the range offers a softer impression. The top wines come from two monopoles, Clos de l'Olive (a 5 ha *clos* purchased in 1951) and Clos de l'Echo (the only vineyard actually in the town of Chinon). The style is rounded but with a mineral underlay: the epitome of Cabernet Franc, and you would swear that barrique aging had been used to achieve this complexity of texture. Crescendo is a second wine from Clos de l'Echo that continues to be matured in (new) barriques.

Azay-le-Rideau
Chinon
Chinon, Clos de l'Echo
www.coulydutheil-chinon.com

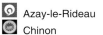

94 ha; 500,000 bottles

Loire:Touraine

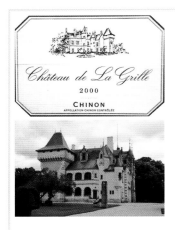

Château de La Grille

Château la Grille was owned by the Gosset family (of Gosset Champagne) until it was sold in 2009 to Jean-Martin Dutour, who also owns three other properties: Domaine de la Perrière, Domaine de Roncé, and Château de St. Louand, making him the largest owner of vineyards in Chinon with 150 ha. The properties are used more or less as an ascending hierarchy (although with a little overlap between the special cuvée of one Château and the regular cuvée of the next Château). Altogether there are 10 principal cuvées. Domaine de la Perrière (on recent alluvial soils in the valley) is directed towards easy drinking wines; Domaine de Roncé (on an ancient terrace) is more tense and tannic; Château de la Grille (coming from relatively homogeneous limestone and clay) is a vin de garde in the middle of the range (50% matured in barriques and 50% in cuve); and Château de St Louand (calcareous terroir on the plateau) is matured entirely in new barriques. It's really only when you get to Château de la Grille that you see the typicity of Cabernet Franc breaking out. This is a mainstream Chinon, as opposed to the Château de Saint Louand which is distinctly in an international style. At Château de la Grille, half of the 27 ha surround the château; the other half is on a slope across the nearby autoroute, planted almost entirely in Cabernet Franc. There's been a large investment here, with a new gravity-feed winery underground, and a modern tasting room.

⊙ Chinon

🍾 Chinon, Château de la Grille

www.chateaudelagrille.com

🚶 ⅏ G

27 ha; 150,000 bottles

Domaine Huët

Founded in 1928 by Victor Huët, together with his son Gaston, this is the most famous domain in Vouvray. Gaston's son-in-law Noël Pinguet became the third winemaker. With Gaston in ill-health, the domain was sold to the Hwang family, who are interested in sweet wines and also have a domain in Tokaji. Noël Pinguet retired in 2012 amid reports of disagreements about style and quality. Hugo Hwang and his sister Sarah now run the property. "The goal of the domain is to make sweet wine, that is the tradition," says Hugo, "but it changes from year to year." The domain has three vineyards. The 5 ha of Le Haut Lieu were the origin of the estate; Clos du Bourg (one of the oldest vineyards in the region) was added in 1953; and Le Mont was added in 1957. All the vineyards are on the slope of the Première Côte running up from the river. There is a range of wines, from dry to fully sweet, from each vineyard; the usual balance is about 40% dry to 60% in various sweet styles (demi-sec, moelleux, and moelleux Première Trie). The sweet wines are the glory of the domain, but terroir shows through all: the moelleux most clearly typify the classic acid-sweet balance of Vouvray. These are very fine wines, which certainly can stand up to dessert wines produced anywhere in the world by the point 1er Trie moelleux is reached. Cuvée Constance is a selection of the most botrytized berries, made only occasionally. About 20% of production goes into méthode traditionelle and pétillant sparkling wines.

⊙ Vouvray

🍾 Vouvray Moelleux, Le Mont

www.huet-echansonne.com

▦ ⅏ G 🗀

30 ha; 100,000 bottles

Domaine Charles Joguet

The winery was originally a farm, before Charles Joguet converted it exclusively to viticulture when he came back to Sazilly from art studies in Paris in 1959. Following the model of Burgundy, he decided to see what effect terroir would have in Chinon, and introduced cuvées from different vineyards. Charles retired in 1997, and since then the domain has been owned by the Genet family. "He was quite an innovator, some things worked, some didn't," recalls current winemaker Kevin Fontaine. Joguet had the first stainless steel tanks in the Loire: today they are the standard. The focus remains on cuvées from different terroirs, although there have been some changes in the vineyard holdings. The style here tends to freshness, with increasing fruit density and structure going up the scale; the wines are never aggressive or heavy. Ascending the hierarchy of the red cuvées, Cuvée Terroir (from sandy soils), Les Petites Roches (an assemblage from several parcels), and Cuvée de la Cure (from clay and gravel terroir around the church) are relatively straightforward. The other terroirs are clay and limestone. There's a step up with Les Charmes, but the best three cuvées, Les Varennes du Grand Clos (which has some sandstone), Clos du Chêne Vert (a warm spot), and Clos de la Dioterie (the oldest vineyard) have the most interest. The one to try first is Clos du Chêne Vert for an elegant balance that makes it more approachable. The white Clos de la Plante Martin is one of the finest white Chinons.

Les Varennes du Grand Clos
CHINON
CHARLES JOGUET

Sazilly
Chinon
Chinon, Clos du Chêne Vert
www.charlesjoguet.com
38 ha; 150,000 bottles

Domaine Frédéric Mabileau

There are at least ten producers with the name Mabileau in St. Nicolas de Bourgueil, but Frédéric Mabileau is by far the best known. Vineyards are mostly in St. Nicolas de Bourgueil, but there are some in Bourgueil. The domain started in 1988 with a 2 ha vineyard and then expanded; Frédéric's father passed on 15 ha when he retired in 2003. The vineyards in St. Nicolas are on the typical sandy-gravel soils of the appellation. They have been managed organically since 2007, and all harvest is manual. There are three cuvées from St. Nicolas: Les Rouillères (which comes from the original vineyard) is the largest in volume; Les Coutures comes from the base of the slope; and L'Eclipse is an assemblage from old vines (50 to 60 years old) in various parcels on the slope. In addition there is a Bourgueil from gravel terroir (Les Racines), an Anjou red (from parcels of Cabernet Franc just to the west of the appellation of St. Nicolas de Bourgueil), Chenin Blancs from Saumur and Anjou, a Cabernet Sauvignon from Anjou, and a rosé de Loire. The lower level wines are matured in cuve, and the top cuvées for nine months in barrique. They require two or three years to come around. The usual style is fresh. "I want my wines to be representative of the appellation, giving off crisp fruit aromas, and easy to drink... we must have drinkability in St. Nicolas de Bourgueil," Frédéric says. The estate bottlings are supplemented by a small negociant activity that is separate from the domain.

FRÉDÉRIC
MABILEAU
LES ROUILLÈRES
ST NICOLAS DE BOURGUEIL

St. Nicolas de Bourgueil
St. Nicolas de Bourgueil, Les Coutures
www.fredericmabileau.com

30 ha; 150,000 bottles

Loire:Touraine

Vouvray

12 ha; 55,000 bottles

Domaine du Clos Naudin

In spite of the shabby appearance of the buildings (just up the street from the much grander quarters of Domaine Huët), Clos Naudin has a good reputation for its sweet white wines. Dating from 1923, the domain has been run by Philippe Foreau since 1983. Located in the northeastern part of Vouvray, generally south-facing, the vineyards are almost entirely situated on perruches—clay soils with a high siliceous content—which makes the wines austere and closed when young. (Hermetic is the word used in French descriptions.) They are said to require a long time to open out into elegance. The domain is one of the most traditional in Vouvray. Fermentation occurs slowly in the cool cellars and usually lasts two months. There is no chaptalization. Malolactic fermentation is blocked. Wines are matured in 300 liter barriques, almost all old (a couple of new barrels are purchased each year out of the 100 total); they are concerned here to avoid the taste of wood. Production is 60% still wine and 40% sparkling wine. Sparkling wine comes in both nonvintage and vintage cuvées and is exclusively Méthode Champenoise (no pétillant). The division between dry and sweet wines depends on vintage conditions, but the domain is better known for its sweet wines. Made only in warmer vintages, these are characterized as demi-sec, moelleux, and the moelleux reserve. Visitors are nominally welcome, but reception is unreliable, so don't count on a visit.

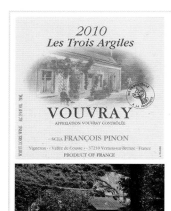

Vernou-sur-Brenne

Vouvray

Vouvray Demi Sec, Trois Argiles

15 ha; 60,000 bottles

Domaine François Pinon

The winery appears a ramshackle affair, on the plateau above Vernou, just north of Vouvray, but the wines are among the most interesting of the appellation. We tasted outdoors in a lean-to porch, just off the winery, besides the family residence. François has forceful opinions about character and aging. "We have bought one or two parcels but the basic idea is to stay with our terroir and we've never tried to go beyond it," he says. There are 6-7 parcels now. When things go well there is a Pétillant and two dry cuvées (coming from clay and siliceous terroirs); sweet wines depend on vintage. Wines are named only by their terroir. On the Silex Noir with 14 g/l residual sugar, for example, the label makes no statement about sweetness. François think that to state demi-sec would give a false impression of sweetness. "The idea is to showcase the minerality of the terroir with a touch of sugar to add complexity." François shows a definite preference for developed flavors as he brings out older vintages back to the 1960s for tasting. The wines are deceptively straightforward when young—the dry wines show the minerality of the local terroir, the sweet wines tend to be more obvious—but wines with ten or twenty years of age show impressive development, yet always retaining freshness. The dry wines may be at their best after a decade, the sweet wines after perhaps twice that time. "My intention is to capture the flavors of Chenin, and as the wines become sweeter, that takes longer aging."

Clos Roche Blanche

At the eastern edge of Touraine, the vineyards were planted by the Roussel family at the end of the nineteenth century; the caves date from 1905. Catherine Roussel took over the domain in 1975 and today runs it together with winemaker Didier Barrouillet (formerly an engineer). They started with conventional viticulture but converted to organic in 1992; they have tried biodynamic treatments but aren't convinced there's a significant difference. The size of the domain has been reduced from its peak of 32 ha to 18 ha today, which includes 12 ha of vineyards around the property (surrounded by woods, creating its own separate ecology), planted with Sauvignon Blanc, Chardonnay, Gamay, Pineau d'Aunis, and Malbec; other parcels in the adjoining villages are planted with Sauvignon Blanc, Cabernets Franc and Sauvignon, Gamay, and Malbec. Soils vary from clay to silex with a limestone subsoil. Production is half red and half white with just a little rosé (from Pineau d'Aunis). There is a small parcel of very old (115-year) Malbec vines, which are used to produce a monovarietal wine at yields that vary wildly from year to year. Most production is in stainless steel, the exception being the cuvée #5 of Sauvignon Blanc which is in old oak vats. The wines are bottled as AOP Touraine. There are six cuvées identified by varietal names, and three others. Cuvée Pif is a blend of 60% Malbec and 40% Cabernet Franc with tiny amounts of Cabernet Sauvignon and Pineau d'Aunis.

Mareuil-sur-cher
Touraine
Touraine, Sauvignon

9 ha; 20,000 bottles

Domaine de La Taille aux Loups

A wine broker at the time, Jacky Blot was regarded as a young Turk when he established Domaine de La Taille aux Loups by buying 7 ha in Montlouis in 1988. His attempts to introduce more precision into the wines were regarded with suspicion, but now he is regarded as a fixed feature of the appellation. Today he has 27 ha in Montlouis, divided among more than 30 parcels, and another 7 ha in Vouvray. Harvest is very extended at the domain, often lasting four or five weeks, as there is an attempt to harvest each parcel at a specific state of maturity. Young vines (less than twenty years of age) are used to make two sparkling wines, a Méthode Champenoise and the pétillant Triple Zero, which has no chaptalization, no dosage, and no liqueur de tirage. Virtually all the still wines, from older vines, are usually given extended maturation in wood, which has been a point of criticism. "I like long élevage in barriques or demi-muids and I hate the white Loire wines that have malolactic fermentation," describes the philosophy of the domain. There are five dry cuvées from Montlouis and three from Vouvray, distinguished by time of harvest, as well as by terroir and vine age, and a series of sweet wines from both appellations extending from demi-sec to liquoreux. In 2003 Jacky expanded into Bourgueil with the purchase of the 15 ha Domaine de la Butte, from which he produces four different cuvées. Visits are stated to be welcome, but visitors risk being ignored.

Montlouis-sur-Loire
Montlouis
www.jackyblot.fr

65 ha; 350,000 bottles

Loire:Touraine

 Chavignol

Sancerre

Sancerre, La Bourgeoise

Sancerre, Les Monts Damnés

www.henribourgeois.com

74 ha; 600,000 bottles

Domaine Henri Bourgeois

One of the largest producers in Sancerre, this family-run domain occupies much of the village of Chavignol, with a hotel, restaurant, tasting room, and modern gravity-feed winery located at the edge of the town where goats used to roam. Called by other vignerons half affectionately and half pejoratively "the American winery," it has a splendid view over the steeply rising vineyard of Monts Damnés opposite. The domain has expanded steadily from its 2 ha in 1950, spreading out from Chavignol. There are eight principal cuvées of white Sancerre, two from Pouilly, and wines from other appellations in the vicinity. Going up the range, the cuvées represent distinct terroirs, mostly matured in a mix of stainless steel and old wood. The top cuvées represent individual plots: I especially like Jadis from forty-year old vines in Monts Damnés, and Chapelle des Augustins from a unique plot of silex on calcareous subsoil. The range is impressive, all the way from quite traditional Sancerre with characteristic grassy notes, to wines from old vines at such ripeness that the flavor profile turns from citrus to stone fruits. Separate cuvées of Pinot Noir have been made since 1962: Les Baronnes and Les Bonnes Bouches are matured in a mixture of new and old oak, and the top cuvée, La Bourgeoise, comes from Vieilles Vignes (over 50 years old) and ages much like Burgundy. Bourgeois have also established Clos Henri in Marlborough, New Zealand, which is roughly equivalent in size.

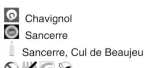 Chavignol

Sancerre

Sancerre, Cul de Beaujeu

4 ha; 30,000 bottles

Domaine François Cotat

The old Cotat domain, run by brothers Francis and Paul from 1947 to 1990, made powerful Sancerre in its own style, which is to say that late harvest sometimes produced wines with residual sugar. François Cotat inherited half of the domain in 1990, and has continued the policy of late harvest. Occasionally the wines have been judged atypical by the AOC. François remains in the old cellars, behind his house, right in the center of Chavignol. "I have no vines more than a kilometer away," he says. He inherited three small vineyards from the old Cotat domain: a hectare each in La Grande Côte, Les Monts Damnés, and Cul de Beaujeu (all Kimmeridgian terroir in Chavignol). He has since added another lieu-dit, Les Caillottes (made since 2005 as previously the wine was declassified because the vines were young). "Unfortunately, Sancerre today is technical wine, but me, I am not at all technical. I don't do anything—the least intervention possible. I am often the last to harvest, I look for full ripeness. I make vins de garde," he says, "They can be kept for up to twenty or thirty years, no problem. The wine is usually closed for the first five years and then begins to open." To make his point, he opens a 1995 Grande Côte that is still full of flavor. As a rule, Les Caillottes is the exception to drink relatively young, Monts Damnés is the most reserved, Cul de Beaujeu is more open, and Grande Côte is the fullest. The style is its own expression of Sauvignon Blanc typicity.

Domaine Pascal Cotat

Brothers Francis and Paul Cotat established a domain in Chavignol in 1947. They shared production, bottling the same wines under their own separate labels. When they retired in 1990, they divided the domain between their sons, Pascal and François. (Part of the reason for the division was a regulation preventing independent producers from selling the same wine under two labels). Pascal makes his wine in new cellars in Sancerre. He got some of the oldest vines when the vineyards were split, and has two vineyards in Chavignol for Sauvignon Blanc production: a single hectare that is half of the Grande Côte lieu-dit (François owns the other half); and 1.5 ha in Les Monts Damnés. Both are on steep north-facing slopes, steep enough that all work has to be manual. Each vineyard makes a separate cuvée. The wine is fermented and matured in old demi-muids; coming from grapes harvested a week later than most in the appellation, it offers rich, full flavors, with significant aging potential. These are not wines to drink young, which would miss most of their complexity and distinction: they need time to develop full richness. They are unctuous without being fat, and rich but very fine, although alcohol can be high. A rosé comes from 4 ha in Sancerre. The 2010 rosé was declassified to Vin de Table because of an argument with the authorities (when Pascal refused to sell the town of Sancerre one of his vineyards to use as a parking lot, the vineyard was declassified).

Sancerre
Sancerre, La Grande Côte

7 ha; 15,000 bottles

Domaine Lucien Crochet

Created by Lucien Crochet from the vineyard holdings of his father and father-in-law, the domain is now run by Lucien's son, Gilles. Much larger than might be suggested by its modest exterior, the winery is a modern facility with sparkling new equipment in the center of Bué. Driving through his vineyards, Gilles points to nuances of terroir much as a vigneron might in Burgundy. The 90 individual vineyard parcels are all in the southern part of the appellation, around Bué, with 29 ha planted to Sauvignon Blanc on various terroirs, and 9 ha planted with Pinot Noir on Kimmeridgian terroir. The house style for whites develops from the mineral, citrus-driven Sancerre to the mélange of stone fruits and citrus in Le Chêne (from the Clos du Chêne Marchand), but the main difference between them is the greater delicacy and subtlety in Le Chêne. Moving from these wines, matured in stainless steel, to the single vineyard Cul de Beaujeu (introduced in 2009), the wine becomes rounder and riper, with more stone fruits than citrus; there is also the added factor of exposure to wood, with half new and half old. Only made in some years, from a plot of vines planted in 1956, the Cuvée Prestige offers a more evidently powerful fruit expression. In reds, the Croix du Roy Sancerre cuvée is a play on the name of Sancerre's famous Clos du Roy; and like its white counterpart, the Cuvée Prestige is made from old vines only in the best years. Its purity could easily come from Burgundy.

Bué-en-Sancerre
Sancerre
Sancerre, Croix du Roy
Sancerre, Le Chêne
www.lucien-crochet.fr

38 ha; 300,000 bottles

Loire: Centre

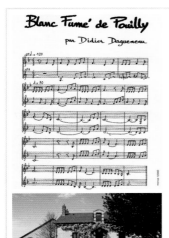

Saint Andelain

Pouilly Fumé

Pouilly Fumé, Pur Sang

12 ha; 50,000 bottles

Domaine Didier Dagueneau

The street address, 5 rue Ernesto Che Guevara, says a good deal about Didier Dagueneau, who created the domain in 1992 with only 3 ha. He rose to prominence as far and away the best (and most expensive) producer in Pouilly. The front office has a charming appearance, but the building just behind is a modern concrete, purpose-built, gravity-feed winery, designed by Didier to optimize wine production. Didier also started the Jardins des Babylone in Jurançon. After he was killed in a light aircraft crash in 2008, his son Benjamin took over as winemaker. The vineyards are in Pouilly except for a half hectare in Sancerre. "We make wines that are true, intended for keeping, they are meant to develop after time," is how Charlotte, Benjamin's sister, who handles the commercial side, describes the style. Blanc Fumé de Pouilly is the only cuvée made by assemblage. Pur Sang comes from 2 ha of clay-flint, with very small pebbles, Buisson Renard comes from 1.5 ha of a thin layer of flint on top of clay, and the most famous, Silex, comes from deep flint at the parcel behind the winery. "It presents the longest potential for aging, but is also the wine that takes longest to develop," Charlotte says. Young vintages of all cuvées are restrained, but there is no mistaking the sheer purity of the underlying fruits: it's worth waiting five years for the full variety of flavors to develop. A mark of greatness is the increase of subtlety with age, with the 1996 Silex showing a delicate balance of truffles and fruits in 2014.

Sury-en-Vaux

Sancerre

Sancerre, Vieilles Vignes

www.vincent-gaudry.com

11 ha; 50,000 bottles

Domaine Vincent Gaudry

This small domain occupies an old building in the village of Sury-en-Vaux. They were bottling when I visited, and the portable bottling line had to be disassembled for us to descend to the cave below for the tasting. Started by Vincent's grandfather (as part of polyculture), the domain has many separate parcels today, and produces three white cuvées every year. Tournebride comes from the vineyard adjacent to the winery; Mélodie de Vieilles Vignes comes from 50-year old vines on clay-calcareous terroir; and Scorpion comes uniquely from silex terroir (the label just says Sancerre, but has an image of a scorpion, which is how Vincent refers to the cuvée). In some years another top cuvée, À Mi-Chemin, is made in tiny quantities (basically one barrel). Tournebride is vinified in stainless steel; the Vieilles Vignes in an equal mixture of stainless steel and wood; and Scorpion entirely in old wood. There's no fixed time for élevage. "I taste, like in the old times, and move it out of barriques into cuve when it tastes right," Vincent explains, but élevage is generally around twelve months. "Tournebride is usually good to drink after two years, the Vieilles Vignes and Scorpion, it's necessary to wait," he says. The house style is refined, elegant, and taut. Tournebride is quite accessible, but the linear purity of the young Vieilles Vignes and Scorpion really needs time to develop. The red is fresh and lively, and comes from a selection massale of the original Pinot Noir grown in Sancerre.

Domaine Philippe Gilbert

One of the larger properties in Menetou-Salon, the domain goes back to François Gilbert, an innkeeper who started making wine in 1768. Two generations ago, in 1959, Paul Gilbert was instrumental in creating the appellation. His son, Jean-Paul, actually reduced the size of the domain slightly; and the current Philippe Gilbert returned to take it over in 1998. At that time, it was two thirds Pinot Noir, due to the enthusiasm of Jean-Paul, who had studied in Burgundy. Today Philippe has increased the proportion of Sauvignon Blanc, and is aiming for an equal division between red and white. Vineyards on clay-limestone soils are scattered throughout the appellation in the villages of Menetou-Salon, Vignoux, Parassy, and Morogues. There are two cuvées of white and two of red. For each color, in addition to the domain wine there is the single vineyard, Les Renardières, (from a 4.7 ha plot divided equally between Sauvignon Blanc and Pinot Noir). There is also a rosé (from a plot of Pinot Noir that doesn't ripen so easily). "I am trying to prove that we have beautiful terroir in Menetou-Salon and we can mature wine for a long time. I want to represent the special elegance of Menetou-Salon; the wines are discrete but unfold slowly," says Philippe. The domain wines are elegant, offering a modern version of the traditional style, but the place to see the aging potential is Les Renardières, offering a ripe, textured expression of Sauvignon.

Menetou-Salon

Menetou-Salon, Les Renardières
www.domainephilippegilbert.fr

28 ha; 120,000 bottles

Domaine De Ladoucette

With 80 ha in the Pouilly Fumé appellation, La Ladoucette is one of the largest producers. Its vineyards include all four soil types of the appellation, flint, sand, chalk, and clay; 90% are planted with Sauvignon Blanc. The youngest and oldest grapes are harvested by hand, the remainder by machine. Grapes are vinified separately from each parcel. The gravity-feed winery was built in 1990. Fermentation takes place in temperature-controlled stainless steel tanks, starting at 12 °C and gradually increasing to 22 °C over the 2-3 weeks of fermentation. After fermentation the wine is matured for 18 months in glass lined cement tanks (the medium reflects the belief that long term maturation in stainless steel would taint the wine with a taste from the steel). No oak is used at the domain. The major part of production is Pouilly Fumé. Baron L is a super-cuvée made from selected lots in the best years. There are also two Sancerres, Comte Lafond which is blended from vines in 5 villages, and is fuller than La Poussie, which comes only from the eponymous village on clay and limestone soil. Both red and rosé are also made from the vineyards at La Poussie. La Ladoucette also owns the Marc Brédif domain in Vouvray. With its large scale of production, this may well be the public face of Pouilly Fumé for many: the standard is reliable if not remarkable. Recent vintages have shown a softening of the style and even a move towards more exotic fruits. The domain is not very receptive to visits.

Saint Andelain

Pouilly Fumé

Pouilly Fumé
www.deladoucette.fr

104 ha; 1,200,000 bottles

Loire: Centre

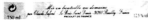

Reuilly

Reuilly, Le Clos des Messieurs

www.claudelafond.com

40 ha; 300,000 bottles

Domaine Claude Lafond

Created by André Lafond in the 1960s with 2.5 ha that he inherited, the domain grew slowly to 6.5 ha. André's son Claude took over in 1977 and further expanded the domain. Today it is run by Claude's daughter, Nathalie. Owning 35 of the 200 ha planted in the appellation, this is the most important domain in Reuilly. There are also further vineyards in Valençay (just over the border in Touraine) and the IGP de Loire. The winery is a somewhat utilitarian modern building on the outskirts of Reuilly, built in 2012. Claude Lafond was instrumental in founding the Chai de Reuilly (which is adjacent and functions as a cooperative to make wines for vignerons to be released under their own labels), but since the new winery was constructed, the domain has been completely independent. Some 60% of production is white. The basic wines are matured in stainless steel, but a mix of stainless steel and barriques is used for the top cuvées. The style is fairly straightforward, with Sauvignon showing its grassy character, but cut by a touch of richness going up the scale as the wines spend longer on the lees and see more oak. The rosés are made from Pinot Gris rather than Pinot Noir. "We've always favored making a rosé from Pinot Gris because it's very delicate," says Nathalie Lafond. The reds tend to be a little tight, with a definite cool climate impression. The top cuvée in each color is called Cuvée André, after the founder.

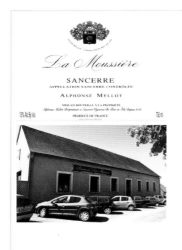

Sancerre

Sancerre, En Grand Champs

Sancerre, Les Romains

www.mellot.com

55 ha; 350,000 bottles

Domaine Alphonse Mellot

Alphonse Mellot occupies a rabbit warren of medieval cellars right under the town center of Sancerre, some dating from the fifteenth century (but modernized recently). Opposite is a modern building with the name of La Moussière, the main cuvée (about half of total). Vineyards in Sancerre include 30 ha in a single plot, and 13 ha of Pinot Noir, with more vineyards (Chardonnay and Pinot Noir) on the IGP Côtes de la Charité. Each cuvée of Sauvignon Blanc is distinct: La Moussière comes from a large block of Kimmeridgian terroir; La Demoiselle from silex; Satellite from Monts Damnés and Cul de Beaujeu in Chavignol (since 2008); Les Romains from a plot of 60-year old vines with flint on the surface and chalk underneath; Edmond comes from 40- to 90-year-old vines; and Generation XIX from 90-year old vines, at La Moussière. Each of the five separate cuvées of Pinot Noir is similarly based on separate parcels, with the top cuvées being En Grand Champs, a 1 ha parcel of 65-year-old vines at the top of La Moussière, and (50 m away) Generation XIX (named for 19 generations of Mellots) from even older vines. Both are true vins de garde. "The spicy quality with notes of fruit is the Sancerre typicity," the Mellots say of their reds. The house style is forceful: the steely roundness of the whites is what Chablis or the Côte d'Or might make of Sauvignon Blanc, and the reds can give the Côte de Nuits a run for its money. All are full of flavor, but always remain in balance.

Vignobles Joseph Mellot Père et Fils

The domain goes back five hundred years to César Mellot and has long been selling wine under its own name. "We are the sole domain to have vineyards in every appellation of the Centre," says Catherine Corbeau-Mellot, who has been in charge since the unexpected death of her husband Alexandre in 2005. All appellation wines come from estate vineyards, with half in Sancerre. Mellot also owns domains Pierre Duret and Jean-Michel Sorbe in Quincy that continue to be run separately. Grapes are purchased to make IGP wines. One of the largest producers in the region, accounting for almost 5% of all production, Joseph Mellot has its headquarters in a modern building constructed in 1990 just outside of Sancerre. "We need to represent the Joseph Mellot spirit, wine should be easy to drink, fresh and pure," is how oenologue Frédéric Jacquet describes the style. "You see terroir more clearly for Sauvignon Blanc with stainless steel," he says, explaining that most wines are vinified exclusively in cuve. More than three quarters of production is white. Except for a few cuvées matured in barrique, the emphasis is on fresh citrus fruits, increasing in intensity as the appellations change from Quincy or Reuilly to Sancerre or Pouilly Fumé. The wines are reliable representations of their appellations: I like the Pouilly Fumés best, with the Domaine des Mariniers and Le Troncsec illustrating the difference between assemblage and a single vineyard.

Sancerre
Pouilly Fume, Domaine des Mariniers
www.josephmellot.com
115 ha; 2,000,000 bottles

Domaine Jonathan Didier Pabiot

This small domain is perched on the heights overlooking the river between Pouilly-sur-Loire and St. Andelain, occupying a small warehouse-like building next to the house. It's a very hands-on operation: Jonathan's wife, Nina, was running the labeling machine when I arrived. "We do everything in the same place," she says. Its history encapsulates change in the region. Didier Pabiot was making a single Pouilly Fumé that was sold in bulk or directly to the clientele. His son Jonathan wanted to try organic viticulture, so Didier gave him a hectare; later he bought a little more land, and started his own small domain. Then Didier decided to go organic after all, and in due course the two domains were joined back together. Yields have come down from 60 hl/ha to 40 hl/ha. The appellation wine is a blend of terroirs; Aubaine and Predilection are single vineyard wines from different calcareous terroirs. All three are vinified in stainless steel with minimal battonage. "Jonathan prefers the wine to take what it wants from the lees, not what we force it to take," explains Nina. Eurythmic comes from the same plot as Predilection but is matured in barrique. The labels of the cuvées say Artiste Vigneron, which is a fair description. House style is delicate and elegant, almost floral. The wines are restrained, even closed, when young; to see the full flavor potential you need to wait three or so years after release. The Pabiots were drinking 2006 and 2007 at home in 2014. The wines are a real bargain.

Pouilly-sur-Loire
Pouilly Fumé
Pouilly Fumé
19 ha; 90,000 bottles

Loire: Centre

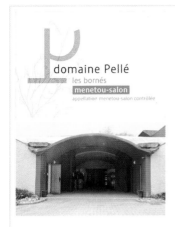

Domaine Henry Pellé

The domain dates from the start of the twentieth century. Three generations later, it was run by Eric Pellé until he died in an accident in 1995, when his wife Anne took over, aided by oenologist Julian Zernott (now in the Languedoc). Paul-Henry Pellé took charge in 2007. Most of Pellé's vineyards in Menetou-Salon are in the village of Morogues, where the 35 ha fall into 25 separate parcels. Another 8 ha are leased on long-term contracts. There are also 5 ha of Sancerre in the commune of Montigny. Production is two thirds white and a third red, with a small amount of rosé. The domain started in a small house across the street which is now used as an office; the modern production facilities were constructed in 1970 and extended in 1998. There are five white cuvées and five reds from Menetou Salon, each representing a single type of terroir, varying from flint to calcareous. "We try to work in Burgundy style, with each plot kept separate. We were the first in Menetou-Salon when my father started to do that in 1981," says Paul-Henry Pellé. Whites are fermented in stainless steel, and mature in varying combinations of stainless steel and wood. Reds are all aged in wood: Paul-Henry has backed off from extraction to go for more elegance, and has moved from barriques to larger 400 liter fûts; there is a little new oak. The style is elegant: whites show Sauvignon typicity in a fresh but round style; reds have precise fruits with good structure, and benefit from aging.

⊙ Morogues
◉ Menetou-Salon
🍾 Menetou-Salon, Les Cris
🍾 Menetou-Salon, Les Blanchais
www.henry-pelle.com
🚶 🏭 G ☙
42 ha; 300,000 bottles

Domaine Vincent Pinard

"We are a very old family estate, winemakers for more than twenty generations, established in Bué since the beginning," says Clément Pinard, who runs the domain today with his brother Florent. There's a modern cave under the family house, and a whole new winery behind for whites. There are 12.5 ha of Sauvignon Blanc and 4.5 ha of Pinot Noir. "The estate has increased in size but we have no plans to grow much more because we want to stay a family estate," Clément says. Vineyards fall into 40 different blocks in Bué: Sauvignon Blanc is planted on the chalkiest soils. Terroir is the driving factor in the white cuvées. Florès is a blend from various calcareous parcels, Clémence from more clay. Nuance comes from 40-year-old vines on very chalky, stony soil. The three single vineyard cuvées are Petit Chemarin (from a late-ripening, west-facing site), Grand Chemarin (with southern exposure), and the famous Chêne Marchand. Harmonie was created in 1989 as an old vines Chêne Marchand with all new oak, but now has a quarter from other sites, and only 15% new oak. The Pinots are divided into the Sancerre from younger vines and the Charlouise from 45-year-old vines (with up to 70% new oak). In exceptional years there is a Vendanges Entières using whole bunches with no destemming. The sweet citrus fruits of the whites are delicate and fragrant, with increasing complexity in the single vineyards; the reds have precise fruits with silky smoothness.

⊙ Bué-en-Sancerre
◉ Sancerre
🍾 Sancerre, Charlouise
🍾 Sancerre, Grand Chemarin
www.domaine-pinard.com
▣ 🏭 G 🍇
17 ha; 100,000 bottles

Domaine Michel Redde et Fils

Michel Redde wanted to be an artist, but started this domain in the hamlet of Les Berthiers. Today it occupies new quarters, built by his son Thierry in 2001, just on the other side of the autoroute. Thierry's son, Sébastien is in charge of the cave, while his brother manages the vineyards. Michel's paintings hang on the wall of the tasting room, which is guarded by an elderly Labrador named Sauvignon. The wines almost all come from Pouilly Fumé, with six cuvées, each representing an assemblage from the same terroirs or a single vineyard, although the domain also maintains 1.5 ha of Chasselas for two cuvées in the Pouilly-sur-Loire appellation. All wines are vinified in the same way, in a mix of foudres and demi-muids, in order to allow terroir to be the sole determining difference. They spend 12 months in wood followed by a year in cuve before release. Although I admire the objective in preserving the old varieties, I'm not entirely sure I find enough flavor interest in the Chasselas. The Sauvignons from Pouilly Fumé all show a very understated style when young, with a faintly citrus character: they tend to be more interesting on nose than palate, which might indicate promise for the future. The revelation at the domain, however, was a tasting of older wines, when the 1996 Pouilly-sur-Loire Cuvée Gustave Daudin put in a creditable performance, and the La Moynerie cuvée of the same vintage from Pouilly Fumé seemed much younger than its age.

Saint Andelain
Pouilly Fumé
Pouilly Fumé, Marjorum
www.michel-redde.com

41 ha; 240,000 bottles

Domaine Pascal & Nicolas Reverdy

Pascal Reverdy took over this family domain in 1985, and moved completely into estate bottling. His younger brother Nicolas joined him in 1993, and after his accidental death in 2007, his wife Sophie came into the domain. The winery has some old, workmanlike buildings in the hamlet of Maimbray. Pascal makes the wine, from 10 ha of Sauvignon Blanc and 4 ha of Pinot Noir. The introductory cuvée in red, white, and rosé is called Terre de Maimbray, as the vineyards are all in the coteaux above Maimbray, on very steep slopes of Kimmeridgian terroir (with inclines of 30-40%, rising up to the plateau at around 300 m elevation at the top). The white Terre de Maimbray is vinified in stainless steel, with six months' élevage on the lees. An old vines cuvée, Les Anges Lots, from vines more than sixty years old, is matured in a large wooden cuve with battonage for ten months. It's richer than the Terre de Maimbray, with stone fruits adding to the citrus, and a sense of restrained power. The red Terre de Maimbray is matured in a mixture of barriques and larger barrels of old wood; it's intended to be a vin de plaisir. Cuvée Nicolas comes from the only vineyard parcel that's not in Maimbray, a plot of pure calcareous terroir in Bué; matured in demi-muids with about one third new, it's intended to be a vin de garde, and shows good purity of fruits with an earthy, mineral, character. The rosé is fresh and savory, made in the tradition of white wine.

Sury-en-Vaux
Sancerre
Sancerre, Les Anges Lots

14 ha; 90,000 bottles

Loire:Centre

Domaine Claude Riffault

The Riffault family was in polyculture involving cereals, goats, and a few vines until viticulture became increasingly important during the fifties. Stéphane Riffault has been making the wine since 2001, in a modern cuverie, constructed twenty years ago, in the hamlet of Sury-en-Vaux. Vineyards are in the northern part of the Sancerre appellation, with about fifty parcels altogether. For the whites, "We've always separated the lieu-dits," Stéphane explains, so each area is vinified separately to make a cuvée representing a specific terroir: of the five cuvées, four come from calcareous terroir, with varying amounts of clay and fossil deposits, one (Les Chailloux) comes from a siliceous plot at the eastern edge of the appellation. Les Boucauds and Les Chasseignes are vinified in a mix of stainless steel and barrels; they have relatively short élevage, and represent half and a quarter of production, respectively. Coming from smaller areas, Les Denisottes, Les Chailloux, and Les Desmalets are vinified entirely in wood, with élevage lasting around 9 months. Stéphane favors 500 liter barrels. The style of the whites is towards precision and clarity of fruits, often subtle and understated when young, except for Les Desmalets, which is more forceful. Red and rosé come from a single 2.5 ha vineyard, La Noue, with the rosé usually coming from the younger vines. The red La Noue tends to be quite tight on release and needs a couple of years to soften.

Sury-en-Vaux
Sancerre
Sancerre, La Noue
Sancerre, Les Chasseignes
www.clauderiffault.com

13 ha; 80,000 bottles

Domaine Vacheron

Located in the center of Sancerre, with old cellars running under the town, Domaine Vacheron is run by cousins Jean-Dominique and Jean-Laurent. The domain wine comes from an assemblage of all their terroirs, but since the first single vineyard wine, Les Romains, was introduced in 1997, they have been moving towards expression of individual terroirs. Jean Laurent's view is that this depends on getting the vigor and the date of harvest right. "At middle vigor you get citrus flavors, which give the most complexity. The window of harvest for Sauvignon Blanc is just four days for each block: you have to be in that time if you want to display varietal character," he says. Les Romains comes from silex; Guigne-Chèvres, Chambrates, and Le Paradis come from different calcareous terroirs. There are also reds from all terroirs, including Belle Dame from silex; its refined character makes you think of Volnay. The house style here is towards precision and elegance in the whites. The same sense of refinement and purity shows for the reds. Both whites and reds from silex show a quality of taut tension; those from calcareous terroirs are broader, but still have that delicate blend of citrus and stone fruits. Both reds and whites age unusually well: top vintages of reds are good for twenty years; and a 1983 appellation Sancerre white was lively and savory in 2014 (quite developed, of course, but with the restrained style offering subtlety). There's a distinctive view of varietal typicity here.

Sancerre
Sancerre, Belle Dame
Sancerre, Le Paradis

50 ha; 250,000 bottles

Domaine Jean-Claude Bessin

The domain is hidden away in the village of Chapelle a few miles outside Chablis. Jean-Claude took over in 1992; his wife represents the sixth generation since the estate started in 1825. Estate bottling started with Jean-Claude. "My father-in-law sold all the juice to negociants. When I took over, I found it frustrating to work on the vines and vinification and sell the juice." Almost half the holdings are in AOP Chablis around Chapelle: the rest are in premier and grand crus. "We don't look to increase the size of the domain, we have the luck to have some vieilles vignes," Jean-Claude says. There is mixed use of wood and cuve, depending on the cuvée, and élevage lasts a year. Chablis AOP is kept in cuve with only a small proportion of barriques. Premier and grand crus are handled the same way with about 60% in barriques, using only old wood. The style here is to bring out the minerality of the fruits. Going up the hierarchy, there is more precision, more reserve or even austerity, but increasing finesse. The single cuvée of Chablis has more character than usual for the AOP, because it comes only from old (about 60-year) vines. The Montmains has more intensity, and then La Forêt (part of Montmains, and matured only in foudre) has increased precision and minerality. Fourchaume shows more open generosity of fruits (usually there are two cuvées, one from vines of 35-45 years, the other from vines over 60 years). Valmur is relatively austere and needs more time to open out.

Chablis
La Forêt
12 ha; 50,000 bottles

Domaine Billaud Simon

The domain originated in a marriage between Jean Billaud and Renée Simon before the second world war, bringing together the vineyards from two viticultural families, and their son Bernard Billaud ran the domain until it was sold to Faiveley in 2014. Behind the gracious old house where tastings are held is a large cuverie, constructed in 1991. Holdings are divided into about forty separate plots, with only six larger than a hectare, but more than half are in premier or grand crus. In winemaking, there are two Billaud Simons. Going round the cuverie, there are lots of stainless steel tanks, and a rather small barrel room with a mix of barriques and demi-muids. The larger group of wines, about 80% of production, comprises Cuvées Haute Tradition; these are vinified exclusively in stainless steel, and range from Petit Chablis to grand crus. The smaller group of Cuvées Prestige has at least some oak maturation, 20% for Chablis Tête d'Or (which comes from a special plot just below Montée de Tonnerre), 10% for Fourchaume, 60% for Mont de Milieu, and 100% for Blanchots. Vaudésir was switched from stainless steel to 100% oak as an experiment in 2011, because it was always too closed previously. I have the feeling that Bernard's heart lies with the stainless steel cuvées, "All oak is old, new oak would be too marked," he says. Freshness is the quality that is most emphasized in tasting, and is marked in the Haute Tradition series, which show traditional zesty character.

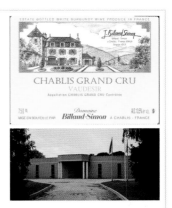

Chablis
Montée de Tonnerre
www.billaud-simon.com
20 ha; 150,000 bottles

La Chablisienne

This important cooperative started in 1923 as a means for individual growers to sell their wines, blending and selling in bulk to negociants. In the 1950s, La Chablisienne made a transition to taking musts, and producing wine for direct sale. It has a splendid modern facility with a constant stream of visitors to its spacious tasting room. Representing 300 growers, today it accounts for around a quarter of all production in Chablis, including cuvées from most of the premier and grand crus. Vinification varies with the level of appellation: Petit Chablis and Chablis are vinified in steel, premier crus in 25% oak, and grand crus in 50% oak. There are three cuvées of Chablis: Finage comes from young vines, Sereine has some old vines, and Venerable comes from vines over 40 years old. There are 12 premier crus and 4 grand crus. The cooperative actually purchased the estate of Château Grenouilles in 2003, which gave it ownership of most of the grand cru of Grenouilles. There are two cuvées: Fiefs de Grenouilles comes from young vines, and Château Grenouilles comes from the old vines, and is the top wine from La Chablisienne, even a little more powerful and aromatic than Les Clos. The differences between the various premier and grand crus stand out—in fact tasting the range offers an unusual opportunity because few producers have so many different crus—and there is good representation of vintage character. The wines are reliable with good typicity.

Chablis
Fourchaume
www.chablisienne.com
1150 ha; 6,000,000 bottles

Domaine Vincent Dauvissat

Dauvissat's approach was epitomized for me the first time I visited, when I asked Vincent how he decided on the length of élevage. Slightly startled, he shrugged, and said simply, "The wine tells me." Without question, this is one of Chablis's top domains, making wines with rare intensity. Fermentation is mostly in cuve, but élevage is in old barriques. "The fact that the wine matures in a container that breathes brings out the terroir for me," Vincent says, "but new oak loses the subtlety of terroir, the delicacy on the finish, I don't like that." Viticulture and vinification are similar for all the cuvées (élevage usually lasts around a year, except for Petit Chablis, which is about nine months). Half of the vineyards are in premier crus and a quarter in grand crus; average vine age is around 50 years. La Forêt and Vaillons are mineral, Preuses the most delicate, and Les Clos verges on austere until it develops that classic edge of anise. Viticulture is biodynamic, but "I'm a peasant, and need to be practical and efficient, so holding to the phases of the moon is tempered by the weather." There is nothing less than exceptional here: on my last visit (in 2014) we were discussing the aging of Les Clos, when Vincent said, "Of course it ages well, but the Petit Chablis also ages, the 2012 will last twenty years. He proved his point by bringing out a 1996 Petit Chablis, which was mature but still lively. Some wines are bottled under the alternative label of Dauvissat-Camus.

Chablis
La Forêt
14 ha; 70,000 bottles

Domaine Jean-Paul et Benoit Droin

This family domain has been passed from father to son for fourteen generations. Benoit has been in charge since the end of the 1990s. A new cuverie was built in 1999 on the road at the foot of the grand crus, but the elegant tasting room remains in the cave under the old family house in town. The domain has grown from 8 ha under Benoit's grandfather to its present size, with a range extending from Petit Chablis to nine premier and five grand crus. Two generations ago the wines had no oak exposure, but oak was introduced in the 1980s, and the domain is now one of the leading producers of oaked premier and grand crus. Petit Chablis (from a single plot on Portlandian soil just above the grand crus) and Chablis (from several plots totaling 9 ha on the other side of the river) are produced in stainless steel. After fermentation in stainless steel, premier and grand crus are matured in a mix of cuves and oak barriques for about 10 months until assemblage just prior to bottling. Oak usage for the crus at first was up to 100%, but "has been reduced from 15 years ago to bring out terroir and elegance," explains Benoit. Today the premier crus (9 ha total) see from 20-40% oak, and the grand crus (4 ha total) from 40-50%. Accentuated by recent vintages, the style is on the fuller side for Chablis, sometimes quite Burgundian, with Montée de Tonnerre usually beating out Montmains as the best premier cru, Grenouilles showing as the fullest grand cru, and Les Clos more austere.

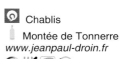
Chablis
Montée de Tonnerre
www.jeanpaul-droin.fr

26 ha; 185,000 bottles

Domaine William Fèvre

The domain owes its present position to William Fèvre, the tenth generation in his family, who built it up to its present size from 7 ha after he took over in 1957. Half of the 90 individual parcels are in premier or grand crus. William was a significant figure in Chablis, trying to maintain quality, and arguing against the expansion of the seventies. With no one to succeed him, he sold to Champagne Henriot in 1998, and Didier Seguier came from Bouchard to run the domain. A large winery at the edge of town has a splendid view of the slope of grand crus, and there's a spacious tasting room and bistro in the town center. The domain produces wines separately from estate and purchased grapes: estate wines state "Domain" discreetly on the label. The style has changed significantly since the takeover: Fèvre used to show new oak, but now there is none. Didier vinifies Petit Chablis in cuve, and uses only 5-10% oak for Chablis. Premier and grand crus have around 40-60% oak, but "nothing gets more than 70% oak, and nothing spends more than six months in oak," he says. After six months in barriques, assemblage is followed by six months more in cuve. The style continues to be on the ripe and powerful side for Chablis, and oak sometimes remains noticeable in young wines (although less so in recent vintages). The impressive range includes six grand crus and eight grand crus, but William would surely have cringed at the latest cuvée, "hipster" Chablis in a bottle that glows in the dark.

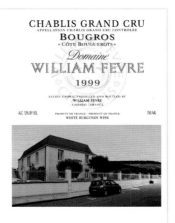

Chablis
Valourent
www.williamfevre.fr

51 ha; 310,000 bottles

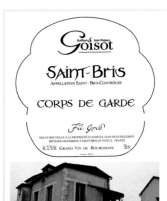

Domaine Guilhem & Jean-Hugues Goisot

This family domain, whose name refers to father and son, occupies a pretty winery building in the center of St. Bris. "We've been in the village since the fifteenth or sixteenth century; members of the family have been innkeepers or tonneliers, but there's always been at least one vigneron each generation," says Guilhem Goisot. "I'm the seventh direct generation to run this domain. My great grandfather planted most of it." The domain includes Bourgogne Aligoté, Irancy, Bourgogne Côtes d'Auxerrois, and Sauvignon de St. Bris. The cuvées represent different soils or altitudes: most of the terroirs are Kimmeridgian, with varying extents of clay, but exposures and altitudes vary. Pinot Noir or Chardonnay are planted on south-facing sites, Sauvignon Blanc is planted elsewhere. There are three different cuvées from St. Bris and five from the Côtes d'Auxerrois. "All the names of the cuvées represent places—we don't use people's names etc." The names are a better indication of sources than the appellation, as Coys de Garde (for example) is Côtes d'Auxerre for Pinot Noir or Chardonnay, but St. Bris for Sauvignon. Vinification is the same for all wines, and the fascinating thing is that the same style of rounded citrus fruits supported by crisp acidity, some more mineral than others, transcends cépage and runs through the Auxerrois and the St. Bris. This makes for a very Burgundian take on the Sauvignon Blanc variety, and as a result, I find the St. Bris cuvées to be the most interesting.

Saint Bris-Le-Vineux

Saint Bris

Sauvignon St. Bris, Exogyra virgula
www.goisot.com

25 ha; 160,000 bottles

Domaine Jean-Pierre et Corinne Grossot

Located in the village of Fleys a little to the east of the town of Chablis, the domain was created by Jean-Pierre Grossot in 1980; previously his parents and grandparents sold grapes to the coop. Today Jean-Pierre works with his daughter Eve, who is taking over winemaking. The vineyards were converted to organic in 2012 (previously viticulture had been lutte raisonnée); in fact, Jean-Pierre was in the vineyards with an organic inspector when I arrived. The major part of the vineyards (13 ha) is in appellation Chablis, giving a cuvée that is about half of all production. A small (1.5 ha) parcel just near the domain, with extremely calcareous soil, is the basis for a separate cuvée, La Part des Anges. There are five premier crus, occupying 5 ha altogether. Almost everything is vinified and then matured on the lees in stainless steel, but Mont de Milieu and Les Fourneaux see a quarter to a third élevage in old oak. The cellar has a mix of tonneaux and barriques. After six months there is assemblage, and then a further eight months in cuve. The style offers fairly direct fruits for the Chablis and the La Part des Anges cuvée, a sense of more complexity with the little-known premier cru Côte de Troemes, and then savory, herbal impressions strengthen going up the hierarchy to Vaucoupin and Fourchaume. At the premier cru level, house style is typified by a fine impression with precision of fruits. Wines are made for enjoyment in the years immediately after release.

Fleys

Chablis

Vaucopin
www.chablis-grossot.com

18 ha; 80,000 bottles

Domaine Laroche

One of the largest producers in Chablis, Domaine Laroche has expanded enormously since Michel Laroche made his first crop from 6 ha in 1967. There is a tasting room in the center of Chablis, and the winery is nearby, behind an old monastery dating from the ninth century. Today the estate includes 62 ha of Chablis AOP and another 21 ha of premier crus. The Chablis St. Martin cuvée under Domaine Laroche comes from the best lots of estate vineyards (roughly 70% of total); the other 30% is blended with purchased grapes and is the simple Chablis cuvée, just labeled Laroche. You have to look carefully at the label to see a difference. Chablis is vinified exclusively in stainless steel; oak is used for premier and grand crus, varying from 15-25% for the premier crus, and around 30% for grand crus. As the largest proprietor of Blanchots, Laroche makes a special cuvée, La Réserve de l'Obédience, based on selecting the best lots by blind tasting: here oak has varied from 30% to 100% over the past few years. Laroche is a modernist not only in style, but in moving to screwcaps. "Michel Laroche was dark red when he saw cork manufacturers because he was fed up with quality," explains Sandrine Audegond at the domain. In fact, premier and grand crus are available with either screwcap or cork, so the buyer can choose. Laroche expanded beyond Chablis, first in southern France and then in Chile and South Africa, before merging with JeanJean to form the Advini wine group in 2010.

Chablis
Montmains
www.larochewines.com

90 ha; 5,000,000 bottles

Domaine Long-Depaquit

"The styles are really different here. The common features of Chablis are freshness and minerality, but Bichot's style is to produce wine with fruity character. We work on the picking date, we don't want to lose the acidity, but we want the wine to show fruit, it needs to speak quickly," says winemaker Matthieu Mangenot. Founded at the time of the French Revolution, Long-Depaquit was purchased by Beaune negociant Albert Bichot in 1968; Bichot built it up from 10 ha to its present position as one of the major estates in Chablis. The splendid château dates from the eighteenth century; a new winery was constructed in 1991 and is presently being renovated and extended. The Chablis is split into two parts: the best selection goes to Long Depaquit Chablis, the rest is labeled as Bichot. Everything is vinified in small tanks of stainless steel; the Chablis and some premier crus remain in cuve. Since the 1990s, the more important premier crus have seen 10-25% oak, and grand crus range from 25% to 100%; oak exposure lasts 6-8 months, after which assemblage is followed by another 9-12 months in cuve. The style is distinctly fruity, and you have to go halfway through the premier cru range really to see minerality. No extremes might be the motto of the house. The house style does have a lovely, smooth, silky balance, with extremely judicious use of oak. Grand crus show their terroir, especially Les Clos and the flagship La Moutonne, a monopole that is essentially part of Vaudésir.

Chablis
Vaillons
www.albertbichot.com

65 ha; 420,000 bottles

Domaine Louis Michel

"Our policy is simply to make wines that represent the terroir of Chablis: fresh, pure and mineral," says Guillaume Michel. This translates to élevage in stainless steel. There has been no oak since 1969, and Louis Michel is now the pre-eminent domain for the unoaked style of Chablis. "My grandfather didn't like the taste of oak, and he didn't have a lot of time to maintain barrels in the cellar," Guillaume explains. The domain stretches out along a street running down to the river. Below the old barrel cellars have been renovated into a snazzy tasting room. The major difference between cuvées is the length of time in cuve before bottling: 6 months for Petit Chablis and Chablis, 12 months for premier crus, and 18 months for grand crus. While lees-aging in steel is common in Chablis, few others achieve the complexity of Louis Michel. Slow fermentation leads to rich extraction. After that, "premier and grand crus wines may be matured on lees but it's not systematic as we want to focus on purity and precision and avoid wines that would be too heavy." The balance of fruity to savory notes changes with each premier cru, but all share a delicious textured background, which often leads to confusion with oak aging. In the grand crus, Vaudésir is rich and savory, Grenouilles is even fuller bodied, and Les Clos shows its usual austerity. These are wines that often can be drunk early, but this misses the complexity that develops later, after say 6 years for premier crus and 10 years for grand crus.

Ⓖ Chablis
Montée de Tonnerre
www.louismicheletfils.com
25 ha; 150,000 bottles

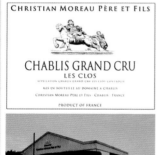

Domaine Christian Moreau Père et Fils

This is nominally a new domain, but Christian Moreau is the sixth generation of winemakers in his family. Christian had been at the family estate of J. Moreau for thirty years when the company was sold to Boisset, but he kept the family vineyards, although grapes continued to be supplied to J. Moreau under contract until 2002, when the new domain started. The domain is housed in a utilitarian warehouse just across the bridge from the town center. "Our goal was to produce top quality Chablis," says Fabien Moreau, who has been involved in the domain with his father since the beginning. "The domain is basically me and my father, with a small vineyard crew. I'm the only person in the cellar." Some grapes are purchased to increase volume for the Chablis, but the premier and grand crus come only from estate vineyards. "I don't like to say there's a Christian Moreau style, I want to respect each terroir," is how Fabien describes their stylistic objectives. Oak is used for premier and grand crus, varying from 30-50% depending on the cru and the vintage. The Chablis and the Vaillons focus directly on fruit, but the Guy Moreau cuvée from a plot of old vines in Vaillons begins the move towards a more structured character, which accentuates through the grand crus. The flagship wine is Clos des Hospices, from a plot in Les Clos, which the Moreau family bought in 1904 from the Hospices; this has always been a big wine for Chablis.

Ⓖ Chablis
Vaillons, Cuvée Guy Moreau
www.domainechristianmoreau.com
12 ha; 100,000 bottles

Domaine Pinson Frères

The Pinsons have been making wine in Chablis since the seventeenth century, but the domain was really created in its present form by Louis Pinson in the 1940s when he focused on producing and bottling his own Chablis. The name changed after his grandsons Laurent and Christophe came into the domain in the early 1980s and increased its size from an initial 4 ha. About half the vineyards are premier cru, and another quarter are in the grand cru Les Clos. A new cuverie was built in 2004 with stainless steel fermentation cuves. The domain is one of the arch exponents of the oaked style: after fermentation wines are transferred to barriques, using 9 months élevage in 1- to 3-year-oak for premier crus, and a year for Les Clos, which includes 10% new oak. There's a special cuvée from Les Clos, Authentique, from older vines, which spends the first 6 months in entirely new oak, followed by 18 months in older oak. The same style at Pinson runs through the Chablis, premier crus, and grand crus. There's a faint note of apples on top of a tendency towards the savory, giving almost a piquant impression. Minerality is in the background. Pinson's premier and grand crus tend to be delicious when released, then after two or three years they close up: do not panic, but it's better not to touch them for the best part of a decade, until they open out again into a full, creamy style that brings a subtle representation of the oak regime.

Chablis

Mont de Milieu

www.domaine-pinson.com

14 ha; 75,000 bottles

Patrick Piuze

As a micro-negociant, Patrick Piuze makes an unusually wide range of cuvées. His winery in the heart of Chablis is an old building bought from Vocoret, larger than it appears at first, as it's connected by a tunnel under the road to caves on the other side. "This was constructed in the period when a Vocoret was the mayor of Chablis, it probably wouldn't be possible today," Patrick explains. What is the driving force to be a negociant in Chablis? "I wasn't born here, I came from Montreal. The only way to express a lot of terroirs is to be a negociant. We try to buy grapes we like from special sites, before we worry about having a specific appellation." Production is 65% Petit Chablis or Chablis; 35% is premier and grand cru. Patrick harvests with his own team. "Choosing harvest date is one of the most important things. We are an early picker. A wine can have only one backbone. 90% of white wines in the world have an alcohol backbone, but we have an acid backbone. Our wines are never more than 12.3%." Petit Chablis is matured in cuve, Chablis in a mixture of cuve and barriques, and premier and grand crus are entirely in barrique. The style gets to full ripeness without excess, with a silky sheen to the fruits, a sense of stone fruits adding to the citrus and minerality of Chablis; yet always with that wonderfully moderate alcohol. A sense of tension counterpoised against elegant fruits runs through the range from premier cru to the more overtly full grand crus.

Chablis

Montée de Tonnerre

www.patrickpiuze.com

0 ha; 150,000 bottles

Domaine François Raveneau

This very discrete domain is identified only by a metal sign above the door. Created in 1948 by François Raveneau from vineyards owned by his and his wife's family, it's the flagship for oak-aged Chablis. Since 1995 the domain has been run by brothers Bernard and Jean-Marie. Most of the plots are very small, less than a hectare each. "My father started with only 3 ha," says Bernard Raveneau, and looking at his daughter Isabelle, adds "We grow only slowly." Élevage is the same for everything from Chablis to Grand Cru, with fermentation followed by aging for a year in old oak. Consistency of style shows from Chablis AOP to the grand crus: fruits give an impression of being textured rather than simply dense, with a savory overlay that turns in the direction of liquorice with time. The Chablis is the most openly fruity. La Forêt (part of Montmains) isn't so much more intense as just shifting the balance from fruity to savory. Butteaux (another part of Montmains) adds more mineral notes as do the Montmains and Vaillons. Chapelot (part of Montée de Tonnerre) is usually more steely and less powerful than the Montée de Tonnerre cuvée, which often approaches the power of the grand crus, where Blanchots is broad, Valmur is precise, and Clos is austere. The steely minerality of the young wines begins to open out after about 5-6 years for premier crus and 8-10 years for grand crus. Raveneau Chablis is virtually unique; unfortunately this is now also true of the price.

Chablis
Chapelot
9 ha; 55,000 bottles

Domaine Servin

The Servin family have owned vines in Chablis since the seventeenth century. Located in old buildings just across the river from the town center, the domain is run today by the seventh generation, François Servin, together with his brother-in-law. Vineyard holdings include an impressive range of the top premier crus as well as some grand crus. The emphasis here is on a fairly straightforward style, with vinification and maturation largely in stainless steel for Chablis and premier crus, and oak used only for grand crus: Les Preuses is vinified in stainless steel but partly matured in oak, and only Les Clos is both vinified and matured in barrique. The wines are attractive and ready for drinking on release, with a citrus fruit spectrum balanced by occasional savory hints and a nice sense of texture to the palate. Servin's general style favors minerality or delicacy over power. In addition to the AOP Chablis, there is a cuvée of Vieilles Vignes from a plot of 50-year old vines in Pargues (at one time considered on a level with the premier crus Montmains and Vaillons, but abandoned during the first world war). The premier crus have more intensity than the AOP Chablis, but I do not see as much distinction between them as I would like, and although there is more intensity at the grand cru level, the only wine that strikes me as having serious aging potential is Les Clos. François also makes wines for a label under his father's name, Marcel Servin.

Chablis
Vaillons
www.servin.fr
35 ha; 250,000 bottles

Domaine de l'Arlot

Although owned by insurance giant AXA, Domaine de l'Arlot is managed like a small proprietor-owned domain. Viticulture follows minimal intervention, and horses are used to work some of the vineyards. Strict pruning ensures low yields, typically about 32 hl/ha. Vinification is traditional. The domain has several monopoles, including the Clos des Forêts St. Georges just up the road, the eponymous Premier Cru Clos de l'Arlot that surrounds the winery in Premeaux, and the Clos du Chapeau across the road in Comblanchien that produces a Côtes de Nuits Villages. There have been some changes in its holdings, with a Beaune Grèves sold, and Vosne Romanée Les Suchots and Romanée St. Vivant purchased. The domain produces an unusually high proportion of white wine for the Côte de Nuits. About a quarter of the Clos de l'Arlot was uprooted from Pinot Noir and replanted with Chardonnay; as a result, about half of the Clos de l'Arlot now produces white wine. The wine from the younger vines has been bottled as Nuits St. Georges Jeunes Vignes. The emphasis here is on elegance and style, with a desire to avoid too oaky a flavor. Of the two red Nuits St. Georges, the Clos de l'Arlot is typically the most elegant, seeing about 30% new oak during maturation, whereas the more muscular Clos des Forêts is matured in about 50% new wood. The white sees only a small proportion of new oak. In spite of changes of winemaker in 2007 and 2011, the style has remained consistent.

Premeaux-Prissey

Nuits St. Georges

Nuits St. Georges, Clos de l'Arlot

Nuits St. Georges, Clos de l'Arlot

www.arlot.com

15 ha; 60,000 bottles

Domaine Arnoux-Lachaux

This started as Domaine Robert Arnoux, in 1858, and was considered to be a typical domain of Vosne Romanée, with strong wines, well structured and concentrated: robust was a common description. Pascal Lachaux, Robert Arnoux's son-in-law, has been running the estate since 1993, and in 2007 changed the name of the domain to Arnoux-Lachaux. There are grand cru holdings in Romanée St Vivant, Echézeaux, Latricières Chambertin, and Clos Vougeot, and some top premier crus, including Suchots, Reignots and Chaumes in Vosne Romanée, and others in Nuits St Georges. Pascal states his objective as being to make elegant wines, and made a revealing comment when we tasted the 2009 Nuits St. Georges, "This is not typical Nuits St. Georges, it is too elegant." That's the direction of the domain these days. This is aided by the new cuverie, right on the N74, with a snazzy tasting room and shop open to visitors. Extending the estate holdings, since 2002 there has been a small negociant activity. Everything is destemmed, there's cold maceration, and then slow fermentation; part of the change in style here may be due to the fact that fermentation now is slower than it used to be. Wines are aged for 16 months in barriques, with 30% new oak for the village wines, 40-60% for premier crus, and 100% for grand crus. There is no fining or filtration. The leading wines are the Romanée St. Vivant and the Vosne Romanée Les Suchots.

Vosne Romanée

Nuits St. Georges, Clos de Corvées Pagets

www.arnoux-lachaux.com

14 ha; 70,000 bottles

  Chambolle Musigny

 Chambolle Musigny, Les Charmes

7 ha; 30,000 bottles

Domaine Ghislaine Barthod

This domain is tightly focused on Chambolle Musigny, where there are nine premier crus as well as the communal wine. The domain started with Marcel Noëllat in the 1920s, became known as Barthod-Noëllat after the union of the Barthod and Noëllat families, and then changed to Barthod after Gaston Barthod took over in the 1960s; his daughter Ghislaine started making the wines in the early 1990s, and has been fully in charge since 1999. The domain has remained the same, except for the recent addition of the Gruenchers premier cru. Ghislaine's husband is Louis Boillot, who left his family domain, started to make wine independently in Gevrey Chambertin, but now also makes wine in Chambolle Musigny. They are located in the heart of Chambolle Musigny, with the winery backing right onto the vineyards. Ghislaine and Louis share the same team for managing the vineyards, but winemaking is independent. All grapes are destemmed at Ghislaine Barthod, then there's a period of maceration before fermentation starts naturally in open-topped wood cuves, with aging following in barriques with up to about 30% new oak for 12-18 months. The regime is the same for all the premier crus. The wines are considered to showcase the characteristic finesse of the commune, with Les Charmes and Les Cras usually at the top of the hierarchy. There is also a Bourgogne Rouge from a vineyard just outside of Chambolle Musigny in Gilly.

  Marsannay-la-Côte

 Chambolle Musigny, Verouilles

 Morey St. Denis
www.bruno-clair.com

23 ha; 100,000 bottles

Domaine Bruno Clair

"The history of the domain is very complicated, it would take hours," says Bruno Clair with a sigh when you ask how it came to be. "My grandfather created the Clair-Daü domain in 1914, but I started all by myself in 1979 by creating my own domain." It's evident that Bruno greatly respects his grandfather, who was clearly a formative influence, but when he died, the vineyards were divided. One daughter sold all her vines to Jadot, the other kept hers, and Bruno's father gave him his third. That's where the grand crus come from. The other vineyards have since been added by Bruno. The domain is located in buildings around a charming courtyard in a back street of Marsannay, but vineyard holdings extend south through Gevrey Chambertin, Morey St. Denis, Chambolle Musigny, Vosne Romanée, Aloxe Corton, and Savigny-les-Beaune. There are five premier crus, mostly in Gevrey, as well as two grand crus (Chambertin Clos de Bèze and Bonnes Mares). Vinification is traditional (with no more than 10-20% whole bunches), and new oak is restrained. "I hate to taste new wood, you won't smell it in my wines, it's up to 50% depending on the cuvée." The style is always smooth and elegant. Fruits show precision, usually more red than black; tannins never stick out. Appellations show their best side; the Morey St. Denis has a silky elegance approaching Chambolle, and the Marsannay has a weight approaching Gevrey. There is refinement right across the range.

Domaine Pierre Damoy

The majority of the domain's holdings are in three important grand crus, Chambertin, Clos de Bèze, and Chapelle Chambertin, but the domain was a significant under-achiever until the current Pierre Damoy took over in 1992. The domain is the largest owner in Clos de Bèze, but sells most of the grapes. Its Clos de Bèze is made from an assemblage of berries from parcels at both ends of the appellation; the vines in the northern parcel are younger; the southern parcel, and the adjacent parcel over the border in Chambertin, were mostly planted in 1973-1974. Pierre Damoy harvests late. "I like ripe berries," he says, although he points out that the late harvest partly reflects the fact that almost all his vineyards are in grand crus. (The domain actually started with the purchase of the Clos Tamisot vineyard, which is a village Gevrey Chambertin, and is the most affordable representation of the domain.) Sometimes there has been a Vieilles Vignes cuvée from a small part of Clos de Bèze. There may also be a Reserve bottling (just two barrels), which is not usually commercialized. In addition to the grand cru wines, there's an unusually refined Marsannay, and a generic Bourgogne that comes from a mix of estate and purchased grapes, and is labeled simply Pierre Damoy (not Domaine). The style tends to be rich and powerful, with quite a bit of new oak usage, ranging from 30% in the Bourgogne, to 50% in Gevrey Chambertin, and 80% or more in the grand crus.

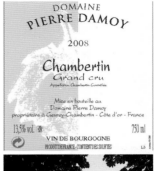

Gevrey Chambertin

Gevrey Chambertin, Clos Tamisot

www.domaine-pierre-damoy.com

11 ha; 38,000 bottles

Domaine David Duband

Chevannes is in the hills of the Hautes Côtes de Nuits at the end of a narrow twisting road. The domain is on the edge of the little village, a large modern warehouse-like building built in 2007. It's a practical facility with winemaking on the upper level and a large storage space on the lower level. Wines come from 25 AOPs, varying from 2 to 40 barrels; grapes are purchased for about 25% of production. David's father created the domain in 1965 when he cut down woods and planted vines on the hillside facing Chevannes. Then he rented vineyards in Nuits St. Georges. David started to make wine in 1991, and took over in 1995. He also makes the wines for Domaine François Feuillet, which has top holdings on the Côte de Nuits, including the old Truchot domain. Wines may be labeled with either name but are the same. David is frankly unimpressed by very old wines and doesn't see the point of extended aging. "I think that a well made wine with mature tannins can be drunk young. I want the wine to be good when it's bottled, I don't want to make wines that are closed when young." The Hautes Côtes de Nuits has 30% new oak, and the premier and grand crus have 40%. The style is silky with a faint glycerinic sheen, and elegant tannins are usually only just in evidence. Red fruits on the light side favor elegance over power, giving a clean impression. Everything is filtered through the prism of Duband's ultra-modern take on Burgundy.

Chevannes

Nuits St. Georges

Chambolle Musigny, Les Sentiers

www.domaine-duband.com

17 ha; 85,000 bottles

Domaine Claude Dugat

It is not often that a mere communal wine from a great vintage is still unready after a decade, but Claude Dugat's Gevrey Chambertin 2002 was still stern and youthful in 2014, although promising to showcase a characteristic smooth sheen of black fruits as it develops over the next decade. This small domain, which has something of a cult following in the Anglo-Saxon world, owns 3 ha and rents another 3 ha, and is managed entirely by Claude and his family. It functions out of the Cellier des Dimes, a thirteenth century building in the heart of Gevrey Chambertin purchased and restored by Claude's father in 1955. A new cave was constructed in 1976. All the wines come from or near Gevrey Chambertin, extending from a Bourgogne Rouge, through the village wine, two premier crus and three grand crus. The key to the style here is the low yield, usually below 18 hl/ha, which is a consequence more of small berries than of the number of grape clusters (aided by a proportion of very old vines). The wines have a strong sense of structure resembling the results of whole cluster fermentation, although here everything is in fact destemmed. After fermentation in concrete for about two weeks, the village wine goes into 50% new oak, and the premier and grand crus into 100% new oak. All the wines are true vins de garde, not for the faint of heart but requiring patience. The family's activities are extended by a negociant label, La Gibryotte.

Gevrey Chambertin
Gevrey Chambertin

6 ha; 24,000 bottles

Domaine Bernard Dugat-Py

This domain is much praised by critics in the U.S. for the density and power of its wine, but sometimes criticized in Europe for over-extraction. Bernard Dugat, a cousin of Claude Dugat, has been making wine since 1975, but has been bottling his own wine only since 1989. The cuverie is located at the foot of the Combe de Lavaux in Gevrey Chambertin, in the remains of the Aumônerie that was constructed in the twelfth century. The winery was renovated in 2004. Until recently the domain was tightly focused on Gevrey Chambertin, where there are three cuvées of village wine, all rather small: Vieilles Vignes, Coeur du Roy (very vieilles vignes of 65-90 years), and the parcel Les Evocelles. There are three premier crus and four grand crus, with the peak being a single barrel of Chambertin. The first white wine of the domain came from a parcel of Morgeots in Chassagne Montrachet purchased in 2004, and Corton Charlemagne was added in 2011. There are other small plots in Vosne Romanée and the Côte de Beaune. There's always a high proportion of whole clusters, new oak runs 60% or more, and élevage lasts 18 to 24 months. If the wines didn't have so much fruit, they would be quite stern, but as it is, Bernard says a minimum of 6-8 years is required before opening. The huge sense of power comes from low yields rather than extraction during vinification, but certainly the style is enormously rich, all dense black fruits hiding the strong structure. Vin de garde is an under statement.

Gevrey Chambertin
Gevrey Chambertin, Coeur du Roy
www.dugat-py.fr

11 ha; 35,000 bottles

Domaine Dujac

"Starting in Burgundy I had the disadvantage of not having many generations before me. But I had the advantage of not having three to ten generations before me," says Jacques Seysses, ironically pointing out that although he was an outsider, this was balanced by not being overly bound by precedents as others were. He started in 1968 by purchasing a small run-down domain, only 4.5 ha, in Morey St. Denis, which had sold off its grapes. Everything had to be developed from scratch, but the domain has been expanding steadily ever since. After a purchase in 2005 of half of the old Charles Thomas domain, the winery had to be expanded. The range now extends from Bourgogne to Grand Cru. Three quarters of the holdings are in premier or grand crus. Jacques's general policy was to use whole bunches for vinification, with little destemming and more or less exclusive use of new oak. Belief in tradition extends to cooling the cellar to delay malolactic fermentation until the Spring. After his son Jeremy became involved in 1999, the style softened, with some destemming, and reduced usage of new oak (40-100% today, depending on the cuvée). The general feeling is that terroir shows better as a result of backing off from using complete stems and new oak, but even so, the style can still be a little severe, coming off best with the grand crus where there is the greatest fruit concentration. In addition to the domain wines, the family has a negociant activity, Dujac Père et Fils.

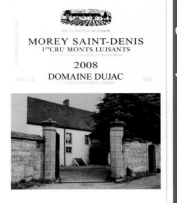

 Morey St. Denis
Morey St. Denis
www.dujac.com

17 ha; 70,000 bottles

Domaine Sylvie Esmonin

Sylvie Esmonin was all but born in Clos St. Jacques—when she was a baby she was left in her cot at the end of the row while her parents worked the vines. "It's full of sentiment for me," she says. The domain is on the road along the base of the Clos St. Jacques, with Sylvie's section of the clos running right up to the house. This is a very hands-on domain: my visit was set for the end of the day because Sylvie was working in the vines during the day. "Working in the vines is my real métier," she says. The domain is mostly in Gevrey Chambertin, but includes Bourgogne, Côte de Nuits Villages, and some Meursault and Volnay Santenots. "It's a little family domain started by my great grandfather," Sylvie explains. The caves below go deep into the rock and are always cool, so the wines develop slowly: when I visited at the start of July, the previous vintage was just at the start of malolactic fermentation. There is some emphasis on whole cluster fermentation, which is around 30% for communal wines with 5-10% new oak, increasing to 50% for the Vieilles Vignes cuvée of Gevrey Chambertin with a third new oak, and then almost complete for Clos St. Jacques with 100% new oak. These are very traditional wines. "I don't want to make wines by technique, I work in the same way as my grandparents," Sylvie says. The style is quite dense, increasing in intensity from Gevrey Chambertin to the Vieilles Vignes to the peak of Clos St. Jacques.

Gevrey Chambertin
Gevrey Chambertin Vieilles Vignes

8 ha; 35,000 bottles

Domaine d'Eugénie

The old René Engel domain produced some of the most elegant wines of Vosne Romanée during the 1990s, with village wines as well as the premier cru Brûlées, and holdings also in Clos Vougeot, Echézeaux, and Grands Echézeaux. Created in the early twentieth century by René Engel, who was an oenologist at the university in Dijon, the domain fell into some neglect under his son in the 1970s, and then revived under his grandson Philippe in the 1980s. After the death of Philippe Engel in 2005, the domain was purchased by François Pinault, owner of Château Latour. In 2009 the domain moved out of its old house in Vosne Romanée into the Clos Frantin property, which was purchased from Albert Bichot and renovated; at the same time, Domaine d'Eugénie exchanged some of its vines in Vosne Romanée with parcels from Bichot. Some replanting has occurred, and the domain is presently being converted to biodynamic viticulture. Vinification is conventional: a few days cold maceration is followed by fermentation, and then wines go into oak depending on appellation: 40% new oak for the village wines, 50% for the premier crus, and 70% for the grand crus. Regarded as a rising new domain, Domaine d'Eugénie is more a demonstration of the reincarnation of an old domain resulting from unlimited investment. The high price paid to purchase the domain, reportedly €25 million, has been reflected in increased price for the wines.

Vosne Romanée
Vosne Romanée
www.domaine-eugenie.com
7 ha; 20,000 bottles

Maison Faiveley

Dating from 1825, Maison Faiveley is one of the major domains in Burgundy, with almost half of its vineyards on the Côte d'Or in premier and grand crus. Based in Nuits St. Georges, the focus has been on red wines, but recently the domain has expanded further into the Côte de Beaune and into white wines. Faiveley also has significant holdings on the Côte Chalonnaise, especially in Mercurey, and even produces Chablis. The style of the reds has always been sturdy, but became more extracted and harder in 1993. "For a long time Faiveley was famous for vins de garde for long aging, but we thought it should be possible to produce wines for aging that would be more drinkable young," says Jérôme Flous, explaining that after Erwan Faiveley (then aged 25) took over from his father François in 2004, he started to soften the style. A Faiveley vertical shows the old style before 1993, the heavily extracted style until 2006, and since then a more forward fruity style. Picking is faster so fruit is fresher, fermentations have been shortened and there is less maceration; pressing is gentler with a new vertical press, and the barriques are higher quality. By way of compensation for the increased softness, new oak usage has increased about 10%, and up to 15% for village wines, 15-40% for premier crus, and 40-100% for grand crus. The best known wine is perhaps the Clos des Cortons monopole. The reds are back on form, and I admit I've always found them more interesting than Faiveley's whites.

Nuits St. Georges
Clos des Cortons
www.domaine-faiveley.com
122 ha; 1,300,000 bottles

Domaine Fourrier

Founded by Fernand Pernot in the 1930s, the domain became known as Pernot-Fourrier when his nephew Jean-Claude Fourrier joined, and then Domaine Fourrier when Jean-Marie Fourrier took over in 1994. The focus is on Gevrey Chambertin, with five premier crus as well as village and grand cru wine. Jean-Marie does not believe in manipulation in the vineyard or winemaking, but says he would call himself more a biologist than a minimalist. He harvests at 100 days after flowering plus or minus five days, and believes that people who harvest very early in warm years or very late in cool years do not necessarily get full ripeness. His philosophy is also a little different from the usual Burgundian approach. "In Burgundy many producers make a difference in how they handle village, premier cru, and grand cru wines, but this does not make any sense, the difference should rest on the terroir," he says. Jean-Marie uses 20% new oak for all cuvées, more to renew the barrels than to add flavor. All of his vines are old, typically around 50 years. The style is fine and precise for Gevrey Chambertin, and there's a clear gradation going from the village wines, which have that slightly hard edge to the palate that's typical of Gevrey, to premier crus such as Goulots, which is more mineral, Champeaux which is earthier, and Clos St. Jacques whose ripe opulence reinforces the impression that it should have been a grand cru. The impression is modern, but continuing to respect Gevrey's typicity.

Gevrey Chambertin
Gevrey Chambertin, Champeaux

9 ha

Domaine Geantet Pansiot

This domain was founded relatively recently (in Burgundian terms) when Edmond Geantet married Bernadette Pansiot in 1954 and started to work on 3 ha of Gevrey Chambertin and Bourgogne. The domain increased to 7 ha by 1977 when their son Vincent joined. Vincent has been running the domain since 1989, and Fabien, the third generation, joined in 2006. Vineyard holdings have continued to increase, remaining focused on Gevrey Chambertin, where there are six cuvées extending from village to grand cru, and Chambolle Musigny, where there are two premier crus and a vieilles vignes cuvée. After destemming and sorting, berries go directly into the fermentation cuves (they are not crushed); after fermentation, élevage lasts 13 months, with 30% new barriques, 30% one-year barriques, and 40% two-year oak used for all cuvées. The appellation wines and premier crus are quite mainstream, with a touch of that typical hardness of Gevrey accompanying high-toned aromatics, but the Charmes Chambertin can be rather powerful. At lower level, there are Marsannay, Ladoix, Côte de Nuits, and Bourgogne. There's also some Bourgogne Blanc and even a rosé. Vincent's daughter has a small negociant business under the name of Emilie Geantet, for which she makes wine in conjunction with her father, with winemaking following the same principles as at Geantet-Pansiot. Prices have tended to remain relatively reasonable.

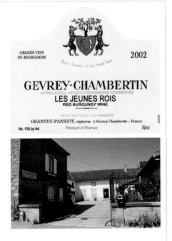

Gevrey Chambertin
Gevrey Chambertin, Vieilles Vignes
www.geantetpansiot.com

13 ha; 70,000 bottles

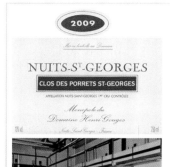

Domaine Henri Gouges

This is one of the most traditional producers in Nuits St. Georges, and the first time I visited, the premises matched my expectations. But a new cuverie was constructed in 2007—in a large courtyard behind the unassuming house—whose existence you would scarcely imagine from the street. Things have not changed with regards to winemaking, however, because "it is the grapes that count." The old cement tanks were moved into the cuverie. The most significant change is that pumping has been eliminated; everything is gravity driven now. Pierre Gouges says that changes in style are due more to the current age of the vines than anything else; the new cuverie maintains better freshness, so the wine is fruiter, perhaps also due to the lack of pumping. Gouges used to be known for a rather tough style when young, requiring time for the tannins to soften. The changes in the new cuverie have lightened the style, and certainly I notice increased purity of fruit, but although the wines are more accessible, still they are not really intended for early drinking. Most of the wines come from Nuits St. Georges, including six premier crus as well as the village wine. Les Pruliers is perhaps the most refined, and Les St. Georges the strongest. In addition to the reds, there are also two white wines, from Clos des Porrets St. Georges and Les Perrières, which come from a mutation of Pinot Noir observed in the Perrières vineyard. This is now known as the Gouges clone of Pinot Blanc.

Nuits St. Georges
Nuits St. Georges, Les Pruliers
Nuits St. Georges, Les Perrières
www.gouges.com
15 ha; 50,000 bottles

Domaine Jean Grivot

The Grivots have an interesting record of buying and selling vineyards advantageously. Coming from the Jura in the seventeenth century, they purchased vineyards at Arcenant (over the mountain from Nuits St. Georges). Just before the Revolution, Joseph Grivot sold these vineyards in order to purchase in Vosne Romanée. In 1919 his son Gaston sold the lesser holdings in order to buy part of Clos Vougeot, running up from the N74 where a splendid entrance gate with a view of the château was built. More recently Jean Grivot purchased a tiny holding in Richebourg. Since 1987, the domain has been run by his son, Etienne. At almost 2 ha, Clos Vougeot is the largest parcel; parcels in five premier crus of Vosne Romanée and three premier crus of Nuits St. Georges, as well as communal plots, are all under a hectare, sometimes much less. Altogether there are around twenty different cuvées. Vines are replaced individually as necessary, and the average age is around 40 years. Vinification starts with complete destemming, followed by 5 days cold maceration, with fermentation lasting just over two weeks. Élevage lasts 18 months, with 25% new oak for communal wine, 30-60% for premier crus, and 40-70% for grand crus. The style has seemed relatively light in the past, with a spectrum of red rather than black fruits, which can pay off by bringing elegance rather than power to grand crus such as Clos Vougeot, but I find more overt fruits in the young wines of more recent vintages.

Vosne Romanée
Vosne Romanée, Bossières
www.domainegrivot.fr
15 ha; 72,000 bottles

Burgundy:Côte de Nuits

Domaine Robert Groffier Père Et Fils

The domain is located on the main road through Morey St. Denis, but its vineyards are in Chambolle Musigny to the south or Gevrey Chambertin to the north. It dates back to the nineteenth century, but most of the vineyard holdings were acquired by Jules Groffier in the 1930s; it was his son Robert who started domain bottling after 1973. A high proportion of the vineyards are in premier or grand cru. Robert has officially retired (but remains involved), and his son Serge and grandson Nicolas now run the domain. There's a hectare of Gevrey Chambertin and half hectare of Clos de Bèze, but the main holdings are in three premier crus of Chambolle Musigny, including Les Amoureuses (where Groffier has the single largest holding, with three parcels that total 20% of the cru), and also grand cru Bonnes Mares. Vines are trained in the Cordon Royale instead of the more usual Guyot, in order to reduce yields; the objective is "to seek concentration in the berries and not in the cave." The Groffiers are late pickers, so the style tends to be full and rich. I might go further and describe it as powerful, smooth, and modern. Policy on destemming has gone to and fro, and now varies with the vintage; usually there are some whole clusters. Cold maceration is followed by fermentation at unusually high temperature. Since the late 1990s, new oak has been moderate, up to a half for the top cuvées. The rising reputation of the domain has been accompanied by a commensurate increase in prices.

Morey St. Denis
Chambolle Musigny
Gevrey Chambertin

8 ha; 35,000 bottles

Domaine Anne Gros

I still remember some splendid wines from the old Louis Gros domain in the fifties and sixties. In the way of French inheritance, the domain became divided into several parts, today represented by Gros Frère et Soeur, Jean Gros, Michel Gros, A. F. Gros, and Anne Gros. After a decade during which production was sold to negociants, Anne Gros and her father François effectively restarted his part of the domain in 1988 (as Anne et François Gros, not to be confused with A. F. Gros!), and then changed the name to Anne Gros in 1998. The best holdings, totaling about 3 ha in Clos Vougeot, Chambolle Musigny, and Echézeaux, come from Louis Gros. Today about half the domain is AOP Bourgogne, divided between vineyards on the other side of the N74 from Vosne Romanée, and more recently planted vineyards on the Hautes Côtes de Nuits. There is white as well as red Bourgogne. Vinification is conventional, in cement for reds and stainless steel for whites, with fermentation lasting up to two weeks. There is a focus on new oak, with 30% for regional wines, 50% for communal wines, and 80% for grand crus. The style is well structured at all levels, with Hautes Côtes de Nuits showing above its appellation level, and Clos Vougeot balanced between its intrinsic fleshiness and the structure of Côtes de Nuits. Anne is married to Jean Paul Tollot (of Tollot-Beaune in Savigny-lès-Beaune) and in 2008 they extended their winemaking into a joint domain in Minervois.

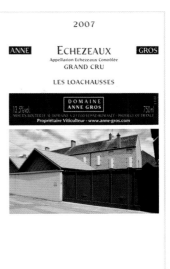

Vosne Romanée
Vosne Romanée, Les Barreaux
www.anne-gros.com

7 ha; 35,000 bottles

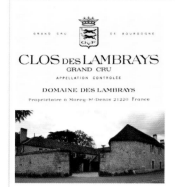

Domaine des Lambrays

The domain is effectively synonymous with the Clos des Lambrays, a 9 ha vineyard in Morey St. Denis. References to Cloux des Lambrey go back to 1365. It was divided between 74 owners after the Revolution, but re-united in 1868. The domain owns all but a tiny parcel at the bottom. Clos des Lambrays was classified as premier cru in 1936 because its owner did not submit the paperwork to become a grand cru. The estate was some-what neglected until a change of ownership in 1979, when Thierry Brouin came as winemaker. The clos was promoted to grand cru in 1981. The domain also produces two other red cuvées: Les Loups is a blend from young vines of the clos together with plots in two premier crus, and there is a communal Morey St. Denis. There are also two Puligny Mon-trachets from tiny plots in Caillerets and Folatières. Occasionally there is a rosé (from less ripe grapes selected out during sorting). Winemaking is traditional, with fermentation of whole bunches irrespective of vintage. I would describe the style as upright. Younger vintages can seem tight, and older vintages soften slowly, with fruits moving from cherries towards strawberries, but not evolving in a savory or tertiary direction in the first couple of decades. The focus is on purity and precision of fruit. Running counter to the modern trend, these are definitely not wines for instant gratification: it remains to be seen how that will play under the aegis of LVMH, who purchased the estate in 2014.

Morey St. Denis
Clos des Lambrays
www.lambrays.com
11 ha; 40,000 bottles

Dominique Laurent

A pastry chef before he went into wine, Dominique Laurent makes wine as a negociant under his own name in Burgundy (and also now owns a few vineyards). He became famous for the technique of using 200% new oak, meaning that the wine is racked from new oak barrels into a second set of new oak barrels. Attempts to discuss his methods are firmly re-buffed. "Like any artisan, I have no wish or need to discuss; my experiences and research are secret and from a commercial point of view can't be explained, you understand my position?.. I have even less wish to discuss a subject which has caused me so much criticism from the most stupid people... You'll have to give just another opinion based on tasting." Recently, Dominique appears to have decided that 100% new oak is enough, because he has supplies of higher quality oak; he selects the trees himself in the Tronçais forest. Insofar as it's possible to form any single opinion, my impression is that sometimes the approach works, and sometimes it overwhelms the wine. An interesting comparison is between the Gevrey Chambertin premier cru Clos St. Jacques from Laurent with that from Sylvie Esmonin, from whom he buys the grapes. In 2002, the Laurent wine was richer and rounder, but in 1999 the fruits could not show through Laurent's oak. Focused on Gevrey Chambertin (although not necessarily the same cuvées every year), the Laurent wines are always powerful.

Nuits St. Georges
Gevrey Chambertin
Gevrey Chambertin, Ca-zetiers
7 ha; 300,000 bottles

Domaine Leroy

Maison Leroy was a negociant, but Henri Leroy also acquired a half share in Domaine de la Romanée Conti. Henri's daughter, Lalou Bize-Leroy, ran Maison Leroy and distributed DRC wines until a disagreement caused her to leave DRC in 1992. Domaine Leroy was founded in 1988 by purchasing the vineyards of Charles Noëllat in Vosne Romanée; Takayashima of Japan is a sleeping partner. Headquartered in an unassuming house in Vosne Romanée, the domain has a small winemaking facility, with open-topped wood fermenters. All wines go into new barriques, as they have the character to stand up to, and indeed, require, new oak. Yields are minuscule here: "25hl/ha is, for me, the absolute maximum for a grand cru," Lalou says. The domain has been biodynamic since its creation: Lalou is a fervent believer to the point of following the lunar cycle to apply the preparations. Vinification is traditional. "Jamais, jamais, jamais" was the response when I asked if destemming is used. The wines show an intensity and concentration across the range that would put most producers to shame; the character of each appellation is magnified by sheer purity of expression. There was a look of surprise when I asked whether Lalou would call her wines "vins de garde" as though the question was simply too obvious to be worth answering. She also owns Domaine d'Auvenay in Saint Romain, a small domain inherited from her father, which is run on the same principles.

Vosne Romanée
Nuits St. Georges
Meursault-Blagny, Premier Cru
www.domaineleroy.com

22 ha; 40,000 bottles

Domaine du Comte Liger-Belair

The domain as such was created in 2000 by Louis-Michel Liger-Belair, but the name goes way back into the history of Vosne Romanée, starting with the purchase of vineyards in 1815, when General Liger-Belair returned from the Napoleonic wars. In the mid nineteenth century, Comte Liger-Belair owned parts of La Tâche and La Romanée, as well as parts of several premier crus in Vosne Romanée and elsewhere. Most of the holdings were sold when the estate was dispersed in the early 1930s, but Louis-Michel started his domain with 1.5 ha that remained, adding another 1.5 ha in 2002. Other vineyards are rented in Vosne Romanée and Nuits St. Georges. The smallest parcel from which a single cuvée is made is 0.12 ha. La Romanée remains a monopole of the domain, and is its most important cuvée. There's a focus on old vines, with most plantings varying from 60 to 90 years old; the domain may be young, but attitudes are quite traditional: "We don't make Pinot Noir, we make Burgundy." The style here tends to elegance, almost delicacy, with concern to avoid over-extraction. Since the domain started, there's been a change to longer cold soak before fermentation starts and less maceration after fermentation; pumping-over is used rather than punch-down. Wine is kept on the lees, without racking, once malolactic fermentation has finished. The strength of the wines (mostly from Vosne Romanée, after all) calls for reliance on largely new barriques for maturation.

Vosne Romanée
Vosne Romanée, Petits Monts
www.liger-belair.fr

11 ha; 30,000 bottles

Nuits St. Georges

Vosne Romanée

Meursault, Les Charmes
www.pasmarchand.com

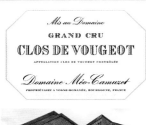

12 ha; 120,000 bottles

Maison Marchand-Tawse

"I'm from Montreal, I came to Burgundy thirty years ago, I was a régis-seur in Pommard at Comte Armand, then I was with Vougeraie for seven vintages. In 2006 I decided to create my own label," says Pascal Mar-chand. "I started by renting premises, and making 5 wines and 1,000 cases." Starting as a negociant, Pascal expanded by forming a partnership in 2010, and the firm became Marchand-Tawse. About three years ago Pascal bought his own space in the center of Nuits St. Georges, with buildings surrounding a handsome courtyard, a large warehouse-like fa-cility on the other side of the street, and extensive cellars underground. After forming Marchand-Tawse, Pascal has acquired some vineyards, with about half in Bourgogne and the rest divided between villages and premier or grand crus. Today production is about half from his own vine-yards and half from purchased grapes (where half are premier or grand cru, and most of the rest are communal). Altogether there are about 60 wines, many in small quantities, sometimes only 1-3 barrels. 30% is white; about half is Côte de Beaune and half is Côte de Nuits. At the moment, all the wines have the same label but Pascal says that, "In the long run I want to distinguish between the negociant parts and the wines from our own vineyards." There's a family resemblance between the wines going from Nuits St Georges to Vosne Romanée to Gevrey Cham-bertin: refinement is the common feature that runs through all.

Vosne Romanée

Nuits St. Georges, Les Boudots
www.meo-camuzet.com

14 ha; 65,000 bottles

Domaine Méo-Camuzet

From its inception until fairly recently, the domain was essentially rented out, as founder Étienne Camuzet and his successors were not resident in Burgundy. In 1988, Jean-Nicolas Méo took over the estate, reclaimed the vineyards, and started bottling wine. (He was helped by Henri Jayer, who had been farming many of the vineyards.) Modernization is shown by the rather striking glass front that has been added to the old building. Produc-tion is divided between the domain (60% of grapes) and purchased grapes. The domain has some remarkable holdings: six grand crus and ten premier crus as well as villages and Hautes Côtes de Nuits. The par-cel of Clos Vougeot was originally bought by Étienne Camuzet together with the château itself (which he owned until it became the headquarters of the Confrérie). Most of the holdings are in Nuits St. Georges or Vosne Romanée. Individual cuvées have characters differing from appellation stereotypes. "Our Vosne is more structured and our Nuits is more femi-nine, it all depends on the plot," says Jean-Nicolas. Vinification varies with the cuvée, for example, with varying extents of destemming. The petit vins (Bourgogne or Marsannay) have up to 10% new oak, village wine 50%, premier crus 60% or more, and grand crus 100%. The style can be a little stern when the wines are young, but is generally full bod-ied. Most of the wines are red, but there is a white from the Clos Saint Philbert vineyard in the Hautes Côtes de Nuits.

Domaine Denis Mortet

There's a sad history to this domain, which has continued to develop its style in recent years. The domain was founded by Denis Mortet in 1991, with vines he obtained when his father retired. (The other half of the family inheritance became Domaine Thierry Mortet.) The domain more or less doubled in size when Denis took over the Guyot estate in 1993. His focus was on working the vineyards to reduce yields and obtain ripe berries, and the result was that wines tended to be somewhat ripe and powerful in what was often regarded as the new wave style. He was known for bringing as much care and attention to his communal vines as to the grand crus. His well known description was that the wines should be "a pleasure to drink young or old." Denis died young in 2006 after taking his own life as the result of depression. The wines now are made by his son Arnaud. Holdings include 14 different appellations; the most important are in Gevrey Chambertin, extending from Le Chambertin, several premier crus, and a variety of communal plots (which may be bottled as one or more cuvées). There's a strong use of new barriques, with most of the premier and grand crus seeing 100% new oak; communal wines see about 60% new oak, and even the Bourgogne has 30-40%. Whether because the vineyards are maturing, the work in the vineyards is more detailed, or vinification is more precise, there is agreement that the wines show increasing finesse.

🔍 Gevrey Chambertin
🍶 Gevrey Chambertin, Les Champeaux
www.domaine-denis-mortet.com

12 ha; 70,000 bottles

Domaine Jacques Frédéric Mugnier

In the early nineteenth century the Mugniers developed a successful business in liqueurs in Dijon. In 1863 they purchased the Château de Chambolle Musigny, an imposing Château at the foot of the hill, and they acquired the vineyards that form the basis of the domain. All the vineyards were in Chambolle Musigny until their last purchase, the Clos de la Maréchale in Nuits St. Georges, in 1902. This vineyard was leased to Faiveley and reverted to Mugnier only in 2004; now it is their largest single property. The vineyards are not formally organic, but there is no use of fertilizers, herbicides, or pesticides. All the wines are red, except for a white that was introduced at the Clos de la Maréchale. Frédéric Mugnier was an airline pilot until he started to run the domain full time in 2000. Soon he was forced to expand, building a new cuverie under the courtyard of the Château, when the domain was tripled by the reversion of the Clos de la Maréchale. The Chambolle Musigny and the two premier crus, Les Fuées and Les Amoureuses, are the quintessence of elegance, textbook examples of the "femininity" of Chambolle. The Clos de la Maréchale follows the same style but is more obviously structured. "It took me years to realize that the best way to vinify the different terroirs was to make all the wine exactly the same," says Frédéric, and today all the wines get the same 15-20% new oak. Freddy says he would be happy to be described as a minimalist but would prefer "essentialist."

🔍 Chambolle Musigny
🍶 Chambolle Musigny
www.jfmugnier.com

14 ha; 45,000 bottles

Domaine Sylvain Pataille

After studying in Bordeaux, Sylvain Pataille returned to Burgundy and became a consulting oenologist in 1997 (including Roumier and Groffier among his clients); he still consults for several domains, but in 2001 he established his own domain, starting out with a hectare. The domain focuses exclusively on Marsannay and its environs, producing red, white, and rosé. In addition to Marsannay, there's AOP Bourgogne from vineyards just to the north in Chenôve (which Sylvain comments had a higher reputation when it used to be known as part of the Côte de Dijon). Most of the vineyards are rented on long term contracts. Altogether there are 8 reds, 5 whites, and 2 rosés. In addition to communal Marsannay cuvées of all three colors, there are several red cuvées from individual lieu-dits of Marsannay (there are presently no premier crus in the Marsannay appellation, but perhaps Sylvain's efforts will result in some lieu-dits being promoted). Sylvain is a modernist in the context of Marsannay. Vinification is in stainless steel and fiberglass tanks, and élevage usually uses a maximum of 30-35% new oak for 12-18 months. The reds are round, the whites are crisp, and the rosés have unusual character. Sylvain is actually a fan of Aligoté, and his largest vineyard is 3 ha of Bourgogne Aligoté. The best of the lieu-dits in Marsannay are Les Longeroies and Clos du Roy, but the top wine of the domain is L'Ancestrale, a cuvée from a 1 ha plot of vines planted in 1946.

Marsannay-la-Côte

Marsannay, Clos du Roy

13 ha; 50,000 bottles

Domaine Henri Perrot-Minot

I started off on the wrong foot when I visited Perrot-Minot by mistakenly going to the new winery across the N74, but Christophe Perrot-Minot was typically charming about it, and the next day we had a splendid tasting in the cellars of the old domain in the center of Morey St. Denis. Christophe is the fourth generation, and worked as a wine broker before making his first vintage in 1993. The domain originated with Domaine Maume Morizot, which was formed by his great grandfather, but the estate was subsequently divided into four parts in 1973. Christophe is quite hands on, spending his mornings in the vineyards; when I arrived, he had just returned from the green pruning. The key here is a combination of old vines and low yields, 20-30 hl/ha for everything, even the Bourgogne. Everything is destemmed except for four cuvées: grapes are cut one by one from the central stem—Christophe calls this destructuration. The house style is faintly spicy and nutty with perfumed hints. Smooth palates show round fruits with silky tannins, never any rough edges; the overall impression is ultra-modern, with a silky approachability even in Gevrey Chambertin or Vosne Romanée, but there's structure behind. Yet when I asked Christophe if he regards himself as a modernist, he was a bit indignant. "For me this is traditional, not modern. It's not that I'm looking for drinking young, I'm looking for elegance, balance, and concentration, but it must be natural, it must come from the berries."

Morey St. Denis

Morey St. Denis, La Riotte

www.perrot-minot.com

13 ha; 65,000 bottles

Domaine Ponsot

William Ponsot established the domain in 1870 with the vineyards that are still at its heart: the premier cru Monts Luisants and the grand cru Clos de La Roche in Morey St. Denis. Jean-Marie Ponsot came into the domain in 1942 and took over in 1957, expanding the domain by marriage, and becoming mayor of Morey St. Denis. Laurent Ponsot, who took over in 1981, expanded the domain further with arrangements to manage vineyards in premier and grand crus going north into Gevrey Chambertin and south into Chambolle Musigny. The new winery is an impressive building extending several storeys underground, allowing all operations by gravity feed. There's now a range of wines in Morey St. Denis and Gevrey Chambertin ranging from the communal to grand crus. Vinification is "non-interventionist," in vineyard and cellar. "I am not a minimalist winemaker, I am the laziest winemaker, I let nature do the work," Laurent says. He harvests late in order to get maximum ripeness: usually he is the last in the village. Laurent uses no new oak, regarding it as a fashion that panders to some critics, the wines are not filtered, and there is minimum use of sulfur. The style is full and round. Mont Luisants is one of the rare white wines produced in the Côte de Nuits, but is unique in consisting largely of Aligoté—probably the only high class production from this grape in Burgundy. Ponsot's vineyard in Clos de la Roche was the origin for the now-famous Dijon clones of Pinot Noir.

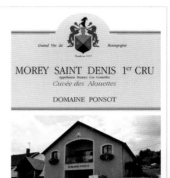

Morey St. Denis

Morey St. Denis, Premier Cru

Morey St. Denis, Monts Luisants

www.domaine-ponsot.com

10 ha; 50,000 bottles

Domaine de La Romanée-Conti

"The typicity of Pinot Noir first is to be Burgundian," says Aubert de Villaine, who has been at the domain since 1965, and indeed DRC is generally acknowledged as the epitome of both Pinot Noir and Burgundy. Ever since the vineyards of Romanée Conti were reunited by Aubert's grandfather, Edmond, who created the Domaine de la Romanée Conti in 1912, and then acquired all of La Tâche in 1933, this has been Burgundy's top domain. With monopoles of Romanée Conti and La Tâche, and major holdings in Romanée St. Vivant, Richebourg, Grands Echézeaux, and Echézeaux, DRC dominates the grand crus of Vosne Romanée. There is also a small holding in Le Montrachet. The focus is not on power, but on subtlety of expression. "Romanée Conti has a character of softness and length in the mouth that makes it special compared to other wines. But it's a question of taste; some people might prefer Chambertin or La Tâche for their greater body," Aubert explains. Viticulture is organic, the vineyards are perpetuated by selection massale using stock that goes back to Romanée Conti before it was replanted in 1945, and vinification is traditional (with no destemming). A horizontal tasting here is an exploration of nuances in expression at the most refined level, but it is fair to say that Romanée Conti and La Tâche are sui generis. The wines are of course fabulously expensive, and unfortunately are now bought more for investment than drinking.

Vosne Romanée

Richebourg

www.romanee-conti.com

29 ha; 80,000 bottles

Domaine Georges Roumier

The domain originated in 1924 when Georges Roumier obtained vine-yards in Chambolle Musigny by marriage. The wines have been estate bottled since 1945. His son, Jean-Marie, took over in 1961, and the domain is now run by Christophe, who joined his father in 1981 and took over in 1990. Expanded from the original holdings, the heart of the estate still lies in Chambolle Musigny, and includes vineyards in the two grand crus, Bonnes Mares and Le Musigny (a really tiny holding, giving only 300 bottles), and in three important premier crus, Les Amoureuses, Les Cras, and Les Combottes. The average age of vines is around forty years. There is a little white wine in the form of Corton Charlemagne (only a hundred cases). The style is on the sturdy side for Chambolle Musigny, and the wines usually require some time to open up: the monopole of Clos de la Bussières from Morey St. Denis, for example, can be positively hard when first released, but give it a decade and it acquires a silky sheen. Some of that initial hardness may be due to the practice of not necessarily destemming—only the village wine is always destemmed, otherwise each vintage is judged separately. A short cold maceration is followed by fermentation under 30 °C and warm post-fermentation maceration. New oak is usually around 25% (perhaps 30% for the grand crus). The corollary of making wines in traditional style requiring time to open out is that they are correspondingly long-lived.

Domaine Armand Rousseau

Armand Rousseau is the doyen of Chambertin, widely acknowledged to set the standard with his premier and grand crus. The domain is the largest single owner of Le Chambertin and has a substantial parcel in Clos de Bèze, as well as holdings in three other grand crus and three premier crus in Gevrey Chambertin. The eponymous Armand Rousseau was involved in the drive to domain bottling in the 1930s; today his grandson Eric is in charge of the domain. Its increasing success in rising into the stratosphere with DRC and Leroy was indicated by the throes of construction when I visited, with the small courtyard being excavated in order to construct a new cave underground. With better capacity for storage, Rousseau won't have to sell all the wine at the vintage. As is evident from the generally soft style, there is usually at least 90% destemming. (In 2009, whole clusters were increased to 15-20%.) Vinification is the same for all wines; the only difference is in the use of new oak. Both Chambertin and Clos de Bèze have their élevage in 100% new oak; Clos St. Jacques is 60-70%. All wines spend 20 months in barrique. "I am completely against over-extraction of color and material. I prefer Pinot Noir with elegance. If you go too far, you eliminate the effects of terroir," Eric Rousseau says. The style here is consistent across the range, with increasing concentration as you go from the village wine to Clos St. Jacques, and then up to Chambertin or Clos de Bèze.

Domaine du Clos de Tart

This splendid domain is synonymous with the largest grand cru mono-pole in Burgundy, occupying a single plot on the slope running up behind the Maison. It has had only three owners since it was created by nuns in 1141. After the Revolution in 1789 it was acquired by Marey-Monge, and then it was sold to the Mommessin family in 1932. The Mommessins also owned a negociant business (since sold to Jean-Claude Boisset). Clos de Tart went through a difficult period until Sylvain Pitiot became the winemaker in 1996. The vineyard unusually is planted with rows in north-south orientation across the slope, and Clos de Tart has its own nursery for selecting vines for propagation by selection massale. There are two cuvées. Until vines are 25 years old, production is declas-sified into La Forge des Tarts (labeled as premier cru). In addition, lots may be assigned to La Forge on the basis of blind tasting. Usually La Forge is about a quarter of production, but there have been extreme vin-tages where there has been much less La Forge or no Clos de Tart. Although this is a genuine clos (entirely surrounded by walls), soils vary extensively, and it is divided into 23 plots, which are vinified separately. Vinification matches the plot, in some cases with complete destemming, in others with partial or entire whole clusters. Only new oak is used. There is no difference in winemaking between La Forge and Clos de Tart, but La Forge is less structured and ready to drink sooner.

Morey St. Denis
Clos de Tart
www.clos-de-tart.com

8 ha; 23,000 bottles

Domaine Trapet Père et Fils

Located right on the N74 in Gevrey Chambertin, Domain Louis Trapet was established in 1870, and was one of the major suppliers to negoci-ants until estate bottling started in the 1960s. Its extensive holdings made it the most important domain in Gevrey Chambertin, but it was divided in 1993 as the result of inheritance issues. One half was renamed as Do-maine Trapet Père et Fils. (The other part gave rise to what is now Domaine Rossignol-Trapet: it can be interesting to compare the styles of the two domains since the holdings are so parallel.) Trapet Père et Fils is presently run by Jean-Louis Trapet, and has holdings in some of the best terroirs of Gevrey Chambertin, including almost 2 ha of Le Chambertin, with vines going back to 1919. The other grand crus are Latricières Chambertin and Chapelle Chambertin, and there are three premier crus, as well of course as the communal Gevrey Chambertin, which is the largest production of the house. There are also Marsannay and Bour-gogne. Vinification uses partial (typically 70%) destemming, cold maceration before fermentation in open top vats, with 30-70% new oak used for élevage of 15-18 months depending on the appellation. The style is structured, but not especially powerful. At its best, it may be very smooth, but it can be austere when young. There is also a Domaine Tra-pet in Alsace, as Jean-Louis's wife, Andrée, comes from Alsace and took over her parents' vineyards in 2002.

Gevrey Chambertin
Gevrey Chambertin
www.domaine-trapet.com

15 ha; 50,000 bottles

 Chambolle Musigny
 Chambolle Musigny
 Musigny Blanc

13 ha; 36,000 bottles

Domaine Comte de Vogüé

One look at the fifteenth century entrance, and you can see this is a really old domain: ownership has not changed since 1450. Comte de Vogüé is by far the most important holder of Musigny, with 7 of the 11 ha. A small part (0.65 ha) makes the Musigny Blanc, although since 1994, when the vineyard was replanted, it has been declassified to Bourgogne Blanc. "It seems a bit brutal to declassify grand cru to Bourgogne, but we didn't have any choice," says François Millet, who has been making the wine here since 1986. "We declassify young vines (everything under 25 years) from (red) Musigny into Chambolle Musigny premier cru," he explains, adding, "I don't consider this to be a second wine, it's a younger Musigny." The domain also has a large holding in Bonnes Mares, and some Chambolle Amoureuses and village Chambolle Musigny. François has strong views on winemaking. "Grapes are destemmed and used as whole berries. I've never used whole bunches. The question I ask is, if we have whole berries, why should I use whole bunches?" And as for oak, "I have chosen to be a winemaker not a forester." There is 15% new oak in Chambolle Musigny, 25% in premier crus, and 35% in grand crus. The best single word to describe the de Vogüé wines is soignée: they give a silky impression of infinite smoothness, ranging from the precision of Chambolle Musigny, to the sheer elegance of the firmer premier cru, the classic seamless Amoureuses, and the weight of Musigny.

 Premeaux-Prissey
 Nuits St. Georges
 Vougeot, Les Cras
 Clos Blanc de Vougeot
www.domainedelavougeraie.com

44 ha; 100,000 bottles

Domaine de La Vougeraie

One of the newest, and most rapidly growing, domains in Burgundy, Domaine de la Vougeraie brings together several old domains under a new name. The driving force is Jean-Charles Boisset, who together with his sister Nathalie, has become Burgundy's largest producer by acquiring Bouchard Aîné in Beaune, Ropiteau Frères in Meursault, Antonin Rodet in Mercurey, Château de Pierreux in Beaujolais, and J. Moreau in Chablis, and several other houses. These continue to run independently, but Domaine de la Vougeraie amalgamates holdings from four old domains: Claudine Deschamps (the original Boisset family estate in Premeaux, where a new winemaking facility has now been constructed), Pierre Ponnelle, Louis Voilland, and L'Héritier Guyot. Starting in 1999, winemaker Pascal Marchand went for a powerful style, and then the style is supposed to have lightened after Pierre Vincent took over as winemaker for 2006. He uses 30% new oak for the village wines, 40% for the premier crus, and 50% for grand crus, with an élevage of 18 months. However, I still find the wines to be on the powerful side: the white Clos Blanc de Vougeot, for example, shows a mass of new oak and is all up-front power, compared with the more classic style it used to have when made by L'Héritier Guyot. But you could say the same of many wines in Burgundy, so the fair comment may be that these are definitely wines in the modern style.

Domaine Robert Ampeau et Fils

The imperatives of winemaking, or to be more precise, of commercializing the wines, are unusual at Robert Ampeau. The focus is on whites, which often are released only several years after the vintage, when the wines of other producers may be past their best. A visit with Robert Ampeau was a completely different experience. It started in the cellars in a back street of Meursault with a long discussion, or perhaps monologue, on the state of France and world affairs: only slowly did it turn to actually tasting the wines. Since Robert's death in 2004, Michel Ampeau has been making the wines. There are holdings in ten premier crus, including four in Meursault. The wines are meant to age, or perhaps more to the point, have reached an interesting stage of maturity when released. The Meursaults show a classically nutty flavor spectrum, and in the era before premox overtook white Burgundy, used to peak around fifteen years of age and hold until twenty. The top whites are the premier crus from Meursault, Les Charmes and Les Perrières, which show great ripeness, with complex layers of flavor on a seamless palate. Among reds, the Volnay Les Santenots premier cru tends to earthiness, but the surprise and the bargain are the wines from lesser appellations: La Pièce Sous le Bois from Blagny and the Savigny-lès-Beaune age much longer than you might expect, in the general soft, earthy style of the house. The domain is remarkable for its ability to produce high quality in lesser years.

Meursault
Savigny-lès-Beaune
Meursault, Les Charmes

10 ha; 50,000 bottles

Domaine du Marquis d'Angerville

The domain takes its name from the Marquis d'Angerville, who inherited the estate in 1906, but its origins go back at least a century earlier. The Marquis was involved in re-establishing the estate as a leading producer of Pinot Noir after the ravages of phylloxera, and during the 1930s became one of the leaders of the grower movement against the large negociants who dominated Burgundy at the time, initiating the move to estate bottling. After 1952, his son Jacques d'Angerville built up the estate's reputation for the sheer precision and elegance of its wines. It's a measure of the commitment to Pinot Noir that a low-yielding, small-berried clone developed from their vineyards is now known as the d'Angerville clone. Jacques was succeeded by Guillaume d'Angerville in 2003. Most of the holdings are in Volnay, with a roll call of premier crus, headed by the monopole Clos des Ducs, adjacent to the domain, which occupies a splendid nineteenth century maison, just behind the church in Volnay. Other top holdings include Caillerets and Taillepieds. The wines always had a wonderful taut precision under Jacques d'Angerville, but seem since then to have become broader and less focused. One change in winemaking has been the introduction of a small proportion (up to 20%) of new oak. Guillaume has expanded his operations by purchasing two estates in the Jura in 2012, followed by another in 2014: wines are labeled as the Domaine du Pélican.

Volnay
Volnay, Les Caillerets
www.domainedangerville.fr

15 ha; 55,000 bottles

MAZIS-CHAMBERTIN
GRAND CRU
BY OLIVIER BERNSTEIN

2007

○ Beaune

🍷 Gevrey Chambertin, Ca-
zetiers

www.olivierbernstein.com

7 ha; 25,000 bottles

Olivier Bernstein

"It's interesting to have someone like me here, in the most conservative region of France, as I'm not from here, I'm not obliged to make wine," says Olivier Bernstein, who comes from a musical background, but became a micro-negociant in 2007. Olivier makes 3 premier crus, 7 grand crus, and village Gevrey Chambertin in a renovated building in a back street of Beaune. Production focuses on reds from the Côte de Nuits. Quantities are small but not miniscule. "There are 4-8 barrels of each wine, I like to have at least four barrels, I don't want to bottle one barrel, that's a nonsense," Olivier says. The boundary between negociant and domain has blurred as Olivier was able to buy 2 ha in 2012, but this doesn't make much difference as he farms all the plots himself anyway. "So I don't really like to be called a negociant," he says. Winemaking is modern, with maturation entirely in new barriques, although Olivier says, "It's not the new wood that's interesting for me, it's the oxygenation." Except for Chambolle Lavrottes, vines are 40-80 years old. "We only have very old vines because they are much better than recent plantings." The style is finely structured, with Lavrottes the lightest, Gevrey Chambertin remarkably pure, Clos de la Roche and Clos de Bèze very tight when young, and fleshiness only just showing on Clos Vougeot behind that tight, precise house style. These beautifully balanced wines should come into their own about six years after the vintage.

Savigny-les-Beaune 1ᵉ Cru
Les Marconnets
APPELLATION CONTROLEE

Simon Bize & Fils
SAVIGNY-LES-BEAUNE · CÔTE D'OR

○ Savigny-lès-Beaune

🍷 Savigny-lès-Beaune, Les
Fourneaux

🍷 Savigny-lès-Beaune, Les
Vergelesses

www.domainebize.com

22 ha; 100,000 bottles

Domaine Simon Bize

The Bize family arrived in Savigny in the middle of the nineteenth century. Simon Bize worked at other domains, and little by little built up his own domain. His son took over after the first world war; and his wife (known as Grandma Bize) was a dominant influence. Estate bottling started in 1926, but complete estate bottling only happened a generation later. Patrick Bize started in 1978, and took over in 1988; he expanded the domain with additional vineyards, and built a new cuverie. Under his leadership—sadly he died in 2013—the domain became a reference for Savigny. You enter in a charming courtyard that appears almost residential, but behind is a huge warehouse facility with an extensive barrel room underneath. Vineyards are mostly in Savigny-lès-Beaune, where there are six premier crus in red and one in white. There's also a little Corton and Corton Charlemagne, and Latricières Chambertin. Overall production is 70% red. Reds are vinified as whole clusters in large wooden vats (there is some destemming in some years), fermentation is relatively warm, élevage lasts about a year, but there is no new wood. Whites are pressed, go into stainless steel to settle, and then into barriques to ferment. Although vinification is traditional, the style of the reds is modern, almost slick, with a crowd-pleasing suppleness, and never any evident tannins; even lesser vintages leave an opulent impression. I find the reds more successful than the whites.

Burgundy: Côte de Beaune

Domaine Jean-Marc Boillot

This domain started with a family division. Jean-Marc Boillot had made 13 vintages at the family domain, when he left in 1984 after a disagreement with his father, Jean Boillot, because he was unable to make the sort of wines he wanted. After four years as winemaker at Olivier Leflaive, while also making his own wine from a couple of rented hectares, he became independent. He now has half the vineyards from his paternal grandfather, Henri Boillot, plus some vineyards from his maternal grandfather, who was Etienne Sauzet. The domain is run from his grandfather's house in Pommard. Holdings are split more or less equally between Puligny Montrachet (including four premier crus and some Bâtard Montrachet) and reds from Pommard, Beaune, and Volnay. The style is undeniably rich and powerful (and interestingly has been so successful that the family domain, now called Henri Boillot after Jean-Marc's brother, subsequently moved in the same direction). Whites see 25-30% new oak, reds get 50% new oak. For me, the style comes off better in whites than reds, where sheer power can overwhelm the delicacy of an appellation such as Volnay. The Pulignys tend to be powerful rather than mineral. Whether red or white, this is very much a domain in the modern idiom. In 1998 Jean-Marc extended his activities into the Languedoc, where he produces IGP d'Oc wines under the labels of Domaine de la Truffière and Les Roques.

🔘 Pommard
🍾 Puligny Montrachet
www.jeanmarc-boillot.com
🚫 ⚒ Ⓖ ✲
10 ha; 50,000 bottles

Domaine Bonneau du Martray

The most aristocratic domain in Corton, Bonneau du Martray has a single block of 11 ha between Pernand and Aloxe Corton. The domain has no other vineyards, and makes just two wines. The winery is located in the center of Pernand-Vergelesses, where its buildings have been renovated and there is a stylish tasting room underneath. Jean-Charles le Bault de Morinière abandoned his architectural practice in Paris to take over Bonneau du Martray only in 1993, although he was present for all vintages after 1969. "You can find Corton Charlemagne producers all around the hill and this produces big differences in the wines—exposition, slope, style of producer," he says, "We have all the variations between Pernand and Aloxe." The single cuvée of Corton Charlemagne is an assemblage from 90% of the estate; the rest is a red Corton coming from four blocks. Jean-Charles is an enthusiast for biodynamics. "The texture is different, it sits on the mid palate, there is a more mineral style, more clarity, purity, volume." The Corton Charlemagne is barrel fermented, spends 12 months in élevage with about a third new oak, and is transferred to stainless steel with all the fine lees for 6 months. "My wines show well in the year after bottling, then they shut down. In the past they used to shut down so much you could not see anything. They still shut down but since 2005 they have been more approachable and understandable, they never become invisible. They open up after 3-4 years," he says.

🔘 Pernand Vergelesses
🔵 Corton Charlemagne
🍾 Corton Charlemagne
www.bonneaudumartray.com
🚫 ⚒ Ⓖ ▱
11 ha; 53,000 bottles

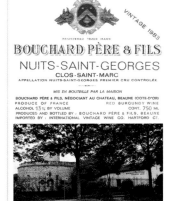

 Beaune

🍷 Beaune, Grèves Vigne de l'Enfant Jésus

🍾 Beaune, Clos St. Landry
www.bouchard-pereetfils.com

130 ha; 600,000 bottles

Domaine Bouchard Père et Fils

Dating from 1731, this is one of the oldest estates in Burgundy and today is one of the largest negociant-growers. (Another member of the family founded Bouchard Aîné in 1750, a separate producer now owned by Jean-Charles Boisset.) Bouchard is the largest owner of premier and grand crus on the Côte d'Or, and these total two thirds of the estate holdings. The domain is housed in the Château de Beaune, a fifteenth century fortress within the walls of the old city of Beaune (with very impressive cellars underneath), but holdings extend right through the Côte de Beaune and Côte de Nuits and the areas to their south. The Bouchard family remained in control for more than two centuries, but at the end of the period, the wines were distinctly under performing. Bouchard was sold to Joseph Henriot Champagne in 1995, and has been revived by new investment, including the construction in 2005 of a new gravity flow winery just north of the city. On the Côte d'Or, around a third of production comes from estate vineyards, with the majority from purchases of grapes. Among the best-known wines are some of the premier cru vineyards in Beaune, the Clos St. Landry (a monopole which produces one of the rare whites from Beaune), and Grèves Vigne de l'Enfant Jésus (a red with more power than usually found in Beaune). There is no doubt about the improvement since Henriot took over, but I still don't find the wines as compelling as those of other comparable negociant-growers.

🍾 Meursault

🍾 Meursault, Les Tessons
www.michelbouzereauetfils.com

12 ha; 65,000 bottles

Domaine Michel Bouzereau et Fils

French inheritance laws explain why there are so many Bouzereau domains in Meursault. "Bouzereau has been important in Meursault for seven generations, although it's only four generations we've been concerned exclusively with viticulture. In my grandfather's time we had four domains, now we have five domains with the name Bouzereau. I have my grandfather's domain, but the vines have been shared at each generation, of course, so we have all the appellations," says Jean-Baptiste Bouzereau. Domain Michel Bouzereau has 14 appellations, 11 in white and 4 in red. A splendid modern underground cave was constructed in 2008. Jean-Baptiste says, "I look for elegance and finesse, and to harvest mature but not too mature to keep freshness." There is 15-30% new wood, with higher levels used for premier crus. The whites are Meursault and Puligny, the reds are Volnay, Pommard, and Bourgogne. The three lieu-dits from Meursault show a range from the breadth of Tessons to the tension of Limousin (which is just next to Puligny). The three Meursault premier crus show breadth, with complexity increasing from Charmes and Genevrières to Perrières, the last two along the lines of what a Meursault grand cru might offer if one existed. The Puligny premier crus, Champs Gain and Caillerets, are more tightly wound. What you see here across the whole range is how purity of the fruits highlights the characters of the individual terroirs.

Domaine Jean-François Coche Dury

One of the great names of white Burgundy, Coche Dury is by far the most difficult to taste in depth, partly because quantities are so small, partly because Jean-François Coche verges on the reclusive. Jean-François retired officially in 2010, with his son Raphaël taking over, but the domain is no more approachable (it accepts visits only in the winter). Vineyards come from the old Coche family holdings plus those brought by Jean-François's marriage to Odile Dury in 1975. About half are in Meursault, with the rest spread around Puligny Montrachet, Auxey-Duresses, Monthelie, and Volnay. Appellation Meursault is the largest holding at just over 4 ha, and the wine puts most growers' premier crus to shame. (Apparently not all bottlings are the same, because some lieu-dits may be bottled separately, but not identified.) The style shows steel and minerality, then going past the smoke and gunflint, the layered palate offers the richness of the Côte d'Or, with precisely delineated fruits, and evident but beautifully integrated oak. The modest alcohol level contributes to elegance. This is the only wine I know to achieve this forceful elegance apart from top flight Puligny. Even more intense, the premier crus (Caillerets and Perrières) are vanishingly rare, and the Corton Charlemagne is almost an endangered species. This is as good as it gets. The Puligny comes from lieu-dit Enseignères, and there are also reds from Meursault and premier cru Volnay.

Meursault

Meursault

9 ha; 45,000 bottles

Domaine Bruno Colin

Colin-Deléger used to be one of the most reliable estates of Chassagne Montrachet, where Bruno worked with his father Michel from 1993 until the domain was divided between Bruno and his brother Philippe. Michel retired in 2003. (Michel Colin held on to three parcels, and continued to make Chassagne en Remilly, Puligny Les Demoiselles, and Chevalier Montrachet under the Colin-Deléger label. Philippe's wines are well thought of, but haven't achieved as high a reputation as Bruno's.) Located in the old buildings of the original premises in the heart of the village, Bruno focuses on white wine from Chassagne Montrachet, including seven premier crus, plus a little Puligny premier cru and some St. Aubin. There is also some Pinot Noir in Bourgogne and Chassagne Montrachet. With a total of 30 different parcels, each holding is small, in fact, the only parcel larger than a hectare is the Pinot Noir in Chassagne. Altogether there are nineteen cuvées (twelve are premier crus). Fermentation for the whites starts in stainless steel and then is transferred to barriques. Both red and whites use 30% new oak, with élevage for 12 months for whites below premier crus and for Bourgogne rouge; everything else has 18 months. When Bruno was involved in making the wines at Colin-Deléger, the style was never to excess, always very measured, so these are not flamboyant wines, but are always solid representations of their appellations.

Chassagne Montrachet

Chassagne Montrachet

8 ha; 60,000 bottles

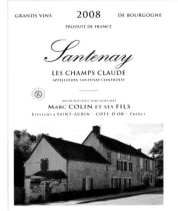

Saint Aubin

St. Aubin, en Remilly

www.marc-colin.com

17 ha; 130,000 bottles

Domaine Marc Colin et Fils

Starting with 7-8 ha, Marc Colin began to make wine with his brother Jacques around 1970, and created the domain in 1979. Marc retired in 2008, and the domain is now run by his sons Damien and Joseph, and their sister Caroline. (The domain was larger until brother Pierre-Yves, who had been the winemaker together with his father, took out his 6 ha share to run separately as Domaine Pierre-Yves Colin-Morey.) Winemaking is centered in some old buildings in the main street of St. Aubin, and a bit farther along is a modern tasting room. The Colins own about half the vineyards, and the other half is rented. About 80% is Chardonnay, with the rest split between Aligoté and Pinot Noir. There are 12 different cuvées from St. Aubin, and also Chassagne and Puligny Montrachet. "As we look more and more for finesse, freshness, and minerality, we have reduced new oak and battonage," Damien says. "St. Aubin has 15% new oak, whereas eight years ago it was 30%. St Aubin is cooler so we always have freshness and minerality. Puligny is sometimes like St. Aubin but can be more floral. Chassagne is usually a bit fatter." The house style is elegant and precise. The St. Aubins are unusually fine for the appellation, but the Puligny shows a touch more tension, and the Chassagne is indeed fatter. It would be good policy to drink St. Aubin and the Chassagne lieu-dit first, while waiting for the Puligny and Chassagne premier crus to come around.

Pommard

Pommard, Clos des Epeneaux

www.domaine-comte-armand.com

10 ha; 40,000 bottles

Domaine Comte Armand

One of the key domains in Pommard, Comte Armand carries as a subtitle, Le Domaine des Epeneaux, reflecting its holding of the monopole of Clos des Epeneaux, one of the best premier crus in Pommard. The same family has owned the domain since before the Revolution; the present Comte Armand is a lawyer in Paris. The domain was devoted exclusively to Pommard until it expanded in 1994 with the purchase of vineyards in Volnay and Auxey-Duresses. The wines increased in elegance under winemaker Benjamin Leroux, who started at the domain when he was fifteen, took over winemaking in 1999 (when he was 23), and stayed until 2014, when he left to make his own wine as a micro-negociant. There's an emphasis on natural winemaking, with chaptalization avoided where others might succumb, and filtration avoided entirely. "I'm not making wine, I'm growing fruit," said Benjamin, describing the philosophy. "I'm not trying to be minimalist, it's just common sense. I'm trying to grow good grapes, if you have to do lots of things in winemaking you are not growing good grapes." He's a strong believer in the importance of local conditions. Vineyards are perpetuated with selection massale from each site, with Pommard and Volnay treated differently, as he believes the vines have adapted to each site. The top wine here is always the Clos des Epeneaux, which expresses the generosity of Pommard. The red Auxey-Duresses premier cru is very fine.

Burgundy: Côte de Beaune

Domaine Vincent Dancer

Since the domain was founded in 1996 with vineyards inherited from Vincent's mother in Chassagne and his father in Puligny Montrachet, Vincent has built a reputation as a rising star; indeed, the wines are on their way to achieving cult status. Vincent grew up in Alsace, but after studying engineering went to Burgundy, where his family owned plots that were being rented out. He took them over and founded the domain, which continues with just the original parcels. All holdings are very small, including lieu-dits and premier cru Les Perrières in Meursault, two parcels in Chassagne's top premier cru, Morgeots, La Romanée and Tête du Clos, and a plot in Chevalier Montrachet so small as to make only one barrel. Vincent is reserved to the point at which detailed information is hard to come by, but he's proud of becoming the first producer in Chassagne to become organic, and he practices a minimalist approach with no battonage, fining, or filtration. New oak is about 25% for the village wines, 50% for the premier crus, and is new for the single barrique of Chevalier Montrachet. The great reputation here is for the whites, where the new wave style is poised between minerality and opulence; going from the lieu-dits in Meursault to the premier cru in Chassagne, the balance shifts towards greater texture and more minerality. There are also reds from Chassagne (from Morgeots, no less), and from Pommard and Bourgogne.

Chassagne Montrachet

Chassagne Montrachet, Les Corbins

www.vincentdancer.com

4 ha; 21,000 bottles

Maison Joseph Drouhin

Joseph Drouhin started as a negociant in Beaune in 1880. When his son Maurice took over in 1918, he began the move to becoming a negociant-grower by buying vineyards in Beaune's Clos des Mouches and in Clos Vougeot. Today one of the larger negociant-growers, and one of the few still in the old city of Beaune, Drouhin remains located in its old cellars, some dating back to the twelfth or thirteenth centuries. The firm is presently run by four siblings of the fourth generation. Drouhin has also invested in Oregon, where it produces both Pinot Noir and Chardonnay in Willamette Valley. Winemaker Véronique Drouhin oversees the harvest in Beaune and then flies to Oregon to make wine there. The range in Burgundy extends from the entry-level Laforêt Bourgogne (both red and white) to the top Grand Crus of both Côte de Beaune and Côte de Nuits. Wines come from around 90 appellations, all across the Côte d'Or, and stretching to Chablis and to Beaujolais. Vinification is traditional, with partial destemming (decreased since 2005), fermentation in open-topped containers, and pump-over or punch-down depending on conditions. Oak is handled lightly, almost always using less than 30% new wood. The Drouhin style is elegant, yet clearly devoted to bringing out the fruits. Clos des Mouches is always a textbook example of Beaune, for either red or white. Otherwise, the top whites are the Pulignys, and the top reds are the grand crus from Gevrey Chambertin.

Beaune

Beaune, Clos des Mouches

Chassagne Montrachet, Marquis de Laguiche

www.drouhin.com

80 ha; 3,600,000 bottles

Meursault

Meursault

3 ha; 20,000 bottles

Domaine Arnaud Ente

Arnaud Ente is sometimes described as a rising star in Meursault, but as evidenced from the price of his wines, he is now solidly established with something of a cult following. Although there are vineyards in the family, they have been run by other members. Arnaud started working at Coche Dury, then in 1991 began producing wine from vineyards rented from his father in law. Individual vineyard holdings are tiny, with nothing as much as a hectare, and most well under half a hectare. This tiny domain is run by Arnaud, his wife Marie-Odile, and two workers. Initially the wines were made in an opulent style from grapes picked quite late, but since 2000 a policy of earlier picking has focused more on bringing out minerality (and also results in moderate alcohol). Impressions of gunflint and salinity are reminiscent of Coche Dury, but the palate still has a more opulent sheen. The affordable wines are Aligoté, Bourgogne Blanc, and Meursault, mostly vinified in demi-muids. The village Meursault comes mostly from the clos of En l'Ormeau, where production is divided into three cuvées: Meursault AOP, Clos des Ambres (old vines), and La Sève du Clos, from very old (around 100 year) vines. There is also some Meursault premier cru Goutte d'Or and a Puligny Les Referts, as well as a little Volnay premier cru. Oak is fairly restrained these days, down to 20% new barriques for the top cuvées compared with 35% in the early years, reflecting the change of focus.

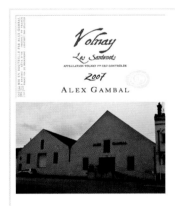

Beaune

Beaune, Grèves

Saint Aubin

www.alexgambal.com

4 ha; 60,000 bottles

Maison Alex Gambal

There's an unexpectedly modern warehouse building behind the extended façade on the ring road around Beaune, although the cellars underneath date from 1800. The building was originally part of Bouchard Aîné, and then was sold off and became an art gallery; Alex Gambal bought it in 2003 and renovated the building to become a gravity-feed winery. An American who came to Beaune because of his interest in wine, and leaned the business by working with broker Becky Wassermann, Alex has been slowly making the transition from negociant to grower. "I started in the business in 1997 as a classic negociant buying semi finished wine, then the next year I started buying grapes. Then I started buying vineyards. We now have 4 ha which are just about a third of our production. I'm planning to add 8 ha which would triple the domain," Alex says. There's a wide range of wines from Bourgogne to premier and grand crus from all over the Côte d'Or, with a little more white than red. Everything is destemmed, then fermentation with indigenous yeast is followed by élevage of up to 16 months. New oak is 10-15% for Bourgogne, 20-25% for village wines, a third for premier crus, and 50-100% for grand crus. "But the percentage of new oak is not so important as the barrels you are using, it's a matter of how the oak and toast interact with the juice," Alex says. Style tends to a light elegance rather than power, but always with a sense of underlying structure.

Maison Louis Jadot

Maison Louis Jadot is one of the most important negociant-growers in Burgundy, with more than half of their holdings on the Côte d'Or consisting of premier or grand crus. They produce more than a hundred different wines. They have also expanded significantly to the south, buying some top producers in the Beaujolais and Pouilly-Fuissé. The firm originated as a negociant in 1859, and was run by the Jadot family until it was purchased by their American importer, Kobrand, in 1985. The old cuverie in the center of Beaune was replaced in 1995 by a modern building on the outskirts, which was expanded further in 2010. Most (60%) of Jadot's production in the Côte d'Or is from estate vineyards; the rest is purchased as grapes from more than 200 growers (on rare occasions they buy finished wine; sometimes they will exchange wine with a grower in order to get a barrel of a specific appellation.) Jacques Lardière was in charge of Jadot's winemaking since 1970 and believes in minimal intervention. "The impression that you can determine quality by controlling winemaking is crazy, you need to have the confidence to work with Nature and allow the terroir to express itself. It is man who makes the mistakes," he says. One of Burgundy's major figures, Jacques retired in 2012, and it remains to be seen what will happen at Jadot post-Lardière. In the meantime, Jacques is making the wines at Jadot's latest venture, the Resonance Vineyard in Oregon.

 Beaune

Chambolle Musigny, Les Baudes

Puligny Montrachet, Clos de la Garenne

www.louisjadot.com

134 ha; 8,000,000 bottles

Domaine Antoine Jobard

The Jobards go back five generations in Meursault, but the two Jobard domains of today date from the division of the Pierre Jobard domain in 1971 between two brothers. Originally one half was known as Domaine François Jobard. When François's son Antoine joined in 2002, the name was changed to François and Antoine Jobard, and then in 2007 it was changed to Antoine Jobard when François nominally retired. The domain is adjacent to the lieu-dit En La Barre (which can be relied upon to outperform the village level). François was famous for his reserve; Antoine is somewhat more forthcoming. The domain is exclusively white wine, and all Meursault except for one very small parcel in Puligny Montrachet. The cuvées in Meursault include two lieu-dits, and four premier crus. (There was some red in Blagny, but it's been replaced with Chardonnay.) Going back to François, the reputation of the domain was for bucking the trend to big, buttery Meursaults and producing a taut, mineral style. Fashion has now caught up, so the Jobard Meursaults are more in the mainstream. Élevage is long (18-24 months), but uses little new oak, "maximum 20%," says Antoine. There is little battonage. "We make wines that are more reserved," is Antoine's description. The minerality of the style gives an impression moving in the direction of Puligny, yet there is a glossy sheen to the palate, with a sense of richness at the end. Current vintages show a lovely balance between minerality and opulence.

Meursault

Meursault, en la Barre

6 ha; 30,000 bottles

🔘 Meursault

🍾 Meursault, Les Narvaux

G **N**

8 ha; 47,000 bottles

Domaine Rémi Jobard

The nameplate at the entrance to the domain still says "Charles et Rémi Jobard" but the domain is now known as Rémi Jobard. The domain started with Charles, when he inherited half of the Pierre Jobard domain in 1971, and has been less well known than the domain of his brother François. The domain has been making strides since it was handed on to Charles's son Rémi, who started making wine in 1991. The main focus of the domain (and its reputation) rests with the estate vineyards in Meursault, especially the premier crus Poruzot-Dessus and Genevrières, but production has been expanded by a small negociant business, and there is also red wine from Monthélie and Volnay. New presses have been installed to allow slower and gentler pressing. Fermentation is unusually slow: "We have a special system in which it's done outside, so the cold weather blocks its progress in October-November," Rémi explains. The style minimizes oak influence by using barrels of Austrian oak (from Stockinger); élevage lasts a year, with only 20% new for the whites, 30% for the reds. "This respects the natural aromas of the wine," Rémi says. There are foudres as well as barriques. The style is quite modern, but at least at the level of the premier crus, the impression is rich, although more in the direction of an opulent glycerinic sheen than the old butter and nuts. The mineral edge of the New Meursault shows underneath. Alcohol on the high side gives an impression of late picking.

🔘 Volnay

🍾 Volnay, Vendanges Sélectionnées

🍾 Beaune, Les Aigrots
www.domainelafarge.fr

G

12 ha; 55,000 bottles

Domaine Michel Lafarge

This is one of the most distinctive domains in Volnay. The Lafarge's have been making wine since the nineteenth century, and started estate bottling in the 1930s. The winery is at an unassuming address in a back street of town, and the rambling cellars underneath are ancient. Vineyards are in 38 separate parcels, divided roughly into a third each of Bourgogne, village wines, and premier crus. In addition to Volnay and its premier crus, which are the heart of the domain, there are holdings in Beaune (white as well as red), Meursault, and Pommard. The style here is traditional in making no concessions to the current trend for immediate gratification: a vertical tasting of Lafarge shows that these wines need time, as you dig back far enough for the sheer purity of the fruits to be able to shine though. The wines are taut, precise, and elegant when they come around. Although keeping up with the latest thinking in converting to biodynamics, Frédéric Lafarge points out that this is in line with their care for the soil and the vines. "We did not fall for the fad of clonal fashions or the heavy fertilization in the 1960s," he says, "and part of the reason for our quality is that the plants are obtained by selection massale in which each generation has continued the match of terroir and cépage." The Lafarge Volnays can typify the crystalline purity of the appellation, but I would not try to drink any except the very lightest vintages within the first decade. The style of the whites is as lean as the reds.

Domaine Comtes Lafon

Dominique Lafon's great great grandfather started the domain. "The big step was when my father took over in 1956, but he was also an engineer, it was not his main job. The vineyards were under a sharecropping agreement, so my father was not managing them himself. I took over in 1984 and stopped the sharecropping. The contracts are for 9 years, so it was 1993 until I took all of them over." The domain has been expanded by splitting the purchase of the Labouré-Roi vineyards with Dominique's friend Jean-Marc Roulot, and Dominique has put his stamp firmly on the domain. "All the work we've done has been focused on a move towards elegance. We use just enough new oak for each vineyard, but I don't want to taste it in the wine. The objective was to get the wines to my taste." The domain has become one of the reference points for Meursault with a splendid array of lieu-dits and premier crus, but the reds from Volnay show the same hallmark elegance and precision. The village Meursault is a blend of various plots, sometimes including declassified lots from premier crus. Clos de la Barre comes from the vineyard next to the winery and captures the house style. "There's always more tension here," says Dominique. Another lieu-dit, Desirée, is always fatter. Terroir shows itself in the approachability of Bouchères, the roundness of Poruzots, power of Genevrières, steely backwardness of Charmes, and smoky, stony, depth of Perrières. Lafon also owns a domain in Mâcon.

 Meursault

 Meursault, Clos de la Barre
www.comtes-lafon.fr

16 ha; 70,000 bottles

Domaine Hubert Lamy

The domain is located just off the main street in St. Aubin in a work-manlike building that feels somewhat like an oversize converted garage. The Lamy's have been making wine in St. Aubin since the seventeenth century, and today Olivier Lamy is making some of the best wine in the appellation. Hubert Lamy started bottling his own wine in 1973, when the domain was created with 8 hectares; it increased significantly during the 1990s. All wine has been estate bottled since Olivier took over in 1996. Now there are 47 parcels altogether, with holdings also in Puligny-Montrachet, Chassagne-Montrachet, and Santenay. More than three quarters of plantings are Chardonnay. Some parcels of Pinot Noir have been replanted with Chardonnay. "My father started the switch to white wine in 1970," says Olivier, "It's not the terroir, it's not the typicité, it's commercial. But this is a return to the situation of many years ago, when production was white." Winemaking uses 2-3 days' cold maceration, followed by a two-week fermentation, and then 12-18 months in fûts or demi-muids (for some of the reds, which Olivier regards as a return to tradition) before assemblage. There is usually 20-30% new oak; less is used for wine from young vines. The most interesting wines here are white (it was a good decision to focus on Chardonnay), and the best from St. Aubin is usually the premier cru Les Murgers des Dents de Chiens. The domain is considered to be one of the benchmarks of St. Aubin.

 Saint Aubin

Saint-Aubin, Les Murgers des Dents de Chiens
www.domainehubertlamy.com

19 ha; 110,000 bottles

 Beaune

Corton, Château Corton Grancey

Corton Charlemagne
www.louislatour.com

50 ha; 6,000,000 bottles

Maison Louis Latour

This is one of the most important growers and negociants in Burgundy, with major vineyard holdings extending all over the area, a large negociant activity in Burgundy, and significant holdings elsewhere in France, notably the Ardèche. Overall Louis Latour is the largest holder of grand crus on the Côte de Nuits. In Corton, it is a major owner of Corton Charlemagne, with 10 ha. The company is still family owned, presently run by Louis VII. Quality is always reliable, even if in recent years a certain tendency to play it safe seems to have resulted in more sense of house style and less variation among appellations. In whites, the Corton Charlemagne is one of the most powerful expressions of the appellation, in line with a house style for whites that tends to rich and powerful. The reds include Chambertin, but the best known is Château Corton Grancey, named for the Château that was built in 1834. This is not a specific parcel, but a selection of the best lots from Corton each year. I've usually found the whites to be more interesting than reds, with the notable exception of Château Corton Grancey. In reds, Louis Latour remains controversial for its belief in pasteurization at bottling, which some critics believe impedes aging, but a vertical of Château Corton Grancey identifies it as one of the more ageworthy Cortons. Expansion under Louis VII has included the purchase of Simonnet-Febvre in Chablis, and large holdings in Beaujolais (including Domaine Henry Fessy).

Beaune

Gevrey Chambertin, Cazetiers

Chassagne Montrachet, Morgeots
www.lucienlemoine.com

0 ha; 30,000 bottles

Lucien Le Moine

Located in a street just outside the town center, from outside the premises look like a run down property, but the interior has been handsomely renovated, practical rather than flashy, but with a certain contemporary flair. Lucien Lemoine is the creation of Mounir and Rotem Saouma, who have been making wine here since 1998. It's perhaps Burgundy's top micro-negociant. The name reflects Mounir's past experience (Lucien, meaning light, is a translation of Mounir, and Le Moine, the monk, refers to the fact that Mounir learned winemaking in a monastery). There are typically around 35 different wines each year, extending from the basic Bourgogne to the premier and grand crus that form the main focus. The production scale is tiny: just one to three barrels (less than 1,000 bottles) from each cru. The approach to winemaking is direct: let the wine have a slow and very long fermentation, and keep it on full lees for élevage. "We have very cold cellars so we never complete fermentation before ten months after harvest," Mounir explains. There's minimal manipulation at bottling, and the wines often have a little residual carbon dioxide, and so need decanting. For me, these wines are completely natural, with a wonderful purity of fruit allowing terroir to show itself at every level of the range. They are expensive and hard to find, but an eye opener as to the potential for minimal manipulation. Since 2009 there has also been a winery in the Rhône called Clos Saouma.

Domaine Leflaive

One of the leading producers in Puligny Montrachet since the 1920s, under Anne-Claude, who took over in 1990, Domaine Leflaive has risen to the absolute summit. Anne-Claude was one of the first in Burgundy to convert to biodynamic viticulture (after an experiment to compare wine from vineyard plots treated organically or biodynamically); whether or not biodynamics are responsible, the wines have simply gone from strength to strength. The domain's style is the quintessence of Puligny: ripe (but never over-ripe) stone fruits, tempered by a steely, mineral structure. New oak is moderate: "What's important for us is to give the wine no more oak than it can take," says manager Antonin Lepetit. The same style runs with increasing intensity from the village wine through the premier crus, a roll call of the most famous names in the appellation, with Les Folatières, Les Combettes, Le Clavoillon (the largest holding and almost a monopole), and Les Pucelles (often of grand cru quality in Leflaive's hands). There are four of the five grand crus: Chevalier Montrachet, Bâtard-Montrachet, Bienvenues-Bâtard-Montrachet, and a tiny holding in Le Montrachet itself. Unfortunately, with the rise to fame the wines have become so expensive that they are for the most part simply out of reach. But at the other end of the range, Mâcon-Verzé (under the subsidiary label of Domaines Leflaive) was added in 2004, and Anne-Claude has just bought a domain in the Loire.

Puligny Montrachet

Puligny Montrachet, Le Clavoillon

www.leflaive.fr

24 ha; 130,000 bottles

Maison Olivier Leflaive Frères

Officially retired, but in practice evident everywhere, Olivier Leflaive is a force of nature. He was involved in managing Domaine Leflaive from 1982 to 1994, started as a negociant in 1984, and this became his full time activity from 1994. More recently he has acquired vineyards (including an inheritance of some that had been part of Domaine Leflaive). (The domain wines are indicated as Récolte du Domaine on the label). Given the family history, the focus is on white wine. His first winemaker was Jean-Marc Boillot, who now runs his own domain, and since 1988 Frank Grux has been the winemaker. "In terms of philosophy and character of wine, I was born in Leflaive style which is finesse and elegance," Olivier says. The house style shows good extraction and the wines are flavorful, first showing fruit, but then with a savory edge behind. They are reliable and consistent. In addition to the main focus on Chassagne and Puligny Montrachet, there are also wines from Chablis and some reds from the Côte de Beaune. Olivier is known as a small, quality negociant, but in fact, including the estate and negociant activity, wine is made overall from around a hundred hectares, so this has grown into a sizeable operation. But Olivier has extensive control of the vineyards, and says firmly, "I am a winemaker, not a negociant." The entrepreneurial spirit has shown itself also in the establishment first of a restaurant in the village square in Puligny Montrachet, and most recently in a hotel.

Puligny Montrachet

Puligny Montrachet

www.olivier-leflaive.com

15 ha; 650,000 bottles

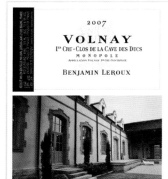

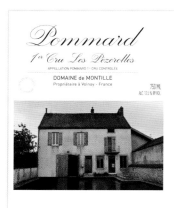

Beaune

Savigny-lès-Beaune

Chassagne Montrachet,
Morgeots
www.benjamin-leroux.com

4 ha; 90,000 bottles

Maison Benjamin Leroux

Benjamin Leroux started his negociant company in 2007, but continued to be the winemaker at Comte Armand in Pommard until 2014, when he became a full time negociant. He rents a rather cavernous space in a large old winery just off the ring road around Beaune. He has now managed to purchase his first vineyards. "Seven years ago, everything came from grape purchases, today it is the strong majority, and ideally in the future it would be half," he says. "Everything is under the same name, I don't distinguish between domain and negociant." Production is half white and half red, with grand cru about 10%, and premier cru and village about 30% each. "I started with lots of regional villages and where I grew the most was premier and grand cru." There are 30 different wines altogether; the largest cuvées are the Bourgogne and Auxey-Duresses, a few thousand bottles each, but others may be as small as only a single barrel. Vinification depends on the vintage. "We are wrong if we destem every year and wrong if we always do vendange entière; you have to adjust to the vintage," Benjamin says. For whites, the house style shows citrus fruits with faintly piquant lime on the finish and a suspicion of herbal savory notes that will add complexity as the wine ages. The reds are always ripe with good supporting structure, often with an approachability in a firm style that makes you think of Pommard, where Benjamin started.

Volnay

Volnay, Taillepieds
www.demontille.com

20 ha; 140,000 bottles

Domaine Hubert de Montille

The great reputation of this old domain started after Hubert de Montille took over in 1947, when it had been reduced to 3 ha in Volnay. A lawyer by profession, he continued to practice law as well as to run the domain. His son Etienne joined in 1983, took over the cellars in 1990, and has been in charge since 1995. The domain has expanded all over the Côte d'Or, and has three quarters of its holdings in premier and grand crus, mostly red. There's been a softening of style with the change of generations. "Hubert's winemaking style was highly extracted and more austere," says winemaker Brian Sieve at Deux Montille, a negociant activity created to complement the domain by producing white wines. Deux Montille is run by Etienne's sister, Alix (who is married to Jean-Marc Roulot, another famous white winemaker). Alix's interest in white wines extends into Côte Chalonnaise and Chablis. Wines for both domain and negociant have been made in a single spacious facility in Meursault since 2005 (previously the domain was vinified in Volnay and the negociant in Beaune). "There are no style differences between the negociant and the domain: everything is handled in exactly the same way," Brian explains. There's extensive use of whole clusters for reds; new oak varies from 20-50%, and is usually higher for the Côte de Nuits. The domain is known for the purity of its wines, and the style is precise and elegant, showing textbook illustrations of differences due to terroir.

Domaine Pierre Morey

"The domain is very old," says Anne Morey, who has been making the wine since 1998. "The Morey family arrived in France in the fifteenth century, and started in Chassagne. They moved to Meursault just after the Revolution." Production is two thirds white and a third red. "We work four villages, Puligny, Meursault, Pommard and Monthelie, and make 7 white and 5 red wines." The cuverie was extended in 2010 to allow gravity-feed winemaking. "We want to produce vins de garde, with long élevage sur lies, we keep lots of lees. Malo occurs late because we have very cold cellars." Whites are fermented in barrique, with 40-50% new wood as the maximum for grand crus. Battonage is done only up to malolactic fermentation. For the reds everything is destemmed. "But I have the impression that you deprive the grapes of something by destemming, I dream of being able to adjust destemming to the vintage and to use a proportion of vendange entière." The reds are precise and the whites tend to a tight, steely character, not surprising as Anne's father Pierre was winemaker at Domaine Leflaive as well as running his own domain. In addition, there is a negociant activity, Morey-Blanc, which is almost entirely white, and was started in 1992, to replace vineyards when the contracts expired on plots rented from Lafon. Today this is being cut back a bit. "It can be frustrating not to work the vines," Anne says, but the style is similar to Pierre Morey itself.

Meursault

Meursault, Les Tessons

www.morey-meursault.fr

10 ha; 50,000 bottles

Domaine de La Pousse d'Or

I remember the wines of Pousse d'Or from the early nineties as among the most elegant in Volnay, with an indefinably delicate expression of Pinot Noir. Then with Gérard Potel's death in 1997 the domain somewhat fell out of view. Patrick Landanger, who had been an engineer and inventor, bought the domain. He started by employing a general manager, but "he was told that if he wanted to regain confidence he would need to make the wine himself. So he went to oenology school... The first vintage he made was 1999, which was well received," explains commercial manager Marleen Nicot. There's been major investment in a new building that houses a gravity-feed winery, with three levels built into the side of the hill. Patrick is still inventing, as seen in a new glass device that has replaced bungs in barrels (so topping up is required less often). Production is focused on red wine. The heart of the domain remains the premier crus from Volnay, but Patrick has expanded, first by purchasing two vineyards in Corton, and then by adding a village wine and four premier crus in Chambolle Musigny. The only white comes from a vineyard purchased in Puligny Montrachet. For all the premier crus there is one third new oak, one third one-year, and one third two-year; grand Crus have 40-45% new oak. Larger barrels (350 liter) are used for the white wine. The wines from Volnay give a precise yet intense expression; the Chambolles seem a little rounder and more feminine.

Volnay

Volnay, Clos de la Bousse d'Or

www.lapoussedor.fr

18 ha; 90,000 bottles

 Meursault

 Clos Vougeot

 Meursault, Clos de Mazeray

www.prieur.com

21 ha; 100,000 bottles

Domaine Jacques Prieur

The domain was founded by a couple in the silk business in Lyon; they gave it to their nephew, Jacques Prieur, who became a significant figure in Meursault. In 1988, most of his children decided to sell their share to the Labruyère family. "We come from Moulin-à-Vent where we have owned 14 ha for 7 generations," Edouard Labruyère explains. "I was a courtier in Bordeaux until I came here to run the domain in 2008. My goal was clear. Jacques Prieur is fantastic in terms of terroir—we own 9 grand crus and 14 premier crus. I asked the team to make wines that represent the terroir. The signature of Prieur was too evident in the bottle, we were more known by the label than the terroir. I wanted to change that." Behind the stone façade is a modern cuverie, with separate facilities for red and white. "We modernized everything in 2009, no renovation had been made since 1958." Production is half red and half white. Meursault Clos de Mazeray is the only village wine in the portfolio. Vinification is traditional, with limited destemming and fermentation in open wood vats. Ageing is 18-24 months with no racking. "I stopped battonage for whites in 2008. I believe we have enough natural richness, I didn't want to add more fat." The reds of the Côte de Beaune have an unusual elegance, while those from the Côte de Nuits tend to be sterner. The whites are relatively sturdy, but good representations of their appellations. Labruyère also owns Château Rouget in Pomerol.

 Pernand Vergelesses

 Savigny-lès-Beaune, Les Fourneaux

 Pernand Vergelesses, Clos du Village

www.domaine-rapet.com

20 ha; 80,000 bottles

Domaine Rapet Père et Fils

Located right by the church in the center of the village of Pernand-Vergelesses, this is a very old domain, going back at least to the mid eighteenth century. Originally its vineyards were all around the village; that remains true of the whites, which come from Pernand-Vergelesses, its crus, and Corton Charlemagne, but today the reds are scattered all over the Côte de Beaune, coming from Pernand-Vergelesses, Aloxe Corton, Savigny-lès-Beaune, and Beaune. Around 1980 when Vincent's grandfather died, the vineyards weren't in great shape, so most of the domain was replanted, using a mixture of clones and selection massale; the domain has increased just a little in size since then. Vincent takes a thoughtful approach to viticulture and vinification. When asked how things have changed since he took over, he says that working the soil is better, there's better canopy management, and vendange vert is done when necessary. A sorting table was introduced in 2004, there's no pumping in the cuverie, and nitrogen is used when bottling the whites to avoid premox. There's a real focus on improving each stage to get quality in viticulture and vinification. "The style of the grand années remains the same, it's the style of the minor years that has changed," he says. "The wine used to require three years, now it's drinkable straight away." The whites can be quite full; there's always some proportion of whole cluster for the reds, giving a structured background to the generally silky style.

Domaine Guy Roulot

The domain was established by Jean-Marc Roulot's parents in the fifties, but, "I wanted to be an actor—I went to Paris—it wasn't entirely successful but it didn't work so badly, I was a professional actor for ten years. When my father died we employed a régisseur, then my cousin Grux managed the vintages until 1988, and then I came back to run the estate," Jean-Marc explains. "I still spend 20% of my time acting, but it's no different from having another estate; it takes less time than making Beaujolais." The domain is famous for its focus on the lieu-dits of Meursault. "My father had no premier crus, but he wanted to distinguish the different lots—he was one of the first to do this—and the style was defined by the decision to separate the cuvées." Jean-Marc has lengthened élevage to 18 months, with 12 months in barrique followed by 6 months in cuve, all on the lees. "The wine needs something to eat." There's no new oak for Bourgogne Blanc or Aligoté, village is 15-18%, and premier crus are 25-33%. The domain increased by 3 ha when Jean-Marc obtained half the vineyards of the old Labouré-Roi domain. The focus is on Meursault, with 6 lieu-dits and 4 premier crus, but there are also Bourgogne, Auxey-Duresses, and Monthelie (in red as well as white). Aided by an emphasis on early picking, the style is crisp and elegant, with moderate alcohol. "In 2009 we were among the first in the vineyard. I don't like high alcohol, I'm very comfortable with 12.5-12.8%."

Meursault
Meursault, Les Tessons
15 ha; 85,000 bottles

Domaine Etienne Sauzet

When Etienne Sauzet founded the domain in the 1930s he was a negociant in gateaux as well as a vigneron. "It's bizarre but his deuxième métier allowed him to buy vines. It was common in that period when things weren't too good to use the second job to buy vines," explains Benoît Riffaut, who married Etienne's granddaughter; management of the domain jumped a generation when he took over in 1974. Now his daughter and son-in-law are involved. He's supposed to retire next year but plans to carry on unofficially. "It's impossible to stop when you are used to this métier. I won't be in charge but I'll be here," he says. The domain has a complicated organization because it was divided among three siblings in 1991, and formally functions as a negociant buying grapes from the various parts, but little by little the original vineyards are being reincorporated into the domain. All cuvées come from Puligny, except for the Bourgogne, which comes from vines just outside the appellation. The village wine comes from 7 plots spread around the village, and there are 9 premier crus—that's our specialty," says Benoît. Backing off from new oak has changed the style a bit: today it is often 20-25%, and the maximum is 30% for the grand crus. "Vanilla and aromatics of oak are artificial for us," says Benoît. I remember vanillin in the wines from two decades ago, but today the style shows a steely minerality, with emphasis on richer stone fruits as opposed to citrus increasing up the hierarchy.

Puligny Montrachet
Puligny Montrachet, Les Champs Canet
www.etiennesauzet.com

10 ha; 100,000 bottles

Domaine Tollot-Beaut et fils

The domain was founded in Chorey-lès-Beaune just around the time of phylloxera. Very much a family affair, it's run today by a group of family members headed by Nathalie Tollot. With the sale of the other large individual producer in Chorey (Château de Chorey), Tollot-Beaut is really the only major producer dedicated to Chorey. For many years Tollot-Beaut was synonymous with good value wines from the appellation, but in fact the Chorey and generic Bourgogne account for only about half the vineyards. Other holdings extend into Savigny-lès-Beaune, Beaune (including premier crus Grèves and Clos du Roi), and Aloxe Corton (including small plots of Corton grand cru and Corton Charlemagne). The Chorey-lès-Beaune red, which is the principal cuvée, is an assemblage from all three areas of Chorey. The best wine from Chorey comes from the lieu-dit of Pièce du Chapitre, a monopole of Tollot-Beaut since 2001. Most of the other holdings outside Chorey are small enough that the wines represent individual plots. All grapes are destemmed, but vinification varies with the year. Prefermentation maceration is used only in good years. Cultivated yeasts are used in difficult years, indigenous in good years. All wines are treated the same, with 16-18 months in barrique; the proportion of new oak depends on the cuvée, extending from around 20% for village wines to 60% for grand crus. I've always found the style to be very reliable, with no disappointments.

◎ Chorey-lès-Beaune

🍾 Savigny-lès-Beaune, Les Lavières

▣⚔G✑
24 ha; 150,000 bottles

Domaine Anne-Marie et Jean-Marc Vincent

The cellars date from the fourteenth century, but this is a new domain. The vines belonged to the family, but they were not vignerons. "Jean-Marc's father was an engineer in Colmar. Jean-Marc didn't want to follow that and went to oenology school at Dijon in 1993. We were in Nuits St Georges before we came here, we didn't know what we were getting into," says Anne-Marie, a fraction ruefully. Established eighteen years ago, this remains a very hands-on operation: Anne-Marie had a second job until 2000, and the first real employee was hired only in 2009. "When we started all the equipment was old and we had to replace everything, but we did it slowly," Anne-Marie recollects. For the first two years, grapes were sold to negociants, but since then all production has been estate-bottled. There are separate cellars for whites and reds in the heart of the village (the old cellars were purchased by Ann-Marie's grandfather in 1950). There's the same élevage for all cuvées, with about 25% new oak. The whites have an intriguing blend of fruits and herbs when young, which strengthens to a delicious savory quality as they age. The reds are round, with a touch of tannin showing for the first couple of years, and the premier crus are quite Beaune-like. You might think that given their delicious quality when young, these wines don't need to age, but they do benefit from time in the bottle, becoming deeper with time, and peaking a few years after the vintage.

◎ Santenay

🍾 Santenay, Passetemps

🍾 Santenay, Beaurepaire

▣⁂G
6 ha; 30,000 bottles

Domaine Stéphane Aladame

The domain is located in a group of old buildings around a courtyard, just above the town of Montagny. "I created the domain in 1992 when I bought 2.5 ha from a vigneron who was retiring. I was eighteen at the time," recollects Stéphane Aladame. Since then, it's been built up slowly to its present size, and now there are six cuvées of Montagny premier cru plus a Crémant. There are no vines in Montagny village, but Stéphane has a negociant activity to produce Montagny AOP. Cuvée Decouverte is an assemblage of premier crus from young vines (less than 20 years old), vinified in cuve for 10 months, with some lees. Cuvée Selection Vieilles Vignes comes from four different premier cru parcels (older than 40 years), and is matured 60% in oak with 10% new. Most of the premier crus are matured in proportions of old barriques and cuve, but the premier crus with the oldest vines (Les Coères at 45 years and Les Burnins at 90 years) are matured exclusively in old barriques. The style tends to elegance, with smooth fruits, and a characteristic catch of lime at the end, reflecting the emphasis on maintaining freshness and precision. "I don't look for wines with too much maturity, too heavy. I harvest relatively early and want to keep acidity. I may have a degree less of alcohol, usually it's 12.5-13%. I look for minerality rather than richness," Stéphane says. Fruit concentration and the sense of texture resulting from oak exposure intensify going up the hierarchy.

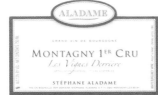

Montagny lès Buxy
Montagny
Montagny, Les Maroques
www.aladame.fr
G N
8 ha; 40,000 bottles

Château de Chamirey

The vineyards of this estate are all in Mercurey, concentrated around the rather splendid château, which was added to the estate two generations ago in 1931. The fifth generation of the Devillard family run the estate today. Across from the château is a modern winery, with a spacious tasting room and restaurant. Vineyards are two thirds red to one third black, with 15 ha in premier crus. The whites are fruit-driven and nicely rounded, very attractive for short or mid-term drinking, but not likely to be especially long-lived. The village wine is matured in 400 liter casks to preserve its minerality, with no new oak; the top white is a premier cru, the monopole La Mission, and is aged for 15 months in barriques with one third new oak. The wines, especially the reds, have evident notes of ripeness approaching over ripeness, so it was not a surprise to hear that, "We are always the last in Mercurey to harvest, we pick very late" (for both reds and whites). The red Mercurey comes from several plots, six from the village AOP, and includes two from premier crus, to increase quality, which has an influence especially in cooler years. Premier cru Ruelles is a monopole, but the top red is Les Cinq, a blend of the best lots from each of the five premier crus (production is small, only 1,900 bottles in 2010). In addition to Château de Chamirey, the Devillards own Domaine de Perdrix in Nuits St. Georges, and Domaine de la Ferté just to the south in Givry.

Mercurey
Mercurey, Clos du Roi
Mercurey, en Pierrelet
www.domaines-devillard.com
G
37 ha; 200,000 bottles

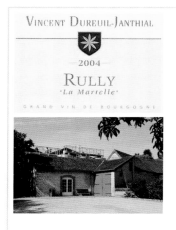

Domaine Vincent Dureuil-Janthial

The range and quality of wines justify this estate's reputation as the most important domain in Rully. At the back of the town, a tasting room in a charming house on one side of the street is run by Vincent's father, and a practical winery, more or less a warehouse, extends along the opposite side of the street. The domain was started by Vincent's grandfather; Vincent took over twenty years ago when he was 24. The holdings are a bit complicated: Vincent has 3 ha in his own name, his father has some, his father-in-law has 1 ha (premier cru in Nuits St. Georges), and 6 ha are rented on long term contracts. "There's no land for sale in Rully, so it's impossible to buy more vineyards," Vincent explains. Vineyards are organic, because "biodynamic is just too expensive for the Côte Chalonnaise." The 16 cuvées come mostly from Rully, with many premier crus, which we tasted not according to terroirs, but in order of vine age, which Vincent evidently views as a more important determinant of quality. The oldest vineyard is in Meix Cadots (the Vieilles Vignes cuvée, planted in 1920, now giving yields of 30 hl/ha.) "For the money it would be better to plant new vines and get 55 hl/ha, but it's four generations of work," Vincent says ruefully. The style shows minerality and precision. The whites are the glory of the domain, at their best a lesser man's Puligny. Reds show the limitations of the Chalonnaise, but with characteristic precision for Rully and earthy breadth for Mercurey.

Rully

Rully, Maizières

Rully, Margotés

dureuiljanthial-vins.com

20 ha; 100,000 bottles

Maison Paul et Marie Jacqueson

The long building that dominates the street has just been built; previously the domain was in much smaller space across the road. Marie Jacqueson's grandfather started the domain in 1946 with some vines from his parents. He had another job, working for a domain in Mercurey, but slowly he bought vines. Her father took over in 1972, and Marie took over in 2006. Vineyards continue to be added, and the domain has now almost doubled in size from when Marie's father started. The domain is principally in Rully but also has some Bouzeron and Mercurey. Overall it is 60% white. There are 18 different cuvées from Bourgogne Aligoté through Rully premier cru in whites and reds, and a Passetoutgrains— "We have everything," Marie says. "Our specialty with the Bouzeron is the élevage of Aligoté entirely in fûts (but no new wood, of course)." The heart of the domain lies in the Rully premier crus, Grésigny (with the oldest vines of the domain, planted by Marie's grandfather 60 years ago), La Pucelle, Raclot, and Les Cordères in white, and Les Naugues and Les Cloux in red. "All the white Rully premier crus are treated the same way and have 20% new oak. Any differences are due to terroir," Marie says. For reds there is complete destemming and 25% new oak. The house style with whites is quite fat, more stone fruits than citrus, with a texture on the palate approaching the style of the Côte d'Or. Reds can be tight at first, then broaden and become earthy after a year or so.

Rully

Rully, Cloux

Rully, Margotés

www.domainejacqueson.fr

14 ha; 80,000 bottles

Domaine Joblot

Run by brothers Jean-Marc and Vincent Joblot, this domain produces mostly red wine from Givry, with a small proportion of white. Jean-Marc's daughter Juliette is now taking over as winemaker; she is also involved with Domaine Lienhardt in Comblanchien, run by her partner Antoine Lienhardt. Functioning more or less out of the family property, Joblot is widely considered to be a point of reference for the appellation. Vineyards in the northern part of Givry are three quarters in premier crus, the best of which are Clos du Cellier aux Moines (the oldest known vineyard in Givry) and Clos de la Servoisine. There are 8 cuvées altogether, 3 white and 5 red (including one red and one white Givry AOP; the rest are premier cru). One unusual feature here is that date of harvest is determined by acidity levels, so the wines have not succumbed to the fashion for increasing ripeness or over-ripeness. With painstaking viticulture, yields are kept low and there is intense selection of grapes at harvest. Grapes are destemmed, and there is long cool maceration before fermentation. There's extensive use of new oak, but the brothers are very fussy about the extent of toast (it should not be too much); barrels come from a long-standing relationship with François Frères. Vinification is the same for all wines, with the stated aim of minimal intervention to ensure that differences between the cuvées are due solely to terroir. Oak can be evident in young wines, so do not try to drink before, say, three years.

Givry

Givry, Cellier aux Moines

14 ha; 65,000 bottles

Domaine Michel Juillot

Located on the main road through Mercurey, the tasting room of this domain seems continually thronged with visitors. The domain is now in its fourth generation, under Laurent Juillot since 1988 (although his father, Michel, a well known character in the town, remains in evidence). It's expanded greatly under the last two generations, from 6 ha when Michel took it over in 1963. Two thirds of the vineyards are in Mercurey, mostly red, with a significant proportion in premier crus; in addition there are holdings in Rully and Bourgogne, and also some in Aloxe-Corton and Corton. The range is wide, but the real interest here is to compare the premier crus, vinified in the same way for either whites or reds, to demonstrate terroir. Vinification is traditional, with élevage in barriques for 12 months for whites and 16-18 months for reds. For whites, new oak (25%) is used only for the three premier crus; for reds, new oak varies from 15% for the Mercurey to 35% for the five premier crus. The barriques come mostly from the Vosges. There's an unusual policy of holding stocks from older vintages. The reds tend to start out a little hard, which is typical of Mercurey, but soften in an earthy direction after a couple of years; they tend to peak around five or six years after the vintage. The whites in my view tend to be more successful; the Mercurey AOP is a bit straightforward in its flavor spectrum, but the premier crus show a nice sense of reserve to the stone and citrus fruits.

Mercurey

Mercurey, Clos Tonnerre

Mercurey, Vignes de Maillonge

www.domaine-michel-juillot.fr

33 ha; 180,000 bottles

Domaine Bruno Lorenzon

In a back street of Mercurey, the domain itself has a rather dilapidated appearance; at the main entrance there's a notice directing you to the office around the back, which as likely as not will be closed also. Perhaps that is because Bruno Lorenzon is in the vineyards, following up on his favorite saying, "Great berries are 90% of the work." This small domain is now in its third generation under Bruno, who took over in 1997, after prior experience in foreign countries (he has made wine in South Africa and New Zealand as a consultant), and a stint with the tonnellerie in Mercurey (with whom he remains associated). Bruno runs the domain together with his sister Carline. Barriques come from the tonnellerie (there is 20-40% new wood for whites and 15-40% for reds). Élevage lasts from 9 to 18 months. Vineyards are almost exclusively in Mercurey, almost all in premier crus, with 4 ha of red and 1 ha of white (including 6 red and 5 white premier crus); there are also Montagny and Corton Charlemagne. The main holding is a large block (3.7 ha) in the center of the steep limestone slope of the Champs Martin premier cru. This is planted with both Pinot Noir and Chardonnay. The style is modern, tending to good color and extraction. It reaches its peak in the vieilles vignes cuvée Carline from Champs Martin (aged for 19 months in 40% new oak), which tends to have more power rather than greater typicity compared with the regular cuvée.

Mercurey

Mercurey, Les Champs Martin

www.domainelorenzon.com

5 ha; 20,000 bottles

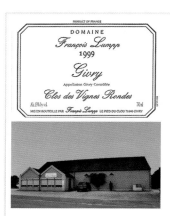

Domaine François Lumpp

Created when François, who had been making wine in Givry since 1977, split from his brother at the family domain in 1991 to create his own domain, this is considered to be one of the most reliable domains in Givry. (His brother's domain is Vincent Lumpp.) It is headquartered in a workmanlike building on the main road through town. Starting with 3.5 ha, the domain has slowly expanded. Today there are 7.5 ha of red and 2 ha of white. The vineyards are exclusively in Givry; there's a village white cuvée and premier cru, and six red premier crus. In fact, the majority of production is in premier crus. François and Isabelle Lumpp have replanted most of their vineyards with closer spacing to reduce yields (using a really dense 11,000 vines per hectare, with vines coming by selection massale from the Côte d'Or). The stated aim is to harvest at "just ripe," rather than over-ripe. The various premier crus are distinguished by position on the slope, with Pied de Clou at the bottom, next to the winery, Crausot at the top, and the best, La Vigne Rouge and Clos du Cras Long, coming from mid-slope. The 2 ha of Vigne Rouge are the most recent acquisition of the estate (in 2007). New oak barriques can be found in the cellar, up to about 30%, but the aim is that the taste of oak should not be evident in the wine. Following plantings in Givry, the focus is on reds, but the domain has an equally high reputation for its whites. Reception can be on the chilly side for visitors.

Givry

www.francoislumpp.com

9 ha; 45,000 bottles

Domaine François Raquillet

François Raquillet is proud of being the eleventh generation in a line of vignerons passing from father to son since the seventeenth century. The domain was formally established in 1963, and François joined his father in 1984; he took over together with his wife Emmanuelle in 1990. By reducing yields (by removing buds at bud break) and modernizing vinification, in particular increasing the emphasis on the quality of oak barrels (using barriques for reds, and 500 liter barrels for whites, with new oak now up to 30%), François revitalized the domain, which is now considered a reference point for Mercurey. Holdings are closely focused on the appellation, with vieilles vignes village level white and red, and then a lieu-dit and premier cru white, and four premier cru reds. The estate vineyards in Mercurey have 8 ha of Pinot Noir and 2 ha of Chardonnay, with an average vine age of 35 years. They are supplemented with purchases of grapes from vineyards that François harvests himself, extending the range to a Bourgogne red, and white Rully premier cru and Meursault. After sorting, reds are fermented in concrete, whites in the 500 liter barrels, with little battonage. Élevage lasts a year, longer for the top premier crus. The red premier crus can show unusual minerality and precision for Mercurey. Although the domaine nominally welcomes visits, in practice visitors are likely to find a notice redirecting them to the communal tasting room in the town if they want to try the wines.

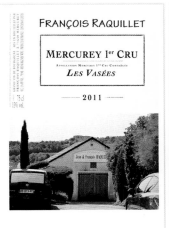

Mercurey

Mercurey, Les Veleys

www.domaine-raquillet.com

10 ha; 50,000 bottles

Domaine Aubert et Pamela De Villaine

In addition to running Domaine de la Romanée Conti, Aubert Villaine, together with his wife Pamela, makes wine at this domain in the Côte Chalonnaise. The Villaines purchased and revived the domain in the seventies, expanding it from its original 8 ha. The domain has been managed since 2000 by Aubert's nephew, Pierre de Benoist. Almost half of the domain's vineyards are in Bouzeron, planted with Aligoté Doré on the tops of the slopes; Chardonnay and Pinot Noir are planted lower. The Aligoté makes the Bouzeron appellation wine. Aubert became one of the spokesmen for Aligoté when he was involved in obtaining appellation status for Bouzeron, and the domain wine is one of the flagships for the appellation, showing citrus fruits, sometimes a touch spicy, light and attractive. The Chardonnay and Pinot Noir are the basis for the various Bourgogne Côte Chalonnaise bottlings, Les Clous and Les Clous Aimé in whites, Les Clous, La Fortune, and La Digoine in reds. There is also a white from Rully. For the Bourgogne and Rully, the house style for Chardonnay shows as a delicious acidity balancing between citrus and stone fruits with a nicely textured finish: both the Les Clous and Les Clous Aimé are a cut above the usual generic Bourgogne Blanc. Among the reds, I prefer the Mercurey to the Bourgogne cuvées. The wines came exclusively from the Côte Chalonnaise until a small parcel was purchased in Santenay in 2011.

Bouzeron

Mercurey, Les Montots

Bourgogne, Les Clous

www.de-villaine.com

23 ha; 110,000 bottles

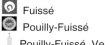

Fuissé

Pouilly-Fuissé

Pouilly-Fuissé, Vers Cras
www.joseph-burrier.com

46 ha; 380,000 bottles

Château de Beauregard

One of the top domains—perhaps the top domain—in Pouilly-Fuissé, Château Beauregard occupies a cluster of old buildings a mile or so out of the town of Fuissé. Beauregard is the largest producer in Pouilly-Fuissé, and also has holdings in Beaujolais. "I feel like a true producer of South Burgundy, I do not see any difference between Beaujolais and here," says Frédéric-Marc Burrier, who is president of the growers association. In that capacity, he is deeply committed to the development of premier crus for the appellation, and his own wines certainly reflect nuances of terroir. There are two communal wines coming from younger and older vines, and then a series of eight single vineyard wines representing different *climats*. These are probably the most ageworthy wines in Pouilly-Fuissé, with the top cuvées maturing for thirty years or so. Winemaking is traditional. "There has been no change here, I am making wines just like my father and grandfather," says Frédéric-Marc. "I am the last to use a mechanical press," he adds, explaining that in his opinion the excessive clarity achieved by pneumatic presses can cause early aging. Wines are fermented in barrique, stay in cask for a year, and are racked only at the end. The same 10-15% new oak is used for all cuvées. Beauregard is known as a white wine producer, but the reds from the top crus of Beaujolais have an unusual refinement and elegance that lifts them well above the usual impression of Gamay.

Mâcon

Viré-Clessé

Viré-Clessé, Vieilles Vignes
www.vireclessebonhomme.fr

10 ha; 80,000 bottles

Domaine André Bonhomme

Aurélien Bonhomme's great grandfather planted 4 ha, and his grandfather was the first to bottle his own wine locally. Since 2001, Aurélian and his parents have run the domain, which presently consists of 35 different parcels in Clessé and Viré. Chickens run around the elegant courtyard. The house is at one side, with a rather striking aviary outside the winery, which is partly under reconstruction; at the other side is a workmanlike warehouse, built three years ago, small but with everything packed in. There's a couple of hectares behind the house, with the remaining vineyards scattered around the hills of Viré and Clessé. Estate production is expanded by purchases of grapes harvested with their own pickers; "80,000 bottles would be a large number for 10 ha!", Aurélian says. All the wines are Viré-Clessé except for a little Mâcon Villages (sold in the U.S.) and some Crémant de Bourgogne. The classic part of production is about five wines. Style varies across the range. Les Pierres Blanches (vinified in stainless steel) and Les Brenillons (vinified in foudres) are intended for relatively early consumption, within five to seven years. Cuvée Spéciale (the major part of production) is a blend using both stainless steel and (old) oak; and Vieilles Vignes increases oak usage to 70%, with less than 20% new oak. These are intended to age for fifteen years or so. Where oak is used, "We are moving from barriques to 400 liter casks to get more harmony," Aurélian explains.

Domaine Daniel et Martine Barraud

Established in 1890, the domain is now run by the fourth and fifth generations, with Daniel and Martine Barraud helped by their son Julien. The domain is located on the slope of the Roche de Vergisson, facing the famous formation of the Roche de Solutré, at the northernmost and highest point of Pouilly-Fuissé. Most of the vineyards are in Pouilly-Fuissé, around Vergisson, but there are also wines from St. Véran and Mâcon. Although the domain is small, the focus is on single vineyard wines, with no less than six cuvées from Pouilly-Fuissé, two St. Vérans, and different wines from various villages in Mâcon. All harvesting is manual (sometimes involving several passes through the vineyard), grapes from each parcel are vinified separately, with immediate pressing, brief settling, and then fermentation and malolactic in barrique, followed by élevage for 10-15 months, and bottling without fining or filtration. Use of new oak depends on the cuvée. The Pouilly-Fuissé Alliance Vergisson is a blend from several parcels; the single vineyard cuvées range from La Roche (the most mineral from 35-year old vines growing at the highest altitudes) to En Bulands (from 80-year-old vines, always the last to be harvested, and the richest). The St. Véran En Crèches is fruity from a southeast-facing vineyard, whereas Les Pommards comes from older vines (planted in 1963) on a northeast-facing slope, and is matured in oak. The style of the Pouilly-Fuissés is a classic representation of the appellation.

Vergisson

Pouilly-Fuissé

Pouilly-Fuissé, Les Crays

www.domainebarraud.com

11 ha; 60,000 bottles

Domaine Ferret

Now part of Jadot's expansion into southern Burgundy, Domaine Ferret started as a family business in 1840. In the present era, Mme. Jeanne Ferret, who took over after 1974 when her husband died, was one of the first to focus on single vineyards. There was some modernization when her daughter, Colette, took over in 1993. In 2006, when Colette died, there was no family to inherit; Jadot had been buying must from Ferret for fifty years, and bought the estate in 2008. There is a lovely courtyard with the old winery just close to the church, and the vineyards of Le Clos and Les Perrières are on the slope right behind, but wine is now made in a new gravity-feed cellar built a few hundred meters away. The old cellar had the capacity only to vinify 10 ha worth of grapes, because Mme. Ferret sold the rest, but now all the grapes are vinified in the new cellar. Mme. Ferret divided the wines into three groups: communal, Tête de Cru, and Hors Classe. In the communal wines, Autour de Fuissé comes from around Fuissé, and Sous Vergisson comes from Vergisson. As Tête de Crus there are Le Clos, Clos de Prouges, and Les Perrières; and as Hors Classe there are Les Ménétrières and Tournant de Pouilly. Mme. Ferret used to prefer the fuller weight of wines from Fuissé rather than the more delicate wines of Vergisson, and usually harvested late to increase power. Since Audrey Braccini took over as winemaker for Jadot, harvesting has moved earlier, and the style has lightened.

Fuissé

Pouilly-Fuissé

Pouilly-Fuissé, Le Clos

www.domaine-ferret.com

19 ha; 80,000 bottles

Fuissé

Pouilly-Fuissé

Pouilly-Fuissé, Le Clos
www.chateau-fuisse.fr

36 ha; 150,000 bottles

Château-Fuissé

The Vincent family have been making wine here since 1862: Antoine Vincent, who took over from his father in 2003, is the fifth generation. There are more than a hundred vineyard plots, mostly in Fuissé with some in Pouilly. Holdings have changed little since the addition of Les Combettes twenty years ago. Soils are heterogeneous. "Even in Les Clos, which is 2.5 ha based on limestone soil just behind the winery, there are differences from top to bottom, so the top is vinified in 1- or 2-year-old barriques to respect the minerality, but at the bottom we can use more new oak," Antoine says. Vinification varies with the vintage: malolactic fermentation depends on the acid balance, and some vintages have extensive battonage while others have little. About 20 lots are vinified individually; the single vineyards remain separate, but others are blended. There are two cuvées at Pouilly-Fuissé village level, Tête de Cuvée and Vieilles Vignes (from 50- to 80-year-old vines in nine plots planted by Antoine's grandfather). There are three single vineyard bottlings, Les Brûlées (relatively powerful), Les Combettes (relatively delicate), and Le Clos (one of the top cuvées of the appellation). The overall style is firm and full-flavored. In addition to Pouilly-Fuissé, there's some St. Véran and Mâcon, and most recently some Juliénas from Beaujolais (Domaine De La Conseillère). There's also a negociant business under the Vincent Signature label with a comparable range of wines.

Milly Lamartine

Mâcon

Mâcon-Milly-Lamartine
www.comtes-lafon.fr

21 ha; 140,000 bottles

Domaine Héritiers du Comte Lafon

This is not, as its name might suggest, an old domain inherited in the Comte Lafon family, which for several generations has run a top domain in Meursault. In fact, it was an existing domain in Milly Lamartine that Dominique Lafon purchased and renamed in 1999, when he was the first producer from the Côte d'Or to expand into Mâcon. Further vineyards in Uchizy were added in 2003. The latest addition to the range in 2009 was Viré-Clessé, coming from the vineyards of Château de Viré. Today the vineyard holdings are divided into three roughly equal parts in Milly-Lamartine, Chardonnay-Uchizy, and Viré-Clessé, so that now the domain produces Mâcon, Mâcon-Villages, Mâcon-Milly-Lamartine, and Viré Clessé, together with five single vineyard wines. Production is typically Mâconnais, with the basic wines aged in stainless steel, and some large wood containers used at the upper end. Dominique describes his objectives as, "I'm not going down to Mâcon to make little Meursault. I'm going to make great Mâcon." The wines are perhaps a little richer than typical for the region, but retain subregional character with the Viré-Clessé, for example, more powerful than the Mâcons. The top wine is the Clos de la Crochette in Mâcon-Chardonnay, a 2.6 ha vineyard originally planted by monks at the Abbey of Cluny. Prices are around a tenth of Lafon's more famous wines from Meursault, but comparisons would be foolish.

Domaine Saumaize-Michelin

Located in view of the famous rock of Vergisson, the domain goes back some generations under the name of Saumaize, but is called Saumaize-Michelin to reflect Roger Saumaize's partnership with his wife Christine (formerly Michelin). The domain started with 4 ha which Roger received from his father when he returned from military service in 1977. (His brother also has a domain under the name of Jacques and Nathalie Saumaize.) Roger constructed a new cellar, opposite the family house, in 1991. Wines come from Mâcon, St. Véran, and Pouilly-Fuissé, with 14 cuvées altogether. Two cuvées under the name Fleur, a Mâcon Villages and Pouilly-Fuissé, are vinified in cuve, the rest in barriques, with 10-25% new oak. Élevage lasts 10 months. The St. Véran is divided into Les Crèches and a Vieilles Vignes cuvée. The wines from Mâcon and St. Véran are generally considered to exceed the quality level of the appellations, but the cuvées from Pouilly-Fuissé are the most interesting; the domain made its first cuvée from an individual parcel in 1985, but following the general trend, the Saumaizes are now introducing more individual cuvées with different origins. Among them, Pentacrine is a blend, Vignes Blanches comes specifically from the village of Vergisson, and Ampélopsis is the top cuvée made by blending the best barrels from each area. Given élevage for two years, Ampélopsis is a big wine for Pouilly-Fuissé.

 Fuissé

 Pouilly-Fuissé

Pouilly-Fuissé, Vignes Blanches
www.domaine-saumaize-michelin.com

9 ha; 50,000 bottles

Domaine La Soufrandière

Only a single hectare at the time, the estate was purchased by the Bret family in 1947, but until the late 1990s, grapes were sold to the cooperative. Today the domain is run by three brothers, who produced their first vintage from La Soufrandière in 2000; they created the negociant business of Bret Brothers in 2001. Overall production is divided equally between estate and negociant activity. A modern cave was built in 2000, and doubled in size in 2011. Each wine for Bret Brothers comes from a single grower (harvested by Soufrandière's pickers); specializing in micro-cuvées (from 900 to 4,000 bottles), they make about 18 bottlings. Estate vineyards are around the property, which looks out over the Saône Valley from just behind the Vinzelles village at 225 m elevation. The 4 ha of Pouilly Vinzelles (Les Quartz) are just behind the house, immediately to the west is the small plot of Les Longeays, and there's a hectare of Macon Vinzelles coming from the bottom of the slope, below Pouilly Vinzelles. Wines are aged for a year in barriques: "All barrels are old, 5-15 years, we don't want any new oak," says Jean-Philippe Bret. The estate wines become increasingly subtle going up the hierarchy. Mâcon-Vinzelles is overtly fruity, Pouilly-Vinzelles shows more restraint and adds some citrus, Les Longeays shows more variety and restraint, and Les Quarts becomes hard to place between stone and citrus fruits. The Bret Brothers wines, which cover a wider range, are a little less intense.

 Vinzelles

Pouilly-Vinzelles

Pouilly-Vinzelles, Les Quarts
www.bretbrothers.com

6 ha; 30,000 bottles

 Clessé

 Viré-Clessé

Mâcon, Cuvée Tradition
www.bongran.com

27 ha; 60,000 bottles

Domaine Jean Thévenet

Headquarters for the three domains under Jean Thévenet (not to be confused with Jean-Paul Thévenet in Beaujolais or Jean-Claude Thévenet at Pierreclos) is a modern utilitarian warehouse in Clessé. There is the unusual policy here of dividing the vineyards according to terroirs into domains, so each domain represents one terroir (defined by the proportion of clay to calcareous soil). All are in Viré-Clessé. Domaine de la Bongran, the largest and best known, was the first of the domains, started two generations back, and then expanded by Jean Thévenet, who was one of the first to introduce organic methods in the region. Domaine Emilian Gillet (the original family name) was founded in 1988 with vines that had been rented. And the smallest, Domaine de Roally, was purchased when its owner retired in 2000 by Gauthier Thévenet, Jean's son. All three domains are worked in similar ways, but with differences resulting from their characters: fermentation is slower, and élevage is longer for Domaine de la Bongran, so its wines are released later than the others. The wine from Domaine de la Bongran has an exotic quality, the fruits are pushed to the limits of ripeness, and there's a distinct impression of sweetness (the 2006 had 5.5 g/l residual sugar). Perhaps this is the terroir of ripeness. "Wines from this terroir always have residual sugar. But if it's balanced, you don't feel it," says Jean Thévenet. Sometimes there's even a late harvest, botrytized wine.

Sologny

Mâcon

Pouilly-Fuissé, La Roche

Chablis, Montée de Tonnerre
www.verget-sa.fr

0 ha; 360,000 bottles

Maison Verget

"In a good year we make about 55 different wines at Verget. Most of the wines are based on grapes from several growers although for Côte d'Or it may be from a single grower because quantities are small," explains Jean-Marie Guffens. "The philosophy is to make wine that is as good as possible within very complicated rules of the region. Taking in mind that we always prefer precision—we try to make the wines as pure as possible." Verget buys only grapes or must, with the range of cuvées changing from year to year. All wines stay in wood for 8 months and in concrete for 8 months. "You see terroir more clearly if you treat all wines the same," Jean-Marie says. Created in 1990, Verget is now part of a trilogy of holdings, also including the Guffens-Heynen domain in Mâcon (established in 1979), and Château des Tourettes (purchased in 1997 in the Lubéron). Verget's range includes southern Burgundy (Mâcon, St. Véran, and many cuvées from Pouilly-Fuissé), Chablis (from village wines to Grand Cru), and the Côte d'Or. Verget demonstrates Jean-Marie's view of the potential of an appellation rather than others' historic view of it, with flavorful Pouilly-Fuissé and ripe, intense, Chablis. The wines from the Guffens-Heynen domain really show what can be done in the region. They have a flavor interest and complexity and texture that in a blind tasting might well be taken for a higher level appellation; in fact it is that deep texture, reminiscent of the Côte d'Or, that for me is Verget's trademark.

Domaine Louis et Claude Desvignes

Devoted exclusively to Morgon, the domain is built around a courtyard just off one of the oldest streets in the village of Villié-Morgon. "We are at least the eighth generation, perhaps more because records were lost in the Revolution," says Louis-Benoît Desvignes. We had our tasting in an old cave. "This is the barrel cellar, but we don't use any barrels in my family, we think cement tanks are more interesting for what we are looking for. We have a lot of interesting flavors in the soils of Morgon, we want to preserve them. The wine is left alone in tank for 10 months or more with no racking until bottling," Louis-Benoît explains. Depending on the vintage, there may be four or five cuvées, including the Côte du Py, where the Desvignes have 5 ha, half on the top of the hill and the rest in parcels lower down. A Vieilles Vignes cuvée comes from two small parcels of hundred-year-old vines on the hill. House style shows a linear purity to the fruits; some people might be inclined to call this minerality. The cuvées reflect their terroirs. The Vieilles Vignes has concentration as well as purity, and I might be inclined to place it in Moulin-à-Vent in a blind tasting or perhaps to think about Pommard. The Javernières, from a parcel in Côte du Py, has a softer impression than the Côte du Py itself: "They used to say 'Pinoté' to mean that some wines have a Burgundian character, and this is a very good example," says Louis-Benoît. Indeed, the subtlety of the cuvées is reminiscent of a tasting in Burgundy.

 Villié Morgon

Morgon

Morgon, Côte de Py
www.louis-claude-desvignes.com

11 ha; 50,000 bottles

Georges Duboeuf

Duboeuf's headquarters at Romanèche-Thorins, on the eastern edge of the Beaujolais near Moulin-à-Vent, represent a vast enterprise, signposted as Hameau Duboeuf, with a museum, tasting room, bookshop, and all the facilities you could want. Hameau Duboeuf makes it sound smaller than it really is: there are villages in the Beaujolais that are smaller than this. Signifying the discrepancy between Duboeuf and other producers, the vast winery occupies more than 6 ha—around the size of the average producer in Beaujolais. Duboeuf produces Gamay everywhere it is grown in France, including Beaujolais, Mâconnais, Pays d'Oc, Côtes du Rhône, Ardèche, and Touraine. Famous for his tasting ability, Georges still tastes every wine that is bottled. "I spend two hours tasting every day," he says. The vast range extends from Nouveau, through Beaujolais and Beaujolais Villages, to the Crus. The Flower series is the best known, but there is an increasing number of individual cuvées indicated by the origin of the grower. The model remains as it started, as a negociant buying grapes (for whites the grower presses the grapes and Duboeuf takes the must). The top line, Cuvée Prestige, is an assemblage of the best lots, depending on the year, but is available only in France. The house style (insofar as a style can be defined for such a wide range) is for open, forward fruits, giving a fresh impression on the palate with supple tannins in the background. The Fleurie is perhaps the epitome of this style.

 Romanèche-Thorins

Beaujolais

Fleurie, Rein de Gré
www.duboeuf.com

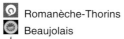

 0 ha; 22,000,000 bottles

Beaujolais

Villié Morgon

Morgon

Morgon, Côte du Py

16 ha; 100,000 bottles

Domaine Jean Foillard

One of the founder members of the "gang of four" who modernized Beaujolais, Jean Foillard took over his father's domain in 1980. The house (and winery) is an old farm that Jean and Agnes Foillard renovated, on the main road out of Villié-Morgon, close to the Côte du Py; it now also offers bed and breakfast for visitors. Most of the vineyards are in Morgon, with the largest holding on Côte du Py; there's also a vineyard in the lieu-dit Corcelette in the north of Morgon that was inherited from Agnes's parents. There are smaller holdings in Fleurie, and just outside Morgon in Beaujolais (which is the source for the Beaujolais Nouveau). There are six cuvées altogether, with three from Morgon. Vinification is traditional (using semi-carbonic maceration), but maturation occurs in old barriques (for Côte du Py) or foudres (for Corcelette). No sulfur is added during vinification. The Morgons are distinguished by terroir and vine age: the Morgon *tout court* is an assemblage; cuvée Corcelette, the lightest of the single vineyard wines, comes from 80-year-old vines on sandstone; Côte du Py, by far Foillard's best known cuvée, comes from vines of varying age on schist and granite; and cuvée 3.14 (which carries a jazzy pi sign on the label, and has been made since 2003 only in the best vintages) comes from the oldest vines (a hundred years old) on the Côte du Py. The Foillard wines have a lightness of touch that has often led to comparisons with Chambolle Musigny.

Romanèche-Thorins

Moulin-à-Vent

Moulin-à-Vent, Clos de Thorins

www.chateau-des-jacques.fr

85 ha; 320,000 bottles

Château des Jacques

For years, Château des Jacques, under the ownership of the Thorin family, produced a single wine that was the best in Moulin-à-Vent, quite Burgundian in its capacity to develop with age. The estate was purchased by negociant Louis Jadot in 1996, and then in 2001 Jadot extended the range by adding the Bellevue estate in Morgon. The wines are vinified following Burgundian practice (destemming and avoiding carbonic maceration) and spend several months maturing in barriques, including new oak (varying from 25% to 100% depending on the cuvée). Winemaker Guillaume de Castelnau seems to be trying to spark a renewal of the region with what he views as a return to tradition. "In 1916, a bottle of Moulin-à-Vent fetched the same price as a bottle of Chambolle-Musigny. In 1895, nine coopers lived in the village and made barrels for all the local growers. There was no such thing as carbonic maceration," he says. Today the Moulin-à-Vent and Morgon are at the base of a hierarchy, with a series of five single vineyard wines from Moulin-à-Vent, and three from Morgon. Jadot divide these into Clos and Grands Clos, with the top wines being the Côte du Py in Morgon, and a trio in Moulin-à-Vent: Grand Clos de Rochegrès (at the top of the slope opposite the windmill), Clos du Grand Carquelin (a sandy parcel with lots of manganese in the soil), and La Roche (right under the famous windmill). The single vineyard wines account for about a third of production.

Domaine Paul & Eric Janin

"There's neither minor wine nor grand wine. My cuvées express first of all their terroirs of origin," says Eric Janin. There are five cuvées: Beaujolais Villages, both red and white, under the name of Domaine des Vignes des Jumeaux, and three Moulin-à-Vents, one a blend from five plots, another representing a selection of lots from the lieu-dit Le Tremblay, and the third from old vines in the lieu-dit Les Greneriers. Old is a relative term here as the vines in Le Tremblay are more than forty years old, and those in Les Greneriers go over eighty years. Whether press reports attributing the quality to the high manganese in the soils are to be believed is uncertain, but the style focuses on precision. "Discrete" is the word that is often used to describe both the producer and the wine. Production is always small here, but when yields were especially low in 2012 there was only a single Moulin-à-Vent, with the lots from Le Tremblay and Les Greneriers declassified into the single bottling. The Beaujolais Villages comes from old vines on soils that are relatively heavy in clay. The domain started in the 1930s when the plot in Le Tremblay was purchased, and then in 1967 the plot in Les Greneriers was added. Eric Janin started working with his father Paul in 1983 and is now fully in charge. Vinification is traditional, using whole bunches, and maturation in old foudres lasts 8 to 11 months, depending on the cuvée, except for Greneriers, which matures in demi-muids.

Romanèche Thorins
Moulin-à-Vent
www.domaine-paul-janin.fr

8 ha; 40,000 bottles

Domaine Jean-Claude Lapalu

Jean-Claude takes Beaujolais to the extremes of late picking and high alcohol. Usually in Beaujolais an elevated alcohol level indicates chaptalization, but here it indicates extreme ripeness. In the 2009 vintage, some of the wines were labeled at 14.5% alcohol. (Levels came back down to 13% in 2011.) Aside from the Beaujolais Villages Vieilles Vignes cuvée, the emphasis is on Brouilly and Côte de Brouilly, where there are eight separate parcels of vines. Viticulture is biodynamic, and yields are low, usually under 35 hl/ha. There are wines from each cru, cuvées from Vieilles Vignes, and the Croix de Rameaux from a single parcel near the winery in Brouilly. Altogether there are six cuvées. Jean-Claude took over the domain from his father in 1996. Grapes had previously been sold to the cooperative, but Jean-Claude started making wine in 2000. His wines are unusual for Brouilly, which usually isn't particularly well distinguished from Beaujolais Villages, but here there is distinctly more structure. Vinification is traditional, but there is reduced use of carbonic maceration for Côte de Brouilly and Croix des Rameaux, which are matured in old barriques. There are experiments with maturing wine in amphorae. Winemaking follows natural precepts, including minimal use of sulfur, but the style is quite different from the "gang of four", giving a much richer impression. Some critics have described the style as "Beaujolais meets Priorat."

Saint Étienne la Varenne
Brouilly
Brouilly, Vieilles Vignes

12 ha; 60,000 bottles

Beaujolais

Domaine Marcel Lapierre

The name of Marcel Lapierre became a symbol of the revival of "serious" wine in the Beaujolais. The domain itself existed before the Revolution, but took its modern form after phylloxera under Marcel Lapierre's grandfather. It was among the first in the region to bottle its own wine. Marcel Lapierre initiated the move away from the image of Beaujolais as following semi-industrial techniques for making cheap and cheerful wine. Located in the town of Villié-Morgon, the domain is divided into two separate sets of buildings; we tasted the wines in a courtyard surrounded by buildings constructed just after the Revolution. Today the domain is run by Mathieu Lapierre, who is continuing his father's focus on natural winemaking. The domain is completely in Morgon, but some of the production from young vines is declassified to Vin de France; "Young Gamay is very productive," explains Mathieu. When the year is sufficiently good there is a Vieilles Vignes bottling; this is the cuvée Marcel Lapierre. Sulfur is always low, but some cuvées are bottled entirely without any. There's always a difference. "There's no rule, it depends on the vintage whether the wine with or without sulfur has more generosity," Mathieu says. My impression most often is that keeping sulfur down increases expression of fruit purity. Certainly the house style is towards a certain linear purity of fruits, quite tight and precise when young, and needing some time to open out.

Villié Morgon
Beaujolais
Morgon
www.marcel-lapierre.com

16 ha; 105,000 bottles

Domaine Coudert Clos de La Roilette

The winery is located on a high point with views over the towns of Fleurie and Moulin-à-Vent. A workmanlike group of buildings is surrounded by vineyards; about half of the holdings are here, with the rest in Fleurie except for 1 ha about 15 km away in Brouilly. Alain Coudert's father bought the domain in 1967, a small part of a 100 ha estate that was being sold. "We have a terroir that is a little different from the rest of the commune; it's granite but it's older and more decomposed. And when you get up to the border with Moulin-à-Vent, the soils have more clay and give more structured wine," Alain explains. (Before the appellations were created, some of the wine had actually been labeled as Moulin-à-Vent.) To get a more typical Fleurie Alain usually includes lots from the other holdings. There are usually three cuvées of Fleurie: Clos de Roilette is an assemblage, Cuvée Tardive is a Vieilles Vignes, coming from 80-year-old vines close to the winery (tardive indicates that the wine is intended for aging), and Griffe de Marquis comes from the same vines as Cuvée Tardive, but is matured in barriques of 6-year wood for one year. Cuvée Christal, made in some years, is the antithesis of Tardive: made from young vines for early drinking. Vinification is traditional (using semi carbonic maceration). The house style is relatively sturdy: the wines are firmer than you usually find with Fleurie, and, at least when young, do not have that open fleshiness.

Fleurie
Fleurie

13 ha; 55,000 bottles

Domaine des Souchons

The domain has been in the family since 1752 and has vineyards in 47 parcels scattered all over the Morgon appellation. The winery is in a functional group of buildings on the main road outside Villié Morgon. They describe the domain as "resolutely Morgon." "We vinify separately and blend at assemblage," says Baptiste Condemine, who started to modernize things when he came into the estate in 2008. "We should have more cuvées, my father did one, I do two, we should have five. We understand all the different *climats* of Morgon." In addition to the estate wines coming from Morgon, a small negociant activity (SARL 1752) extends the range into the other crus as well as Beaujolais and Beaujolais Villages. In Morgon, the general bottling is cuvée Lys (extended by a bottling under screwcap called cuvée Tradition that's overtly for current drinking). The second major cuvée is Claude Pillet, which Baptiste introduced in 2009, named for his grandfather. This is a Vieilles Vignes bottling, coming from vines that are more than a hundred years old at Javernières on the Côte du Py. Vinification starts in concrete for one month, then the wine is pressed off into barrel before fermentation has completed; fermentation is followed by MLF, and then a third is racked off to barriques of new oak, and the rest is matured in cuve. From the 2012 vintage there is potentially a new cuvée, matured entirely in barriques, from the Grand Cras terroir.

Villié Morgon

Morgon

Morgon, Cuvée Claude Pillet

www.domaine-souchons.com

14 ha; 80,000 bottles

Domaine des Terres Dorées

The domain is located almost at the southern tip of Beaujolais, but the best known wines come from holdings of the crus in the north. Jean-Paul Brun's grandfather created the domain. "It's always been a zone of polyculture here; my father practiced polyculture. I took over the domain with 4 ha and stopped the polyculture and started to plant white varieties, and then in the 1980s I planted Pinot Noir." Today there are 9 ha of Chardonnay, 1 ha Roussanne, and 2.5 ha Pinot Noir; the rest is Gamay. The Chardonnay can be labeled as Beaujolais Blanc or Bourgogne, the Pinot Noir is Bourgogne AOP, and the Roussanne is a Vin de France. The Gamay includes 17 ha in crus, including Moulin-à-Vent, Fleurie, and Côte de Brouilly. Beaujolais l'Ancien comes from very old vines. The crus are managed by lutte raisonnée but in the south the domain is organic. Vinification is entirely conventional (with no semi carbonic maceration). The house style here shows serious wines, without any of the false aromatics that can pump up young Beaujolais and make it superficially attractive when young, but which don't really age in an interesting way. These wines follow the Burgundian model, and even if Gamay mostly doesn't lend itself to making true Vins de Garde, they move in that direction. Jean-Paul has expanded his production into negociant territory: "To satisfy the demand from people looking for 'true Beaujolais'," he says. He also makes some late harvest botrytized wines.

Charnay

Beaujolais

Fleurie

47 ha; 300,000 bottles

Beaujolais

Château-Chalon

Château-Chalon

www.berthet-bondet.net

11 ha; 40,000 bottles

Domaine Berthet-Bondet

Jean Berthet-Bondet started the domain in 1985; his family was not pre-viously in wine. "I was attracted by wines and agronomie, I started, I worked abroad, my family had always liked Château-Chalon. The price of vineyards was attractive. People were pulling out vineyards; it was possible to buy." The Berthet-Bondets bought a sixteenth century house with caves underneath, and built a modern winery. Vineyards are pres-ently being converted to organic. The domain has 11 ha, mostly rather broken up, half in Château-Chalon and half in Côtes de Jura. It is more or less equally divided between Chardonnay and Savagnin. There is 1 ha of Poulsard and Trousseau and a tiny parcel of Pinot Noir. The aim is to look for finesse rather than rusticity. Initially there was only wine, under voile in traditional manner, but now there is a Crémant (unusually char-acterful for the region), a red, and a range of both "classique" (modern) and "tradition" (oxidized under voile) white wines. The type of wine is stated only on the back label, as ouillé or vinifié sur voile. The classique wines include Chardonnay or Savagnin from the Côtes de Jura; the oxi-dized wines are an assemblage of Savagnin and Chardonnay from Côtes du Jura (the Tradition cuvée), Savagnin from Côtes de Jura, and Vin Jaune from Château-Chalon. There is also a Vin de Paille and a Macvin. I find the oxidized styles more interesting than the classique, and the best wine by far is the Château-Chalon.

Arlay

Château-Chalon

Château-Chalon

www.cavesjeanbourdy.com

10 ha

Domaine Jean Bourdy

This is surely one of the most, if not the most, traditional domains in the Jura. Jean-François Bourdy is the fifteenth generation. The house was originally just a kitchen and bedroom, and the sixteenth century caves below are still in use. The vineyards are in Arlay except for some in Châ-teau-Chalon. "We have documentation for the production methods for all the old wines, and we follow exactly the same procedures as a hundred years ago; no experimentation or new things," says Jean-François. Bottles have been kept since the eighteenth century, and the library now has 3,000 bottles; vintages for sale go back to the nineteenth century. How many cuvées do you make, I asked? "We don't make cuvées. We make separate wines: red and white from the Côtes de Jura, Vin Jaune from Château-Chalon, and Vin de Paille, and Macvin, including one made by a (written) recipe from 1579 (which includes spices and herbs). The tradi-tion in the Jura is to have an extended range, but there are no cuvées or vins de cépage." The tradition at Bourdy is to keep wines for at least four years in old tonneaux before bottling; there are no young wines here. "Never, never, never any new oak: it would be an error because old oak is neutral." The red ("Our village is considered the leader for vin rouge") is traditional to the extent of cofermenting Pinot Noir, Poulsard, and Trousseau; the Côtes de Jura is Chardonnay; the Vin Jaune from Château-Chalon is the most concentrated of all the wines.

Domaine Ganevat

After working for eight years in Burgundy, Jean-François took over the domain in 1998. Ganevat's cellars run under a row of houses in the main street of a hamlet at the southern tip of the Jura. Extended little by little, the caves are old at one end, but run into a new extension. Vineyards are in many separate parcels. Jean-François has increased the size of the domain, but only a little, and has adopted Burgundian methods for viticulture and vinification. Almost all wines are made in the modern style (ouillé). The domain has all five cépages authorized for Côtes de Jura, and also other cépages, which go into Vins de France. In fact, Jean-François is acquiring a reputation for rescuing little known indigenous varieties as well as for a general quality exceeding the usual character of Côtes de Jura. The wines offer good expressions of the typicities of the varieties for the region, but for some reason, I was not blown away by them in the way their reputation would have led me to expect, perhaps because all the wines in an extensive tasting were the 2012 vintage from barrel: they may just need more time to express themselves. Bottled wines develop a character of minerality and salinity that is not evident in barrel samples. Those I like best are the Chardonnays from limestone terroirs, which although matured in barriques, resemble unoaked Chablis, at their best perhaps richer and more concentrated. The reds taste sturdier than you would expect from the use of carbonic maceration.

Rotalier

Côtes de Jura

Côtes de Jura, Cuvée Florine, Chardonnay

10 ha; 40,000 bottles

Domaine Macle

The Macle family come from barrel makers, and practiced polyculture when they came to Château-Chalon in 1850. In the 1960s they turned exclusively to wine, although the sixteenth century caves make the domain feel much older. Now regarded as one of the oldest producers, the domain has choice vineyard holdings, often on extremely steep slopes. Production here is focused exclusively on white wine; Jean Macle was regarded as one of the most knowledgeable producers of the oxidized style. He was followed by his son Laurent in 1995. The vineyards are divided into 8 ha of Chardonnay in Côtes de Jura and 4 ha of Savagnin in Château-Chalon. Alcoholic fermentation is followed by malolactic fermentation in cuve; then the wine is matured in barriques from Burgundy. There are four wines: the Côtes de Jura (80% Chardonnay and 20% Savagnin), Château-Chalon, a Crémant, and Macvin. Jean Macle's reputation verged on reclusive, and with Madame Macle as the gatekeeper, it was always difficult to make appointments here, which may add to the mystique, but the domain is widely regarded as a reference point for Château-Chalon. Jean Macle's stated view was that Château-Chalon should not be drunk until 10 years after release, which is to say sixteen years after the vintage. The wine is then expected to last for a half century. All wines were produced in the traditional oxidized style until Laurent Macle introduced the first ouillé wine in 2007.

Château-Chalon

Château-Chalon

12 ha; 40,000 bottles

Jura-Savoie

Domaine Louis Magnin

Louis and Béatrice Magnin have acquired a high reputation since taking over this family domain in Savoie in 1973, when it consisted of only 4 ha. Located near Montmélian, in the valley of the Combe de Savoie, right under the massive mountain of Bauges, vineyards are on steep slopes. The domain is certified organic but follows biodynamic principles. A new cave was constructed in 2006. The wines represent the traditions of Savoie: in the whites are Roussette de Savoie, Vin de Savoie Jacquère, and Chignin-Bergeron (100% Roussanne); there is a special cuvée, Grand Orgue, from the two oldest parcels of Roussanne. The reds are the Vin de Savoie Gamay and Arbin Mondeuse. The two major cuvées of the house are the regular Mondeuse (more than half of production), and the Roussanne (around a third). Jacquère and Roussanne are vinified in stainless steel, while the Roussette uses a small proportion of 500 liter barrels. There are three cuvées of Arbin Mondeuse: La Rouge, vinified in steel and then matured in a large old wooden fermenter; La Brova, matured in barriques; and the Vieilles Vignes: there is also a special cuvée, Tout un Monde, from the oldest Mondeuse vines. Occasionally there are sweet wines. The domain made its reputation for its specialty of producing Mondeuse as a serious wine, although the variety is inevitably on the rustic side, especially when young, but the top cuvées become more elegant if given time.

 Arbin
 Arbin Mondeuse
 Chignin-Bergeron, Grand Orgue
www.domainelouismagnin.fr

8 ha; 30,000 bottles

Domaine Jacques Puffeney

Having started as a cheese maker, and then slowly building up the domain with vineyards around the town of Arbois (starting from a tiny plot owned by his father), Jacques Puffeney is regarded as a seminal producer in the region, sometimes called "the Pope of the Jura." After fifty years of making wine, still working alone, it became necessary to reduce the size of the domain in 2012, and with no one to succeed him, in 2014 Jacques sold to Guillaume d'Angerville (of Volnay), who will presumably include the vineyards in his Jura Domaine du Pélican. Holdings have been divided between red and white, with all the traditional varieties. Puffeney is known especially for his Trousseau, with his location in Montagny Les Arsures considered a prime site for the variety. Winemaking is traditional, with natural yeasts, extended aging in old foudres, and minimal use of sulfur. The whites have no topping up and so develop in the oxidized style, but show a subtle hand, almost something of a half way house between the full traditional style and the modern. The Chardonnay, for example, has a mineral quality with a touch of those delicious savory notes of fenugreek. There are almost a dozen cuvées in all, including several special cuvées: Sacha, which is a blend of Chardonnay and Savagnin; Poulsard "M", which comes from vineyards in the home village; the Trousseau Les Bérangères, which comes from a tiny plot of 35-year-old vines planted by selection massale; and of course Vin Jaune.

 Montigny lès Arsures
 Jura
 Arbois Trousseau, Les Bérangères

6 ha; 35,000 bottles

Domaine Rolet Père Et Fils

The estate was created in 1945 by Désiré Rolet, and today is run by four siblings of the second generation, Bernard (viticulturalist), Guy (wine-maker), Pierre and Éliane (marketing). This is the second largest, and most extended, domain in the Jura. It's a go-ahead operation with a tasting room in the center of the town of Arbois. About half the vines are more than fifty years old; the others are regarded as young vines. Plantings are divided roughly equally between white and black varieties. There are vineyards in Arbois (at 36 ha comprising just over half), the Côtes de Jura (21 ha), and most recently an addition of 3 ha in l'Etoile. There is a correspondingly large range of wines. The nine white wine cuvées comprise four Arbois, four Côtes du Jura, and an Étoile; they include Savagnin, and blends of Savagnin with Chardonnay, in both ouillé and oxidized styles. The Étoile is pure Chardonnay. The reds mostly come from Arbois, including separate monovarietal cuvées for Pinot Noir, Poulsard, and Trousseau, as well as Les Grandvaux (an equal blend of Pinot Noir and Poulsard), and a classic assemblage of all three. There are also several Crémants, as well as Vin Jaune and Vin de Paille from Arbois (and of course Macvin). The modern facility includes stainless steel cuves and barriques, including some new wood, which are used depending on the cuvée. The wines are regarded as being among the most reliable of the Jura.

 Arbois
www.rolet-arbois.com

62 ha; 350,000 bottles

Domaine André et Mireille Tissot

One of the most interesting producers in the Jura, Stéphane Tissot has built a great reputation since he took over the family domain a few years ago. It started with 10 ha in 1950 with Stéphane's grandfather, who was a vigneron. The focus is on terroir. "Land is not expensive, although vines of quality cost more." There are 42 ha in Arbois, 2 ha in Château-Chalon, and 6 ha on Côtes de Jura. Vineyards are a mix of large holdings and some very small parcels. All the vineyards are maintained by selection massale. Plantings are split equally between black and white grapes, but there is less red wine production because many of the black grapes, from the less interesting terroirs, go into Crémant, which is a quarter of production. There are 36 cuvées altogether. Chardonnay is vinified by parcel to give seven different cuvées. There are three Vin Jaunes. "We look for finesse and elegance, there are many people who look for power." It's very lively here, there are lots of experiments. One of Stéphane's most common words is experimentation, and if there's one word to describe Tissot, it's originality. Most of the white wine production is Chardonnay, and the house style offers a smoky, spicy introduction, following to a palate varying from mineral to more opulent depending on the terroir, with a finish that tends to a savory impression in the direction of tarragon. The whites have a distinctive savory orientation. The reds are light and fresh, and at their best can show an earthy character.

 Montigny lès Arsures
Jura
Arbois Vin Jaune, La Vasée
www.stephane-tissot.com

50 ha; 140,000 bottles

Jura-Savoie

Château Carbonnieux

One of the largest properties in Pessac-Léognan, Château Carbonnieux was rescued from disrepair by Marc Perrin in 1956. His grandsons Eric and Philbert run the domain today. The estate has a history of ups and downs: it was successful and as large as 115 ha in the seventeenth century, fell into disrepair and was sold to the Benedictines, then brought back up to 50 ha and gained high repute in the eighteenth century. The major vineyards are in a very large block of gravel terraces sloping down from the château. Black grape varieties are only just over half of all plantings. The terroir varies from the most gravelly at the top to clay-limestone at the bottom, so Cabernet Sauvignon and Sémillon tend to be planted higher up, and Merlot and Sauvignon Blanc lower down. The white wine is barrel fermented, and spends 10 months in barriques with about one third new oak; the red has fermentation and malolactic in cuve before transferring to barrel for 18 months. The style of the wines is understated if not a little lightweight for Pessac-Léognan: they are best enjoyed in the immediate to mid term. The red shows an approachable style that is soft on the palate. I sometimes find the white a little bit lacking in character. Tour Léognan is a second wine that comes from younger vines; Croix de Carbonnieux is another second wine directed principally to the restaurant trade. The Perrins also own Châteaux Haut-Vigneau and Lafont Menaut in Pessac-Léognan.

 Léognan

Pessac-Léognan

2 Château La Tour Léognan

www.carbonnieux.com

92 ha; 500,000 bottles

Domaine de Chevalier

Dating from the eighteenth century, Domaine de Chevalier has a contiguous block of vineyards surrounded by a pine forest; 45 ha are black and 5 ha are white. The estate fell into disarray during the nineteenth century and was revived at the start of the twentieth century under the Ricard family. Present owner Olivier Bernard purchased it in 1983. Maintaining its traditional style of precision and elegance, the red wine has tended to fall out of favor with those who advocate powerful wines in the modern idiom. "The idea here is to keep the authentic taste, the typicity of Domaine de Chevalier is not the technique of making Cabernet Sauvignon, it is to express the terroir. It's possible to transform Cabernet Sauvignon or other wines with technology, but it's a crime," says manager Rémi Edange. Black plantings are 65% Cabernet Sauvignon and 30% Merlot, with 4% Petit Verdot and almost no Cabernet Franc, "because there is no chalk in the soil." The division between grand vin and the second wine makes no concessions: all barrels are tasted by a group of five, and all must agree for a barrel to be included in the grand vin. The white wine is widely acknowledged to be one of Bordeaux's most elegant: around 70% Sauvignon Blanc to 30% Sémillon, it spends 18 months in oak, but with only 30% new oak. One of my favorite Graves, the exquisite red remains under appreciated. The second wine is well-structured and elegant. A third wine is sold as Pessac-Léognan AOP.

Léognan

Pessac-Léognan

2 L'Esprit de Chevalier

www.domainedechevalier.com

50 ha; 200,000 bottles

Château de Fieuzal

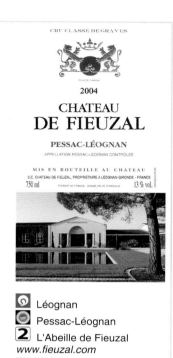

Named after the owners immediately prior to 1851, this grand old estate was divided after the de Fieuzal's sold it, into Château de Fieuzal and Château Haut Gardères, and the two halves were reunited in the 1990s, when the Bank Populaire purchased first Château de Fieuzal (in 1994) and then a year later followed with Château Haut Gardères. The Bank sold the estate to the Quinn family in 2001, and they appointed Stephen Carrier as winemaker. Originally from Champagne, he worked in Napa Valley before coming to Lynch Bages in Bordeaux. Hubert de Boüard has been a consultant since 2006. The vineyards are divided into 65 ha of black grapes and 10 ha of white grapes, located on a gravel plateau. The wines had a dull patch in the early 2000s, but seem now to be coming back on form. There has been investment in a new state of the art winery, which was completed in 2012. Fermentation takes place in stainless steel, and maturation is in barriques, usually with about 50% new oak. The red is a roughly equal blend of Cabernet Sauvignon and Merlot, while the white is an equal blend of Sauvignon Blanc and Sémillon. My impression of both red and white is that they are wines that usually please in the short term, and the white can certainly be delicious. The red is pleasant, but recent vintages don't really seem to have enough stuffing for long term aging. The white has the higher reputation, and usually sells for about 25% more than the red.

Léognan
Pessac-Léognan
L'Abeille de Fieuzal
www.fieuzal.com

75 ha; 140,000 bottles

Clos Floridène

This is one of the few domains outside of Pessac-Léognan that can be easily recommended in the Graves. It's named for its owners, Denis and Florence Dubourdieu, who also own Châteaux Haura in the Graves, Reynon in Cadillac, and Doisy-Daëne (the oldest property in the family portfolio) and Cantegril in Barsac. Well known as a consulting oenologist, and for his research at the University of Bordeaux, Denis Dubourdieu has been a driving force behind the revival of white Bordeaux because of his work on vinification of Sauvignon Blanc. Clos Floridène started with 2 ha in 1982, and then expanded by purchasing neighboring properties, including Château Montalivet, which was used as Clos Floridène's second wine, but has now been supplanted by Drapeau de Floridène. The vineyards are located on the plateau at Pujols sur Ciron, near Sauternes. Clos Floridène, Drapeau de Floridène, and Montalivet are all AOP Graves in both red and white; there is also a rosé Clos Floridène under AOP Bordeaux. Most of the vineyard is planted with white varieties. The white Clos Floridène has more or less equal proportions of Sauvignon Blanc and Sémillon; the red is three quarters Cabernet Sauvignon to one quarter Merlot. These are, as you would expect, impeccably made wines; they offer reasonable value, although flavor profiles are rather direct, and they do not rise to the level of interest of the whites or reds from Pessac-Léognan.

Béguey
Graves
Drapeau de Floridène
www.denisdubourdieu.com

42 ha; 145,000 bottles

Léognan

Pessac-Léognan

2 La Parde de Haut-Bailly
www.chateau-haut-bailly.com

G

30 ha; 120,000 bottles

Château Haut Bailly

Located on a slight rise just above Léognan village, Haut Bailly vies with Château Pape Clément for third place in Pessac-Léognan, behind Haut Brion and Mission Haut Brion. Its recent history started when a Belgian wine merchant, Daniel Sanders, bought and restored the property. His son, Jean Sanders, took over in 1979, but was subsequently forced to sell by inheritance issues. The estate was purchased by a New York banker, but Jean Sanders remained involved, and the manager today is his daughter Véronique. Unusually for Graves, only red wine is produced here; the style is full bodied for the area. Increasing selection has reduced the grand vin to about half of production. It is matured half in new oak and half in one-year oak. In addition to the second wine, there is also an AOP Pessac-Léognan from the estate, consisting mostly of press wine and lots from young vines. A neighboring château, La Pape, was recently purchased, but is run independently. The glory of the estate is a 4 ha plot immediately around the château, planted around a century ago, and including all six of the black Bordeaux varieties intermingled. This is at least partly responsible for Haut Bailly's power. "We considered doing a garage cuvée from the old vines in 1995, but decided it would change the character of Haut Bailly. We bottled one barrique from old vines, and it showed as stronger in tannins but not as complex as the Haut Bailly itself," says winemaker Gabriel Vialard.

Léognan

Pessac-Léognan

2 Le Clarence de Haut Brion
www.chateau-haut-brion.com

G

51 ha; 145,000 bottles

Château Haut Brion

Vines may have been grown in the vicinity since Roman times, and the earliest reference to production at the estate dates from 1423, placing this as one of the oldest châteaux in Bordeaux. The family fortune was made by Arnaud de Pontac in the fifteenth century, and Pontac ownership continued to the end of the seventeenth century. Haut Brion was famous in London by then. It was the only château outside the Médoc to be included in the 1855 classification. After 1922, the château went through a difficult period until it was eventually purchased by the American banker Clarence Dillon in 1934. The terroir is a gravel mound, varying in depth from 1 to 7 meters, with an undulating pattern of clay subsoils. There is just a little more Merlot than Cabernet Sauvignon in the vineyards, which have 90% black grapes. Vinification is conventional, with malolactic in cuve. "Performing MLF in barrel gives a standardization of taste, which is not what we are looking for," says Director Jean-Philippe Delmas. The second wine is made by selection. All the grand vin goes into new oak for twenty months. Haut Brion's white (roughly equal parts of Sauvignon Blanc and Sémillon) has been Bordeaux's best known dry white for a long time, challenged only by Mission Haut Brion Blanc. It has a full, oaky, style. The style of the red is less overtly powerful than the Médoc: to call it delicate would perhaps be to overstate the case, but its character is to let aromatic complexity show.

Château Malartic Lagravière

The splendid château claims to be located on one of the oldest wine-producing sites in Bordeaux. Its name comes from proprietors in the nineteenth century. It stayed in the same family from 1860 to 1990, but by the end of this period, little attention was being paid to it. It was sold to Laurent-Perrier, who in turn sold it on in 1997 to Alfred-Alexandre Bonnie. New winemakers and consultants were appointed, the size of the estate was doubled, the winery was replaced with a hi-tech gravity-feed installation, and there was significant replanting in the vineyard, including an increase in the proportion of Merlot. The main vineyards are located around the château on a high, gravel plateau, and the château is classified for both red and white wine. Just under 15% of the plantings are white. The white is a classic blend of 80% Sauvignon Blanc to 20% Sémillon, designed more for short term consumption than for aging. The red is a more or less equal blend of Cabernet Sauvignon and Merlot, with a little Cabernet Franc and Petit Verdot, but usually strikes me as more Cabernet-driven; consistent in style, it drinks well in the mid-term. In some vintages, saignée is used to produce a rosé. "Malartic is a typical Pessac-Léognan with good balance and elegance. It's feminine relative to the Médoc," says Séverine Bonnie. The holding company of Vignobles Malartic also owns another château in Pessac-Léognan, Château Gazin-Rocquencourt, as well as Bodega Diamandes in Argentina.

 Léognan
Pessac-Léognan
2 La Réserve de Malartic
www.malartic-lagraviere.com

55 ha; 150,000 bottles

Château La Mission Haut Brion

"Mission is always more immediately charming, with Haut Brion you have to work harder to catch everything," says Jean-Philippe Delmas, the third generation of Delmas's to be the Director for Haut Brion and Mission Haut Brion. La Mission is not quite as old as Haut Brion, but monks were making wine here in the seventeenth century. Since 1983, La Mission has been under the same ownership as Haut Brion, sharpening the question of the nature of the difference between the two wines. Vineyards of the two châteaux run more or less contiguously across two small hills, and plantings are very similar, with just a little less Cabernet Franc at La Mission. The only difference in the vineyards is that Haut Brion is planted at 8,000 vines/ha and La Mission is planted at 10,000/ha (but with replanting Haut Brion's density is being increased). Vinification is the same at both. Although Haut Brion was classified in 1855 and La Mission was not (its price at the time was below the range of the classed growths), it's a fascinating exercise to compare a vertical tasting of the two wines side by side today. Personally, I usually prefer Haut Brion in more vintages, but it's a close-run thing. Perhaps that easy charm of La Mission comes from a slightly fuller, less delicate, structure. With the whites, Mission Haut Brion (previously known as Laville Haut Brion) is the only close challenger to Haut Brion. There's a joint white second wine, La Clarté de Haut Brion, for Haut Brion and La Mission.

 Pessac
Pessac-Léognan
2 La Chapelle de la Mission
www.mission-haut-brion.com

26 ha; 85,000 bottles

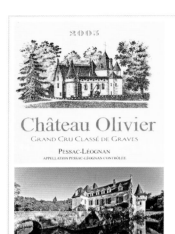

 Léognan
Pessac-Léognan
2 Le Dauphin d'Olivier
www.chateau-olivier.com

60 ha; 280,000 bottles

Château Olivier

For once, Château is not a misnomer, as a genuine castle (with parts dating back to the thirteenth or fourteen century) is protected by a moat at the center of a vast domain of 220 ha including forest and pastures as well as vineyards. It's been in the hands of the de Bethmann family since it was purchased by Alexandre de Bethmann, then mayor of Bordeaux, in 1886, but the vineyards were leased to the negociant Eschenauer until 1987. It's only in the past decade that the wines have begun to live up to their potential. Following a survey of soil types in the estate, the vineyards were reorganized in the 2000s: some parcels planted on clay were taken out, and new plantings were undertaken on some forested land with gravel soils (which had been planted with vines two centuries ago). A new winery was built in 2002. The domain is classified for both red and white wine, and about 20% of plantings are white, split more or less equally between Sauvignon Blanc and Sémillon. The whites are well made but the reds have more potential. A roughly equal blend of Cabernet Sauvignon and Merlot, they offer an understated, elegant style in the old tradition of Graves, generally peaking in about a decade. The domain has eschewed the modern trend to high extraction and lots of new oak. One third new oak is used, with some 500 liter tonneaux as well as barriques. A difference here from other properties in Graves is that wine production is only one of the agricultural activities of the estate.

Pessac
Pessac-Léognan
2 Le Clémentin du Pape-Clément
www.pape-clement.com

46 ha; 220,000 bottles

Château Pape Clément

"The order in Graves has always been Haut Brion and Mission Haut Brion, then Pape Clément, then the others," says Bernard Magrez, who now owns about forty producers in seven countries, ranging locally from AOP Bordeaux to Grand Cru Classé. Pape Clément, which he inherited by marriage, is by far the most important. Taking its name from Pope Clément V in 1305, the estate is now surrounded by the suburbs of Bordeaux: at one time there was a risk it would be torn up for housing. Quality slipped until Bernard took over in 1985 when both viticulture and vinification were renovated. Merlot was increased to make the wine rounder, but then later cut back for a more elegant style. Plantings today are balanced roughly equally between Cabernet Sauvignon and Merlot, with a little Cabernet Franc and Petit Verdot. White varieties are about 10%. Pape Clément now seems to me to be one of the more powerful, modern styles in Graves, for both red and white, but Bernard disagrees: "The typicity is the terroir, that we can't change, this is what gives character to the wine. One can't make a wine international. The wine is easier to drink young but that won't stop it aging." There is substantial use of new oak, and the richness of the white is emphasized by its equal proportions of Sauvignon Blanc and Sémillon. The style comes over full force in great vintages, when sometimes winemaking seems to triumph over terroir, but shows to advantage in lesser vintages.

Château Smith Haut Lafitte

From a rather average property run for almost a century by the Bordeaux negociant Eschenauer, Smith Haut Lafitte has turned into a major enterprise since the Cathiards (well known skiers who developed a chain of sports shops) took over in 1991. Subsequently they developed the Caudalie Spa and hotel at the site, as well as acquiring Château Cantelys nearby, and more recently Château le Thil Comte Clary. Rumors that the spa is more profitable than the winery are hard to believe given the rise of Smith Haut Lafitte. Style is influenced by the market: "We have to listen to our consumers (sometimes). The Americans showed what they like, now the Chinese. There is an influence because we want our wine to be referred, we want to make wine that pleases our customers," says Daniel Cathiard. My impression is that the style of the red started to become more international, meaning softer, rounder, more overtly fruit driven, with the 2005 vintage. "Warmer vintages mean our wines are riper, fuller, more alcoholic—but the Americans like it," says Daniel. New oak exposure is usually around 50%. Yet the style is refined, and manages to retain typicity of Pessac-Léognan. The white is unusual in being essentially Sauvignon Blanc, softened by the inclusion of a small amount of Sauvignon Gris. The best known second wine, Les Hauts de Smith, has more Merlot and is sold mostly to restaurants, but there is another, Le Petite Haut Lafitte, with more Cabernet, for export markets.

Martillac
Pessac-Léognan
2 Les Hauts de Smith
www.smith-haut-lafitte.com

67 ha; 200,000 bottles

Château La Tour Martillac

The Bordeaux negociant Alfred Kressmann bought this property in 1929 (partly out of competition with rival Eschenauer who owned nearby Smith Haut Lafitte), and subsequently his son Jean took charge of it for the next forty years. The firm of Kressmann has now been absorbed by the CVBG conglomerate, but La Tour Martillac is still owned by the Kressmann family, and is run today by Tristan and Loïc Kressmann. When it was purchased in 1929, the property had only around 12 ha of mostly white plantings: the Kressmanns expanded the vineyards and introduced black varieties. Most of the vineyards are on the gravel plateau around the château; they were further expanded in the 1990s, mostly with Cabernet Sauvignon and Merlot, and the proportion of red wine increased towards its present three quarters. The white has historically had an unusually high proportion of Sémillon (between 50% and 60%), but recent vintages have returned to a more traditional regional blend, with up to 70% Sauvignon Blanc, making it distinctly crisper. The red varies from one half to two thirds Cabernet Sauvignon, and unusually for Graves, has included some Petit Verdot since 1997; it is matured in 30-50% new oak for 15-20 months. The red is classic for Graves, showing black fruits with a smoky background and relatively soft palate, best enjoyed in the mid-term. It's a good value for the region. The second wine comes from the younger vines.

Martillac
Pessac-Léognan
2 Château Lagrave-Martillac
www.latour-martillac.com

45 ha; 290,000 bottles

Château d'Armailhac

Château d'Armailhac was originally part of the Ségur estate in the early eighteenth century. It occupied the center of the estate, with the vineyards that were to become Mouton Rothschild to its north, and those of Pontet Canet to its south. It was purchased by Dominique d'Armailhacq in the early eighteenth century, and renamed as Château Mouton-d'Armailhacq. The d'Armailhacq family continued to own the property, but due to financial difficulties, part of the estate, the Carruades plateau, was sold to Château Lafite in 1845. (Mouton, whose vineyards were all but intertwined with d'Armailhacq, also tried to buy it.) D'Armailhacq was ranked as a fifth growth in the 1855 classification, and stayed in the family until it was sold to Baron Philippe de Rothschild in 1933. The Baron changed the name to Mouton-Baron-Philippe. More recently it was changed back to d'Armailhac (without the final 'q'). There were 75 ha of vineyards when the estate was purchased by the Rothschilds, but this dropped to 32 ha by 1960, and now has recovered to 50 ha. Plantings are almost three quarters Cabernet, but an unusually high proportion is Cabernet Franc, maintained because they are very old vines. The style is relatively sturdy, and a certain robust quality accentuates with age: there's the power of Pauillac, but not the finesse of the top wines. D'Armailhac is usually reckoned to be comparable to Clerc Milon in the hierarchy of Rothschild wines, placing after Mouton and Petit Mouton.

Pauillac
www.chateau-darmailhac.com

60 ha; 240,000 bottles

Château Beychevelle

Beychevelle originated in a vast estate known as the Château de Médoc in the fifteenth century. In 1587 the estate became the property of the Duc d'Epernon, who appears to have given it its name, originating in the custom that ships sailing past the estate lowered their sails (baisse voile) in respect to the Duc, who was the Governor of Guyenne. Large parts of the estate were sold off in 1642, creating Châteaux Branaire and Ducru Beaucaillou. The vineyards of today's Beychevelle were probably established around the start of the eighteenth century. The estate covers 250 ha, of which 90 ha are planted, including 74 ha in the St. Julien appellation and another 13 ha in the Haut Médoc. Beychevelle and its second wine come from St. Julien; there is also an Haut Médoc AOP. Most of the wine intended for Beychevelle is matured in new oak; and about 20% new oak is used for Amiral. Although the terroir is mostly gravel based, Beychevelle has one of the highest proportions of Merlot in the area. "We are trying to go towards more Cabernet Sauvignon in the blend. But it takes time," says Director Philippe Blanc. "We'd like to see the Cabernet reach 65% here." Classified as a fourth growth in 1855, Beychevelle has more or less maintained that position ever since, generally reflecting the finesse and elegance of St. Julien. In contrast with the usual emphasis on Merlot in second wines, the Amiral tends to have more Cabernet than the grand vin.

Saint Julien Beychevelle
St. Julien
Amiral de Beychevelle
www.beychevelle.com

90 ha; 640,000 bottles

Château Branaire Ducru

Château Branaire originated when some parcels were split off after the Beychevelle estate was sold in 1642. After a reorganization in 1680, Jean-Baptiste Braneyre (Seigneur of Duluc) purchased the part that became Château Branaire. His descendents owned the château through the Revolution, and were the proprietors in 1855 when it was classified as a fourth growth. A more distant branch of the family, the Ducrus, inherited a few years later, and the name changed to Branaire-Ducru. (Past ownership is now indicated by Dulac-Ducru under the name of the château on the label.) The Ducrus remained in charge until the sale to Jean-Michel Tapie in 1919. Branaire-Ducru was considered a perennial underachiever through most of the twentieth century. The most recent change was the sale to Patrick Maroteaux in 1988. There's been a steady program of improvement, with a gravity feed winery constructed in 1991, a nursery established to allow the vineyard to be propagated by selection massale, and focus on avoiding manipulation in vinification. The vineyards, which are dispersed in many parcels, are dominated by Cabernet Sauvignon. Recently there's been a move towards later harvesting. The style is very much mainstream St. Julien: generally elegant rather than powerful. If I have a criticism, is that's the wines show well when young, but may lack the structure needed for really long term aging, although they are good in the medium term.

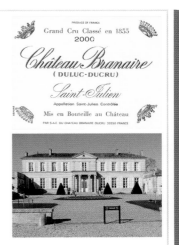

Saint Julien Beychevelle
St. Julien
2 Duluc de Branaire-Ducru
www.branaire.com

60 ha; 300,000 bottles

Château Brane Cantenac

At its origins in the early eighteenth century, what we now know as Brane Cantenac was called Château Gorce after its proprietor; by 1735 wine was being sold under this name. A measure of the high regard in which it was held was that when it was purchased in 1833 by Baron Hector de Brane, he sold what was then known as Brane-Mouton (and is now Mouton Rothschild) in order to finance the purchase. Baron de Brane, known as the Napoleon des Vignes at the time, was an influential figure in viticulture during the period. Brane Cantenac fitted comfortably into the middle of the range of second growths at the time of the 1855 classification. At the end of the nineteenth century it encountered the usual difficulties due to problems with oïdium and phylloxera followed by economic depression, and the modern era started when it was purchased by the Lurton family in 1925. When the Lurton holdings were divided among the family in 1992, Brane Cantenac became the property of Henri Lurton. Although the wines show the typicity of Margaux, they do not seem quite to maintain the concentration of a second growth, but seem really more like a third growth, and indeed this is the price level at which the market presently places them. This may be partly a function of size: this is one of the larger estates in the Médoc. Of course, Margaux should never be a heavy wine, but I sometimes feel that Brane Cantenac is a little too lightweight.

Cantenac
Margaux
2 Le Baron de Brane
www.brane-cantenac.com

85 ha; 250,000 bottles

Bordeaux: Médoc

St. Estèphe
2 Marquis de Calon
www.calon-segur.fr
55 ha; 300,000 bottles

Château Calon Ségur

The origins of Calon Ségur are ancient; the name goes back to a local stronghold known in Roman times as Calones. By the eighteenth century, it was owned by the Marquis Nicolas-Alexandre de Ségur, known as the Prince des Vignes, who also owned Lafite and Latour. The origin of the heart on the label of Calon Ségur is his declaration that "I make my wine at Lafite and Latour, but my heart belongs to Calon." As a third growth, Calon Ségur has always played second fiddle to Châteaux Montrose and Cos d'Estournel, the second growths of St Estèphe, although its price level in the present market places it well up the third growths. During the twentieth century, Calon Ségur belonged to the Capbern-Gasqueton family; the last proprietor was Philippe Capbern-Gasqueton, and then after his death, the property was run from 1995 by Mme. Capbern-Gasqueton. Visiting was difficult, and the estate became somewhat fixed in its ways. The wines are perhaps best described as robust, sometimes slipping over into the hardness that can mark St. Estèphe. The 1970s were disappointing; even the 1982 is workmanlike rather than interesting. There does not seem to have been any attempt to move towards the more modern style that has overtaken most of Bordeaux. Nothing wrong with tradition, of course, but there's a certain lack of pizzazz. It's uncertain whether and how the style may change as the result of the sale in 2012 to the insurance company Suravenir Assurances.

Moulis-en-Médoc
Moulis
2 Oratoire de Chasse Spleen
www.chasse-spleen.com
113 ha; 500,000 bottles

Château Chasse Spleen

Chasse Spleen is the largest château in Moulis-Listrac. It was Château Gressier Grand Poujeaux until 1820, when it was divided: one part remained known as Gressier, and the other part became Chasse Spleen. The Merlauts bought it in 1976; they bought Gressier Grand Poujeaux in 2003, but the châteaux continue to run independently. There are five wines: Chasse Spleen (which uses all four black grape varieties), Oratoire de Chasse Spleen (a second wine from young vines), Heritage de Chasse Spleen (an Haut Médoc from vineyards owned by the château immediately outside the Moulis appellation), Gressier Grand Poujeaux, and Blanc de Chasse Spleen. Almost all plantings are black grapes, with just 3 ha for the white. The Château is located on the gravel terroir of the Grand-Poujeaux plateau (which it shares with rival Château Poujeaux), and accordingly is heavily dominated by Cabernet Sauvignon (three quarters of plantings). Merlot is planted on areas where the soils are clay-limestone. The best wine in Moulis-Listrac, one of the few to compare with those of the great communes along the Gironde, Chasse Spleen was a leading Cru Bourgeois until it withdrew from the classification, but in any case most critics consider it of Grand Cru Classé quality. The style is firm—a very proper claret—and if it does not have the weight of the wines of the great communes, that is a reflection of its terroir and the slightly cooler climate inland.

Château Clerc Milon

Château Clerc Milon appears to have been established early in the nineteenth century by Jean-Baptiste Clerc, reflecting in its name the village of Milon in the northwest of Pauillac. It was classified as a fifth growth in 1855, still under the management of M. Clerc. The estate was split into two parts and sold in 1877, and the smaller part won the right by legal action to use the name of Clerc Milon; it was then called Château Clerc-Milon-Mondon after its new owner. The estate deteriorated as it passed through a series of proprietors until (consisting of only 10 ha) it was finally sold to Baron Philippe de Rothschild in 1970. For a while, it was known as Clerc Milon Rothschild. It's been expanded under Rothschild ownership, and the vineyards now consist of more than two hundred parcels scattered around the Pauillac commune. In spite of its ownership, it has never achieved the reputation of the better known classed growths of the commune. Significant change is afoot here, however, with adjustment of the varietal mix to more Merlot, construction of a new winery, and optical sorting of grapes, all combining to bring what was a rather robust, even sometimes hard, style, into a more modern idiom. This has been reflected in a new label to show the new winery. The major challenger for Clerc Milon in the Rothschild stable is d'Armailhac, which has always shown better when young, but recent vintages of Clerc Milon show a new softness on release.

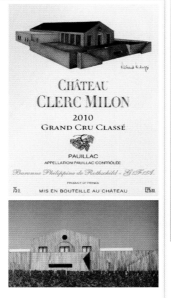

Pauillac
www.chateau-clerc-milon.com

41 ha; 160,000 bottles

Château Cos d'Estournel

The exotic appearance of Château Cos d'Estournel makes it the most striking château in the Médoc. One of the last of the Grand Cru Classés to be established, it owes its origins to Louis-Gaspard d'Estournel. Inheriting vineyards close to the village of Cos, he started to produce wine, and had a rapid success with exports, especially to India, for which he was called the Maharajah of St. Estèphe. In 1830, he imported the famous pagodas from Zanzibar that surmount the château. Cos d'Estournel was classified as a second growth in 1855. The modern era starts with its purchase by Fernand Ginestet in 1917. The château stayed in the same family until very recently, passing from Ginestet to his grandson Bruno Prats. In 1998 the Prats family sold Cos d'Estournel to The Taillan Group, who in turn sold it to Michel Reybier in 2000. Reybier made a massive investment in an eye-catching new cuverie. Jean-Guillaume Prats continued to make the wine until he left in 2012. The wine is as showy as the château, and is considered by many to be more Pauillac in style than St. Estèphe (Château Lafite Rothschild is adjacent). "Global warming is a key component in the evolution of Cos, we are now producing wines which have extraordinary levels of phenolic ripeness," Jean-Guillaume told me just before he left. I find the wines attractive when young, full of ripe Cabernet flavor, but I seem to be alone in worrying that they will not have the longevity I look for in St. Estèphe.

St. Estèphe
Les Pagodes de Cos
www.estournel.com

90 ha; 450,000 bottles

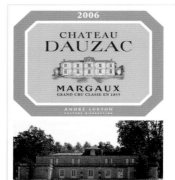

 Labarde

Margaux

2 La Bastide de Dauzac

www.chateaudauzac.com

45 ha; 230,000 bottles

Château Dauzac

Château Dauzac claims that the first vines were planted there in the twelfth century, although it was not until Thomas-Michel Lynch arrived in 1740 that it became established in the form of the Château that was recognized in 1855 as a fifth growth. It declined as it passed through various ownerships, until the first attempts at revival were made when Alain Miailhe of the old Bordeaux wine family purchased it in 1966. He sold it to Félix Chatelier in 1978, who in turn sold it to the present owners, the MAIF insurance group, in 1988. André Lurton had a minority share, and his daughter Christine Lurton-de-Caix was in charge until he sold his share in 2014, making MAIF the sole owner. Laurent Fortin came to run the estate, which in fact is rather grand, extending over a total area of 120 ha. A new winery was built in 2004. The vineyards are close to the river, all in Margaux AOP except for 3 ha classified as Haut Médoc. Only Cabernet Sauvignon (65%) and Merlot are grown. Dauzac remains one of the least known classified growths, and seems to be casting about a bit to establish its identity. The second wine, La Bastide, comes from younger vines and sandier plots. Since 2013 there has also been Aurore de Dauzac, another wine from an equal blend of younger vines of Cabernet and Merlot, with the same stated intention of being easier to drink. The revival still seems to be a work in progress. The wine from the Haut Médoc part of the estate is labeled as Château Labarde.

 Cantenac

Margaux

2 Initial de Desmirail

www.desmirail.com

30 ha; 160,000 bottles

Château Desmirail

Jean Desmirail founded the estate at the end of the seventeenth century and his family owned it until the middle of the nineteenth. M. Sipière, the régisseur at Château Margaux, was the owner in 1855, when Desmirail was classified as a troisième cru. There were several changes of ownership until Desmirail disappeared when Château Palmer acquired the vineyards in 1957, although the name was used for Palmer's production in the terrible vintage of 1963. (The château itself was sold to Marquis d'Alesme, so Desmirail is now made in some workmanlike buildings in Cantenac.) Lucien Lurton had been assembling plots from Château Palmer and others in Margaux, and selling the wine without classification, but then acquired the rights to the name Desmirail from Palmer; he labeled the wine as Château Desmirail from 1981. "Without the name it would have been difficult to rise above the cru bourgeois level," says his son Denis Lurton, who took over in 1992. There's been an effort to reassemble some of the original holdings of Desmirail; the estate now has 11 ha in Arsac, 10 ha in Cantenac, and 9 ha in Soussans, corresponding to about two thirds of the original holdings. Cabernet Sauvignon has decreased from a peak of 85% to around 60% today, to make the wine more approachable. The style shows the typical delicacy of Margaux. The second wine (also sold as Château Fontarney) is made by declassification, and represents about 40% of production.

Château Ducru Beaucaillou

The name refers to the beautiful pebbles (beaux caillou) in the vineyard. At one time, it was supposedly known as Maucaillou (bad pebbles), until it was decided that pebbles were good: an early example of marketing speak, perhaps. By the 1855 classification, there was no question about Ducru's status as a second growth. Soon after, the château was bought by negociant Nathaniel Johnston. Ducru Beaucaillou remained firmly in the second growths, but the Johnstons were forced to sell the property in the 1920s. It was purchased by the Bories in 1941, when it was in poor condition. In 1970, Jean-Eugène Borie purchased an additional 32 ha from Château Lagrange; this could have been included in Ducru Beaucaillou but it was bottled as Château Lalande Borie; in effect it is now the third wine, as a second wine, Croix de Beaucaillou, was introduced in 1995. "It's a descending hierarchy, Ducru may be declassified to Croix, which may be declassified to Lalande Borie: but never the reverse," says manager René Lusseau. There was an awkward patch in the late eighties, when TCA contamination led to some corked wines; but aside from that, Ducru Beaucaillou has had no threat to its position as a super-second. Vineyards are all around the château in a single block, sloping down to the Gironde. Plantings are exclusively Cabernet Sauvignon (75%) and Merlot, and this is probably the most refined wine of St. Julien. I would describe it as exquisite rather than powerful.

Saint Julien Beychevelle

St. Julien

La Croix de Beaucaillou

www.chateau-ducru-beaucaillou.com

75 ha; 260,000 bottles

Château Duhart Milon Rothschild

Château Duhart Milon Rothschild is located near the village of Milon in the northwest corner of Pauillac. There is no information about M. Duhart, who presumably gave his name to it. The first information about wine production at Duhart Milon dates from the eighteenth century, and by the nineteenth century it was well known. The château was bought in the 1830s by Pierre Castéja, who was the proprietor at the time of the 1855 classification, when it became a fourth growth. After Castéja's death, the estate was run for the family by André Delon, at the time also the manager of Léoville Lascases. Financial difficulties caused the usual depredations, and some of the vineyards were sold off, including 15 ha that went to Château Batailley. Things got steadily worse as the property kept changing hands, until it was bought in 1962 by the Rothschilds of Château Lafite. At the time, the estate consisted of only 17 ha, but under the Rothschilds the existing vineyards were replanted, and there was a great expansion as new vineyards were purchased. Dominated by Cabernet Sauvignon, the vineyards are close to Lafite, but at lower elevation, and with a more northern exposure. In spite of physical proximity and similarities in winemaking, the wine does not at all resemble Lafite: it is solid where Lafite can be ethereal, and robust rather than powerful. Benefiting from the halo cast by its famous neighbor, it prices above its classification.

Pauillac

Moulin de Duhart

www.lafite.com

71 ha; 336,000 bottles

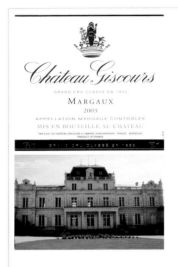

 Labarde

Margaux

2 La Sirène de Giscours

www.chateau-giscours.fr

86 ha; 400,000 bottles

Château Giscours

In 1552, land described as vineyards was sold for 1,000 livres. Not much is known about its history until it was seized and sold as a result of the French Revolution. The château itself was constructed in 1847. After its classification as a third growth in 1855, Giscours declined fairly steadily until it was purchased in 1952 and renovated by Nicolas Tari. Forty years later, in 1990, Tari sold the vineyards to Eric Albada Jelgersma, a Dutch supermarket magnate (who also bought Château de Tertre). The wine is generally regarded as a little robust for Margaux, resulting from its location at the southern border of the appellation, just north of neighboring classified growth La Lagune (nominally in the Haut Médoc, but sometimes grouped with Margaux). Giscours also owns 60 ha nearby in the Haut Médoc (formerly Château du Thil, now the Haut Médoc de Giscours). There was a scandal in 1999 when some of the Haut Médoc wine was added to the second wine of Giscours, and oak chips were used: the winemaker was changed and Giscours's reputation has now recovered. Although there have been significant renovations in both viticulture and vinification, the style has remained steady: somewhat full bodied, never out of balance, but not fully displaying Margaux's elegance. It shows best for consumption in the medium term. Chunky is sometimes used as a description, but Giscours continues to maintain the market position of a third growth.

Saint Julien Beychevelle

St. Julien

2 Château Peymartin

www.domaines-henri-martin.com

50 ha; 290,000 bottles

Châteaux Gloria (& St. Pierre)

Gloria is one of the best known unclassified châteaux because of its history. With a longstanding ambition to own a classified growth, but unable to buy one, Henri Martin purchased 6 ha of vineyards in St. Julien in 1942. Parcels were subsequently bought, one at a time, from most of the classified growths in St. Julien, including Beychevelle, Léoville Poyferré, Gruaud-Larose, Léoville Barton, St. Pierre, Lagrange, Ducru Beaucaillou, Talbot, Pichon Baron, and Duhart Milon, making a patchwork quilt of vineyards throughout the appellation. So if terroir was the criterion, Château Gloria would be a classified growth. Never included in any classification, Gloria prices anyway with the lower tier of classified growths. The actual château stands where there used to be a shed on the land of Château Saint Pierre Bontemps. Henri Martin was in fact able to buy Château St. Pierre (a fourth growth) in 1982, when it was quite run down, and he managed to reconstruct it by assembling vineyards in the same way as for Gloria. The two châteaux are adjacent, share a cuverie, and remain under common ownership. Curiously, Gloria always seems to me to show less breed than St. Pierre: it can show fine fruits with a structured impression, but has a lightweight character which is too easily dominated by the tannins. The style is similarly lean at St. Pierre, but there usually seems to be a touch more concentration and a greater sense of refinement.

Château Grand Puy Lacoste

Grand Puy means a small hill, and the château is at the top of a mound, with vineyards in a single block running down from the building. Plantings are 75% Cabernet Sauvignon, 20% Merlot, and 5% Cabernet Franc. Grand Puy Lacoste and Grand Puy Ducasse resulted from splitting a single estate, and both were given fifth growth status in 1855, although Lacoste has generally been better regarded than Ducasse. After reaching 90 ha in the 1920s, the estate declined to 25 ha as it passed through changes of ownership. Renovation started in 1978 when the Borie family acquired a half share; they subsequently took over the estate completely. The facilities have been slowly renovated. François-Xavier Borie is conscious of its history: "There's an inheritance and it's a slow process to change, we think in terms of decades, not years," he says. One of the best of the fifth growths, Grand Puy Lacoste prices at third growth level. There is 75% new oak for the grand vin, and 35% for the second wine. A clear lineage shows through the vintages, with a refined, elegant style emphasized by the fine texture of tannins. The 1990 is beginning to lose fruit, the 1995 remains in perfect balance, and the 2000 is now at its peak, if anything a touch more developed than the 1995. The style comes through even the lushness of the 2009 vintage. I regard Grand Puy Lacoste as a half way house between the traditional power of Pauillac and the elegance of St. Julien. The Bories also own Haut Batailley.

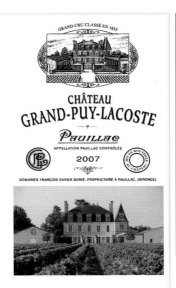

Pauillac
Lacoste Borie
www.grand-puy-lacoste.fr

55 ha; 300,000 bottles

Château Gruaud Larose

"Gruaud used to be the best wine in St. Julien," said owner Jean Merlaut as we looked over the vineyards from the tower on the estate. "In the forties, Lascases was not so good, Poyferré was not so good. In moments like this we can see the 1855 classification was very well done, because when people renovate the vineyards they return to form." The estate originated around 1725, and by the 1750s sales of wine were recorded in the records of Tastet & Lawton. The estate was legally divided into two parts in 1845, but was classified as a second growth in 1855. Desiré Cordier bought one half in 1917, and then reunited the estate by buying the other half in 1935, making it one of the largest estates in the area. It remained firmly in the class of second growths. Sold by Cordier in 1993, it came under its present ownership by the Merlauts in 1997. There's been a steady program of improvement. Cordier's style was for a very dry, firm, character, sometimes described as masculine. "Since I have been here we have planted more Cabernet Sauvignon. In 1999 it was 57%, now it is 61%," says Jean Merlaut. "But it takes 30 years to change the vineyards. I started in 1997; in ten years time there will be 70% or so Cabernet Sauvignon." He sees this as representing a return to form. "In the nineties the style of Gruaud was far more classical—what we make now is more like the first part of the twentieth century." The style is still typical St. Julien, but perhaps less restrained than it used to be.

Saint Julien Beychevelle
St. Julien
Sarget de Gruaud Larose
www.gruaud-larose.com

82 ha; 600,000 bottles

St. Estèphe
2 Château MacCarthy
www.larobefendue.com
66 ha; 330,000 bottles

Château Haut Marbuzet

Haut Marbuzet was often considered to be the top château in the Cru Bourgeois classification (it was one of the nine Cru Bourgeois Exceptionnel in the top level of the original classification). It originated as an offshoot when the large Domaine de Marbuzet, owned by the MacCarthy family, was split into many parts in 1854 as the result of an inheritance crisis. Current ownership dates from 1952, when Hervé Duboscq, a negociant who often purchased the wines, bought the estate, at the time all but derelict. A subsequent program of vineyard purchases (including Châteaux MacCarthy-Moula, Chambert-Marbuzet, and MacCarthy, now used to describe the second wine) eventually led to the recreation of the original Domaine de Marbuzet under the name of Haut Marbuzet. (Château Marbuzet is a different property, owned by Michel Reybier of Cos d'Estournel.) Today Haut Marbuzet is run by Hervé's son, Henri. Reflecting a high content of clay in the soils, plantings of Merlot are relatively high (usually 40% in the grand vin). Harvesting is late, to achieve high ripeness. The wine is known for its oaky taste, resulting from the use of only new oak, a policy introduced in the 1970s (and at the time considered controversial, to say the least). The style might be considered a bit flashy for St. Estèphe, certainly it is on the rich side, but its success is indicated by the fact that Haut Marbuzet easily prices with the classified growths.

Lansac
Margaux
2 Blason d'Issan
www.chateau-issan.com
53 ha; 300,000 bottles

Château D'Issan

Château d'Issan stands on the site of a fifteenth century fortress. By the early eighteenth century it had established a high reputation, and in 1855 was classified as a third growth. It was sold to the owner of Château Brane-Cantenac in 1866, and stayed in good shape until after the next sale in 1914. It then declined fairly steadily. The modern era starts with its purchase in 1945 by Emmanuel Cruse of the Cruse wine dynasty, who began to renovate it. D'Issan is still owned by the Cruse family (it is now the only classed growth château they own, although at various times they have owned Pontet-Canet, Rauzan-Ségla, and Haut-Bages-Libéral). From a minimal size at the time of acquisition, the vineyards have now been expanded to more than the original size. Plantings have changed from 70% Cabernet Sauvignon, 30% Merlot to 65%/35%, but Emmanuel Cruse says, "This is more to match cépage to terroir than an attempt to change the taste of the wine." The second wine is usually around 40% of production, the exact amount being determined by the proportion of young vines, on which it is based. There's also a series of other wines including a third wine, an Haut Médoc, and a Bordeaux Supérieur (from land close to the Gironde). Some of the vineyards in the Haut Médoc were reclassified as Margaux in 2007. The grand vin is in the tradition of Margaux, elegant rather than powerful, understated rather than obvious. It's generally felt to justify its third growth status again.

Château Kirwan

Sir John Collingwood, a local merchant, purchased the Kirwan estate in 1710 and established it as a working vineyard. Its name came later from the marriage of his daughter to Mark Kirwan. It established an early reputation, and was one of the vineyards visited by Thomas Jefferson in his travels through the Médoc (he referred to it as Quirouen). The estate was seized in the Revolution but subsequently restored to its owner. It was classified as a third growth in 1855. This is one of the rare châteaux whose vineyards today remain similar to those in 1855. It changed hands a couple of times before coming under the ownership of Schröder & Schÿler, one of the old negociant firms of Bordeaux, who still hold it today. They did not pay much attention to it, and it remained an underachiever, however, until Michel Rolland was engaged as oenologue in 1991. (It was his first venture on the Left Bank.) With viticulture and vinification taken in hand, the wines were greatly improved, although there was criticism that the style became fuller, fruitier, and too oaky to represent the typicity of Margaux. Michel Rolland stopped consulting for Kirwan in 2007, and since then the style has backed off somewhat to a more traditional restraint. Recent vintages have been true to the style of Margaux, generally understated, but while good, none has struck me as great. These are wines for medium term enjoyment rather than long-term cellaring.

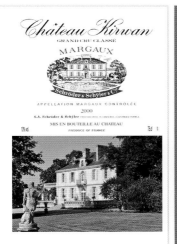

🅞 Bordeaux

🅜 Margaux

2️⃣ Les Charmes de Kirwan

www.chateau-kirwan.com

37 ha; 200,000 bottles

Château Lafite Rothschild

The name Lafite comes from the Gascon term 'la hite', which means 'hillock'. The first reference to Lafite dates from 1234; vines may have already been planted when Jacques de Ségur established the Lafite vineyard in the late seventeenth century as part of the great Ségur Seigneurie. Lafite's reputation dates from these beginnings, and it was recognized as one of the four first growths as soon as the concept of individual Crus arose. The Rothschilds acquired the property in 1866. Vineyards fall into two major parts: the main estate around the château; and the Carruades plateau just to the southwest (added in 1845). Carruades de Lafite is used to name the second wine of Lafite, however, rather than a wine from the plateau. "Part of the vineyard produces Lafite every year, whether it has young or old vines, the terroir is so extraordinary. There is a part that makes Carruades every year. And there's a part that can go either way," says manager Charles Chevallier. In addition to the grand vin and second wine, adjacent Château Duhart Milon is part of the Lafite portfolio, and there are also wines under the broader appellations of Pauillac or Médoc (sold as the Barons de Rothschild Collection). Domaines Baron de Rothschild also owns Châteaux L'Évangile in Pomerol and Rieussec in Sauternes. Lafite's reputation is nonpareil: it expresses a unique combination of elegance with supple power, and with age develops seamless layers of flavor, achieving an ethereal impression in top vintages.

🅞 Pauillac

2️⃣ Carruades de Lafite

www.lafite.com

112 ha; 540,000 bottles

Saint Julien Beychevelle
St. Julien
2 Les Fiefs de Lagrange
www.chateau-lagrange.com

118 ha; 750,000 bottles

Château Lagrange

One of the oldest established châteaux in the Médoc, this was known in the Middle Ages under the name of Maison Noble de Lagrange Monteil. It was one of the largest wine estates in the Médoc, around 120 ha at the time of the 1855 classification, when it was given third growth status. Passing through a series of proprietors who seemed to lack commitment, by 1974 the area under vines was down to as little as 39 ha. In 1983 the château was sold to the Suntory group, who have made major investments. The vineyards have been replanted. Facilities, including 92 cuves of stainless steel in a huge cuverie built in 2008, give an almost semi-industrial impression. Over 25 years on, construction continues. The vineyards are in a single block, but soils are quite varied. "Lagrange is more a unit in terms of administration than geography. There are four types of terroir, more or less representing points of the compass," says director Bruno Eynard. The best terroir is white gravel in the northwest quadrant used for Cabernet Sauvignon and Merlot; ferrous soils with large pebbles in the southeast are used for Cabernet Sauvignon and Petit Verdot. Other areas have clay or sand and are used for Merlot. Since 2006, the proportion of Cabernet Sauvignon has been increasing, but to my mind the wine has all the same moved to a lighter, more modern, fruit-forward style, making it one of the more "international" properties in St. Julien. The second wine comes from a mostly separate set of parcels.

Ludon Médoc
Haut Médoc
2 Moulin de La Lagune
www.chateau-lalagune.com

90 ha; 350,000 bottles

Château La Lagune

Vineyards were established at La Lagune by 1724, when there are records of wine being sold, although the reputation of the château dates from the ownership of Jouffrey Piston from 1819. Classified as a third growth in 1855, it is one of the five Grand Cru Classés that are not in one of the four famous communes; in fact, it is the first château you come to driving up to the Médoc from Bordeaux. It's a living illustration of the power of the 1855 classification, because it declined throughout the first half of the twentieth century until in 1954 there were only 4 hectares left. Revived following its purchase by Georges Brunet in 1954, it was sold to Champagne Ayala in 1961, and then passed to its present owners, the Frey family, when they acquired Ayala in 2000. The Freys kept La Lagune when they sold Ayala (in order to finance the purchase of Jaboulet in the Rhône). A new winery was constructed in 2003. Caroline Frey is the winemaker. The grand vin was half of production in 2010; the second wine, Moulin de La Lagune, comes from young vines, and has now been supplemented by a third wine, Mademoiselle L (coming not from La Lagune itself but from adjacent vineyards). The style at La Lagune can be masculine compared with the châteaux in Margaux to its immediate north. Quality and sense of character have improved greatly in recent vintages, where the style tends to be quite firm, but shows increasing precision with age.

Château Lascombes

Château Lascombes originated in the division of a large estate in the mid eighteenth century and was classified as a second growth in 1855. After the Revolution, the estate was purchased by negociant Nathaniel Johnston. A revolving series of proprietors presided over a continuous decline, until the château was on the verge of extinction when it was rescued by a syndicate headed by Alexis Lichine in 1951, but Lichine was never able to bring it to real second growth status. It was sold to Bass Charrington in 1971, and although nominally there was more investment, it remained a perennial under-achiever. In 2001 it was acquired by Colony Capital, an American pension fund group for €50 million; another €50 million was invested over the next decade, before it was sold for €200 million in 2011 to MACSF, a French pension fund group. The change in style has been as dramatic as any in Bordeaux, partly due to changes in the vineyard, partly to winemaking. Tasting at the château, the 1995 and 2005 seem like night and day. "This demonstrates the change," says Dominique Befve, who was hired as winemaker from Lafite. Soil surveys led to replacing 12 ha of Cabernet Sauvignon on clay terroirs with Merlot, which no doubt contributes to the change to a warmer style. Michel Rolland is a consultant, and there has been an increase in intensity and richness, making Lascombes one of the more "international" styles in the Médoc. Only new oak is used. The second wine is based on selection.

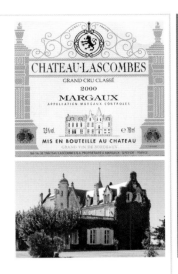

 Margaux

2 Chevalier de Lascombes
www.chateau-lascombes.com

84 ha; 320,000 bottles

Château Latour

A major estate in the seventeenth century, Latour was established as one of the top four wines of Bordeaux by the early eighteenth century. After the French Revolution, ownership passed to the negociant firms of Barton & Guestier and Nathaniel Johnston, but by 1844 the original owners, the Ségur family, had bought back a controlling share. In 1855, there was no question but that Latour was a first growth. Descendents of the family ran the château until 1962, when it was sold to a British syndicate. Then in 1993 it was sold to François Pinault, owner of a French luxury goods group, for $120 million—which given subsequent events looks like a bargain. Consistently the longest-lived wine of Bordeaux, Château Latour has not, by and large, passed through the bad patches that the other first growths of the Médoc have suffered; although Latour was dilapidated when it passed into British ownership in 1962, the wines of the fifties and sixties were probably the best in Bordeaux. The top vintages remain impressive even today. The second wine, Forts de Latour, was introduced in 1966; and the generic Pauillac, produced occasionally in the seventies or eighties, became a regular feature in 1990. The masculine style of Latour runs through all the wines, even the Pauillac. It's one of the clearest expressions of Cabernet Sauvignon in the Médoc. "The style of Latour, this incredible length, backbone, refinement, is better expressed by Cabernet Sauvignon than Merlot," is how manager Frédéric Engerer puts it.

 Saint Martin du Puy

Pauillac

2 Les Forts de Latour
www.chateau-latour.fr

65 ha; 420,000 bottles

Château Léoville Barton

Léoville Barton is the smallest of the three Léovilles (about one quarter of the original estate). Hugh Barton, of negociant Barton & Guestier, bought the estate in 1826, following his purchase of Langoa Barton a few years earlier. Léoville Barton was classified as a second growth in 1855, together with the other Léovilles (Langoa Barton was classified as a third growth). Léoville Barton and Langoa Barton both remain in the Barton family, presently run by Lilian Barton, who has been taking over from her father, Anthony, who started at the estate in 1951 with his uncle Roland, but took over completely only in 1986. The two Barton châteaux hold the record for the longest period under single family ownership among the Grand Cru Classés. I always think of Léoville Barton as a very proper claret, the quintessence of St. Julien, with elegance and freshness counterbalancing ripe fruits. The blend remains consistent from year to year, with about three quarters Cabernet Sauvignon. There is a little more Merlot in Langoa Barton. There are no tricks here to enhance ripeness by artifice in the vineyards or cellar, and Anthony Barton is known for picking early to maintain freshness. He regards 13% alcohol as the upper limit. These are food wines. The policy of producing eminently drinkable wines and selling them at a fair price means that Léoville Barton has not risen into the super-seconds, but the wine has stayed true to its traditions, although taking advantage of technical developments.

Saint Julien Beychevelle

St. Julien

2 La Réserve du Léoville Barton

www.leoville-barton.com

50 ha; 240,000 bottles

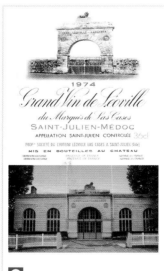

Château Léoville Lascases

The Léoville estate originated as part of the seigneurie of Calon. Vines were established by the end of the seventeenth century on a gravel mound surrounded by swamps. Under the Delon family, ownership goes back to the Marquis Las Cases, whose great grand daughter married André Delon. The current owner, Jean-Hubert, is the fifth generation. The best and largest part of the original Léoville estate, over the past 20 years Léoville Lascases has surged ahead of the other second growths to become a leading member of the super seconds. Michel Delon, the previous owner, expressed the ambition of bringing its price to parity with the first growths, and occasionally came close. The fierce reputation of the proprietors is epitomized by the motif of Léoville Lascases, a lion rampant that sits on the gate at the entrance to the vineyards, with the motto "I do not attacked unless provoked." The heart of Lascases is the 55 ha of L'Enclos, a single block running down to the river (adjacent to Château Latour), which is the major source for the grand vin. The average blend is about three quarters Cabernet Sauvignon, with the rest split between Merlot and Cabernet Franc. To the west, Clos du Marquis was vinified separately from 1902, subsequently became the second wine of Léoville Lascases, and now is made as a separate wine again. The new second wine is Le Petit Lion de Lascases. The Delons also own Châteaux Potensac in the Médoc and Nénin in Pomerol.

Saint Julien Beychevelle

St. Julien

2 Le Petit Lion du Marquis de Las Cases

www.leoville-las-cases.com

98 ha; 540,000 bottles

Château Léoville Poyferré

Split off from the Léoville estate in 1815, Léoville Poyferré was classified as a second growth in 1855, when its price was the same as that of Lascases (Barton was lower). The estate was sold in 1866 and run by the Lalande family until it was sold to the Cuvelier negociant family around 1920. Léoville Poyferré declined in reputation during the sixties and seventies; indeed, at one time it became known as Voie-Ferré, after the railway, reflecting a metallic taste in the wines. Didier Cuvelier took over in 1979 and started a program of modernization. During the eighties the reputation began to be restored. Didier brought in Michel Rolland as consultant in 1994. "When I hired Michel Rolland, everyone laughed, and said, ho ho, he's from the right bank," he recalls. The main change in the wine, he considers, has been in the maturity of the tannins. Replanting has almost doubled the vineyard area, with Cabernet Sauvignon increasing from 30% to 65%. Didier also owns Château Moulin Riche, whose relationship with Léoville Poyferré has been slightly muddled. "For a long time, Moulin Riche was regarded as the second wine of Léoville Poyferré, but today it is made from its own terroir and a new second wine, Pavillon de Poyferré, in effect has been used for declassified lots from both Moulin Riche and Léoville Poyferré since 1995," Didier explains. In the past two decades, Léoville Poyferré has turned towards a more modern representation of St. Julien, suppler and softer.

 Saint Julien Beychevelle
St. Julien
2 Pavillon de Poyferré
www.léoville-poyferre.fr
80 ha; 380,000 bottles

Château Lynch Bages

The vineyards appear to have been established in the mid eighteenth century, and the château was classified as a fifth growth in 1855. Its modern history starts when it was acquired by Jean-Charles Cazes, a local insurance agent who was investing in the wine trade. From 1934 he rented the vineyards as a tenant, and then purchased them in 1938. His son, André, added Château Haut Bages Averous to the portfolio, and this became the second wine of Lynch Bages. The estate is dominated by almost three quarters Cabernet Sauvignon. Following the modern trend, the second wine has been renamed Echo de Lynch Bages, and a third wine (a Pauillac AOP) has been introduced. There is also a white wine, which originated by a mistake when a nursery sent Sauvignon Blanc vines instead of Cabernet Sauvignon. Lynch Bages demonstrates the greatest disparity between official status and actual status among the classed growths. It has been placed with the second growths at least since the second half of the twentieth century, and today market price places it firmly in the super seconds. "The wine we produce is an opulent hedonistic Pauillac, and has not changed, but we have been producing much better wine since the 1980s, based on the investments made in the seventies," says Jean-Charles Cazes (great grandson of the first Jean-Charles). The wine is classic Pauillac, relatively powerful, but never over the top. It ages well: I still remember the 1961 from only a few years ago.

 Pauillac
2 Echo de Lynch Bages
www.lynchbages.com
110 ha; 480,000 bottles

Margaux

2 Pavillon Rouge du Château Margaux

Pavillon Blanc du Château Margaux
www.chateau-margaux.com

94 ha; 400,000 bottles

Château Margaux

Under the name of La Mothe de Margaux, the estate dates from the twelfth century, but wine production did not start until the sixteenth. By the end of the seventeenth century, the estate included 265 ha, more or less equivalent to its size today, with vineyards occupying about a third. Under the same ownership as Haut Brion, it was well known in England by the eighteenth century (the 1771 vintage was the first claret to appear in a Christies' catalogue). Established as one of the top four growths, there was no question about Margaux's position as a first growth in 1855. It was comfortably established at the top of the hierarchy when it was sold to Frédéric Pillet-Will in 1879. Some of the Pillet-Will bottlings, including the 1900, remain famous to this day. A syndicate took over after his death and ran the estate until the Ginestets obtained control in 1949. At this point, however, lack of investment began to tell, and the wines are generally acknowledged as falling below first growth standard through the 1960s and 1970s (the 1959 was excellent, however). Greek supermarket magnate André Mentzelopoulos purchased the château in 1979, but died in 1980, leaving the château to be managed by his daughter, Corinne. Emile Peynaud was brought in as consulting oenologue and there was a continuing program of investment. Since 1982, the wine has regained the very top level, showcasing the classic elegance of Margaux. Unusually for the Médoc, there is also a significant production of white wine.

Bordeaux

St. Estèphe

2 Prieur de Meyney
www.meyney.fr

51 ha; 280,000 bottles

Château Meyney

One of the châteaux acquired by Désiré Cordier in 1919, this Cru Bourgeois remained in the Cordier portfolio together with Gruaud Larose and Talbot until the group was split up in a sale in 2005. While part of the Cordier holdings, Château Meyney (like Château Talbot) was never quite able to come out from under the shadow of Gruaud Larose. Today it is owned by the investment arm of Crédit Agricole (which also owns Grand Puy Ducasse in Pauillac and other châteaux). As witnessed by the date of 1662 set in iron at the entrance, this is an old wine-producing property; it was originally a monastery. Château Meyney was always one of the best Cru Bourgeois in its appellation, although it chose not to remain in the most recent classification. Typifying St. Estèphe, the wine is classically based on Cabernet Sauvignon (although it has an unusually high proportion of Petit Verdot, usually around 10%). The vineyards are in a single block overlooking the Gironde, located between Châteaux Montrose and Phélan Ségur. There's a deep streak of blue clay under much of the vineyard. Under the previous management, the wine always had that touch of dryness on the finish marking the Cordier style, but recent vintages seem to have become softer. There's cold maceration before fermentation, part of the wine undergoes malolactic fermentation in new barriques, and it spends 16-18 months maturing in barrique, with 30-40% new oak. New oak is reduced to 10-15% for the second wine.

Château Montrose

One of the last of the Grand Cru Classés to be established, Château Montrose dates from 1815, and was classified as a second growth in 1855. It has been fortunate in a series of committed proprietors: the Charmolües owned it from 1896 until it was sold to the Bouygues brothers in 2006. Always one of the most long-lived wines of Bordeaux, Montrose has remained true to its roots. Even with a recent softening, it is as traditional as you can get, with a massive, solid, structure underneath the fruits. Vineyards are in a contiguous block on a gravel outcrop close to the Gironde, where the gravel goes down a couple of meters to iron-rich subsoil. Soils are relatively homogeneous, although Merlot is planted where there is more clay closer to the river. The blend changes little from year to year. Vineyards were recently expanded substantially by a purchase from adjacent Phélan Ségur (a Cru Bourgeois). This has increased production, although only one third of grapes from the new vineyard go into the grand vin. Montrose used to epitomize the tradition that a wine would be too tough to taste when young; that has changed, and there is now more obvious fruit in the young wine, but it would still be vinicide to drink in its first decade. "We are making better balanced wines, less austere than earlier vintages, which perhaps were too masculine," manager Nicolas Glumineau said in 2011. By contrast, La Dame de Montrose is mostly based on Merlot and is more approachable.

 St. Estèphe

2 La Dame de Montrose

www.chateau-montrose.com

95 ha; 325,000 bottles

Château Mouton Rothschild

Château Brane-Mouton was owned by Baron Hector de Brane in 1833 when he sold it to finance his purchase of Château Gorce, which he renamed Château Brane-Cantenac. A few years later, in 1853, it was purchased by Baron Nathaniel de Rothschild of the English branch of the Rothschild family, who renamed it as Château Mouton Rothschild. At that time it was firmly established as the best of the second growths, and was duly classified as such in 1855. It remained in this position until the start of the twentieth century, when its price moved to parity with Lafite and the other first growths. Baron Philippe de Rothschild became the first member of the family to manage the property personally when he took it over in 1922. During fifty years of campaigning for promotion to first growth, the château's motto was, "First I cannot be, Second I disdain, I am Mouton." Promotion finally came in 1973. The company also owns Châteaux Clerc Milon and d'Armailhac. It was run by Baron Philippe's daughter, Baroness Philippine, a great figure in Bordeaux until she died in 2014. Often one of the most powerful wines of Bordeaux, Mouton Rothschild can age for decades, becoming less opulent but without much loss of its remarkable density. The second wine represents a lower proportion of production than other classed growths, but Mouton seems none the worse for it. Mouton Cadet is a brand whose only connection with the great château is common ownership.

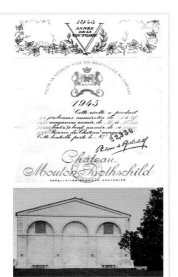

Pauillac

2 Le Petit Mouton

www.chateau-mouton-rothschild.com

82 ha; 320,000 bottles

Château Palmer

Château Palmer was founded by General Charles Palmer, an Englishman, when he bought Château de Gascq and its 82 hectares of vines in 1816. It was sold in 1853 to the Péreire banking family, which was forced to sell the estate in 1938, when it was purchased by a consortium of two wine families, the Dutch Mählers and the German Sichels. Its reputation has been well above its official third growth status for many years. It came to fame when the 1961 vintage was generally acknowledged to be comparable to the first growths; indeed, for a while Palmer 1961 sold at auction at prices above the first growths. It is presently a leading member of the group of super seconds. Most of the vineyards are in a contiguous series of blocks around the château with two further separate plots within a kilometer. Winemaker Thomas Duroux explains its unique character: "Due to the enthusiasm of a past manager, a unique feature of the vineyards is the equal proportion of Cabernet Sauvignon and Merlot, which unusually is planted on the best gravel terroirs as well as clay." Undoubtedly the next best wine in the appellation to Château Margaux, Palmer is famous for showing an almost fleshy warmth without any loss of precision. Until 1997, the second wine, La Réserve du Générale, was produced by declassifying lots from Palmer. Then it was replaced by Alter Ego de Palmer, which is now treated as a separate brand, based on selecting lots with more forward fruit.

Margaux
2 Alter Ego de Palmer
www.chateau-palmer.com
55 ha; 200,000 bottles

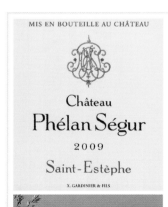

Château Phélan Ségur

This has long been regarded as one of the best Cru Bourgeois. The estate dates from 1804, when it was created by Bernard Phélan; a subsequent marriage is responsible for the Ségur part of the name (not connected with the famous Seigneurie de Ségur). The estate has been owned by the Gardinier family (of Champagne Lanson) since 1985. It was in some disarray at the time of purchase, but a new winery was constructed in 1988, and the estate was expanded in 2002 by purchasing the 25 ha of neighboring Château Houissant. Then it contracted in 2010 by selling 22 ha to Château Montrose (long ago these were actually part of the Montrose estate). The impact of this change in sources is not entirely clear, but the blend of 55% Cabernet Sauvignon to 45% Merlot does not seem to have changed. The style is traditional, relatively restrained, sometimes tight, giving a good representation of St. Estèphe at the Cru Bourgeois level, meaning that fruit is not always immediately obvious and some patience may be required before it emerges. In addition to the second wine, which is named for an early proprietor, there is a third wine (Croix Bonis, mostly Cabernet Sauvignon from parcels of young vines), and a rosé. In an attempt at a modern style, there were reports in 2008 of a super cuvée, Feé des Roses, coming from the oldest vines, but this seems to have been abandoned. The château is only part of the Gardinier family holdings, which include three star restaurants and hotels.

St. Estèphe
2 Frank Phélan
www.phelansegur.com
70 ha; 325,000 bottles

Château Pichon Longueville Baron

The grand estate of Pichon Longueville was divided into two more or less equal parts in 1850. Wines were not actually produced under separate labels for some years after the split, so there was in fact no experience of the wines produced by the individual estates when both were classified as second growths in 1855. Pichon Baron was sold to the Bouteiller family in 1933 and continued to have a good reputation until the 1960s, when after the death of Jean Bouteiller it went into decline. One of the early examples of revival by corporate investment, Pichon Baron was sold to insurance company AXA in 1987, when there were only 33 ha of vineyards remaining. AXA invested in winemaking and expanded the vineyards, not entirely successfully since some of the acquisitions proved not to be of top quality and now are used for the second wine, the Tourelles de Longueville. The grand vin comes from the vineyards closer to the château itself. The style of the wine is distinctly Pauillac: powerful, but smooth. It seems more muscular than Pichon Lalande. "There is an overall objective for style. The grand vin is Cabernet style for sure, looking for elegance and finesse, although there can be austerity when young," says Director Jean-René Matignon. Recent vintages display the wine at full power, and the status of Pichon Baron has been rising into the super-seconds. The wine has moved towards a more modern style, but without betraying the appellation.

Pauillac
2 Tourelles de Longueville
www.pichonlongueville.com

73 ha; 400,000 bottles

Château Pichon Longueville Comtesse de Lalande

The modern era started at Pichon Lalande when the Miailhe brothers, Edouard and Louis, from an old family of courtiers, purchased the château in 1925. After a difficult period in the seventies, the estate passed to Édouard's youngest daughter, May-Éliane Lencquesaing in 1978. The vineyards doubled in size, and the estate rose steadily in reputation. The Miailhe era ended when the estate was sold to Roederer Champagne in 2006. Pichon Lalande is one of the trio at the heart of the super-seconds in Pauillac and St. Julien (its close rivals being Léoville Lascases and Ducru Beaucaillou). The vineyards visible from the château are in fact those of neighboring Château Latour: Pichon Lalande's vineyards are on the other side, in large blocks extending to St. Julien. The new owners have started a major program of further investment, initiated while Sylvie Cazes (sister of Jean-Charles Cazes at Château Lynch Bages) was Director. The current director is Nicolas Glumineau, who came from Château Montrose in 2012. Aside from improvements in viticulture and vinification, the main change will be an increasing emphasis on Cabernet Sauvignon, but this is likely to take some years to accomplish. The style of Pichon Lalande is influenced by an unusually high proportion of Merlot (which is why "Cabernet years" are not necessarily top years for the château): unmistakably Pauillac all the same, and with a sheen that I would describe as polished.

Pauillac
2 Réserve de la Comtesse
www.pichon-lalande.com

89 ha; 450,000 bottles

Pauillac

2 Les Hauts de Pontet-Canet

www.pontet-canet.com

82 ha; 540,000 bottles

Château Pontet Canet

At the start of the eighteenth century, Jean-François de Pontet, who was the governor of the Médoc, assembled several parcels of land to form the vineyards of Pontet. Some years later his descendants added vineyards in the region of Canet. The châteaux's reputation was high in this period, but in 1855 it was classified only as a fifth growth. Purchased by the Cruse negociant house in 1865, it stayed in the Cruse family until they were forced to sell by the scandal of 1973, but by then there had been a decline in quality. Pontet Canet was purchased by Guy Tesseron, a cognac merchant who had married into the Cruse family, and already owned Château Lafon Rochet. Michel Rolland was engaged as consultant during the 1990s. Current winemaker Jean-Michel Comme says, "We are looking for more and more purity in the wines. Today they have finer tannins and more concentration." He attributes the improvement to biodynamics, for which Jean-Michel and proprietor Alfred Tesseron have made Pontet Canet a leader in Bordeaux. Young wines show the power of Pauillac with something of the elegance of St. Julien, developing seamless layers of flavor with age. Reflecting the steadily improving quality of the wine, price has been moving up towards the super-seconds. The second wine comes from younger parcels and has more Merlot. It was declassified to Vin de France in 2012, but this reflects more on the AOP panel than the château.

Ordonnac

Médoc

2 La Chapelle de Potensac

www.potensac.com

84 ha; 320,000 bottles

Château Potensac

North of St. Estèphe, beyond the Haut Médoc, Château Potensac makes one of the best wines of the Médoc AOP. It was one of the châteaux originally classified as Cru Bourgeois Exceptionnel, but which withdrew from the most recent classification. A large estate, long owned by the Delons of Léoville Lascases (long means more than two centuries), Potensac produces wine in the style, if without quite the concentration, of the communes to its south. It's close to the Gironde on a natural high point. Soils are similar to St. Estèphe, with a lot of limestone and gravel, and a fair amount of red clay. Dominated by an impression of Cabernet Sauvignon (although Merlot is typically about half the blend), it can be austere in lesser vintages, but very good value in good vintages. The wine is made by the team from Léoville Lascases. Tasting a vertical of Château Potensac over the past decade offers a view of the effects of global warming on wine production, from the classic wines of the mid nineties with fresh acidity and herbaceous notes to the wines of the last decade, soft and supple in 2009 and 2010. Excepting 2003, Potensac is remarkably consistent across vintages, generally offering a refined impression. It's a wine that develops slowly, losing fruit rather than turning tertiary, but a good vintage lasts twenty years, and the overall impression is really quite classic: unmistakably claret, and well above expectations for the lowly appellation.

Château Prieuré Lichine

Wine was being sold by Le Prieur de Cantenac in the eighteenth century for 1000 livres per tonneau. As property of the church, the estate was seized in the Revolution, divided, and sold to a M. Durand. The estate then was sold to the Pagès family, became known later as Château Prieuré and subsequently as Prieuré-Cantenac, and decayed as it passed through a long series of owners. Its modern history starts when it was purchased by the American wine merchant Alexis Lichine in 1952 for a bargain sum. By the time of purchase, the vineyards were reduced to a mere 11 ha, and Lichine set about reconstructing the estate by purchasing further vineyards whenever possible. (He later was also part of a syndicate that bought Château Lascombes.) By 1974 Prieuré-Lichine was back up to 57 ha (well above its size at the time of the 1855 classification). Lichine's willingness to entertain tourists and sell wine directly was regarded as all but scandalous. The estate was inherited by his son, Sacha Lichine, but sold to the Ballande mining group in 1999 to become part of their growing portfolio of wine investments. A modern concrete winery now sits besides the traditional château, and a new cuverie was added in 2014. Stéphane Derenoncourt became the consulting oenologue. The style has changed from its former slightly austere character, to a much more fruit forward, "international" style. The wine is undoubtedly technically better, but the style is quite full for Margaux.

Margaux
2 Le Cloître de Prieuré-Lichine
www.prieure-lichine.fr

80 ha; 300,000 bottles

Château Rauzan-Gassies

The Rauzan estate was created in 1661; Rauzan-Gassies and Rauzan-Ségla were formed when it was split in 1766. Rauzan-Gassies is the smaller part. The château itself became part of Rauzan-Ségla, so wine is made in a relatively modern building. Rauzan-Gassies passed into the Quié family when Paul Quié, a wine merchant in Paris who sold Algerian wine, invested in Bordeaux. In 1942 he bought Croizet Bages and then in 1946 followed with Rauzan-Gassies. He had a Parisian view that the vineyard was more an investment than a principal occupation; it was not until his son took over in 1968 that the property was managed directly. Today it is run by the third generation of winemaker Jean-Philippe and his sister Anne-Françoise. The estate consists of about 17 individual parcels, all in Margaux. The grand vin is about three quarters of production and is dominated by Cabernet Sauvignon (ranging from 60-85% in recent vintages) and matured in 55% new oak. The second wine, Le Chevalier de Rauzan-Gassies, uses 25% new oak. There are some unusual features in both viticulture and vinification. Machine harvesting contrasts with the common emphasis on manual work at most châteaux; and in the cellar, malolactic fermentation is initiated by inoculation at the start of alcoholic fermentation. Rauzan-Gassies was considered to produce wines that tend to be a bit rustic for Margaux, but lately has become more precise.

Beychac et Caillau
Margaux
2 Le Chevalier de Rauzan-Gassies
www.rauzangassies.fr
29 ha; 150,000 bottles

Château Rauzan-Ségla

Pierre des Mesures de Rauzan created the Rauzan estate in 1661, and it was split as the result of inheritance issues to form Rauzan-Ségla and Rauzan-Gassies in 1766. Both the Rauzans were classified as second growths in 1855. The estate was purchased in 1903 by Fréderic Cruse of the Cruse negociant, but Cruse's half century of ownership was not particularly distinguished. Rauzan-Ségla's reputation declined until Cruse sold it in 1956; then it was managed by the negociant firm Eschenauer. Some improvements were made, but it was still relatively run down, and real renovation came only with its acquisition by the Wertheimer brothers of Chanel in 1994. Everything is new, from 15 km of drainage in the vineyards to a fermentation facility. "The only old part of the property today is the nineteenth century barrel room," says John Kolasa, who came from Château Latour to manage the vineyards in 1994. (He also manages the other Wertheimer property, Château Canon in St. Emilion). The wine remains true to the traditions of Margaux. Scots by origin, John has trenchant opinions about modern technology. "There is very traditional vinification, we are not modern style," he says. Today's wine is refined and elegant, a very good impression of Margaux's typicity in the current era. It now places in the Margaux market just after Château Margaux itself and Palmer. My only question is how well the wines will age in the long term.

Margaux
2 Ségla
www.chateaurauzansegla.com
66 ha; 220,000 bottles

Château Sociando Mallet

Is Sociando-Mallet the most under valued estate in the Médoc? That's a difficult judgment, but there's no doubt the wine is of classed growth quality, although the estate is a relatively recent creation that has never been included in any classification. Just north of St. Estèphe, it is located on a slight rise with a good view over the Gironde. Proprietor Jean Gautreau is a person of strong, not to say iconoclastic, opinions. The first person in his family to be involved in wine, he purchased the property in 1969 when it had a mere 5 ha of vines, mostly Cabernet Sauvignon. "Cabernet was planted in the wrong places, it was an absolute nonsense," he says. As he expanded the vineyards, the original vines were pulled out and Cabernet Sauvignon was planted in more appropriate locations. Today there is just over half Cabernet Sauvignon. Jean does not believe in green harvests, and holds that well managed vineyards can perfectly well make quality wine from yields of 50 hl/ha. "Vendange vert is more to increase the price than the quality; the garage wines were a catastrophe for Bordeaux. What is a grand wine of Bordeaux? Finesse and elegance in the aroma and taste," he states. "I'm contre-courant," is his general position. The wines are full, smooth, and elegant, more like a cross between Pauillac and St. Julien than neighboring St. Estèphe. A special cuvée, called Jean Gautreau, which can be 100% Cabernet Sauvignon, is selected from the top barrels.

Saint Seurin de Cadourne
Haut Médoc
2 La Demoiselle de Sociando-Mallet
www.sociandomallet.com
85 ha; 550,000 bottles

Château Talbot

Château Talbot takes its name from John Talbot, Earl of Shrewsbury, although his only connection with it appears to have been his involvement in the war in Aquitaine in the fifteenth century. During the eighteenth and nineteenth centuries the estate was owned by the Marquis d'Aux de Lescout, and was known as Talbot d'Aux. It was classified as a fourth growth in 1855. The negociant Desiré Cordier purchased the estate in 1917. Cordier also owned second growth Gruaud Larose and cru bourgeois Château Meyney; all three were bottled in characteristic squat bottles with the Cordier imprint. The Cordiers sold up in 1993, but kept Château Talbot, which was also the family home. The vineyards are in a single large block of mostly gravel terroir. The Cordier style has always been rather dry, and while Cordier owned both Gruaud Larose and Talbot, there was a marked resemblance between the wines, with Talbot somewhat seeming the poor man's Gruaud. Château Talbot is priced more or less in line with its original classification as a fourth growth, but even though it has been freed of the shadow of Gruaud Larose, it seems somehow to have failed really to establish its own reputation in the next tier in St. Julien. The style has remained quite traditional, but recently there have been investments in both vineyard and winery in an effort to increase precision; and the 2010 is the best result since the outstanding 1986. There is also a white wine, Caillou de Talbot.

Saint Julien Beychevelle
St. Julien
2 Connétable de Talbot
www.chateau-talbot.com

105 ha; 500,000 bottles

Château La Tour Carnet

There are many châteaux described as "La Tour" in Bordeaux, but La Tour Carnet started its history as an actual fortress. Access is by a bridge across the moat. It's not clear when production of wine actually began, but during the eighteenth century the château came into the hands of the de Leutken family, who held it through the 1855 classification, when it became a fourth growth. Subsequently owned by a Bordeaux negociant, it declined significantly, with the vineyards much reduced. The château was sold in 2000 to become part of the portfolio of Bernard Magrez, owner of many properties, including Château Pape-Clément in Graves as well as châteaux on the right bank. "There were problems, it took three years to improve the quality of the wines. It's once again the terroir that counts, now it's getting back to produce wine at the level of the terroir," he says. Vineyards are largely in a single parcel, but even so the terroirs are quite varied. The proportion of Merlot has been increased, and is now more than half. "Cabernet Sauvignon used to be harvested too early, which gave the wine a structure that was a little rustic," Bernard says. With Michel Rolland as consultant, the style, if not completely international, is certainly more opulent. The smooth ripeness of the fruits is very much in the modern idiom, but vintage is always evident, from the opulent 2009, to the more reserved 2010, to the classic impression of 2011. It's certainly back up to Grand Cru Classé quality.

Saint Laurent Médoc
Haut Médoc
2 Douves de Carnet
www.latour-carnet.com

115 ha; 450,000 bottles

Sainte-Colombe

Côtes de Castillon

www.derenoncourtconsultants.com

10 ha; 20,000 bottles

Domaine de L'A

Stéphane Derenoncourt is known worldwide as a consulting oenologist. He is especially prominent on Bordeaux's right bank, where he established Domaine de l'A in the satellite area of Castillon in 1999. Loans from local vignerons enabled him to buy a couple of hectares of south-facing calcareous terroir on a high point, and he built the first cuverie with the help of some friends. Planting density was increased by interspersing additional rows between the existing rows of vines, the vineyard was later expanded by buying two more plots, and the mix was brought to 80% Merlot and 20% Cabernet Franc. Stéphane believes that Castillon has the potential to rival St. Emilion, and sets out to prove it with his domain. Together with Château d'Aiguilhe (for which he consults), it's become one of the defining properties for the appellation. What typicity do you want in Domaine de l'A, I asked? "Expression calcaire. I love calcaire, it's the rock that gives the best transformation for red wine," Stéphane says. "On calcareous soil, Merlot is fresh and gives flowers and minerality or salinity." The first vintage was 2000. The style is well structured, although it can be a little lacking in generosity in difficult years. It needs time, beginning to develop after five or six years, with minerality showing as a touch of gunflint. When young, fruits are dense and quite extracted. The 65% new oak can be quite evident, and the style is a little sturdy.

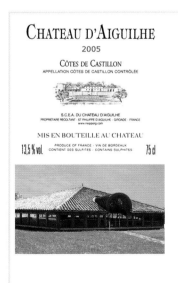

Saint Philippe d'Aiguille

Côtes de Castillon

2 Seigneurs d'Aiguilhe

www.neipperg.com

70 ha; 220,000 bottles

Château d'Aiguilhe

Stephan von Neipperg of Château Canon La Gaffelière in St. Emilion was ahead of his time when he purchased Château d'Aiguilhe in 1998. It's an old estate that at one point had 400 ha of vines. The name, which means needle or peak, reflects its location on a rocky outcrop, just across the boundary with St. Emilion. The place was run down when Stephan purchased it. "When I took over we preserved 27 ha of old vines, we took out 16 ha of poor Cabernet Franc and Sauvignon," he says. The planting mix is now 80% Merlot and 20% Cabernet Franc; there is no Cabernet Sauvignon because, "We are on chalk, and chalk and Cabernet Sauvignon is a disaster." The average vine age of 30 years reflects a large gap between the preserved old vines and the new plantings. The estate extends over 110 ha and includes a ruined fourteenth century fortress. Old buildings have been restored and a new cuverie constructed. Stéphane Derenoncourt, of Domaine de l'A, is the consulting oenologist. Coming mostly from young vines, the second wine is about a third of production. The grand vin has a nicely structured impression coming from the Cabernet Franc (and 50% new oak). There can be quite a mineral impression when young, and it develops quite slowly, reaching a peak after about ten years, but staying fresh and lively. It's an interesting contrast with Clos de l'Oratoire, a grand cru St. Emilion in the Neipperg portfolio, which is lighter and rounder, but without Aiguilhe's mineral depth.

Château Angélus

From the magnificent set of bells (programmed to play your national anthem on arrival) to the vast entrance hall with a vaulted wooden roof set to rival the largest in Europe, it is evident that no expense was spared in constructing the new château, which took more than two years to build. It's so massive and convoluted that you are left wondering where to find the working winery. Before there was just a cuverie, but Hubert de Boüard wanted to build a Château. The Boüard's have owned Angelus since 1782. The vineyards are in a large single holding, facing south on a gentle slope. Angélus uses 27 ha; 12 ha are not classified and are used for Carillon. The vineyard was expanded in the sixties and seventies, but the proportions of 50% Merlot, 47% Cabernet Franc, and 3% Cabernet Sauvignon have not changed since Hubert's grandfather planted the vineyards, focusing on Cabernet Franc to produce more structured wine. The large amount of Cabernet Franc is "just like it is at Cheval Blanc and Ausone." Hubert changed the style after he came to Angélus in 1979, reducing yields and improving quality. All this was rewarded with promotion to Premier Grand Cru Classé A in 2012 (and commemorated by being engraved in stone at the entrance to the new building). Merlot is vinified in stainless steel to preserve fruit, but Cabernet Franc in concrete, malolactic occurs in barrique, and Angélus matures in 100% new oak for up to two years. The wine has all the refinement of ripe Cabernet Franc.

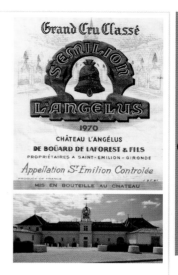

◯ St. Emilion
2 Le Carillon de L'Angélus
www.angelus.com
🔲 ⚒ G
39 ha; 100,000 bottles

Château Ausone

Ausone is a small property, with a very discrete access just besides the town of St. Emilion. About a quarter of its vineyards are immediately around; the rest are on the surrounding slopes. Now clearly one of the top wines of St. Emilion, every drop a first growth, Château Ausone had a chequered history for the last quarter of the twentieth century. A family dispute led to arguments about who was in charge, with constant disagreements about routine issues such as date of harvest, but this was resolved when (following a legal action) Alain Vauthier took over the estate in 1995. Since then the wine has gone from strength to strength. The unusually high proportion of Cabernet Franc, which is just over half of plantings, is the driving force for Ausone's style. "In the top terroirs I have more Cabernet Franc than Merlot," Alain says. "It's the Cabernet Franc that makes Ausone," says Maitre de Chai Philippe Baillarguet. There's an ongoing experiment with Cabernet Sauvignon; enough has been planted to make four barriques. At the moment it goes into the second wine, "but it's almost sure some will go into the grand vin when the vines are older," Philippe says. The style shows purity of fruits, balance rather than excess, structure for aging, and that indefinable quality: breed. The mark of Ausone is constant questioning in viticulture and vinification as to what will make the best wine. The Vauthier family also owns two other châteaux in St. Emilion, Moulin St. Georges and Fonbel.

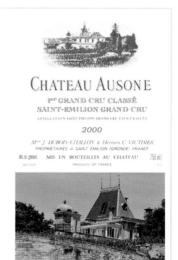

◯ St. Emilion
2 Chapelle D'Ausone
chateau-ausone.fr

8 ha; 24,000 bottles

St. Emilion

2 Petit Bécot de Beauséjour

www.beausejour-becot.com

22 ha; 70,000 bottles

Château Beauséjour Bécot

"This estate has belonged to my family since the French Revolution," says Juliette Bécot. Her grandfather owned a 5 ha property called Château La Carte, which he worked at weekends. At the end of the sixties, he purchased Beauséjour, which together with La Carte was 12 ha, and renamed Beauséjour Bécot. Juliette's father, Gérard, bought Trois Moulins, the highest point in St. Emilion, in the seventies; he thought it was the highest quality terroir, but Beauséjour was demoted in 1986 because of its inclusion, and it wasn't until 1996 that it regained its status as a Premier Grand Cru Classé. "It was hard during this period because the consumer doesn't understand why you lost your classification. The positive side was that we had to make a lot of effort, we introduced green harvest and sorting earlier than other châteaux," Juliette now says. Located on the plateau close to the town, Beauséjour's vineyards have 70% Merlot, but are changing. "In 1995 we bought 2.4 ha of La Gomerie which has 100% Merlot, and after the last classification we were allowed to include it in Beauséjour Bécot, so we have more Merlot," Juliette explains. The first blend including La Gomerie was 2012. The Merlot is typically very ripe, so expect to see Beauséjour become just a little richer in style in the future. "Beauséjour Bécot brings the structure, La Gomerie the fat," is how Juliette describes it. Juliette also bought an estate in Castillon in 2001, where she makes wine under the label of Joanin Bécot.

St. Emilion

2 Croix de Beauséjour

www.beausejourhdl.com

7 ha; 25,000 bottles

Château Beauséjour Duffau Lagarrosse

One of the smallest Premier Grand Cru Classés, this has been owned by the same family since 1847 and is now in the hands of the seventh generation, but is managed by Nicolas Thienpont. The estate has not changed since it was created in 1869 by dividing the 14.5 ha of the original Beauséjour. This part has the original house, and under the château are extensive limestone caves from the Roman era. The estate lies in an amphitheater protected from the north wind, with a plateau falling off to the south and southwest. Plantings are one third Cabernet Franc and two thirds Merlot. Five zones in the vineyards are vinified separately. Vinification is in concrete vats. Grapes are destemmed but not crushed, indigenous yeast start fermentation in three days, and it lasts 10-12 days. Both pump-over and punch-down are used depending on the lot. "It's not the usual approach in Bordeaux but it suits us very well," says winemaker David Suire. The small vat room looks a bit old fashioned, very WYSIWG, with no glitzy renovation here. Lots go into new or old wood depending on character, and MLF occurs in barriques. There is 60-65% new oak for the grand vin and no new oak for the second wine. "For us the most important determinant between grand vin and second wine is the terroir," David says. The first racking after malo is the main point of selection. The style is mainstream for St. Emilion, which is to say focused on the ripeness of Merlot, but can be a little sturdy.

Château Bélair-Monange

With vineyards divided between the limestone plateau and the slopes near Château Ausone, this should be one of the top châteaux of St. Emilion. As Château Belair, however, it was never very successful, perhaps due to the idiosyncrasies of its former owner. Purchased by Moueix in 2008, the name was changed to Bélair-Monange in memory of Christian Moueix's grandmother, and an enormous program of investment began, with vineyards extensively replanted, and the château rebuilt. Yet there was scarcely a chance to see the effects before Moueix announced that Bélair-Monange was to be merged with Château Magdelaine close by. Owned by Moueix since 1952, Magdelaine has been impeccably run, and has been one of my favorite St. Emilions. Although its proportion of Merlot was the highest in St. Emilion at 90%, the wine has always been refined and elegant. Perhaps for that reason, it was never completely successful in the marketplace. The fig leaf for the merger is that the complementary character of the two properties will allow a better wine to be made than either alone. "We have big ambitions for Bélair-Monange," says Frédéric Lospied at Moueix. Certainly the combined property will have vineyards as impressive as any in St. Emilion. From 2012, the wine from the combined properties is labeled as Bélair-Monange; whether it will follow Magdelaine's discrete style remains to be seen. In the meantime, Magdelaine 2009 and 2010 are still available.

St. Emilion
www.moueix.com

24 ha; 50,000 bottles

Château Canon

Overlooking the Church, all around the lieu-dit of Saint Martin at the top of St Emilion, are gateposts marked Château Canon. Most lead into vineyards or annex buildings; entrance to the château itself is blocked by building works as it is in the last stage of an extensive restoration. "When we got here there were many problems—which is why no one wanted to buy it—we've been here since 1996 and we only broke even two years ago. Things go very quickly down and it takes a long time to come back. It's taken twenty years to get to where we wanted," says John Kolasa, who took over when the Wertheimer brothers (of Chanel) added Canon to their holding of Rausan-Ségla in Margaux. The vineyards have been three quarters replanted; the cellars, which were contaminated with TCA, have been completely rebuilt. The 4 ha estate of Curé Bon was incorporated in 2000, and more recently the adjacent 12 ha estate of Matras has been added; in due course it will become the second wine. At one point, Canon went up to 80% Merlot while replanting, but now it's back to 65%. "The vines get stressed up here, they get more minerality, the wines will last for years," John says. "I see more Cabernet Franc when I taste Canon than there really is. It's all to do with the terroir, it's the stress on the limestone." Comparing the 2001 and 2011, I see a clear lineage: fine and elegant, never blowsy, more the precision of Cabernet Franc than the roundness of Merlot, a real connoisseur's wine.

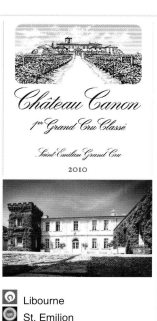

Libourne
St. Emilion
2 Croix de Canon
www.chateaucanon.com

29 ha; 90,000 bottles

Château Canon La Gaffelière

Comte Stephan de Neipperg, to give him his full title, came from Mont-pellier in 1983 to take over Canon La Gaffelière, which his father had bought in 1969. At the time, it was a St. Emilion Grand Cru Classé with a middling reputation. In 2012 it was promoted to Premier Grand Cru Classé, and today Vignobles Neipperg owns four châteaux in St. Emilion, and other properties in Castillon and Pessac-Léognan, as well as outside France. The coat of arms is the distinguishing mark on all the brands. The improvements at Canon La Gaffelière include replanting the vineyards, restricting yields, and renovating the winery, which is a practical building just below the town of St. Emilion. Lying at the base of the Côtes, the south-facing vineyards are 55% Merlot, 40% Cabernet Franc, and a little Cabernet Sauvignon. "Cabernet Franc is difficult in St. Emilion, but if it's good, it makes outstanding wine," Stephan says. "Here we never take the Cabernet Franc out, it's all perpetuated by selection massale. For me it's very important that we are not working with the clones, it's about com-plexity not volume." Vinification is in wooden vats, followed by malolactic in barrique, with 80-100% new oak for the grand vin. The wine has gone from strength to strength since the mid nineties, with the high proportion of Cabernet Franc always conveying a sense of finesse; in fact, although Cabernet Franc is the minority grape, I usually feel it is the dominant aromatic influence.

St. Emilion
2 Neipperg Selection
www.neipperg.com
20 ha; 65,000 bottles

Château Cheval Blanc

Since Cheval Blanc was created by splitting off from Figeac in the 1830s, it's been a defining property in St. Emilion. Yet located adjacent to Pomerol, it is atypical, with mostly gravel soil types. Plantings are 60% Cabernet Franc to 40% Merlot. However, "people who say that Merlot is for clay and Cabernet Franc is for gravel don't understand Cheval Blanc. It's exactly the opposite here," says technical director Pierre Clouet. There's also a small amount of Cabernet Sauvignon: "This is like salt and pepper, we need it." Cheval Blanc was purchased in 1998 by Bernard Arnault of LVMH, and there has been massive investment in a new, rather controversial winery, completed in 2011. "We respect the nine-teenth century patrimony but we are in the twenty-first century and we wanted to build something modern," Pierre explains. The new building has a living roof with a garden, and a cellar equipped with special tanks to handle each of the 45 plots. "We don't want to change the style of Cheval, it was decided two centuries ago. But we want to have more precision, more resolution, more pixels," Pierre says. "The philosophy is that 100% of each plot goes into Cheval or into Petit Cheval. So we pro-duce each plot with the intention of making Cheval, but in any year there may be plots that don't succeed." There is also a third wine. The compel-ling richness of the grand vin is offset against a background of finely structured black fruits stopping just short of impressions of tobacco.

St. Emilion
2 Petit Cheval
www.chateau-chevalblanc.com
36 ha; 200,000 bottles

Château Clinet

It's been all change at Clinet since the Laborde family purchased the property in 1999. Previously, Clinet was a family property before being sold to an insurance company in 1991. With Michel Rolland as consultant, the style was distinctly full bodied. Ronan Laborde came to run the property after his father purchased it, and in 2004 the building was extended into a very modern winery with huge windows looking out over the vineyard. At the time of purchase, there were 8.6 ha with 80% Merlot, 15% Cabernet Sauvignon and 5% Cabernet Franc. Ronan changed the balance to more Merlot, and then added some vineyards (close by in Feytit) that are all Merlot, so the plantings are now 90% Merlot. "What we are always looking for here is the creamy touch that is brought by the Merlot, we don't extract too much," Ronan says, explaining that he has backed off from the opulent style of the former ownership. The grand vin sees 60% new oak. Fleur de Clinet is not strictly a second wine; it has declassified lots from Clinet, but also includes juice and berries purchased from other growers in Pomerol. In addition, there is a Bordeaux AOP simply called Ronan, made in a rented facility while a new winery is being constructed for it. I have found recent vintages of Clinet to be relatively restrained, but in a clean, soft, modern style. "This typifies the style of Clinet I would like to produce," says Ronan about the 2008, which has supple, slightly aromatic, round black fruits.

 Bordeaux

Pomerol

2 Fleur de Clinet

www.chateauclinet.com

12 ha; 40,000 bottles

Château La Conseillante

La Conseillante has been owned by the Nicolas family since 1871 (not related to the wine merchants). It's had the same 12 ha for three centuries. Vineyards are on gravel soils adjacent to St Emilion; actually one third of the vineyards are in St. Emilion. Plantings are 80% Merlot and 20% Cabernet Franc. "La Conseillante is not entirely typical of Pomerol, which is known for power and richness; we are known for elegance and silky tannins. We can mix in one bottle the roundness of Pomerol and Merlot with the elegance of Cabernet Franc. We don't want to compete for the biggest wine of the vintage, we want to preserve our elegance, and the silky tannins. That's why we are not considered to be a Parker wine," says winemaker Jean-Michel Laporte. Cabernet Franc is mostly planted on gravel, and Merlot on clay, but there is some Merlot on gravel. "I think a lot of people only realized the importance of Cabernet Franc a few years ago, but at La Conseillante we've always known its importance. I could have 60% Merlot to 40% Cabernet Franc to match the soils, but I'm very happy with Merlot on gravel, it's very elegant." A new building was constructed in 2012 to replace the old cuverie, and the striking circular vat room is full of concrete vats of varying sizes. No doubt it's due largely to the gravel, but I've always found La Conseillante to be one of the most elegant wines of Pomerol; although it's more Merlot than Cabernet in style, it's well structured, and never goes to excess.

Pomerol

www.laconseillante.fr

12 ha; 45,000 bottles

St. Emilion
www.maltus.com

4 ha; 10,000 bottles

Le Dôme (and other boutique wines)

Since arriving from Britain twenty years ago, Jonathan Maltus has become one of the largest landholders in St. Emilion, with the purchase (and expansion) of Château Teyssier followed by Château Laforge, but he offers one of the most direct views of terroir in St. Emilion with his four single vineyard wines. These fall into two pairs, Le Carré and Les Astéries (just over 1 ha each) and Vieux Château Mazerat and Le Dôme (about 4 ha each). Le Carré and Les Astéries are 200 yards apart; Le Carré was planted in 1956, but the vines at Les Astéries are about 90 years old. Both are 80% Merlot. Le Carré is plush, structured and rich, but Les Astéries is all tension, finer and tighter, with a great sense of precision. "Les Astéries is the least Maltus-like wine I make. Our wines are accused of being North American in style," Jonathan says. He bought Vieux Château Mazerat in 2008; it's surrounded on three sides by Canon, on the fourth by Angelus. Le Dôme, which used to be part of Vieux Château Mazerat, was purchased previously in 1996. "It's the biggest expression of Cabernet Franc in Bordeaux," Jonathan says. (Plantings are 75% Cabernet Franc.) Vieux Château Mazerat can start off quite stern, with a fine-grained structure waiting for tannins to resolve. Le Dôme is more supple and elegant, with that taut, filigree impression of Cabernet Franc; it takes several years for complexity to emerge. In addition to St. Emilion, Jonathan also makes wine in California and Australia.

Pomerol
www.eglise-clinet.com

6 ha; 25,000 bottles

Château L'Église Clinet

This property originated in 1882 as a joint venture merging plots from Clos l'Eglise and Château Clinet. The wines were sold as Clos l'Eglise Clinet until the name changed to Château l'Eglise Clinet in 1954. Until 1983, when Denis Durantou took over, the property was part of a family holding with other agricultural interests, and was managed by Pierre Lasserre of Château Clos René on a profit-sharing arrangement. The wine is typically 85% Merlot and 15% Cabernet Franc. The property got off unusually lightly from the great winter freeze of 1956, and so has a greater proportion of old vines than is common in Pomerol. Denis has a slightly unusual attitude towards winemaking: harvesting is relatively early, bunches are selected in the vineyard but there is no sorting at the winery, and special tanks are used for fermentation to increase contact between juice and cap. There is no second wine here (La Petite Eglise is sometimes incorrectly described as the second wine, but is based on a blend of lots from young vines and purchased grapes). The result is a wine that does not go to the extremes of opulence that often characterize Pomerol: I often find a slightly mentholated quality that gives an impression the wine came from a cooler year than was really the case. Well structured for Pomerol, the wine supports long aging: the 1952 (made well before the Durantou era, of course) was still lively in 2014. There's a definite sense of grip to the style.

Château L'Évangile

Lying between Châteaux Pétrus and Cheval Blanc, l'Évangile occupies prime terroir of iron-rich clay and gravel. One of the oldest properties in Pomerol, it dates back to 1741. At the start of the twentieth century, it was considered one of the top estates in Pomerol. From 1862, the property was owned by the Ducasse family, until Château Lafite Rothschild acquired a major share in 1990. The vineyards were renovated and a second wine was introduced. The Rothschilds did not gain full control until a few years later, when they purchased the remaining share, after which they built a new winery (completed in 2004). Greater distinction is now made between parts of the vineyard with differing terroirs, there's more sorting, and new oak has increased to 100%. The vineyards were more or less constant for two hundred years, until in 2012 the Rothschilds purchased an additional 6 ha from neighboring Château Croix de Gay: most of the production from the extra land goes into the second wine, but around 1 ha is added to the grand vin. L'Évangile has always been an opulent wine, and under the Rothschilds the opulence has become even more overt. The contrast between the 2000 and 2005 vintages is striking: the 2000 is not the blockbuster you might expect from the reputation of the vintage, but is still quite tight, with a sense of tense black fruits. The 2005 is presently full of high-toned aromatics that would not be out of place on a cult Cabernet from Napa.

◎ Pomerol
2 Blason de l'Évangile
www.lafite.com
▨ ⚒ G
22 ha; 60,000 bottles

Château Figeac

Until the nineteenth century, Figeac was an enormous estate, extending from St. Emilion into Pomerol. Several of today's famous châteaux lie on parts of the original estate, including neighboring Cheval Blanc, and La Conseillante in Pomerol. The estate came by marriage to the Manoncourt family in 1892, and into the hands of Thierry Manoncourt in 1947. Since then, Figeac has been regarded as one of the top châteaux of St. Emilion; at the top of Premier Grand Cru Classé B, its official standing was just below the two châteaux (Cheval Blanc and Ausone) classified as group A. With its equal proportions of Cabernet Sauvignon, Cabernet Franc, and Merlot, Figeac is sui generis, without doubt the right bank's leader in Cabernet Sauvignon. Perhaps fashion has partly overtaken Figeac with the rise of the extremely lush style of modern St. Emilion, as in the reclassification of 2012, Pavie and l'Angélus were promoted over Figeac into class A. Thierry's son-in-law, Eric d'Aramon, who managed the estate at the time, said, "We are not looking for high alcohol. I was the latest to pick 20-30 years ago, now I'm in the average." Although current vintages are more approachable than those of the past, this is still a wine that benefits more from age than other St. Emilion's. The 1966 showed a brilliant delicacy in 2014. Eric was replaced in a family coup in 2013, and it remains to be seen whether the subsequent appointment of Michel Rolland as consultant will change Figeac's unique style.

◎ St. Emilion
2 Château La Grange Neuve de Figeac
www.chateau-figeac.com
 ⚒ G
39 ha; 200,000 bottles

Néac

Lalande-de-Pomerol

Château la Fleur St. Georges

www.lafleurdebouard.com

25 ha; 100,000 bottles

Château La Fleur de Boüard

One of the most influential people in St. Emilion, Hubert Boüard has fingers in many pies. He has seen Château Angélus promoted to Premier Grand Cru Classé A, is a consulting oenologist for more than 60 other châteaux, and owns Fleur de Boüard in Lalande de Pomerol (purchased from an insurance company in 1998) as well as Château Bellevue in St. Emilion. Plantings are 80% Merlot (with 15% Cabernet Franc and 5% Cabernet Sauvignon), but that is more or less the only thing that is typical about the château relative to Lalande de Pomerol in general. Fleur de Boüard has its own winemaking team, and a modern gravity-feed winery. Technique is somewhat different from Angélus, using délestage (rack and return) with tronconique tanks, producing a wine that is soft and rich. It matures for 12-33 months in barriques including 75% new oak. The super-cuvée, Le Plus de Boüard, only 3-4,000 bottles, was made for the first time in 2000. It's based on selection; "even during one pass through the vineyards there is selection between Fleur and Plus," says Laurent Benoît at Angélus. Fleur de Boüard is extremely powerful for Lalande de Pomerol, with forward black fruits, smoky aromatics, and lots of evident new oak. It needs quite a long time to calm down. Le Plus is the same squared (only the 2000 is at all ready now). These are by far the most expensive wines of the appellation, but whether they are the best depends on what you want from Lalande de Pomerol.

Libourne

Pomerol

19 ha; 60,000 bottles

Château La Fleur-Pétrus

La Fleur Pétrus was the first property Jean-Pierre Moueix purchased, in 1950. The property is named for the original vineyard block, lying between Château Lafleur and Pétrus. There are two other major plots, one between Le Pin and Trotanoy, the other just outside the town. In 2013, the cuverie was moved from the original château near Pétrus to a building opposite the church in Pomerol (it's the original Presbytery of the church), on a block purchased in 2005. This places it more or less in the center of the vineyard holdings. The vineyard area has roughly doubled since the original purchase, and the style of Fleur Pétrus has changed as additional blocks were purchased; 4 ha were bought from Le Gay in 1995, and the most recent block came in 2009 from Château Guyot. There are three types of soil: light clay at the new château, heavier clay near Pétrus, and gravel terroir near Trotanoy. The impression at the new château is workmanlike rather than glitzy, with concrete vats and a practical barrel room. "La Fleur Pétrus is probably the lightest of the Moueix properties," says export manager Frédéric Lospied. Winemaking is traditional and moderate, with up to 50% new oak for 14-20 months depending on the vintage. The blend is typical for Pomerol, with 80-90% Merlot, but the style is not at all heavy: it can give quite an elegant impression, with a good sense of freshness. Following general Moueix policy, there is no second wine.

Châteaux Fombrauge & Magrez-Fombrauge

The rather grand property of Château Fombrauge, with its long history, was only a Grand Cru in St. Emilion until it was promoted to Grand Cru Classé in 2012. To what extent this reflects the improvements in the wine brought about since Bernard Magrez purchased the estate in 1999, and to what extent it represents glory reflected from Magrez-Fombrauge is hard to determine. Somewhat of a specialist in reviving under-performing châteaux, Bernard made considerable investments in replanting the vineyards, renovating the chais, and generally improving the property. Magrez-Fombrauge started as a micro-cuvée in 2000, when the best lots were selected from three plots (producing only 6,000 bottles). Similar "Cuvées d'Exception" are made, each in tiny amounts, from several of Magrez's properties, but Magrez-Fombrauge has become independent. "It was a cuvée but now it's a different Château, it's not vinified at Fombrauge," Bernard explains. Château Fombrauge is located at Saint Christophe des Bardes, where the soils are calcareous clay, but also has vineyards to the southeast at Saint Etienne de Lisse on limestone and molasses, and then vineyards at Saint Hippolyte, with more of a clay terroir. Some 2.4 ha at Saint Hippolyte now provide the basis for Magrez-Fombrauge. While Château Fombrauge has the style of a typical St. Emilion, Magrez-Fombrauge has the high extraction, richness, and alcohol, of a garage wine. All Magrez wines are modern, but this is über-modern.

St. Emilion
2 Le Cadran de Fombrauge
www.fombrauge.com

58 ha; 200,000 bottles

Château Fontenil

This property has been owned since 1986 by Michel Rolland, the famous flying winemaker who advises many châteaux on the Right Bank. Purchased as a country home, the property came with vineyards on the typical terroir of clay over limestone. With Michel's expertise, Château Fontenil probably makes the best wine in Fronsac, a satellite of Pomerol. But the château's fame comes as much from an incident in 2000, when Michel decided to protect the vines from rain by placing plastic sheeting between the rows, so the water would run off instead of soaking the roots. INAO was not amused, and refused to allow the wine to have the appellation label, so it was declassified to a separate cuvée, called Defi de Fontenil, and labeled as Vin de France. (A similar incident at Château Valandraud led to the creation of Interdit de Valandraud.) Because the best plots in the vineyard were protected, Defi de Fontenil became a special cuvée. The technique was so effective—"the grapes were considerably sweeter with more advanced maturity," Michel says—that it was repeated it in 2001 and 2004. Coming from the same plots, and still labeled as Vin de France, Defi de Fontenil has become the flagship cuvée (although plastic sheeting is not usually used); a notch below, Château Fontenil remains in the Fronsac AOP. How do they compare? Both start with overt fruits, but Fontenil closes up to become more classic in mid life, while Defi de Fontenil has greater warmth and aromatic complexity,

Fronsac
www.rollandcollection.com

9 ha; 45,000 bottles

Lansac
Côtes de Bourg
www.fougas.com

17 ha; 80,000 bottles

Château Fougas

Jean-Yves Bechet bought Château Fougas in 1976, and in 1993 started to produce the Maldoror cuvée from a single hectare; it was only 10% of production. The estate was converted to biodynamic viticulture, quality improved, and slowly Maldoror was increased to its present proportion, about 90% of production. The "regular" cuvée is called the Prestige. In effect Maldoror has gone from a special cuvée to becoming the grand vin. Its proportion of 25% Cabernet Sauvignon is more or less constant each year; the Cabernet vines are now about forty years old, which no doubt contributes to the quality. "Cabernet Sauvignon is difficult here, but when we get ripe Cabernet Sauvignon, its taste is extraordinary, with lots of structure," says Jean-Yves. I don't think I would describe the wine as claret, because it doesn't quite have that tang of dominant Cabernet Sauvignon, but it seems more like a half way house between right bank and left bank than a typical right bank wine. The wine is matured for up to eighteen months in 50% new oak. There's good structure with the fruits, although there isn't quite the power of the Cabernet Sauvignon-dominated wines of the Médoc. "If you like powerful wines, drink between three and seven years, if not they will age much longer," is Jean-Yves's view. Certainly the wine ages well; tertiary development starts after a decade, and the inaugural vintage was just beginning to fade gently in 2012. This is one of the top wines of the Côtes de Bourg.

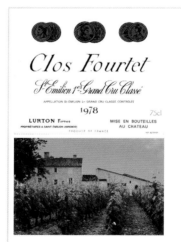

St. Emilion
Closerie de Fourtet
www.closfourtet.com

20 ha; 100,000 bottles

Château Clos Fourtet

Opposite an old entrance to St. Emilion, surrounded by stone walls, Clos Fourtet originated as a fort. Owned successively by negociants Ginestet and Lurton, quality was a bit erratic, until Pierre Lurton (now Director at Cheval Blanc) became winemaker. The estate was purchased in 2001 by Philippe Cuvelier, a businessman enthused by Bordeaux, who later also bought Château Poujeaux in Moulis. Clos Fourtet's vineyards are in two blocks: the *clos* of 14 ha extends from the town walls to the west; another 6 ha are farther to the north. The grand vin mostly comes from the first block, which has the classic terroir of a thin layer of clay over limestone. The 6 ha block is not as good, and mostly goes into the second wine. Three other properties in St. Emilion have recently been added to the portfolio: Les Grands Murailles (adjacent to Clos Fourtet), Château Clos St Martin, and Côte de Baleau. A large part of Clos Fourtet was replanted in 2001, so today the vines are mostly relatively young. Although Merlot is always at least 85%, recent vintages seem to be quite stern when young, with structure more evident than usual for St. Emilion. One feature here is that the rest of the blend is usually Cabernet Sauvignon (typically around 10%), so Cabernet Franc is rarely more than 5%. (Until 1999, the blend was usually only Merlot and Cabernet Sauvignon.) "We try to make the wine with freshness. We are not looking for opulence, we don't want too much extraction," is how Matthieu Cuvelier describes the wine.

Château La Gaffelière

"We didn't want to impress visitors, it's not Disneyland here," says Alexandre Malet Roquefort, going around the small winery, renovated in 2013, and packed with equipment including purple fermentation cuves in an interesting conical shape. The Malet Roqueforts have been making wine here since the sixteenth century. One of the most traditional wines in St. Emilion, La Gaffelière was languishing when Alexandre and his father decided to bring it up to speed in 2004. Production was halved, and Stéphane Derenoncourt became consulting oenologist. Vineyards are around the château, running from the slopes below Ausone to the plain beyond. The Cabernet Sauvignon was taken out in 2005, and a planting program was started in 2006. Cabernet Franc from the bottom of the hill was replaced with Merlot and replanted at the top of the hill. "Previously everyone put the best parcels into Merlot, now we know to make the best wine it's necessary to put the best parcels into Cabernet Franc," Alexandre explains. Although plantings are 70% Merlot, I have always found Gaffelière to be one of the more restrained wines in St. Emilion. "The DNA of Gaffelière is really classic, it's one of a small group in St. Emilion that didn't change its style in recent years. We like wine that is fruity, not too extracted. The style of Gaffelière should not change with me or my children. I want them to realize they must make wine as it should be, not as they would like it to be." The revival is well under way.

St. Emilion
Clos La Gaffelière
www.chateau-la-gaffeliere.com
23 ha; 80,000 bottles

Château Le Gay

Under common ownership since the late nineteenth century, Château Le Gay was run in tandem with Château Lafleur. The last joint owners were two sisters who lived at Le Gay, and contracted with Moueix to make the wine. In 2002, the estate was left to five cousins in the family; in order to keep Château Lafleur, they were forced to sell Le Gay to pay estate taxes. Moueix were interested but were outbid by Catherine Péré-Vergé, the daughter of the late industrialist Jacques Durand, who developed Cristal d'Arques. The reported price was $25 million. "It's absolutely too expensive, and it makes no sense. You can never get a return on investment with such prices," Christian Moueix said at the time. Catherine Péré-Vergé already owned Château Montviel, a less well-known Pomerol, and now also owns Châteaux La Violette, Tristan, and La Gravière under the rubric of Vignobles Péré-Vergé. There was a massive program of investment at Le Gay, with a new winery constructed next to the old house, and some additional vineyards planted (on one of the few remaining plots of unplanted land in Pomerol, near Château Lafleur). Le Gay is now decidedly in the modernist camp: vinification starts with a long soak; punch-down increases extraction during fermentation, and there is even some barrel fermentation; micro-oxygenation is used; and the wine is aged for up to 20 months in all-new oak. Michel Rolland is the consultant oenologist.

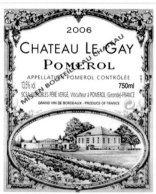

Pomerol
Manoir de Gay
www.montviel.com
10 ha; 24,000 bottles

Libourne
Pomerol
www.moueix.com
5 ha; 18,000 bottles

Château Hosanna

There is no château, only vineyards. One of the newest properties in Pomerol, Château Hosanna owes its origin to the deconstruction of Château Certan-Giraud after it was purchased by Moueix. The best vineyards were split off to become Château Hosanna in 1999, 4 ha were sold to Château Nénin, and the rump became Château Certan-Marzelle. The terroir is essentially red gravel with a base of clay and *casse de fer,* and a drainage system was installed to satisfy concerns that water had been a problem. The vines are middle aged, with an average around 40 years. "Hosanna is unusual for Moueix; with 30% Cabernet Franc it's the highest. The goal was to make the Cheval Blanc of Pomerol," says Frédéric Lospied of Moueix, but he's quick to add, "this is a joke." (However, you might consider that the choice of the name Hosanna implies a certain ambition for the wine.) Would you consider Hosanna to be a garage wine, I asked? "That would be pejorative. We would agree with the distinction that Château La Fleur Pétrus is an assemblage of terroirs but Hosanna is a single vineyard wine." The Moueix view is that Hosanna's high content of Cabernet Franc makes it a more feminine wine than Pétrus or Trotanoy. The wine is matured in 50% new oak for 18 months. It's been made every year from 1999 to 2012, but there was no production in 2013 because yields were simply too low. Hosanna is always very expensive, if not yet a rival to Pétrus.

Mouillac
Pomerol
2 Les Pensées de Lafleur
5 ha; 20,000 bottles

Château Lafleur

This tiny property has a reputation in inverse proportion to its size. In the same family since it was founded in 1872 by the proprietor of Château Le Gay, it was previously owned by two sisters who lived at Le Gay. The wine was made by Moueix until the sisters leased the property to their nephew Jacques Guinaudeau in 1985, and then in 2002 Jacques purchased it. The "château" is a somewhat obscure farmhouse with a tiny vineyard adjoining Pétrus. There is surprising variation in terroir for such a small property, from gravel over clay to sandy gravel. Pensées de Lafleur started as a second wine in 1987, but since 1995 has come 90% from a lower strip of deeper soils running along the southwest edge of the vineyard. "A large part of our identity comes from the high proportion of Cabernet Franc," says Baptiste Guinaudeau. Usually about 55% Cabernet Franc, Lafleur has a restrained character distinct from the average Pomerol. The focus in winemaking is to avoid too much extraction. "We don't use the word extraction, we want to infuse," says Baptiste. "Cuvaison is only 12-15 days, which is short for Bordeaux, because the wine is already well structured." Élevage sees some restraint. "We love barrels but we hate oak; 80% is aged in 6-month barrels, the rest is new oak." This is old-fashioned Bordeaux in the best sense—elegant rather than powerful or jammy, with moderate alcohol and restrained wood. The Guinaudeaus also make wine at Grand Village in Fronsac.

Château Larcis Ducasse

Larcis Ducasse has belonged to the same family since 1813, but as they are absentee owners, everything depends on the management. The wine was a reliable, if not very exciting, representation of St. Emilion at the Grand Cru Classé level until Nicolas Thienpont was asked to take over in 2002. More detailed attention paid off, and the château was promoted to Premier Grand Cru Classé in the reclassification of 2012. The facility itself seems a little old-fashioned, but was ahead of its time, as it took advantage of the slope to build a natural gravity feed system. Cement cuves are underneath grape reception, and élevage lasts 14-17 months in 60% new oak, using both barriques and 500 liter barrels (for lots from the warmest plots). Vineyards are located in prime terroir, with 15% of the plots on the limestone plateau, and the rest descending down terraces on the Côte Pavie slope to the south, with very calcareous terroir of molasses of white clay. "Going up the terraces, there's a distinct change of character. Merlot is not the same on each terrace. There's a contrast between the spot, which is warm, and the soil, which is cool. So we get good ripeness but at the same time keep freshness. There's good aromatic complexity but good acidity also," is how winemaker David Suire describes the situation. This is not a flamboyant example of St. Emilion; the wine is on the reserved side, in cooler vintages showing an almost savory or herbal touch, which in warmer vintages shows as minerality.

Saint Laurent-des-Combes
St. Emilion
www.larcis-ducasse.com

10 ha; 28,000 bottles

Château Latour à Pomerol

For many years under the same ownership as Pétrus, this small estate has remained unchanged since it took its present form after the division of the Chambaud estate in 1917, when it was inherited by Mme. Edmond Loubat (who later acquired Pétrus). She added some vineyards, and in due course, in 1961, Latour à Pomerol and Pétrus passed to her niece, Lily Lacoste. Mme Lacoste sold her stake in Pétrus to Moueix, but kept Latour à Pomerol until 2002, when she donated it to a Catholic charity. However, since 1962 it has been managed by Moueix; as now there is no owner with an interest in wine production, to all intents and purposes today this is another estate in the Moueix portfolio. The vineyards lie in two separate areas, with 5 ha consisting of gravel soil on a clay subsoil, in the best area close to the church of Pomerol, the rest elsewhere on lighter, sandier soils. (There isn't much information about what wine was produced from these parcels before they became Latour à Pomerol.) The rather gracious château is on the main parcel, Les Grandes Vignes, and takes its name from a tower at one end of the building. Vines have an average age of forty years. The wine is a typical Pomerol with 90% Merlot, matured for 18 months in 50% new barriques. Given the small scale of production, there is no second wine. The grand vin is full-bodied, ripe, and rich, opulent and powerful rather than elegant, needing time to develop, but lasting for up to thirty years.

Libourne
Pomerol
www.moueix.com

8 ha; 30,000 bottles

St. Emilion
www.neipperg.com

5 ha; 10,000 bottles

La Mondotte

Is La Mondotte a garage wine, I asked Stephan von Neipperg? "I never understood why they call it a garage wine," he says. "La Mondotte has been completely independent since 1996. It is now a classified growth. You cannot talk about a first growth being a garage wine." Its independence is almost an accident. "I tried to bring La Mondotte into Canon La Gaffelière in the classification of 1996, but they told me, it's different, you have to see if you can age 15 years. Well, now we have shown it." Whereas Canon La Gaffelière is at the foot of the town, La Mondotte is well to the east on the limestone plateau. The vines are 65-100 years old; some are even on their own roots by marcottage from grafted vines. Following its rejection in the classification of 1996, a cuverie was constructed on the property, and the wine was vinified separately. It's aged entirely in 100% new oak. It now has the same classification as Canon La Gaffelière! The similarity to the garage wines lies in the tiny scale of production and the intensity, the sheer richness, of the wine, with deep black fruits on the palate, cut by chocolaty tannins, very much the iron fist in the velvet glove. Yet with a quarter Cabernet Franc to the three quarters Merlot, it avoids the jammy quality of some garage wines and remains a real wine. You have to wonder what would have happened if wine of this character had in fact been incorporated into Canon La Gaffelière.

Libourne
Pomerol
2 La Fugue de Nénin
www.chateau-nenin.com

25 ha; 110,000 bottles

Château Nénin

One of the largest estates in Pomerol, with a high reputation in the late nineteenth century, Château Nénin was a distinct under-performer by the time the Despujol's, who had owned it since 1847, sold it to their cousins, the Delons of Château Léoville-Lascases, in 1997. The best that could be said is that the wine was somewhat four-square. Unusually for Pomerol, the château is quite grand, with a surrounding park, and it is used now as a hospitality center. Just north of the village of Catusseau, the vineyards lie around the château, with soils of sand-clay on a subsoil of *casse de fer*, and were restructured immediately after the purchase, with significant replanting, especially to replace vines that had been planted on poor rootstocks after the great freeze of 1956. Drainage systems were installed, manual harvesting replaced machine harvesting, and the winery was modernized. A second wine was introduced immediately. The vineyards were expanded by acquiring 4 ha in 1999 from Château Certan-Giraud. Plantings are 70% Merlot, 20% Cabernet Franc, and 10% Cabernet Sauvignon. Today the wine goes through alcoholic and malolactic fermentation in stainless steel, and is then aged in barriques with about a quarter to a third new oak. Improvement in the wine was not instantaneous, but it started to come back on form in the mid 2000's. It might be fair to say that it focuses on power rather than finesse. Michel Rolland is the consulting oenologist.

Château Pavie

When Château Pavie and adjacent Pavie Decesse came on the market in 1997, supermarket magnate Gérard Perse, who had bought Château Monbousquet in 1993, acquired Pavie Decesse. When Pavie had not sold a year later, "He decided to change his life, he sold the supermarkets and left Paris to build up Château Pavie," says Gérard's son-in-law, Henrique da Costa. Since then, it's been a steady upward path, culminating in promotion to Premier Grand Cru Classé A (now engraved in stone over the entrance to the massive new building, which took five years to build). Inside the new facility are vast vat and barrel rooms, with separate fermenters for each plot. The vineyard is in a single block facing south, running down from the château. Merlot has been decreased from 70% to 60% (now with 25% Cabernet Franc and 15% Cabernet Sauvignon). "This may be the best place in St. Emilion for Cabernet," Henrique says. The transition to a very lush, extracted, New World style, laden with new oak, since Perse bought Pavie is controversial, generally loved in the U.S. but not in the U.K.; although vintages tasted during my visit seemed more measured, one still questions what this says about Bordeaux. The major part of Pavie Decesse was incorporated into Pavie in 2012, leaving a rump of 3.5 ha, so it's difficult to assess its future. In addition to owning several châteaux in St. Emilion, Perse Vignobles produces Esprit de Pavie, which is a Bordeaux AOP from the estates in Castillon.

St. Emilion
Arômes de Pavie
www.chateaupavie.com

37 ha; 120,000 bottles

Château Pavie Macquin

Surrounded by limestone terraces, overlooking the grand church at St. Emilion, Pavie Macquin is located right in the heart of the limestone plateau. Access is by a very steep twisting one track path that requires much maneuvering even for small cars. There are old buildings behind and a stylish tasting room in front, built two years ago as an extension of an old maison. Vineyards are all in one holding except for two parcels. Everything in the field of view is part of Pavie Macquin; just over the hill is Pavie. "Pavie Macquin was on the verge of being declassified under the previous management," says Nicolas Thienpont, who was appointed in 1994 to run the estate for the absentee owners (who are descendants of Albert Macquin). The château has made great strides under Thienpont management, and was promoted to Premier Grand Cru Classé in the reclassification of 2006. The elevated location means that maturation is slow, and this is always one of the last châteaux to harvest. There is 60% new oak during élevage. I would say that since the reclassification, most vintages show a sense of increased elegance, partly because the wine tastes as though it has more Cabernet Franc than it really does (it's actually 80% Merlot). Winemaker David Suire says there's one area that's planted with Merlot but you would think it was Cabernet Franc from its refinement. "Pavie Macquin has a certain power but is always fresh, we look for grand purity and definition," is Nicolas's view.

St. Emilion
Les Chênes de Macquin
www.pavie-macquin.com

15 ha; 80,000 bottles

 Pomerol

[2] Le Jardin de Petit Village

www.petit-village.com

11 ha; 42,000 bottles

Château Petit Village

This property was not exactly neglected during the twentieth century, but it was owned by proprietors who, although located merely on the other side of the Gironde, did not have it at the forefront of their attention. First it was owned by the negociant Ginestet, and then it passed by inheritance to Bruno Prats of Cos d'Estournel. Its revival began when it was sold in 1989 to AXA (owners of Château Pichon Baron in Pauillac and Château Suduiraut in Sauternes). Extension of the Château for a new winery in 2005 has given a distinctly modern impression. Located on the gravel plateau that extends from St. Emilion, its vineyards occupy a triangle, with Châteaux Le Pin, Vieux Château Certan, and La Conseillante at the apices. Part of the character of the wine was ascribed to an unusually high proportion (for Pomerol) of 17% Cabernet Sauvignon. This was recently discovered to be a mistake: a large plot of old vines that had escaped the frost of 1956, thought to be Cabernet Sauvignon, was discovered really to be Cabernet Franc. They are rather sniffy about this at the château. "We do not feel that speaking about Cabernet Sauvignon here is relevant to the style and personality of the wines from Petit Village," says Marie-Louise Schÿler of AXA, so it is unclear whether any future change is planned in reaction to the discovery. No doubt the age of the vines contributes in any case to the sense of structure in the wine, which generally does not have as much opulence as usual for Pomerol.

 Libourne

Pomerol

www.moueix.com

12 ha; 30,000 bottles

Pétrus

The most famous wine in Pomerol, and often the most expensive wine in Bordeaux, the fame of Pétrus goes well back into the twentieth century, when Mme. Edmond Loubert bought shares progressively from 1925 until she became sole owner in 1949. The Moueix involvement started when Jean-Pierre Moueix became sole agent in 1943. He was left a small portion when Mme Loubert died, and in 1964 he bought a majority interest from one of the heirs, subsequently expanded into full control. The "château" was famously shabby, but was renovated about five years ago to become quite showy. It sits on an oval-shaped hill with shallow topsoil over deep blue clay—the famous buttonhole where the clay comes close to the surface. Its ability to store up water in the winter gives a good reserve for the summer and is part of Pétrus's unique character. "On this soil the Merlot develops a high degree of tannins, but they are not aggressive," says Elisabeth Jaubert at the château. There was a small section of Cabernet Franc from 1957-2010, but now the wine is 100% Merlot. Grapes are destemmed and cooled on arrival, fermented in concrete, transferred to stainless steel for malolactic, and then into barriques, with about 50% new oak. Vinification is by plot, but plots are defined by vine age. "Obviously we don't make Pétrus from 100% of the grapes. The last time that happened was 1975," Elisabeth says, "but there will no second wine." The combination of power and elegance is sui generis.

Le Pin

The pine tree that gave its name to the property still towers over it, although the old house has been replaced by a contemporary jewel of a winery. When Jacques Thienpont started Le Pin in 1979, he had no idea it was going to become one of the most famous—and at one time the most expensive—wines of Pomerol. The tiny vineyard of 1.2 ha is located between Vieux Château Certan (owned by the Thienpont family) and Trotanoy. The original plan was to add it to Vieux Château Certan, but the family did not want to pay the price, so Jacques bought it together with his uncle and his father, and became responsible for the winemaking. Later Jacques bought his uncle's and father's shares. In 1984 he added the adjacent plot. The team at Vieux Château Certan looks after the vines. There's no second wine, but there is selection, and barrels that don't make it are relegated to generic Pomerol. Jacques also makes Trilogia, a blend of three vintages. Variety in terroir is shown by the range of individual barrels from rich and full (but tight) to super-smooth elegance. The blend belies the monovarietal composition by its refinement. Longevity is indicated by the fact that the 1998 was at a point of perfect balance between mature and primary influences in 2014. Intending to repeat his success, Jacques has bought Château Haut Plantey, a derelict property with good terroir on St Emilion's limestone plateau, renamed it as L'If, and plans to make it the Le Pin of St. Emilion.

 Pomerol

  G

3 ha; 7,000 bottles

Château Roc de Cambes

This is by far and away the most expensive wine from the Côtes de Bourg. When François Mitjavile purchased Château Roc des Cambes in 1987, it was pretty dilapidated, but it had good terroir and old vines—the story often told is that François put his finger in the soil and decided to buy the property. Merlot is the driving force, and the wines are usually 80% Merlot to 20% Cabernet Sauvignon. "The terroir is homogeneous and there are few differences between the plots where Cabernet and Merlot are planted. There are difficulties with Cabernet Sauvignon because it ripens late and requires dry conditions. In dry years we get a superb maturity of Cabernet Sauvignon, we like the effect of having the Cabernet Sauvignon, but it's more a matter of the aromatic complexity it brings than the structure. This terroir is perfect for Merlot," says Nina Mitjavile. As at the Mitjavile's other property, Château Tertre Rôteboeuf in St. Emilion, all the efforts go into the single wine. The young wines at Roc des Cambes are pretty forceful, more evidently so than those of Tertre Rôteboeuf, perhaps because the fruits in St. Emilion are so much richer as to hide the structure. But as the wines age, there seems to me to be something of a convergence in style, with Roc des Cambes becoming more like Tertre Rôteboeuf in its overall balance. The 2000 vintage of Roc de Cambes unusually had equal proportions of Cabernet and Merlot, and (showing well in 2013), remains my favorite.

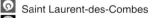 Saint Laurent-des-Combes

Côtes de Bourg
roc-de-cambes.com

10 ha; 45,000 bottles

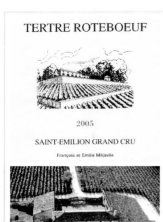

2005

SAINT-EMILION GRAND CRU

François et Emilie Mitjavile

 St. Emilion
www.tertre-roteboeuf.com

6 ha; 27,000 bottles

Château Le Tertre Rôteboeuf

François Mitjavile marches to the beat of his own drum: a discussion with him at the château tends to take a philosophical direction, but always returns to issues of style and quality. Tertre Rôteboeuf is generally regarded as one of the top wines of St. Emilion, but it is not a Grand Cru Classé. "The classification has a dead weight, I prefer something more alive. Classification is a very good thing but it is static. I had too much pride to apply and am very content to remain outside it," François explains. The château produces only the grand vin: it is one of the few at this level to have no second wine. In fact, François does not believe in second wines. "With a homogeneous terroir, it is more interesting not to make a selection for a second wine, because production of a single wine best expresses the variations of the vintage, as the fruits ripen differently every year. A second wine is more suitable for properties which have heterogeneous terroirs," he says. Pruning follows a cordon system as opposed to the Guyot that is common in St. Emilion, and there is no green harvesting. Picking is late to get full ripeness. The wine of Tertre Rôteboeuf is in the modern idiom, with full fruits matured in 100% new oak, but François believes that tannins are often confused with quality. "Too powerful tannins are an error... Garage wines are grotesque. I prefer to call them 'vins de bois conservé' [wines of preserved wood]." All that said, the wines tend to be among the more powerful of the appellation.

CHÂTEAU TROPLONG MONDOT
GRAND CRU CLASSÉ
SAINT-EMILION GRAND CRU
ALC 13.5 %VOL.   2001   750ML
MIS EN BOUTEILLE AU CHATEAU

St. Emilion
2 Mondot
www.chateau-troplong-mondot.com

30 ha; 80,000 bottles

Château Troplong Mondot

Situated on a high point (106 meters) on the limestone plateau a couple of miles to the east of the town of St. Emilion, Troplong Mondot has a view all the way across to the spire of the church in the town. The château preceded the vineyards and dates from the eighteenth century. The property has been in the hands of the Valette family, originally wine merchants from Paris, since 1936. Essentially unchanged since they were created in the nineteenth century, vineyards are in a single block around the château, on a southwest-facing slope. They are planted with 90% Merlot; the rest is divided between Cabernet Franc and Cabernet Sauvignon. Average vine age is about 30 years. The soil is a mixture of clay and limestone. Advised by Michel Rolland, yields are low and the harvest is late, followed by traditional vinification, and élevage for 12-24 months in 75% new oak (the rest is one-year old oak). From a middle of the road reputation, the wine improved to the point of promotion to Premier Grand Cru Classé in 2006. "Our wine is complex, tannic, difficult to drink when young," Christine Valette used to say. "It needs explanation and a certain knowledge." Indeed, the wine can show a tannic bite when young, although this is usually followed by soft black aromatics. Under Christine, who inherited the property in 1981, the château expanded its activities with a guest house and a gourmet restaurant. The future is uncertain as Christine sadly died young in 2014.

Château Trotanoy

A long avenue of trees leads to the modest château that is Trotanoy, but in Moueix's discrete fashion, there is no sign at the entrance. The property was bought by Jean-Pierre Moueix in 1953. It dates from the eighteenth century, when its name originated as a shortening of Trop Ennuie (referring to the difficulty of working the soils). This is a warm, gravelly area, protected enough that many of the vines survived the great freeze of 1956. Underneath the gravel, or the black clay of some parts, is the famous *casse de fer* (iron-rich subsoil). Average vine age today is about 40 years. Trotanoy is usually the first of the Moueix estates to be harvested. The combination of old vines, microclimate, and terroir makes for a powerful wine. "Trotanoy is the most massive of the Moueix properties," says export manager Frédéric Lospied. Élevage lasts about 20 months in barriques with 50% new wood. Perhaps these days Trotanoy is a little more restrained, or rather a bit more precise, than it used to be. The wines of the sixties and seventies were splendid, with the 1961 showing dense black structure, and the 1970 and 1971 all opulence. Recent vintages show good grip and underlying structure to balance the richness of the fruits, which are 90% Merlot. Christian Moueix might describe Trotanoy as the "poor man's Pétrus," but the style is not the same, upright versus broad, gravel versus clay, even a little austere when young. A wine of real character, this is always one of the top Pomerols.

 Libourne
Pomerol
www.moueix.com

7 ha; 25,000 bottles

Château Trottevieille

One of the oldest estates in Pomerol—the name refers to an old lady who lived there in the fifteenth century—Trottevieille claims to have some of the oldest vines in Bordeaux including Cabernet Franc surviving from before phylloxera. (A special cuvée from these vines was produced in 2004.) Trottevieille is one of several properties owned by the Castéja family (of the Borie-Manoux negociant), and recently they have been trying to improve the quality, which in the past has tended to be a little rustic. At one time Trottevieille was the only Premier Grand Cru Classé to the east of St. Emilion. In a single block around the Château on the limestone plateau, the vineyards have red clay on top of the limestone. There's a substantial proportion of Cabernet Franc, usually a little over 40% in the grand vin, and also a small amount of Cabernet Sauvignon, so the wine is less dominated by Merlot than the average for St. Emilion. Vinification is standard: cold soak, fermentation, and maturation in new oak for up to 18 months. Major improvements have occurred since 2002, when the second wine was introduced (although it's usually only around 10% of production). One of the other châteaux owned by Philippe Castéja is Batailley in Pauillac, and in spite of the evident differences between left bank and right bank, there seems to me to be a similar sturdy character in the styles of the two properties. These are solid wines, and can be good value, but I don't usually find them really exciting.

St. Emilion
La Vieille Dame de Trottevieille
www.trottevieille.com

10 ha; 36,000 bottles

Château Valandraud

Valandraud embodies St. Emilion's development over the past twenty years. Jean-Luc Thunevin came from Algeria, opened a wine shop, became a negociant, and began buying land. From his first plot of 0.6 ha (near Pavie Macquin) he made the first vintage of Valandraud in 1991 in the garage adjacent to his house, only 1,200 bottles. (Valandraud is a play on his wife's maiden name.) Everything was done by hand, from deleafing in the vineyard to destemming before vinification. "I was the first garagiste. We protected the fruits, took precautions against oxidation, introduced green harvest, leaf pulling. Everyone does it now," Jean-Luc says. The defining year was 1995, when 200% new oak was used (racking from new oak into new oak). The wine made a great reputation, achieving a price to match the first growths, although its super-extraction and oakiness were controversial. Ageability was questioned. "Happily we can now make wines that are good now and age well. When I started people said Valandraud would not last more than ten years, but now it has lasted thirty years," Jean-Luc points out. The original terroir was undistinguished, but subsequent purchases have built up more extensive vineyards in the area of St. Etienne to the east, and now there is even a real château. The movement has been validated, or come full circle, with the inclusion of Valandraud as a Premier Grand Cru Classé in 2012. Today it's just 100% new oak, and the style is less flamboyant.

 St. Emilion

2 Virginie de Valandraud

www.chateau-valandraud.com

9 ha; 35,000 bottles

Vieux Château Certan

One of the oldest properties in Pomerol, Vieux Château Certan has been held by the Thienpont family since 1924, and they are proud of its history. "It's exactly the same as it was in 1745," says Alexandre Thienpont, who has been running the property since 1985. Vineyards are in a single block around the château, some on buttonhole clay similar to adjacent Pétrus. They are divided into 23 plots that are vinified separately. Plantings are 60% Merlot, 30% Cabernet Franc, and 10% Cabernet Sauvignon, with Merlot on clay, and the Cabernets on areas of gravel. Unusual for Pomerol, the high proportion of Cabernet gives Vieux Château Certan a distinctive restraint, with a balance in the direction of St. Emilion. Fermentation in wooden vats is followed by élevage for 18-22 months. "Because alcohol is getting higher now, new oak was reduced from 100% in 2008, to 80% in 2009 and 2010, to 67% today," Alexandre explains. Alexandre's son Guillaume has been involved since 2011 and the style is changing further as a result: "It is more focused on concentration (as opposed to power) and he would regard the wine we are tasting (the 2006) as old fashioned." So picking is now a little bit later, there is a saignée, and there is a touch more pump-over. Vieux Château Certan can be a relative bargain: because ownership is spread among 44 members of the Thienpont family, there is a constant need for cash flow to generate dividends, so the wine is always priced to sell quickly.

Pomerol

2 La Gravette de Certan

www.vieuxchateaucertan.com

14 ha; 50,000 bottles

Château Climens

Climens is an old property, originating in the sixteenth century. It was in the same hands for almost a century before Lucien Lurton purchased it in 1971. Since 1992, it has been run by his daughter Bérénice. Located on the highest point of Barsac, vineyards extend around the château in a single block. "The vineyards have never changed," says manager Frédéric Nivelle. The soils are very fine, never more than half a meter deep. "We produce only sweet wine. The reason is that because the soils are atypical we have only one grape: Sémillon. So it would be difficult to produce dry wine. The encépagement is old; when we bought in 1971, there was only a little Sauvignon Blanc and it was never good enough to put in Climens, so we took it out." The approach is typically Sauternaise. "We never select the harvest by plot, we select by botrytis (and this is equally true for the second wine). Selection is by time, morning versus afternoon, each day. At the end of harvest there are 15-25 different lots of wine, each is a few barrels. Alcoholic fermentation takes place in barrels, with 30-40% new oak. The aging protocol is the same for everything. The second wine is not necessarily less botrytized. Many people prefer Cyprès for the first few years when it's more open, and Climens is closed." Usually a bit richer than the average Barsac, perhaps more like Sauternes, Climens is in that select group of half a dozen châteaux ranked immediately behind Château d'Yquem.

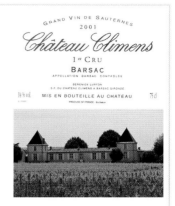

Barsac
Les Cyprès de Climens
www.chateau-climens.fr
30 ha; 30,000 bottles

Château Coutet

Coutet has an interesting history. It started out as a fortress built by the English in the thirteenth century. The first record of wine being produced here is 1643. After the Revolution, the owners married into the Lur Saluces family and Coutet was in fact vinified at Yquem. (There's a wonderful myth that the two are connected by very long underground tunnel.) The property was used as a horse farm until the Saluces family sold it in the 1920s to the Guy family, who manufactured vertical presses (still present in the winery); and it was purchased by the Baly family in 1977. Today it is run by Philippe Baly and his niece Aline. The vineyards are relatively homogeneous clay soils on top of limestone, planted with 75% Sémillon, 23% Sauvignon Blanc, and 2% Muscadelle. There are 6-8 passes through the vineyard. Fermentation starts in tank, and then the must is transferred to barriques. Élevage for Coutet is in 90-100% new oak; the second wine is 70% new. The style is sumptuous. Cuvée Madame is a special cuvée (named to honor Mme. Rolland, the last owner in the Guy family) that comes from very old Sémillon in two parcels, made only in top vintages (using the old Guy vertical press), and amounting to only a thousand bottles or so. The latest addition to the range is Opalie, only 3-4,000 bottles of a dry white wine that's a blend of equal parts of Sauvignon and Sémillon. "It comes from specific rows in some of the best parcels; it's not a first pass of the vineyard in general," Aline Baly explains.

Barsac
Chartreuse de Coutet
www.chateaucoutet.com
39 ha; 42,000 bottles

 Barsac
www.denisdubourdieu.com

18 ha; 50,000 bottles

Château Doisy-Daëne

The Doisy estate was originally a single property in Barsac, but was divided into three parts in the early nineteenth century. Since 1924, Doisy-Daëne has been owned by the Dubourdieu family, today headed by oenologist Denis Dubourdieu. Other properties in the portfolio include Château Cantegril and Clos Floridène, not far away in the Graves appellation. The terroir of Doisy-Daëne is typical for Barsac: the so-called red sands consisting of red clay over calcareous subsoil. Three wines are produced here: the two sweet wines are the eponymous Doisy-Daëne and a super-cuvée called l'Extravagant de Doisy-Daëne; and there is also a dry white, Grand Vin Sec du Château Doisy-Daëne. The château wine is a mainstream Barsac, on the lighter side as is often true for Barsac compared with Sauternes, and in good years showing the classic flavor spectrum of botrytis. It is usually 95% Sémillon. L'Extravagant is something different. Made only in top years since the first vintage in 1990, it comes from an extremely late harvest (in November), and there is never more than half a dozen barriques. It has extraordinary levels of sugar, and is splendid to taste, but in all honesty I'm not sure I wouldn't prefer the château cuvée if I had more than a glass at a meal. The dry white comes exclusively from Sauvignon Blanc, and is fermented and matured in new oak; in fact, it originated in the previous generation with Pierre Dubourdieu, who was known for experimenting with vinification.

Barsac
2 Petit Védrines

27 ha; 80,000 bottles

Château Doisy-Védrines

This is the largest part of the original Doisy estate, created in the early eighteenth century and broken into three parts in the middle of the nineteenth century. The Védrines portion stayed with the original proprietors (whose name it reflects), but was sold to the Boireau family in 1851. It came by inheritance (through the female line) from the Boireaus to the branch of the Castéja family that now runs the major Bordeaux negociant, Maison Joanne. The estate was expanded from the original holding by a purchase in 2001 of an additional 6 ha (presently used for the second wine). The estate has been managed since 2004 by Olivier Castéja, recently elected as President of the Crus Classés of Sauternes and Barsac. Located between Châteaux Climens and Coutet on the high point of the Barsac plateau, the vineyards are planted with 85% Sémillon and 15% Sauvignon Blanc. Vinification typically starts in cuve and then is transferred to barrique for 16-18 months; new oak has been cut back from 100% in the 1980s to 50% in the 2000s. The style is on the rich side for Barsac—in fact this is usually one of the richest and most full-bodied wines in the appellation—and it is labeled as Sauternes rather than Barsac. The high sugar level is intended to counteract a natural high acidity. I find recent vintages to be more aromatic than usual, providing a nice counterpoise to the richness, which in the past has sometimes been overwhelming.

Château de Fargues

The ruined fourteenth century fortress, presently being painstakingly restored brick by brick, dominates the view of Château de Fargues. "There were certainly already vines here when Clement V built the château, and it came into the lur Saluces family by marriage in 1472," says Alexandre lur Saluces. De Fargues was not included in the Sauternes classification in 1855 because it was producing red wine during the nineteenth century. It was not until the 1930s that Alexandre's uncle replanted the vineyards with Sémillon and Sauvignon Blanc; the first vintage was 1943, bottled in 1947. "I restored everything at Yquem, and then I started again when I came here in 2004 (after LVMH took over Yquem)," Alexandre says. "I want to continue my family tradition of making great Sauternes." There were no facilities for winemaking, and the wine is made in a building constructed in 2006, small but modern, with stainless steel tanks and pneumatic presses, and a neat barrel room. Vineyards are being replanted and extended; the objective is to bring the proportion of Sauvignon Blanc up to 20%. The terroir at de Fargues is relatively homogeneous, clay with limestone underneath, and gravel on top. The difference in the microclimate from Yquem is that harvest is usually a week later. Subtle is not a word I often use to describe Sauternes, but de Fargues is all lightness of being, balancing botrytis, sweetness, acidity, fruits, and offering a fantastic combination of richness and delicacy.

 Fargues
 Sauternes
www.chateau-de-fargues.com

29 ha; 15,000 bottles

Bordeaux: Sauternes

Château Guiraud

One of the largest estates in the area, Château Guiraud has a slightly chequered history. Its name comes from an eighteenth century owner, and it subsequently passed through several hands before ending up with the Narby family in 1982. Xavier Planty became the régisseur, and then in 2006 bought the estate as part of a syndicate including Olivier Bernard from Domaine de Chevalier in Graves and Stephan von Neipperg of Château Canon La Gaffelière in St. Emilion. The vineyards are divided into 85 hectares used to produce Sauternes, and 15 ha for dry white Bordeaux. There's a relatively high proportion of Sauvignon Blanc, which is 35% of the plots for the grand vin. Both sweet and white wines are barrel-fermented, with one third new oak, one third one-year, and one third two-year. Techniques such as chaptalization or cryo-extraction are not used. The second wine, Petit Guiraud (formerly Le Dauphin de Guiraud), is described as a "modern Sauternes," vinified in a mixture of stainless steel and barriques. The dry white, G de Guiraud, comes from plots that reverse the proportions of varieties, and is 70% Sauvignon Blanc. Production is split on average between 100,000 bottles of grand vin, 40,000 bottles of second wine, and 30,0000 bottles of G de Guiraud. The Sauternes is in the mainstream, with the usual vintage variations in botrytis levels, of course, but I usually find the style to be a little in the direction of rusticity.

 Saint Ciers de Canesse
Sauternes
2 Petit Guiraud
www.chateauguiraud.com

100 ha; 170,000 bottles

 Bommes

Sauternes

2 La Gourmandise de
Clos Haut-Peyraguey
*www.bernard-
magrez.com/en/content/clos-
haut-peyraguey*

17 ha; 19,000 bottles

Clos Haut Peyraguey

This estate originated when the Lafaurie property was divided as an inheritance in 1879; the main and lower part became Lafaurie Peyraguey, and the small upper part became Clos Haut Peyraguey. Both parts retained the classification of 1855 as premier cru. Bordering Yquem, Clos Haut Peyraguey is one of the smallest premier crus in Sauternes. Together with adjacent Château Haut Bommes, the property was purchased by the Pauly family in 1914, and held for a century, until it was sold to Bernard Magrez in 2012. Jacques Pauly made the wine until 2002, when his daughter Martine took over. Hautes Bommes was used in effect as a second wine until Gourmandise was introduced in 2004. The terroir is quite complex, divided into a gravel area, part with more clay, and a sandier sector. Altogether the main vineyard is divided into more than 20 plots, with more in the 5 ha of Haut Bommes. Plantings are strongly dominated by Sémillon, which is 95%. Grapes go into pneumatic presses, the juice is settled briefly, and then goes directly into new or one-year barriques (typically about half are new). Under the Pauly regime, the objective was to achieve elegance. I have usually found the wines a little slow to develop. Before this purchase, Bernard Magrez had been trying to purchase an estate in Sauternes for his portfolio to satisfy growing demand for sweet wine in Asia, so it remains to be seen whether he will maintain the same style or will go for a more obvious, richer, style.

 Bommes

Sauternes

2 La Chapelle de Lafaurie-
Peyraguey
*www.chateau-lafaurie-
peyraguey.com*

36 ha; 60,000 bottles

Château Lafaurie Peyraguey

Château Lafaurie was one of the top classified growths in 1855, rated third, just below Yquem. A few years later, in 1879, the property was divided. Representing about three quarters of the estate, the main part became Château Lafaurie-Peyraguey; the smaller part became Clos Haut-Peyraguey. Both parts remained premier crus. The estate was purchased by the negociant house of Cordier in 1917. Lafaurie became part of the Suez group when they took over Cordier in 1984; they invested in renovating the vineyards and cellars. Then the estate was acquired in 2014 by Silvio Denz, chairman of Lalique and owner of several other châteaux in Bordeaux including Faugères and Peby-Faugères in St. Emilion. "I wouldn't pay above market price," is all that Silvio would say about the purchase. Vineyard parcels are dispersed all around the commune of Bommes, with a major block of 12 ha in a walled clos around the château; another major block of 5 ha is higher up the slope, facing Clos Haut Peyraguey. Plantings are heavily (93%) Sémillon. I have found the wines to be relatively light in recent vintages, with middling levels of botrytis, and it will be interesting to see what changes result from the new ownership. Silvio's stated objective is to concentrate sweet wine production on the 17 ha of parcels on the best terroirs at the core of the estate, and to increase dry wine production from the rest of the estate. Change is afoot, as Sherlock Holmes might have said.

Château Rieussec

During its lengthy history, Château Rieussec has gone from one extreme to another. It belonged to a Carmelite monastery before it was confiscated at the French Revolution. It became part of Lafite Rothschild's portfolio in 1984 (Charles Chevallier was the manager before he left to run all of Lafite). Officially classified as a premier cru, Rieussec is well established as one of the handful of châteaux in the second tier, ranking below Yquem. Although standing on a (relatively) high point, just beneath Yquem, the entire property is under drainage; there are also some leased vineyards elsewhere in Fargues. Plantings are 90% Sémillon. Harvest is usually a few days before Yquem, then grapes are pressed gently for 24 hours, and juice is run off straight into barrels for fermentation, which lasts around three weeks (the cellar is warmed to help the process). Fermentation is stopped when alcohol reaches 13.5-14%. After tasting in January, lots are assigned to either the grand vin or second wine, blended in tank, and then the wine goes back into barrel, remaining for two years for the grand vin and one year for the second wine. The second wine is slightly lower in alcohol and sweetness, but does not necessarily have less botrytis. The dry white ("R" de Rieussec) is 20% of production. It comes from plots that don't usually give good botrytis; in fact, they are treated against botrytis and harvested earlier (usually early in September as opposed to the others which go through October).

Fargues
Sauternes
2 Carmes de Rieussec
www.lafite.com

93 ha; 120,000 bottles

Château Sigalas Rabaud

Originally there was a single Château Rabaud, which was classified as a premier cru in 1855. Later in the century it expanded by acquiring the vineyards of a second growth château. The estate was split into two parts in 1903, Sigalas Rabaud and Rabaud Promis, and then the two parts were effectively reunited in 1929 as they were managed together by the negociant Ginestet. The estate was again split in 1949. Château Rabaud Promis has roughly two thirds, and Sigalas Rabaud has just under a third of the original property. Both parts remain premier cru. Since 1949 there have been ups and downs in the fortunes of the owning family, the de Lambert des Granges; the negociant Cordier took a stake in the property and had a hand in management from 1995 until 2008, but today it is run by oenologist Laure de Lambert-Compeyrot, daughter of owner Gérard de Lambert. The de Lamberts view the property as one of the few major Sauternes châteaux still to be family-owned. It is the smallest classified growth in Sauternes, with relatively homogeneous gravel terroir in one holding, facing south or southeast; it is mostly planted with Sémillon but a small amount of Sauvignon Blanc is planted on the areas that are richer in clay. The grand vin is typically 85% Sémillon, but in some years has been close to 100%. The name of the second wine changed from Cadet de Sigalas to Lieutenant de Sigalas; Demoiselle de Sigalas is a dry white Bordeaux, introduced in 2009.

Bommes
Sauternes
2 Le Lieutenant de Sigalas
www.chateau-sigalas-rabaud.com

14 ha; 30,000 bottles

 Fargues
Sauternes
2 Castelnau de Suduiraut
www.suduiraut.com

92 ha; 135,000 bottles

Château Suduiraut

The name goes back to 1580, and the impressive estate covers 200 ha of fields and forests. This is one of the small group of châteaux ranking immediately below Yquem, although it hasn't always fulfilled its potential. I still remember the astonishing quality of the 1900, drunk to celebrate the millennium in 2000. Between that wine, fresh and lively, full of deep, complex flavors at its centennial, and today, there have been disappointments, especially mid-century. Since the property was purchased by AXA in 1992, there has been significant investment. Plantings are 90% Sémillon and 10% Sauvignon Blanc. "I think Sémillon is the best grape," says manager Pierre Montégut. "Sauvignon Blanc is interesting to make a tropical style with fresh finish, but for me it lacks body. I don't want to make a heavy wine, but to have capacity to age you need to have a good body." The second wine, Castelnau, was created in 1992. "It was a classic second wine from lots that weren't good enough for grand vin. But since 2001 it's come mostly from different lots, it's more approachable, a little lighter and more drinkable. In 2009 we separated the half for Castelnau again. Les Lions de Suduiraut has more minerality and freshness, it's a style for young people, you have the impression of less sugar." Suduiraut uses 50% new oak for 18 months; other wines are up to 30% new oak for 12-15 months. Production is usually 50% Suduiraut, 25% of each of the other sweet wines, and a little dry wine, S de Suduiraut.

 Sauternes
www.yquem.fr

103 ha; 100,000 bottles

Château D'Yquem

Château d'Yquem has been making sweet wine since the Middle Ages, and the vineyards have existed more or less in their present form since about 1600. The method of picking successive *tries* dates back to the early nineteenth century. D'Yquem's supreme quality in Sauternes was recognized in 1855, when it was the only Château to be classified as Premier Cru Supérieur. The Château was in the hands of the Saluces family for many generations until it was sold to LVMH in 2004 (against the wishes of Alexandre de Lur Saluces, who now runs another family property, Château de Fargues). With a typical 90 days of fog per year, botrytis is very reliable. Quality is enforced by stringent selection in picking only berries above Brix 360 (20% potential alcohol). If a vintage is not considered good enough, no Yquem is produced, as in 1974, 1992 and 2012. Yields are roughly 8 hl/ha (the limit for Sauternes is 25 hl/ha), which roughly corresponds to one glass per vine. Vinification is organized at Yquem by days rather than by plot, that is, each day's pick goes into vinification as one lot, so at the end of the period there will be as many lots to blend as there were days of picking. Artificial aids are not common, although cryoextraction was used in two days in 2004. All wine is fermented in new oak, and then spends an average of 3 years in barrel, being topped up every two weeks and racked every 3 months. Of course, Yquem is generally acknowledged to be peerless.

Domaine L'Ancienne Cure

From the village at the top of the hill, you get a panoramic view of the domain. Its vineyards extend all the way from the winery at the top, which takes its name from the thirteenth century church in the village, to a tasting room geared for tourists passing along the main road at the bottom. The stone and metal winery building seems somewhat dilapidated outside, but it's all modern equipment inside, with stainless steel tanks for fermentation, and barriques for élevage of the more powerful wines. The domain was founded by Christian Roche's grandfather when he started to bottle his own wine, although production continued to be split between estate and cooperative. The domain owes its present position to Christian, who is clearly a mover and shaker. "We were too limited by size, it was necessary to expand the domain," he says. The emphasis is on whites, which are three quarters of plantings. There are 3 red cuvées, 3 dry white cuvées, 3 Monbazillac, and 1 rosé and 1 moelleux. They are divided into three brand lines: Jour de Fruit (introductory line); L'Abbaye (mid range); and L'Extase (top of the line). Everything is AOP, Bergerac Rouge or Sec for the dry red or white, Côtes de Bergerac for moelleux, and Monbazillac for fully sweet. There is also a negociant line of wines from Pécharmant. Christian is a late picker, but the style is quite delicate for the dry whites, and verges on savory for the sweet whites; the reds are a little heavier.

🄖 Colombier
Bergerac
Monbazillac, l'Abbaye
Bergerac Sec, l'Abbaye
www.domaine-anciennecure.fr

47 ha; 180,000 bottles

Château Barréjat

Denis Capmartin is the sixth generation to run this old family domain, which has some of the oldest vines in France, just near the charming house and terrace. There's a workmanlike winery behind, and viticulture and vinification are modern, focused on bringing out fruit flavors. When phylloxera struck, Denis's great great grandfather pulled out all the vines, leaving just two small parcels of 4 ha. Up to 200 years old, about 80% Tannat and 20% Cabernet Sauvignon, these pre-phylloxera vines are the basis for the Cuvée de Vieux Ceps (a blend of varieties) and l'Extrême (the best parcel of old Tannat). When Denis took over in 1992 there was only one cuvée of Madiran, but he introduced the vieille vigne cuvées, and divided the major production into two cuvées: Tradition and Seduction are exactly the same blend of 60% Tannat with 40% Cabernet Sauvignon or Franc, but are matured differently, Tradition in cuve and Seduction (introduced in 1996) in barriques. The wines are powerful, in the typical style of the appellation and varieties, but Denis has really mastered the tannins. Tradition still shows a little of the old style Tannat, but Seduction has nicely rounded fruits; and the cuvées from the old, pre-phylloxera vines, really are special in their concentration. There are also dry and sweet white wines under the Pacherenc AOP, and Chardonnay, Cabernet Franc, and rosé under the IGP Côtes de Gascogne, not to mention an Armagnac.

🄖 Maumusson Laguian
Madiran
Madiran, Seduction
www.chateaubarrejat.com

37 ha; 200,000 bottles

Monein

Jurançon

Jurançon, Symphonie de Novembre

Jurançon Sec, Seve d'Automne

www.jurancon-cauhape.com

43 ha; 260,000 bottles

Domaine Cauhapé

Henri Ramonteu created this domain in 1980, and it is now the largest independent property in Jurançon. "I started with 1 ha, I had to pull it up and replant because the vineyard had been used just to make wine for family consumption," Henri recollects. The estate is an example of the polyculture that's common in the region, with more than 50 ha of corn (and other crops); vineyards extend up to 22 km from the winery. A modern facility has several buildings packed with stainless steel tanks. Sweet wines are matured in barrique. The domain used to produce red wine (as Béarn AOP), but now is exclusively white. "Initially I had to master moelleux, in 1982 I started a sec cuvée. I achieved a certain success because of the aromatic style, then I slowly developed new cuvées," Henri says. Dry wine is as important as sweet here, with style determined by harvest date. Chant des Vignes and Geyser are harvested early; harvested in mid October, Seve d'Automne has more depth of flavor and texture. La Canopée (100% Petit Manseng) is harvested in November at the same time as the moelleux, and has something of the flavor spectrum of the sweet wines. The sweet wines have names reflecting harvest dates: Ballet d'Octobre, Symphonie de Novembre, and then Noblesse du Temps and Quintessence, followed by Folie de Janvier (the last three are 100% Petit Manseng, and only made in some years). The top cuvées here don't increase in sweetness, but show greater complexity.

Vieux

Gaillac

Vin de France, Causse Toujours

Vin de France, Zacmau

www.causse-marines.com

12 ha; 50,000 bottles

Domaine de Causse Marines

Hidden away just outside Vieux, the domain is not particularly well signposted because Patrice Lescarret and Virginie Maignien don't want to be interrupted by cellar door sales. It's very hands-on: Patrice does the grafting himself (he's adamant about not using clones), and when I arrived Virginie was pruning in the vineyard. We had lunch under the trees in a charming garden behind the house, and went through the range of wines, which are now mostly Vin de France. "Since I set up here in 1993 there have been problems with the AOP, and in 2003 and 2004 I stopped using the AOP. Now only the three basic wines are labeled with the appellation, and everything else is labeled as Vin de France," Patrice explains. "Gaillac has special grapes and my objective is to make authentic wine." This is defined as coming from local varieties: whites use Len de l'El, Ondenc and Mauzac; reds use Duras, Braucol, and Prunelard. There is also some Syrah. The dry whites are Les Greilles (a blend in Gaillac AOP), Zacmau (100% Mauzac), and Dencon (100% Ondenc). The reds are Les Peyrouzelles (a Gaillac blend), Rasdu (100% Duras), and Causse Toujours (Syrah and Prunelard). There are several moelleux cuvées, and in exceptional years a fully botrytized cuvée, Folie Pure. The vin de voile is a solera. The style is fresh, with light fruits supported by good acidity, varying between more and less aromatic varieties, but the same intent to avoid heaviness characterizes all the wines.

Château du Cèdre

The Verhaeghe family came from Belgium as refugees during the first world war; Pascal's grandfather was an agricultural worker who married a local girl, and their son took the domain into viticulture. At first he sold wine to negociants, then when Cahors became an AOC, he began to bottle his own wines. Pascal and his brother Jean-Marc took over from their father in 1993. The Cahors vineyards are 90% Malbec, with 5% each of Merlot and Tannat. In addition, there are a couple of hectares with white grapes. There is also a small negociant business, dating from 1995 when they lost the whole crop to hail, and had to buy grapes. There are three cuvées of Cahors and two IGPs under the Cèdre label. Produced from young vines, Château du Cèdre is the only cuvée that is not 100% Malbec. Le Cèdre and the Vieilles Vignes GC come from the same areas, but there are differences in vine age and the proportions of foudres, barriques, and new oak used in élevage. All cuvées are based on blends between vineyards in the third terrace and the calcareous Tran area. "I wanted to make cuvées from each terrace, but we decided there is more complexity in making an assemblage," Pascal says. The general style becomes more refined as you go up the hierarchy, with a big step up from château wine to Le Cèdre, and then GC shows left bank-like style needing time to resolve, with the difference from Le Cèdre more in texture than flavor; it reaches a peak after about fifteen years.

 Vire-sur-Lot
Cahors
Cahors, Le Cèdre
www.chateauducedre.com

29 ha; 120,000 bottles

Domaine Cosse Maisonneuve

Coming from north of Paris because she had always wanted to work on the land, Catherine Maisonneuve created the estate with her partner Mathieu Cosse in 1990. Very isolated and completely surrounded by woods, the domain is at the end of a valley, occupying a sort of amphitheater with vineyards all around, rising up to the surrounding woods. Wine is made in a utilitarian warehouse. Different cuvées are made from the top, middle, and bottom of the slope to display the effects of terroir on Malbec. "It's the noble cépage, it's perfectly adapted to the climate here," Catherine says. The bottom is gravel, the middle is more calcareous, and the top is clay over limestone. Wines from the three cuvees taste increasingly refined going up the slope. The difference is due to the tannins, which become increasingly finer-grained. Le Combal from the bottom (12 months élevage) is chewy and a little hard, Lafage from the middle (16 months élevage) shows more precision, and then Les Laquets from the top (24 months élevage) is fine and precise and almost perfumed. Aside from a small proportion of Le Combal that has élevage in cuve, everything is matured in barrique. From a nearby site with yet more clay and limestone comes La Marguerite, the finest of all. There is some new oak in Les Laquets and 100% in La Marguerite. All the Cahors are 100% Malbec. In addition, there are monovarietal Vin de France cuvées of Merlot, Gamay, and Cabernet Franc.

Cahors
Cahors, Les Laquets

19 ha; 60,000 bottles

Southwest

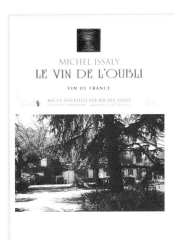

Domaine Guirardel

Jurançon

Bi dé Casau

🔾 Monein
⬤ Jurançon
🍾 Jurançon, Bi de Prat
www.domaine-guirardel.fr
▦ ♨ G ♣
6 ha; 20,000 bottles

Domaine Guirardel

Located at the end of a one track road, the domain has vineyards in a single block running down a very steep slope into the valley, planted with 4 ha Petit Manseng and 1 ha Gros Manseng, and then 1 ha of Gros Manseng on the other side. The estate has been in Françoise's family for 400 years; the original house is a single room, used for vinification for the past 200 years, and now the tasting room. The centuries' old buildings are packed with modern equipment. The ancient facility has even been converted to gravity feed by cutting a hole to allow the press to stand on a higher floor above the vats on the ground floor. The bottle cellar is where the cows used to be kept. Françoise and Pierre took over six years ago, increasing plantings, and adding new cuvées. Pierre, who has a questioning eye, has been experimenting to get fresher wines, and dry wines with a spectrum more like the sweet. Pierre describes the Jurançon Sec as a "moelleux without sugar. You can see it's not a typical dry wine, it's the same color as the moelleux," he says. Tradiciou is the cuvée that goes back to Françoise's father. Bi de Casau has been made since 2008 by selecting barrels of Gros Manseng with the most freshness. "We want a half dry effect in the wine, which isn't allowed in Jurançon, but this is our false half dry wine," says Pierre. Bi de Prat, Marrote, and Confit de Manseng are 100% Petit Manseng and come from the end of the vineyard, with Confit picked last. The style tends to be quite spicy.

MICHEL ISSALY
LE VIN DE L'OUBLI
VIN DE FRANCE
MIS EN BOUTEILLE PAR MICHEL ISSALY

🔾 Sainte-Cécile-d'Avès
⬤ Gaillac
🍾 Gaillac, Le Sang
🍶 Gaillac, Quintessence
www.michelissaly.com
▦ ♨ G ♣
6 ha; 12,000 bottles

Michel Issaly

Michel Issaly is the sixth generation at this family domain. "We are in the center of the historical part of the Gaillac appellation. I want to make authentic wine," Michel says, defining authenticity as terroir, climate, and preservation of old cépages. The domaine has a single holding running across two valleys, with a friable, very deep limestone base, more calcareous on the top half, more clay on the bottom half, and differences in the microclimates. Average vine age is 40-50 years. "Unfortunately half of my vines are clonal," Michel says unhappily (they were planted by his father). 2013 was his 30th vintage. "I worked for many years conventionally before I had enough experience to work like I do now. I don't like too much temperature control for the reds, I want to respect the vintage. In a hot year fermentation should be hotter. The wine should be a photograph of vintage and cépage," Michel says. "I have pulled my wines out of the appellation because they say they are oxidized. Only two of my cuvées are Gaillac." These are Combe d'Avès (Duras and Braucol) and Le Sang (90% Braucol and 10% Prunelard). Le Grand Tertre reverses the proportions, and another Vin de France, Le Peche de la Tillette, is a blend of four varieties, including a little Merlot. They are fresh, with some herbal impressions. Les Cavaillès is a spicy dry white from Mauzac, Len de l'El, and Ondenc; and Le Vin de l'Oubli is a vin de voile from Mauzac. Quintessence is a sweet white in an oxidative style.

Les Jardins de Babylone

The heart of this tiny estate is a spectacular 2 ha terraced vineyard of Petit Manseng. Didier Dagueneau (famous for his Pouilly Fumé) bought the property, close to Pau, in 2002, in order to make dessert wine, and called it the Jardins de Babylone for its perpendicular appearance. "The Petit Manseng was already planted, but there was nothing here but the vines, as all the grapes had been sold to the coop," says manager Guy Pautrat. The winery was constructed as a group of small buildings just opposite. Didier decided also to make a dry wine, so he planted another hectare nearby with the old lost varieties, Camaralet, Lauzac, and Petit Courbu. Where did he find them, I asked Charlotte Dagueneau? "Papa 'liberated' them from a nursery of old cépages," she explains. Production is split more or less equally between sweet and dry wine, with just one cuvée of each. The first vintage was 2002, but it was spoiled by problems with corks, and the first commercial release was 2004. The style here brings the same intensity to bear, whether dry or sweet, that characterizes the Dagueneau wines in Pouilly Fumé. The flavorful dry wine ranges from perfumed to savory depending on the vintage. The sweet wine is matured in a variety of barrel sizes, including French 300 liter and 600 liter, and Austrian 600 liter, each with its own character, as barrel samples show. Once bottled, piquant apricots show lots of concentration on the palate, with impressions of truffles increasing as the wine ages.

 Aubertin

Jurançon

Jurançon

3 ha; 6,000 bottles

Château Lagrézette

By far the most imposing property in Cahors, with a fifteenth century château at the center, Château Lagrézette has vineyards extending as far as the eye can see around the château, planted with 70% Malbec, 26% Merlot, and 4% Tannat. The wide variety of soils ranges from stony, clay and limestone, to pebbles, sand and silt. Château Lagrézette produces four wines, with Michel Rolland as consulting oenologue. Chevaliers Lagrézette is a light, earlier maturing wine made from young vines, and matured in old barriques, but I find it a little tight and rustic. Château Lagrézette is the domain's premium production each vintage, matured like the prestige cuvées in new barriques, and conveying a rather stern impression. Prestige Dame Honneur is produced only in small quantities in the best vintages. These cuvées all come from blends of Malbec and Merlot, with the proportion of Malbec increasing along the hierarchy. Le Pigeonnier comes from a 2.7 ha parcel of Malbec around the old pigeon loft, located near the château. The top cuvées are rich and chocolaty, but with a tendency to high-toned aromatics. Although this rather splendid large property has a spacious tasting room and is nominally open to visits, it is not very welcoming: when I turned up for my appointment, the tasting room was deserted, and a phone call elicited the response, "You have the wrong sort of appointment and I am going home in ten minutes." Caveat visitor!

 Caillac

Cahors

Cahors, Château Lagrézette
www.chateau-lagrezette.com

90 ha; 300,000 bottles

Southwest

Jurançon

Jurançon, La Magendia
www.jurancon-lapeyre.fr

18 ha; 60,000 bottles

Clos Lapeyre

Clos Lapeyre is tucked away up a long access road in the foothills of the Pyrenees; it feels quite isolated and much higher than it really is, as you are surrounded by peaks, but it's only 400 m elevation. Originating as a domain with the traditional polyculture, it has focused exclusively on viticulture since 1985, when Jean-Bernard Larrieu, grandson of the founder, constructed the first vinification facility. The tasting room is in a charming old house, but just behind is a modern winery, on the edge of a very steep vineyard that Jean-Bernard was busy replanting when I arrived. Vineyards are in many separate parcels, increased about 50% in 2004 by purchase of the nearby Nays-Labassère domain. There are three dry wines and four sweet wines, divided into three ranges. Lapeyre has one dry and one sweet cuvée, and is matured in cuve to emphasize fruit. More complex, La Magendia and Vitage Vielh each spend 1 year in barrique. Then there are the cuvées exceptionelle, either dry or sweet depending on the year. The cuvées are based on varying proportions of Gros and Petit Manseng. The sweet wines come from late harvest of grapes with passerillage, but for the cuvée exceptionelle Vent Balaguer, this is augmented by drying the berries further in the sun. "It's very, very concentrated, almost like a digestif." The dry wines are slightly perfumed, with something of the impression of apricots that characterizes the sweet wines. The sweet wines can be quite herbal, showing truffles as they age.

Aydie

Madiran

Madiran, L'Origin

Pacherenc de Vic-Bilh,
Château d'Aydie
famillelaplace.com

58 ha; 6,000,000 bottles

Famille Laplace

François Laplace's grandfather established the domain in 1962, when the Madiran appellation had all but disappeared. Initially confined to the area around the house, vineyards today are located in three different parts of Madiran. "We believe it's always more interesting to make an assemblage. Yes, a terroir is a terroir, but in a warm year St. Lanne will do better, in a wet year Aydie and Moncaup will make the best wine," François says. Madiran is only a third of total production, as most is IGP, made from purchased grapes in a new building full of large stainless steel tanks. There are three cuvées of Madiran, all from estate grapes. The wines are all labeled Famille Laplace. Matured mostly in cuve, the classic cuvée, L'Origine, is Tannat with 30% Cabernet Franc. "When I say classic it's not necessarily a wine of terroir. It's vinification to have simple fruits, not tannin, with a fresh equilibrium. It's true this doesn't have the old typicity of Madiran, but for today's consumer this is a good accompaniment to a meal," says François. "We are looking for Tannat with fruits not tannins." The other two cuvées comes from the slopes of all three locations and are 100% Tannat. Odé d'Aydie is matured in a mixture of foudres and cuves. Château d'Aydie is used as the name for the top wine, and is matured in barriques and foudres. Tight when young, Odé and Château d'Aydie become elegant with age. There are also dry and sweet white wines under the Pacherenc de Vic-Bilh appellation.

Château Montus

By far the largest producer in Madiran, Alain Brumont owns Château Bouscassé (a family property which he took over in 1979 and expanded), Château Montus (founded in 1980), Torus (a blend from young vines of Bouscassé and Montus together with a cooperative), and other domains in Vignobles Brumont. Almost 15 km apart, Bouscassé and Montus are virtually at opposite ends of the appellation. Before Alain bought Montus, it was a farm; he planted the vineyards, and the first wine was made in 1985. The focus is on Tannat. "Tannat made the great Bordeaux, I was very aware of it. I could see that we have very original terroir. I had a chance; because no one was interested in the terroir, I was able to buy vineyards," Alain says. Across the courtyard from the château, a huge new vinification facility has been built into the hillside in three storeys. Underground is a vast barrel room; above is a facility packed with stainless steel tanks, which Alain calls the Church of Tannat. Torus is soft and approachable, Bouscassé has more structure and depth (especially the Vieilles Vignes cuvée), and Montus is full force, with four intense cuvées. Château Montus itself is a blend of Tannat and Cabernet Sauvignon, with 12 months in barrique; Cuvée Prestige is 100% Tannat with up to 24 months élevage; XL is extended for 30 months; and La Tyre is a single vineyard wine from the best plot, given 18 months élevage. All require years to develop. There are also dry and sweet whites.

Maumusson
Madiran
Madiran, Cuvée Prestige
www.brumont.fr

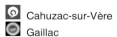

220 ha; 800,000 bottles

Domaine Plageoles

The domain originated in 1805 and is now run by Bernard Plageoles, the sixth generation. There's building work everywhere, with a modern tasting room in front of the buildings. The old cellars, under the original family house, are now used for the vin de voile. Behind is a practical warehouse with cement cuves. The domain owes its present reputation to Bernard's father, Robert, who made a huge effort to rescue the old varieties of Gaillac. "We wanted to use the old cépages to avoid the programmed wines," Robert says. The Plageoles believe that you can express the terroir only with single cépages, so all the wines are monovarietals. Altogether there are around fourteen different varietal cuvées. "The only cépage we have that isn't local is Syrah," says Bernard, who took over from his father about ten years ago. Red wines come from Prunelart, Mauzac Noir, and Verdanel, as well as Braucol, Duras, and Syrah. Dry whites come from Ondenc and Mauzac Vert, and sweet wines from Mauzac Roux, Muscadelle, Ondenc, and Loin de l'Oeil. There's also a vin de voile from Mauzac Roux, which is unusually powerful, and would be easy to mistake for Palo Cortado sherry. The white I like best is the dry Mauzac, which seems to offer something of the same impression as Gewürztraminer, in smelling sweet but tasting dry. The reds are light and fresh. The old varieties are no longer allowed in Gaillac AOP, so some of the wines are Vin de France.

Cahuzac-sur-Vère
Gaillac
Gaillac, Mauzac
www.vins-plageoles.com

25 ha; 90,000 bottles

Southwest

 Laroin

Jurançon

Jurançon Sec

www.domainedesouch.com

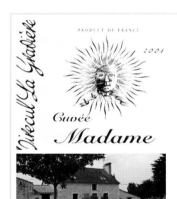

6 ha; 20,000 bottles

Domaine de Souch

This small domain started as a retirement project when Yvonne and René Hegoburu purchased a ruined house on the top of a hill just across the river from Pau for their retirement. The property has about 20 ha, half of which are woods. The plan was to plant a vineyard, but René died before this could be accomplished. Although Yvonne had been involved in administration at Château de Viaud in Pomerol, she had not made wine, but in 1987 she planted a small vineyard, running down the slope from 325 m elevation. Vines had been grown on the site in the seventeenth century by Jean de Souch, for whom the domain is named, but had perished with phylloxera. Known today as one of the grand characters of the region, Yvonne now runs the domain together with her son Jean-René. Plantings are 70% Petit Manseng, 20% Gros Manseng, and 10% Courbu. The blend of the Jurançon Sec follows the vineyard plantings, while the Jurançon has equal proportions of Petit and Gros Manseng. Both are matured in stainless steel. The Jurançon cuvée Marie Kattelin (named after Yvonne's granddaughter) is 100% Petit Manseng, and is directly pressed from partially destemmed grapes into barriques. It's been described as a "monster of concentration," and is usually one of the richest wines of the appellation. From time to time there are other cuvées, including Pour René, matured in 100% new barriques. The rich sweet wines classically show notes of truffles as they develop.

 Monbazillac

Monbazillac

www.tirecul-la-graviere.fr

8 ha; 12,000 bottles

Château Tirecul La Gravière

There isn't much doubt that Château Tirecul La Gravière is the best producer in Monbazillac. In the nineteenth century, it was one of 17 grand crus, but production collapsed after phylloxera, and when the AOC was created in 1936, the system of grand crus was not perpetuated. Located on a hill with the Dordogne only a couple of miles away, the site gets botrytis reliably in the mornings, and then the fog blows off in the afternoons. When Bruno Bilancini came here in 1992, grapes were being merged with another property, so he recreated the name of Tirecul La Gravière. Bruno uses only Sémillon and Muscadelle. "When we arrived here there was a small amount of Sauvignon Blanc. The problem is that its maturity is very different from the others." Production is almost entirely Monbazillac, divided between Les Pins (from young vines, which means less than 25 years here), the Château wine (vines aged up to 80 years), and Cuvée Madame (selected berry by berry, made only in exceptional years). A Bergerac Sec (dry white) is made in some years from plots that did not get botrytis. Bruno's policy goes to extremes: the Monbazillac comes exclusively from 100% botrytized grapes, the Bergerac Sec (if any) comes from zero botrytis. These are distinctive wines, very much their own style, spicy in hot years, more herbal in cooler years. "Tirecul needs to wait 8-10 years to develop complexity. It depends less and less on sugar as it ages, and becomes more elegant," Bruno says.

Clos Triguedina

A family property since 1830, Clos Triguedina has been built up into the most important producer in Cahors: since Jean-Luc Baldès, the eighth generation, took over in 1990, he has expanded the domain from its original 22 ha and introduced several new cuvées. "I have stabilized the size. Our mission is to occupy the pole place," he explains. "There are no negociants in Cahors, so we are obliged to do everything, to work out the techniques for viticulture and vinification and to commercialize," he adds. Just outside the extensive cuverie, Triguedina has the oldest Malbec vines in France, planted by Jean-Luc's grandfather who was a nurseryman. There are vineyards on the second, third, and fourth terraces. Vinification is in stainless steel, with élevage in barriques, except for Le Petit Clos, which is effectively an approachable second wine (80% Malbec), but even so is nicely structured. Clos Triguedina is a 100% Malbec classic blend from all terraces, with a strong but fine character. Trilogie comprises a box of three wines, one from each terrace: Au Coin de Bois (2nd terrace) is the most approachable and New World in character; Les Galets (3rd terrace) is more reserved; and Petits Cailles (4th terrace) is the finest in structure. Probus comes from old vines, and is the Vosne Romanée of Cahors. The New Black Wine is effectively a single vineyard cuvée from a 1.3 ha plot of old vines, and is rich but supple. There's also some white wine, rosé, and a sparkling rosé made from Malbec.

Puy l'Évêque

Cahors

Cahors, Clos Triguedina

www.jlbaldes.com

65 ha; 400,000 bottles

Vignoble des Verdots

The large new winery was built in 2003 to replace the old cuverie in the village. Below the tasting room is an underground barrel room, which David Fourtout excavated himself, with raw rock exposed at the ends, and a well in the middle revealing a stream below. The whirlwind that is David Fourtout came into the domain in 1992 when there were only 10 ha of vineyards, but lots of cows. Expanding, David invested in better vinification, aiming for more precision. "It's easy to get tannins and structure here, and I wanted to work my tanks in order to get softer tannins," he says, showing off stainless steel tanks that imitate wood tronconique cuves, made by an old school friend in the next town. Angles vary so that tanks are used according to the desired degree of extraction. David is an enthusiast for the latest equipment—fantastic is his favorite description. With mostly red wine, the estate is exclusively AOP, largely Bergerac and Côtes de Bergerac. Clos de Verdots is the historic range from the 1970s. David started the barrique-aged Château Les Tours de Verdot in 1992, and Grand Vin de Verdot (matured in new oak) in 1995. The top of the line is Le Vin (made only some years). "We try to have a distinct style in each range," he says. Styles extend from forward and fruity to strong structure. There's a common tendency to power, but fruits for the reds become more supple and complex, with intensity increasing along the hierarchy. Whites are relatively savory, with nutty overtones.

Conne-de-Labarde

Bergerac

Côtes de Bergerac, Chateau Les Tours de Verdots

Bergerac Sec, Grand Vin les Verdots

www.verdots.com

45 ha; 250,000 bottles

Southwest

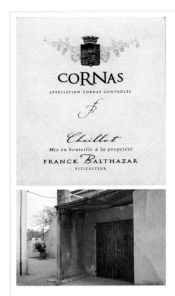

 Cornas

🔘 Cornas

🍾 Cornas, Chaillot

4 ha; 10,000 bottles

Domaine Franck Balthazar

This must surely be the smallest domain I visited in the Rhône. It started with 1.2 ha in 1931, and since Franck Balthazar took over from his father, René, in 2002, he has tripled it. Franck does all the work in the vineyards himself. The wine is made in a small cellar with a dirt floor round the back of the church in the village. The domain consists of three parcels in Cornas, Chaillot (1.7 ha), Mazards (0.4 ha), and Legre (1.7 ha), and also some recently planted vines in St. Péray. In 2011 there was a bottling under the Côtes du Rhône label from the young vines, which were very productive that year. Usually the Casimir bottling from Cornas comes from the young vines in the plot at Legre, which Franck replanted; it's warm, round, and nutty. At the other extreme, the Chaillot bottling comes from old vines replanted at the end of the nineteenth century just after phylloxera (some of this holding was inherited from Franck's uncle, Noël Verset); this makes an earthier, stonier, impression, with the intense, brooding black fruits of old vines. The objective here is "to make wines with purity of fruit, not technological wines. I don't want any aggressivité in my tannins," Franck says. Everything is matured in old demi-muids. For all the intention to maintain tradition, the well-delineated fruits give an impression of precision, with tannins certainly tamed. The older vines offer a more concentrated impression than the young vines, but the same purity of style shows through.

🔘 Larnage

⚫ Crozes-Hermitage

🍾 Crozes-Hermitage, Cuvée Louis Belle

🍾 Crozes-Hermitage, Terres Blanches

www.domainebelle.com

26 ha; 80,000 bottles

Domaine Belle

Up in the hills of Larnage at about 100 m elevation in the heart of the original Crozes Hermitage appellation, Domaine Belle occupies a utilitarian building surrounded by vineyards. The domain has expanded significantly in Crozes Hermitage, where it's still possible to buy land. "It's impossible in Hermitage," Philippe Belle says. The focus is decidedly on terroir. "We have always vinified by terroir. Why? Because we have very specific terroir, the only one here of white clay. Each terroir has its specificity and it's necessary to adapt to it. The white clay of Larnage is known for bringing freshness," says Philippe. If I had to choose a single word to describe the wines of Domaine Belle, it would be finesse. At all levels the wines show precision, increasing as you go from Crozes Hermitage to St. Joseph to Hermitage, but the refined style is always evident. The three cuvées from Crozes Hermitage make the case most forcefully: from the plain of Chassis, Les Pierelles is the most fruity; Cuvée Louis Belle from white clay terroir around the winery in Larnage has a fresh impression; and Roche Pierre from granitic terroir is taut. Coming from the heart of St. Joseph, between Tournon and Mauves, the St. Joseph is more elegant yet; and with the Hermitage you reach a true vin de garde, with long keeping power, but also elegance. These are textbook illustrations of the effects of terroir on Syrah. There are also excellent whites from Crozes Hermitage and Hermitage.

Maison Chapoutier Vins Fins

I left Chapoutier feeling slightly confused as to why I felt they might have lost their way. On previous visits, the wines were interesting all across the range. Now they seem more to be going through the motions. Chapoutier is both a large grower, with vineyards all across the Northern Rhône (the firm is the single largest owner of Hermitage), and a major negociant business handling wines from the entire Rhône. Chapoutier is a major believer in single vineyard bottlings, and it's always been true that with Hermitage, the single vineyard wines are vastly more interesting than the blended cuvée, Monier de la Sizeranne; but the most recent vintages of Sizeranne seem somewhat rustic, which should never be the case for Hermitage. Chapoutier's top vineyard in St. Joseph, Les Granits, has in the past has produced some splendid wines, both red and white, almost worthy of Hermitage, but recent vintages seem lacking in character. This is against a background of real interest in viticulture, with Chapoutier perhaps qualifying as the largest producer in France to be biodynamic, but I cannot find interest in the generic wines, or real conviction in the single vineyard wines, in the present releases. Perhaps expansion has been too rapid (Chapoutier now has interests elsewhere in France, and also in Portugal and Australia). The tasting room in the old headquarters in Tain l'Hermitage is thronged with visitors, although most wines now are made in a large modern facility away from the town.

Tain L'Hermitage
Hermitage
St. Joseph, Les Granits
www.chapoutier.com

179 ha; 330,000 bottles

Domaine Jean-Louis Chave

The entrance to the most famous domain of Hermitage is quite deceptive, just a simple front door with a plate saying Gérard Chave on what appears to be an ordinary residence in the main street of Mauves. The doorway opens into a courtyard surrounded by winery buildings, with a rabbit warren of old cellars underneath. Jean-Louis Chave is widely acknowledged as a master of assemblage, and his Hermitage comes from a blend of plots on the hill that changes according to the year. His red is one of the longest-lived wines of Hermitage, and the white is equally fine. Some years there is also a limited bottling of Cuvée Cathelin, representing an alternative assemblage. In fat years this may perpetuate the tradition of Hermitage for strong structure more forcefully than the regular bottling. Wines from each plot are matured separately, in old barriques, with less than 20% new oak, until assemblage after about eighteen months. The white is mostly barrel-fermented and matured in oak, but a small part is kept in cuve. There is now St. Joseph from an old family vineyard that's being replanted, as well as St. Joseph (Offerus) produced under the negociant label of JL Chave selections, which also produces a characterful Crozes Hermitage (Silène). Vineyards are maintained by replacing vines individually as necessary by selection massale. "The grape is a vector for the soil to express itself. What I want is that what comes from Rocoule goes back to Rocoule," says Jean-Louis.

Mauves
St. Joseph
Hermitage

27 ha; 45,000 bottles

Domaine Auguste Clape

The domain was created when Auguste Clape left the Languedoc after the riots of 1907 and began to buy land in Cornas. Winemaker Olivier Clape is the third generation to produce wine under the domain name; his grandfather started bottling in 1955, his father Pierre-Marie took over, and then Olivier followed. Most of the vineyards are behind the village of Cornas, "not too high up," and there are also small plots in St. Péray and the Côtes du Rhône. This is a traditional domain, with vinification in concrete tanks, and maturation in old foudres for 22-24 months. "The main difference between my father and grandfather was the date of picking," says Olivier, "and my father had lower yields. We don't want to have too much acidity because we keep 100% stems, so we pick a bit late." There are two cuvées from Cornas. Introduced in 1998, Renaissance comes from young vines: young here means half from 12-16 years, giving yields of 36-38 hl/ha, the other half from 25-year-old vines on a south-facing site that is one of the warmest in Cornas. The traditional cuvée, labeled only with the appellation name, comes from older vines with lower yields, at 26-32 hl/ha. Tasting barrel samples from the various plots that go into the Cornas, there is a clear increase in aromatic complexity from 35-year-old vines to 80-year-old vines. The assembled Cornas is a vin de garde; give it sufficient time and you will see what Cornas is all about. The domain remains the reference point for Cornas.

Cornas
Cornas
9 ha; 30,000 bottles

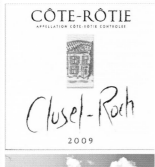

Domaine Clusel Roch

The winery is in what appears to be a modest house in a residential area. The principal production is Côte Rôtie, and there is also a little Condrieu. There are 5 ha in Côte Rôtie and 1 ha in Condrieu. Recently 2.5 ha were acquired in the Coteaux du Lyonnais (located north of Côte Rôtie), where plantings are Gamay and the wine is similar to Beaujolais. From the several parcels in Côte Rôtie there are four cuvées: one general blend, one from young vines (La Petite Feuille), and two lieu-dits. There is partial destemming (0-50% depending on the year), stainless steel fermentation, pump-over and punch-down, 20-30 days' total maceration, and two years in barrique, with a little new oak but not too much (less than 20%). The Côte Rôties are 100% Syrah except for the classic (general) bottling which has a little Viognier. The old vines are perpetuated by selection massale, and Guillaume Clusel has been involved in a project to propagate old Serine vines. The measure of the house is subtlety of approach. La Petite Feuille and the Côte Rôtie blend are not as interesting as the bottlings from the lieu-dits, Les Grandes Places and Les Vallières. Guillaume attributes the subtlety of the wines to time of harvesting. "We harvest just at maturity without sur-maturity," he says. The Condrieu shows equal subtlety, a fine demonstration that Viognier does not have to be taken to excess. The Gamays from the Coteaux du Lyonnais are nice, but not exceptional.

Ampuis
Côte Rôtie
Côte Rôtie, Viallière
www.domaine-clusel-roch.fr
8 ha; 25,000 bottles

Domaine Jean-Luc Colombo

Jean-Luc Colombo was regarded as a young Turk, if not a revolutionary, when he started to buy land on the higher Cornas slopes in the 1980s, not to mention introducing new oak into his cuvées. The 12 ha of estate vineyards in Cornas are broken up into 25 different parcels. The modernist approach extends to complete destemming—Syrah is a very tannic variety," says Laure Colombo. "When my parents were criticized for making more sophisticated wine, people would say, this wine is not typical," she recollects. But Jean-Luc has won the argument as his approach is now common in Cornas. The bulk of production is through a negociant business, with around thirty wines, the biggest line being the Côtes du Rhône. The style of the negociant wines is direct and fruity: these are well made wines for immediate consumption, but they do not have the interest of the wines from the estate vineyards, especially when you move to single vineyard cuvées. These are modern wines in the sense that the fruit clearly comes first, but I would not accuse Jean-Luc, at least not today, of being a modernist in the sense that the wines show excess new oak: the oak is judicious, just showing on the youngest vintages, but well integrated after, say, five years. If the wines do not always rise to the heights that you would really like to see, they are true to type in reflecting vintage, with the 2006 Cornas Les Ruchots, for example, giving a more reserved impression than the more exuberant 2009.

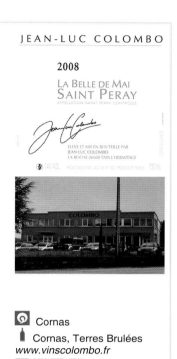

Cornas
Cornas, Terres Brulées
www.vinscolombo.fr

12 ha; 100,000 bottles

Domaine Combier

Maurice Combier came to Pont de l'Isère to grow apricots and other fruit in 1962, and became known as Maurice Le Fou (Crazy Maurice) when he turned to organic agriculture in the 1970s. Grapes from the domain were sold to the cooperative. His son Laurent studied viticulture and joined the domain in 1989. At that point the estate had 5 ha of vines and 15 ha of peaches and apricots. Laurent moved the domain into viticulture, built a cave, and started to produce wine. Most of the vineyards are around Pont de l'Isère (in the Crozes Hermitage AOP about four miles south of Hermitage); there are also smaller holdings across the river in St. Joseph. Cuvée Laurent Combier is an introductory blend that comes from rented vineyards. Cap Nord is a new line, started in 2010, from parcels in the north of the Crozes Hermitage and St. Joseph appellations. The Domaine Combier Crozes Hermitage cuvées are blends from several estate parcels in the vicinity of Pont de l'Isère. The top cuvées come from the Clos des Grives, a 9.5 ha vineyard just next to Alain Graillot's estate; this has the oldest vines of the domain, 4 ha that were planted in 1952. The red is pure Syrah, the white is 95% Roussanne. Grapes are destemmed and fermented in stainless steel; then they are matured in cuve for Cuvée Laurent Combier, in old barriques for the domain, and in barriques with about a quarter new oak for Clos des Grives. Laurent Combier also is a partner in a domain (Trio Infernal) in Priorat (Spain).

Lanoraie
Crozes-Hermitage
www.domaine-combier.com
30 ha; 150,000 bottles

Northern Rhône

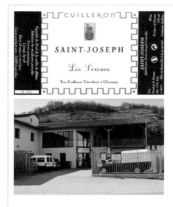

Cave Yves Cuilleron

This family domain was created by Yves's grandfather when he planted vines in 1920. He started in bottling in 1947. When Yves took over the domain in 1987, there were 4 ha; today vineyards have expanded considerably from the original holdings in St. Joseph and Condrieu to Côte Rôtie, Cornas, and St. Péray. "Now it is difficult to buy land, but when I started there was plenty of land for sale," Yves says. The modern tasting room just off the main road is thronged with visitors. With a reputation in the region for producing wines in a more modern style, Yves is also one of the entrepreneurs behind the Vins de Vienne. Cuilleron produces 25 different wines. "In each appellation there are several cuvées. You can make cuvées by lieu-dit or by style. I prefer the second because many parcels are very broken up, and very small, so I make cuvées de style, some more fruity, some more structured coming from an assemblage of parcels with the same character." All plots are vinified separately. The AOP wines are matured in barriques. There's been some retreat on the amount of new oak, which today is less than 20% except for the vins de garde. Whites have 9 months élevage and reds have 18 months. It's not surprising that with 25 different cuvées there should be some variety, and style here depends on the level. The introductory cuvées from each appellation tend to be fruity; the more advanced show more of a mixture of influences with savory notes on nose and palate.

 Chavanay
Condrieu
Côte Rôtie, Bassenon
St. Joseph, Saint Pierre
www.cuilleron.com

56 ha; 350,000 bottles

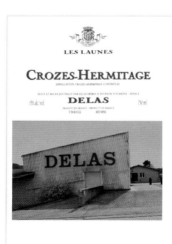

Maison Delas Frères

Delas was founded as a negociant of Hermitage in 1834, and after its acquisition by Champagne Deutz in 1977, came under the ownership of Champagne Roederer when Roederer acquired Deutz in 1993. It presently functions out of a utilitarian building constructed fifteen years ago across the road from the original site, just under the hill of Saint Epine, which is the top cuvée from St. Joseph. The estate vineyards break down into 10 ha in Hermitage (including 8 ha in Les Bessards), 17 ha in Crozes Hermitage, and 2 ha in St. Joseph. About half of production comes from the estate vineyards; the other half is a negociant business based on purchased grapes. Many of the domain bottlings are identified as Domaine des Tourettes. Production is largely red, with only about 10% white. The style here tends towards a silky refinement, running through the best reds from Crozes Hermitage, St. Joseph, and Hermitage. Even at the lower levels, the wines are finely balanced, which is to say following the traditions of the region as opposed to pandering to a style for jammy fruits. They are all recognizably from the Northern Rhône, with typicity of the individual appellation, in which freshness is balanced by a sheen of glycerin in the house style. Delas also has a range of wines from the Southern Rhône; richer but less refined, these typify the difference between south and the north. The wines are always reliable, although of course the top cuvées from the better appellations have the most interest.

Saint Jean de Muzols
St. Joseph
St. Joseph, François de Tournon
Condrieu, Clos Boucher
www.delas.com

29 ha; 1,500,000 bottles

Maison Michel Ferraton Père & Fils

The domain started in 1998 when Michel Ferraton left Chapoutier. After he had a serious accident in 2007, the firm was bought by Chapoutier, although it continues to run independently. Chapoutier does have an influence however: Ferraton has the same belief in emphasizing bottlings of individual *climats* rather than a single assemblage, and also has biodynamic vineyards in Hermitage, Crozes Hermitage, and St. Joseph. "Our philosophy is to express the different terroirs found in the Northern Rhône. We want to show the different typicities we find in St. Joseph, the difference between granite and other soils, or in Cornas the difference between elevations," says manager Olivier Goni. There are five different cuvées from Hermitage: two are from assemblage of various plots, and the others come from Méal, Dionnières, and a blend of Méal and Dionnières; there are two cuvées from each of the other appellations. There is also a negociant business, principally for wines from the Southern Rhône, but also including Côte Rôtie, and this is much larger than the production of estate wines. The greatest part of the business is the negociant wine from Côtes du Rhône and Crozes Hermitage. The style is towards freshness rather than exuberance; "We look for discretion and elegance," says Olivier. The reds are relatively restrained, and the whites fulfill the aim of maintaining freshness; there is good weight on the palate, but they are wines to drink in five years rather than hold for ten.

Tain L'Hermitage
Hermitage
Hermitage, Les Miaux
St. Joseph, La Source
www.ferraton.fr
13 ha; 350,000 bottles

Domaine Pierre Gaillard

There's a distinctly thoughtful air at this domain, tucked away on the plateau above the medieval village of Malleval. Pierre Gaillard has an interest in the old Roman wines—each year he makes a wine in an amphora using different experimental procedures—and he was instrumental in reviving the old vineyards at Seyssuel when he started the Vins de Vienne. Although committed to preserving the character of the region, in winemaking he is a modernist, using around 20% new oak for his St. Joseph and Côte Rôtie. All wines are matured in barriques but there is no new oak for the whites, "Because the whites have minerality but not acidity." His first vineyard showed typical lateral thinking. "The first land I bought was in Chavanay, I wanted to make a Viognier, but there was no land in Condrieu. This was probably not included in Condrieu because it is east-facing, but I heard it had made good Viognier before." There's an impressive range of wines here, with 48 cuvées altogether, made to a high standard with each typical of its appellation, from the round Côte Rôtie, to the fresh St. Joseph, and the slightly stern Cornas. Wines from Pierre's daughter Jeanne are also available under the Gaillard name, and Pierre has expanded into Faugères (Domaine Cottebrun) and Banyuls (Domaine Madeloc), "Just for pleasure, around here it is all Syrah, I wanted the experience of other varieties. Here we could not expand. My passion is to understand terroir."

Malleval
St. Joseph
St. Joseph, Les Pierres
www.domainespierregaillard.com

25 ha; 125,000 bottles

Northern Rhône

Domaine Jean-Michel Gerin

The family has been involved in wine in Ampuis for six generations, but Jean-Michel created the domain in 1983 with one small parcel on Côte Rôtie; it has been expanding ever since. His sons Michaël et Alexis are now involved. The original vineyard holdings were all close to Ampuis, with 7 ha in a dozen separate plots in Côte Rôtie and another 2 ha in Condrieu. The major Côte Rôtie, Champin le Seigneur, is an assemblage from all the sites, but mostly from the Côte Brune, and includes 10% Viognier. In addition there are single vineyard bottlings from the *climats* Grandes Places (since 1988), which is considered Gerin's top wine, La Landonne (since 1996), and La Viallière (planted only in 2003, with the first vintage in 2009). These are all exclusively Syrah. Another site on Côte Rôtie, Les Lezards, is presently being planted. There is a single Condrieu, La Loye. More recently, a St. Joseph red has been added, together with Syrah and Viognier under the IGP Collines Rhodaniennes. (There's also a collaborative venture with two other producers from southern France to make wine at a 6 ha domain in Priorat, Spain.) The style here is modern, with destemming, and maturation in barriques including lots of new oak for 18 months. Grandes Places and La Landonne use 100% new barriques, La Viallière uses 100% new demi-muids, and other wines use varying proportions. There is frequent battonage. The Condrieu uses a mix of stainless steel and one-year barriques.

Ampuis
Côte Rôtie
Côte Rôtie, Le Seigneur
www.domaine-gerin.fr

12 ha; 100,000 bottles

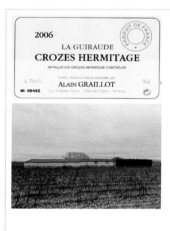

Domaine Alain Graillot

Alain Graillot is one of the new generation who came into winemaking in search of something different from the corporate world. He established his domain in Crozes Hermitage in 1985. Self taught as a winemaker since there was no wine in the family background, he rapidly acquired a reputation for his thoughtful approach, which maintains tradition, for example by manual harvesting rather than the mechanization that is common in Crozes Hermitage. The heart of the domain consists of vineyards on the Plain de Chassis in the southern part of Crozes Hermitage, more or less centered on the cellars, which are located just outside the town of Pont de l'Isère between Tain l'Hermitage and Valence. In addition, there is a small vineyard at Larnage in the hills to the north of Crozes Hermitage, on granite terroir, and also two tiny parcels in St. Joseph. The top cuvée is a barrel selection from Crozes Hermitage, made only in top years, La Guiraude. Production is mostly red, but the white Crozes Hermitage, a blend of 80% Marsanne with 20% Roussanne, has acquired a high reputation. Wines are aged in 1- to 3-year-old barriques. The wines have a reputation for moderation, which is a contrast with Alain's more recent involvement with winemaking elsewhere, notably with wines from Australia and Morocco now associated with his name. Since 2008, the wines at Alain Graillot have been made by his son Maxime, who also makes wines at his own domain, Domaine des Lises.

Pont de l'Isère
St. Joseph
St. Joseph

21 ha; 100,000 bottles

Maison Guigal

The entire atmosphere in the Northern Rhône changed when Marcel Guigal introduced single vineyard cuvées from Côte Rôtie in the 1970s. His father had founded Maison Guigal in 1946; today his son Philippe has taken over as chief winemaker. Estate vineyards now extend all over the Northern Rhône, with top sites in Hermitage and St. Joseph coming from the purchase of the old Grippat estate, adding the Vigne de l'Hospice (St. Joseph) and Ex Voto (Hermitage) to the La Landonne, La Mouline, and La Turque vineyard cuvées from Côte Rôtie. With a current production of 6.5 million bottles, Guigal is the most important negociant in the Northern Rhône, although the majority of the negociant business, including 3.5 million bottles of Côtes du Rhône, comes from the Southern Rhône. Guigal has also purchased Vidal Fleury (which remains independently run), where Étienne Guigal worked before founding Maison Guigal. All this has been accomplished while retaining a concern for quality and character. For example, "I've never been a big fan of Grenache Blanc," says Philippe. "Thirty years ago my dad was struggling to get Viognier, it was only 5% then, but today the white Côtes du Rhône is 60% Viognier. It took thirty years, but we achieved it." A splendid new headquarters has been constructed across the road, connected to the original winery by a tunnel. (The winery covers 3 ha.) Guigal has the rare distinction of being a quality leader in both estate and negociant wines.

🕤 Ampuis
⬤ Côte Rôtie
🍾 Côte Rôtie, Château d'Ampuis
🍾 Crozes Hermitage
www.guigal.com
🚶 🏭 G N
50 ha; 6,500,000 bottles

Domaines Paul Jaboulet Aîné

"We are the smallest of the big negociants," says winemaker Ralph Garcin. Jaboulet is a great old name, famous from the mid-twentieth century for its blended Hermitage, La Chapelle, but quality had slipped by the time the Frey family (of Château La Lagune in the Médoc) took it over in 2006. The new owners have started a forceful expansion, increasing estate vineyards from the 80 ha at the time of takeover, adding vineyards in Châteauneuf-du-Pape as well as in the Northern Rhône. "For every appellation in the Rhône we have a minimum of two wines, one from the estate and one from the negociant. We look for more consistency in the negociant line," says Ralph. Differences between wines here are due to intrinsic character, as fermentation and élevage are similar for the whole range; new oak is presently around 20% but will decrease to about 15%. "We are looking for freshness and elegance even if it is a warm spot like Châteauneuf-du-Pape," Ralph says. Jaboulet is organic and is going biodynamic. I was impressed with the progress when I tasted a range of domain wines from recent vintages: La Chapelle is good once again (although I have my doubts about Petit Chapelle), the white Chevalier de Sterimberg is right on form, and there are interesting wines from Crozes Hermitage, St. Joseph, and Condrieu. I was less certain about the Châteauneuf-du-Pape (but I almost always have reservations about Southern Rhône wines from Northern Rhône producers).

🕤 Tain L'Hermitage
⬤ Hermitage
🍾 St. Joseph, Domaine de la Croix de Vigne
🍾 Hermitage, Chevalier de Sterimberg
www.jaboulet.com
🚶 🏭 G N 🍇
115 ha; 200,000 bottles

Northern Rhône

Ampuis

Côte Rôtie

12 ha; 55,000 bottles

Domaine Jamet

Until the eighties, the family business was polyculture, mostly concentrating on growing apricots. Once the focus switched to grapes, Joseph Jamet became regarded as one of the most traditional producers in the appellation, and the style was continued when he retired in 1991 and his sons Jean-Paul and Jean Luc took over. Two thirds of Jamet's vineyards are in Côte Rôtie, spread around 26 different parcels in a variety of lieudits, three quarters in Côte Brune and a quarter in Côte Blonde. Vines range from 25 to 50 years old; there is only Syrah. Some parcels are vinified and aged separately, while others are blended. Some are destemmed while others are not; there are significant differences from year to year. Wines are matured in a mixture of barriques and demi-muids, with a trend towards increasing the proportion of demi-muids in recent years. New oak is around 20%. The philosophy here is to represent the domain with one wine; "My philosophy, it's assemblage," says Jean-Paul. "I don't like to focus on a wine, a parcel, or a year," but there is a cuvée, Côte Brune, made from a single 0.5 ha parcel in the best years. In fact, this was the sole production when Joseph Jamet started the domain; now it is only 5%. There are also both red and white Côtes du Rhône, from the one third of vineyards outside Côte Rôtie. However, as of 2013 the brothers have split, with Jean-Paul retaining the domain, and Jean-Luc creating a new domain based on the Lancement parcel in Côte Rôtie.

Ampuis

Côte Rôtie

Côte Rôtie

6 ha; 26,000 bottles

Domaine Jasmin

This typical small domain on Côte Rôtie, now in its fourth generation since Patrick Jasmin gave up cross-country motorcycling to take over from his father Robert in 1999, has eleven separate parcels spread over nine lieu-dits, with terroirs of both schist and granite. Including some additional leased vineyards, the average vine age is over thirty years. The vineyards are coplanted with 95% Syrah and 5% Viognier; the proportion of Viognier in the finished wine varies, depending on the vintage. Propagated by selection massale in the estate vineyards, the Syrah is the old Sérine selection. Parcels are vinified separately, the wine is racked into barriques for malolactic fermentation, and then all the wine goes into a single assemblage to make the unique Côte Rôtie, which is matured for two years in a mixture of barriques and demi-muids, with around a quarter new oak. In addition, there is a Vin de Pays de Collines Rhodaniennes, which comes from vineyards below Côte Rôtie. Robert Jasmin was known for his traditional approach (he was considered to be one of the holdouts for the old style, together with Auguste Clape and Joseph Jamet), but there has been some modernization in recent years, with destemming introduced and a saignée to concentrate the must. The style tends towards elegance rather than power, with freshness evident, even a touch lean at times, but with complex aromatics and oak not at all evident. This is tradition at its best.

Domaine Michel et Stéphane Ogier

Michel Ogier sold his grapes to Chapoutier and Guigal until 1983, when he started to bottle his own wine from his tiny 3 ha vineyard in Côte Rôtie. His son Stéphane spent five years studying viticulture and oenology in Burgundy, and then returned home to join the domain in 1997. "That is why great Burgundy, along with Rhônes, are my preferred red wines," he says. One of his main objectives was to increase the estate to a more economic size, and he added vineyards in several lieu-dits in Côte Rôtie, and at La Rosine just above Côte Rôtie, as well as planting Syrah farther up the river at Seyssuel. His most recent acquisition was a hectare in Condrieu. Renamed Domaine Michel & Stéphane Ogier, the domain now produces a variety of cuvées. Côte Rôtie is presently a blend from 10 parcels in the appellation; the IGP Collines Rhodaniennes comes from La Rosine; and the L'Âme de Soeur cuvée comes from Seyssuel. There are two prestige cuvées from Côte Rôtie, Lancement from Côte Blonde, and Belle Hélène, a selection from old vines that is aged exclusively in new oak. There is also a small negociant activity producing a Côtes du Rhône from Plan de Dieu (the area in the southern Rhône between Vacqueyras and Cairanne). Most production is red, but there is a Viognier from La Rosine, as well as the Condrieu. The style of the wines is modern (with about 30% new oak in the regular Côte Rôtie), and you might call the top cuvées very modern.

Ampuis
Côte Rôtie
www.domaine-ogier.fr
13 ha; 80,000 bottles

Domaine André Perret

The Perret family were vignerons in Chassagne Montrachet until they relocated as a result of the second world war. His father and grandfather cultivated fruits, and André abandoned a career as a biologist to start the domain by renting a vineyard in the Coteau de Chéry lieu-dit of Condrieu. Then he obtained a tiny area of his own vines from his uncle. Initially in 1983 the domain consisted of just 1 ha in Condrieu. It's been built up slowly since then, but remains a small domain today, with the winery in what looks like a residence just off the main road in Chavanay, although in fact a new cave was constructed in 1995. Today the AOP vineyard holdings are split between St. Joseph and Condrieu, and there are also 2 ha planted within the IGP on the plain. Basically André plants Viognier in the warmest spots (to make Condrieu) and Syrah, Marsanne, or Roussanne elsewhere (to make St. Joseph). The interest here is in terroir: "I'm a Burgundian, I respect terroir," André says of his bottlings from lieu-dits in Condrieu. The Coteau de Chéry, which is still the top cuvée, and the old vines Les Grisières bottling of a red St. Joseph, are the most interesting wines. The style is quite fine, and both the Condrieu and St. Joseph are good representations of the appellations. The white St. Joseph is an equal blend of Marsanne and Roussanne, and gets about 10% new oak. "It's not typical but the Roussanne makes the wine finer," André says.

Chavanay
Condrieu
St. Joseph, Les Grisières
Condrieu, Chéry

13 ha; 55,000 bottles

Mercurol
Crozes-Hermitage
Hermitage, Cuvée Emilie
www.domaineremizieres.com

34 ha; 150,000 bottles

Domaine des Remizières

This family domain (also known as Cave Desmeure) started with 4 ha in the late 1960s; originally Alphonse Desmeure sold half the wine to the cooperative and the other half to negociants, but domain bottling started in 1973. Philippe Desmeure took over in 1996 and was responsible for enlarging the estate; now he has been joined by his daughter Emilie. The first vineyards were in Crozes Hermitage, and then Hermitage and St. Joseph were added. Production is all from estate vineyards except for a Cornas made from purchased grapes. The operation is still expanding, as witnessed by the building materials and cranes everywhere when I visited. The wines are all well made, but to my mind they seem to risk becoming superficial: it's difficult to get a feeling of character, or a personality behind them. Quite a bit of new oak is used (100% for the red Hermitage, 50% for the white). No white grapes are used in the red wines. "It's not needed any more," Emilie explains. The consistent house style shows something of an impression of glycerin on the palate, giving almost a sense of sweetness on the finish; this can verge on oppressive in the less expensive cuvées, but is more pleasing at the higher end where there is sufficient balancing structure. The top wines are named for the current generation: Cuvée Christophe is a red Crozes Hermitage from old vines on the slopes (whereas the entry level cuvée comes from the plain); the top red Hermitage is called Cuvée Emilie, as is the white Hermitage.

Ampuis
Côte Rôtie
Côte Rôtie, Ampodium
www.domainerostaing.com

10 ha; 40,000 bottles

Domaine René Rostaing

The modest premises consist of a purpose-built concrete facility with a cellar underground, off a small courtyard behind the family residence in Ampuis. Although the domain started with under a hectare in 1971, today the vineyards consist of 25 separate parcels in Côte Rôtie and Condrieu; there is also now a small domain in the Languedoc (Puech Noble). (Why expand into Languedoc? "For experience of other grape varieties and terroir. It's easy to buy land in Languedoc, here it's impossible.") There are three cuvées from Côte Rôtie: Ampodium (the general bottling), La Landonne (from a 2 ha plot), and Côte Blonde, which is the best, but most tannic, wine. The mark of the house, for both Condrieu and Côte Rôtie, is subtlety. "When I describe my vinification, winemakers become very excited because they think I have a secret," René says, "but I have no secret. The only secret is no intervention. If you have too much intervention in vinification, you make a factory wine." René uses a rotary fermenter, which in other hands might lead to too much extraction, and alcohol is usually no more than 13%. There is no destemming: this is a puzzle given the evident gracefulness and elegance of the wines. "If you respect the grape, it's not necessary to destem," is all René will say about it. Both barriques and demi-muids are used for aging, and there is a very little new oak. However it is achieved, the style is old school elegance rather than modern power.

Domaine Marc Sorrel

The domain was started in 1928 by Marc Sorrel's grandfather, Félix; grapes were sold to the cooperative until his son, Henri, started domain bottling in 1979. Marc took over in 1984. When Henri Sorrel died, the domain was divided between Marc and his brother, Jean-Michel (whose domain is called J.M.B. Sorrel). Marc subsequently acquired some plots in Crozes Hermitage, but this remains one of the smallest quality domains in the region; the key vineyard holding is the 2.5 ha in top sites on the hill of Hermitage. There are two red and two white cuvées of Hermitage. The principal cuvées—just labeled with the appellation name—are blends from Les Plantiers and Les Greffieux. The prestige red cuvée is called Le Gréal, to reflect its origins in an assemblage from Le Méal and Les Greffieux, and includes 10% Marsanne. The prestige white cuvée comes from Les Rocoules. The red and white Crozes Hermitage both come from the hills around Larnage. The wines were uneven for the first few years after Marc took over, but have certainly bounced back since then. The approach has been traditional. Everything is aged in oak (up to 24 months for the top cuvées); the whites are barrel-fermented. Only old oak was used until 2004, when new oak, generally up to a quarter, was introduced. The style has been riper since the 2000 vintage, when Marc switched to harvesting later. Both reds and whites offer fine examples of fruit purity. Most of the production is exported.

 Tain L'Hermitage
Hermitage
Hermitage, Les Rocoules
www.marcsorrel.fr

4 ha; 15,000 bottles

Domaine Eric Texier

Switching from a career as a nuclear engineer, Eric Texier apprenticed at Verget in Burgundy, and then became a negociant; now he is becoming a grower. "My first intention was to make Burgundy—which is difficult if you're not from the area or a millionaire. I was buying wine from the old growers in the northern Rhône, and when I found it was difficult to get land, one of the vignerons sent me to Brézème. The style was very similar to what I used to get from Cornas: light precise Syrah. I bought grapes in 1998-1999, then rented land, and bought land later." Eric now owns vineyards in St. Julien en Saint Alban as well as Brézème, both small appellations at the southern tip of the northern Rhône. Plantings include southern varieties as well as Syrah and Viognier. From Saint Alban, Grenache is blended with 20% Clairette for the Chat Fous cuvée, which offers a rare opportunity to see a cool climate Grenache. Eric has some very old plots of Syrah in both Brézème and Saint Alban, old enough that the vines look different compared to modern Syrah. Half the vines in these vineyards are on their own roots. The production goes into the Vieilles Vignes cuvées. The Vieilles Vignes white Brézème, which comes from old Roussanne, is aged for 20 months in clay. Other wines are aged in old barriques: "Oak taste is disturbing, I deeply hate oak." Brézème is a cool climate and gives elegant, precise wines with a supple structure, which fits with Eric's love of the Burgundian style.

 Charnay
Brézème
Brézème, Vieilles Vignes
Brézème
www.eric-texier.com

12 ha; 85,000 bottles

Northern Rhône

 St. Péray

Cornas

8 ha; 35,000 bottles

Domaine du Tunnel

It's unusual to find top domains headquartered in St. Péray, which has been painfully making the switch from sparkling to still wines, and has had some trouble establishing its identity, but this is where Stéphane Robert established his domain in 1994, after an apprenticeship with Jean-Louis Grippat in Tournon. (The name of the domain comes from an old railway tunnel that runs underneath.) Starting with leased vineyards, Stéphane slowly built up the domain with his own holdings in Cornas, St. Joseph, and St. Péray. The largest holding is in Cornas, with parcels in fifteen different sites, including some vineyards from the old Marcel Juge domain, which added some very old vines to the portfolio. Stéphane's stated objective is to produce wine with intensity rather than oak flavors, so the wines are matured in old (4- to 6-year) barriques. The St. Joseph comes from parcels in Tournon, Glun, and Mauves, in the heart of the original St. Joseph appellation. The St. Péray includes a varietal Roussanne bottling (somewhat of a contrast with the usual amorphous flavors of the appellation). As well as the appellation wine from Cornas (a blend from many parcels), there is the Cornas Vin Noir (a real vin de garde coming from vines that are around a hundred years old). The style is clean and modern in the sense that there's none of the animal notes that used to characterize Cornas, but traditional in the sense that the wines aren't overly influenced by oak.

Condrieu

Condrieu, Terrasses de l'Empire

www.georges-vernay.fr

20 ha; 100,000 bottles

Domaine Georges Vernay

The domain has been run by George Vernay's daughter, Christine, together with her husband Paul Ansellem, since 1997. The original holdings consist of vineyards in the heart of the Condrieu appellation (in the commune of Condrieu itself), and vineyards in Chavanay that make St. Joseph. More recent additions are some plots in Côte Rôtie and some Syrah and Viognier in the IGP. The domain has a high reputation for its Condrieus, which show a subtle, elegant style. There are three cuvées. The largest is Les Terrasses de l'Empire, which comes from the lieu-dits St. Agathe and La Caille. Chailles de l'Enfer is a smaller production, coming from La Caille, and is more reserved. Coteaux de Vernon is regarded as one of the defining cuvées for the appellation, coming from a 2 ha plot of old vines (50- to 80-year) on biotite (a type of granite); located in the center of the appellation, this is considered to be one of the best sites in Condrieu. This was the original vineyard holding when the domain was created. The Côte Rôtie, Blonde du Seigneur, is softened with 5% Viognier. All the wines are matured in barrique, with about one quarter new oak for the top cuvées. The Condrieus are barrel-fermented. The two cuvées from St. Joseph are both relatively fruity and forward. There's also a Côtes du Rhône, Sainte Agathe, from vineyards near Condrieu, several IGP Syrah cuvées (Maison Rouge, Fleur de Mai, and De Mirbaudie) and an IGP Viognier. The domain is not particularly receptive to visits.

Maison Vidal Fleury

Founded in 1781, Vidal Fleury is one of the old-line negociants in the Northern Rhône. In fact, it's the oldest negociant still in business. Starting in Ampuis, it expanded into other regions of the Rhône in the 1920s. The wines had a good reputation until the late seventies (I remember some excellent Côte Rôties from the sixties), when they began to be regarded as dull, especially after Joseph Vidal died in 1976. By the 1980s Vidal-Fleury was in difficulties, until it was purchased by Marcel Guigal in 1984; his father had been the chef de cave until he left to establish Maison Guigal. Vidal Fleury continues to run independently (although its best vineyards on Côte Rôtie, including La Turque, are now part of the Guigal portfolio). It has benefited from new investment since the take-over, including the construction in 2009 of a massive new winery in Ampuis, which the locals describe as looking like an ancient Egyptian temple. Vidal Fleury remains a sizeable negociant business (although only about 15% of the size of Guigal itself), making reliable wines from about twenty different appellations all over the Rhône. Packaging and style have been modernized. "We saw an opportunity when we opened the new winery," says winemaker Guy Sarton du Jonchay. "We tried to make a wine that's more modern, more fruity." It's an open question whether the style is more modern than Guigal, but it is fair to say that Vidal Fleury does not rise to the same heights as Guigal.

Tupin et Semons
Côte Rôtie
www.vidal-fleury.com

12 ha; 1,000,000 bottles

Les Vins de Vienne

His interest in the vineyards from Roman times led Pierre Gaillard to start Vins de Vienne together with Yves Cuilleron and François Villard. They began in 1996 by replanting the old vineyards at Seyssuel, just north of Vienne, and then expanded into a negociant business in 1998. They moved to an industrial building close to the Rhône on the outskirts of Chavanay in 2009. There are more than thirty different wines now, divided into three lines. Archeveque comes from their own vineyards in St. Péray, Cornas, St. Joseph, Condrieu, and Côte Rôtie, as well as the original vineyard in Seyssuel (where Vins de Vienne now owns the ancient château of the archeveque that appears on its label). It's been difficult to acquire vineyards, especially with Condrieu and Côte Rôtie, so some are leased rather than owned. The negociant wines are divided into two series. Amphora d'Or is the higher level, all with élevage in barriques, typically for 9 months. Amphora d'Argent is the lower level series. The two lines are separate and come from different vineyards (there is no declassification). Vins de Vienne has become a sizeable negociant, but the best wines remain those under the IGP label from the original vineyards at Seyssuel that were the impetus for starting the operation. Those in the Archeveque series offer a good representation of each appellation. The wines of the Amphore d'Or negociant series are distinctly more "serious" than the more approachable wines of the Amphore d'Argent series.

Chavanay
Condrieu
IGP Collines Rhodaniennes, Sotanum
Hermitage, Amphore d'Or
www.vinsdevienne.com

18 ha; 450,000 bottles

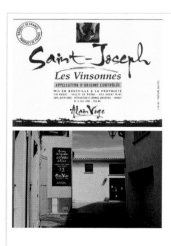

Saint Michel-sur-Rhône
St. Joseph
www.domainevillard.com

30 ha; 185,000 bottles

Domaine François Villard

François Villard describes himself as a former chef who was passionate about wine, started by qualifying as a sommelier, and then moved into viticulture and oenology. He planted his first vineyard in 1989 in a small plot in Condrieu. The domain has grown to produce several cuvées from Côte Rôtie, Condrieu, St. Joseph, and St. Péray, as well as several IGPs or Vins de France from declassified lots or from vineyards outside the appellations. The winery was constructed in 1996, then expanded in 2002, and again in 2013. Altogether François makes red appellation wines from about 14 ha, and white wines from about 11 ha; about 5 ha are in the IGP Collines Rhodaniennes. With around twenty different cuvées, most of the wines are produced only in small amounts, a few thousand bottles at most. The style is rich and modern, although recently it has backed off a bit from new oak. Whites are barrel-fermented; reds are fermented in open-topped wood fermenters or stainless steel. Usually for reds there is only partial destemming. The style is described as looking for optimal ripening, which in practice means that the whites are often harvested late enough to show a touch of botrytis. In addition to his own domain (relying upon owned and leased vineyards and some purchased grapes), François was one of the gang of three (together with Pierre Gaillard and Yves Cuilleron) who created Vins de Vienne. He's regarded as one of the most enterprising producers in the region.

Domaine Alain Voge

Alain Voge is a family estate, run by Alain Voge together with Alberic Mazoyer. "Alain started in the sixties when the small appellations in the Northern Rhône were in very different circumstances from now. The surfaces were decreasing except where the negociants had an interest. Until the seventies, Alain managed a nursery and was a distiller. Things have changed in the last twenty years. It's become possible now to sell Cornas for high prices; this was absolutely impossible before," Alberic says. Alberic has been a friend of the family for more than twenty years, and came from Chapoutier in 2004 to help with the domain. Behind the modern tasting room at the end of an alley in the center of Cornas is a modern winery (built twelve years ago), small but packed with everything necessary for fine wine production. Everything is aged in barrique, but there is limited use of new oak. Barriques are kept for up to 8 years for the reds, and up to 3 years for the whites. There are 7 ha in Cornas, 4 ha in St. Péray, and 1 ha in St. Joseph, spread among many small parcels. Alain Voge makes both white and sparkling wines from St. Péray, and reds from Cornas and St. Joseph; for me, the Cornas was the most interesting, especially the Vieilles Vignes, which comes from ten parcels of vines from 30-60 years old, all on granite terraces. Most of the white (95%) is Marsanne, and about 80% is barrel fermented. The style at Alain Voge is pretty taut; in some vintages it can veer towards angularity.

Cornas
Cornas, Vieilles Vignes
www.alain-voge.com

12 ha; 55,000 bottles

Domaine Paul Autard

Located in the sandy area just at the northeastern edge of the Châteauneuf-du-Pape appellation, the domain has 10 ha within the AOP and another 13 ha just outside. Plantings are similar for both, with more than 70% Grenache, the rest being Syrah and Mourvèdre. The same elegant style runs through both the Châteauneuf-du-Pape and the Côtes du Rhône. Current winemaker Jean-Paul Autard, the fourth generation, who took over in 1997, thinks a lot of the elegance comes from destemming. "This allows us to do a lot of maceration because you're not obliged to stop because of extraction from the stems." The Côtes du Rhône does not see wood, and is bottled in April following the vintage. The Châteauneuf-du-Pape has élevage in barriques, one third new. The cuvée La Côte Ronde uses 100% new oak for 17 months. Cuvée Juline offers a new twist: since 2008 it has been fermented in special barriques, made by Seguin Moreau, standing up with the top open; when fermentation is over, the missing end is put on, the barrel is put on its side, and élevage continues in the same barrique. Jean-Paul is an arch modernist, but the style comes off, with unusual elegance for the Côtes du Rhône, refinement for the Châteauneuf-du-Pape, and a really modern, more oak-driven impression for the cuvées. Precision and purity of fruits are not descriptions that are usually at the forefront for Châteauneuf-du-Pape, but they are the most common terms found in my tasting notes here.

Courthézon

Châteauneuf-du-Pape

Châteauneuf-du-Pape, La Côte Ronde

www.paulautard.com

23 ha; 100,000 bottles

Château de Beaucastel

Given as a wedding present to Pierre Perrin when he married into the family of an olive oil merchant in 1909, Beaucastel is now the jewel in the crown of the Perrin holdings, which extend widely over the Southern Rhône. Pierre's son, Jacques, built up the estate, and it is run by his sons, François and Jean-Pierre, and their children. The major part of their 330 ha in the Southern Rhône is Vieille Ferme, a vast enterprise making a million bottles per year of red and rosé Ventoux, and white Lubéron. The Côtes du Rhône (called Coudelet) comes partly from vineyards at the Beaucastel estate, just across the appellation boundary. The vineyard occupies a vast, flat, stony area, with average vine age of 50-80 years. Château Beaucastel is well known for its commitment to maintain all the traditional grape varieties in Châteauneuf, but more to the point in terms of style is that the red is based on a high proportion of Mourvèdre (30%) with an equal proportion of Grenache. Red wine vinification uses a system of flash heating invented by Jacques Perrin. Unusually for Châteauneuf, the white is driven by Roussanne (80%), and there is also the famous Vieilles Vignes Roussanne bottling from a 2 ha plot of 90- to 100-year-old vines. Recently the style of the reds seems to have become more modern; the leathery, animal impressions of the eighties and nineties have been replaced by more direct, forward, fruits. I find them technically better but less interesting, although maybe more to popular taste.

Courthézon

Châteauneuf-du-Pape

Châteauneuf-du-Pape

www.beaucastel.com

94 ha; 300,000 bottles

⊙ Châteauneuf-du-Pape
🍷 Châteauneuf-du-Pape
www.beaurenard.fr

61 ha; 200,000 bottles

Domaine de Beaurenard

This is a family-owned domain, where Daniel Coulon and his brother represent the seventh generation. The 30 ha of vineyards in Châteauneuf-du-Pape are spread among more than 25 separate parcels (there are also vineyards in Rasteau and the Côtes du Rhône). The Coulons are committed to biodynamic viticulture, and because the vineyard holdings are so broken up, they have to be quite forceful sometimes to stop treatments from their neighbors from encroaching. They are committed to maintaining all thirteen varieties and do their own selection and grafting. Fermentation occurs in stainless steel or wood, and the wine matures in foudres (with the only break from tradition being the use of a small proportion of barriques). Bottling is done by the phases of the moon. In both Rasteau and Châteauneuf there is a regular bottling and special cuvée. The Rasteau is quite appealing, and the special cuvée, called Les Argiles Bleues after a 2 ha plot of clay terroir, is more sophisticated. The red Châteauneuf, based on 70% Grenache, has good structure when young, but quickly becomes more supple. The real mark of elegance comes with the Boisrenard special cuvée (not made every year), from vines planted in 1902; the red is elegant (based on 60% Grenache), and the white is quite unctuous, showing its barrel-fermentation and maturation in oak. There used to be 10 ha for Boisrenard, but the need to replant has reduced the plot to 6 ha.

⊙ Châteauneuf-du-Pape
🍷 Châteauneuf-du-Pape,
Marie Beurrier
10 ha; 16,000 bottles

Domaine Henri Bonneau

Henri Bonneau is a living legend in Châteauneuf. It's all but impossible to arrange a visit to the old cellars, located in the center of the town (with a permanent sign saying "cave fermé"), which are filled with decrepit-looking barrels. The vineyards are broken up into many plots. This is the quintessential Grenache-driven domain, but one note of distinction is that the vines are (relatively) young, between 30 and 50 years old: Henri does not like very old vines, and believes that the useful life span is fifty years. Typically there is not much detailed information about breakdown of grape varieties, but Grenache is probably more than 90%; the rest is estimated to consist of Mourvèdre, Counoise, and Vaccarèse. Henri is famous for picking late and achieving a high degree of ripeness. Fermentation in concrete cuves is followed by maturation in old barriques. Winemaking is famously traditional. In addition to the regular cuvée, there are the Cuvée Marie Beurrier and Cuvée des Célestins, produced when vintage conditions are deemed appropriate. The decision is taken only at the time of bottling, which may be several years after the vintage. This must surely be the longest élevage in the appellation. Bonneau distinguishes his three cuvées as "good, very good, and grand vin." With Jacques Reynaud no longer on the scene at Château Rayas, Henri Bonneau is now by far the most idiosyncratic producer in Châteauneuf-du-Pape.

Domaine Les Cailloux

Disentangling the different wines made by André Brunel can be confusing. There's a Côtes du Rhône under the label Domaine André Brunel. There's another from Domaine de la Becassonne, a small estate just to the east of the Châteauneuf-du-Pape AOP, which makes exclusively white wine. The Brunel business is 40% negociant and 60% from estate holdings in the Côtes du Rhône (11 ha) and Châteauneuf-du-Pape (22 ha). "We are a classical family of Châteauneuf-du-Pape, we have had wines in our family for 300 years," says Fabrice Brunel. The jewel of the holdings is the Châteauneuf-du-Pape, Domaine Les Cailloux, whose Le Centenaire was one of the first special cuvées, with only 300 cases from an 0.80 ha parcel. Les Cailloux's nominal address is in the town of Châteauneuf-du-Pape, but I went to a utilitarian warehouse on the outskirts in Sorgues to meet Fabrice, who has come into the business to take over the commercial side and let his father concentrate on what he likes best—"he's happiest driving his tractor through the vineyards," Fabrice says. The Châteauneuf is fairly full bodied and shows its dominant Grenache component in the old tradition of the appellation. Le Centenaire originated as a special cuvée to celebrate the hundredth anniversary of the vineyard. "Since then, the wine from Centenaire has always been vinified separately, and at assemblage we decide whether to bottle it separately or include it in the general Châteauneuf," Fabrice explains.

Châteauneuf-du-Pape

Châteauneuf-du-Pape

domaine-les-cailloux.fr

33 ha; 400,000 bottles

Domaine Clos du Caillou

Located at Courthézon at the northeast boundary of Châteauneuf, Clos du Caillou is an oddity: it's virtually an enclave surrounded by Châteauneuf vineyards, but only 8 ha of the domain are classified in the AOP, the rest being Côtes du Rhône. The reason lies in the history of the domain: when Châteauneuf was classified in 1936, the owner of the time refused admission to the authorities, so the vineyards were not classified, although they almost certainly otherwise would have been included in Châteauneuf. The present ownership dates from 1956, with additional vineyards planted in 1995. Black grape plantings are 80% Grenache. The main cuvée was known originally simply as Clos du Caillou but now is called Les Safres: this is 95% Grenache and aged conventionally in old foudres. Les Quartz comes from old vines Grenache (85%) and Syrah, sourced from two specific vineyard parcels. It's aged in a mixture of tronconique cuves and foudres. The top cuvée, La Réserve, has 60% Grenache, 20% Mourvèdre, and 20% Syrah, and is matured in a mixture of concrete vats and new and old demi-muids. There's a matching range of Côtes du Rhône: the main cuvée is called Le Bouquet des Garrigues; Le Clos du Caillou comes from the most interior parcels; Les Quartz comes from parcels very close to those used for the old vines Grenache in the Châteauneuf Les Quartz; and La Réserve is a selection of the best lots. There are also whites from both Châteauneuf and Côtes du Rhône.

Courthézon

Châteauneuf-du-Pape

Châteauneuf-du-Pape, Les Safres

www.closducaillou.com

53 ha; 180,000 bottles

Château Fortia

One of the oldest producers in Châteauneuf-du-Pape, Château Fortia was making wine in the mid eighteenth century. By the twentieth century, it was owned by Baron Roy de Boiseaumarié, who was instrumental in establishing the appellation system in France, and responsible for Châteauneuf-du-Pape becoming one of the first AOCs. Just southeast of the town, the domain remains in the hands of the Boiseaumarié family. The building is a genuine château, dating from the nineteenth century (some of the cellars date from the fourteenth century). The vineyards are in a single block around the château. The traditional red Châteauneuf is 80% Grenache to 20% Syrah; the special cuvée, La Cuvée du Baron, reduces the Grenache to 50%, with 45% Syrah and 5% Mourvèdre. The latest innovation, unusual for the region, almost reverses the proportions of the traditional cuvée, and really focuses on Syrah; the Cuvée Réserve has 85% Syrah and 15% Mourvèdre. Winemaker Pierre Pastre says, "We found some old bottles in the cellar, they were remarkable, and my father-in-law finally remembered he had done an experiment with pure Syrah one year. So I have made a cuvée of Syrah with Mourvèdre, because I think Grenache doesn't do well with Syrah." There is also a white, in which malolactic fermentation is blocked to retain freshness. Aside from the new cuvée, the approach is traditional, and aging for all wines is exclusively in foudres.

Châteauneuf-du-Pape
Château Fortia
www.chateau-fortia.com

30 ha; 100,000 bottles

Domaine de La Janasse

The domain is located in Courthézon but has more than fifty separate vineyard parcels scattered around the Châteauneuf appellation, with a corresponding variety of terroirs. Founded in 1967, grapes were originally sold to the cooperative, but Aimé Sabon built a cellar and started domain-bottling in 1973; since 1991 the domain has been run by his children Christophe and Isabelle. There are 15 ha in Châteauneuf-du-Pape, with other holdings in Côtes du Rhône and IGP Orange. The Tradition cuvée consists of 80% Grenache, 10% Syrah, and 10% Mourvèdre; Cuvée Chaupin comes exclusively from Grenache planted in 1912 in the northern part of the appellation a (slightly cooler location); and the cuvée Vieilles Vignes is a blend based on 85% Grenache, from vines that are more than eighty years old. Wines are matured in a mixture of (mostly) foudres and barriques, some new, with the most new oak used in the Vieilles Vignes. The style here is definitely Grenache-dominated, tending to forceful aromatics; it would be fair to describe the wines as modern. His American importer describes Christophe as a "self-proclaimed defender of Grenache." The regular white cuvée is a blend of Grenache Blanc, Clairette, and Roussanne, but the white Cuvée Prestige comes from old vines, 60% of which are Roussanne. Unusually for the region, the whites go through malolactic fermentation. The Côtes du Rhônes follow the style of the Châteauneufs.

Courthézon
Châteauneuf-du-Pape
Châteauneuf-du-Pape, Tradition
www.lajanasse.com

70 ha; 250,000 bottles

Domaine de Marcoux

Sisters Sophie and Catherine Armenier have run this domain since 1993; Sophie handles vinification and Catherine manages the vineyard. In addition to 19 ha in Châteauneuf, they have some Côtes du Rhône and also some plots for Vin de France, both near the winery but across the appellation boundary, and an 8 ha domain in Lirac, which they purchased in 2010. They would like to buy more Côtes du Rhône; in fact they found the vineyard in Lirac when looking for Côtes du Rhône. The winery is at the north of Châteauneuf-du-Pape (actually quite close to Orange) but the vineyards are mostly in the south, although with some in the east at La Crau, and in the west, so terroirs range from galets to sandy to calcareous. Each area is vinified separately. Everything is completely destemmed, and only pumping-over is used for extraction; some barriques are used for Syrah and Mourvèdre but most élevage is in cuve. The style here is quite fine, but distinctly rich, with alcohol often pushing up well over 15%. I like the purity of the fruits, but find a slightly sweet touch to the finish (most likely derived from the high alcohol), sometimes to be a little disconcerting. The Vieilles Vignes is always distinctly more forceful than the regular bottling, partly due to extra concentration from the old vines, and partly because the proportion of Grenache is higher. The wines take five or six years to come into their own, and by a decade usually begin to show some tertiary complexity.

Châteauneuf-du-Pape
Châteauneuf-du-Pape
www.domainedemarcoux.com

30 ha; 40,000 bottles

Clos du Mont-Olivet

Mont Olivet is owned by a branch of the Sabons, an old Châteauneuf winemaking family. This domain was founded by Séraphin Sabon in 1932; it later became one of the first estates to bottle its own wine, and is run by the fourth generation today. (In the early 1950s, the vineyards that are now part of Roger Sabon were split off.) There are 28 ha of vineyards spread throughout the Châteauneuf appellation in many small holdings, with further vineyards about twenty miles to the north in the Côtes du Rhône. In Châteauneuf, the domain is driven by Grenache, whereas in the Côtes du Rhône, plantings are divided more or less equally between Grenache and Syrah. The traditional Châteauneuf has 80% Grenache. Le Petit Mont is effectively a second wine, produced from young vines, and is 95% Grenache. (Does this imply an even more Grenache-driven future at Mont Olivet?) A special cuvée, the Cuvée de Papet, is produced in some vintages from 80- to 100-year-old vines in the walled vineyard of Montolivet in the eastern part of the appellation, and the grape mix here has varied from 75% to 95% Grenache. Winemaking is traditional, with only partial destemming, and all cuvées matured in neutral foudres. The single white is fairly mainstream, although sometimes I find it to lack character (admittedly this is a criticism I have of many white Châteauneufs.). The style of the reds is sturdy and ageworthy, not overdone, although the Cuvée de Papet is more exotic.

Châteauneuf-du-Pape
Châteauneuf-du-Pape
www.clos-montolivet.com

47 ha; 200,000 bottles

Châteauneuf-du-Pape
Châteauneuf-du-Pape,
Cuvée des Cadettes
www.chateau-la-nerthe.com
90 ha; 280,000 bottles

Château La Nerthe

The history of La Nerthe goes way back to when it was known as La Ferme de Bourguignon. In the sixteenth century it began to be known as La Nerthe. By the seventeenth century there were 25 ha of vineyards. "At this time, Châteauneuf-du-Pape was not known, but La Nerthe was already known; by the end of the nineteenth century people were talking about the quality of La Nerthe," says winemaker Christian Voeux. Current ownership dates from 1985. It's a large domain, extended by a 21 ha purchase in 1991, with a higher than usual proportion (15%) of white wine. Surrounded by galets, the Château sits on the western edge of the famous La Crau plateau; vineyards are in two large blocks. The special cuvée, Cuvée des Cadettes, is made only in some years by a selection from the best old vines of the Château (around 100 years old); it is a blend of Grenache, Syrah, and Mourvèdre like the main cuvée of La Nerthe. The style is relatively restrained, usually with around 55% Grenache in La Nerthe, and a little less in Cuvée des Cadettes. There's also a cuvée from young vines (young in this context means less than 20 years), the Clos de la Granière. In addition to the white La Nerthe, there is also the cuvée Clos de Beauvenir, which carries more obvious wood. The mark of the house style is freshness. "I always look for freshness and natural acidity to safeguard the fruit," Christian says. The wines achieve more subtlety than is common in Châteauneuf.

Châteauneuf-du-Pape
Châteauneuf-du-Pape
www.clos-des-papes.fr
37 ha; 60,000 bottles

Domaine Clos des Papes

The Avril family has long been established in Châteauneuf-du-Pape, and has sold wine under the name of Clos des Papes since the end of the nineteenth century. Vineyards are concentrated around the town of Châteauneuf-du-Pape, but the 24 different parcels extend throughout the appellation. (The domain takes its name from a plot close to the ruined castle in the town.) There are 5 ha outside the appellation, which are used to make a Vin de France, Le Petit Vin d'Avril (usually a blend across vintages). Clos des Papes is a traditional domain in the sense of producing only one cuvée of red and one of white, a policy established by Paul Avril, who ran the estate from 1963 to 1987, and believed in "one estate, one wine." Yields are kept low, less than 28 hl/ha. Grenache is only about two thirds of the blend, with a high proportion of Mourvèdre (20%); the rest is essentially Syrah with very small amounts of Vaccarèse, Counoise and Muscardin. The white is a more or less equal blend of five varieties (Clairette, Bourboulenc, Grenache Blanc, Roussanne and Picpoul). The domain has been run by Vincent Avril since 1987. Style is partly determined by Vincent's five years at school in Burgundy, which gave him a taste for moderation. Vincent introduced destemming, for example. He's been known to say, "I take it as a compliment when people tell me that Clos des Papes makes a wine almost in the style of a Burgundy!"

Domaine du Pegau

This is a relatively recent domain, created by Paul Féraud (a school friend of Henri Bonneau) and his daughter Laurence in 1987 (although the estate has existed under the name of Domaine Féraud since the eighteenth century). Initially there were only 7 ha. Today there are 21 ha of plantings in 11 separate vineyard parcels throughout the Châteauneuf appellation; and in 2012 the Férauds purchased another estate at Sorgues, just to the south of the appellation, now known as Château Pegau, which has 25 ha in the Côtes du Rhône Villages, 5 ha in Côtes du Rhône, and another 11 ha used for Vin de France. There are also negociant wines under the Féraud name. Vinification of the Châteauneuf-du-Pape is quite traditional with no destemming. There are several cuvées: all the reds are 70% or 80% Grenache. The regular cuvée is called Réservée and spends 18 months in foudres; there is also a white. There are two special red cuvées. The Cuvée da Capo, made most years, comes from a plot on La Crau and follows the same regime as the regular bottling, but is a selection of the best lots (usually one foudre). The Cuvée Laurence is also based on selection, but the wine matures much longer, for 36 months in foudres or old barriques, depending on the vintage: it is intended to be a long-lived, traditional style. Alcohol is high, and the style is lush and robust. Domaine du Pegau is widely considered to be a standard bearer for the traditional style of Châteauneuf-du-Pape.

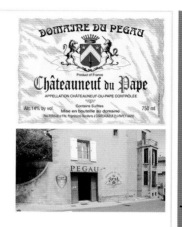

○ Châteauneuf-du-Pape

🍷 Châteauneuf-du-Pape, Réservée

www.pegau.com

🟦🏭 **G N**

63 ha; 90,000 bottles

Château Rayas

Château Rayas is a legend, not just for its wine, but for the idiosyncratic behavior of its proprietors. The British importer used to tell the story of how he turned up for a visit to find the place deserted, and then as he was driving away, saw Louis Reynaud climbing out of the ditch where he had been hiding. Two proprietors later (after Rayas passed on to Louis's son Jacques and then to Jacques's nephew Emmanuel), it is still difficult to arrange to visit Rayas, but when you get there, it turns out the stories are true about the contrast between the primitive old cellars and the quality of the wine. There is no arguing with the quality of Rayas: the red is made exclusively from Grenache, but it does not slide over the edge into jamminess. The second wine, Pignan, comes from a separate plot. The white Rayas, although less well known than the red, is equally remarkable, especially as it comes from a blend of the undistinguished Grenache Blanc with Clairette: it has a wonderful savory quality, redolent of the garrigue of the south. But there is something of a split personality here, because Château de Fonsalette, a medium size property in the Côtes du Rhône, is also owned and made at Rayas (and a remarkable price it is too, for a Côtes du Rhône). And under the same ownership is the much larger Château des Tours, where a Vacqueyras is made from Grenache and Syrah, and a Côtes du Rhône from a blend of Grenache with Cinsault and Syrah. Perhaps the cobwebs are for show.

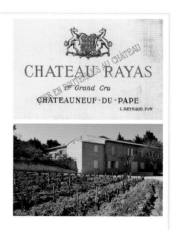

○ Châteauneuf-du-Pape

🍷 Châteauneuf-du-Pape, Pignan

www.chateaurayas.fr

🚫🏭 **G**

13 ha; 70,000 bottles

Châteauneuf-du-Pape

Châteauneuf-du-Pape, Réserve

www.roger-sabon.com

18 ha; 73,000 bottles

Domaine Roger Sabon

Séraphin Sabon was making wine at the start of the twentieth century, and this domain was founded in 1952 by his son Roger Sabon with 15 ha of Châteauneuf-du-Pape. Today the vineyards fall into 13 separate parcels, and also include holdings in Lirac and Côtes du Rhône. Production focuses on reds: the 5% of white production is vinified in one large wooden cask. The Côtes du Rhône and also a Vin de France are fermented in cement and made to be fruity and easy to drink. Lirac and Châteauneuf-du-Pape are fermented in stainless steel. The wine rests six months in cuve, then after assemblage is matured in foudres or demi-muids for a year. "Our approach is a little different in that each cuvée has a style and we try to maintain that style each year. It's not necessarily the same parcels in each cuvée every year," says winemaker Didier Negron. Three cuvées are made in roughly equal amounts. With Les Olivets, the objective is to have a traditional wine that's ready to drink soon; it is 80% Grenache, 10% Syrah, and 10% Cinsault. The Réserve is richer and more structured, and Prestige is more powerful, intended to be a vin de garde. These were among the first special cuvées made in Châteauneuf (in 1981 and 1982), and were received with some suspicion at the time. In addition there is Le Secret des Sabon, a special cuvée coming from hundred-year-old vines planted by Séraphin Sabon. There's increasing power going up the scale; I like the balance of Réserve best.

Châteauneuf-du-Pape

www.domaine-solitude.com

91 ha; 100,000 bottles

Domaine de La Solitude

One of the oldest domains in Châteauneuf-du-Pape, La Solitude was purchased as a dowry for marriage into the Barberini family, which changed its name to Barberin in Châteauneuf in 1604. The wine was being sold as Vin de la Solitude before the French Revolution, and the domain claims to have been bottling its own wine by 1815. The domain is still run by direct descendants of the Barberin family, the current owners being brothers Jean and Michel Lançon, who took over in 1980. This is now a sizeable domain, with the vineyards divided between Châteauneuf-du-Pape and Côtes du Rhône. The 38 ha in Châteauneuf are in a single block to the east of the town. Plantings are a little unusual. Whites are almost a quarter, based on Grenache Blanc and Roussanne, with a little Clairette and Bourboulenc. Red plantings in Châteauneuf are about 60% Grenache, 15% Syrah, 10% Mourvèdre, and 5% Cinsault, with small amounts of all the other varieties. The Côtes du Rhône is almost entirely red, with 40% Grenache and 40% Syrah. The basic cuvée is called Tradition; special cuvées were introduced in 1999, and are made most years: Cuvée Barberini is made in both red (80% Grenache) and white (80% Roussanne); Réserve Secrète (from selected lots) and Cuvée Cornelia Constanza (an old vines Grenache) are two additional red cuvées. There's a fair use of new oak barriques, and the wines make a modern impression, with strong fruit aromatics.

Domaine Pierre Usseglio

Francis Usseglio started producing wine from leased vineyards in 1948. His son Pierre took over the vineyards and purchased plots to establish Domaine Pierre Usseglio in 1966. Pierre's brother Raymond established another domain, Domaine Raymond Usseglio, shortly after. Now with 17 vineyard parcels in three separate areas of the appellation, with half of the vines older than eighty years, Domaine Pierre Usseglio is presently run by brothers Jean-Pierre and Thierry. There are regular cuvées of both red and white Châteauneuf-du-Pape (called Cuvée Traditionelle), the Réserve des Deux Frères which is a selection of lots, usually 70% Grenache and 30% Syrah, aged in a mixture of foudres and barriques, and the cuvée that made the domain famous, the Cuvée de Mon Aïeul, which was introduced in 1998 from a 2 ha plot planted in 1926. (Subsequently some grapes have also been sourced from other plots.) This is a Grenache-dominated cuvée (usually 90% today), enormously rich and dense, matured in a mix of wood and stainless steel. All of the wines of the domain show strong Grenache influence, in a modern style, but the Cuvée de Mon Aïeul is the über-Châteauneuf, with forceful, high-toned aromatics. The focus on super-richness was reinforced in 2007 by the Not for You cuvée from a single barrique coming from 95-year-old Grenache vines. The domain has expanded and there are now also wines from Lirac, Côtes du Rhône, and Vin de France.

Châteauneuf-du-Pape
Châteauneuf-du-Pape
www.domaine-usseglio.com

28 ha; 80,000 bottles

Domaine de La Vieille Julienne

The domain was created in 1905, but did not begin bottling until the 1960s. Jean-Paul Daumen, the fourth generation, took over in the 1990s. Located to the north, the 10 ha of vineyards in Châteauneuf-du-Pape are in three blocks at the edge of the appellation. There are also 5 ha in the Côtes du Rhône. Grapes are destemmed, vinified in concrete, and matured in foudres. Until recently, there were only two cuvées of Châteauneuf-du-Pape: the regular bottling and Le Réservé, made only in some years (when the oldest vines—more than a hundred years old—achieve something special, says Jean-Paul). Since 2012 there have also been wines based on selection. "I still pick parcels separately, but I make a true parcel selection for my wines, versus just blends," Jean-Paul explains. Les Trois Sources comes from two areas (clay-limestone and galets); Les Haut Lieux comes from the more elevated vineyards. Like the Châteauneuf, the Côtes du Rhône is dominated by old Grenache; it comes from vineyards in the lieu-dit Clavin just over the border from the vineyards in Châteauneuf-du-Pape (literally on the other side of the D72). There is no white Châteauneuf, but there is a white Côtes du Rhône, which includes grapes from the small amount of white plantings in Châteauneuf. In addition, there's a negociant business under the Daumen name (which includes declassified lots from young vines at Vieille Julienne as well as those purchased from other sources).

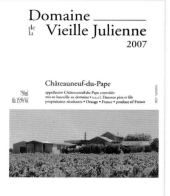

Orange
Châteauneuf-du-Pape
Châteauneuf-du-Pape
www.vieillejulienne.com

15 ha; 40,000 bottles

Domaine Le Vieux Donjon

A relatively recent domain, Vieux Donjon originated when Marcel Michel started estate-bottling in 1966, but took its present form from the combination of vineyards from two families after the marriage of Marie José and Lucien Michel in 1979. Mostly in the northern part of the appellation on the galets, with the rest on sandier soils in the south, the vineyards have been in the families for generations, and include a good proportion of very old Grenache vines. Plantings include one hectare of white grapes. The domain is now run by the next generation, Marie José and Lucien's daughter Claire Fabre. The philosophy of the domain remains quite traditional, and there is only a single red and a single white wine; Vieux Donjon is one of the few prominent houses that have withstood the trend to special cuvées. The red has a more or less average mix of 75% Grenache, 10% Syrah, 10% Mourvèdre, and 5% Cinsault. The white is 50% Grenache Blanc with the rest from Clairette, Bourboulenc, and a little Roussanne. Vinification is traditional, with grapes partially destemmed and all varieties fermented together in concrete tanks, followed by maturation in foudres. There is no new oak. This is very reliable, mainstream Châteauneuf-du-Pape, solid and sturdy, sometimes described as old school; it's always a safe bet in a restaurant, although it does not usually rise to the heights. The wine is recognized as one of the better values from the appellation.

Châteauneuf-du-Pape
Châteauneuf-du-Pape
www.levieuxdonjon.com

15 ha; 50,000 bottles

Domaine du Vieux Télégraphe

The heart of Vieux Télégraphe is the vineyard on the stony soil of the La Crau plateau in the southeastern part of the appellation. Production follows classic lines, with 90% red and 10% white. Established by Hippolyte Brunier in 1898, this remains a family business, today run by Daniel Brunier and his brother. The Bruniers also own Domaine La Roquette (bought in 1986), which has 30 ha in the more western parts of Châteauneuf, including the stony Plateau de Pielong and the sandy Pignan district. In addition, they bought Les Pallières in Gigondas in partnership with Kermit Lynch, and they make wine in Ventoux. All production is from their estates. "Oh no, we don't want to expand into the negociant business, we are growers, it's so frustrating to buy grapes and wines," says Daniel Brunier. The philosophy is to produce a single wine for each domain. There is a joint second wine, Télégramme, for Vieux Télégraphe and La Roquette, made from young vines or occasional declassified cuvées. The red Vieux Télégraphe has 65% Grenache, 15% Mourvèdre, 15% Syrah, and 5% Cinsault, from vines with an average age of 50 years. The red wines of both domains are made by fermentation in stainless steel, transfer to concrete tanks for 9 months, and maturation in foudres of old oak for 8-12 months. The wines are neither fined nor filtered. Vieux Télégraphe is distinguished by a restraint that allows graceful aging for years: the 1985 was still vibrant when I visited in 2013.

Bédarrides
Châteauneuf-du-Pape
Châteauneuf-du-Pape, La Crau
www.vignoblesbrunier.fr

72 ha; 280,000 bottles

Domaine Les Aphillanthes

Daniel Boulle is committed to the Côtes du Rhône, with ten or more different cuvées, including plain Côtes du Rhône, Côtes du Rhône Villages, and wines from named villages. Recently 10 ha was added in Rasteau to replace a vineyard that was lost in Cairanne. The fourth generation of winemakers, Daniel took over the estate in 1987, but until 1999, he sold the grapes to the cooperative. A winery was built the following year. At 25-30 hl/ha, yields are significantly lower than the 45 hl/ha limit for the Côtes du Rhône. Most of the cuvées are blends based on Grenache, with Syrah, Mourvèdre, Carignan, and other varieties in lesser proportions depending on the location, but there are some monovarietal wines. The Cairanne L'Ancestrale du Puits and the Rasteau are almost pure (90%) Grenache. The Côtes du Rhône is a blend of Grenache, Carignan, and Mourvèdre, the Villages Vieilles Vignes is Grenache and Mourvèdre, and the Cuvée des Galets is GSM. The Côtes du Rhône Le Cros is pure Syrah. The Cuvée 3 Cépages is equal parts of Grenache, Syrah, and Mourvèdre; it is partly harvested as a field blend (very late, when the Mourvèdre is ripe, so the Syrah and Grenache are extremely concentrated). The top cuvées are matured in oak, with Le Cros the only cuvée to use barriques. The style is rich and powerful, often with alcohol levels pushing 15%, and the wines have been compared with Gigondas and Châteauneuf-du-Pape.

Travaillan

Côtes du Rhône

Côtes du Rhône, Plan de Dieu, Cuvée des Galets

45 ha; 100,000 bottles

Domaine des Bernardins

The domain takes its name from the Bernardin monks who used to own the property. It's been in the hands of the Castaud family for five generations, since the nineteenth century (they still have a bottle of Muscat from 1847 in the wine library). Louis Castaud was involved in obtaining appellation status for Beaumes de Venise in 1955, and today the domain is run by his granddaughter Elisabeth together with her husband Andrew Hall. Production is about three quarters Muscat Beaumes de Venise, coming from plantings of three quarters Muscat à Petits Grains Blanc and one quarter Muscat à Petit Grains Noir. In addition to the regular bottling, which tends to a style that is richer, fuller, and more aromatic than average (and which has some aging potential), there's a multivintage cuvée called Hommage, the name intending to imply homage to the style of wine Louis Castaud used to produce in the 1930s: rich, full, dark, and intense in a Rancio (oxidative) style. It's more like an Oloroso Sherry or Rivesaltes than the usual Muscat de Beaumes de Venise, and has won high praise. When production is sufficient, there may also be a dry Muscat cuvée (an IGP) called Le Doré des Bernardins (the grapes are harvested together with those for the sweet wine, but fermentation is allowed to proceed to completion). Red wine for the Beaumes de Venise and Côtes du Rhône comes from 5 ha planted with 70% Grenache, 25% Syrah, and 5% Cinsault. There is also a Grenache-based rosé.

Beaumes de Venise

Beaumes de Venise

www.domaine-des-bernardins.com

23 ha; 100,000 bottles

Domaine La Bouissière

Thierry Faravel and his brother Gilles run this domain, which was created by their father in 1978. The first vines had been planted earlier, when Antonin Faravel was chef de culture at the negociant Amadieu, and he worked on the plot at weekends, selling grapes to Amadieu until he started the domain. Just over half the vineyards today are in Gigondas, almost all at relatively high elevations in the Dentelles, with the rest in Vacqueyras, Beaumes de Venise (but sold to the cooperative), and also some plantings for Vin de France. The winery is in a small building (looking like an ordinary garage from the outside) on the outskirts of Gigondas, with a small tasting room in the town. The wines tend to a solid rich, ripe impression, with the Gigondas showing a little more restraint and increase in refinement over the Vacqueyras. "What is important for me is the typicity of the traditional cuvée as that represents the house," Thierry says. The cuvée Font de Tonin is a prestige cuvée from older vines, with a tighter balance that is really refined for Gigondas; there are usually around 400 cases, but it is not made every year. Part of the difference is due to the fact that the traditional cuvées are blends of Grenache and Syrah, but the Font de Tonin is a blend of Grenache and Mourvèdre. Also, the traditional cuvées are matured in foudres—Thierry has moved back to foudres to preserve the fruit better—but with its greater weight, the Font de Tonin remains in barriques.

 Gigondas
 Gigondas
17 ha; 45,000 bottles

Domaine Brusset

This is a family domain, with its winery in Cairanne where Laurent Brusset's grandfather started, although now there are vineyards in five appellations. Initially grapes were sold to the cooperative, and then Laurent's grandfather began to bottle himself. "He had the three colors (red, white, and rosé) so he could sell to restaurants," says Laurent, recollecting a somewhat different era. Laurent's father expanded the domain, and in 1986 bought 18 ha on the Dentelles: it took twenty years to construct the vineyard, with 68 terraces. More than half the vines of the domain (around 35 ha) are still in Cairanne, with Gigondas the next largest holding. "It was difficult to buy vineyards 10 years ago, but with the *crise*, it has become easier. We are strictly an estate business, no negociant activity," says Laurent. The style here tends towards supple fruits. "People think of Gigondas as a vin de garde with rustic tannins, but it can be more delicate and velvety. A new generation of vignerons like more delicate wines," says Laurent. A major part of the range consists of entry level wines, coming from Côtes du Rhône or Ventoux, sometimes with a touch of carbonic maceration to bring out fruitiness and make for immediate approachability. Even at the top end, represented by the two cuvées from Gigondas, the style is distinctly modern and supple. The wine with potential for aging, the cuvée Les Hauts de Montmirail, comes from the highest vineyard in the Dentelles.

 Cairanne
 Côtes du Rhône Villages Cairanne
 Gigondas, Les Hauts de Montmirail
www.domainebrusset.fr

87 ha; 300,000 bottles

Domaine du Cayron

Founded in 1840, and until recently run by Michel Faraud for thirty years, the domain is now run by his three daughters, Roseline, Delphine, and Cendrine Faraud, who are the fifth generation. It's located in a small utilitarian building in the main street of the village of Gigondas, with cramped cellars. The vineyards in Gigondas are spread over twenty separate parcels, with an average vine age of 45 years. Usually individual vines are replaced as necessary, but the highest vineyard in the Dentelles, on the Côte du Cayron, has been pulled out, and new terraces are being constructed for replanting. The domain has 70% Grenache, 14% Syrah, 11% Cinsault, and a little Mourvèdre. The policy has been consistent for decades: only a single cuvée is made. This is widely regarded as a domain whose wines define the classic traditions of Gigondas. "We do traditional vinification with vendange entière, everything goes through alcoholic then malolactic fermentation, pressing with an old bench press, and assemblage more or less directly after the MLF in February. Everything goes into foudres for 12 months," Delphine says. The foudres are quite old, although two were replaced in 2011: this makes for a slight increase in freshness compared with samples from the old foudres. For all the reputation for tradition (most commentators refer to the massive structure and richness of the wine), I find the sense of precision and elegance quite evident from foudre samples to finished wine.

Gigondas
Gigondas
www.domaine-cayron.com

16 ha; 60,000 bottles

Domaine le Clos des Cazaux

This family estate is now run by brothers Jean-Michel and Frédéric Vache. The building has a slightly shabby appearance, with old enameled tanks at the entrance, and a small bottling line in the back. Almost all the vineyards have been in the family for the past fifty years; more than half are in Vacqueyras, with some in Gigondas; there are also some Côtes du Rhône and Vin de France. Plantings are similar in Vacqueyras and Gigondas, with 50-60% Grenache, lots of Syrah, and a little Mourvèdre. "The Syrah was planted in Gigondas in the sixties when grandfather created the vineyard, but in Vacqueyras we've been replacing a lot of the Grenache with Syrah," says Jean-Michel, who is really concerned about the effects of warmer vintages. "We are making wine to match food, so our objective is to get balance, always balance, we are frightened by alcohol. A good balance for a Grenache-based wine is 13.5%, 14% maximum, and a good balance for a Syrah wine is 13-13.5%. To make outstanding wine at 15% is really rare," he says. There are pleasing herbal overtones to the cuvées Saint Roch and des Templiers from Vacqueyras, and La Tour Sarrasine from Gigondas. The focus on Syrah has brought an unusual degree of refinement to the Cuvée des Templiers. Up one step, the Prestige cuvée from Gigondas comes from old vines of Grenache; and the Grenat Noble from Vacqueyras is a rare sweet Grenache with botrytis (made every three or four years).

Vacqueyras
Vacqueyras, Cuvée Saint Roch
www.closdescazaux.fr

48 ha; 120,000 bottles

Domaine de Coyeux

The domain has one of the most spectacular views in the region, with vineyards at an average altitude of 260 m at the foot of the Dentelles de Montmirail, overlooking the town of Beaumes de Venise. Yves and Catherine Nativelle started with the purchase of a 7 ha estate in 1976, and continued to add vineyards, building up the domain to comprise one of the largest estates in the area, all in a contiguous block. The soil is an outcrop of Trias (deep soils of decomposed rocks, rich in iron). Most of the plantings are Muscat, and the focus is really on the dessert wine, which is the most important single product. The first Muscat de Beaumes de Venise was produced in 1982; in fact, the production of Muscat de Beaumes de Venise (including the cuvée Les Trois Fonts) accounts for around 10% of the total production of the appellation. Besides Muscat, the other plantings are black grapes, consisting of 50% Grenache, 20% Syrah, 20% Mourvèdre, and 10% Cinsault, used to produce red Beaumes de Venise, Gigondas, and Côtes du Rhône Villages. There's also a dry Muscat, labeled as IGP Méditerranée. The domain stands out as one of the relatively few to produce estate-bottled wine in Beaumes de Venise (most wine in the appellation is produced by negociants). There is no mistaking the character of the Muscat, but the style of the wine is relatively light and straightforward. Like all Muscat, it's best drunk young, within a couple of years of the vintage.

Beaumes de Venise
Beaumes de Venise
120 ha; 350,000 bottles

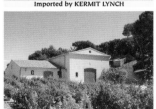

Domaine de Durban

Situated above the town of Beaumes de Venise with a panoramic view over the vineyards, the domain is best known for its sweet Muscat de Beaumes de Venise, but also produces dry red wine from Beaumes de Venise and from neighboring Gigondas, varietal white wines of Chardonnay and Viognier in the IGP Vaucluse, and rosé. Production of Beaumes de Venise is split more or less equally between sweet wine and dry wine. Jacques Leydier bought the property (which according to records going back to 1159 had been a fortified farm in the Middle Ages) in a state of complete disrepair in 1960; today it is run by his grandsons, Henri and Philippe. The soils are a mixture of Trias (an unusual soil type, very rich in iron, that's characteristic of the area) and clay-limestone. Beaumes de Venise can be made only from Muscat à Petits Grains Blanc or Noir, and the Leydiers believe that the quality of their Muscat partly derives from the fact that the domain grows only Muscat à Petits Grains Blanc, whereas most producers grow Muscat à Petits Grains Noir. It may also be a factor that most vineyards are located lower down, on the plain, and Domaine de Durban is one of the few above the village. The VDN is vinified in stainless steel, neutral spirits are added to stop fermentation with at least 110 g/l of residual sugar, and the wine is matured in cuve for about five months until it is bottled. Domaine de Durban is widely considered to produce the best sweet wine of the appellation.

Beaumes de Venise
Beaumes de Venise
www.domainedurban.com
33 ha; 250,000 bottles

Domaine des Espiers

Philippe Cartoux created this domain in 1989 with 2 ha in an area where his family had owned vines in the nineteenth century. For the first few years the wine was sold to negociants, until Philippe felt it was good enough to bottle under the estate name. The vineyards are planted with two thirds Grenache and one third Syrah (with a little Mourvèdre), producing Gigondas (3 ha), and Côtes du Rhône Sablet (2.5 ha), and Côtes du Rhône (4 ha). Vines are planted at higher density than usual for the area (5,400 vines per hectare compared to the normal 3,500). The objectives of the domain are a little different from usual. Philippe describes them as more Burgundian or more like the northern Rhône than the south. The Gigondas and Côtes du Rhône Sablet are blends exclusively of Grenache and Syrah; the Mourvèdre goes into the Côtes du Rhône (both red and rosé). The focus is on red wine, but there's a white Côtes du Rhône (50% Roussanne and 50% Clairette) from a small plot in Sablet. Côtes du Rhône Sablet is vinified in cement cuves. The Gigondas is matured in old demi muids, but the Gigondas Cuvée des Blaches is aged in barriques (including about 15% new oak) for 12 months; it comes from old vines (around 40 years age), harvested at super-ripeness, and uses higher fermentation temperatures to get maximum extraction. The wines are correspondingly robust and powerful, sometimes quite spicy. Showing some exuberance, they are intended for drinking young.

Vacqueyras
Gigondas
p.cartoux.free.fr
10 ha; 50,000 bottles

Domaine Gourt de Mautens

It's ironic that Jérôme Bressy was one of the producers who helped Rasteau obtain promotion to a separate appellation, but has been forced by the rules of the new appellation to withdraw his wines. Committed to preserving the old varieties of the region, he planted Picardin to include in his white, and Vaccarèse, Counoise, Carignan, Cinsault, and Terret to include in the red. The problem is not so much with the varieties themselves, but with the fact that their proportions exceed the permitted limits. (Rasteau allows up to 12% Picardin in white, and up to 15% in total for the indigenous black varieties; and Syrah and Mourvèdre must be at least 20%.) The Syndicat ruled that his wines should be excluded from 2012, but in response he labeled all his wines as IGP Vaucluse from 2010. The grapes from this family domain (with vines 30- to 100-years old) were sold to the cooperative until Jérôme took over in 1996, making wine in temporary space until the cave was constructed in 1998. One cuvée is produced in each color. The vast majority is red, matured in a mix of concrete, foudres, and demi-muids for 24 to 36 months. Jérôme mentions Jacques Reynaud of Château Rayas and Henri Bonneau of Châteauneuf-du-Pape as his models. "Rasteau isn't yet a great appellation like Châteauneuf-du-Pape," he says, "it has fifty years of history with sweet wine, and the history of dry wine has just started." Expelling one of its top producers will not help.

Rasteau
IGP Vaucluse
www.gourtdemautens.com
13 ha; 18,000 bottles

La Martinelle

It is not so easy to find producers to recommend in Ventoux, but Corinna Faravel (who is married to Thierry Faravel of Domaine la Bouissière in Gigondas) has been making waves with her winery, La Martinelle. Corinna started by making white wine in Germany's Nahe region, but became interested in the red wines of the Rhône. In 2001, she purchased vineyards at Martinelle, on the other side of the Dentelles from Gigondas and Vacqueyras. The first years were difficult, with torrential rains in 2002 and a hailstorm destroying the crop in 2003. So the first vintage was 2004, made in rented space: a cellar was constructed at Lafare in 2009. The main production is Ventoux in red, white, and rosé, but there are also cuvées from Beaumes de Venise and Vin de France. A small vineyard in Beaumes de Venise was purchased in 2008, and has old vines of Grenache and some Syrah. Another source of old vines Grenache comes from a vineyard just to the south, and this is the basis of the Vin de France, which may also include grapes from the other vineyards; the exact blend varies with the year, and does not necessarily follow appellation rules. All the red wines are driven by Grenache, typically with about three quarters in each blend. The Ventoux has Syrah, Mourvèdre, Carignan, and small amounts of other varieties, including some white grapes. The Beaumes de Venise red has a quarter Syrah, and Syrah is usually the other important grape in the Vin de France.

Lafare
Ventoux
www.martinelle.com

12 ha; 40,000 bottles

Domaine de La Mordorée

This must be one of the more widely dispersed domains in the southern Rhône. Although based in Tavel, it has 38 different vineyard parcels in several different appellations. It was only in 1986 that Francis Delorme and his son Christophe decided to focus on winemaking and to expand their vineyards. Christophe's brother Fabrice joined in 1999, and Christophe is the winemaker today. Starting with 5 ha, they now have holdings in Lirac, Tavel, Châteauneuf-du-Pape, and Côtes du Rhône. The wines are divided into two lines in most appellations, the introductory cuvée, La Dame Rousse, and the top cuvée, La Reine des Bois. In Châteauneuf-du-Pape there is a super cuvée, La Plume du Peintre, produced only in some vintages from hundred-year-old Grenache vines. Viticulture was lutte raisonnée because Christophe was worried about the high use of copper in organic cultivation, but with newer techniques reducing use of copper, the domain became organic in 2007. Everything is destemmed, and fermentation is at relatively high temperature to bring out structure. The wines tend to be powerful and aromatic. The Châteauneuf cuvées are well regarded, but it's in Lirac and Tavel that the domain really makes its mark by producing wines well above the usual appellation level. The Tavel cuvées are complex blends (60% Grenache plus Cinsault, Syrah, Bourboulenc, Clairette, and Mourvèdre in La Dame Rousse); 48 hour cold maceration gives high color and strong aromatics.

Tavel
Châteauneuf-du-Pape, La Reine de Bois
Tavel, La Dame Rousse
www.domaine-mordoree.com

55 ha; 220,000 bottles

Domaine de L'Oratoire Saint-Martin

This is not a typical domain of the Côtes du Rhône on the plain. Vineyards are on steep slopes to the northeast of Cairanne, close to the hills of Rasteau, on pebbly soils with a high content of clay and active limestone. White varieties and Syrah are planted on slopes at Douyes around 200 m altitude with northeast exposure; other varieties (mostly Grenache and Mourvèdre) are planted on the slopes at St. Martin with south exposure. The Alary family has been making wine for three centuries (since 1692) and the vineyards have a good proportion of old vines. Yields are low, typically around 25 hl/ha (the oldest vines are not being replaced, even though yields are down to 15 hl/ha). Brothers Frédéric and François have been running the domain since 1984, with Frédéric making the wine and François managing the vineyards. Most of the vineyards are in the Côtes du Rhône Cairanne AOP, with a few in Côtes du Rhône. Three quarters of production is red. Two introductory-level cuvées are produced from the Côtes du Rhône. There are three cuvées from Cairanne: Réserve des Seigneurs is Grenache based, and matured in tank; Haut-Coustias is Mourvèdre, with Grenache and Syrah as the minor components, and is matured in foudres; and Les Douyes (formerly called Cuvée Prestige) is Grenache and Mourvèdre from hundred-year-old vines, matured in foudres for 18 months. The wines are often compared with Châteauneuf-du-Pape.

Cairanne
Côtes du Rhône Villages Cairanne
www.oratoiresaintmartin.fr

25 ha; 100,000 bottles

Domaine Les Pallières

Les Pallières is a 135 ha estate, with 25 ha planted with vines in a natural amphitheater at elevations of 250-400 m in the Dentelles. The underlying clay-sandy terroir is partially covered with calcareous rocks, becoming rockier with altitude. Owned by the Roux family for a century, originally the estate was planted with olive trees; subsequently they were replaced with grapevines. In 1998 the estate was purchased by a partnership between Domaine de Vieux Télégraphe of Châteauneuf-du-Pape and the American importer Kermit Lynch. About 80% of the vines are Grenache, but there's also some Syrah, Mourvèdre, Cinsault, and Clairette. About 5 ha were replanted, but the remainder are old vines. A new gravity-feed winery was constructed by 2002. The wine is made by the same team that produces Vieux Télégraphe. There are two cuvées. Terrasse du Diable comes from 40-year old vines, running up to 400 m on a north-facing slope. Some white grapes are included. "The softening effect of Clairette (and some reduction in alcohol) is what we are looking for, and it brings some minerality," says Daniel Brunier of Vieux Télégraphe. Les Racines comes from 75-year-old vines and tends to have a more brooding presence, with an unusual sense of tension for a Grenache-based wine. It's one of the top wines from Gigondas (but in some vintages I prefer Terrasse du Diable for greater freshness, although both cuvées tend to show high alcohol). There's also a rosé, le Petit Bonheur (Vin de France).

Gigondas
Gigondas, Terrasse du Diable
www.les-pallieres.com

25 ha; 80,000 bottles

Domaine de La Réméjeanne

Located on the west side of the Rhône, approaching the foothills of the Cevennes, the domain is well away from the main plain of the Côtes du Rhône. Vineyards on the slopes facing east are Côtes du Rhône, while the warmer sites facing southeast are Côtes du Rhône Villages; altitudes range from 200 to 280 m. The combination of altitude and exposure to the mistral gives the wine better freshness than is usually found in Côtes du Rhône. Soils are calcareous, with clay and sandstone. Réméjeanne was founded in 1960 when François Klein returned from Morocco and purchased 5 ha of vineyards. Grapes were sold to the cooperative, the vineyards were expanded, and then the domain was created when estate bottling started in 1975. It includes 2 ha of olive trees and 0.5 ha of figs as well as vines. Rémy Klein took over from his father in 1988, continued to expand the domain, and has been helped by his son Olivier since 2009. There are about ten cuvées; all the reds are blends, varying from 80% Grenache to 80% Syrah. Winemaking is modern: grapes are destemmed, there is cold maceration, and after fermentation the wines are matured in cuve (except for the cuvées Les Eglantiers (mostly Syrah) and Les Prunelles (pure Bourboulenc), which go into demi muids). The white Côtes du Rhône, Les Arbousiers, is a blend of the usual suspects (Viognier, Roussanne, Marsanne, Bourboulenc and Clairette). The style is generally straightforward.

Sabran
Côtes du Rhône
www.domainelaremejeanne.com

38 ha; 140,000 bottles

Château de Saint Cosme

Château de Saint Cosme claims an origin going back to 1490. The estate vineyards are in Gigondas, with an average vine age of 60 years, and Louis Barruol (the fifteenth generation) added a negociant business in 1997. The Gigondas offers a mainstream representation of the appellation; the Valbelle cuvée is a blend of 80-year-old vines, including 10% Syrah as well as the predominant Grenache, from a mixture of terroirs, and gives more sense of restraint and finesse. Saint Cosme is unusual in offering several bottlings from individual vineyards, all 100% Grenache from old vines. "There's no established tradition here, it's a pretty open debate whether you are for cuvées or lieu-dits. When I taste my lieu-dits, I think it would be a shame to blend. On this issue Gigondas remains a pretty young place," says Louis. "I've tried all my plots as separate wines. I keep those separate that work by themselves, but others can be good but need blending." Le Claux comes from 90-year-old vines on a 1 ha lieu-dit of clay and limestone terroirs; it offers significantly more flavor variety than the Gigondas as such. Le Poste comes from vines that are a mere 60 years old on a limestone-marl terroir, but is more refined than Le Claux. Hominis Fides comes from 80-year-old vines on a terroir of limestone and sand, and reflects the terroir in a lighter, subtler way. All the cuvées have significant (30%) new oak, and once this wears off, offer a rare impression of the effects of terroir on Grenache.

Gigondas
Gigondas, Le Claux
www.saintcosme.com

22 ha; 115,000 bottles

Domaine Le Sang des Cailloux

The domain originated when a single large property owned by the Ricard brothers was divided between them in 1975. Serge Férigoule's ambition was to be a winemaker, and after qualifying in oenology at Montpellier, he took charge of the vineyards at the domain in 1979. He became a partner in the domain in 1982, and then took over when M. Ricard retired in 1990. A new cuverie was built in 2001. The name of Sang des Cailloux means blood from the stones. The wines became Vacqueyras AOC when Serge took over, as the appellation was created that year. Sang des Cailloux is now widely considered one of the leading estates of Vacqueyras. The vineyards are located on the stony Plateau des Garrigues, underneath the Dentelles de Montmirail. The traditional red cuvée confusingly alternates its name each year to have the name of one of Serge's three daughters, Floureto, Doucinello, and Azalaïs: but it remains the same 70% Grenache and 20% Syrah with small amounts of Mourvèdre and Cinsault. It is matured for six months in foudres. There is also a Vieilles Vignes cuvée, Lopy, which is three quarters Grenache, from vines over sixty years old, to one quarter Syrah. The style is generally powerful. The single white cuvée is less than 10% of production and is a blend of six varieties. Serge is famous not only for his wine, but for his handlebar moustache; since 1999 he has shared the winemaking with his son Frédéric.

Sarrians
Côtes du Rhône
Vacqueyras
www.sangdescailloux.com
18 ha; 60,000 bottles

Domaine Santa-Duc

Behind Santa-Duc's modern tasting room, located across the main road below the village of Gigondas, is a lively enterprise with a negociant activity as well as production of domain wines. Almost half the domain vineyards are in Gigondas, but there are also holdings in Vacqueyras, Rasteau, other parts of the Côtes du Rhône, and (most recently) Châteauneuf-du-Pape. "For twenty years I was a candidate to buy every plot that came up in Châteauneuf-du-Pape," says Yves Gras, who is the fifth generation at the domain. Local character is expressed as freshness in the Côtes du Rhône Villages Roaix, which is quite classy for its appellation, there is a more robust impression in the Vacqueyras and Gigondas, and a sheen of finesse to the Châteauneuf-du-Pape. "My model looks to Burgundy with minerality and freshness, and good acidity," says Yves. "We are trying to keep alcohol levels down by picking earlier and changing grape handling," he adds, but the levels are now pushing 15%. However, the objective of retaining freshness has been achieved. There are three cuvées from Gigondas: Tradition, Santa Roc (intended to be a fresher style), and Prestige du Garrigue (which comes from around the winery). The Prestige is an unconventional blend of Grenache with Mourvèdre: "They are very complementary because Grenache is oxidative and early, and Mourvèdre is reductive and late." The vines have a minimum age of 50 years and the wine is not made every year.

Gigondas
Gigondas, Prestige des Hauts Garrigues
www.santaduc.fr
28 ha; 110,000 bottles

⊙ Rasteau

🍾 Rasteau

www.domainelasoumade.fr

🚶 🍷 G

27 ha; 110,000 bottles

Domaine La Soumade

The Roméros have been involved in wine in the region for a long time, but the domain as such is relatively new, founded by André Roméro in 1979; he has been estate bottling all the production since 1990. His son Frédéric has been involved since 1996. A new winery was constructed in 2002, when Stéphane Derenoncourt of Bordeaux was engaged as consulting oenologist. Domaine La Soumade is considered to be one of the leading producers in the appellation: the wines are a good demonstration of Rasteau's typicity vis à vis Gigondas and others. Almost all the vineyards are in Rasteau, with just 1 ha in Gigondas (close to the Dentelles). Soils are blue clay on limestone. There are three cuvées from Rasteau: Cuvée Prestige (matured in a mix of foudres and cement) and Cuvée Confiance (matured in foudres) are both 70% Grenache, 20% Syrah, and 10% Mourvèdre; Fleur de Confiance comes from a specific vineyard parcel and is 90% Grenache and 10% Syrah, matured in demi-muids. Yields decline along this hierarchy from 35 hl/ha to 25 hl/ha to less than 18 hl/ha. The Gigondas is 70% Grenache to 30% Syrah. There are also two cuvées of Côtes du Rhône, one based on Grenache, but the other (Les Violettes) based on Syrah. There is no production of white wine, but a little Viognier is included in the reds. The range of appellation wines finishes with a rosé and VDN. The style is distinctly on the rich side: these are wines for people who like a really powerful style.

⊙ Loumarin

⬤ Côtes du Rhône Villages

🍾 St. Joseph

www.tardieu-laurent.com

▦ 🍷 N

0 ha; 90,000 bottles

Maison Tardieu-Laurent

It's not easy to visit or gain information about the Tardieu Laurent negociant, which started as a collaboration between Dominique Laurent (from Burgundy, and noncommunicative if not secretive) and Michel Tardieu in 1994. Today it's run by Michel Tardieu, and has now become a family firm, with Bastien and Camille Tardieu joining their father. Michel is known for traveling constantly in the region to taste in each appellation. Since Dominique Laurent left, the concentration of new oak has been reduced. The firm is located in the southern Rhône and has been advised by well-known oenologue Philippe Cambie since 2000. The wines are divided into three groups: Vieilles Vignes (always from vines more than fifty years old), Grandes Bastides (vieilles vignes from certain domains), and Vins à Façon, which is a special range developed for general distribution to the wine fairs. There are approximately fifty different cuvées from all over the Rhône, with the range headed by four Châteauneuf-du-Papes in the Southern Rhône, and both red and white Hermitage in the Northern Rhône. The Vieilles Vignes are regarded as points of reference in each appellation. They seem to me to offer unusual fruit purity, lifting the wines above the general level of the appellation, whichever it might be. The future is somewhat uncertain because supplies have been dwindling as more growers turn to bottling their own wines and there is increased competition for grapes with larger negociants.

Château des Tourettes

Château des Tourettes was the last addition to Jean-Marie Guffens's trio of properties, after the Guffens-Heynen domain and the Verget negociant in Mâcon. Guffens-Heynen dates from 1976, Verget from 1990, and Château des Tourettes was purchased in 1997. The domain was run down and required much replanting. It's in the Lubéron, but the varieties do not completely conform to appellation regulations, so the wines are labeled under the IGP Vaucluse. Grape varieties include Chardonnay, Roussanne, Marsanne, Viognier, Syrah, Grenache, and Cabernet. Jean-Marie is never one to accept the traditional view, or as he might express it, to accept traditional limitations, and the aim here is to show freshness and precision in the wines, not the most common objective in the region. The red shows the aim of the house even more clearly than the whites: I would describe it as more like the northern than the southern Rhône. Grande Trilogie is the name for the blended cuvée, both red and white. Plateau de l'Aigle is a Chardonnay that shows as quite mainstream, with less aromatics than Grande Trilogie. There is also a range of whites from named varieties, including blends of Chardonnay-Viognier, Roussanne-Viognier and Marsanne-Roussanne. The style is modern with significant usage of new oak. I am not sure where one would place the wines in a blind tasting, but it would probably be in a more important appellation than the Lubéron.

🔄 Apt
⬤ Lubéron
🍾 IGP Vaucluse, Grande Trilogie
🍾 IGP Vaucluse, Plateau de l'Aigle
www.chateaudestourettes.com

20 ha; 120,000 bottles

Jean-Michel Alquier

The winery is located in the center of town, with the cellar just opposite the family house. "I am the fifth generation on the property," says Jean-Michel. His grandfather left the area to become a negociant in Paris, but his father, Gilbert, returned, and began to renew the vineyards in the 1960s, with a focus on Syrah. "This was how the domain began to acquire its present reputation," Jean-Michel explains. The domain was split after Gilbert's death between Jean-Michel and Frédéric Alquier, and it's Jean-Michel's wines that are now considered to be a leading light of the appellation. There's only one hectare for white grapes. For red wines, vineyards are divided according to position on the slope (all south-facing) to make three cuvées: La Première (half Syrah) comes from the base of the slope where the soils are deepest; Maison Jaune comes from the slope and is more structured, although it's 70% Grenache; and Les Bastides comes from the top of the hill and is always very ripe, although it's 70% old vines Syrah. All the wines are matured in barrique. The style here is modern, but the wines display it in different ways. La Première has a freshness you would not have seen in Faugères ten or twenty years ago, satisfying the objective of being ready to drink soonest. Maison Jaune has a smoothness and elegance that shows the progress of recent years. And Les Bastides has structure rather than simple expression of overt fruit, requiring at least a decade to begin to open up.

🔄 Faugères
🍾 Faugères, La Maison Jaune

12 ha; 50,000 bottles

Languedoc

Langlade
IGP de Gard
IGP de Gard
IGP de Gard
www.rocdanglade.fr

10 ha; 35,000 bottles

Roc d'Anglade

Winemaking is a second career for Rémy Pédréno. He had been a computer programmer for nine years when he discovered wine, and started by making a single barrique in his parents' garage. He became the winemaker when René Rostaing (from Côte Rôtie) wanted to make wine in the south in 1998, and then in 2002 he bought his own vines and became independent. The winery has two storeys, located under the family residence. Vineyards are in various parcels in the vicinity. Rémy is an enthusiast for Carignan, to the point that his wines are labeled as IGP de Gard because he wants to include more Carignan than is permitted in the AOP. He makes his point with the concentration and elegance of an experimental Vieilles Vignes cuvée of Carignan from 2007. In the regular cuvée, the red is around half Carignan, with Grenache, Syrah and (in recent vintages) Mourvèdre. It's a wine that's very expressive of vintage, from a positively Burgundian 2002, to a savory 2004 with mineral overtones, and then a more typically southern 2011, but all vintages show a sense of reserve and elegance. "If you asked me to produce a wine to show why I chose this métier, this is the wine I would show today," Rémy says about his 2002 vintage. The rosé is based on Mourvèdre, and the white on Chenin Blanc, a good example of breaking out of the southern straightjacket by moving to more northern varieties. The white has lots of character, developing in a savory, mineral direction.

Montpeyroux
Languedoc-Montpeyroux
Languedoc, Les Cocalières
www.aupilhac.com

25 ha; 130,000 bottles

Domaine d'Aupilhac

Sylvain Fadat is the fifth generation of vignerons in the family, but was the first to bottle his own wine in 1989. At that time the domain was still involved in polyculture, but since 1992 it has been concerned exclusively with viticulture. Its headquarters are in an unassuming house along what used to be the route for the stagecoach through Montpeyroux. But behind the house is a winery full of modern equipment. The main vineyards are at Aupilhac (close to Montpeyroux), including some extending directly behind the property, but there is another vineyard at Cocalières, with an elevation of 350 m, where Sylvain planted vines on a steeply terraced hillside in 1998. The focus is on traditional Southern varieties: Carignan, Grenache, Cinsault, Mourvèdre, and Syrah for the reds, with Roussanne, Marsanne, Grenache Blanc, and Vermentino for the whites. It was the reds that established the reputation of the Domaine, all made by traditional methods of vinification. The wines are mostly labeled as Languedoc (formerly Coteaux du Languedoc), with the best cuvées in the category of Languedoc-Montpeyroux. Sylvain is known as somewhat of a specialist in Carignan, and Le Carignan, a monovarietal cuvée from 60-year-old vines, is one of the domain's best-known wines. (It's an IGP Mont Baudile, as is the monovarietal Cinsault.) It's a sign of progress in the area that Sylvain was a trendsetter in 1990 but is now one of several good producers in Montpeyroux.

Domaine Les Aurelles

Wine is in the family background as Caroline Saint Germain comes from Cognac, but the creation of Les Aurelles in 1995 was a new career for Basil Saint Germain. He was influenced by two years spent at Château Latour. "I chose this particular area because the first wine of the Languedoc I tasted came from here, and because the terroir seemed to resemble Château Latour, with an area of gravel," he says. Vineyards are located where alluvial deposits created a deep layer of gravel; plantings are Carignan, Mourvèdre, Syrah, and Grenache, with some Roussanne for white wine. The winery is a modern concrete bunker constructed on a high point in Nizas in 2001. The domain is committed to organic viticulture to the point of including a statement on the back label certifying the absence of pesticides. Yields are low, under 25 hl/ha for reds and under 18 hl/ha for white. Basil is a devotée of Carignan, and has planted new vines as well as buying all the old vines he can find. There are three cuvées of red and one white. After the entry level Déelle (a blend that changes with vintage), come Solen (Grenache, Carignan, and Syrah) and Aurel (Mourvèdre, Syrah, and Grenache). These express vintage: Solen shows its best qualities in cooler years, while Aurel really requires warmer years for the Mourvèdre's character to emerge. The white Aurel is Roussanne. The style is moderate, in line with Basil's purpose: "I want above all to make a wine to have with food not to win competitions."

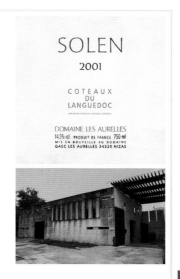

 Nizas

 Languedoc-Pézenas

Languedoc-Pézenas, Aurel
www.les-aurelles.com

9 ha; 25,000 bottles

Château La Baronne

The Lignères have the unusual characteristic of being medically qualified, although their main interest is now wine. The domain was founded by André and Suzette in 1957, and is now run by their three children. Visits start at the headquarters in Moux, where wines for all their three domains are bottled. Château La Baronne is the most important; nearby are Las Vals and Plo de Maorou. Vineyards lie between Moux and Fontcouverte under the lee of calcareous mountains, with elevations around 100-200 m making for late harvests. Black varieties are 90% of plantings. The winery has a mix of all sorts of cuves: concrete, stainless steel, and wood. There are also experiments with amphorae (made by a local potter from clay from the same terroir as the wines). Vineyards are in Corbières, but several monovarietal cuvées are bottled as IGP Hauterive, including Notre Dame (Syrah), and Las Vals (Mourvèdre for red and Roussanne for white). The most interesting of the monovarietals is Pièce de Roche, from a 4 ha plot of Carignan planted in 1892. Carignan is a focus of the domain, occupying more than a third of the vineyard area. It figures in the blends under the Corbières AOP: Les Lanes (Grenache and Carignan), Les Chemins (Grenache, Syrah and Carignan), and Alaric (Syrah, Carignan, and Mourvèdre). There's a focus on low sulfur, and Les Chemins de Traverse is a cuvée bottled without added sulfur. "We are looking for light extraction," is how Paul Lignères describes the style.

 Moux

Corbières

Corbières, Alaric
www.chateaulabaronne.com

90 ha; 250,000 bottles

Cabrerolles

Faugères

Faugères

www.domaineleonbarral.com

33 ha; 90,000 bottles

Domaine Léon Barral

This committed biodynamic domain is well known for its natural wines, and when I arrived, Didier Barral was about to set out to move his cows to new pasture. He has a herd of around 40 cows, not to mention some horses and pigs; during summer they graze on pastures near the vineyards, then during winter they are allowed into the vines. "We do polyculture, to get balance you have to have polyculture," explains Didier, under the enquiring gaze of the cows, some of which are a recreated medieval breed. Didier founded the domain in 1993 (it is named after his grandfather). It consists of many vineyard parcels, varying from 0.3 to 5 ha in size, with many old vines. The vineyards look quite old fashioned, with the vines pruned in gobelet style as free-standing bushes. "This makes a parasol for the sun, which is important. I don't think a trellis is well adapted to the climate," Didier maintains. Back in the cave, a stone building in the hamlet of Lenthéric, a tasting of barrel samples runs through many varieties, each still separate in barrique. Each variety shows its character through the prism of a highly refined style—even Carignan. The single white cuvée is based on the old variety of Terret Blanc and is an IGP Pays d'Hérault. The three reds cuvées are Faugères, the Faugères Jadis, and the Faugères Valinière, the first two being half Grenache, but the last more than three quarters Mourvèdre. Fine, tight, and precise would be a fair description of house style.

Félines-Minervois

Minervois

www.boriedemaurel.fr

35 ha; 200,000 bottles

Domaine Borie de Maurel

A young domain, this was founded in 1989 by Sylvie et Michel Escande (who abandoned a nautical career) as part of the return to the land movement in the Languedoc. The domain is located in the heart of Minervois, by La Livinière, one of the Crus of the Languedoc. The Escandes started by buying 5 ha of vineyards and a rather dilapidated house. Steady expansion has made this one of the larger domains in the area, and the next generation, Gabriel and Maxime, are now involved. Vineyards are on steep slopes, and significant heterogeneity in the terroirs (roughly divided between warmer sandstone and cooler limestone) is matched by the diversity of grape varieties, many vinified as monovarietals. All the wines are under the Minervois label, coming from different varieties or blends: Rève de Carignan and Sylla (100% Syrah) use carbonic maceration for softening the flavor profile, while Maxime (100% Mourvèdre) and Belle de Nuit (100% Grenache) are vinified conventionally. The Sylla cuvée was the wine that made the reputation of the domain in the early nineties. The introductory wine, Esprit d'Automne, is a blend of Syrah, Carignan, and Grenache, while the Minervois La Livinière, La Feline, is a blend of two thirds Syrah with one third Grenache and a little Carignan; it's matured a third in barriques and two thirds in cuve. Most production is red, but there is a white, La Belle Aude, which is 90% Marsanne and 10% Muscat.

Borie La Vitarèle

Cathy and Jean-François Izarn bought this 100 ha estate, located up a dirt track a few miles from the village of Causses-et-Veyran in 1986. It was mostly virgin land, and has been gradually built up to its present size, with vineyards in several separate parcels. Plantings are 40% Syrah and 40% Grenache, with smaller amounts of Merlot, Mourvèdre, Carignan, and white varieties. "We look for concentration but we don't want anything massive. We want refinement more than power," is how Jean-François explained his objectives. "We use very little new oak, we want to respect the terroir. I like to represent the unique character, the particularité of each terroir. It's more interesting to make cuvées from each terroir in a Burgundian way rather than to follow the Bordeaux model and make a grand vin and second wine." In reds, there is an introductory cuvée, Les Cigales: "This is my equivalent to rosé, I don't like rosé but this is easy to drink." The three cuvées from specific terroirs become progressively richer: Terres Blanches comes from calcareous soils, Les Schistes comes from schist on the slopes, and Les Crès comes from galets. Midi Rouge is the grand wine of the domain, made in small amounts from a blend of varieties and terroirs. The style is rich, in the direction of the generosity of Châteauneuf-du-Pape, something of a modern take on the tradition of the Languedoc. Sadly, Jean-François died in an accident in April 2014, but Cathy continues to run the domain.

 Causses-et-Veyran

St. Chinian

St. Chinian, Les Schistes
www.borielavitarele.fr

19 ha; 60,000 bottles

Mas Cal Demoura

Isabelle and Vincent Goumard took over Mas Cal Demoura in 2004 on the retirement of Jean-Pierre Jullien, who had created the estate in 1993. Vincent was a consultant in Paris before he took up wine as a second career. The winery is a small practical facility packed with equipment. Vineyards are in two main groups on either side of Jonquières. The majority have clay-calcareous soils, and are planted with black grapevines, including all five varieties of the appellation; the rest have calcareous pebbles and are where the white varieties are planted, mostly Chenin Blanc (going back to an experiment of the 1990s), with smaller quantities of the usual southern varieties. Wines are matured in a mixture of demi-muids and barriques (except for the more aromatic white varieties, which are vinified in cuve). There are three red cuvées, two whites, and a rosé. L'Infidèle is the principal red cuvée, a blend of all five varieties. Coming from a selection of pebbly parcels, Les Combariolles is mainly Syrah and Mourvèdre, and is the most structured wine of the house. At the other extreme is Feu Sacré, based on old vines Grenache. In the whites, L'Etincelle is half Chenin Blanc, but the top white wine, Paroles de Pierres, is three quarters Chenin with Roussanne making up most of the rest of the blend. The style varies quite a bit through the reds, but tends to be smooth and harmonious. The whites have a fresh character far removed from the old amorphous phenolics of the south.

 Jonquières

Terrasses du Larzac

L'Infidèle

IGP Pays d'Hérault, Parole de Pierres
www.caldemoura.com

14 ha; 45,000 bottles

Languedoc

Lagamas

Languedoc-Montpeyroux

Languedoc, Campredon
www.alainchabanon.com

17 ha; 55,000 bottles

Domaine Alain Chabanon

After qualifying in oenology at Bordeaux and Montpellier, and serving an apprenticeship with Alain Brumont in Madiran, Alain Chabanon returned to his roots in the Languedoc where he purchased vineyards between Jonquières and Montpeyroux. His first vintage was 1992 (only 2,500 bottles). A new winery was built in 2001. Originally the domain was called Font Caude (named for a nearby warm spring), but now the wines are labeled as Domaine Chabanon. Alain produces a wide range of wines, including Languedoc, IGP d'Oc, and Vin de France, from vineyards spread over several communes just below the Terrasses de Larzac. Under IGP and Vin de France are wines from varieties that aren't common in the region, including Chenin Blanc and Vermentino (Trélans is a blend of two thirds Vermentino to one third Chenin Blanc), and Merlot (this is the well-regarded Merle aux Alouettes cuvée); the Languedoc AOP wines are Grenache-Syrah-Mourvèdre or Syrah plus Mourvèdre. In fact, the first wine of the domain was the l'Esprit de Font Caude blend of equal proportions of Syrah and Mourvèdre. There are nine cuvées altogether, the idea being to demonstrate the characters of the very different plots. "This is not a range from petit vin to a grand vin, it's several different choices to suit different tastes, sometimes at the same price so that consumers aren't tempted to choose by cost. Of course, some are ready to drink today and others need three years," Alain explains.

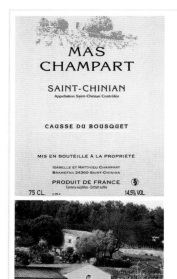

St. Chinian

St. Chinian, Causse du Bousquet

16 ha; 40,000 bottles

Mas Champart

Isabelle and Mathieu Champart moved from Paris to take over an old farm in 1976; with no experience in winemaking, grapes were sold to the cooperative until 1988 when they began to bottle their own wine. A winery was constructed in 1995. Since they took over, they have expanded the estate from its original 8 ha, sometimes by buying abandoned vineyards of old vines. In addition to the vineyards, the property includes another 8 ha of other fruits and crops. The vineyards comprise around twenty small plots on limestone hills, at altitudes between 200 m and 300 m. Grenache is grown on the higher locations, Syrah on north-facing slopes, and Mourvèdre on the clay-limestone terraces. The wines come in all three colors of St. Chinian, with three different red cuvées: going up the scale, Côte d'Arbo is a classic blend aged in vat (a lively introductory wine); Causse de Bousquet is two thirds Syrah with Mourvèdre and Grenache, aged partly in vat and partly in barrel (this is the major wine of the domain); and Clos de la Simonette is almost three quarters Mourvèdre (the rest is Grenache) aged in demi muids. The white St. Chinian is a conventional blend of local varieties. The Champarts' interests include some grapes that aren't allowed in the St. Chinian AOP, so there's an unusual IGP d'Oc which is a blend of 70% Cabernet Franc to 30% Syrah, and a white IGP Pays d'Hérault made from 80% Terret and 20% Grenache Gris.

Coume del Mas

This domain was created by Philippe and Nathalie Gard in 2001 (after Philippe consulted for several domains in Chablis and Pomerol), when they purchased vineyards mostly around the lieu-dit of Coume del Mas, but with outlying plots scattered all over the hills surrounding Banyuls-sur-Mer. The domain expanded from its original 2 ha to its present thirty parcels. The focus was to find old vines, and the majority of plantings are old bush vines of Grenache. The domain produces both the VDN (sweet) Banyuls and also the dry style of Banyuls Blanc, dry red under the Collioure AOP, and a rosé. Altogether there are about eight cuvées; sweet wines are about 20% of production. The flagship wine is Quadratur, a blend of Grenache, Carignan and Mourvèdre that spends 12 months in oak. By contrast, Schistes is a monovarietal old vines Grenache that is fermented and matured exclusively in stainless steel. Given the amount of manual (or equine) labor required to maintain the vines, the Coume del Mas domain has now reached its size limit, but has become quite a wide-ranging enterprise as another set of wines comes from Mas Christine, a separate property leased nearby in the Côtes de Roussillon appellation. In addition, Philippe runs a negociant business, Tramontane Wines, in association with winemaker Andy Cook, who is also a partner in Mas Christine. The Consolation range comes from selections from Coume del Mas, Mas Christine and other sources.

 Banyuls-sur-Mer

Banyuls

www.coumedelmas.com

15 ha; 40,000 bottles

Mas de Daumas Gassac

Aimé Guibert was looking for a country house when he purchased the estate in 1970. The geographer Henri Enjalbert, a family friend, suggested that the Gassac valley, with red glacial soils and a microclimate of cool nights, was suitable for wine production. Emile Peynaud from Bordeaux became a consultant, and the creation of the domain pioneered the production of high quality wine in Languedoc. Today the domain has about 50 small individual vineyards separated by the original garrigue. Based on Cabernet Sauvignon, but with many subsidiary varieties, the red wine is by no means a typical Cabernet. "We are not looking for the modern jammy fruity style. We belong more to the Bordeaux 1961 attitude—wine with 12.5% alcohol and good acidity," says Samuel Guibert. Older vintages seem to alternate between Atlantic austerity and the spices and herbs of the Mediterranean garrigue, with long aging potential: the 1982 and 1983 vintages were still vibrant in 2013. Current vintages are more forward but less complex. The white is based on a blend of Chardonnay, Viognier, and Petit Manseng, with the balance from many other varieties. In addition to the regular cuvées, there is now a cuvée Emile Peynaud in some vintages; made from the oldest Cabernet Sauvignon vines in one of the original vineyards, it is powerful in the modern idiom. Moulin de Gassac is a negociant line that includes purchased grapes. Success is indicated by the constant stream of visitors to the tasting room.

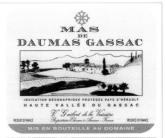

Aniane

IGP Pays d'Hérault

IGP Pays d'Hérault

www.daumas-gassac.com

40 ha; 205,000 bottles

Languedoc

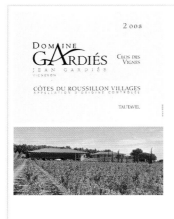

Domaine Gardiés

Jean Gardiés took over the family domaine in 1990. Previously the wine had been sold off in bulk, but he started bottling in 1993. A new wooden winery was built at Espira de l'Agly in 2006. Vineyards are located in two somewhat different terroirs, on the chalky-clay soils of Vingrau (where the family originated), and the black schist of Espira de l'Agly north of Perpignan. The older vines are at Vingrau, with newer plantings at Espira de l'Agly. The major plantings are black varieties, on the south- and east-facing slopes, with some white varieties on north-facing slopes in Vingrau at higher altitudes to retain freshness. Black varieties are Grenache and Carignan; whites are Grenache Blanc and Roussanne. There are four series of wines. The introductory wines, red, rosé, and white, are Côtes du Roussillon, blended from various holdings. Both red and white Le Clos des Vignes come specifically from Vingrau (the red is a Côtes du Roussillon Tautavel). The top of the line reds come from lower yields; La Torre is based on a blend dominated by Mourvèdre from Espira de l'Agly; and Les Falaises is dominated by Carignan from Vingrau. Although production has decreased, there is also a series of sweet wines from Rivesaltes, including a Muscat de Rivesaltes: "These sweet wines are a difficult sell outside of France, which is a pity as it's a unique tradition to the Roussillon," Jean says. Most of the wine is sold to restaurants in France.

Espira de l'Agly
Côtes du Roussillon Villages
www.domaine-gardies.fr
40 ha; 100,000 bottles

Domaine Gauby

The entrance to Domaine Gauby is an intimidating one-car-wide track along the ridge above a valley just outside Calce, 30-40 km northwest of Perpignan, at an elevation around 350-450 m. Half of the valley is given over to vineyards, the other half remaining in its natural state to maintain the ecosystem: "We practice polyculture, I don't believe in monoculture. We've planted cereals, olive trees, and almond trees," says Gérard Gauby. In 2003, winemaking moved from a garage in the town of Calce to a purpose built chai under the family house in the middle of the valley. Soils are based on deep, friable schist at the bottom of the valley with calcareous components higher up. Plantings are two thirds red. The whites are IGP Côtes de Catalanes and the reds are AOP Côtes du Roussillon Villages. Tasting here is an exercise in understanding extreme precision and elegance, reinforced by moderate alcohol, rarely above 12.5% yet always fully ripe. When tasting, Gérard instructs you not to swirl the wine but to let the complexity of the aromas "montent tranquillement." The whites are remarkable for their freshness. The reds extend from the classic blend of Vieilles Vignes, to the Grenache-based La Roque from old vines. Coume Gineste comes from friable schist, and Muntada comes from the same terroir as La Roque but is based on Syrah. The deepest red is La Founa, based on a complex mix of prephylloxera vines. Almost nothing here is less than exceptional for the region.

Calce
Côtes du Roussillon Villages
Muntada
Coume Gineste
www.domainegauby.fr
43 ha; 90,000 bottles

Domaine de La Grange des Pères

Laurent Vaillé established his domain in 1989 on ungiving terroir of hard limestone by dynamiting and bulldozing to clear land for planting. The winery is actually in the middle of uncultivated fields with not a vine in sight, but the Syrah and Cabernet vineyards are fairly close by, the main difference being that Cabernet is planted in the cooler exposures. Mourvèdre is 4-5 km away, on a rather hot south-facing plot covered in galets. The red wine for which the domain is famous is a blend of 40% Syrah, 40% Mourvèdre, and 20% Cabernet Sauvignon. "The Cabernet Sauvignon is like salt in food. I do not want Cabernet Sauvignon to dominate my assemblage," says Laurent. Vines are grown low to the ground. Yields are always very low, often below 25 hl/ha. There are only two wines here, one red and one white. Laurent is a perfectionist: "Any lot that isn't satisfactory is discarded, I don't want to make a second wine." Laurent refuses to draw any distinction between vins de garde and wines to drink now, but in my view the red wine needs considerable age to show its best. The 1994 showed a seamless elegance in 2012, with a subtlety comparable to a top northern Rhône. The 2000 vintage was still dense and rich at this point; and it was vinicide to drink the 2008 or 2009, because sheer power and aromatics hid much of their potential. Only 10% of production, a white wine is based on Roussanne with smaller amounts of Marsanne and Chardonnay.

Aniane
IGP Pays d'Hérault
15 ha; 30,000 bottles

Domaine de L'Hortus

The winery occupies a new, purpose-built building surrounded by carefully tended vines. The domain is in the center of Pic St. Loup, where its first vines were planted right under the cliffs of Mount Hortus. There was nothing here in 1979 when Jean and Marie-Thérèse Orliac started to construct the estate, which has been built up, little by little with many separate parcels. Now their sons Yves and Martin are involved. This is a very lively enterprise: the family gathers for lunch each day at the winery, and conversation to say the least is spirited. There are three red cuvées, two whites, and a rosé. The entry-level wines are labeled as Bergerie de l'Hortus, and are intended for relatively rapid consumption. The Grande Cuvée label of Domaine de l'Hortus indicates wines that are intended to be more vin de garde. The Clos du Prieur red comes from the most recent acquisition, ten years ago, of a vineyard in Terrasses de Larzac, about 20 miles to the west (where the climate is distinctly more Continental). "The vineyards have reached their size: there are no new plantings planned. It's the story of the 2000s; we replanted some abandoned vineyards, but now we have finished," says Jean Orliac. The style is modern. ""We look for wines that aren't too powerful but have some finesse," says Martin Orliac. The Bergerie wines are very approachable, but I find the Grand Cuvée more mainstream, while the restraint of Clos du Prieur is attractive and ageworthy.

Valflaunès
Pic St. Loup
Pic Saint Loup, Grand Cuvée
www.domaine-hortus.fr
77 ha; 350,000 bottles

Languedoc

Domaine Ledogar

Four generations of Ledogars have been making wine in Corbières, but it was only when Xavier Ledogar decided he wanted to become a vigneron that his father, André, decided to create his own domain (initially called Domaine Grand Lauze, renamed Domaine Ledogar in 2008). They purchased an old building in 1997, and made the first vintage in 1998. Xavier's younger brother Mathieu joined the domain in 2000. The domain is committed to producing natural wine, and as a result has run into the usual difficulties with the *agrément* for the AOP; so although 80% of their vineyards are in Corbières and 20% in IGP, some of the wines are labeled as Vin de France. Within Corbières, plantings are mostly Carignan (11 ha), Mourvèdre (2.5 ha), Syrah (2.5 ha), or Grenache (2 ha); the rest consists of Maccabeu and Cinsault, and a small amount of white varieties. Yields are low, at 25-35 hl/ha. In addition there are some IGP vineyards that André had planted with Cabernet Sauvignon and Marselan. There are some plots in Corbières of very old Carignan and Grenache, within which are some other old varieties of the area. The top wines of the domain come from Carignan or Carignan-dominated blends. Rather spicy, the Corbières is a conventional blend, but Tout Natur, a Vin de France blend of Carignan with Mourvèdre, would make a fine Corbières if it had the agrément. Coming from very old vines, La Mariole is a monovarietal Carignan with a rare precision.

 Ferrals lès Corbières
  Corbières
  Vin de France, La Mariole
www.domaineledogar.fr
19 ha; 40,000 bottles

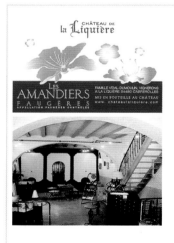

Château de La Liquière

The modern tasting room is located in an old castle in the center of the town of Cabrerolles. The vineyards are in many different parcels scattered throughout all four villages of Faugères. "The domain has increased since the 1960s but now we have decided not to grow any more," says François Villard, whose grandparents established the domain. Vinification by parcel produces 50 different lots, and it's only later that the decision is made on which to bottle as separate cuvées and which to blend together. There are five red cuvées, three whites, and two rosés. The entry level line goes under the name of Les Amandiers and is matured in concrete and steel. The white Cistus has a few months maturation in new oak barriques, new because the period is short; and then the barriques are used to mature the red wine. Amandiers comes from wines at lower altitudes, and Cistus from those higher up, so there's a correlation at Liquière between the top of the hill and the top of the scale. A Vieilles Vignes red cuvée comes from a blend of old vines of Carignan and Grenache; and the Nos Racines cuvée comes from a 110-year-old plot of Carignan that's planted in a field blend with some other old varieties. It's a paradox that these are the oldest vines but the wine seems the most modern in the range. The house style is round and smooth and elegant (although of course there is some stylistic variation from the entry level to the top wines).

  Cabrerolles
  Faugères
  Faugères, Cistus
www.chateaulaliquiere.com
65 ha; 280,000 bottles

Clos Marie

The winery is a tiny property in the center of the little town of Lauret where Françoise Julien and Christophe Peyrus make the wine. The estate was worked by Christophe's grandfather (who made wine) and father (who sent grapes to the coop), but Françoise and Christophe created Clos Marie as a domain when they decided to produce wine in 1992. They began with 8 ha, and today there are various parcels scattered around Lauret in the Pic St. Loup AOP. There are four red cuvées, two whites, and one rosé. Terroir is the main criterion for distinguishing the cuvées—even in Pic St. Loup there are variations of terroir, says Françoise—but there are also differences in assemblage and age of vines (with one cuvée coming from young vines). The objective is for Clos Marie to be mineral with freshness and precision. "It's very important to keep alcohol low to maintain freshness; we do vendange vert and pick relatively early," explains Françoise. Viticulture is organic with some biodynamic treatments. Each parcel is vinified separately. "Originally each variety was vinified separately, but then we found we got better results with cofermentation." Wines are matured in oak, but there is no new wood. The style here is a long way from the old stereotype of the region: both reds and whites are light and fresh, in particular the red Metairies du Clos, which comes from old vines. Alcohol levels are moderate for the region. This is a standard bearer for the new style of the Languedoc.

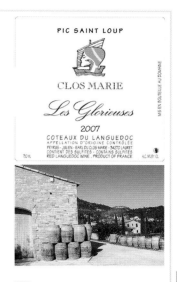

Lauret

Pic St. Loup

Pic Saint Loup, Metairies du Clos

23 ha; 95,000 bottles

Domaine du Mas Amiel

The history of this large domain, located just outside Maury, is somewhat chequered; won in a game of cards from the Bishop of Perpignan in 1816, it became the property of a bank when the owners were ruined in 1909, and then in 1999 was sold to its present owner, who has set about renovating the vineyards (several hectares are replanted each year) and chais. Its fame was established for sweet fortified wines, but in the past couple of decades it has been making a transition to a point at which half the wines are dry. The old cellar is used for maturing traditional wines, but now there is a new cellar with temperature-controlled cuves for the new lines of dry wines. The vineyards are on slopes surrounding the winery, generally on soils of schist. There are dry whites and reds under the AOP Côtes de Roussillon, and recently four cuvées of dry red wines from old vines and single vineyards have been introduced under the new Maury Sec label. The sweet wines divide into the modern Vintage line and the traditionally oxidative Classique line. Oxidative wines start out with a year in glass demi-johns in the sun, and then mature in large foudres. Vintage-dated VDNs are produced about once every decade; other Classique wines come from a blend of two or three vintages, and are labeled by their average age as 15-year or 20-year. Although no longer in fashion, the sweet wines remain a benchmark; the dry wines have yet to catch up.

Maury

Maury, Vintage

www.masamiel.fr

170 ha; 350,000 bottles

Languedoc

Mas Jullien

Mas Jullien was started by Olivier Jullien in 1985 (the same year the AOC of Coteaux du Languedoc was created), when he was twenty. (His father, Jean-Pierre, was a grower who sent his grapes to the coop. He started Mas Cal Demoura next door after Olivier's success, and later sold it.) The winery has grown into a collection of buildings, with a tasting room to accommodate the constant trek of visitors. From a small start with 3 ha of rented vines, the domain has expanded into many separate holdings with various soil types, with many changes in the vineyard holdings over the years. Olivier is still buying and selling vineyards to balance the terroirs: there is a sense of restless movement here, with Olivier often giving the impression he wants to be off to the next thing. Based on the traditional Southern varieties of Carignan, Grenache, Cinsault, Syrah, and Mourvèdre, there are three red cuvées (all Terrasses de Larzac AOP). The principal cuvée is called simply Mas Jullien. The introductory wine is Les Derniers Etats de l'Ame (a reference to an earlier cuvée, L'Etat de l'Ame, which Olivier had proposed to stop producing, but resumed after protests). Its constitution changes from year to year. The top wine, Carlan, is a parcel selection from terroir of schist (in some years there are also other parcel selections). The single white cuvée, a blend of Carignan Blanc and Chenin Blanc, is IGP Pays d'Hérault. There are also a rosé (with the varieties changing each year), and a dessert wine, Cartagène.

Jonquières
Terrasses du Larzac
Languedoc, Mas Jullien

20 ha; 70,000 bottles

Domaine de Montcalmès

His grandfather produced wine, but his father sold grapes to the coop, until Frédéric Pourtalié took over the domain in 1998, after working elsewhere in the south, with internships at Grange des Pères and Alain Graillot. His first vintage was in 1999, just 5,000 bottles for the domain. The entrance to the winery is quite unassuming, just an ordinary building off the main street in Puéchabon, but behind are extensive caves packed with stainless steel tanks for fermentation and barriques for maturation. Vineyards are planted in many parcels on a variety of terroirs in Terrasses de Larzac. (The size of the domain was reduced when Frédéric's partner, Victor Guizard, left in 2010 to form Domaine St. Sylvestre with his wife Sophie.) Blending is the focus here. "We vinify each cépage from each terrace in order to understand the terroir, but it takes 15 years, so as yet there aren't any single vineyard wines," Frédéric says. Montcalmès is planted with 60% Syrah, 20% Grenache, and 20% Mourvèdre; there is also a white (from a hectare divided between Roussanne and Marsanne). Wines are matured in 1- to 3-year-old barriques for two years, and bottled by the waning moon without filtration. The variety of terroirs provides Grenache varying from broad fleshiness to steely structure, and the house style is for a precise, harmonious elegance, very much a representation of the modern style of Languedoc. The red is labeled as Terrasses du Larzac, the white as Languedoc.

Puéchabon
Terrasses du Larzac
Terrasses du Larzac
www.domainedemontcalmes.fr

23 ha; 60,000 bottles

Château Pech Redon

Pech Redon is a truly unique location, on the site of an old Roman villa, several miles along a dirt track at the end of a large rocky plateau surrounded by impressive calcareous cliffs. The environment could not be more different from the seaside town of Narbonne, which is the official postal address. Christophe Bousquet bought the domain in 1988 upon the death of the previous owner, Jean Demolomben, a negociant in Narbonne. It's very isolated, but that was part of the appeal for Christophe. Regarded as a young Turk at the time, he is now one of the most established producers in the La Clape AOP. Pech Redon is at the highest point in La Clape (Pech Redon means "rounded peak"), and its elevation (about 200 m) makes it cooler and fresher than the rest of La Clape. All the wines are AOP La Clape (Christophe was much involved in its creation: he is president of the local producers' association). There is a classic Languedocian mix of the five black grape varieties (and also some whites). The terroir is relatively homogeneous, so differences between cuvées are due more to assemblage and élevage. The L'Epervier white cuvée is fresh and lively, but the main focus here is on the red cuvées, which ascend from Les Cades (8 months in cuve, fresh and lively, based on Syrah, Grenache, Cinsault, and Carignan), to L'Epervier (the flagship wine, 18 months in cuve, from Syrah, Grenache, Mourvèdre, and Carignan), and the weightiest, Centaurée (classic GSM, 24 months in oak fûts).

 Narbonne
 La Clape
La Clape, L'Epervier
www.pech-redon.com
30 ha; 50,000 bottles

Domaine Peyre Rose

To say that Peyre Rose is a bit tricky to find is an understatement. It's not easy to spot the entrance to the narrow unpaved track in Saint Pargoire that winds for several kilometers until it reaches the domain. "Follow the telegraph poles," the instructions say, but the faint of heart might well lose confidence along the way. It's entirely understandable that Marlène Soria used to come here on vacation for the savage quality of the countryside. She purchased 60 ha of garrigue, and then in 1970 planted some vines to make wine for personal consumption. The domain started later, with some plantings of Syrah in the 1980s, followed in 1985 by Mourvèdre and Grenache. Almost all of the plantings today are black varieties, with Syrah dominant, and just 3 ha of Rolle and Roussanne. This remains an intensely personal operation, with Marlène making the wines single-handed in the cave. Until 2002, everything was vinified in cuve, but since then about a quarter has been matured in foudres. Aging is quite extended here, with at least 7-8 years of élevage. A tasting at Peyre Rose in 2013 focused on current releases: 2003 and 2004. This is not your usual economic model. The wines move from the fleshy sex appeal of Marlène #3, to the more classic balance of Clos des Cistes (80% Syrah and 20% Grenache, the only wine really to show any restraint), and Clos Léone (80% Syrah and 20% Mourvèdre), but the general style is for intense, very ripe, exuberant fruits.

 Saint Pargoire
 Languedoc
Coteaux du Languedoc, Clos des Cistes
23 ha; 32,000 bottles

Languedoc

Calce

IGP Côtes Catalanes

Côtes Catalanes, Le Clot

www.domaineolivierpithon.com

18 ha; 35,000 bottles

Domaine Olivier Pithon

"My family were vignerons in the Loire, and I never thought of doing anything else," says Olivier Pithon. "After studying wine in other regions, I looked for vines, and I liked the varieties and area here at Calce." The winery entrance is a garage door in what looks like a residence in the main street of Calce, but inside is a small winemaking facility, crammed with equipment. Starting with 7 ha the first year, the domain has slowly expanded, and now includes white grapevines as well the original black. The vineyards are in the area that used to be the Vin de Pays Coteaux des Fenouillèdes (the name refers to the fennel that grows naturally on the hillsides); they are all labeled as IGP Côtes de Catalanes. "The regulations for AOP are just too strict with regards to encépagement," Olivier says. There are three white cuvées and three red. The entry level wines, Mon P'tit Pithon, both red and white, come from purchased grapes: everything else comes from the estate. The top white wine, D18, is a blend of Grenache Gris and Blanc. The reds are the real heart of the domain, with Laïs based on a blend of Carignan and Grenache (it replaced two previous cuvées, La Coulée and Saturne); Le Pilou is a 100% Carignan from 100-year-old vines on calcareous terroir; and Le Clot (bottled only in magnums) is based on Grenache from schist. Olivier describes house style by saying, "The idea with the reds is to get elegance without aggressive tannins."

Prieuré Saint Jean de Bébian

The winery sits on the site of a Roman villa, where perhaps vines were grown long ago, but the modern story starts with M. Roux, who sourced Syrah from Chave, Grenache from Château Rayas, Mourvèdre from Domaine Tempier, and Roussanne from Château Beaucastel. The estate was bought in 1994 by Chantal Lecouty and Jean-Claude Lebrun (formerly of the Revue du Vin). Karen Turner came as winemaker in 2004, and stayed on when the estate was sold to Russian owners in 2008. The top wine is labeled Grand Vin du Languedoc; the red has a high proportion of Syrah and Mourvèdre, and the white is more than half Roussanne. A second wine, La Chapelle de Bébian, is made in all three colors; the red is half Grenache, and the white is half Grenache Blanc. With more of an eye on the market, a new entry level line has been introduced under the name La Croix de Bébian. In addition, there is a Cabernet Sauvignon under the label L'Autre Versant. Even after some softening, the reds remain somewhat counter to the trend for instant gratification. "I have the impression that no one in Languedoc wants tannins any more, but I want them. One of the most important things about Bébian is that it's one of the few wines in Languedoc that ages well. It's probably best at 10-20 years after the vintage," Karen says. In my view, even La Chapelle isn't really ready after five years, and Prieuré does not open out until after ten years, making it one of the region's more ageworthy wines.

Pézenas

Languedoc

Languedoc, Le Prieuré

www.bebian.com

33 ha; 120,000 bottles

Château Puech Haut

This is quite a grand estate, surrounded by vineyards, with a long drive flanked by olive trees. There's a spacious tasting room in a nineteenth century house, with a large barrel room on display just behind. But when Gérard Bru purchased the property in 1985, the land was mostly bare garrigue. There were 80 ha in the estate at the start, and then twenty years later this was increased to 200 ha, which makes it one of the larger properties in Languedoc. Most (100 ha) of vineyards are in Saint Drézéry (just northeast of Montpellier), but there are some additional plots in Pic St. Loup. Red, white, and rosé are produced in the entry level line, Prestige, and in the flagship line, Tête de Beliér. The Prestige red is more than half Grenache; the Tête de Bélier is three quarters Syrah, with smaller amounts of Grenache and Mourvèdre. There's also a Loup St. Pic red and occasional production of special cuvées. The style is full and powerful, with Châteauneuf-du-Pape as the model, to judge from the recent employment of Rhône oenologue Philippe Cambier as consultant. "Over the past four or five years the style has changed to be more Languedocian—warmer," says Alain Asselin in the tasting room. The whites have gone in a different direction. "Originally they were like all the others of the Languedoc—heavy," Alain says. The objective of a more mineral style for whites has been pursued by a Burgundian style of vinification, but they still show southern aromatics.

◎ Saint Drézéry
◉ Languedoc
🍷 Languedoc St. Drézéry, Tête de Bélier
www.chateau-puech-haut.com
🚶 🏭 G N
115 ha; 1,000,000 bottles

Domaine de La Rectorie

Located in an old chapel in the center of Banyuls, this domain goes back to the start of the nineteenth century. Grapes were sent to the coop until 1984, when Marc and Thierry Parcé decided to produce their own wine. Today Thierry runs the domain together with his son Jean-Emmanuel, while Marc runs an associated negociant, Les Vins Parcé-Frères. Vineyards are scattered in small plots all around the steep hills of Banyuls. Plantings focus on Grenache. The sweet wines of Banyuls are only around 15% of production, with the main focus on dry red wines under the Collioure label. "It's often said that the wines of the south are too strong, too heavy, but we want to show they can have elegance," says Jean-Emmanuel. The red Collioure cuvées are L'Oriental (matured for a year in foudres, but with a modern impression), Côté Mer (matured in barriques and foudres, but fresh and approachable), and Montagne (the most complex assemblage and the most elegant impression, with the least Grenache, matured in barriques and foudres for 18 months). Under the Banyuls label there are three cuvées of fortified wines: Thérèse Reig comes from an early harvest, with sweet, ripe, black fruits; Léon Parcé is harvested later from select parcels and has an intriguing mix of savory and sweet influences; and the new cuvée, Pierre Rapidol, is matured for six years before release to show an intense, oxidized style. Under the IGP Côte Vermeille there is a dry Rancio wine, the Pedro Soler cuvée.

◎ Banyuls-sur-mer
◉ Banyuls
🍷 Collioure, Montagne
🍾 Banyuls, Cuvée Léon Parcé
www.la-rectorie.com
 🏭 G N
30 ha; 80,000 bottles

Languedoc

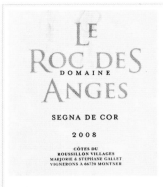

Domaine Le Roc des Anges

Coming from the northern Rhône after working at Yves Cuilleron and Pierre Gaillard, Marjorie Gallet cut short an apprenticeship at Domaine Gauby when the chance came to purchase her own vineyards in 2001. Roc des Anges started with 10 ha. Vineyards are around Montner, a village in the Agly valley in the far south of Roussillon. Originally located at Tautavel, the cave was moved to Montner in 2008, and her husband Stéphane came from nearby Mas Amiel to join Marjorie. (The name Montner derives from Monte Negro, reflecting the dark color of the schist; near Maury, this used to be part of the Vin de Pays Coteaux Fenouillèdes before it was abolished.) The focus is on traditional Mediterranean varieties (Carignan, Grenache, and Macabeo, supplemented by a little Syrah), planted on soils based on the dark schist. Plantings are about two thirds black to one third white. Wines are matured in a mixture of concrete and old wood. The whites are IGP Pyrénées Orientales, with Iglesia Vella coming from pure Grenache Gris, and the Vieilles Vignes coming from 70-year-old vines, mostly Grenache Gris. L'Oca Blanc comes from Macabeo. The reds are Côtes du Roussillon Villages. Segna de Cor comes from young vines; the Vieilles Vignes is a blend from old Grenache and Carignan (vines over seventy years old) plus some younger Syrah; and Vignes Centenaires Carignan cones from 3 ha of very old Carignan. There's also a rosé and a passerillé dessert wine.

Montner
Côtes du Roussillon Villages
IGP Catalanes, Vignes Centenaires Carignan
www.rocdesanges.com
28 ha; 60,000 bottles

Château Rouquette Sur Mer

Faithful to its name, Château Rouquette sur Mer is on the sea, overlooking Narbonne Plage. A family domain since the 1940s, this is a large estate; vineyards surround the property and run down towards the sea, but altogether around 50 separate parcels are scattered all over La Clape, making for significant heterogeneity in the soils. Château Rouquette is definitely on the oenotourism circuit, with a professional tasting room open almost every day, and a constant stream of visitors, many bringing their own containers to be filled with one of the three colors right out of the spigot in the tasting room. There are wines at all levels from Vin de France to IGP to AOP, with the range extending all the way from the bulk wines to special cuvées. It would be easy to be put off by the touristic atmosphere in the tasting room, but the special cuvées are in fact the antithesis of the bulk wine, with something of a concentration on Mourvèdre, which is a minor component in Cuvée Henry Lapierre (matured in new barriques), but is three quarters of Clos de la Tour. The top wine is Cuvée Absolute, where only 2,000 bottles are produced from a selection of the best lots, with the parcels and varieties changing each year, but Mourvèdre was always dominant in my tastings. The wide range makes it hard to define house style here, but at the level of cuvées, the animal quality of Mourvèdre stands out. A dessert wine, Vendanges d'Automne, is made from late harvest Bourboulenc in some years.

Narbonne
La Clape
La Clape, Clos de la Tour
www.chateaurouquette.com
55 ha; 200,000 bottles

Château La Tour Boisée

This old family domain dates from 1826. A person of strong opinions ("AOC says something—it is controlled—but AOP is nothing, it is a trick to talk about Protégé"), current proprietor Jean-Louis Poitou, who took over in 1982, tries to maintain tradition, growing 17 grape varieties in his many parcels. "We can take a Burgundian approach and identify a place for each variety," he says. He's been trying to reintroduce some of the old Gris varieties that used to be grown in the area. About 70% of production is red, with the rest divided between white and rosé; 60% of the wines are Minervois; the others, including monovarietals and some unusual combinations of varieties, are in one of the local IGPs. The difference is due more to the regulations of the AOPs and IGPs than quality. "Our IGP wines are worked in the same spirit as AOP with similar yields, 40 hl/ha for the IGP, and 30 hl/ha for the AOP." The whites of Minervois are blends of the usual southern varieties, but the IGP Coteaux de Peyriac is a Chardonnay. There's a range of red monovarietals in the IGP, but the most interesting wine here is the red Minervois Marie-Claude, a blend of Syrah, Grenache, and Carignan. A late harvest wine from Marsanne, Minervois Noble, has some botrytis as well as passerillage, and matures for ten years in old tonneaux. In addition to the wines that are labeled as Château Tour Boisée, there's also an entry level line (including red, white, and rosé) under the label of Domaine Tour Boisée.

 Laure-Minervois
 Minervois
Minervois, Marie-Claude
www.domainelatourboisee.com
85 ha; 300,000 bottles

Château de La Tuilerie

Located just outside Nîmes, which has changed its allegiance from Languedoc to Rhône, Château de la Tuilerie has a foot in both camps, as it produces both AOP Costières de Nîmes and IGP d'Oc. Purchased by Chantale Comte's father in 1955, it's been a leader in improving quality in Costières de Nîmes. "When I started thirty years ago, the region made vins de café, more like Beaujolais. I could see that if we waited with harvest—they were harvesting green berries—you could make great wine. There were no barriques in Costières, we were the first," Chantale says. In both AOP and IGP, Château de la Tuilerie has entry level wines (the Château wine for AOP and Celebration for IGP) and higher level wines (Eole for AOP and Alma Soror for IGP). The vineyards are in fact almost all in the Costières de Nîmes, except for some tiny plots in the IGP. They are on the oldest soils of the appellation, rather poor with lots of pebbles. The IGP line is extended with some varieties that aren't allowed in the AOP, but the focus in reds is on Syrah. "I have tried to make wines in the spirit of the Rhône, especially the Syrah of the northern Rhône," Chantale says. I find the whites—which are barrel-fermented in new oak—to be generally more interesting than the reds; the Eole white (a blend of many varieties) is rich but fresh, with a real density and texture supporting good development with age. The château also produces olive oil, and rums from a property on Martinique.

 Nîmes
Costières de Nîmes
Costières de Nîmes, Eole
www.chateautuilerie.com

66 ha; 400,000 bottles

Languedoc

Casalabriva

Corsica

Ministre Imperiale

Général de la Revolution

www.domaine-abbatucci.com

20 ha; 100,000 bottles

Domaine Comte Abbatucci

Abbatucci is a dominant name in Ajaccio (capital of Corsica), going back to Jean-Charles Abbatucci, who was one of Napoleon's generals. Today his descendent, also named Jean-Charles, runs Domaine Abbatucci. Although the domain is located within the Ajaccio AOP, all the wines are labeled as Vins de France. This started with the production of wines based on old varieties that are not allowed in the AOP. Collecting vines from abandoned vineyards around the island, Jean-Charles's father, Antoine Abbatucci, planted a set of these varieties between 1963 and 1976; today they form the basis for the top wines of the estate, the Cuvée Collection, which includes wines coming from around eighteen indigenous varieties. The wines are named after Abbatucci's military ancestors. Most are blends, but there are also two monovarietals. Made in small quantities (around 1,500 bottles of each per year), these are among the most expensive wines in the Vin de France category. Under the Faustine brand name, varieties are more conventional, with the red blended from Sciacarello and Nielluccio (Sangiovese), the rosé from 70% Sciacarello and 30% Barbarossa, and the white from Vermentino. The Faustine wines used to be AOP Ajaccio but are now also labeled as Vin de France. There is also an entry-level range of all three colors that is sold only locally. With a strong savory influence, the whites are far more interesting than you would expect from the warm climate of Corsica.

Patrimonio

Corsica

Patrimonio, Grotte di Sole

Patrimonio, Haut de Carco

14 ha; 50,000 bottles

Domaine Antoine Arena

This is one of the most important domains in the appellation system on Corsica. It was founded when Antoine Arena returned to Corsica from the French mainland and took over the family vineyards. He had been studying law at Nice University, but returned to Corsica as a reaction to the violent protests that occurred on the island in the mid 1970s. When he started in 1980, the family property consisted of only 3 ha, but he has expanded it considerably by planting new vineyards. The vineyards are on difficult sites, with steep slopes and high rock content (which had to be cleared before vines could be planted). The soils are calcareous with varying amounts of clay. Plantings are split more or less equally between red and white; the reds are Nielluccio (Sangiovese), the whites are Vermentino. There's also a hectare of the local variety Bianco Gentile, which Antoine has had a hand in reviving, and a little Muscat. The wines are monovarietal, and the various cuvées represent single vineyards, including Grotte di Sole (the original family vineyard with the oldest vines), Carco (and the more recently planted, very steep, Haut Carco), and Morta Maio (the name of the hamlet where the domain is located). Cuvée Zero is a Nielluccio with no sulfur (and sulfur is kept very low on the other cuvées). Whites are aged for up to eight months on the lees, reds for up to two years, with no use of oak. The whites have a delicious open quality; the reds offer a light Pinot-ish expression of Sangiovese.

Domaine de La Bégude

The Tari family's involvement in wine started in Algeria, moved to France where they owned Château Giscours in Margaux from 1954 to 1995, and began in Provence when they founded Domaine de La Bégude in 1996. Wine had been made here in the sixteenth century; the barrel room is an ancient chapel from the seventh century. Today's estate covers 500 ha at an elevation of 400 m, at the peak of the Bandol appellation, overlooking the Mediterranean. The exposure ensures high diurnal variation and brings freshness to the wines. Vineyards are divided into twenty separate parcels. Most of the production is red Bandol, but the parcel at the very top of the estate, La Brûlade, makes a special cuvée (only 1,500 to 2,000 bottles). The Bandol is 90% Mourvèdre; La Brûlade is 95% Mourvèdre. The use of new oak has backed off a bit, now usually a third to a quarter, with either barriques or demi-muids used depending on the year. There is also a rosé Bandol, or at least there was, until 2012 when it became a Vin de France. "For several years, obtaining the *agrément* for our rosé became a battle. It was difficult to maintain the anonymity of our rosé, identifiable by its color among the transparent wines (of the appellation)," says Guillaume Tari. With the right to use the AOP denied because the wine was too dark, the rosé became a Vin de France called l'Irréductible. Production of rosé is slightly greater than production of red wine. The domain also produces olive oil.

 Le Camp du Castellet

Bandol

www.domainedelabegude.fr

17 ha; 35,000 bottles

Château de Bellet

Perhaps because it really is a château and carries the name of the appellation, this is by far the best known producer in Bellet, and is regarded as a flag-bearer for the appellation. The residence of the Barons of Bellet since the sixteenth century, and long owned by the de Charnacé family, the property was sold in 2012 to a real estate conglomerate, Française REM, who also own 30 other domains in France. REM also simultaneously purchased the neighboring producer, Les Coteaux de Bellet. Ghislain de Charnacé remains the winemaker (with Les Coteaux de Bellet now incorporated into Château de Bellet). The merger greatly increased the size of the estate, making Château de Bellet the (relatively) giant producer of the appellation: its vineyards total about half of the appellation. Following the merger, there has been some reconstruction, with a new winery under way. Typically for the appellation, the reds are based on Folle Noire, the rosé on Braquet, and the whites on Rolle (Vermentino). The top wines are matured in barriques, the others in cuve. The Baron G label is used to indicate a higher level than the regular Château de Bellet, but now some new cuvées are being introduced (the La Chapelle white and Agnès red). It remains to be seen what the effect will be on quality. The attitude here is somewhat commercial as attempts to visit are rebuffed with a firm statement that, "The Château is private, but you can come to the tasting room and buy some wine if you want."

Nice

Bellet

Bellet, La Chapelle

www.chateaudebellet.com

20 ha; 35,000 bottles

Provence

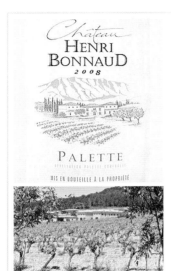

Château Henri Bonnaud

There are basically two games in town at Palette: Château Henri Bonnaud is the smaller, with around a quarter of the appellation, compared to Château Simone's three quarters. Just outside Aix-en-Provence, the estate is run today by Stéphane Spitzglous, who named it Château Henri Bonnaud in memory of his grandfather, who created the domain in the 1920s. Henri Bonnaud restructured the domain more or less in its present form in 1953; in 1992 a program of replanting was started; and in 1996 Stéphane took over. Born on the domaine, Stéphane grew up there with his grandfather, but describes himself as self-taught. With Mont Sainte Victoire looming over the vineyards, the soil is limestone and gravel. There are 14 ha in Palette and another 10 ha in Côtes de Provence. Red wine is three quarters of production. There are three main wines from Palette: a powerful red (Mourvèdre, Grenache, and old vines Carignan) that is not to be drunk too young, rosé (Mourvèdre, Grenache, Cinsault), and white (Ugni Blanc and Clairette). There's also a micro-cuvée, called Quintessence, in red and white. The red Palette is aged in a mixture of barriques and larger casks: the red Quintessence (the same varieties as Palette with some Syrah added) is matured exclusively in barriques. The wines from Côtes de Provence are labeled as Terre Promise: the red is Grenache, Carignan, and Syrah, the rosé is Grenache and Cinsault, and the white is Vermentino; they are matured in stainless steel.

 Le Tholonet
Palette
Palette
www.chateau-henri-bonnaud.fr

24 ha; 70,000 bottles

Clos Canarelli

Located at Figari at the southern tip of Corsica, Clos Canarelli has a terroir of poor red soil on a granite base, exposed to high winds from the Gulf of Figari that create dry, even harsh, conditions. The wines are made in a totally modern gravity-feed winery including the latest innovations. Like other top producers on Corsica, Canarelli is marked by a determination to preserve the old indigenous varieties. After abandoning economics to take over the family estate from his grandfather in 1993, Yves Canarelli left the cooperative and replanted some of the vineyards, replacing Cinsault, Alicante, and Grenache with indigenous varieties such as Carcajolu Neru and Biancu Gentile, which make monovarietal wines that must be relegated to the Vin de France label (but nonetheless are the domain's top wines). The red Tarra d'Orasi is a field blend of Sciacarello, Minustello, and Cinsault from a half hectare plot of pre-phylloxera vines (probably around 140 years old) that Yves discovered. There are also more conventional wines under the Corse-Figari AOP, including a Vermentino and a blend of Nielluccio (Sangiovese) with Syrah and Sciacarello, as well as rosé. Most of the wines are matured in old oak foudres, but two wines (made in very small quantities) have their élevage in amphorae. The reputation of the domain was established by the freshness of the whites, but I find the reds even more interesting for their variety of expression.

 Figari
Corsica
Figari, Amphora
28 ha; 100,000 bottles

Château d'Esclans

The slightly shabby appearance of Château d'Esclans, a nineteenth century villa built on a Tuscan model, belies its reputation. Sasha Lichine, formerly of Château Prieuré Lichine in Margaux, purchased the property, in the Fréjus area of Côtes de Provence, in 2006 with the avowed aim of "making the best rosé in the world." Patrick Léon came from Château Mouton Rothschild to become winemaker. Soils are varied; on the hillsides there's clay and chalk, while lower down are gravel and sand. Plantings include many old vines, with seven grape varieties: Cinsault, Grenache, Merlot, Mourvèdre, Vermentino, Syrah, and Tibouren, but the rosés are dominated by Grenache. Stainless steel is used for the entry level rosé, Whispering Angel, and there is some oak exposure for the estate wine, d'Esclans. The two top rosés, Les Clans and Garrus, are fermented and matured in a mixture of cuve and demi-muids. Made in an aperitif style, Whispering Angel stormed to immediate success on its introduction. The higher level wines have increasing savory character; unusually for rosé, Les Clans and Garrus have aging potential (indeed Garrus requires some age). Grapes for Whispering Angel come mostly from outside sources, but the other wines are sourced from estate grapes. Whether Garrus is the best rosé in the world is debatable, of course, but it is certainly the most expensive. Under the Déesse label there is also a red and a white. Sasha also makes wines under the Lichine label.

La Motte
Côtes de Provence
Côtes de Provence, Esclans
www.chateaudesclans.com

47 ha; 550,000 bottles

Domaine Gavoty

The label is somewhat gaudy, but Domaine Gavoty has a good reputation, especially for its rosés, which are three quarters of production. The domain was founded by Philémon Gavoty just after the Revolution, in 1806, and today is run by Roselyne Gavoty, the eighth generation. Its top cuvée, Clarendon (used for all three colors), takes its name from the pseudonym of an earlier proprietor, Bernard Gavoty, who was also the music critic of Le Figaro. The large estate (which includes 150 ha of woods as well as the vineyards) is located on the plateau of Cabasse, more or less in the center of Provence. Individual vineyards within the estate are surrounded by woods. Soils are a mixture of clay and limestone (the latter predominating on the slopes). The climate is more extreme than usual. The red cuvée Tradition is a blend of Syrah, Cabernet Sauvignon, and Grenache; Hautbois Solo is Syrah; and Clarendon (not made every year) is Syrah and Cabernet Sauvignon. The whites are 100% Rolle (Vermentino), aiming at a mineral style. But the main interest is with the rosés: "Our most fragile child is the subject of mockery and requires special attention to be accepted, and even admired." Cuvée Tradition is a blend of Cinsault, Syrah, and Rolle, Melopée is a blend of Syrah and Cabernet Sauvignon, while Clarendon is a warmer blend of Grenache and Cinsault. In addition, there are IGP du Var wines under the Le Cigale label.

Cabasse
Côtes de Provence
Côtes de Provence, Cuvée Clarendon
www.gavoty.com

45 ha; 270,000 bottles

Provence

La Cadière d'Azur

Bandol

Bandol

www.gros-nore.com

16 ha; 70,000 bottles

Domaine du Gros'noré

Before Alain Pascal started Domaine du Gros'noré in 1997, he and his father used to sell their grapes. The domain was constructed from a mix of existing vineyards and new plantings on additional land. Average vine age is now 40 years. Soils are clay and limestone. Hands-on has another meaning here: Alain not only built the winery himself, but continues to handle all the grapes as the harvest comes in. A small underground cave is packed with tanks and foudres, compact but workmanlike. "It's necessary to stay on the human scale," he says, explaining why he wants the domain to remain around its present size. Most of the vineyards are in the vicinity of the winery, and are farmed organically. "I have always worked like this," Alain says, "but I don't need certification." Production is mostly red, with about 75% Mourvèdre in the estate cuvée, which is an assemblage from all the vineyards. There's a small production of a special cuvée, Antoinette, which fills a single foudre; this is 95% Mourvèdre from a single hilltop vineyard. Vinification is traditional, with reds matured in foudre for the required 18 months. However, the wines have become softer since the debut of the domain, and the house style of current vintages shows a supple, furry impression on the finish. Does that change anything? "No, if it's good when young, it will be good when old," is Alain's view. The rosé comes from younger vines, and has increased in proportion recently as the result of some replanting.

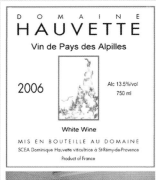

Saint Rémy de Provence

Côtes de Provence

Les Baux-de-Provence, Cornaline

16 ha; 35,000 bottles

Domaine Hauvette

Dominique Hauvette extended a vacation in Provence in 1980 into the purchase of a 2.5 ha vineyard in 1988. She has slowly expanded the domain, learning oenology along the way, including a degree in Montpellier. Just outside St. Rémy de Provence, the winery is a workmanlike warehouse building. Vineyards are in many separate parcels. Committed to biodynamic viticulture and natural vinification, the domain has an impressive array of egg-shaped fermenters. The two whites are IGP des Alpilles; Jaspe is 100% Roussanne; and Dolia is a blend of Marsanne, Roussanne, and Clairette from older vines. They show a full flavored, viscous style, with a savory flavor spectrum reminiscent of Châteauneuf-du-Pape. The rosé follows a similar style, tasty on the palate if not quite savory. "Our rosé is original, it's a white wine made from red grapes, a Blanc de Noirs," says Dominique. The rosé and two reds are AOP Baux de Provence. Cornaline is a blend of Grenache, Syrah, and Cabernet Sauvignon; Améthyste comes from old vines of Cinsault, Carignan, and Grenache. There are strong views about avoiding over-powerful wines, so there is a careful watch on grape maturity in the vineyard, followed by efforts to avoid excess extraction. "We try to control extraction with the reds, we use only punch-down—we tried pumping-over but there was too much extraction." The house style for reds is flavorful in the direction of savory, with alcohol levels that are relatively moderate for the region.

Domaine de L'Hermitage

This domain encapsulates in miniature the revival of Bandol. When Gérard Duffort purchased the property in 1974, it was derelict, without even running water, and the vineyards were in ruins. The name comes from the Chapelle de Beausset-Vieux, just above the domain. The estate has an elevation around 300 m, looking out southwest over the appellation. Vineyards were replanted on terraces with dry stone walls (the traditional restanques). Soils vary from calcareous clay with high mineral content just under the ridge at Le Beausset to finer clay nearer Le Castellet. The first white and rosé were produced in 1978, followed four years later by the red. An additional plot of old vines was purchased in 1982. In spite of its recent origins, the approach of the domain is quite traditional, focusing on single cuvées in each color. The red is softened by including around 20% Grenache with the Mourvèdre. The rosé and white come from the usual blends. Harvest is as late as possible to obtain maximum ripeness, in September for the Grenache but not until early October for the Mourvèdre. Vinification is traditional, with extended cuvaison, and the red spends eighteen months in tonneaux. The Dufforts also own Château La Moutète, in Côtes de Provence (purchased in 1988, also requiring renovation, and now producing red and rosé), and in addition there is an IGP from the Var, Les Trois Chênes. Olivier Duffort took over from his father in 2003.

 Bandol
 Bandol
www.domainesduffort.com

32 ha; 120,000 bottles

Château Sainte Marguerite

Just inland from the coastal town of La Londe, this domain was created in 1929 and purchased by the Fayard family in 1977. The first owner had unusually sophisticated tastes, which is how Grenache and Cabernet Sauvignon came to be planted. Sainte Marguerite became one of the cru classés in 1955. 50 ha of vineyards are in the 120 ha estate surrounding the winery, which is a workmanlike warehouse-like facility; there are more vineyards elsewhere in La Londe. The soils are a fairly homogeneous schist and clay. "This gives finesse and minerality," says Jean-Pierre Fayard. Production is 70% rosé with the rest split between red and white. There are three lines: the entry level Grande Réserve (red, rosé, and white); the "M" de Sainte Marguerite (the flagship rosé); and the premium Symphonie (red, rosé, and white). The rosés are based on Grenache, with some Cinsault and Syrah; the reds are based on Syrah and Cabernet Sauvignon; and the whites are Rolle (Vermentino). Some barriques are used for reds and whites but not for rosé. "All the rosés are matured in cuve, we experimented with barriques but I'm not persuaded; it changes the character of the wine too much," Jean-Pierre says. Rosés and whites are pressed directly; there is no malolactic fermentation, and battonage is used to increase roundness. The house style is light and slightly aromatic; these are wines to be enjoyed in their youth.

La Londe-Les-Maures
Côtes de Provence
"M" de Marguerite
www.chateausaintemarguerite.com
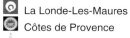
85 ha; 600,000 bottles

Provence

🌍 Saint Rémy de Provence
⚫ Les Baux-de-Provence
🍷 Vin de France, Clos Milan
🍷 Vin de France, La Carrée
www.domaine-milan.com
🚶 🍷 G 🐝
15 ha; 60,000 bottles

Domaine Henri Milan

A tasting at Henri Milan is a convivial experience. Everyone working at the winery joins in to give an opinion. Robert Milan founded the domain in 1956, and Henri took over in 1986. Henri's strong opinions lead to wines of distinctive character. They are all now labeled as Vins de France as Henri does not want to be constrained by AOP rules. "I want to be free, I would like to label them as Vin de France Libre," he says. There is a strong emphasis on natural wine, especially on reducing sulfur. Two whites, Papillon and Grand Blanc, come from assemblage of many varieties, planted together and cofermented, the difference being that Papillon has no added sulfur. The house style for whites is towards savory—that combination of herbs and spices with a sense of the garrigue is hard to pin down. The peak of the whites is the 100% Roussanne La Carrée, a penetrating example of varietal typicity. The reds are different blends, most based on Grenache and Syrah, sometimes with other varieties. Le Papillon red, like the white, is bottled without sulfur. Le Vallon is a single vineyard wine from a small parcel near La Carrée. The most expressive of vintage is Clos Milan, a Grenache-Syrah blend, which in hot years shows southern generosity but in cool years a more northern freshness. Le Jardin is the most unusual, a 100% Merlot coming from terroir of blue clay that achieves real elegance. The decision to leave the appellation system to make more interesting wine has paid off handsomely.

🌍 La Londe-Les-Maures
⚫ Côtes de Provence
🍷 Côtes de Provence, Clos Mireille Coeur de Grain
🍷 Côtes de Provence, Clos Mireille Blanc de Blancs
www.domaines-ott.com
🚶 🍷 G 🍇
182 ha; 850,000 bottles

Domaines Ott

Started by Marcel Ott at the beginning of the twentieth century, Domaines Ott remained family owned until it was sold to Champagne Roederer in 2004, but Jean-François Ott still manages the group of three estates. Clos Mireille (at La Londe-Les-Maures, near the sea) has 50 ha of vines, with a mixture of schist and clay soils. Château De Selle is an inland estate near Draguignon, with 64 ha of vines on chalky hillsides, at an elevation around 300 m. Château Romassan is located in the center of the Bandol appellation, and has 60 ha. Each property has its own style, but the name of Domaines Ott is better known than any of the individual estates, and was identified with a flagship rosé well before such quality was common in Provence. All three properties produce rosé: they are quite distinct, with Château de Selle the softest, Clos Mireille showing a savory touch, and Château Romassan the faint austerity of Bandol. People who recognize Domaines Ott by the unusually shaped bottle introduced by Marcel Ott in the 1930s, which is used by all three estates, are sometimes confused by the differences between the rosés as they do not realize they are tasting wines from different properties. Clos Mireille also produces a white wine, while Château de Selle and Château Romassan also produce red wines. Based on Sémillon, the Clos Mireille Blanc de Blancs has more character than most white Provence. There's also a less expensive line, called Domaines Ott Selection.

Château de Pibarnon

"We have 50 ha now, but there were only 3.5 ha when my parents bought the property in 1977," says Eric de St. Victor. "They were looking for an estate, and couldn't afford Burgundy, but they tried the wines of the area and liked them." Today there are many small plots, scattered around the hills at elevations around 300 m where the soil has a lot of active limestone. The Château itself is high up a winding precipitous road, and you can see across to Bandol and the Mediterranean from the vineyards above. The château wine is 90-95% Mourvèdre, close to the limit for the appellation. It has become increasingly refined since 2000. "The last of the old fashioned style of Pibarnon was 1998; since then there has been less extraction and power, we are not looking for muscular or international wines." Quality was further improved by the introduction in 2003 of the second wine, Restanques de Pibarnon, a blend of Mourvèdre with 30% Grenache, coming from a mixture of specific plots and declassified lots; its proportion increased in 2010. Pibarnon's reputation rests on the reds, but the rosé and white are also good representations of modern Bandol. The style of the Château Pibarnon red is extremely refined, with precise fruits and taut, fine-grained tannins. It tends to close down about a year after bottling, and then opens up again after another five years. It develops slowly: the 2001 was showing the first faint signs of development in 2013.

La Cadière d'Azur

Bandol

Bandol, Château de Pibarnon

www.pibarnon.com

48 ha; 180,000 bottles

Domaine Richeaume

Domaine Richeaume nestles under the ridge of the long rocky escarpment of La Croix de Provence, with vineyards extending towards the mountains on red, stony soil. Sylvain Hoesch has taken over from his father, Henning Hoesch, who constructed the modern winery in the early 1970s, in concrete built into the hillside on the site of a former Roman villa. Winemaking is completely modern, producing fresh whites and elegant reds. Some changes occur with the passage between generations, for example, there is ongoing discussion as to whether or not to perform malolactic fermentation for the whites. Most production is red, with 7% white, and 2-7% rosé depending on the vintage. The Blanc de Blancs is made from Vermentino and Clairette; there's also a Viognier and a Sauvignon. There are various blends of Cabernet Sauvignon, Grenache, and Syrah, and some monovarietals. The top wine, Columelle, is a Cabernet Sauvignon-Syrah blend, with a little Merlot; it's at its best after about five years. The style has become more Mediterranean. "For a long time they worked the vines around here as though they were Bordeaux, but that was an error, these are not the same cépages and it is not the same climate," explains Sylvain. The wines have made a complete transition of label, having started as Côtes de Provence, then moving to Vin de Pays Bouches du Rhône, and ultimately to Vin de France, as AOP and IGP requirements became too restrictive.

Puyloubier

Côtes de Provence

Vin de France, Columelle

www.domaine-richeaume.com

30 ha; 80,000 bottles

Provence

Domaine Saint André de Figuières

This domain is a newcomer, created by Alain Combard after he left Domaine Laroche in Chablis in 1991 after spending 22 years there. Returning to his origins in Provence, and starting with 16 ha at La Londe les-Maures, he built the domain up to its present size. A plot of an additional 25 ha adjacent to the original domain was purchased in 2003; and a new winery was constructed in 2009. Even before Alain acquired it, the original estate was organic (dating from 1979), and the entire domain remains organic today. There are ten different grape varieties, and average vine age is around 35 years. In typical Provençal style, the vineyards are surrounded by pine and oak trees; thin soils lie on top of the typical schist of La Londe. Coming from Chablis, Alain's first reputation was made with a white, a barrel-fermented Vermentino. This was followed by red and rosé, and a sparkling rosé (l'Atmosphère) made by Méthode Champenoise from Cinsault and Grenache. There are three lines of dry wines: Les Confidentielles (conventional blends of southern varieties), Vieilles Vignes (Mourvèdre for the red and rosé, Vermentino for the white), and Signature, a negociant line (each cuvée carries the name of one of Alain's children). The avowed objective of the domain is to make a rosé whose quality matches the whites and the reds. All the wines are labeled as Côtes de Provence La Londe, except for an IGP intended for easy drinking.

La Londe-Les-Maures
Côtes de Provence
www.figuiere-provence.com
65 ha; 850,000 bottles

Château Sainte Roseline

Surrounded by woods, Sainte Roseline is an old domain, created by the Bishop of Fréjus in the fifteenth century. A program of cultural attractions and other events has made this a center of oenotourism, with a twelfth century abbey on the property, and an impressive tasting room worthy of Napa Valley. Unusually for Provence, rosé is only just over half of production; there is 30% red and 15% white. The rosé comes from Grenache, Cinsault, Tibouren, and Mourvèdre. The red comes from Syrah, Cabernet Sauvignon, and Carignan. "There is no Grenache in the red because we are looking for more structure," says proprietor Aurélie Bertin Teillaud. All wines are vinified and aged in oak. The house style for whites and reds is quite firm, overlaid by evident new oak. The rosé is a rare example that seems like a wine first and a rosé second, and the top rosé cuvée is refined: it's a wine to accompany food more than to be enjoyed as an aperitif. When the Teillauds bought Château Sainte Roseline twenty years ago, there was only one rosé cuvée (now known as the Lampe de Méduse, presented in a special bottle), but they introduced Cuvée Prieure in 1996, and then the premium La Chapelle line in 2007. The rosé and white La Chapelle are produced every vintage, but the red is produced only in top vintages. The Teillauds also own Château des Demoiselles, and a negociant business producing Perle de Roseline and Harmonie de Roseline (a blend of estate and purchased grapes).

Les Arcs-sur-Argens
Côtes de Provence
Côtes de Provence, Cuvée Prieure
www.sainte-roseline.com
100 ha; 4,500,000 bottles

Clos Saint-Vincent

This small domain is one of the eight producers in the appellation of Bellet. It's more or less average size for the appellation—there isn't room for anything substantial on the hillsides outside Nice. It was purchased by the Sicardi and Sergi families in 1993 (Joseph Sergi is the current winemaker), who then set about renovating the estate. Vineyards were expanded, viticulture became biodynamic, and grape varieties focused on the typical choices of Vermentino (called Rolle here), Braquet, and Folle Noire. The rosé comes from the Braquet, while the reds come mostly from the Folle Noire, and correspondingly have a tendency to give a somewhat rustic impression. Coming from Vermentino, the two whites, Le Clos and Vino di Gio (the latter produced in very small quantities), are the most interesting wines here, achieving a good deal more expression and concentration than is usually found with this variety. With good acidity supporting savory impressions on the palate, Le Clos does not at all resemble Vermentino as produced in Italy. For vinification, grapes are sorted, and there is skin contact for a period, followed by fermentation in barrique. Le Clos spends a year in barrique with battonage before it is bottled without filtration. Clos Saint-Vincent is also the last producer in Bellet still practicing distillation to produce marc. The wines are mostly sold in the local area, although it is easier said than done to arrange to visit.

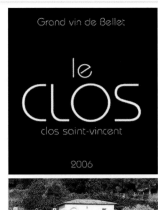

Bellet

Bellet, Le Clos

www.clos-st-vincent.fr

10 ha; 20,000 bottles

Château Simone

Château Simone is well known for the difficulty of obtaining an appointment to visit; perhaps this is because the Rougiers, who have been making wine here for a couple of centuries (since 1830), have close to a monopoly of the Palette AOP, accounting for 80% of its production. Located close to Aix-en-Provence, vineyards are on calcareous soil, at elevations around 200 m, rather unusually facing north. This is responsible for a restraint in the wines that distinguishes them from others of the region. Most of the vines are more than 50 years old. Harvesting is manual, fermentation takes place with indigenous yeasts, and the wine is matured first in small (20-30 hl) foudres of oak for 8 months (whites) or 18 months (reds) and then in barriques of various ages for a year before bottling. The white is based on 80% Clairette, with 10% Grenache Blanc, 6% Ugni Blanc, and some other varieties. The black cépages are 45% Grenache, 30% Mourvèdre, 5% Cinsault; the remaining 20% is a mix of varieties including Syrah, Castets, Manosquins, and Carignan. Priced only slightly below the red and white, a rosé is made from the same varietal blend as the red wine; it is matured like the reds in oak. The wines are widely distributed all over Provence and have the reputation of being among the best in the local AOP system. A second wine has now been introduced for white and rosé under the label of Les Grands Carmes de Simone.

Meyreuil

Palette

Palette

www.chateau-simone.fr

19 ha; 100,000 bottles

Provence

Domaine Tempier

Perhaps the most famous domain in Bandol, this estate originated at the end of the eighteenth century. The house dates from 1834, and just behind is the small, somewhat cramped, working winery. In the 1940s, Lucien Peyraud (who married a Tempier daughter in the third generation) was instrumental in reviving Mourvèdre in Bandol. Domaine Tempier's original wine was the Cuvée Classique; the red is three quarters Mourvèdre, the rosé is half Mourvèdre, and the white (made in tiny amounts) is based on Clairette. The recent fame of the domain comes from the single vineyard bottlings, introduced in 1969. Migoua is a 6.5 ha site in Le Beausset-Vieux, planted mainly with Mourvèdre, but also with some Cinsault and Grenache. La Tourtine is a 7 ha site in Le Castellet, with more Mourvèdre. The cuvée Tourtine comes from the south-facing slopes; cuvée Cabassaou, which is 95% Mourvèdre, comes from a parcel at the base of the slope, which is a sheltered warm spot. Tasting through the single vineyard wines, the measure is increasing precision and refinement rather than power. The tannins become finer grained and the wines show more elegant structure from Migoua (with the broadest spectrum) to Tourtine and Cabassaou (close to one another, but with Cabassaou a bit more varied in flavor). Fine but dense when young, flavor variety really begins to develop after about ten years (perhaps nearer twenty for Tourtine); this is Mourvèdre at the peak of its expression.

Le Plan du Castellet
Bandol
Bandol, Migoua
www.domainetempier.com
40 ha; 170,000 bottles

Domaine de Trévallon

The name of Domaine de Trévallon reflects its construction from three valleys, where separate vineyards were planted after the land was cleared in 1973 by dynamiting limestone rocks in the hills surrounding the domain. Located near Saint Rémy de Provence, the vineyards are on soils that remain rather stony with a mixture of sand and gravel. Individual parcels are surrounded by woods. There are 2 ha for the white wine, a blend of 45% Roussanne, 45% Marsanne and 10% Chardonnay; it is barrel-fermented and aged in oak for one year. The major plantings are nine plots of Syrah and nine of Cabernet on essentially similar terroirs. This gives an unusual assemblage for a red wine in France of 50% Cabernet Sauvignon and 50% Syrah; whole bunches of grapes are fermented in stainless steel and aged in oak, mostly in foudres with a small proportion of barriques, for two years before assemblage. The style is somewhere between Bordeaux and Hermitage; although Syrah is usually more obvious than Cabernet, this varies with the year. The vineyards are located within the AOPs of Coteaux d'Aix and Les Baux de Provence, but the wines use proportions of cépages that are not permitted within the AOP rules, so they are bottled as IGP des Bouches du Rhône. (For the whites, Marsanne is not permitted in the AOP; for the reds, Coteaux d'Aix permits up to 30% Cabernet Sauvignon and Les Baux de Provence permits up to 20%.) Reception can be on the chilly side if you visit the domain.

Saint Étienne du Grès
IGP des Bouches-du-Rhône
www.trevallon.com
17 ha; 50,000 bottles

Domaine de Triennes

This large estate on a south-facing hillside just south of Aix-en-Provence started as a collaboration in 1989 between two winemakers from Burgundy, Jacques Seysses from Domaine Dujac and Aubert de Villaine from Domaine de la Romanée Conti. It is at relatively high elevation (above 400 m) with soils of clay and limestone; its location between two mountain ranges keeps the nights relatively cool, so there is more diurnal variation than usual for the region. (The domain was previously named Domaine du Logis-de-Nans; it was in disarray when purchased, and was renamed Triennes after the Roman festival in honor of Bacchus.) Many of the existing vines were grafted over to new varieties. The emphasis is a little different from the usual focus in Provence on rosé, as there are five wines: two reds, a rosé, and two whites. Les Auréliens is the label for the basic wines of the domain, a blend of Cabernet Sauvignon and Syrah for the red, and mostly Chardonnay with some Vermentino and Viognier for the white. The Saint Auguste red is a blend of selections of the best lots of Syrah, Cabernet Sauvignon and Merlot. (This was originally called the Aurélien Reserve, but the name had to be changed because Reserve was not allowed in Vin de Pays.) The Sainte Fleur white is a Viognier. The rosé is based on Cinsault (around 70%), blended with some Grenache, Syrah, and Merlot. As the varieties are not typical for the Provence AOP, the wines are labeled as IGP du Var or Méditerranée.

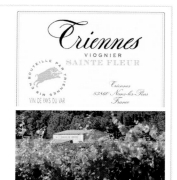

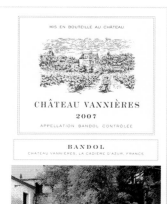

Nans les Pins
IGP de Var
www.triennes.com

38 ha; 250,000 bottles

Château Vannières

"I've always wanted to make just one wine—Château Vannières. I don't like the idea of multiple cuvées; there is one cuvée for each color," says Eric Boissieux. The family background is wine, and Bandol has been the focus since Eric's grandfather bought the domain in 1956. This is a large estate, with the vineyards in a single holding around the winery. Production is split between red and rosé, with only a small amount of white. Eric is a great believer in Mourvèdre and the unique character it brings to Bandol. The red has 95% Mourvèdre, the maximum allowed by the appellation: it would be 100% Mourvèdre if the rules permitted. The rosé is made by a mixture of saignée from Mourvèdre (to increase concentration of the red) and direct pressing of Cinsault and Grenache. Everything is destemmed, and there is long cuvaison for the reds, with a month's maceration followed by élevage for up to two and a half years in a mixture of foudres and barriques; rosé is matured solely in cuves of stainless steel or concrete. Consistency between vintages is noticeable here, and the bottled wines age slowly: comparison of the 2009 and 2003 reds, for example, shows a glacial pace of development, with the same very fine-grained structure supporting dense black fruits, and refreshing uplift on the palate. House style brings out a taut refined character, a bit of a contrast with Eric's view that, "There are no modernists in Bandol, it's stayed in the classic style."

La Cadière d'Azur
Bandol
Bandol
www.vannieres.com

33 ha; 160,000 bottles

Provence

Vineyard Visits

The profiles indicate which producers accept visits, but this list suggests those who may provide a particularly good starting point for each region. There's a bias towards larger producers as they more often have dedicated tasting rooms, while at the smallest you may be tasting in the cellars and spitting on the floor, but all are especially welcoming and helpful. Of course, all make lovely wines. It always helps to call ahead to make an appointment; you may get a tour of the facilities as well as a tasting.

Alsace	Maison Hugel, Domaine René Muré, Maison Trimbach, Domaine Paul Blanck
Champagne	Larmandier-Bernier, Nicolas Feuillatte, Ruinart, Taittinger
Loire: Muscadet	Domaine de L'Ecu, Domaine Pierre Luneau-Papin
Loire: Anjou	Domaine Baumard, Domaine du Closel, Domaine Richou
Loire: Touraine	Domaine de La Charmoise, Maison Couly-Dutheil, Domaine François Pinon, Catherine et Pierre Breton
Loire: Sancerre	Domaine Henri Bourgeois, Domaine Alphonse Mellot, Vignobles Joseph Mellot, Domaine Vacheron
Burgundy: Chablis	Jean-Paul et Benoit Droin, Domaine William Fèvre, Domaine Laroche, Domaine Louis Michel
Burgundy: Côte de Nuits	Domaine Arnoux-Lachaux, Domaine Fourrier, Domaine Mugnier
Burgundy: Côte de Beaune	Bouchard Père, Marc Colin, Joseph Drouhin, Louis Jadot, Olivier Leflaive
Burgundy: Chalon-naise	Château de Chamirey, Domaine Dureuil-Janthial, Domaine Michel Juillot
Mâcon	Château de Beauregard, Château-Fuissé, Domaine La Soufrandière
Beaujolais	Louis et Claude Desvignes, Georges Duboeuf, Coudert Clos de La Roilette
Jura-Savoie	André et Mireille Tissot, Domaine Louis Magnin
Bordeaux: Left Bank	Smith Haut Lafitte, Pichon Lalande, Rauzan-Gassies
Bordeaux: Right Bank	Château Teyssier (see Le Dôme), Pavie Macquin
Southwest	Domaine L'Ancienne Cure, Château du Cèdre, Château Tirecul La Gravière, Clos Triguedina, Vignoble des Verdots
Northern Rhône	Domaine Belle, Jean-Luc Colombo, Yves Cuilleron, Pierre Gaillard, Maison Guigal, Domaine Jaboulet
Southern Rhône	Domaine Paul Autard, Château de Beaucastel, Château La Nerthe, Domaine du Vieux Télégraphe, Domaine Santa-Duc, Château de La Tuilerie
Languedoc	Jean-Michel Alquier, Mas de Daumas Gassac, Château de La Liquière, Château La Tour Boisée
Provence	Domaine Henri Milan, Domaines Ott, Château de Pibarnon, Domaine Richeaume, Château Sainte Roseline

Bibliography

Stephen Brook, *Bordeaux. People, Power and Politics* (Mitchell Beazley, London, 2001)

Stephen Brook, *The Complete Bordeaux, 2nd edition* (Mitchell Beazley, London, 2012).

Clive Coates, *An Encyclopedia of the Wines and Domaines of France* (University of California Press, Berkeley, 2000).

Clive Coates, *The Wines of Burgundy* (University of California Press, Berkeley, 2008).

Charles Cocks & Edouard Féret, *Bordeaux et ses vins classés par ordre de mérite, 19th edition* (Editions Féret, Bordeaux, 2014).

Roger Dion, *Histoire de la Vigne et du Vin en France. Des Origines aux XIX Siècle, 1st edition* (CNRS Editions, reprinted 2010).

Hubrecht Duijker, *The Bordeaux Atlas and Encyclopedia of Châteaux* (Ebury Press, London, 1997)

Benoît France, *Grand Atlas des Vignobles de France* (Solar, 2002).

Jacqueline Friedrich, *A Wine and Food Guide to the Loire* (Henry Holt & Co, New York, 1996).

Jacqueline Friedrich, *Earthly Delights from the Garden of France* (Friedrich, Paris, 2013).

Pierre Galet, *Cépages et Vignobles de France : Tome 3, Les Vignobles de France, parts I and II, 2nd edition* (Tec & Doc Lavoisier, 2005).

Rosemary George, *The Wines of the South of France. From Banyuls to Bellet* (Faber & Faber, London, 2001)

Harry Karis, *The Châteauneuf-du-Pape Wine Book* (Kavino, Roermond, Netherlands, 2009).

Marcel Lachiver, *Vins, Vignes et Vignerons. Histoire de Vignoble Français* (Fayard, Paris, 1988).

Benjamin Lewin, *Claret & Cabs: the Story of Cabernet Sauvignon* (Vendange, 2013).

Benjamin Lewin, *In Search of Pinot Noir* (Vendange, 2011).

Benjamin Lewin, *What Price Bordeaux?* (Vendange, 2009).

Benjamin Lewin, *Wine Myths and Reality* (Vendange, 2010).

John Livingstone-Learmonth et al., *Gigondas: Its Wines, Its Land, Its People* (Editions Bottin Gourmand, Paris, 2012).

John Livingstone-Learmonth, *The Wines of the Rhône*, 3rd edition (Faber & Faber, London, 1992).

John Livingstone-Learmonth, *The Wines of the Northern Rhône* (University of California Press, Berkeley, 2005).

Jasper Morris, *Inside Burgundy* (Berry Bros, London, 2010).

Remington Norman, *Grand Crus* (Kyle Cathie, London, 2010).

Remington Norman, *Rhône Renaissance* (Wine Appreciation Guild, San Francisco, 1996).

Edmund Penning-Rowsell, *The Wines of Bordeaux, 6th edition* (Penguin Books, London, 1989).

David Peppercorn, *Bordeaux, 3rd edition* (Mitchell Beazley, 2003).

Jancis Robinson, Julia Harding and José Vouillamoz, *Wine Grapes* (Penguin, London, 2012).

Michel Smith, *Les Grands Crus du Languedoc et du Roussillon* (Editions Renault, Cap d'Agde, 2006).

Tom Stevenson, *Christie's World Encyclopedia of Champagne & Sparkling Wine* (Sterling Epicure, London, 2014).

Tom Stevenson, *The Wines of Alsace* (Faber & Faber, London, 1993).

Paul Strang, *South-West France. The Wines and Winemakers* (University of California Press, Berkeley, 2009).

Paul Strang, *Languedoc-Roussillon: The Wines and Winemakers* (Mitchell Beazley, London, 2002).

Preface

[1] Le Monde, May 28, 2004, p. 15.

Chapter 1: France

[1] Attributed by Jonathan Fenby, *On the Brink* (New York: Arcade Publishing, 1999) to a recollection by U.S. Secretary of State Madeleine Albright of a French response to a proposal for European cooperation.

[2] Average production in cases from 2007-2011:

Southwest	41 million (9%)
Bordeaux	66 million (15%)
Loire	34 million (8%)
Alsace	13 million (3%)
Champagne	32 million (7%)
Burgundy	18 million (4%)
Beaujolais	10 million (2%)
Rhône	41 million (10%)
Provence	23 million (5%)
Languedoc	152 million (35%)

Source: FranceAgriMer

[3] Prices calculated from net receipts in the region, that is, representing return to producers, so significantly less than retail price per bottle.

[4] The price of wines in France in 1795:

Bordeaux-Lafite 29
Clos Vougeot 29
Jurançon 26
Cahors 24
Champagne 21
Bordeaux Blanc 18
Burgundy 16 (livres/bottle)

Prices from a sale of assets seized in the French Revolution. The most expensive wines were sweet foreign wines (from Tokaji, Cyprus, Malaga, and Jerez) at a range of 37-75 livres. Lafite and Vougeot were at the top of the French list (Claire Desbois-Thibault et al., *Le Champagne. Une histoire franco-allemande*, PUPS, Paris, 2011, p. 151).

[5] Kermit Lynch, *Adventures on the Wine Route* (Noonday Press, New York, 1988), p. 179.

[6] It's a basic principle of the AOC system that wine from higher-level appellations can always be declassified to lower level appellations. So if a producer decides that wine produced from a district vineyard isn't really good enough (or if in the past the authorities decided he had produced too much wine), the wine can be sold instead under the regional appellation.

[7] Some large producers have wines in all categories, but most producers focus on one category According to the agricultural census of 2000, 25% of the producers of AOC wines also produced a Vin de Pays wine (Jean Strohl et al., January 2005, Agreste #157: La Statistique Agricole, Service Central des Enquêtes et Études Statistiques, Paris).

[8] 94% of IGP d'Oc production is varietal-labeled (Vins du Pays d'Oc, 2012).

[9] Varietal-labeled IGP can be made from one or two varieties; when a single variety is named, it must comprise 100% of the content (although general E.U. law requires only 85%).

[10] France produces more than 450 million cases of wine each year (with another 70 million produced for distillation into brandy). 315 million cases (70%) are red or rosé (the official figures do not distinguish between them), 90 million (21%) are white, and 40 million (9%) are sparkling (of which 75% is Champagne). Some 250 million cases (54%) are AOC, 164 million cases (35%) are IGP, and 53 million cases (11%) are Vin de France (FranceAgriMer).

[11] Forum Vinexpo, Académie Amorim, 2005.

[12] Data from Charles Cocks, *Bordeaux,* and FranceAgriMer. The proportion of vineyards making quality wine was estimated to be less than 10% before 1939 (Gilles Laferté, *La Bourgogne et ses vins: image d'origine contrôlée,* Belin, Paris, 2006, p. 18.).

[13] Production figures include wine for distillation into Cognac, which averages 16% of total. The average proportion of AOP wine over the past 10 years increases from 46% to 55% if Cognac is excluded. Data from FranceAgriMer.

[14] The nominally allowed yield is the *rendement de basse*. There is a provision for allowing it to be increased to recognize special conditions in any year, for example, when there has been a larger crop of high quality. However, an increase of up to 20% has generally been allowed every year, irrespective of conditions (Lewin, *Wine, Myths, and Reality*, p. 373).

[15] The original system for approval for the AOC was that the wine would be submitted to a panel of producers from the appellation. This has been replaced for the AOP by consideration by a panel of outside "experts," supposedly more objective. The usual criticism is that no one knows what the standard is supposed to be and it is erratic.

[16] FranceAgrimer 2009.

[17] http://www.causse-marines.com/#box3;

accessed July 2013.

[18] Occasionally wines are excluded for unusual reasons, the most famous case being the use of plastic sheeting to protect vines against rain, which led to separate bottling of wine from those vines as the cuvées Defi de Fontenil (2000, 2001 et 2004, at Château Fontenil) and Interdit de Valandraud (2000, at Château Valandraud).

[19] The trend is growing nationally. In 2000, 10% of wines that could have been AOC were labeled as Vin de Pays, largely in the various appellations of the south (Jean Strohl et al., January 2005, Agreste #157).

[20] Regulations usually call for pesticide treatment to stop a significant period before harvest, but Pascal Chatonnet of the Excell laboratory in Bordeaux reported at a conference in February 2013 that only 10% of 300 wines analyzed from Bordeaux and the Rhône were without detectable levels of pesticides.

[21] Numbers include only certified vineyards and those converting to certification, and there are others that follow organic practices without being certified. As of 2012, there were 40,500 ha certified as organic, with another 24,000 at various stages of conversion. This corresponds to 4,927 organic producers (Agence Bio.)

[22] As barrel samples in January 2013.

[23] I have heard this story several times in Bordeaux. As I have been unable to confirm it directly, it may well be apocryphal, but it does capture the spirit of the era.

[24] However, green pruning is no longer used at Pétrus, "because we are not looking for concentration of sugar now, we are looking for concentration of flavor," says Elisabeth Jaubert.

[25] FranceAgriMer, 2012.

[26] Named for Jean-Antoine Chaptal, a chemist who was Minister of the Interior under Napoleon, and proposed the addition of sugar to increase alcohol strength in a book on winemaking.

[27] Potential alcohol is calculated by assuming that all the sugar in the grapes is converted to alcohol.

[28] As many as 2.5 million barrels were constructed each year at the start of the twentieth century. The number declined to about 10% of that by 1980, and then steadily increased with the growing demand for new oak in winemaking. Today it is probably around 1.2 million (calculated from data in Jean-Paul Lacroix, *Bois de Tonnellerie*, Gerfaut, 2006, p. 65).

[29] The impetus for the move to screwcaps came from Australia and New Zealand, where the quality of imported corks was absolutely dire, causing a significant proportion of wine to be rapidly spoiled by oxidation.

[30] 90% of Ugni Blanc is in Charentes. There are also 3,400 ha in the Pyrenees, 3,000 ha in Provence, and 900 ha in Aquitaine (FranceAgriMer, 2010).

[31] Chardonnay: Burgundy 14,800 ha; Languedoc 12,200 ha; Champagne 9,800 ha; Rhône 1,900 ha; Loire 1,500 ha (FranceAgriMer, 2010).

[32] Sauvignon Blanc: Languedoc 7,400 ha; Aquitaine 7,100 ha; Loire 6,500 ha; Pyrenees 2,300 ha; Burgundy 1,500 ha (FranceAgriMer, 2010).

[33] The Loire has 4.6 million cases of Muscadet, 3.3 million cases of Chenin Blanc, and 1.4 million cases of Sauvignon Blanc. Burgundy is divided into 4 million cases of Chablis, 2 million cases from Côte d'Or, and 5.7 million cases elsewhere. In Alsace, the major varieties of Riesling, Gewürztraminer, and Pinot Gris account for 6.7 million cases of the total (FranceAgriMer, 2012).

[34] Hectares of white grape plantings ("quality" varieties in italics) (FranceAgriMer, 2010):

Ugni Blanc	83,892
Chardonnay	44,593
Sauvignon Blanc	26,839
Muscadet	12,364
Sémillon	11,693
Chenin Blanc	9,828
Colombard	7,790
Muscat Petits Grains	7,620
Grenache Blanc	4,976
Viognier	4,395
Vermentino	3,569
Riesling	3,490
Gewürztraminer	3,145
Gros Manseng	2,919
Macabeo Blanc	2,628
Muscat Alexandria	2,610
Clairette	2,405
Auxerrois	2,351
Mauzac	1,991
Aligoté	1,952
Folle Blanche	1,770
Chasselas	1,648
Muscadelle	1,589
Piquepoul Blanc	1,455

Terret Blanc	1,451
Sylvaner	1,399
Roussanne	1,352
Marsanne	1,341
Pinot Blanc	1,292
Jacquère Blanc	1,027
Petit Manseng	1,019
Chasan	801
Chasselas	794
Baco Blanc	773
Len De L'El Blanc	640
Bourboulenc Blanc	596
Savagnin	481
Sauvignon Gris	*463*
Carignan Blanc	411
Altesse Blanc	356
Villard Blanc	309
Danlas Blanc	254
Total	262,271

[35] Hectares of black variety plantings in 2011 (FranceAgriMer):

Merlot	115,746
Grenache	84,753
Syrah	58,632
Cabernet Sauvignon	52,747
Carignan	48,714
Cabernet Franc	34,895
Gamay	30,443
Pinot Noir	29,738
Cinsault	18,584
Pinot Meunier	11,088
Mourvèdre	9,363
Malbec	6,155
Alicante Bouschet	2,544
Muscat Hamburg	3,504
Tannat	2,914
Aramon	2,877
Pinot Gris	2,617
Caladoc	2,464
Marselan	2,375
Grolleau	2,350
Grenache Gris	1,699
Fer	1,610
Nielluccio	1,589
Villard Noir	1,320
Negrette	1,227
Plantet	1,105
Duras	923

Petit Verdot	862
Alphon Lavallee	829
Sciaccarello	773
Tempranillo	766
Chambourcin	758
Jurançon Noir	706
Aubun	648
Chenanson	506
Grolleau Gris	454
Tibouren	445
Counoise	443
Pineau D'aunis	435
Lledoner Pelut	433
Abouriou	364
Portan	311
Poulsard	311
Mondeuse	299
Egiodola	271
Clairette Rosé	260
Cardinal Rg	217
Gamay de Bouze	215
Couderc	214
Trousseau	172
Total	554,801

[36] Merlot: Aquitaine 76,000 ha; Languedoc 31,000 ha; Provence 2,600 ha; Pyrenees 2,300 ha (FranceAgriMer, 2011).

[37] FranceAgriMer, 2010.

[38] Cabernet Sauvignon: Aquitaine 28,000 ha; Languedoc 18,000 ha; Rhône, Pyrenees, Loire, about 1,000 ha each (FranceAgriMer, 2012).

[39] Pinot Noir: Champagne 11,650 ha; Burgundy 11,000 ha; Alsace 1,500 ha; Loire 1,300 ha (FranceAgriMer, 2012).

[40] Grenache: Provence 40,000 ha; Languedoc 34,000 ha; Rhône 11,000 ha; Pyrenees 1,000 ha (FranceAgriMer, 2012).

[41] Cinsault in the Languedoc declined from 20,000 ha in 2000 to 10,000 ha in 2011; there are presently also 8,000 ha in Provence (FranceAgriMer 2000, 2012).

[42] Which probably has around a thousand varieties.

[43] The vineyards survived phylloxera but were destroyed in the second world war. They were revived in 1955 under the name of Listel, and today there are 2,000 ha.

[44] In 1851 the old lake was connected to the river Aude by a canal and tunnel to provide a sufficient supply of fresh water. The flooding is managed by an extensive irrigation network.

[45] Varieties and style are similar to Madiran, although it has taken the past twenty years to reach a quality level for promotion to AOP.

[46] The averages summarized in the section heading come from Bordeaux.

[47] Locations of isotherms based on data in GHCN (Global Historical Climatology Network) Monthly Version 1.

[48] This example is from Bordeaux. Harvest dates are from the Fédération des Grands Vins de Bordeaux; temperature data are from the weather station at Merignac.

[49] Benjamin Lewin, *Wine Myths and Reality*, p. 30.

[50] In the case of Burgundy, the increase resulting from later harvesting to obtain grapes with higher sugar is partially offset by avoiding the need to chaptalize. Even so, Burgundy is now found at up to 13.5% alcohol whereas the limit used to be around 12.5%.

[51] Sugar production depends on heat and light, and until the point at which the grapevine shuts down (over 30°C), is proportional to temperature. Anthocyanin (color) production, which correlates with phenolic development, is more a function of time, and shows less dependence on temperature. Indeed, whereas sugar continues to increase between 20 °C and 30 °C, anthocyanins decrease.

[52] The corollary is that going back to the old system and determining harvest on the basis of the Brix (sugar level) or the sugar/acid ratio, would yield unripe grapes if a level was set equivalent to 12.5% or 13% alcohol.

[53] Averages for the 2010 vintage, based on a survey by the author.

[54] The 690 cooperatives have 84,000 grower-members cultivating 331,855 ha and producing 200 million cases of wine. They produce 50% of dry still wine and 36% of Champagne (www.coopdefrance.coop accessed February 2012). The major cooperative groups are: Val d'Orbieu, Champagne Nicolas Feuillatte, Union Auboise, UVDCR-Cellier des Dauphins, Union Champagne, Alliance Champagne, Producteurs Plaimont, Vignerons Catalans, Bestheim.

[55] FranceAgriMer statistics for 2010. The Loire stands out as an exception where cooperatives have never taken hold.

Loire	12%
Burgundy	29%
Aquitaine	29%
Champagne	37%
Alsace	38%
Beaujolais	39%
Provence	62%
Languedoc	72%
Rhône	76%

[56] http://www.umvin.com, accessed July 16, 2013.

[57] According to FEVS (Fédération des Exportateurs des Vins et Spiritueux), negociants are responsible for 70% of all French wine and for 80% of exports.

[58] Val d'Orbieu is an organization of 11 cooperatives and other domains. It has 1591 growers with 10,334 hectares de vignes, and produces 170 million bottles with a value of €190 million.

[59] The median size for AOP is 15 ha; the median size for IGP is 10 ha (FranceAgrimer, 2012).

[60] Regional averages are: Languedoc 12 ha; Bordeaux 12 ha; Rhône 7 ha; Champagne 2.5 ha; Loire 10 ha; Burgundy 7.5 ha; Alsace 3.7 ha (FranceAgrimer, 2013).

[61] The largest groups with negociant interests devoted largely to wine are Groupe Castel, Grand Chais de France, Groupe Advini, Taillan, Val d'Orbieu, Baron Philippe de Rothschild, Boisset la Famille des Grand Vins, and CVBG Dourthe Kressmann. Pernod-Ricard, which also has major interests in wine inside and outside of France, had its basis in spirits. More specialized, LVMH owns some of the most individual Bordeaux châteaux and Champagne houses as part of its luxury goods portfolio.

[62] Cooperatives vinify 39% of AOP wines and 71% of IGP wines (FranceAgrimer, 2012).

Chapter 2: Burgundy

[1] Denis Morélot, *Statistique de la Vigne dans le Departement de la Cote-d'Or* (Ch. Brugnot, Dijon, 1831), p. 158.

[2] CNRS (Délégation Paris Michel-Ange) *Burgundy Wine Has Long History In France: Remains Of Gallo-Roman Vineyard Discovered In Gevrey-Chambertin.* ScienceDaily, March 16, 2009. Retrieved September 9, 2010, from http://www.sciencedaily.com /releases/2009/03/090310084846.htm

[3] Dion, *Histoire de la Vigne,* p. 142.

[4] Jean-François Bazin, Histoire du vin de Bourgogne (Jean-Paul Gisserot, Plouédern, France, 2002), pp. 12-13.

[5] Jean-François Bazin, *ibid.,* p. 14.

[6] Côte d'Or has two meanings. Describing wine production, it refers specifically to the

narrow strip of land running from Dijon to the south of Beaune. But the term also describes one of the Départements (political and administrative units) of France. Official statistics for wine production for the Côte d'Or refer to the whole Département. Burgundy, in the sense of what can be included in Bourgogne AOC, covers four Départements: Côte d'Or, Saône-et-Loire (including the Côte Chalonnaise), Yonne (including Chablis), and Nièvre (no significant vineyards).

[7] Dion, *Histoire de la Vigne*, p 286.

[8] In fact, it was counter-productive, and resulted in a general decline in Burgundy's importance as a wine-producing region (Tim Unwin, *The Wine & the Vine*, Routledge, London, 1996, p. 17).

[9] In 1485, the authorities in Dijon complained to Charles VII about the increasing encroachment of Gamay (Camille Rodier, *Le vin de Bourgogne, 3rd edition,* Damidot / Laffitte reprints, Dijon, 1948, p. 14).

[10] Gilles Laferté, *La Bourgogne et ses vins: image d'origine contrôlée* (Belin, Paris, 2006), p. 19.

[11] The overall decline in planted areas was 12%, but it was only 2% in the Côte d'Or (Robert Laurent, *Les vignerons de la "Côte d'Or" au XIXe siècle,* Société Les Belles Lettres, Publications de l'Université de Dijon, Paris, 1958, tome I, p. 360).

[12] BIVB, 2012.

[13] Just near Chablis, there is Sauvignon Blanc in the appellation of St. Bris.

[14] Giving an exact number for grand and premier crus is a little tricky because of the use of overlapping names.

[15] The difference was only about 3.5 fold in mid nineteenth century (Gilles Laferté, *La Bourgogne et ses vins: image d'origine contrôlée,* Belin, Paris, 2006, p. 23). It is more than ten fold today, and furthermore is much more influenced by the name of the producer.

[16] Christophe Lucand, *Négoce des vins et propriété viticole en Bourgogne durant la Seconde Guerre Mondiale* (Ruralia, 16/17, 2005).

[17] The exceptions are St. Romain, Marsannay, and Chorey-lès-Beaune.

[18] J. Lavalle, *Histoire et Statistique de la Vigne,* (Picard [Phenix Editions, 2000 reprint], Dijon, 1855), pp. 150-159.

[19] Benjamin Lewin, *In Search of Pinot Noir,* pp. 45-47.

[20] Anthony Hanson, *Burgundy, 1st edition* (Faber & Faber, London, 1982), p. 132.

[21] A fair amount of domain bottling was performed by mobile bottling plants, transported on the back of a truck (ibid., p 130).

[22] DRAAF Bourgogne, Agreste 157, 2013.

[23] Hectares owned and total production by the leading producers in the Côte d'Or.

Producer	Village	Premier	Grand
Louis Jadot	75		75
Bouchard Père	12	74	12
Louis Latour	48	15	27
Faiveley	37	16.5	10.5
Joseph Drouhin	32	19	4
Vougeraie	20	8	4
Patriarche	10	?	

Information provided by the producers.

[24] Clive Coates, *Côte d'Or: A Celebration of the Great Wines of Burgundy* (University of California Press, Berkeley, 1997), p. 114.

[25] Originally the limits applied to labeling rather than production. So if you were producing wine in a grand cru with a limit of 35 hl/ha but actually you produced 60 hl/ha, you could label wine as the grand cru until reaching the 35 hl/ha limit. The rest of the production could still be sold, but had to be labeled according to the limits for the lower parts of the appellation hierarchy. You might label the next 5 hl/ha as village wine, to reach a village limit of 40 hl/ha, the last 10 hl/ha as Bourgogne to reach the limit of 50 hl/ha for the region, and then the rest would have to be sold outside the AOP. So there could be a whole range of bottles, labeled from Vin de Table to Grand Cru Burgundy, but all containing exactly the same wine. The rules were changed in 1974 so that the limits actually applied to production, but they were increased. As a practical matter, the nominal limits are the *rendement de base* (base yield), and an additional 20% is usually allowed.

[26] Charles Arnoult, representative from Dijon to the constitutional assembly, suggested Côte d'Or in preference to Département de Seine-et-Saône or Haute-Seine (Jean-François Bazin, *Histoire du vin de Bourgogne,* op. cit., p. 41).

[27] Suggested by Richard Olney, *Romanée Conti* (Rizzoli, New York, 1995), p. 1.

[28] There were 1,200 ha of vines at Dijon in 1892. (Claude Chapuis, *La Mémoire des Coteaux,* Editions de Bourgogne, Dijon, 2010), pp. 26, 54).

[29] James Wilson, *Terroir* (Wine Appreciation Guild, San Francisco, 1998), p. 111.

[30] Recently renamed the D974 in a fit of mad French bureaucracy. Locally everyone still calls the quality line the N74.

[31] Reds and whites were equally well regarded. Those of Clos Vougeot sold for the same price in the seventeenth and eighteenth centuries (J. Lavalle, *Histoire et Statistique de la Vigne*, op. cit., pp. 55, 119, 154).

[32] Declassified to Bourgogne Blanc since 1994 when the vineyard was replanted.

[33] Distribution of premier and grand crus:

Commune	premier	grand
Gevrey Chambertin	26	8
Morey St Denis	20	4
Chambolle Musigny	24	2
Vougeot	4	1
Flagey-Echézeaux/ Vosne Romanée	14	8
Nuits St Georges	37	0

[34] Jean-François Bazin, *Chambertin* (Jacques Legrand, Paris, 1991), p. 92.

[35] The three premier crus in Flagey-Echézeaux are Les Beaux Monts (partly in Vosne Romanée itself), Les Rouges, and en Orveaux.

[36] "Il n'y a point à Vosne de vins communs" (Abbé Courtépée, *Description Générale et Particulière du Duché de Bourgogne*, Chez Frantin, 1775).

[37] But the vineyard was under contract, with the wines made by Bouchard Père until 2005, after which it reverted to Liger-Belair.

[38] La Grande Rue lies between La Tâche and Romanée Conti so there isn't much doubt about the potential quality of the land, although the general feeling is that the Lamarche wines have not been up to grand cru quality.

[39] Echézeaux is a relatively modern concept, going back to a failed attempt to limit it to the 3.5 ha *climat* of Echézeaux du Dessus. The grand cru was then defined as including eleven *climats* in the vicinity, although in previous classifications, several of the *climats* had been placed one level lower. It's an indication of its reputation that it used to be sold as Vosne Romanée premier cru (Allen D. Meadows, *The Pearl of the Cote, The great wines of Vosne Romanée*, Burghound Books, Winnetka, California, 2010, p. 96).

[40] The original distinction between Grands Echézeaux and Echézeaux may have been no more than that very long rows of vines ran continuously, and those at the far end were known as Grands Echézeaux.

[41] The legend has since been transmogrified into saying that the top was reserved for the Pope, the middle for bishops, and the bottom for monks, but does not appear to have any factual basis. In fact, it is not clear whether the monks actually vinified separate cuvées (Denis Morelot, *Statistique de la Vigne*, op. cit., p. 25.) There is also a story that a nineteenth century proprietor, Jules Ouvrard, tried making separate cuvées, and that in fact that from the bottom was preferred at a blind tasting (Jean-François Bazin, *Clos Vougeot*, Jacques Legrand, Paris, 1987, p. 80).

[42] When the official map was prepared in 1861, a proposal to divide Clos Vougeot into two parts, "tête de cuvée" for the best and "première cuvée" for the rest, was defeated by the proprietor: "Undoubtedly all the parts are not the same; but if we follow this path, it will not be possible to stop with two divisions, but there should be at least 5 or 6" (quoted in Rolande Gadille, *Le Vignoble de la Côte Bourguignone,* Les Belles Lettres, Dijon, 1967, p. 200).

[43] Benjamin Lewin, *Breaking Ranks*, Decanter, July 2010, pp 48-51.

[44] Some of the vineyards to the east of the N74 included in the original appellation in 1936 were removed in 1964 (Jean-François Bazin, *Chambertin,* Jacques Legrand, Paris, 1991, p. 50).

[45] Benjamin Lewin, *Breaking Ranks*, Decanter, July 2010, pp 48-51.

[46] Dr. Lavalle rated it below only Chambertin and Clos de Bèze in 1855. Clos St. Jacques was rated first out of 10 Première Cuvées (J. Lavalle, *Histoire et Statistique de la Vigne*, op. cit., p. 93).

[47] Jean-François Bazin, *Chambertin,* op. cit., p. 88.

[48] Jean-François Bazin, ibid., pp. 72, 86.

[49] Technically Marsannay is not officially within the Côte de Nuits, which ends at Fixin, but this a distinction without a difference.

[50] Based on a survey of prices in the U.S., U.K. and France for vintages 2002-2007, analyzed over the period 2007-2010. Prices for appellations were compared for individual producers in each vintage, and then the data sets were merged on the basis of relative appellation prices. Some very small crus (especially if they are monopoles) are not included because of lack of data.

[51] The Hospice owns 61 hectares, mostly premier and grand crus.

[52] André Jullien, *Topographie de tous les vignobles connus* (Huzard, Paris, 1816), p. 110.

[53] White grapevines were increasingly planted over the first half of the twentieth century to reach the present levels by the times the AOC was introduced in 1936 (Camille Rodier, *Le vin de Bourgogne,* op.

cit).

[54] Clive Coates, *The Wines of Burgundy*, p. 181.

[55] Benjamin Lewin, *Breaking Ranks*, Decanter, July 2010, pp 48-51.

[56] Although I have noticed that Chablis from producers following a richer style is beginning to show the same problems at more or less the same age as the Côte d'Or. I suspect battonage may be involved.

[57] It is named for the village of Kimmeridge on the south coast of England, where the fossil beds are exceptionally rich.

[58] Taking its name from the village of Portland on the English south coast.

[59] See décret in Journal Officiel, January 8, 1967, p. 412-413.

[60] Décret 78-238 of February 27, 1978.

[61] William Fèvre, *Le Vrai Chablis et Les Autres*, 1978.

[62] Premier crus in 1938 were (sub-area names in parentheses):
Mont de Milieu
Montée de Tonnerre (Chapelot)
Fourchaume (Côte de Fontenay, L'Homme Mort, Vaulorent)
Vaillons (Séchet, Beugnons, Les Lys)
Montmains (Forêts, Butteaux)
Côte de Léchet.

Premier crus created since 1978 are:
Beauroy (Troësmes)
Vauligneau
Vaudevey
Vaucoupin
Vosgros (Vaugiraut)
Les Fourneaux
Côte de Vaubarousse
Berdiot
Chaume de Talvat
Côte de Jouan
Les Beauregards.

[63] By the fifteenth century the general reckoning was that Beaune was superior in wet years and Auxerre was superior in dry years (Claude Chapuis, *La Mémoire des Coteaux*, Editions de Bourgogne, Dijon, 2010), p. 41.

[64] Collectif, Vignes et vins de l'Auxerrois (Armançon, 2003).

[65] Jadot, Drouhin, Latour, and Bouchard.

[66] Some producers in the northern part of the region produce red wine as Beaujolais and white wine as Mâcon where the AOPs overlap.

[67] "Red wines from the Département of Saône-et-Loire and from the arrondissement of Villefranche equally have the right to AOC 'Bourgogne'," according to the rules laid down when the AOCs were defined in 1943-1946.

[68] Quoted by Jancis Robinson, *Bust-up in Burgundy*, jancisrobinson.com, July 8, 2009.

[69] If labeled simply Bourgogne, it must have less than 30% Gamay. To be labeled Pinot Noir requires at least 85% of the variety. Basically the change in the law means that a wine labeled Bourgogne can no longer be made principally from Gamay. The appellation Bourgogne Grand Ordinaire is being replaced by Coteaux Bourguignons, which can be used by any red Beaujolais.

[70] Georges Duboeuf & Henry Elwing, *Beaujolais - Vin du Citoyen* (Jean-Claude Lattes, 1989), p. 38.

[71]

	Beaujolais	Villages	Crus	Total
2009	3.5	2.5	2.9	8.9
2008	3.2	2.1	2.6	7.9
2007	4.2	3.1	3.6	10.9
2006	5.4	3.4	3.5	12.3
2005	5.6	3.3	3.0	11.9
2004	6.4	4.0	3.6	14.0
2003	4.3	2.5	2.4	9.2
2002	6.4	3.9	4.1	14.4
2001	7.3	4.0	4.1	15.4
2000	7.3	4.0	4.1	15.4
1999	7.3	4.0	4.1	15.4

Annual production is in millions of cases (FranceAgriMer).

[72] FranceAgriMer.

[73] Michel Deprost, *Beaujolais. Vendanges amères* (Golias, Villeurbanne, 2004), p. 80.

[74] Based on the author's survey of 700 producers.

[75] La Cooperation Viticole Dans La Production En 2010, FranceAgrimer.

[76] Michel Deprost, *Beaujolais. Vendanges amères* (Golias, Villeurbanne, 2004), pp. 103, 104.

[77] Sometimes exceptions are made to allow more economical shipping. Moving the Beaujolais by air is usually necessary outside of Europe (in fact special arrangements have to be made to move such a large volume in such a short time) and this is expensive. In 2008, the authorities agreed to allow two-thirds of the Beaujolais going to the United States to leave earlier in order to be shipped by sea (Emily S. Ruer, *Rolling out the Beaujolais Nouveau*, New York Times, November 20, 2008).

[78] Beaujolais Nouveau was around 13 million bottles out of a total production of 80 million bottles of all Beaujolais until 1970 (Gilbert Garrier, *L'Etonnante Histoire de Beaujolais Nouveau*, Larousse, Paris, 2002, p. 23).

[79] UIVB (Union Interprofessionnelle des Vins du *Beaujolais*).

[80] Japan takes about a million cases of Beaujolais Nouveau, roughly 20% of all Nouveau, and more than a third of exports (UIVB).

[81] The phrase is supposed to have originated when Louis Orizet, the Inspecteur Général of INAO responsible for dealing with frauds, spotted it written on a bar window (Garrier, *op. cit.,* p. 29).

[82] Quoted in Eric Asimov, *Discovering a 'new' and finer Beaujolais*, New York Times, October 4, 2007.

[83] Clive Coates, *An Encyclopedia of Wines*, p 240.

[84] Quote in Gabriel Savage, *Beaujolais forges ahead with classification,* The Drinks Business, March 2013 (at www.thedrinksbusiness.com).

[85] All four were imported into the United States by Kermit Lynch, who coined the term. It may have started as clever marketing, but it stuck.

[86] Quite a bit of Beaujolais is distilled already. And in 2002 the UIVB took a bank loan to reduce the surplus by buying up a million cases, to be variously distilled, turned to vinegar, or declassified to table wine (Michel Deprost, *Beaujolais. Vendanges amères,* Golias, Villeurbanne, 2004, p. 12).

[87] Marquis d'Angerville (from Volnay) has purchased three artisanal producers to form the Domaine du Pélican. Jean-Claude Boisset, who has several brands in Burgundy, purchased Henri Maire, the biggest single vineyard owner in the Jura, and producer of a successful brand of Crémant.

[88] White plantings were only about one quarter in 1958 (Pierre Galet, *Cépages et vignobles de France*, p. 828).

[89] Chardonnay was 73% of white plantings in 1958, compared with 70% today (Pierre Galet, *Cépages et vignobles de France*, 2005, p. 828).

[90] Jean Berthet-Bondet, *Le Château Chalon. Un vin, son terroir et ses hommes* (Meta Jura, Lons-Le-Saunier, 2013), p. 6.

[91] Savagnin originated in northeast France or southeast Germany. It is a parent of both Sauvignon Blanc and Chenin Blanc. It is also related to Pinot Noir (Jancis Robinson, *Wine Grapes,* p. 960).

[92] The first actual use of the term Vin Jaune was not until 1820 (Jean Berthet-Bondet, *Le Château Chalon*, op. cit., p. 7).

[93] Pinot Noir was 1% of black plantings in 1958 today (Pierre Galet, *Cépages et vignobles de France*, p. 828).

[94] Christian D. Brisis, *Vins, Vignes et Vignobles du Jura* (Cêtre, Besançon, 1991), p. 60.

[95] Average growing season temperatures over the three years 2010-2012 were 15.3 °C at Chambéry compared with 16.3 °C for Sancerre or 15.8 °C for Alsace (Goddard Weather Center).

[96] Abymes, Apremont, Arbin, Ayze, Chautagne, Chignin, Chignin-Bergeron, Cruet, Jongieux, Marignan, Marin, Montmélian, Ripaille, Saint-Jean-de-la-Porte, and Saint-Jeoire-Prieuré.

[97] Frangy, Marestel, Monterminod, and Monthoux.

[98] Curiously, the indigenous varieties in Savoie do not seem to have any connection with those in the Valais (in Switzerland) or Val d'Aosta (in Italy), neighboring regions that were originally part of Savoy. (José Vouillamoz & Giulio Moriondo, *Origine Des Cépages Valaisans Et Valdôtains*, 2nd Edition, Editions Du Belvédère, Fleurier, Switzerland, 2011°.

Chapter 3: Bordeaux

[1] Narbonne, close to the Pyrenees, was the major source of wine, imported to Bordeaux via Toulouse.

[2] Pijassou, *Le Médoc*, Tallandier, Paris, 1978, pp. 290-293; Dion, *Histoire de la Vigne*, pp. 121-126.

[3] One of the first mentions of vines in the Bordeaux region was by Pliny, in 71 C.E.

[4] Aubin, *La seigneurie en Bordelais,* Université de Rouen, Rouen, 1989,, p. 18.

[5] "Thin and infertile countryside" was a description used in 1416 and repeated in 1524 by the local authorities (Pijassou, *Le Médoc,* op. cit., p. 314).

[6] Pijassou, *Le Médoc*, op. cit., pp. 304, 477; Thiney, *Fascinant Médoc*, Editions Sud Ouest, Bordeaux, 2003, pp. 166-168.

[7] Today there are fewer than 20 negociants in the vicinity of the Quai des Chartrons. In 1950, there were close to 200 (Réjalot, *Les Logiques du Château*, p. 143).

[8] Benjamin Lewin, *What Price Bordeaux*, p. 204.

[9] Réjalot, *Les Logiques du Château*, Bordeaux University Press, Bordeaux, 2007, pp. 241, 249.

[10] Lewin, *What Price Bordeaux?*, p. 51.

[11] INAO lists Cabernet Sauvignon, Cabernet Franc, Merlot, Malbec, Carmenère, and Petit Verdot as the only permitted black varieties. Sémillon, Sauvignon Blanc, Sauvignon Gris, and Muscadelle are listed as "principal" white varieties, with the lower quality varie-

ties Colombard, Merlot Blanc, and Ugni Blanc listed as "accessory" varieties (CDC Bordeaux Homologation, June 11, 2008).

[12] Estimated proportions of Cabernet Sauvignon are; Pauillac 65%; St. Julien 64%; Margaux 54%; St. Estèphe 53%; Pessac-Léognan 53%; Haut-Médoc and Médoc (excluding communes) 48%; Graves (excluding Pessac-Léognan) 37% (from a survey by the author in 2011).

[13] An increase in total plantings contributes to the increase in proportion of Merlot. The very best areas, identified long ago, are planted with Cabernet Sauvignon. New areas naturally are not such good terroir, and therefore tend to be planted with Merlot.

[14] Paul Massé, *Le dessèchement des marais du Bas-Médoc*. In Revue historique de Bordeaux et du Département de la Gironde (No. 1 pp. 1-44, 1957); Henri Enjalbert, *Les Pays Aquitains*. (Bordeaux: Biere, Bordeaux, Tome I, 1960, p. 171).

[15] James Wilson, *Terroir* (Wine Appreciation Guild, San Francisco, 1998), pp. 187-191.

[16] Bernardin & Le Hong, *Crus Classés du Médoc* (Editions Sud Ouest, Bordeaux, 2010), p. 12.

[17] Of the 1,200 ha in Pauillac, just under 400 ha are north of the town. The Rothschild châteaux account for 250 ha in this part of Pauillac. They do not own châteaux in the more southern part.

[18] The appellations take the names of individual villages, except for Margaux, which includes five communes, so wines in any of Arsac, Cantenac, Labarde, Margaux and Soussans are "Appellation Margaux Contrôlée."

[19] Pontac (Haut Brion), Latour, Lafite, and Margaux were selling at 4-5 times the price of other wine from the Médoc (Pijassou, *Le Médoc*, op. cit., p. 371).

[20] Markham, *A History of the Bordeaux Classification,* John Wiley & Sons, New York, 1997.

[21] The term Grand Cru Classé is now restricted by law to châteaux in Bordeaux.

[22] Benjamin Lewin, *What Price Bordeaux?*, p. 42.

[23] Actually a total of 57 châteaux were classified in 1855, but since then some have been divided, increasing the total number of classified growths to 61. In Sauternes, 21 châteaux were classified.

[24] The only one not to conform completely is Château Margaux, where some of the vineyards are on bedrock rather than gravel; and some people consider that in fact this makes it the best terroir in the Médoc (Wilson, *Terroir*, Wine Appreciation Guild, San Francisco, 1998, pp. 194-198).

[25] Wilson, ibid, pp. 198-199.

[26] Benjamin Lewin, *What Price Bordeaux?*, p. 229.

[27] Benjamin Lewin, ibid., pp. 236-241.

[28] Benjamin Lewin, ibid., p. 87.

[29] The Cru Bourgeois classification was drawn up in 1932 by the Bordeaux wine brokers, under the authority of the Chamber of Commerce and the Chamber of Agriculture. 444 châteaux were ranked into three levels of Cru Bourgeois. The list was never made official but was used for more than 50 years. The Syndicat des Crus Bourgeois du Médoc was established in 1962, and was authorized by a ministerial decree in 2000 to reclassify the Cru Bourgeois. This led to a classification that was published in 2003, with the intention of being revised every 12 years. Disputes led to law cases and a new classification was finally agreed only in 2010.

[30] When the 2003 classification was annulled, The Alliance des Crus Bourgeois decided to create a new certification using Cru Bourgeois, "not as a classification, but as a mark of quality."

[31] There are also some commercial considerations. For example, Château Caronne Ste Gemme was excluded in 2011 because some wine had been sold under conditions that aren't permitted by the classification.

[32] A château must obtain the agrément for its wine to be included in its AOP before it be can submitted for approval for the Cru Bourgeois label.

[33] The original Cru Bourgeois Exceptionnel that have eschewed the new classification are: Chasse Spleen, Haut-Marbuzet, Labégorce Zédé (now Labégorce), Les Ormes de Pez, de Pez, Phélan Ségur, Potensac, Poujeaux, and Château Siran.

[34] In 1997, the worst vintage of the past decade, many châteaux used less than half of their production for the grand vin. In the more normal 2006 vintage, grand vin provided an average 69% of production compared to 31% for second wine. (Based on a survey by the author.)

[35] Benjamin Lewin, *What Price Bordeaux?*, pp. 200-202.

[36] The length of time spent in oak varies from 10-24 months for grand vins, and from 6-18 months for second wines. Most second wines are matured in old oak, but a minority of 10% see no oak at all (Benjamin Lewin, *What Price Bordeaux?*, p. 205).

[37] The grand vins of the left bank on average

have 52% Cabernet Sauvignon, but second wines have 44%. There is less difference on the right bank (Lewin, op. cit, p. 205).

[38] The history of Carruades de Lafite, the second wine of Château Lafite Rothschild, casts an interesting light on this question. This was produced until 1966, when it was discontinued because of confusion among consumers. It was reintroduced in 1974, and represented about a third of the crop made from young vines, but did not use the name of Lafite on the label. However, there was little demand, so in 1985 the wine was again labeled Carruades de Lafite—and demand revived (Edmund Penning-Rowsell, *The Wines of Bordeaux, 6th edition,* Penguin Books, London, 1989, p. 192). Today it sells especially strongly in Asia, where the name of Lafite is magical.

[39] The classification in 1955 included 13 châteaux, all located in Pessac-Léognan. The modification in 1959 gave Cru Classé status to 9 châteaux for white wine, including 7 of the original 13 classified châteaux plus an additional two that are classified only for white wine. The classification has never been changed.

[40] The classified châteaux are larger than average. The overall averages are 23 ha for all châteaux in St. Emilion and 29 ha for all châteaux in the Médoc.

[41] Drinks Business, June 12, 2013.

[42] Isabelle Saporta, *Vino Business* (Albin Michel, Paris, 2014), p.28.

[43] It was revised twice at roughly 15-year intervals (in 1969 and 1986), but since then has been revised more systematically every decade (in 1996, 2006, and 2012).

[44] Like Eskimos having multiple words for snow, at one time St. Emilion distinguished between varieties of Cabernet Franc, with the proportions of Bouchet and Cabernet Franc described separately, although they are in fact the same variety (Henri Enjalbert, *Les grands vins de Saint-Emilion, Pomerol, Fronsac*, Editions Bardi, Paris, 1983, p. 515).

[45] Lewin, *What Price Bordeaux?*, p. 166.

[46] There was 5% Merlot from 1957 to 2010. Because of the global warming trend, "we are thinking of bringing it back," says Elisabeth Jaubert at Pétrus.

[47] It is not particularly wet here, in fact there is slightly less rainfall in Sauternes and Barsac than farther north in Graves (Jeffrey Benson & Alastair MacKenzie, *Sauternes, 2nd edition,* Sotheby's Publications, London, 1990, p. 18).

[48] If the skin breaks and botrytis penetrates into the berry (called gray rot), it makes the grapes susceptible to other, pernicious infections (called sour rot). If either gray rot or sour rot sets in, there is nothing to do but throw away the grapes. Dry spells are the best protection against this happening.

[49] Ron S. Jackson, *Wine Science: Principles, Practice, Perception* (Academic Press, New York, 2000), p. 522.

[50] Tannins are measured by the IPT (Indice des Polyphénols Totaux). IPT was typically about 62 in Bordeaux in 1982, 70 in year 2000, and 78 in year 2005, which suggests roughly a 20% increase of tannin from 5 g/l to 6 g/l over the period.

[51] Wines are listed in descending order of average price for the period 2000-2011. This classification has been based on the Livex data base of prices for vintages from 2000-2011 in February 2014. My previous classifications (in *What Price Bordeaux?* and *Wine Myths and Reality*) were based on en primeur prices on the Place de Bordeaux. There are advantages and disadvantages to both approaches. One disadvantage of using pricing from the Place de Bordeaux is that not every wine trades through the Place, so some wines cannot be placed. Although en primeur prices relate most closely to the basis for official classifications, they show the château's assessment of its own position in reflecting the prices demanded from negociants: sometimes the market subsequently readjusts these prices (up or down).

[52] Michel Delpon, *Vins de Bergerac : le Perigord Pourpre* (Editions Féret, Bordeaux, 2002), p.27.

[53] Robert Plageoles, *Le Vin de Gaillac, 2000 Ans d'Histoire* (Editions Privat, Toulouse, 2000), p. 77.

[54] These grapevines do not seem to have contributed genetic material to the local varieties, which may therefore have originated elsewhere (Olivier Yobrégat, *Cépages principaux, secondaires, oubliés : Etat des lieux de la biodiversité régionale*, V'Innopôle Sud-Ouest, Colloque, Lisle sur Tarn, 2013).

[55] Décret n° 2009-1262 du 19 octobre 2009 relatif à l'appellation d'origine contrôlée "Madiran". The previous regulation in 1997 specified between 40% and 60%.

[56] Data from Vignobles et Jurançon.

[57] Wines can be labeled Vendange Tardive if the grapes have 281 g/l sugar (17% potential alcohol), as opposed to Jurançon, which is 226 g/l (13.5% potential alcohol).

Chapter 4: Champagne

[1] The seven regions defined for Crémant

production are Alsace, Loire, Bourgogne, Bordeaux, Die, Jura, and Limoux.

[2] The process for making sparkling wine was invented in England well before it was tried in Champagne. Two advances in technology were needed to stop bottles from exploding under the pressure of carbon dioxide: stronger glass; and corks. English glass was much stronger than French because of industrial improvements early in the seventeenth century; and corks were (re)discovered in England a century before France. Wine was shipped in barrels to England where there was a healthy bottling trade, and some of it was converted to sparkling wine (Tom Stevenson, *Encyclopedia of Champagne*).

[3] Dion, *Histoire de la Vigne*, p. 643.

[4] Dion, *Histoire de la Vigne*, p. 643.

[5] Typically the sugar content will be 22-24 g/l in the liqueur de tirage, and its fermentation adds an alcohol level of 1.3-1.5%.

[6] Most prestige cuvées are riddled by hand in the old way, not because the results are better, but because it's part of the myth that production is exclusively artisanal. It's ironic that an inferior method is used for the top cuvées.

[7] So wines that are technically extra brut can be labeled as brut.

[8] Extra-Sec is 12-20 g/l; Sec is 17-35 g/l; Demi-Sec is 35-50 g/l.

[9] Dion, *Histoire de la Vigne*, p. 615.

[10] Claire Desbois-Thibault et al., *Le Champagne. Une histoire franco-allemande* (PUPS, Paris, 2011), p. 93.

[11] Dion, *Histoire de la Vigne*, p. 632.

[12] Claire Desbois-Thibault et al., op. cit., p. 85.

[13] Claire Desbois-Thibault et al., op. cit., pp. 164-165.

[14] Claudine Wolikow, *Champagne ! ; Histoire Inattendue* (Editions de l'Atelier, Paris, 2012), p. 52.

[15] Dion, *Histoire de la Vigne*, p. 640.

[16] Pierre Galet, *Cépages et vignobles de France,*, p. 5.

[17] Dion, *Histoire de la Vigne*, p. 644.

[18] Claudine Wolikow, op. cit., p. 123.

[19] The other varieties, all white, are Pinot Blanc, Arbane, and Petit Meslier. A Champagne from Arbane is made today by Moutard-Diligent in some vintages. A Petit Meslier Champagne is produced by Duval-Leroy in some vintages.

[20] Technically a Blanc de Noirs is a Champagne made from black grapes, which means Pinot Noir and Pinot Meunier. But most high quality Blanc de Noirs is made from Pinot Noir.

[21] Champagne-Ardennes consists of the four Départements, Aube, Ardennes, Haute-Marne, and Marne.

[22] Troops had to be called in to restore order. It was said that there were more troops in Champagne than vignerons.

[23] The period became known as the Twenty Year War between Champenoise and Aube.

[24] This differs from a solera because it consists of a single cuvée, whereas a solera has a series of separate scales that are used to replenish one another.

[25] Blending across vintage not only allows producers to even out variations but also enables them to react to market conditions. The significant production statistic for Champagne is not so much the size of the annual harvest as the number of bottles shipped each year. When demand is high, Champagne is matured for the minimum period before releasing to market. When demand is low, base wines may be kept longer before blending, and Champagne may be kept longer in the bottle before disgorging, to avoid flooding the market. This actually means that in periods of low demand, the product is better.

[26] Recensement Agricole, 1958; CIVC 2013.

[27] Benjamin Lewin, *In Search of Pinot Noir*, p. 168.

[28] It is allowed in premier crus, but it stands to reason that the best sites will grow the top grape varieties (Pinot Noir and Chardonnay) if only for economic reasons. Pinot Meunier is discouraged indirectly because the pruning system that is most often used for Pinot Meunier is not allowed in grand cru and premier cru vineyards.

[29] The financial stakes are huge. Vineyards classified for Champagne production can sell for €1 million per hectare. Adjacent land used for other crops, such as beets or wheat, has a value around €6,000 per hectare. If an additional 4,000 ha were added to the Champagne AOC, this would be making a present of €4 billion in land values to the lucky farmers. (Average prices from Valeur Venale, Journal Officiel De La République Française, February 5, 2009.)

[30] Data sources: Marcel Lachiver, *Vins, Vignes et Vignerons,* and CIVC.

[31] Another measure of the leaps and bounds in Champagne is that at the end of the eighteenth century, the largest Maison produced 50,000 bottles; by the middle of the nineteenth century it passed one million, and at the end of the century it reached three million. Claudine Wolikow, op. cit., p. 73.) Today it is 30 million.

[32] The nominal limits have gone up steadily from 12,000 kg/ha in the 1980s to 15,500 kg/ha in 2008.

[33] In 2009, when the yield was apparently a (relatively) low 9,700 kg/hl, it was really 14,000 kg/hl, because the rule was that 9,7000 kg/ha could be used to make Champagne for current consumption, but an additional 4,300 kg/ha could be used to make reserve wines.

[34] The limit is that 14,000 kg of grapes can be harvested from each hectare, and 2,550 liters of must can be pressed from every 4,000 kg of grapes. This is equivalent to 89 hl/ha.

[35] The cuvée is the initial pressing of 2,050 liters; the tail is the second pressing of 500 liters. The total is the limit allowed from 4,000 kg of grapes.

[36] Hugh Johnson, *The Story of Wine* (Mitchell Beazley, London, 2005), p. 180.

[37] Reports of major increases in alcohol or declines in acidity are exaggerated. According to figures that the CIVC has been collecting since 1990, average acidity in the 1990s was 12.27 g/l (tartaric acid equivalent), and the average is 11.4 g/l since then. Alcohol has changed from an average of 9.8% to an average of 9.9%.

[38] Introduced in 1961 for the 1952 vintage.

[39] There are two Oenotheque releases, P2 after at least 12 years, and P3 after at least 18 years.

[40] From 3% of Champagne in 2000 to 9.2% today (CIVC, 2013).

[41] Production of Dom Pérignon is thought to be 4-5 million bottles; production of Cristal is 300,000-400,000 bottles.

[42] CIVC, 2013.

[43] CIVC.

[44] The top five groups between them include 23 houses:

LVMH: Moët & Chandon, Mercier, Ruinart, Montaudon, Veuve Clicquot, Krug.

Boizel Chanoine: Lanson, Burtin Besserat de Bellefon, Boizel, Chanoine, Philipponnat, De Venoge, Alexandre Bonnet.

Vranken-Pommery: Demoiselle, Charles Lafitte, Heidsieck & C° Monopole, Vranken-Pommery.

Laurent-Perrier: Laurent-Perrier, De Castellane, Salon-Delamotte, Lemoine.

Pernod-Ricard: Mumm, Perrier-Jouët.

[45] The name goes back to 1912, when a breakaway group of the less successful producers left the producers' organization. Those remaining in the Syndicat du Commerce des Vins de Champagne decided that they were the grand Marques, and in 1964 officially changed their name to the Syndicat de Grandes Marques de Champagne. But in the early 1990s there was a brouhaha when the members of the Syndicat were asked whether their membership implied production of superior quality. The answers were equivocal: the members failed to agree on any quality standard, and as a result the Syndicat dissolved itself in 1997. At this point, the 24 Grand Marques accounted for 60% of all Champagne production.

[46] The group of Grand Marques defined in 1964 was Ayala, Billecart-Salmon, Bollinger, Canard-Duchène, Delbeck, Deutz, Gosset, Heidsieck Monopole, Charles Heidsieck, Henriot, Irroy, Krug, Lanson, Massé, Mercier, Moët & Chandon, Montebello, Mumm, Perrier-Jouët, Joseph Perrier, Laurent Perrier, Piper-Heidsieck, Pol Roger, Pommery, Prieur, Roederer, Ruinart, Salon, Taittinger, Veuve Clicquot.

[47] The CIVC lists 76 leading Maisons de Champagne and states 10 criteria for being considered a Grande Marque, from which quality of production is significantly absent.

[48] Cooperatives have increased from 7% in 1950 to 37% of the harvest today (France-Agrimer, 2013).

[49] A major part is not commercialized directly, but is supplied to the Maisons as grapes or wine (or finished product).

[50] The name is supposed to reflect the fact that lower pressure gave a creamy rather than pricking sensation. Crémant was originally used to describe Champagnes with lower pressure, but the term is now used only to describe wine made elsewhere.

Chapter 5: Alsace

[1] Stevenson, *The Wines of Alsace*, p. 49.

[2] Precipitation changes from 1,200-1,500 mm at the far, western edge, to around 2,000 mm at the peak of the mountain range, to 650 mm in the vineyards.

[3] Plantings in Alsace:

	1969	1991	2012
Riesling	12%	22%	22%
Pinot Blanc	11%	23%	*7%
Auxerrois			*14.3%
Gewürztraminer	21%	19%	19%
Pinot Gris	5%	7%	15%
Pinot Noir	2%	7%	10%
Sylvaner	27%	18%	7%
Muscat	4%		2%
Chasselas	10%		<1%

Mixed	8%	<1%

* indicates proportions are estimated.
Data source: CIVA.

[4] The only alternative to AOP is Vin de France (about 4% of all production), since there is no IGP.

[5] FranceAgriMer distinguishes between Pinot Blanc (1,111 ha) and Auxerrois (2,289 ha), but the CIVA (Conseil Interprofessionnel des Vins d'*Alsace*) remains in denial, with no mention of Auxerrois in its statistics and a figure of 3,303 ha for Pinot Blanc, curiously almost exactly the sum of the Pinot Blanc and Auxerrois according to FranceAgriMer! (Auxerrois here is a white variety; no connection with its use as a synonym for Malbec in Cahors!)

[6] Crémant has increased from 17% in 1991 to 24% today (CIVA).

[7] Stevenson, *The Wines of Alsace*, p. 6.

[8] In the eighteenth century the predominant variety was Burger, by the nineteenth century it was Knipperlé, but the mark of both is very high yields of flavorless wine (Stevenson, *The Wines of Alsace*, p. 9).

[9] For example, chaptalization was performed by adding sugar in solution, which increases the total volume of must, resulting in significant dilution. This ceased only in 1962.

[10] Proportions in 2012 were: White Alsace 64%, Crémant 23%, Red Alsace 9%, VT/SGN 3%, Grand Cru 4% (CIVA).

[11] Typical recent yields for Alsace average 75 hl/ha, whereas Champagne has reached 89 hl/ha. (Data from Viniflhor based on DGDDI.)

[12] Alsace has 4,400 growers, who include 890 producers. Independent producers account for about 20% of production, cooperatives for 39%, and negociants for 41% (CIVA, 2014).

[13] Grand Crus were created between 1975 and 2007:

1975	Ha	Character
Schlossberg	80.3	Granite
1983		
Altenberg de Bergbieten	35.1	Clay-marl
Altenberg de Bergheim	29.1	Marl-sandstone
Brand	58.0	Granite
Eichberg	57.6	Marl
Geisberg	8.5	Marl
Gloeckelberg	23.4	Granite
Goldert	45.3	Marl
Hatschbourg	47.4	Marl-calcareous
Hengst	53.0	Marl-calcareous
Kanzlerberg	3.2	Marl
Kastelberg	5.8	Schist
Kessler	28.5	Sandstone
Kirchberg de Barr	40.6	Marl-calcareous
Kirchberg de Ribeauvillé	11.4	Marl-sandstone
Kitterlé	25.8	Sandstone
Moenchberg	11.8	Marl-calcareous
Ollwiller	35.9	Marl-sandstone
Rangen	26.7	Marl-sandstone
Rosacker	26.2	Muschelkalk
Saering	26.8	Marne-sandstone
Sommerberg	28.4	Granite
Sonnenglanz	32.8	Marl-calcareous
Spiegel	18.3	Marl-sandstone
Wiebelsberg	12.5	Sandstone
1992		
Altenberg de Wolxheim	31.2	Marl
Bruderthal	18.4	Muschelkalk
Engelberg	14.8	Marl-sandstone
Florimont	21.0	Marl
Frankstein	56.2	Granite
Froehn	14.6	Marl
Furstentum	30.5	Granite
Mambourg	61.8	Marl-calcareous
Mandelberg	22.0	Marl-calcareous
Marckrain	53.3	Marl-calcareous
Muenchberg	17.7	Volcanic
Osterberg	24.6	Marl-calcareous-sandstone
Pfersigberg	74.6	Marl-sandstone
Pfingstberg	28.1	Calcareous-sandstone
Praelatenberg	18.7	Granite
Schœnenbourg	53.4	Marl
Sporen	23.7	Marl
Steinert	38.9	Calcareous
Steingrubler	23.0	Marl-calcareous
Steinklotz	40.6	Muschelkalk
Vorbourg	72.6	Marl-sandstone
Wineck-Schlossberg	27.4	Granite
Winzenberg	19.2	Granite-siliceous
Zinnkoepflé	68.4	Calcareous-sandstone
Zotzenberg	36.5	Marl-sandstone
2007		
Kaefferkopf	68.0	Gneiss

[14] Riesling 41%, Gewürztraminer 38%, Pinot Gris 19%, Muscat 1% (Data from CIVA for 2008).

[15] Muscat Ottonel is actually a hybrid that originated in the Loire between Muscat d'Eisenstadt and Chasselas, so it is really only

half Muscat (Jancis Robinson, *Wine Grapes*, p. 694).

[16] There is a little Pinot Gris left in Burgundy, where it is called Pinot Beurot. New plantings are not allowed, but wine can be made from existing plantings. Here it manages to make a dry wine, which seems perfectly ripe in those examples I have tasted, showing an aromatic profile similar to Alsace, with stone fruits backed by savory mushrooms.

[17] Another closely related variety, Klevner de Heligstein, is the same as Savagnin Rosé, a variant of Traminer from the Jura. It is less spicy and perfumed than Gewürztraminer.

Chapter 6: The Loire

[1] Pierre Brejoux, *Les Vins de Loire, 2nd edition* (Larmat, Paris, 1974), p. 18.

[2] Jancis Robinson, *Wine Grapes*, p. 623.

[3] FranceAgriMer, 2012.

[4] It may be the variety called Plant d'Anjou in the early sixteenth century.

[5] "Pinaud" may have been planted around the Loir in the ninth century, and was common by the twelfth century. It was mentioned in literature in 1183. By the late nineteenth century "Pineau" was on the list of quality black grapes (Emile Turpin, *Les Vignes et Les Vins du Berry* Bourges, Paris, 1907, pp. 325, 331). It was for a long time erroneously thought to be a black variant of Chenin Blanc.

[6] Comte Odart, *Ampélographie universelle ou Traité des cépages les plus estimés dans tous les vignobles de quelque renom, 6th edition* (Tours, 1824), p. 118.

[7] The variety was identified as Bidure, the traditional variety of Bordeaux from the Middle Ages (Jean Barennes, *Viticulture et vinification en Bordelais au moyen-age,* Marcel Mounestre-Picamilh, Bordeaux, 1912, p. 60; Germain Lafforgue, *Le Vignoble Girondin*, Louis Larmat, Paris, 1947, p. 156).

[8] In 1448 the Seigneurie of Menetou-Salon, including the château and its extensive vineyards, was purchased by a highly successful local merchant, Jacques Coeur. It is claimed that both red and white wine were produced, and may have been provided to the court in Paris. Although the wine appears to have been well regarded, there is no reliable evidence on its nature, let alone which cépages were grown.

[9] A legend that Pinot Noir was grown at Saint Satur is unlikely to be true, as Pinot Noir probably did not originate in Burgundy for another century or so.

[10] Depicted in *Les Très Riches Heures du Duc de Berry*, an illustrated manuscript with paintings from the Limbourg brothers dating between 1412 and 1416.

[11] This is scarcely a new situation as in 1827, Cavoleau in his book on wines of France, commented that, "The good wines of Anjou (products of Pineau Blanc) are not valued at what they are worth."

[12] Raphael Schirmer, *Muscadet. Histoire et Géographie du Vignoble Nantais* (Grappes et Millésime, Bordeaux, 2010)

[13] FranceAgriMer.

[14] Vineyards were about €17,000 per hectare in 2000 and are about €7,000 per hectare today (Valeur Venale and SAFER).

[15] Raphael Schirmer, *op. cit.*, p. 78.

[16] Roger Voss, *Wines of the Loire* (Faber & Faber, London, 1995), p. 7.

[17] Raphael Schirmer, *op. cit.*, p. 101.

[18] Melon de Bourgogne was 20% of plantings in 1900, 25% in 1961, and 67% in 2000 (Raphael Schirmer, *op. cit.*, p. 312).

[19] VDQS was abolished as a category, so the VDQS regions had either to apply for promotion to AOP or be demoted to IGP.

[20] These areas were more recently introduced to try to bring some distinction, but with only a couple of hundred of hectares each, production is scarcely significant set against Muscadet de Sèvre et Maine.

[21] Goulaine, Château-Thébaud, Mouzillon-Tillière, and Monnières-Saint Fiacre are expected to be approved soon. Vallet and La Haye Fouassière are still being considered.

[22] Yields for regional Muscadet are limited to 65 hl/ha, for Muscadet de Sèvre et Maine to 55 hl/ha, and for the Crus to 45 hl/ha.

[23] Muscadet sur lie must stay on the lees until it is bottled, but bottling must occur only in one of two periods: between March 1 and 30 June after the vintage or between the following October 15 and November 30. The Crus require longer time on the lees, 17 months for Le Pallet. and 24 months for Clisson and Gorges.

[24] If the wine is in barrique, it's done simply by stirring with a long stick, while in cuve it can be done by dropping in solid carbon dioxide.

[25] This may be a modern view. "Muscadet can be kept well until the tenth year," according to a book of 1937 (Joseph de Camiran, *Le Vignoble du Pays Nantais,* La Presse de l'Ouest, Nantes). "In excellent vintages like those of 1893, 1906, and 1928, one can keep them very much longer."

[26] It must have at least 10 g/l residual sugar.

[27] It must have at least 7 g/l residual sugar, and usually has less than 20 g/l..

[28] Cabernet Franc, Cabernet Sauvignon, Grolleau, Gamay, Malbec, Pineau d'Aunis.

[29] Rosé de Loire can come from Touraine as well as Anjou.

[30] Pierre Galet, *Cépages et Vignobles de France,* p. 1929.

[31] Quoted in http://www.winewisdom.com/articles/savennieres-roche-aux-moines---identity-crisis-or-evolution/, accessed August 2013.

[32] The AOP requires more than 34 g/l residual sugar.

[33] Beaulieu-sur-Layon, Faye-d'Anjou, Rablay-sur-Layon, Rochefort-sur-Loire, Saint-Aubin-de-Luigné, and Saint-Lambert-du-Lattay.

[34] It's unclear whether the name of Quarts de Chaume originated as a description of a specific area within Chaume or for the practice of farmers sharing part of the crop with the landowner.

[35] The regulations were made more stringent when Quarts de Chaume was promoted to grand cru. Previously, yields were limited to 25 hl/ha and the residual sugar required after fermentation was 34 g/l. The new regulations also require a planting density of at least 5,000 vines/hectare, increased from 4,000 (INAO, *Cahier des charges de l'appellation d'origine contrôlée,* February 2011).

[36] It's an ironic comment on the effectiveness of the assessment for the AOC agrément that one producer had their monovarietal Chardonnay accepted without demure, but their Sauvignon Blanc was rejected as atypical (author's interview with château proprietor, April 2006).

[37] Plantings of black varieties in the Loire are:

Cabernet Franc	15,129 ha	(61%)
Gamay	4,650 ha	(19%)
Grolleau	2,213 ha	((9%)
Cabernet Sauvignon	1,283 ha	(5%)
Pinot Noir	1,393 ha	(6%)
Pineau d'Aunis	237 ha	(1%)

Data source: FranceAgrimer.

[38] Previously abandoned, the plateau was purchased by Baptiste Dutheil in 1925, and the southern part was added by René Couly in 1951. The wine was originally called Chinon Moulin-à-Vent after a windmill that was then located in the middle of the vineyard. It was renamed Clos de l'Echo after objections from Beaujolais.

[39] In Jacky Rigaux, *Le Terroir et Le Vigneron* (Editions Terre en vues, 2006).

[40] André Jullien, *Topographie de tous les vignobles connus* (Paris, 1816).

[41] Voss, *op. cit.,* p. 7.

[42] Voss, *op. cit.,* p. 32.

[43] Production in the Loire:

AOP	White 000 bottles	Red 000 bottles	Rosé 000 bottles	Ha	G*	N*
Sancerre	1,500	185	110	2,915	308	21
Pouilly Fumé	870			1,302	156	8
Menetou-Salon	215	82	10	506	80	6
Quincy	130			270	33	3
Reuilly	52	19	15	215	38	4
Coteaux du Giennois	54	27	10	200	33	3
Châteaumeillant		28	16	95	23	
Total	2,821	341	161	5,503	671	45

G* = growers; N* = negociants.

[44] Wilson, *Terroir,* p. 244.

Chapter 7: The Rhône

[1] Named for the flavor resulting from the addition of resin (Dion, *Histoire de la Vigne,* p. 119).

[2] The original mosaic of 28 panels is now in the National Museum of Archeology in Saint-Germain-en-Laye.

[3] John Bowers et al., *A single pair of parents proposed for a group of grapevine varieties in Northeastern France* (Acta Hort 528, 129–132., 2000).

[4] If the evidence that Syrah is a distant descendant of Pinot Noir is correct, it must have originated well after Pinot Noir.

[5] Claudius Roux, *Monographie du Vignoble de Côte Rôtie* (Societie d'Agriculture, Sciences et Industrie, Lyon, 1907), p. 28.

[6] The traditional pruning for Serine on Côte Rôtie was a style called the baguette—somewhat of a long loop—and there are still old vines pruned that way.

[7] Blending red and white wines was not allowed. It now turns out that there is in fact an interesting and useful aspect to this rule,

which is that the Viognier provides factors that help to fix the color from the Syrah; this would not happen if the wines were made separately and then blended.

[8] The limit depends on the appellation.

[9] Livingstone-Learmonth, *Wines of the Northern Rhône*, p. 37.

[10] The maximum plantable area in the appellation is 320 ha.

[11] 8 ha in Condrieu and less than 2 ha in Château Grillet in 1965 according to Livingstone-Learmonth, *Wines of the Northern Rhône*, pp. 151, 155. A commonly quoted figure is that there were 13.7 ha in France in 1971.

[12] Growth was 1971 - 12 ha; 1982 - 14 ha; 1986 - 20 ha; 1990 - 40 ha; 1992 - 60 ha; 2004 - 117 ha (Livingstone-Learmonth, *Wines of the Northern Rhône*, p. 155).

[13] According to the producers' association.

[14] Plantings have increased to 700 ha in the Rhône, with another 1,500 ha in Languedoc, as well as 1,200 ha in Australia and 750 ha in California.

[15] Viognier is related to Syrah, either a half-sibling or an ancestor: the exact relationship is presently unclear. Most likely it originated somewhere in the region of the extreme Northern Rhône

[16] Lewin, *What Price Bordeaux?*, p. 213.

[17] George Ripley & Charles Anderson Dana, *The American Cyclopaedia: A Popular Dictionary of General Knowledge: France (Wines of),* (Appleton, 1874), p. 412

[18] Livingstone-Learmonth, *Wines of the Northern Rhône*, p. 244.

[19] There were 123 ha in the early 1970s (Livingstone-Learmonth, *Wines of the Northern Rhône*, p. 245).

[20] Quoted by Livingstone-Learmonth, *Wines of the Northern Rhône*, p. 245.

[21] Quoted in James Lawther, *Interview with Jean-Louis Chave,* Decanter, April 2004.

[22] Chave does produce a special cuvée, called Cuvée Cathelin, made in small amounts only in some years. "First we make the normal blend as special as possible without compromising, Sometimes you lose something exceptional in the blend, that wouldn't add anything to the blend and might even conflict with it—it's rare which is why we do it only occasionally."

[23] There have been reports that Le Méal is being downplayed—famous vineyard uprooted and replanted, screamed some press headlines in 2009—but the situation has been exaggerated; "We actually replanted 0.5 ha (out of 7 ha) in Le Méal," says Ralph Garcin at Maison Jaboulet.

[24] Production is 3,000-7,000 of each individual vineyard wine, compared to around 30,000 for Monier de la Sizeranne.

[25] Le Pavillon represents a single plot at the top of Les Bessards, but up to 1989 it was a blend from various plots of old vines.

[26] Smaller producers who make a point of specific bottlings are Marc Sorrel (with Rocoule and Le Gréal, a blend of Le Méal and Greffieux), and Michel Ferraton (with Le Méal and Les Dionnières).

[27] For example, the one single parcel wine at Delas, which comes from old vines in Les Bessards, is made only in top vintages. It's night and day compared with the general brand, Marquise de la Tourette, which comes from Les Bessards, L'Hermite, and le Sabot, and is about 30,000 bottles. Les Bessards is about 6,000 bottles when produced.

[28] Plantings of Roussanne are about 10% of those of Marsanne in the Northern Rhône as a whole (FranceAgriMer).

[29] Quoted in Livingstone-Learmonth, *Wines of the Northern Rhône*, p. 256.

[30] Quoted in interview with The Wine Society, September 2012.

[31] Created in 1956, St. Joseph consisted of 6 communes. It was expanded to include a further 20 communes in 1969. In 1986 INAO agreed to a reduction in the areas that were classified for production of St. Joseph from 6,800 ha to 3,400 ha, but producers can continue to sell production from the excluded areas under the St. Joseph label until 2021 (Livingstone-Learmonth, *The Wines of the Rhône*, p. 440).

[32] In terms of total production, the cooperative of Saint-Désirât (which was largely instrumental in the expansion of St. Joseph), is responsible for almost half of production. There are also four other cooperatives.

[33] Roussette is also allowed, but it is unclear whether this is a subvariety of Roussanne or a different variety.

[34] One possible setback to the use of clones is the development in the past twenty years of a disease called Syrah decline, which involves cracking at the site of the graft. This appears to be confined to young vines, but it's not clear whether it's associated with any particular rootstocks or clones of Syrah. The cause is unknown and it's potentially a major threat to Syrah plantings in the Rhône and Languedoc (Ted Rieger, *Syrah Vine Health Issues Explored at UCD Symposium,* Vineyard & Winery Management, Jan/Feb, 2008).

[35] M. Borty's address was 21, rue Longue: today the street has been renamed as rue Placide Cappeau, but the house is still there.

[36] FranceAgriMer, *La Cooperation Viticole Dans La Production En 1996 Et En 2006.*

[37] The individual villages are Cairanne, Chusclan (red and rosé only), Gadagne, Laudun, Massif d'Uchaux (red only), Plan de Dieu (red only), Puyméras (red only), Roaix, Rochegude, Rousset-les-Vignes, Sablet, Saint Gervais, Saint Maurice, Saint-Pantaléon-les-Vignes, Séguret, Signargues (red only), Valréas, Visan.

[38] Yields are 55 hl/ha for Côtes du Rhone, 44 hl/ha for Côtes du Rhône Villages, and 41 hl/ha for individual villages.

[39] They are called "Crus" because technically they are the Crus of the Côtes du Rhône. In practice, however, they are regarded as independent appellations.

[40] Jean-Claude Portes, *Châteauneuf-du-Pape Mémoire d'un village*, Editions A. Barthélemy (Avignon 1993).

[41] With 40% of Mourvèdre, Syrah, Muscardin, and Vaccarèse, 30% Counoise and Picpoul, and 10% Clairette and Bourboulenc (quoted in Karis, *Châteauneuf du Pape*, p 71).

[42] John Livingstone-Learmonth, *The Wines of the Rhône*, p. 328.

[43] John Livingstone-Learmonth, *The Wines of the Rhône*, p. 326.

[44] John Livingstone-Learmonth, *The Wines of the Rhône*, p. 328; Karis, *Châteauneuf du Pape*, p. 75.

[45] There are also colored variants of some of the other varieties, e.g. Terret, which has a propensity to throw off light colored and white grapes.

[46] Although white varietals can legally be included in red Châteauneuf-du-Pape, this practice has all but disappeared.

[47] Harry Karis, *Châteauneuf-du-Pape*, p. 105.

[48] Quoted in Jancis Robinson, *Southern Rhône 2012 Wines*, Financial Times, January 14, 2014.

[49] Don't ask why there are several producer syndicats requiring a Fédération; this appears to be a thorny political issue and some producers tell you darkly that they don't belong to any Syndicat.

[50] John Livingstone-Learmonth et al., *Gigondas: ses vins, sa terre, ses hommes* (Editions Bottin Gourmand, Paris, 2012), p. 92.

[51] After Châteauneuf-du-Pape, Tavel, and Lirac.

[52] John Livingstone-Learmonth et al., *Gigondas*, op. cit., p. 94.

[53] Production averages 450,000 cases from 1,260 ha (Inter-Rhône statistics).

[54] Originally the Muscat was basically a sweet wine made from late harvested grapes that were dried on straw mats. The appellation rules introduce in 1943 specified that the wine had to be fortified. Typically 7-10% of neutral spirits are added to stop fermentation and to bring the final alcohol level to 15%. The wine began to be vintage-dated only in the 1980s.

[55] Reds must have a minimum of 20% Syrah and Mourvèdre combined, at least 25% Grenache, and less than 40% Carignan. Whites have similarly complicated rules for a blend from Bourboulenc, Clairette, Grenache Blanc, Macabeo, Marsanne, Roussanne, Vermentino, and Viognier (Trebbiano was disallowed in 2010).

Chapter 8: Languedoc & Provence

[1] Paul Strang, Languedoc-Roussillon, p. 12.

[2] Olivier Torrès, *The Wine Wars. The Mondavi Affair, Globalization and 'Terroir'* (Palgrave Macmillan, London, 2006), p. 48.

[3] Paul Strang, Languedoc-Roussillon, p. 12.

[4] Geneviève Gavignaud-Fontaine, *Caves coopératives en Languedoc-Roussillon* (LIEUX DITS, Lyon, 2010.

[5] FranceAgriMer Stats, 2012.

[6] Data source: La Direction Régionale de l'Alimentation, de l'Agriculture et de la Forêt (DRAAF) of Languedoc Roussillon.

[7] Plantings of black varieties (ha) today are:

Syrah	40,866	21%
Grenache	38,951	20%
Carignan	31,361	16%
Merlot	28,298	15%
Cabernet Sauvignon	16,889	9%
Cinsault	10,211	5%
Mourvèdre	5,208	2.5%
Cabernet Franc	3,548	2%
Total	193,748	

Data source: FranceAgriMer Stats, 2013.

[8] Coteaux du Languedoc was originally scheduled to expire in April 2012, but was allowed to be used until May 2017.

[9] Languedoc, Languedoc-Cabrières, Languedoc-La Clape, Languedoc-Grés de Montpellier, Languedoc-La Méjanelle, Languedoc-Montpeyroux, Languedoc-Pézenas, Languedoc-Pic Saint Loup, Languedoc-Quatourze, Languedoc-Saint-Christol, Languedoc-Saint Drézéry, Languedoc-Saint-Georges-d'Orques, Languedoc-Saint-Saturnin, Languedoc-Sommières, Languedoc-Terrasses du Larzac, Cabardès, Clairette du Languedoc, Corbières, Corbières-Boutenac, Faugères, Fitou, Limoux, Minervois, Minervois-La Livinière, Picpoul de Pinet, Saint-Chinian, Saint-Chinian Berlou, Saint-Chinian

Roquebrun, Les Aspres, Caramany, Collioure, Côtes du Roussillon, Côtes du Roussillon Villages, Latour de France, Lesquerde, Maury, Tautuvel.

[10] Quoted in C. Gourtorbe, *Aimé Guibert de la Vaissière: "je suis un cul-terreux"*, Terre de Vins, December 1999.

[11] Latour de France, Lesquerde, Caramany, Tautuvel.

[12] Roussillon provides 2% of wine in France but 80% of the fortified wine.

[13] Pierre Torrès, *Histoire de la vigne et du vin en Roussillon* (Editions Trabucaire, Canet, 2012), p.129.

[14] Pierre Torrès, *op. cit.,* p.82.

[15] Pierre Torrès, *op. cit.,* p.119.

[16] Pierre Torrès, *op. cit.,* pp. 24, 26.

[17] Pierre Torrès, *op. cit.,* p.51.

[18] White Coteaux du Languedoc (now simply Languedoc) must be at least 70% Grenache Blanc, Clairette, Bourboulenc, Picpoul, Roussanne, Marsanne, Vermentino and Tourbat. Carignan Blanc, Terret Blanc, Trebbiano, and Maccabeu are also allowed, together with Viognier, which is limited to 10%.

[19] White wine plantings are:

Chardonnay	13,960 ha	31%
Sauvignon Blanc	8,732 ha	19%
Muscat	8,432 ha	18%
Grenache Blanc	4,015 ha	9%
Viognier	3,945 ha	9%
Macabeo	2,167 ha	5%
Picpoul	1,573 ha	3%
Vermentino	1,531 ha	3%
Terret Blanc	1,281 ha	3%
Total	45,636 ha	

Data source: FranceAgriMer Stats, 2013.

[20] 40% of production is consumed within Provence (CIVP).

[21] The white varieties allowed for use in Provence AOPs are Clairette, Ugni Blanc, Bourboulenc Blanc, Sémillon, and Vermentino. The use of the first four have declined in recent years as Vermentino has increased.

[22] Also known as Fuëlla Nera.

[23] The first known regulations date from 1363 (Jean Richard Fernand, *Les Vins De Bandol*, Editions Autres Temps, Gemenos, 2006, p. 12).

[24] Jancis Robinson, *Wine Grapes*, p. 588.

[25] Plantings are Nielluccio – 1,400 ha; Sciacarello – 600 ha; Barbarossa – 680 ha; Vermentino 680 ha (Vins de Corse, 2013).

[26] Quoted in The Drinks Business, May 30 2012.

[27] Vins de Provence, 2013.

[28] Var Matin, August 13, 2012.

[29] Statistically it is blocked more than three quarters of the time everywhere in France except for the Loire and Alsace, where it is usually performed (Claude Flanzy, *Le Vin Rosé*, Editions Féret, Bordeaux, 2009, p. 187).

[30] There's 3% Vermentino in Whispering Angel and 30% in Garrus.

[31] Claude Flanzy, *Le Vin Rosé* op. cit., p. 276.

[32] Other dry rosés are Touraine Rosé (and various subregions of Touraine), Chinon Rosé, Fiefs Vendéen, Coteaux d'Ancenis, Bourgueil Rosé, Coteaux du Loir Rosé.

[33] Rolf Bishel, *Tavel; des Hommes et des Vins* (Editions Féret, Bordeaux, 2011), p. 39.

Chapter 9: Challenge to France

[1] Quoted by Kym Anderson, *Wine's New World* (Foreign Policy, 136, 46-54, 2003), p. 47.

[2] Quoted in *Wine War. Savvy New World marketers are devastating the French wine industry*, Business week cover story, September 3, 2001.

[3] Spain has a greater area of vineyards but many of the vineyards are sparsely planted and scarcely producing.

[4] At Château de la Grille in 2006.

[5] This refers to the number of commercial producers. The total number of declarations of harvest in 2009 was 139,500 but only 92,800 were commercial. In 1995 the corresponding numbers were 291,071 and 162,000, so noncommercial producers have been declining even faster than commercial producers. Data from FranceAgriMer.

[6] Lewin, *What Price Bordeaux?*, p. 104.

[7] At position 24 according to Jean-Pierre de La Rocque, *Les 50 Fortunes du Vin*, Challenge magazine, No, 349, July 2013.

Indexes

Profile Appellation Index

Profile Name Index

General Index